SUBMARINES IN INTERNATIONAL LAW

Submarines in International Law is the first book to explore both the legal history and the contemporary regulation of submarine operations in varied areas of international law. The analysis demonstrates the instances where submarines influenced the development of the law of the sea and the law of armed conflict, as well as highlighting where international law needs to give greater account for submarines in existing bodies of law – including international marine environmental law, the law on the use of force, navigational safety rules, transnational criminal law and international cultural heritage law. Submarine operations range from military and defence uses, to supporting research and commercial seabed industries, to ocean tourism and smuggling of illicit goods. International law regulates all these activities to varying degrees. While submarines may strive to be evasive objects in the ocean, this book demonstrates why they cannot and should not elude the reach of international law.

DR NATALIE KLEIN is a professor at UNSW Sydney's Faculty of Law & Justice, Australia. Australia has nominated Professor Klein as a conciliator under Annex V and arbitrator under Annex VII of the UN Convention on the Law of the Sea. Her research focuses on the law of the sea.

DR KATE PURCELL is a research fellow at UNSW, Sydney's Faculty of Law & Justice, Australia. Her previous publications include *Geographical Change and the Law of the Sea* (2019), a monograph considering the implications of sea level rise for maritime baselines and boundaries in international law.

JACK MCNALLY is a research fellow at UNSW, Sydney's Faculty of Law & Justice, Australia and a practising international lawyer. His practice and research focuses on public international law, international arbitration, the law of the sea and international environmental law.

CAMBRIDGE STUDIES IN INTERNATIONAL AND COMPARATIVE LAW: 197

Established in 1946, this series produces high quality, reflective and innovative scholarship in the field of public international law. It publishes works on international law that are of a theoretical, historical, cross-disciplinary or doctrinal nature. The series also welcomes books providing insights from private international law, comparative law and transnational studies which inform international legal thought and practice more generally.

The series seeks to publish views from diverse legal traditions and perspectives, and of any geographical origin. In this respect it invites studies offering regional perspectives on core *problématiques* of international law, and in the same vein, it appreciates contrasts and debates between diverging approaches. Accordingly, books offering new or less orthodox perspectives are very much welcome. Works of a generalist character are greatly valued and the series is also open to studies on specific areas, institutions or problems. Translations of the most outstanding works published in other languages are also considered.

After seventy years, Cambridge Studies in International and Comparative Law sets the standard for international legal scholarship and will continue to define the discipline as it evolves in the years to come.

A list of books in the series can be found at the end of this volume.

SUBMARINES IN INTERNATIONAL LAW

NATALIE KLEIN
UNSW, Sydney

KATE PURCELL
UNSW, Sydney

JACK MCNALLY
UNSW, Sydney

CAMBRIDGE
UNIVERSITY PRESS

CAMBRIDGE
UNIVERSITY PRESS

Shaftesbury Road, Cambridge CB2 8EA, United Kingdom

One Liberty Plaza, 20th Floor, New York, NY 10006, USA

477 Williamstown Road, Port Melbourne, VIC 3207, Australia

314–321, 3rd Floor, Plot 3, Splendor Forum, Jasola District Centre, New Delhi – 110025, India

Cambridge University Press is part of Cambridge University Press & Assessment, a department of the University of Cambridge.

We share the University's mission to contribute to society through the pursuit of education, learning and research at the highest international levels of excellence.

www.cambridge.org
Information on this title: www.cambridge.org/9781009463423

DOI: 10.1017/9781009463416

When citing this work, please include a reference to the DOI 10.1017/9781009463416

First published 2026

Cover image: Submarine / alxpin / E+ / Getty Images

A catalogue record for this publication is available from the British Library

Library of Congress Cataloging-in-Publication Data
Names: Klein, Natalie (Natalie S.) author | Purcell, Kate (Research Fellow) author | McNally, Jack author
Title: Submarines in international law / Natalie Klein, Kate Purcell, Jack McNally.
Description: Cambridge, United Kingdom ; New York, NY : Cambridge University Press, 2026. | Series: Csil series (cambridge studies in international and comparative law) | Includes bibliographical references and index.
Identifiers: LCCN 2025051661 | ISBN 9781009463423 hardback | ISBN 9781009463447 paperback | ISBN 9781009463416 ebook
Subjects: LCSH: Submarine mines (International law) | Submarines (Ships) | War, Maritime (International law) | Submarine warfare | Maritime law | Law of the sea
Classification: LCC KZ5645.5.S83 K54 2026
LC record available at https://lccn.loc.gov/2025051661

ISBN 978-1-009-46342-3 Hardback

CONTENTS

FIGURES

ACKNOWLEDGEMENTS

Work on this book was made possible through the generous financial commitment from UNSW Sydney's SHARP scheme and we gratefully acknowledge this support.

Natalie Klein also acknowledges the work of several research assistants throughout the life of the project and warmly thanks Varun Rao, Dohyeon Bae, Bram Jan Burger and Madison Durham. She also benefitted from feedback following presentations at the Australian Department of Foreign Affairs and Trade and the UNSW Sydney's Faculty of Law & Justice research seminar series. Thanks to colleagues for the insightful comments at a crucial stage of the book. Natalie also presented preliminary research on this book for the Hungdah Chiu Lecture at the ILA-ASIL Asia-Pacific Research Forum in Taiwan. The latter lecture drew on this work and was published as 'Nuclear Submarines under AUKUS and Implications for International Law in the Indo-Pacific' (2023) 41 *Chinese (Taiwan) Year Book of International Law* 1–18, DOI:10.1163/9789004719934_00.

We also benefited from the comments of numerous colleagues who reviewed different chapters at various stages of the writing. We thank Steven Haines, David Letts, Lucas Lixinski, Rob McLaughlin, Karen Scott, Michael White and Sarah Williams for their generosity in providing feedback. They are of course in no way responsible for any errors or contrary views that remain in the text.

Finally, Natalie, Kate and Jack would all like to thank their respective families for their love, support and forbearance during all the time spent at periscope depth working on this book.

TABLE OF CASES

TABLE OF TREATIES

Page references to key treaties are included in the Index

Treaty between Belgium and the Netherlands relative to the Separation of their Respective Territories, London, 19 April 1839, 88 CTS 427

Declaration Respecting Maritime Law (Déclaration réglant divers points de droit maritime), Paris, 16 April 1856, entered into force 16 April 1856, 61 BFSP 155

Boundary Treaty between Chile and Argentina, Buenos Aires, 23 July 1881, 159 CTS 45

1884 Convention on the Protection of Submarine Cables, Paris, 14 March 1884, 163 CTS 391

Hague Convention (III) for the Adaptation to Maritime Warfare of the Principles of the Geneva Convention of 22 August 1864, The Hague, 29 July 1899, entered into force 4 August 1900, 187 CTS 443

Hague Convention (VI) relative to the Legal Position of Enemy Merchant Ships at the Start of Hostilities, The Hague, 18 October 1907

Hague Convention (VII) relative to the Conversion of Merchant Ships into War-ships, The Hague, 18 October 1907, entered into force 26 January 1910, 205 CTS 319

Hague Convention (VIII) relative to the Laying of Automatic Submarine Contact Mines, The Hague, 18 October 1907, entered into force 18 October 1907, 205 CTS 331

Hague Convention (IX) concerning Bombardment by Naval Forces in Time of War, The Hague, 18 October 1907, entered into force 26 January 1910, 205 CTS 345

Hague Convention (X) for the Adaptation to Maritime Warfare of the Principles of the Geneva Convention, The Hague, entered into force 26 January 1910, 18 October 1907, 205 CTS 359

Hague Convention (XI) relative to Certain Restrictions with regard to the Exercise of the Right of Capture in Naval War, The Hague, 18 October 1907, entered into force 26 January 1910, 205 CTS 367

Hague Convention (XII) relative to the Establishment of an International Prize Court, The Hague, 18 October 1907, 205 CTS 381

Hague Convention (XIII) concerning the Rights and Duties of Neutral Powers in Naval War, The Hague, 18 October 1907, entered into force 26 January 1910, 205 CTS 395

Hague Convention (V) respecting the Rights and Duties of Neutral Powers and Persons in Case of War on Land, The Hague, 18 October 1907, entered into force 26 January 1910, 205 CTS 299

Hague Convention (IV) respecting the Laws and Customs of War on Land, The Hague, 18 October 1907, entered into force 26 January 1910, 205 CTS 277

Declaration concerning the Laws of Naval Warfare, London, 26 February 1909, never entered into force, in (1914) 8(S2) *American Journal of International Law* 88

Convention for the Unification of Certain Rules of Law with respect to Collisions between Vessels, Brussels, 23 September 1910, entered into force 1 March 1913, [1910] ATS 14

Treaty of Peace between Austria-Hungary, Bulgaria, Germany and Turkey, and Russia, Brest-Litovsk, 3 March 1918

Armistice between Germany and the Allied Powers, Compiègne, 11 November 1918, entered into force 11 November 1918, 224 CTS 286

Treaty of Peace between the Allied and Associated Powers and Germany, Versailles, 28 June 1919, entered into force 10 January 1920, [1919] UKTS 4

Treaty of Peace Between the Allied and Associated Powers and Turkey, Sèvres, 10 August 1920, never entered into force, 113 BFSP 652

Treaty between the United States of America and Japan concerning the Yap Island and the Other Islands under Mandate Situated in the Pacific North of the Equator, Washington, 11 February 1922, 12 LNTS 202

Treaty between the British Empire, France, Japan and the United States of America relating to their Insular Possessions and Insular Dominions in the Pacific Ocean, Washington, 13 December 1921, entered into force 17 August 1923, 24 LNTS 193, [1921] ATS 7

Treaty between the British Empire, the United States of America, France, Italy and Japan for the Limitation of Naval Armaments, Washington, 6 February 1922, entered into force 17 August 1923, 25 LNTS 202

Treaty relating to the Use of Submarines and Noxious Gases in Warfare, Washington, 6 February 1922, never entered into force, in Dietrich Schindler and Jirí Toman (eds.), *The Laws of Armed Conflicts* (Martinus Nijhoff, 1988) 877

Treaty relating to Principles and Policies to Be Followed in Matters concerning China, Washington, 5 February 1922, entered into force 5 August 1925, 38 LNTS 277, [1922] ATS 12

Armistice of Mudanya between Turkey, Italy, France and Great Britain, Mudanya, 11 October 1922

Treaty of Peace with Turkey, Lausanne, 24 July 1923, entered into force 6 August 1923, 28 LNTS 11

International Convention for the Unification of Certain Rules relating to the Immunity of State-owned Vessels, Brussels, 10 April 1926, entered into force 8 January 1936, 176 LNTS 199

Inter-American Convention on Maritime Neutrality, Havana, 20 February 1928, entered into force 21 January 1931, 135 LNTS 187

Treaty for the Limitation and Reduction of Naval Armament, London, 22 April 1930, entered into force 31 December 1930, 112 LNTS 65

Convention Regarding the Regime of Straits, Montreux, 20 July 1936, entered into force 9 November 1936, 173 LNTS 213

Exchange of Notes between His Majesty's Government in the United Kingdom of Great Britain and Northern Ireland and the Government of the German Reich regarding the Limitation of Naval Armaments, London, 18 June 1935, entered into force 18 June 1935, [1935] UKTS 22

Procès-Verbal relating to the Rules of Submarine Warfare set forth in Part IV of the Treaty for the Limitation and Reduction of Naval Armament of 22 April 1930, London, 6 November 1936, entered into force 6 November 1936, 173 LNTS 353, [1936] ATS 14

Treaty for the Limitation of Naval Armament, London, 25 March 1936, entered into force 29 July 1937, 184 LNTS 115

Agreement between His Majesty's Government in the United Kingdom and the German Government providing for the Limitation of Naval Armament and the Exchange of Information concerning Naval Construction, London, 17 July 1937, [1937] UKTS 2

Agreement between His Majesty's Government in the United Kingdom and the Government of the Union of Soviet Socialist Republics providing for the Limitation of Naval Armament and the Exchange of Information concerning Naval Construction, London, 17 July 1937, [1937] UKTS 17

Agreement between Germany and Japan Against the Communist International (Komintern), Berlin, 25 November 1936, entered into force 25 November 1936, 140 BFSP 529

Armistice Agreement between the German High Command of the Armed Forces and French Plenipotentiaries, Compiègne, 22 June 1940

Declaration of Panama, Panama City, 3 October 1939 in Matilda F Axton, et al. (eds.), *Foreign Relations of the United States: Diplomatic Papers, 1939, The American Republics* (United States Government Printing Office, 1957) vol. 5, 36

General Declaration of Neutrality of the American Republics, Panama City, 3 October 1939 in (1939) 1 *Department of State Bulletin* 326

German-Turkish Treaty of Friendship, Ankara, 18 June 1941

Charter of the United Nations, San Francisco, 26 June 1945, entered into force 24 October 1945, XV UNCIO 335

Protocol of the Proceedings of the Crimea (Yalta) Conference, Yalta, 24 March 1947, entered into force 24 March 1947, 148 BFSP 80

Treaty of Peace between the Allied and Associated Powers and Italy, Paris, 10 February 1947, entered into force 15 September 1947, 49 UNTS 3

Treaty of Peace between the Allied and Associated Powers and Finland, Paris, 10 February 1947, entered into force 15 September 1947, 48 UNTS 203

Treaty of Peace between the Allied and Associated Powers and Romania, Paris, 10 February 1947, entered into force 15 September 1947, 42 UNTS 3

Treaty of Peace between the Allied and Associated Powers and Bulgaria, Paris, 10 February 1947, entered into force 15 September 1947, 41 UNTS 21

Treaty of Peace between the Allied and Associated Powers and Hungary, Paris, 10 February 1947, entered into force 15 September 1947, 41 UNTS 135
North Atlantic Treaty, Washington, 4 April 1949, entered into force 24 August 1949, 34 UNTS 243
Geneva Convention (I) for the Amelioration of the Condition of the Wounded and Sick in Armed Forces in the Field, Geneva, 12 August 1949, entered into force 21 October 1950, 75 UNTS 31
Geneva Convention (II) for the Amelioration of the Condition of Wounded, Sick and Shipwrecked Members of Armed Forces at Sea, Geneva, 12 August 1949, entered into force 21 October 1950, 75 UNTS 85
Geneva Convention (III) relative to the Treatment of Prisoners of War, Geneva, 12 August 1949, entered into force 21 October 1950, 75 UNTS 135
Geneva Convention (IV) relative to the Protection of Civilian Persons in Time of War, Geneva, 12 August 1949, entered into force 21 October 1950, 75 UNTS 287
Treaty of Peace with Japan, San Francisco, 8 September 1951, entered into force 28 April 1952, 136 UNTS 45
Security Treaty between the United States and Japan, San Francisco, 8 September 1951, entered into force 28 April 1952, 136 UNTS 211
Treaty of Friendship, Cooperation and Mutual Assistance, Warsaw, 14 May 1955, entered into force 6 June 1955, 219 UNTS 3
Treaty of Amity, Economic Relations, and Consular Rights, Tehran, 15 August 1955, entered into force 16 June 1957, 284 UNTS 93
Protocol Modifying and Completing the Treaty for Collaboration in Economic, Social and Cultural Matters and for Collective Self Defence, Paris, 23 October 1954, entered into force 6 May 1955, 211 UNTS 342
Protocol III on the Control of Armaments, Paris, 23 October 1954, 211 UNTS 364
Statute of the International Atomic Energy Agency, New York, 26 October 1956, entered into force 29 July 1957, 276 UNTS 3
Convention on the Territorial Sea and the Contiguous Zone, Geneva, 29 April 1958, entered into force 22 November 1964, 516 UNTS 205
Convention on the High Seas, Geneva, 29 April 1958, entered into force 30 September 1962, 450 UNTS 11
Agreement for Co-operation on the Uses of Atomic Energy for Mutual Defense Purposes, Washington, 3 July 1958, entered into force 27 July 1959, 326 UNTS 3
Antarctic Treaty, Washington, 1 December 1959, entered into force 23 June 1961, 402 UNTS 71
Paris Convention on Third Party Liability in the Field of Nuclear Energy, Paris, 29 July 1960, entered into force 1 April 1968, 956 UNTS 251
Single Convention on Narcotic Drugs, New York, 30 March 1961, entered into force 13 December 1964, 520 UNTS 151
Brussels Convention Supplementary to the Convention on Third Party Liability in the Field of Nuclear Energy, Brussels, 31 January 1963, entered into force 4 December 1974, 1041 UNTS 358

Vienna Convention on Civil Liability for Nuclear Damage, Vienna, 21 May 1963, entered into force 12 November 1977, 1063 UNTS 266

Polaris Sales Agreement between the Government of the United Kingdom and the United States of America, Washington, 6 April 1963, entered into force 6 April 1963, [1963] UKTS 59

Treaty Banning Nuclear Weapon Tests in the Atmosphere, in Outer Space and under Water, Moscow, 5 August 1963, entered into force 10 October 1963, 480 UNTS 43

Treaty on Principles Governing the Activities of States in the Exploration and Use of Outer Space, including the Moon and Other Celestial Bodies, Washington, Moscow and London, 27 January 1967, entered into force 10 October 1967, 610 UNTS 205

Treaty for the Prohibition of Nuclear Weapons in Latin America (Treaty of Tlatelolco), Mexico City, 14 February 1967, entered into force 22 April 1968, 634 UNTS 281

Treaty on the Non-Proliferation of Nuclear Weapons, Moscow, London and Washington, 1 July 1968, entered into force 15 March 1970, 729 UNTS 161

International Convention on Civil Liability for Oil Pollution Damage, Brussels, 29 November 1969, entered into force 19 June 1975, 973 UNTS 3

Convention on Psychotropic Substances, Vienna, 21 February 1971, entered into force 16 August 1976, 1019 UNTS 175

Treaty on the Prohibition of the Emplacement of Nuclear Weapons and Other Weapons of Mass Destruction on the Seabed and the Ocean Floor and in the Subsoil Thereof, Washington, Moscow and London, 11 November 1971, entered into force 18 May 1972, 995 UNTS 115

International Convention on the Establishment of an International Fund for Compensation for Oil Pollution Damage, Brussels, 18 December 1971, entered into force 16 October 1978, 1110 UNTS 57

Agreement between the Government of the United States of America and the Government of the Union of Soviet Socialist Republics on the Prevention of Incidents on and over the High Seas, Moscow, 25 May 1972, entered into force 25 May 1972, 852 UNTS 151

Treaty between the United States of America and the Union of Soviet Socialist Republics on the Limitation of Anti-Ballistic Missile Systems, Moscow, 26 May 1972, entered into force 3 October 1972, 944 UNTS 13

Protocol to the Treaty between the United States of America and the Union of Socialist Soviet Republics on the Limitation of Anti-Ballistic Missile Systems, Moscow, 26 May 1972, entered into force 26 May 1972, 1042 UNTS 424

Convention on the International Regulations for Preventing Collisions at Sea, London, 20 October 1972, entered into force 15 July 1977, 1050 UNTS 16

Convention on the Prevention of Marine Pollution by Dumping of Wastes and Other Matter, London, 29 December 1972, entered into force 30 August 1975, 1046 UNTS 120

International Convention for the Prevention of Pollution from Ships, London, 2 November 1973, entered into force 2 October 1983, 1340 UNTS 62

International Convention for the Safety of Life at Sea, London, 1 November 1974, entered into force 25 May 1980, 1184 UNTS 2

Additional Protocol I to the Geneva Conventions of 12 August 1949, and relating to the Protection of Victims of International Armed Conflicts, Geneva, 8 June 1977, entered into force 7 December 1978, 1125 UNTS 3

Treaty Between the United States of America and The Union of Soviet Socialist Republics on the Limitation of Strategic Offensive Arms (SALT II), Vienna, 18 June 1979, never entered into force, (1979) 18 ILM 1138

International Convention on Maritime Search and Rescue, Hamburg, 27 April 1979, entered into force 22 June 1985, 1184 UNTS 278

Convention on Certain Conventional Weapons which may be deemed to be Excessively Injurious or to Have Indiscriminate Effects, Geneva, 10 October 1980, entered into force 2 December 1983, 1342 UNTS 137

Agreement between the Government of the United States and the Government of the United Kingdom of Great Britain and Northern Ireland to Facilitate the Interdiction by the United States of Vessels of the United Kingdom which are Suspected of being Engaged in Trafficking in Drugs, London, 13 November 1981, entered into force 13 November 1981 (1981) 33 UST 4224 (TIAS No. 10296)

United Nations Convention on the Law of the Sea, Montego Bay, 10 December 1982, entered into force 16 November 1994, 1833 UNTS 397

South Pacific Nuclear Free Zone Treaty (Treaty of Rarotonga), Rarotonga, 6 August 1985, entered into force 11 December 1986, 1445 UNTS 177

Protocol 1 to the South Pacific Nuclear Free Zone Treaty, Suva, 8 August 1986, 1971 UNTS 470

Protocol 2 to the South Pacific Nuclear Free Zone Treaty, Suva, 8 August 1986, 1971 UNTS 475

Protocol 3 to the South Pacific Nuclear Free Zone Treaty, Suva, 8 August 1986, 1971 UNTS 482

Convention on Early Notification of a Nuclear Accident, Vienna, 27 October 1986, entered into force 27 October 1986, 1439 UNTS 275

Convention on Assistance in the Case of a Nuclear Accident or Radiological Emergency, Vienna, 26 September 1986, entered into force 26 February 1987, 1457 UNTS 133

Convention for the Suppression of Unlawful Acts against the Safety of Maritime Navigation, Rome, 10 March 1988, entered into force 1 March 1992, 1678 UNTS 201

Protocol to the Convention of 10 March for the Suppression of Unlawful Acts Against the Safety of Fixed Platforms Located on the Continental Shelf, Rome, 10 March 1988, entered into force 1 March 1992, 1678 UNTS 201

United Nations Convention against Illicit Traffic in Narcotic Drugs and Psychotropic Substances, Vienna, 20 December 1988, entered into force 11 November 1990, 1582 UNTS 95

United States of America-Union of Soviet Socialist Republics Joint Statement on the Uniform Interpretation of Rules of International Law Governing Innocent Passage, Wyoming, 23 September 1989

International Convention on Salvage, London, 28 April 1989, entered into force 14 July 1996, 1953 UNTS 165

Southeast Asia Nuclear Weapon-Free Zone Treaty (Treaty of Bangkok), Bangkok, 15 December 1995, entered into force 27 March 1997, 1981 UNTS 129

Agreement on Illicit Traffic by Sea, Implementing Article 17 of the United Nations Convention against Illicit Traffic in Narcotic Drugs and Psychotropic Substances, Strasbourg, 31 January 1995, entered into force 1 May 2000, 2136 UNTS 61

Treaty on the Final Settlement with Respect to Germany, Moscow, 12 September 1990, entered into force 15 March 1991, 1969 UNTS 115

Treaty between the United States of America and the Union of Soviet Socialist Republics on the Reduction and Limitation of Strategic Offensive Arms (START I Treaty), Moscow, 31 July 1991, entered into force 5 December 1994, (1992) 31 ILM 246

Treaty between the United States of America and the Union of Soviet Socialist Republics on Further Reduction and Limitation of Strategic Offensive Arms (START II Treaty), Moscow, 3 January 1993, never entered into force

Protocol of 1992 to Amend the International Convention on Civil Liability for Oil Pollution Damage, London, 27 November 1996, entered into force 30 May 1996, 1956 UNTS 258

Protocol of 1992 to Amend the International Convention on the Establishment of an International Fund for Oil Pollution Damage, London, 27 November 1992, entered into force 30 May 1996, 1956 UNTS 255

Africa Nuclear-Weapon-Free Zone Treaty (Treaty of Pelindaba), Cairo, 12 April 1996, entered into force 15 July 2009, 35 ILM 698

Comprehensive Nuclear-Test-Ban Treaty, New York, 10 September 1996, never entered into force, UNGA Res. 50/245 (UN Doc. A/50/1027)

Joint Convention on the Safety of Spent Fuel Management and on the Safety of Radioactive Waste Management, Vienna, 9 May 1997, entered into force 18 June 2001, 2153 UNTS 303

Protocol to amend the Vienna Convention on Civil Liability for Nuclear Damage, Vienna, 12 September 1997, entered into force 4 October 2003, 2241 UNTS 270

Rome Statute of the International Criminal Court, Rome, 17 July 1998, entered into force 1 July 2002, 2187 UNTS 3

International Convention on Arrest of Ships, Geneva, 12 March 1999, entered into force 14 September 2011, 2797 UNTS 3

Protocol against the Smuggling of Migrants by Land, Sea and Air, supplementing the United Nations Convention against Transnational Organized Crime, New York, 15 November 2000, entered into force 28 January 2004, 2241 UNTS 507

Convention on the Protection of the Underwater Cultural Heritage, Paris, 2 November 2001, entered into force 2 January 2009, 2562 UNTS 3

Agreement concerning Co-operation in Suppressing Illicit Maritime and Air Trafficking in Narcotic Drugs and Psychotropic Substances in the Caribbean Area, San Jose, 10 April 2003, not entered into force

Protocol to Amend the Convention on Third Party Liability in the Field of Nuclear Energy as amended by the Additional Protocol of 28 January 1964 and by the Protocol of 16 November 1982, Paris, 12 February 2004, entered into force 1 January 2022

United Nations Convention on the Jurisdictional Immunities of States and Their Property, New York, 2 December 2004, not entered into force (UN Doc. A/59/508)

Protocol of 2005 to the Convention for the Suppression of Unlawful Acts against the Safety of Maritime Navigation, London, 14 October 2005, entered into force 28 July 2010, ATNIF 31

Protocol of 2005 to the Protocol for the Suppression of Unlawful Acts against the Safety of Fixed Platforms Located on the Continental Shelf, London, 14 October 2005, entered into force 28 July 2010 (IMO Doc. LEG/CONF.15/22)

Central Asian Nuclear-Weapon-Free Zone Treaty (Treaty of Semipalatinsk in Central Asia), Semipalatinsk, 8 September 2006, entered into force 21 March 2009, 2970 UNTS 91

Nairobi Convention on the Removal of Wrecks, Nairobi, 18 May 2007, entered into force 14 April 2015, [2023] ATNIF 8

Amendment to the Convention on the Physical Protection of Nuclear Material, Vienna, 8 July 2005, entered into force 8 May 2016, 3132 UNTS 136

Agreement on Port State Measures to Prevent, Deter and Eliminate Illegal, Unreported and Unregulated Fishing, Rome, 22 November 2009, entered into force 5 June 2016, 3161 UNTS 377

Treaty on the Prohibition of Nuclear Weapons, New York, 7 July 2017, entered into force 22 January 2021, 3379 UNTS 36

Agreement between the Government of Australia, the Government of the United Kingdom of Great Britain and Northern Ireland, and the Government of the United States of America for the Exchange of Naval Nuclear Propulsion Information, Canberra, 22 November 2021, entered into force 8 February 2022, [2024] ATS 4

Memorandum of Understanding between the Department of Defense of the United States of America and the Ministry of National Defense of the People's Republic of China Regarding the Rules of Behavior for Safety of Air and Maritime Encounters, Washington and Beijing, 10 November 2014.

Agreement among the Government of Australia, the Government of the United Kingdom of Great Britain and Northern Ireland, and the Government of the United States of America for Cooperation related to Naval Nuclear Propulsion, Washington, 5 August 2024, entered into force 17 January 2025, [2025] ATS 5

Agreement under the United Nations Convention on the Law of the Sea on the Conservation and Sustainable Use of Marine Biological Diversity of Areas beyond National Jurisdiction, New York, 19 June 2023, entered into force 17 January 2026 (UN Doc. A/CONF.232/2023/4)

ABBREVIATIONS

ABM	anti-ballistic missile
AIP	air independent propulsion
ASW	anti-submarine warfare
AUKUS	Australia-United Kingdom-United States
COLREGs	International Regulations for Preventing Collisions at Sea
CUES	Code for Unplanned Encounters at Sea
EEZ	exclusive economic zone
FRG	Federal Republic of Germany
GDR	German Democratic Republic
IAEA	International Atomic Energy Agency
ICBM	intercontinental ballistic missile
ICJ	International Court of Justice
IDI	Institut de Droit International
ILA	International Law Association
ILC	International Law Commission
IMO	International Maritime Organization
INTERCO	International Code of Signals
ISR	intelligence gathering, surveillance and reconnaissance
ITLOS	International Tribunal for the Law of the Sea
LOFAR	low-frequency analysis and recording
LPV	low profile vehicle
LTTE	Liberation Tigers of Tamil Eelam
MASS	Maritime Autonomous Surface Ships
MIRV	Multiple Independently Targetable Re-entry Vehicles
NATO	North Atlantic Treaty Organization
NNWS	non-nuclear weapon State
NPT	Treaty on the Non-Proliferation of Nuclear Weapons
NWS	nuclear weapon State
ODAS	ocean data acquisition systems, aids, and devices
PLA	People's Liberation Army
ROV	remotely operated vehicle
SALT	strategic arms limitation talks
SCICEX	SCience ICe EXercise

SLBM	submarine-launched ballistic missile
SOFAR	SOund Fixing And Ranging
SOLAS	Safety of Life at Sea
SOSUS	SOund SUrveillance System
SPSS	self-propelled semisubmersibles
SSBN	ballistic missile submarine
SSGN	guided cruise missile submarines
SSN	attack submarine
START	Strategic Arms Reduction Treaty
SUBOPAUTH	NATO Submarine Operating Authority
TPNW	Treaty on the Prohibition of Nuclear Weapons
UCH	underwater cultural heritage
UMAV	underwater maritime autonomous vehicle
UN	United Nations
UNCLOS	United Nations Convention on the Law of the Sea
WEU	Western European Union
WWI	World War I
WWII	World War II
XLUUV	extra-large uncrewed underwater vehicles

1

Introducing Submarines in International Law

1.1 Introduction

Submarines have, for centuries, occupied a position of fascination, fear and imagination. The early submarine was conceived of by inventor Leonardo da Vinci, whose sketches envisaged a boat able to submerge and attack enemy vessels.[1] English mathematician William Bourne drew up plans for such a vehicle in 1578 and, over the following decades, early patents were filed and designs began to take shape. In 1775, the submarine acquired its first military purpose. George Washington provided the funds for the construction of the three-metre-long *Turtle*, which was designed to affix explosive charges to British ships during the American Revolutionary War. It achieved little success. In 1864, the *H. L. Hunley*, a submarine of the US Confederacy, made the first successful military attack on a vessel, sinking the Union's *Housatonic* warship. The US Navy Submarine Force was founded in 1900, with the British Royal Navy Submarine Service forming soon after. By the time World War I (WWI) commenced, all major powers and a smaller number of other States had an active submarine service.[2] Submarines began to be powered by diesel-electric engines, making them viable instruments of war. As the US Ambassador to the United Kingdom observed in 1917: 'The submarine is the most formidable thing the war has produced – by far – and it gives the German the only earthly chance he has to win.'[3]

During WWI and World War II (WWII), submarines were indispensable in the war effort. The German U-boat force wreaked havoc on its enemies, and Japanese midget submarines were used in attacks on Pearl Harbor and Sydney Harbour. Nuclear-powered submarines commenced operation shortly after WWII, with the USS *Nautilus* entering into

[1] ASC, 'Evolution of the Submarine' <www.asc.com.au/wp-content/uploads/2021/11/Evolution-of-the-submarine.pdf>. See also Thomas Parrish, *The Submarine: A History* (Viking, 2004).

[2] ASC (n 1).

[3] John Terraine, *Business in Great Waters: The U-Boat Wars: 1916–1945* (Pen & Sword Books, 1989) 38.

service in 1955. Since that time, submarine technology and weaponry have advanced significantly, with submarines now serving as among the most expensive, significant and powerful pieces of military technology.

Submarines have also occupied important places in public consciousness. From the legends of Alexander the Great's explorations of the ocean floor using antediluvian submersibles, the futuristic submarine *Nautilus* in Jules Verne's science fiction classic *Twenty Thousand Leagues Under the Sea*,[4] to the more recent *Hunt for Red October*[5] and *Das Boot*,[6] depictions of submarines are well known and indicate an 'unending fascination with underwater seafare'.[7] In 2023, the world was engrossed by the disappearance of the *Titan* submersible near the wreck of the *Titanic*, drawing new attention to the use of submarines for private scientific and leisure purposes.[8]

In contemporary settings, the recent Australia-United Kingdom-United States (AUKUS) alliance, which will see Australia make the first acquisition of nuclear submarines by a non-nuclear power,[9] has sent a ripple through Indo-Pacific geopolitical fault lines. The ongoing use of submarines as an instrument of war has been made apparent by the use of submarine-launched missiles by Russia in the Russo-Ukrainian War,[10] and in tests by North Korea.[11] While submarine warfare has been rather limited since the end of WWII,[12] an increasingly diverse number of States

[4] Jules Verne, *Twenty Thousand Leagues under the Sea* (Penguin, 2018, first published 1870).

[5] Tom Clancy, *The Hunt for Red October* (Naval Institute Press, 1984); *The Hunt for Red October* (Mace Neufeld Productions, 1990).

[6] Lothar-Günther Buchheim, *Das Boot* (W&N, 2004, first published 1973); *Das Boot* (Bavaria Film, 1981).

[7] Linda Maria Koldau, 'Why Submarines? Interdisciplinary Approaches to a Cultural Myth of War' (2011) 4(1) *Journal of War and Culture Studies* 65, 66.

[8] See, e.g., Brad Brooks and Daniel Trotta, 'Titanic Sub: How Is Submersible Tourism Regulated and What's Next for Industry?', *Reuters*, 24 June 2023 <www.reuters.com/world/after-titanic-sub-disaster-industry-faces-scrutiny-2023-06-23/>.

[9] 'Joint Leaders Statement On AUKUS', *Prime Minister of Australia*, 14 March 2023 <www.pm.gov.au/media/joint-leaders-statement-aukus>; 'AUKUS: The Trilateral Security Partnership Between Australia, UK and US', *US Department of Defense*, 15 September 2023 <www.defense.gov/Spotlights/AUKUS/>.

[10] See, e.g., Tomasz Grotnik, 'Russia Deploys Three Submarines Armed with Cruise Missiles to Sea for the First Time', *Naval News*, 30 July 2024 <www.navalnews.com/naval-news/2024/07/russia-deploys-three-submarines-armed-with-cruise-missiles-to-sea-for-the-first-time/>.

[11] See, e.g., Associated Press, 'North Korea Says It Has Tested Submarine-Launched Cruise Missiles', *NBC News*, 29 January 2024 <www.nbcnews.com/news/world/north-korea-kim-jong-un-cruise-missiles-submarine-rcna136105>.

[12] Notable exceptions include the INS *Khukri*, an Indian frigate sunk by the Pakistani *Hangor* submarine during the Indo-Pakistani War (1971), and the Argentine *Belgrano*

have prioritised the capacity to undertake both submarine warfare and anti-submarine warfare in their national defence strategies, evidenced through the proliferation of increasingly powerful and expensive submarines.

A distinct current trend is that military submarines are now operated by a growing and ever more diverse group of States.[13] In particular, it is notable that military submarines are increasingly concentrated in the Asia-Pacific region, as opposed to the past and present great powers and a select few other highly advanced economies.[14] This phenomenon is said to be as a result of economic growth in the region and, as such, can be considered a 'catching up' of the region.[15] Further, Wong estimates that there will be more than 250 submarines operating in the Asia-Pacific by 2030, which raises 'the spectre of unintended escalation of issues rising from unplanned encounters at sea for submarine operators'.[16] There is a clear 'pattern of proliferation' in the region, not only of submarine platforms but also for anti-submarine warfare capabilities.[17] The impetus for these States acquiring submarines is diverse; for the larger economies, it is to preserve sea lines of communication and trade/energy security; for smaller economies, the impetus may lie in submarines' 'utility for covert surveillance and intelligence collection rather than war-fighting purposes'.[18] The extent to which this regional proliferation, as well as submarine proliferation more broadly, is cause for concern has, however, been debated.[19]

Clearly, States recognise the critical security functions of intelligence gathering, surveillance, reconnaissance and power projection of submarines during both times of peace and war, as well as their other non-militaristic State functions in scientific research, environmental

sunk by the British *Conqueror* submarine during the 1982 Falklands War. The United States used submarine-launched tomahawk missiles during the Operation Desert Storm phase of the 1991 Gulf War.

13 Peter Hayes, 'Off the Beach: Underwater Warfare in the 21st Century' (2018) 13(1) *Global Asia* 48, 49–51.

14 Andrew Davies, 'Up Periscope: The Expansion of Submarine Capabilities in the Asia-Pacific Region' (2007) 152(5) *RUSI Journal* 64, 64 (in respect of Asia).

15 Ibid, 65.

16 Kelvin Wong, 'Guardians of the Deep: Singapore Navy Readies for Future Undersea Operations', *Janes*, 1 March 2021.

17 Ridzwan Rahmat, 'Underwater Ambitions: Submarines and Anti-submarine Capabilities in Southeast Asia', *Janes: Navy International*, 17 March 2015.

18 Sam Bateman, 'Perils of the Deep: The Dangers of Submarine Proliferation in the Seas of East Asia' (2011) 7(1) *Asian Security* 61, 62.

19 See, e.g., ibid, 81 (voicing concern).

monitoring and surveying. New uses and applications for submarines are constantly being identified, particularly through their growing acquisition by non-State actors, and submarines increasingly support commercial operations at sea as well as scientific and recreational activities. Private uses of submarines have also extended to less peaceful uses, such as international drug smuggling. The role of submarines is further being enhanced through the development of autonomous or remote-controlled underwater craft, turning what was once science fiction into our new reality. In turn, it is becoming increasingly apparent that each of these unique purposes may point to the operation of different international laws.

The renewed focus on submarines, the further development of submarine technology and their progressively myriad uses, including by non-State actors, inspire inquiry as to the international legal regime applicable to submarines. An initial response may be that the law of the sea, as set out in the United Nations Convention on the Law of the Sea (UNCLOS)[20] and other rules of international law (especially those adopted within the International Maritime Organization (IMO)), applies to submarines as it does to any other vessel operating on the surface. The law of the sea is a critical starting point, as the evolution of rules relating to passage in particular has responded to developments in both submarine technology and the use of these vessels by State actors. An appreciation of the origin of these rules helps to clarify their content; yet it also raises questions as to whether the existing law of the sea remains fit for purpose in view of further developments in submarine technologies and uses, including the increasing use of underwater vehicles by non-State actors, who lack the entitlement to sovereign immunity afforded to States.

The very nature of submarines as *underwater vehicles* prompts a closer scrutiny of the existing rules. A rapid reveal shows that the legal frame for submarines is much more complex than it may seem at first blush. Other areas of international law that are implicated include international nuclear law, international marine environmental law, law of armed conflict and law on the use of force, transnational criminal law, laws relating to navigational safety, the law of salvage and international cultural heritage law. While the law of the sea is a significant context for the regulation of submarine activities, State and non-State uses of

[20] United Nations Convention on the Law of the Sea, Montego Bay, 10 December 1982, entered into force 16 November 1994, 1833 UNTS 397 ('UNCLOS').

submarines also engage distinct subdisciplines of international law and, of course, core rules of international law relating to State responsibility, sources of international law, jurisdiction, immunities and the law of treaties, especially treaty interpretation. It is readily apparent that submarines are not a single legal issue, nor can they properly be folded into the treatment of all other ships at sea in all instances. Instead, the operation of submarines raises distinct and varied legal questions for consideration, which this book seeks to explore and answer.

A key aim of this book is to bring together all the international law rules that apply to the operation of different types of submarines. The military utility of submarines has seemingly allowed for submarines to be overlooked or excluded from explicit regulation in international law. Yet the deployment of submarines carries a variety of risks, including for the submariners on board, the safe operation of surface ships, the peaceful pursuit of other maritime activities, the protection of the marine environment and in international and national security relationships. In light of the lack of explicit focus on submarines typically afforded in existing international law, this book also seeks to indicate a path forwards to respond to ambiguities, gaps and inconsistencies that emerge from the current law. The general inclusion of submarines, along with other marine vessels, will be sufficient in some instances, but certainly not all. Our analysis draws out the specific rules, as well as regulatory gaps and weaknesses, and aims to show why lawyers and policymakers need to focus more on submarines in international law.

In this chapter, we first consider how 'submarine' may be defined for legal purposes in Section 1.2 below. It is readily apparent that submarines are predominantly associated with the navies and defence structures of States and a critical consideration in any legal examination of submarine operations is the sovereign immunity enjoyed by these military submarines. Section 1.3 provides an initial explanation of the relevance of sovereign immunity to the topic, which features throughout the book. To facilitate the book's international legal analysis, Section 1.4 then details a legal taxonomy of submarines. Most notably, we consider how differences in the identity of the operator of a submarine, the nature of its propulsion and the technology equipped to it may implicate different international laws. Following this taxonomy, we introduce in Section 1.5 the international laws applicable to submarines, which will be further detailed in the remainder of the book. The concluding sections of the chapter provide an overview of the book, its contents and further explain its goals.

1.2 Defining the Submarine

It is first necessary to define, with some level of precision, the modern submarine. This task is not an abstract one; it is required to identify the vehicles with which international law is concerned. Definitional clarity is not only critical to drawing the metes and bounds of the applicable international legal regime, but, from an epistemological view, it focusses attention on the diversity of vehicles constituting the contemporary submarine extending beyond the large vehicles used for military purposes with which the term 'submarine' is most frequently associated.[21]

A key definitional challenge exists in distinguishing between '*submarines*' and '*submersibles*'. This difficulty is not a new one.[22] In the literature and in public media, these terms are often used interchangeably and inconsistently. In the law of the United States, a 'semi-submersible vessel' is defined as 'any watercraft constructed or adapted to be capable of operating with most of its hull and bulk under the surface of the water, including both manned and unmanned watercraft', while a 'submersible vessel' is a 'vessel capable of operating completely below the surface of the water, including both manned and unmanned watercraft'.[23] The latter definition would appear to include what has come to be recognised as the modern submarine, though, in practice, submarines are rarely referred to as submersibles. The term 'submersible' typically refers to smaller underwater vehicles, such as bathyscapes, which are not generally capable of travelling long distances or otherwise undertaking autonomous activity independent of a support vessel. This latter understanding of submersibles is sometimes used in this book. The distinction between submarines and submersibles finds support in the dictionary definitions of the terms, which distinguish between the two categories of vessel by defining submarines as 'a vessel, esp. a warship, capable of operating under water', whereas submersibles are 'small submarine[s]', such as those used in 'underwater exploration [and] drilling', which are 'capable of operating

[21] The search for definitional clarity is, however, a vexed task. As Busby observed, terms in the field are not used with consistency. 'Undersea Vehicles', 'Deep Research Vessels', 'Deep Submergence Vehicles', 'Mini-Subs', 'Submersible Vessels', even '*Submarinos*' are synonymous: R Frank Busby, *Manned Submarines* (US Department of Defence, 1976) 2. The quest for a definition is made difficult by jargon alone.

[22] Simon Lake, 'The Submarine versus the Submersible' (1996) 18(2) *Journal of the American Society for Naval Engineers* 533, 534 (observing that 'submarine vessels are broadly distinguished today by the two denominations of "submarine" and "submersible". The difference between these terms has not always been well defined').

[23] 46 U.S.C. § 70502 (United States).

underwater for short periods' and are 'not independently powered, instead relying on batteries that have to be recharged by a support vessel'.[24]

For the purposes of this book, we generally adopt an expansive approach to the use of the term 'submarine', such as to include vehicles capable of submersion regardless of size, level of autonomy, tonnage, weapons system, form of propulsion or status of ownership (i.e., operated by a State or by a private organisation). We use the 'broad term "submarine" to designate all vessels capable of navigating totally submerged'.[25] As such, the midget submarines of WWI and WWII, small maritime autonomous vehicles and research vessels, and the modern, large nuclear-powered cruise missile submarine fall under the same umbrella. While the diverse characteristics of these vehicles may implicate the application of different international laws, the capacity for submersion is crucial and renders each vehicle a 'submarine' with which international law is concerned.

A further issue of nomenclature also warrants clarification. Submarines are sometimes referred to as 'boats', rather than as 'ships' or 'vessels'. Traditional wisdom separates 'boats' and 'ships' by referring to the former as a smaller watercraft capable of being carried by another vessel and the latter as larger vessels. The reference to submarines as 'boats' is somewhat quaint, as many of them are substantially larger than modern surface warships. The reasoning for this quirk of definition is historical, with the classification of submarines as 'boats' coming from a time when submarines were significantly smaller and needed support from a 'mother ship'. Complicating matters further, the names of submarines in the United States are prefixed with 'USS', or 'United States Ship'.[26] This expression is not merely a convention in English. Most famously, German submarines are known in English as 'U-boats', an abbreviation of the German *Unterseeboot* (or 'undersea boat'). Other examples can be found in Dutch (*Onderzeeboot*), Swedish (*Undervattensbåt*) and Russian (*podvodnaya lodka*). In this book, however, we generally refer to submarines,

[24] Rupert Neate, 'Blue Planet Gives Super-Rich their New Toys – Submersibles', 3 February 2018 <www.theguardian.com/business/2018/feb/02/blue-planet-david-attenborough-super-rich-submersibles>.

[25] Lawrence Spear, 'Underwater Torpedo Boats' (1909) XXI(2) *Journal of the American Society of Naval Engineers* 353, 354–356.

[26] Similarly, Australian submarines are prefixed with 'HMAS' (His Majesty's Australian *ship*); UK submarines are prefixed with HMS (His Majesty's *ship*); Canada's are prefixed with 'HMCS' (His Majesty's Canadian *ship*); India's with 'INS' (Indian Naval *ship*).

rather than boats, but emphasise that there is a vast diversity in the types of vehicles constituting the modern submarine, their varied operators and myriad usages and whether they are warships or not (as discussed in Section 1.3).

1.3 Sovereign Immunity and Submarines

A hallmark of submarines has been their military use; from the time of their initial development, submarines were considered as a vital component to a State's naval power. To this day, submarines are predominantly counted as vessels within a State's naval fleet. In Section 1.4, we set out a legal taxonomy of submarines to demonstrate that submarines comprise more than just warships. Yet throughout this book, in seeking to articulate which international laws apply to submarines, their primary use as warships also brings to the fore their sovereign immune status. Sovereign immunity has implications for the application and enforcement of international law,[27] and hence has core relevance for this study. In this section, we seek to explain when submarines enjoy sovereign immunity and provide a preliminary indication of the scope of that immunity. Part II of the book addresses the relevance of sovereign immune status for some submarines in relation to the each of the legal regimes considered.

UNCLOS recognises two categories of sovereign immune vessel. First, Article 95 of UNCLOS provides 'complete immunity from the jurisdiction of any State other than the flag State' to '[w]arships on the high seas'. Article 29 of UNCLOS defines 'warship' as 'a ship belonging to the armed forces of a State bearing the external marks distinguishing such ships of its nationality, under the command of an officer duly commissioned by the government of the State and whose name appears in the appropriate service list or its equivalent, and manned by a crew which is under regular armed forces discipline'.[28] This definition is broadly equivalent to that provided for previously in Article 8(2) of the 1958 Convention on the High Seas,[29] and is largely accepted to reflect customary international

[27] Sovereign immunity derives from the sovereign equality of States and is considered 'one of the fundamental principles of the international legal order': *Jurisdictional Immunities of the State* (Germany v. Italy; Greece Intervening) (Judgment of 2 February 2012) [2012] ICJ Rep 99, para. 56.

[28] UNCLOS (n 20) art. 29.

[29] Convention on the High Seas, Geneva, 29 April 1958, entered into force 30 September 1962, 450 UNTS 1.

law.[30] Importantly, while the term 'warship' may more readily conjure images of surface vessels, there is little debate that it extends to encapsulate submarines.[31] The history of the negotiation of Article 95 of UNCLOS, and the distinction between warships and other ships in earlier instruments of international law (including the 1856 Declaration Respecting Maritime Law,[32] and Hague Convention (VII) relating to the Conversion of Merchant Ships into Warships[33]) suggest that the intention behind the definition of 'warship' was not to exclude certain types of military vessel capable of exercising belligerent rights (such as submarines), but rather was part of 'an effort to outlaw privateering' and to 'limit certain belligerent activities to state ships'.[34] To this end, private fishing and other mercantile vessels that participate in military activities, such as the Chinese 'maritime militia', are not entitled to the sovereign immunity of the State.[35] There is, however, debate as to whether underwater maritime autonomous vehicles (UMAVs) constitute a warship within the meaning of Article 95,[36] and we address this question further in Chapter 14.

Second, Article 96 of UNCLOS affords sovereign immunity to ships on the high seas that are 'owned or operated by a State and used only on government non-commercial service'. UNCLOS does not define the vessels that fall within the scope of Article 96, but examples can be

[30] James Kraska, 'Intelligence Collection and the International Law of the Sea' (2022) 99 *International Law Studies* 602, 627; Bernard H Oxman, 'The Regime of Warships Under the United Nations Convention on the Law of the Sea' (1984) 24 *Virginia Journal of International Law* 809, 810; Ingrid Delupis, 'Foreign Warships and Immunity for Espionage' (1984) 78 *American Journal of International Law* 53, 55, 75. See also Wolff Heintschel von Heinegg, 'Warships' in Anne Peters and Rüdiger Wolfrum (eds.), *Max Planck Encyclopedia of Public International Law* (Oxford University Press, 2015) para. 6; Myron Nordquist (ed.), *United Nations Convention on the Law of the Sea: A Commentary* (Martinus Nijhoff, 1985–2011) vol. 2, para. 95.2 ('*Virginia Commentary*').

[31] Kraska, 'Intelligence Collection and the International Law of the Sea' (n 30) 627; von Heinegg (n 30) para. 68 ('With regard to submarines it may be recalled that the efforts during the beginning of the 20th century to outlaw the use of submarines were in vain. Hence, submarines are warships as long as they meet the requirements of the definition.')

[32] Déclaration réglant divers points de droit maritime, Paris, 16 April 1856, 61 BFSP 155.

[33] Hague Convention (VII) relating to the Conversion of Merchant Ships into War-Ships, The Hague, 18 October 1907, entered into force 26 January 1910, 205 CTS 319.

[34] Simon McKenzie, 'When Is a Ship a Ship? Use by State Armed Forces of Un-crewed Maritime Vehicles and the United Nations Convention on the Law of the Sea' (2020) 21 *Melbourne Journal of International Law* 1, 30–31.

[35] Kentaro Furuya, 'Law Enforcement Measures against Chinese Maritime Militia' (2023) 100 *International Law Studies* 672, 679.

[36] McKenzie (n 34) 29ff.

taken from the commentary to Article 16(2) of the United Nations Convention on Jurisdictional Immunities of States and Their Property: 'police patrol boats, custom inspection boats, hospital ships, oceanographic ships, training vessels and dredgers, owned and operated by a State and used or intended for use in government non-commercial service'.[37] This position was earlier reflected in Article 3 of the 1926 Brussels Convention, which excluded certain State-owned vessels (and their cargoes) from being subject to seizure, arrest or detention by legal processes when operated for non-commercial services.[38] More recently, the 1999 Convention on Arrest of Ships excludes from its scope any warship, naval auxiliary or other ships owned or operated by a State and used only for government non-commercial service.[39] The effect of Article 96 is to extend the grant of sovereign immunity to these types of vessels.

A question of immunity may arise in relation to submersibles that are tethered to or operated from a warship, and whether those craft share the immunity (as well as other rights and duties) of the parent ship. It may be possible to argue that as an extension of a warship, that the associated vessel enjoys the same immunity.[40] Doubts on this position may arise, however, when the vehicle or submarine in question is operating long distances from the parent warship.[41] Rather than consider any connection to another vessel, Kraska has argued, in his examination of maritime autonomous vehicles, that what is dispositive is not whether a vehicle is classed as a ship or not (or seemingly a warship or not), but whether it is State property.[42] Even if it is

[37] United Nations Convention on Jurisdictional Immunities of States and Their Property, New York, 2 December 2004, not yet entered into force (UN Doc. A/59/508).

[38] International Convention for the Unification of Certain Rules relating to the Immunity of State-owned Vessels, Brussels, 10 April 1926, entered into force 8 January 1936, 176 LNTS 199.

[39] International Convention on Arrest of Ships, Geneva, 12 March 1999, entered into force 14 September 2011, 2797 UNTS 3, art. 8(2).

[40] Natalie Klein et al., 'Maritime Autonomous Vehicles: New Frontiers in the Law of the Sea' (2020) 69 *International and Comparative Law Quarterly* 719, 725. This position was set out by Phillimore in 1854: Robert Phillimore, *Commentaries upon International* Law (T&JW Johnson, 1854) vol. 1, 275, cited in James Kraska, 'Sovereign Immunity of Unmanned Maritime Vehicles' in Natalie Klein et al. (eds.), *Maritime Autonomous Vehicles and International Law: Maritime Security Perspectives* (Routledge, 2025) 77, 84.

[41] Klein et al. (n 40) 725. See also Sanjeet Ruhal, 'The Evolving Seascape of Naval Warfare: Unmanned Underwater Vehicles and the Challenges for International Law' (2024) *Journal of Conflict and Security Law* 1, 23.

[42] Kraska, 'Sovereign Immunity of Unmanned Maritime Vehicles (n 40) 77, 83. To this end, Kraska posits: 'In short, if a UMV or other object belongs to a state or is operated on government non-commercial service, it is immune from foreign jurisdiction': ibid, 84.

accepted that State *property* enjoys immunity, there may still be a question as to the scope of that immunity,[43] and whether it is commensurate with the sovereign immunity enjoyed by warships or a lesser status such as functional immunity, which aligns more with the immunity accorded to State agents.[44] The 'complete' sovereign immunity enjoyed by warships is the same as that enjoyed by government vessels operated on non-commercial service.[45]

The unifying factor among Article 95 and Article 96 vessels is that both are operated by States and are not used for ordinary mercantile purposes. UNCLOS thus clearly excludes 'government ships operated for commercial purposes' from the scope of sovereign immunity afforded by the Convention,[46] subjecting them to the same legal regime concerning civil and criminal jurisdiction as merchant vessels when operating in the territorial sea.[47] The distinction between these vessels and those entitled to sovereign immunity 'turns on the nature of the ship's use, not the extent of the state ownership or possession'.[48] The exclusion of government vessels operated for commercial purposes from the scope of sovereign immunity has a long history,[49] and was expressed in Article 1 of the

43 Especially when regard is had to the pre-judgment and post-judgment immunity of State property as set out in Articles 18 and 19 of the Convention on Jurisdictional Immunities (n 37). For discussion see Peter-Tobias Stoll, 'State Immunity' in Anne Peters and Rüdiger Wolfrum (eds.), *Max Planck Encyclopedia of Public International Law* (Oxford University Press, 2011) para. 53.

44 See Rob McLaughlin, 'Some Rules Applicable to Use of Long-Range Underwater Maritime Autonomous Vehicles for Intelligence, Surveillance and Reconnaissance Purposes' in Natalie Klein et al. (eds.), *Maritime Autonomous Vehicles and International Law: Maritime Security Perspectives* (Routledge, 2025) 145, 156, 158.

45 James Kraska, *Maritime Power and the Law of the Sea* (Oxford University Press, 2011) 252–253; Ted McDorman, 'Sovereign Immune Vessels: Immunities, Responsibilities and Exemptions' in Henrik Ringbom (ed.), *Jurisdiction over Ships: Post-UNCLOS Developments in the Law of the Sea* (Brill Nijhoff, 2015) 82, 94. It could, however, be noted that Article 30 of UNCLOS refers to non-compliance by *warships* only and does not reference government vessels on non-commercial service, as happens in Article 31 (as the other exception to sovereign immunity).

46 The heading to Section 3(B) of Part II of UNCLOS (n 20) refers to 'Rules applicable to merchant ships and government ships operated for commercial purposes'. Compare this with the heading to Section 3(C) of Part II, which sets out the rules applicable to 'warships and other government ships operated for non-commercial purposes'.

47 See UNCLOS (n 20) arts. 27, 28.

48 Hazel Fox and Philippa Webb, *The Law of State Immunity* (Oxford University Press, 3rd ed., 2015) 110. McDorman similarly writes '[w]hether or not a particular vessel is one to which sovereign immunity applies is a question of fact much informed by the function of a vessel, physical characteristics and the relationship between the vessel and the flag state': McDorman (n 45) 90.

49 See generally Fox and Webb (n 48) 110–112, 116–118.

1926 Brussels Convention.[50] In relation to submarines, those that are used for commercial exploration and exploitation, or are privately owned, do not enjoy sovereign immunity.

While reference in Articles 95 and 96 of UNCLOS is made to immunities on the high seas, sovereign immunity is also applicable in the exclusive economic zone (EEZ) by virtue of the operation of Article 58(2).[51] The sovereign immunity of warships and other government vessels operated on non-commercial service also applies in the territorial sea, but is subject to two limited exceptions.[52] First, a coastal State may request a warship failing to comply with its laws concerning innocent passage to leave its territorial sea.[53] Second, where a sovereign immune vessel causes loss or damage to a coastal State resulting from its non-compliance with the laws and regulations of that coastal State under UNCLOS, the flag State bears international responsibility.[54] Warships enjoy sovereign immunity in the ports and internal waters of other countries under general international law.[55]

The effect of Articles 95 and 96 of UNCLOS is that States have no jurisdiction to interfere with the operations of other States' sovereign immune vessels, which are unable to be arrested, detained, boarded or subjected to the coercive measures otherwise within the competencies of a coastal State.[56] Whether States may assert prescriptive jurisdiction over sovereign immune vessels when those vessels are within a coastal State's maritime zones, as opposed to immunity applying to both prescriptive and enforcement jurisdiction, has been a matter of debate.[57] Article 236 of UNCLOS, which is discussed further in Chapter 12, has the effect of

50 Convention for the Unification of Certain Rules of Law with respect to Collisions between Vessels, Brussels, 23 September 1910, entered into force 1 March 1913, [1930] ATS 14.

51 *Virginia Commentary* (n 30) vol. 2, para. 95.6(c).

52 UNCLOS (n 20) art. 32, describing them as 'exceptions'.

53 Ibid, art. 30.

54 Ibid, art. 31.

55 *ARA Libertad* (Argentina v. Ghana) (Provisional Measures Order of 15 December 2012) [2012] ITLOS Rep 332, para. 95. Judges Wolfrum and Cot considered that the sovereign immunity of warships in ports and internal waters was established as a matter of customary international law (and not addressed in UNCLOS): Separate Opinion of Judges Wolfrum and Cot, para. 7.

56 Immunity from the prescriptive jurisdiction of non-flag States on the high seas is inapposite because when any vessel is on the high seas it is subject to the exclusive jurisdiction of the flag State.

57 Kraska has argued that '[w]arships and other government vessels are beyond the prescriptive jurisdiction of coastal states, even while in port or in internal waters': Kraska, 'Sovereign Immunity of Unmanned Maritime Vehicles' (n 40) 95. Excluding both prescriptive and enforcement jurisdiction is described by Kraska as the 'purist view':

preventing the application of rules concerning the protection and preservation of the marine environment to sovereign immune vessels. It could be argued that the explicit exclusion of prescriptive jurisdiction in this provision of UNCLOS by implication suggests that prescriptive jurisdiction otherwise exists in relation to sovereign immune vessels. In this vein, Oxman has argued that immunity from enforcement jurisdiction 'does not excuse a warship' from respecting other provisions of the Convention, including rules relating to innocent passage in the territorial sea, nor may they ignore the rights of other users.[58] However, even if a coastal State's law applies, it is not able to enforce those laws against a sovereign immune vessel. It is typically the exercise of enforcement jurisdiction that produces the most tension between States.[59]

Submarines that are classified as warships or government vessels on non-commercial service thus enjoy sovereign immunity throughout ocean areas. Their sovereign immunity does not necessarily preclude the application of international law, as the flag State may still be found internationally responsible for the conduct of its submarines.[60] Instead, States are precluded from the exercise of enforcement jurisdiction (such as arrest or detention of the vessel and its crew) over sovereign-immune, foreign-flagged submarines.

1.4 Legal Taxonomy of Contemporary Submarines

To situate the discussion in this book, this section creates a typology of submarines presently known to be in operation based on the way that they are treated by international law. As discussed immediately above, whether a submarine is entitled to sovereign immunity is of paramount importance for determining the applicable legal regime. The availability of sovereign immunity thus provides a first key marker of distinction in categorising submarines in international law. We further distinguish between submarines depending on their form of power, as international law has specific rules for nuclear energy. Another legal distinction must

ibid, 94. McDorman has instead posited that the 'local state' has prescriptive jurisdiction but no enforcement jurisdiction: McDorman (n 45) 95.

[58] Oxman (n 30) 826–827, a view supported by the language of Article 30 of UNCLOS.

[59] An example being Russia's seizure of three Ukrainian naval vessels. *Detention of Three Ukrainian Naval Vessels* (Ukraine v. Russia) (Provisional Measures Order of 25 May 2019) ITLOS Case No 26. As noted by ITLOS in *ARA Libertad*, 'any act which prevents by force a warship from discharging its mission . . . is a source of conflict that may endanger friendly relations among States': *ARA Libertad* (n 55) para. 97.

[60] UNCLOS (n 20) art. 304. See further arts. 31, 42(5), 110(3).

be made depending on whether there is an operator aboard the submarine or it is remote-controlled or autonomous. The discussion in this section thus elaborates on a legal taxonomy of submarines that informs their regulation.

Considering the critical importance of the status of submarines as sovereign immune vessels (or not), our legal taxonomy initially divides contemporary submarines into two categories: submarines entitled to sovereign immunity (typically referred to as 'military submarines' in this book) and submarines not entitled to sovereign immunity. The former category can be divided into three second-level categories: warships entitled to immunity under Article 95; other vessels in government non-commercial service entitled to immunity under Article 96; and UMAVs. UMAVs are separated out into their own second-level category as they could be entitled to immunity under either Article 95 or Article 96 of UNCLOS.[61] Article 95 submarines can be further taxonomised by their mode of propulsion. In particular, a nuclear-powered submarine attracts the operation of an additional set of international laws compared to conventionally powered submarines. The submarines not entitled to sovereign immunity can be further divided into commercial submarines and UMAVs, both of which may be operated by State and non-State actors, as well as submarines used for criminal purposes by non-State actors such as narco-submarines. This taxonomy is reflected in Figure 1.1 below.

The task of taxonomising the contemporary submarine is constrained by the fact that details as to the characteristics and design of submarines, their ownership and their operational status are not always available. Secrecy often exists around submarines operated for military purposes, and certainly in respect of submarines operated for criminal purposes, of which little information is known unless they are captured or salvaged. Further, little information exists regarding submarines in private ownership as there is no requirement in international law – and often not in domestic law – for such submarines to be subject to central registration. For instance, a submarine may change ownership many times in a year, it may be put in storage and then made re-operational multiple times in a year, or research vessels may be used periodically by States and at other times by non-governmental organisations. These changes in status implicate the operation of different international laws. Further, the pace of technical advancement means that often what is known about certain

[61] See further discussion below in Section 1.4.3. See also Chapter 14.

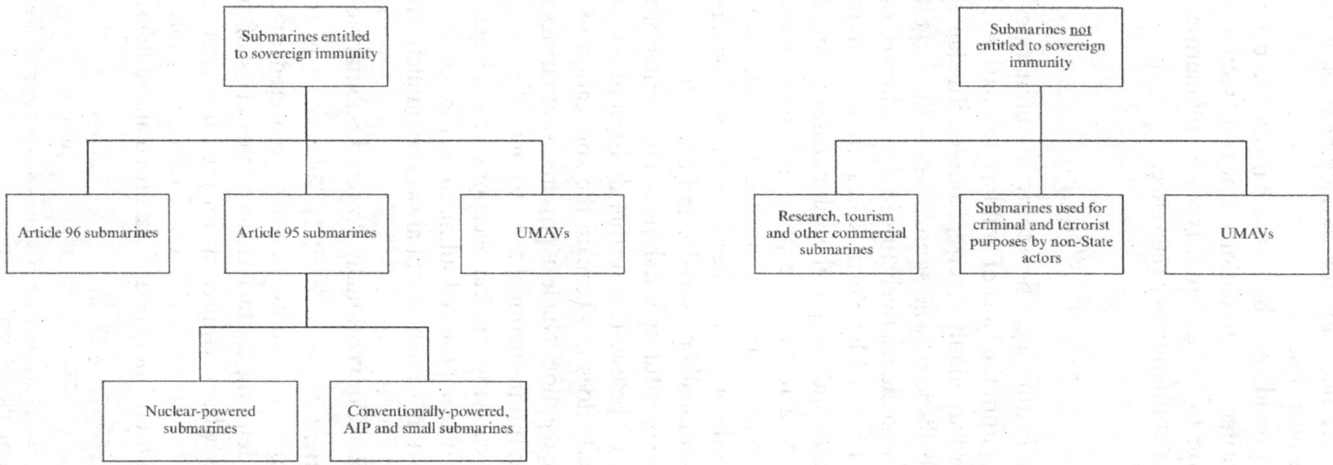

Figure 1.1 Legal taxonomy of submarines.

submarines, or future plans for the development of submarines, may become inaccurate over time.

In addition to providing a basic mechanism for determining how submarines are treated in international law, this section also provides a brief introduction to the different types of submarines presently in operation and their contemporary relevance.

1.4.1 Warships

The first category in this legal taxonomy of submarines is warships, which we include within the label of 'military submarines'. The submarines in this category are highly diverse, from the Russian *Typhoon*-class nuclear-powered ballistic missile submarines – the largest submarines ever constructed[62] – to the relatively tiny midget submarines of the *Yugo*- and *Yono*- classes operated by North Korea. In addition to the obvious characteristics of size and weight, the submarines in this category vary significantly according to their weapons systems (cruise and ballistic missiles carrying conventional and nuclear payloads, as well as torpedoes) and their mode of power (diesel-electric and/or air-independent propulsion ('conventionally powered'), and nuclear).

The submarines constituting warships can be further broken down as reflected in Figure 1.2 below. This further division of sovereign immune submarines generally does not bear on the application of international law, with one key exception. Nuclear-powered submarines are subject to different treatment in international law owing to their mode of propulsion. Submarines carrying nuclear weapons are subject to a broadly similar regime as nuclear-powered submarines, though the type of weaponry carried by a submarine may not always be publicly known.

1.4.1.1 Conventionally Powered Submarines

The most prominent form of military submarine is conventionally powered submarines, also known as diesel-powered or diesel-electric submarines. The defining characteristic of this class of submarines is their diesel engine, which requires air for the process of combustion to take place. As such, these vehicles are required to 'snort' or 'snorkel', a process in which their 'snort masts' are raised above the surface to take

[62] Though note the Russians have since taken delivery and put into service a *longer* (though not heavier) submarine, the *Belgorod*.

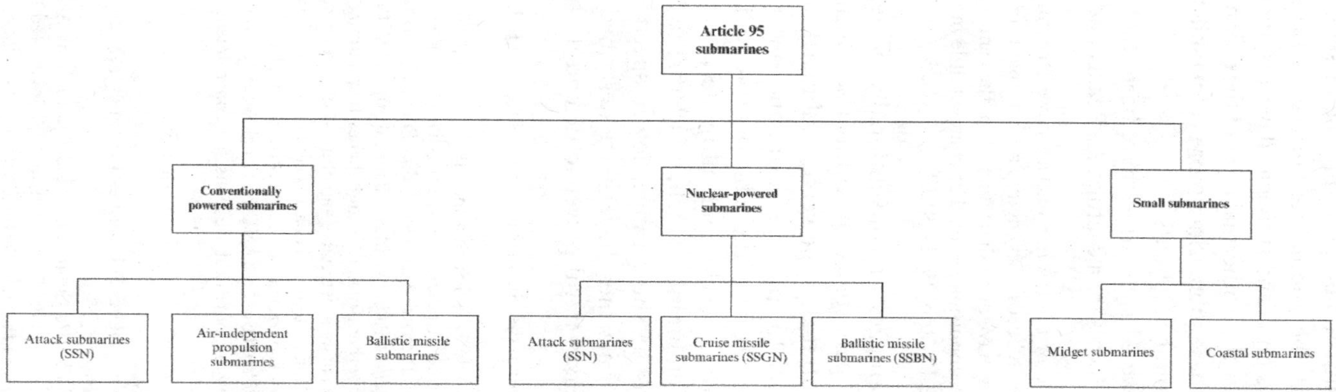

Figure 1.2 Types of submarines considered as warships.

in air and expel exhaust fumes, powering the diesel-electric engines.[63] The requirement that the submarine surface in order to charge its batteries serves as a significant strategic flaw; the inability to sustain extended periods below the isothermal layer of the ocean and the requirement to snort makes these submarines more vulnerable to detection and, accordingly, attack from belligerents.[64]

Conventionally powered submarines have been the backbone of contemporary submarine forces for a century. As Reader and Potter observed:

> Even in today's age of underwater nuclear power the majority of the world's submarines still use diesel engines as their main source of mechanical power, as they have done since the turn of the century. The diesel-electric submarine propulsion system has changed little in concept since the start of the Great War of 1914–1919.[65]

The significant advantages of conventionally powered submarines help to explain their persistence. In comparison to nuclear-powered submarines, conventionally powered submarines are cheaper, quieter, smaller, easier to train crews on, and often are more manoeuvrable in combat.[66] Each of these factors lead to 'improved target-identification-and-attack cycle and ultimately increased mission flexibility, mobility, endurance, reach, and lethality'.[67] As such, despite their limitations of short range, lower speeds and being air-dependent, these submarines have been described as 'one of the best means for a weaker naval power to defend itself from seaborne

[63] Ed Swain, 'Turbocharging the Submarine Diesel Engine' (1994) 4(4) *Mechatronics* 349, 350.

[64] J. Snouck-Hurgronje, 'On the Diesel Submarine' (1977) 122(3) *RUSI* 49, 50; Michael Raska, 'Diesel-Electric Submarine Modernization in Asia: The Role of Air-Independent Propulsion Systems' in Richard Bitzinger (ed.), *Emerging Critical Technologies and Security in the Asia-Pacific* (Palgrave Macmillan, 2016) 91, 96 ('[w]hile snorkels have improved with radar absorbent materials and shapes to minimize their bow wave and wake signatures, they emanate a detectable signature – and are increasingly vulnerable to advanced counter-detection systems'); Sadia Tasleem, 'Pakistan's Nuclear Capabilities and Prospects for Sea-Based Deterrence' in Rory Medcalf et al. (eds.), *The Future of the Undersea Deterrent: A Global Survey* (ANU National Security College, 2020) 43, 46 ('[d]iesel-electric submarines are not ideal weapons for concealment or operations in the deep sea').

[65] G. T. Reader and I. J. Potter, 'Early Submarine Engine Development' (1997) 106(3) *Journal of Engines* 1921, 1921.

[66] See, e.g., Sandra I. Erwin, 'Diesel Submarines Becoming a Main Irritant to US Navy' (2004) 89 *National Defense* 58, 58.

[67] Michael Raska, 'Diesel-Electric Submarine Modernization in Asia: The Role of Air-Independent Propulsion Systems' in Richard Bitzinger (ed.), *Emerging Critical Technologies and Security in the Asia-Pacific* (Palgrave Macmillan, 2016) 91, 91.

invasion by a stronger power . . . [;] they are among the most, if not the most, asymmetric of traditional platforms'.[68]

Within the subset of conventionally powered submarines are two further types of vessel. First, those powered by air-independent propulsion (AIP). These submarines can operate without the need to snort as the oxygen required to complete the process of combustion is stored on board in liquid form. Their engines can operate while the submarine is submerged, leading them to be referred to as the 'poor man's nuclear submarine'.[69] As a result, '[r]ather than being constrained by battery life, the endurance of an AIP-enabled submarine is limited by its stores of pressurized liquid oxygen',[70] leading to an extension of their submerged endurance from days to weeks.[71] The result is a submarine that maintains the substantial advantages of traditional conventionally powered submarines, while significantly alleviating the strategic burden caused by the requirement to have access to air.[72] This different form of propulsion is not, however, legally significant.

Second, conventionally powered submarines have generally not been armed with nuclear weapons. However, North Korea has developed submarine-launched nuclear ballistic missiles, which have been test fired using the State's sole, experimental conventionally powered submarine capable of firing such missiles.[73] Israel's conventionally powered *Dolphin*-class submarines are also speculated to be capable of launching

68 IISS, 'Taiwan's Submarine-building Plan' (2021) 27(1) *Strategic Comments* 1.

69 Wong (n 16).

70 James R. P. Brun, 'A Modern Canadian Submarine Force' (Thesis, Canadian Forces College, 2021) 40, citing Norman Jolin, 'Future Canadian Submarine Capability: Some Considerations' (2015) 11(1) *Canadian Naval Review* 17.

71 For a description of AIP systems, see Tomasz Lus, 'Waiting for Breakthrough in Conventional Submarine's Prime Movers' (2019) 4 *Transactions on Maritime Science* 37.

72 Other advantages were outlined in Raska (n 67) 97 (arguing that AIP technologies 'close the endurance gap between nuclear and conventional submarines . . . promis[ing] significant operational advantages in the prolonged submerged endurance capability . . . lower acoustic, bow wave, and wake signature in the water, and the resulting tactical flexibility coupled with lowered probability of detection and expanded operational capabilities').

73 Josh Smith, 'Imagery Shows N. Korea May Soon Launch New Missile Submarine: Think Tank', *Reuters*, 22 September 2022 <www.reuters.com/world/asia-pacific/imagery-shows-nkorea-may-soon-launch-new-missile-submarine-think-tank-2022-09-21/>; 'North Korea Unveils New Submarine-launched Missile', *BBC News*, 16 January 2021 <www.bbc.com/news/world-asia-55671745>; Choe Sang-Hun, 'North Korea Tests a Submarine-launched Missile', *New York Times*, 7 May 2022 <www.nytimes.com/2022/05/07/world/asia/north-korea-missile-submarine.html>.

nuclear weapons.[74] However, little is known about these submarines and the weapons they are suspected to carry, consistent with Israel's policy of deliberate ambiguity concerning nuclear weapons. These vessels are subject to the regime applicable to nuclear-powered submarines, which is outlined below, on account of the fact that they carry ultrahazardous material (and, where necessary, are referred to in this book as nuclear-armed submarines).

In sum, the persistent use of conventionally powered submarines and their acquisition by an increasingly diverse number of States demonstrates the ongoing relevance and use of submarines as warships. Conventionally powered submarines are exceptionally powerful naval weapons; 'classic "asymmetric" threats that could wreak havoc on a technically superior . . . naval force'.[75] The increasing use of AIP and further innovation in submarine propulsion technology, and a developing ability to carry more dangerous weaponry, indicate an ongoing focus on conventionally powered submarines. It is anticipated that these military submarines are likely to remain among the most numerous class of submarine into the future.

1.4.1.2 Nuclear Submarines

Described as the 'apex predator' of the maritime domain,[76] nuclear-powered submarines are exceptionally powerful and highly sought after. We use the term 'nuclear submarine' to refer to both nuclear-powered submarines and submarines carrying nuclear weapons. A submarine may be nuclear-powered but carry conventional weapons, and as mentioned above, conventionally powered submarines may be nuclear-armed. The key point for the purposes of our analysis is that these submarines carry ultrahazardous nuclear material. Where the

[74] Dan Williams, 'Exclusive: In the Belly of the Whale: Israeli Sub Simulates Strike', *Reuters*, 11 June 2021 <www.reuters.com/world/middle-east/exclusive-belly-whale-israeli-sub-simulates-strike-2021-06-10/>; James Martin Center for Nonproliferation Studies, 'Israel Submarine Capabilities', *Nuclear Threat Initiative*, 15 August 2024 <www.nti.org/analysis/articles/israel-submarine-capabilities/>; H. I. Sutton, 'Israel's Submarine Secret: New Dolphin-IIs Could Have VLS', *Naval News*, 19 January 2022 <www.navalnews.com/naval-news/2022/01/israels-submarine-secret-new-dolphin-class-boat-could-have-vls/>.

[75] Erwin (n 66) 58.

[76] See, e.g., Matthew Knott, 'All Set for the US to Sell Australia Three "Apex Predator" Submarines', *Sydney Morning Herald*, 8 December 2023 <www.smh.com.au/politics/federal/all-set-for-the-us-to-sell-australia-three-apex-predator-submarines-20231208-p5eq5m.html>.

distinction between a nuclear-powered submarine and a submarine carrying nuclear weapons is legally material, we will differentiate the two.

The military submarines within this category differ in significant respects as to their size, displacement and crew. The submarines in this class can be further separated into third-level categories based on their weaponry: attack submarines (SSN), ballistic missile-carrying (SSBN) and cruise missile-carrying (SSGN).[77] SSNs are much like conventionally powered attack submarines, save for their form of propulsion. Their purpose largely replicates that of conventionally powered attack submarines, but with the unique added benefits of longevity of submersion and increased speed and range arising from nuclear-powered propulsion.[78]

Both SSGNs and SSBNs are powerful, armed vehicles. As Lieber and Press note, cruise and ballistic missile 'submarines could fire their missiles from near the enemy's shore and so give the enemy's leaders almost no time to respond'.[79] Further, as Watson observes, these submarines provide 'a significant deterrent advantage over land-based missiles or aircraft systems because of [their] mobility and . . . ability to avoid detection in vast ocean patrol areas, thus remaining invulnerable to a surprise attack'.[80] The primary point of distinction between these two submarines is the type of weapon they launch. SSGNs are equipped with cruise missiles, which are propelled by jet engines, remain low in the atmosphere and are self-guided.[81] They are generally not nuclear-armed, and a number of US SSGNs were previously SSBNs but were converted to comply with international law concerning non-proliferation,[82] in particular the START II Treaty between the United

[77] These submarines are often referred to by their US Navy hull classification code, which has, broadly speaking, entered common parlance as a shorthand way of describing submarines.

[78] Hugh White, 'SSN vs SSK', *The Interpreter*, 29 September 2021 <www.lowyinstitute.org/the-interpreter/ssn-vs-ssk>.

[79] Keir A. Lieber and Daryl G. Press, 'The Rise of US Nuclear Primacy' (2006) 85(2) *Foreign Affairs* 42, 44.

[80] John M. Watson, 'The Strategic Missile Submarine Force and APL's Role in its Development' (1992) 13(1) *Johns Hopkins APL Technical Digest* 125.

[81] Ronald O'Rourke, 'Navy Virginia (SSN-774) Class Attack Submarine Procurement: Background and Issues for Congress' (Congressional Research Service Report RL42318, 26 August 2022).

[82] See generally Ronald O'Rourke, 'Navy Trident Submarine Conversion (SSGN) Program: Background and Issues for Congress' (Congressional Research Service Report RS21007, 2 October 2008).

States and the former USSR.[83] On the other hand, SSBNs are armed with ballistic missiles, which are rocket-powered when initially launched and then follow an unpowered trajectory, reaching greater heights than cruise missiles.[84] Contemporary examples include the US *Ohio*-class, the UK *Vanguard*-class, the French *Triomphant*-class and the Russian *Borei*-class. Unlike SSGNs and SSNs, the purpose of SSBNs is not to engage in sea denial or control per se, but rather to 'remain hidden at sea with their nuclear-armed submarine-launched ballistic missiles . . . perform[ing] a singular mission of strategic nuclear deterrence'.[85] As vehicles armed with nuclear weapons, they are subject to international law concerning nuclear non-proliferation. Each vessel in this class is also subject to the strict requirements of the nuclear non-proliferation regime in respect of nuclear power, including regulation by the International Atomic Energy Agency (IAEA).

The number of States currently operating nuclear-powered submarines is small; six States operate nuclear-powered submarines: China, France, Russia, the United Kingdom, the United States and India. The first five States are 'nuclear-weapon States Party' to the Treaty on the Non-Proliferation of Nuclear Weapons (NPT),[86] whereas India is not a party to the NPT but does possess nuclear weapons. As to the concentration of these submarines among the nuclear-weapon States party to the NPT, Moltz has observed, 'part of the reason for the race to the sea among new nuclear powers may be the international demonstration effect. The most advanced navies in the world (US, French, and British) now operate only nuclear-powered submarines, sending a potent signal to other states that nuclear power is better'.[87]

[83] Treaty between the United States of America and the Union of Soviet Socialist Republics on Further Reduction and Limitation of Strategic Offensive Arms (START II Treaty), Moscow, 3 January 1993, never entered into force. See further Chapter 6, Section 6.4.2.

[84] Center for Arms Control and Non-Proliferation, 'Fact Sheet: Ballistic vs Cruise Missiles', April 2017 <https://armscontrolcenter.org/wp-content/uploads/2017/04/Ballistic-vs.-Cruise-Missiles-Fact-Sheet.pdf>.

[85] Ronald O'Rourke, 'Navy Columbia (SSBN-286) Class Ballistic Missile Submarine Program: Background and Issues for Congress (Congressional Research Service Report R41129, 28 March 2025) 2. See also Charles D. Sykora, 'SSGN: A Transformation Limited by Legacy Command and Control' (2006) 59(1) *Naval War College Review* 42.

[86] Treaty on the Non-Proliferation of Nuclear Weapons, Washington, Moscow and London, 1 July 1968, entered into force 5 March 1970, 729 UNTS 161. These States are nuclear weapon States by virtue of Article IX of the Convention, which defines nuclear-weapon States as those that had 'manufactured and exploded a nuclear weapon or other nuclear explosive device prior to January 1967'.

[87] James Clay Moltz, 'Global Submarine Proliferation: Emerging Trends and Problems', 31 March 2006 <www.nti.org/analysis/articles/global-submarine-proliferation/>.

Von Hippel argues that there are two reasons that only a select few States operate nuclear submarines: cost and mission.[88] First, as to cost, not only are nuclear-powered submarines expensive to construct vis-à-vis conventionally powered submarines, but they are also dependent on costly domestic nuclear industries. Second, as to mission, nuclear submarines 'enhanc[e] a maritime power's blue-water and power-projection capabilities'[89] due to their ability to remain, in theory, submerged permanently. 'Blue-water capability' or a 'blue-water navy' refers to the operation of naval forces in the oceanic waters farthest from land, (i.e., beyond areas of national jurisdiction and into the high seas) such that the navy is 'oceangoing, capable of more than purely littoral operations'.[90] Not all States need or wish to have this mission capability.

To these factors, one may further add that the development of nuclear submarines is a legally fraught exercise. The provision of highly enriched uranium from a nuclear-weapon State party to the NPT to another State, or the generation of highly enriched uranium by an NPT State party, implicates the operation of international legal obligations under the NPT, requiring that State to seek approvals through the IAEA due to the nuclear proliferation risk involved.[91] As Yu and French note, 'many SSNs use highly enriched uranium . . ., which can be used to provide

88 Frank von Hippel, 'Mitigating the Threat of Nuclear-Weapon Proliferation via Nuclear-Submarine Programs' (2019) 3(1) *Journal for Peace and Nuclear Disarmament* 133, 139–141.

89 Jihoon Yu and Erik French, 'Should the United States Support a Republic of Korea Nuclear Submarine Program?' (2020) 73(1) *Naval War College Review* 84, 101. See also Gareth Jones, 'United Kingdom Submarine Nuclear Propulsion' (2021) 7(3) *British Journal for Military History* 101, 102 (observing that '[t]he nuclear-powered submarine enables [States] to project military power in ways not possible by conventional means').

90 Robert C. Rubel, 'Talking about Sea Control' (2010) 63(4) *Naval War College Review* 38, 44ff. See also, e.g., Nicholas D Kristof, 'The Rise of China' (1993) 72(5) *Foreign Affairs* 59, 66 (describing a 'blue-water navy' as one comprised of 'ocean-going vessels, rather than just coastal ships'); David Scott, 'China's Indo-Pacific Strategy: The Problems of Success' (2019) 6(2) *Journal of Territorial and Maritime Studies* 94, 103 (simply describing a 'blue-water navy' as one that 'operates on the oceans').

91 Australia entered into what is known as an Article XIV Agreement with the IAEA as part of its Comprehensive Safeguards Agreement. Australia sought to have the strictest safeguards in place so that any subsequent State that would similarly develop nuclear-powered submarines would be required to align with the standard set in Australia's agreement with the IAEA: IAEA Director General, 'Statement in Relation to the Agreement between Australia, the United Kingdom and the United States Related to Naval Nuclear Propulsion', *IAEA*, 15 August 2024 <www.iaea.org/newscenter/pressreleases/iaea-director-general-statement-in-relation-to-the-agreement-between-australia-the-united-kingdom-and-the-united-states-related-to-naval-nuclear-propulsion>.

the fissile material for a nuclear weapon'.[92] These implications, which have become apparent through the development of AUKUS,[93] are significant and further demonstrate how the law relating to submarines is necessarily entwined with and dependent on a number of other areas of international law, including nuclear non-proliferation law.

In addition to the States currently operating nuclear-powered submarines, there are several States that have ambitions, whether likely or not, to operate such vehicles. Australia and Brazil appear likely to operate SSNs in the medium term. In 2021 and 2025, Australia, the United Kingdom and the United States entered into agreements through which the latter two States agreed to provide Australia with the necessary designs and technical know-how to acquire and operate nuclear-powered submarines.[94] The States are presently cooperating with the IAEA with respect to the implications of the provision to Australia of highly enriched weapons-grade uranium on their obligations under international non-proliferation law, and the first submarine is expected to be launched in the 2030s.[95] For its part, Brazil has harboured ambitions of developing its own indigenous nuclear-powered submarines since the 1970s, with its Submarine Development Program (known as PROSUB) seeking to fulfil the State's goal of possessing a 'large submarine naval force, composed of both conventional and nuclear-powered submarines'.[96] These ambitions have been repeatedly beset by difficulties in the process of production and design, as well as in the enrichment of uranium to the necessary levels.[97] Neither Australia nor Brazil has the intention to arm

[92] Yu and French (n 89) 86–87.

[93] Australian Submarine Agency, 'AUKUS and Non-Proliferation' <www.asa.gov.au/sites/default/files/documents/2024-10/NonProliferation-Factsheet.pdf>.

[94] Agreement between the Government of Australia, the Government of the United Kingdom of Great Britain and Northern Ireland, and the Government of the United States of America for the Exchange of Naval Nuclear Propulsion Information, Canberra, 22 November 2021, entered into force 8 February 2022, [2022] ATS 4; Agreement among the Government of Australia, the Government of the United Kingdom of Great Britain and Northern Ireland, and the Government of the United States of America for Cooperation related to Naval Nuclear Propulsion, Washington, 5 August 2024, entered into force 17 January 2025, [2025] ATS 5 ('2024 AUKUS Agreement').

[95] See above n. 93.

[96] Israel de Oliveira Andrade, et al., *Brazilian Nuclear-Powered Submarine: National Defense and Technological Externalities* (IPEA Discussion Paper No. 232, October 2020) 7.

[97] Andrea de Sá, 'Brazil's Nuclear Submarine Program: A Historical Perspective' (2015) 22(1) *The Nonproliferation Review* 3; Antônio Ruy de Almeida Silva and José Augusto Abreu de Moura, 'The Brazilian Navy's Nuclear-powered Submarine Program' (2016) 23(5–6) *The Nonproliferation Review* 617 (see especially 622ff). On the Brazilian

their nuclear-powered submarines with nuclear weapons, though the possession by these States of what is likely to be weapons-grade uranium[98] has raised significant concern from the civil society sector and other States in relation to non-proliferation and the NPT.[99] As this book went to press, US President Trump approved South Korea's development of nuclear-powered submarines in US shipyards. Other States, including Canada and Iran have, at various times, expressed a desire to operate nuclear-powered submarines,[100] but those ambitions do not appear to be, at least at present, viable.

1.4.1.3 Coastal Submarines and Midget Submarines

Beyond conventionally powered and nuclear submarines, there are several other types of submarine operated by States that are entitled to sovereign immunity and are otherwise not subject to a different legal regime. Most notable are the two categories of 'small' or 'mini' submarine: midget submarines and coastal submarines. These submarines are not only the smallest in terms of displacement and size, but also in raw number and number of State users. Categorisation is difficult but some sources suggest that midget submarines are those submarines with

program generally, see de Oliveira Andrade et al. (n 96). The Brazilian Government expects its first nuclear-powered attack submarine, the *Álvaro Alberto*, to be completed in 2029 and commissioned in 2034: Government of Brazil, 'Brazil is Developing Nuclear-Powered Submarine', 24 June 2022 <www.gov.br/en/government-of-brazil/latest-news/2022/brazil-is-developing-nuclear-powered-submarine>. The submarine is based on the French *Scorpène*-class conventionally powered attack submarine through agreement between Brazil and France; notably that agreement does not extend to the nuclear power: Xavier Vavasseur, 'Brazil's Nuclear-Powered Submarine Project SN-BR Making Progress', *Naval News*, 6 December 2021 <www.navalnews.com/naval-news/2021/12/brazils-nuclear-powered-submarine-project-sn-br-making-progress/>.

[98] Though note that under the terms of the 2024 AUKUS Agreement (n 94) Australia is to be provided with 'welded Power Units', meaning that it will not possess weapons-grade uranium at the time at which it is enriched (and lacks an enrichment facility of its own): art. IV(B).

[99] See, e.g., ICAN Australia, *Troubled Waters: Nuclear Submarines, AUKUS and the NPT* (ICAN, July 2022). For legal considerations see Frank von Hippel, 'Mitigating the Threat of Nuclear-Weapon Proliferation via Nuclear-Submarine Programs' (2019) 3(1) *Journal for Peace and Nuclear Disarmament* 133, 133–136; Jeffrey Kaplow, 'The Canary in the Nuclear Submarine: Assessing the Nonproliferation Risk of the Naval Nuclear Propulsion Loophole' (2015) 22(2) *The Nonproliferation Review* 185.

[100] See von Hippel (n 99) 137–138; Eugenio Pacelli Lazzarotti Diniz Costa, 'Brazil's Nuclear Submarine: A Broader Approach to the Safeguards Issue' (2017) 60(2) *Revista Brasileira de Política Internacional* 1.

a displacement of under 100 tons,[101] while others suggest that 150 tons[102] or 250 tons is a more appropriate marker.[103] Other definitions focus on the number of crew as one of the defining features of the midget submarine, namely that they only carry one or two crew.[104] Such a definition becomes somewhat antiquated when one considers that contemporary midget submarines generally accommodate up to eight personnel.[105]

Though they are no longer as pervasive as they once were, midget submarines remain a versatile element of modern military operations.[106] North Korea continues to operate *Yugo*- and *Yono*- class midget submarines,[107] and Iran operates the *Ghadir*/*Qadir*-class submarine.[108] Pakistan,[109] Thailand[110] and India[111] are in the stages of developing their own indigenous midget submarines, while Indonesia is actively considering their acquisition.[112] Commentators have suggested that a new generation of midget submarines could be valuable in future conflicts in the South China Sea.[113]

For the purposes of this taxonomy, it suffices to say that midget submarines specialise in surprise attacks and reconnaissance missions, are small in size and with limited crew, and generally work with a parent ship or parent submarine such that they do not have the accommodations or technical capacity to undertake extended independent seafaring.

[101] B. Tyurin, 'Midget Submarines' (1983) 3 *Militaertechnik* 164.
[102] *Oxford English Dictionary* (online at April 2025) 'midget submarine'.
[103] IISS, 'Principal Naval Definitions' (2022) 122 *The Military Balance* 516, 516.
[104] *Oxford English Dictionary* (online at April 2025) 'midget submarine' (small submarine . . . often carrying a crew of only one or two, and used in surprise attacks [and] surveillance'); *Macquarie Dictionary* (online at April 2025) 'midget submarine' ('a small submersible, typically operated by one or two men, and supported by a mother ship or submarine, and sent on short expeditions to release torpedoes and mines . . . ').
[105] Eight for the *Yono*-class; seven for the *Ghadir* class; six for the *Yugo*-class.
[106] Thomas Withington, 'Revival of the Midget Submarine' (2010) 31(3) *Naval Forces* 32, 32.
[107] See generally 'North Korea – Navy', *Janes World Navies*, 17 April 2025.
[108] See, e.g., Jeremy Binnie, 'Iran Announces Launch of Two More Ghadir Midget Subs', *Janes Defence Weekly*, 30 November 2018.
[109] Prakash Panneerselvam, 'Pakistan's New Midget Submarine: Emerging Challenge to India in the Arabian Sea', *The Diplomat*, 29 April 2020 <https://thediplomat.com/2020/04/pakistans-new-midget-submarine-emerging-challenge-to-india-in-the-arabian-sea/>; Ridzwan Rahmat, 'Changing Tack: Pakistan Navy Transforms Amid Increasing Indian Ocean Rivalries', *Janes International Defence Review*, 25 August 2022.
[110] 'Thailand – Navy', *Janes World Navies*, 5 July 2024.
[111] Mrityunjoy Mazumdar, 'Building Up: India's Intensifying Effort to Construct Its Own Warships', *Janes Defence Weekly*, 4 August 2022.
[112] 'Indonesia – Navy', *Janes World Navies*, 23 April 2025.
[113] Giunio Santi, 'Has the Time Come for Midget Submarines?' (2022) 148(10) *USNI Proceedings* 1436.

Due to their size, they are conventionally powered.[114] It is important to define the midget submarine not just by reference to its size but instead by its purpose. Otherwise, the definition would encapsulate the large majority of commercially-operated submersibles, which are, generally speaking, as small in size as the modern military midget submarine. The term 'midget submarines' refers only to the State-owned and operated craft with military missions so as to capture the sovereign immunity to which these submarines are entitled.

'Coastal' submarines are generally larger than midget submarines but smaller than the deep ocean going military submarines.[115] They include the German-built *Type 209*, which is operated by a number of States particularly in South America and Asia; the concept *Andrasta*-class;[116] the Iranian *Fateh*-class,[117] which has the more limited purpose of operating in the littoral, shallow waters of the Persian Gulf;[118] and the North Korean *Sang-O*-class[119] and forthcoming *Sang-O II* class.[120] It has been suggested that the 'coastal submarine' term 'does not describe just any small submarine; it identifies a specific type of boat designed to operate in coastal shallows, follow the contours of the seabed, and slip into harbors covertly to deliver weapons or combat swimmers'.[121] As a matter of international law, the size of the coastal submarine vis-à-vis other military submarines is unlikely to be of consequence. As with 'midget' submarines, their status as sovereign immune vessels (due to being warships or otherwise State-owned and operated for non-commercial purposes) is the legally significant distinction.

[114] With the notable exception of the 400t (so not technically midget) NR-1, which was used for research and reconnaissance purposes. Russia is attempting to create nuclear-powered midget submarines under Project 09787: 'Russian Federation – Navy', *Janes World Navies*, 17 April 2025.

[115] IISS (n 103) 516.

[116] Ridzwan Rahmat, 'DSA 2014: DCNS Pushes Andrasta as Littoral Submarine for Southeast Asia', *Janes Navy International*, 17 April 2024.

[117] Jeremy Binnie, 'Iran Commissions Fateh Submarine', *Janes Defence Weekly*, 18 February 2019.

[118] Caleb Larson, 'What You Need to Know about Iran's Fateh Class Submarine', *National Interest*, 7 January 2022 <https://nationalinterest.org/blog/reboot/what-you-need-know-about-iran%E2%80%99s-fateh-class-submarine-198972>.

[119] IISS (n 103) 281; Thomas Withington, 'Revival of the Midget Submarine' (2010) 31(3) *Naval Forces* 32, 33.

[120] That is to say with its torpedoes removed: Joseph S Bermudez Jr and Karl Dewey, 'North Korea Modernises Submarine Fleet', *Janes Intelligence Review*, 9 February 2016.

[121] Santi (n 113).

1.4.2 Other Sovereign Immune Submarines

Submarines operated by a State for government and non-commercial purposes are entitled to immunity under Article 96 of UNCLOS. The types of submarines within this category include (but are not limited to) those used for government research purposes (such as for cartographic mapping and surveying); submarines operated by coastguards, domestic police forces, customs authorities and other government bodies; and training submarines. Some submarines may be entitled to immunity under Articles 95 and 96 because the operation of a submarine may serve both a militaristic purpose meeting the requirements of the warship definition and also have other purposes (particularly in relation to surveying and cartographic research, which submarines necessarily undertake as part of their process of navigation). The type of crewing of the vessel may be quite different; a 'warship' has uniformed, commissioned officers and crew whereas other government vessels have (or may include) civilian officers and crew. The essential point, however, is that these submarines must not be operated for commercial or mercantile purposes such as the exploitation of the natural resources of the continental shelf.

The most prominent form of submarine that would be covered by sovereign immunity as stipulated in Article 96 is the research submarine. Critical for the purposes of our taxonomy is whether these vessels are government-owned and operated for non-commercial purposes and the specific activities being undertaken. The regulation of research submarines is examined in connection with the rights and duties exercised by States in the EEZ in Chapter 8.

1.4.3 Underwater Maritime Autonomous Vehicles

The label of 'maritime autonomous vehicles' is a 'catch-all term for a variety of vehicles that operate on the surface of, below and above the ocean autonomously (with no human intervention) or varying levels of remote control'.[122] UMAVs may be launched not only from submarines,

[122] Natalie Klein, 'Maritime Autonomous Vehicles and International Laws on Boat Migration: Lessons from the Use of Drones in the Mediterranean' (2021) 127 *Marine Policy* 104447. See also the definition adopted by the US Department of Navy, *Unmanned Campaign Framework*, 16 March 2021, 7 ('"Unmanned" refers to the spectrum of autonomy from remote to autonomous can be platform, system or subsystem specific'). To this end, maritime autonomous vehicles remove human operators from situations 'that pose a high risk of injury, death, or capture of onboard human operators – so-called "three

but also from surface vessels, as well as from land installations and bases on the coast. UMAVs may be tethered to a vessel or operate separately; the key feature of legal relevance is the lack of a master and crew on board the UMAV.

The international legal regime applicable to UMAVs is impacted by two key factors. First, to the extent the UMAV is a *vessel* (as opposed to equipment or a maritime autonomous system) operated by a State for militaristic or other non-commercial purposes, it is likely to be entitled to the immunities afforded under either Article 95 or Article 96 of UNCLOS. However, there is a live question as to whether any UMAV is a 'vessel' or 'ship' or not. This question is an important one as different international law rights and obligations accrue depending on this characterisation. Second, whether a UMAV can be classified as a 'warship' or not in light of the definition under Article 29 of UNCLOS, which assumes a commanding officer and crew aboard the vessel, has been questioned. We examine these debates in Chapter 14.

1.4.4 Submarines Not Entitled to Sovereign Immunity

While submarines used for military purposes are undoubtedly the most prominent type of submarine, there are a significant number of submarines in non-military service, operated both by States (including through their militaries) and by non-State actors for varied, non-governmental, purposes. These submarines are not entitled to sovereign immunity. As will be discussed in later chapters, there was some anticipation of private or commercial use of submarines and allowance was made for this in early law. However, such sustained commercial use has not yet eventuated.

These submarines remain the concern of international law, even if they are not sovereign immune vessels, and can be further divided by their purpose. Without attempting to create an exhaustive list, these subcategories include narco-submarines and other submarines used for criminal purposes, research submarines, tourist submarines and other submarines owned by high net-worth individuals for leisure purposes. UMAVs that are privately owned or operated for non-governmental purposes also fall within this branch of the taxonomy.

D" missions, meaning missions that are dull, dirty or dangerous': Ronald O'Rourke, 'Navy Large Unmanned Surface and Undersea Vehicles: Background and Issues for Congress' (CRS Report No R45757, 18 October 2022) 1–2.

1.4.4.1 Narco-Submarines

Submarines used for the transport of drugs are commonly referred to as narco-submarines and are examined in Chapter 13. These non-government submarines have been and continue to be used by criminal groups and sub-State actors for the transportation of drugs,[123] causing 'considerable alarm'.[124] Early (possibly the first) narco-submarines were designed and constructed by the Revolutionary Armed Forces of Colombia (FARC) in the 1990s with the purpose of transporting cocaine to the United States.[125] These initial narco-submarines were constructed out of fibreglass and wood; today, narco-submarines can be fully submergible and self-propelled with diesel engines. As Olson and others observe:

> The use of what are essentially mini-submarines is a relatively new phenomenon dating to the late 1990s when a clandestine factory for the first subs was discovered in rural Colombia. Today's semi-submersibles are 45 to 82 feet in length and are made of fiberglass or steel. They have a range of 2,000 miles and can carry up to seven metric tons of cocaine. US officials estimate that over 60 submarines move over 300 metric tons of cocaine per year. Most of the subs leave Colombia's and Ecuador's Pacific Coastlines.[126]

[123] Jafar Javan and Almut Wieland-Karimi, 'Foreword' in United Nations System Staff College (ed.), *Understanding a New Generation of Non-State Armed Groups* (UNSSC, 2015) 7.

[124] United Nations Office on Drugs and Crime, *Transnational Organized Crime in Central America and the Caribbean: A Threat Assessment* (UNODC, September 2012) 32.

[125] See, e.g., Michelle Jacome Jaramillo, 'The Revolutionary Armed Forces of Colombia (FARC) and the Development of Narco-Submarines' (2016) 9(1) *Journal of Strategic Security* 49, 49; Victor Asal and Justin V. Hastings, 'When Terrorism Goes to Sea: Terrorist Organizations and the Move to Maritime Targets' (2015) 27(4) *Terrorism and Political Violence* 722, 735 (noting that '[d]rug traffickers have developed maritime capabilities that can take advantage of sea routes, such as the submarines that ply the waters from the western coast of South America up into Central America, several of which were reportedly built by the Revolutionary Armed Forces of Colombia and seized in September 2011'); Rob McLaughlin and Natalie Klein, 'Maritime Autonomous Vehicles and Drug Trafficking by Sea: Some Legal Issues' (2021) 36 *The International Journal of Marine and Coastal Law* 389, 392–393. For a US perspective, see Brian Wilson, 'Submersibles and Transnational Criminal Organizations' (2011) 17(1) *Ocean and Coastal Law Journal* 35.

[126] Eric L. Olson, David A. Shirk and Andrew Selee, *Shared Responsibility: US-Mexico Policy Options for Confronting Organized Crime* (Woodrow Wilson International Center for Scholars, October 2010) 80. See also Daniel Rojas-Sanchez, Samuel Rivera-Paez and German Afanador, 'Submersibles and Drug Trafficking' in Edward R. Lucas et al., *Maritime Security: Counter-Terrorism Lessons from Maritime Piracy and Narcotics Interdiction* (IOS Press, 2020) 47, 51 (observing that '[t]he Colombian-made submersibles are between 14 and 24 meters long, are usually crewed by four, and can transport up

These submarines have been used to considerable success; the US Drug Enforcement Administration has estimated that 30 per cent of drugs imported to the United States by sea are transported by narco-submarines originating from South and Central America.[127] Such submarines have also been used for smuggling operations into Europe and West Africa.[128]

There is no consistent definition of narco-submarines as they are defined not by their size or by their characteristics, but rather by their purpose. They may, though, be distinguished as self-propelled semi-submersibles (SPSS) and low-profile vehicles (LPVs), and fully submersible vehicles.[129] The former are 'designed to escape detection by riding low in the water. They do not fully submerge'.[130] Only an estimated 14 per cent of such vessels are detected,[131] and, in the event of detection, the vehicles are often intentionally scuttled leaving the detecting navy or coast guard to rescue the smugglers while the evidence sinks to the seabed. Due to their inability to fully submerge, the extent to which such vehicles may qualify as a submarine in international law may be contested.

Rarer are the narco-submarines capable of full submersion. Over time, narco-submarines have become increasingly sophisticated both in terms of their design and the technologies carried on board.[132] Plans for the use of fully submersible vessels for smuggling purposes are not new; Colombian cartels reportedly attempted to purchase submarines from

to 20 tons of cocaine. In most cases, submersibles protrude only a few centimetres above the surface of the water').

127 Rear Admiral Charles Michel, 'Hearing on Border Security Threats to the Homeland: DHS's Response to Innovative Tactics and Technique' (Written Statement before the Subcommittee on Border and Maritime Security House Committee on Homeland Security, US House of Representatives, 19 June 2012) 3 <https://homeland.house.gov/files/Testimony-Michel.pdf>.

128 Carsten Weerth, 'Cocaine Smuggling by Help of Narco-Submarines from South America to Africa and Europe: A Call for A Higher Awareness of an Existing Smuggling Pathway'(2020) 2 *Customs Scientific Journal* 33, 42.

129 Jacome Jaramillo (n 125) 50 fn 6 (noting that '[t]he term narco-submarines is commonly used to describe all types of vessels (low profile vessels, self-propelled semi-submersibles and fully submersibles)').

130 See H. I. Sutton, 'Narco Subs 101', *Covert Shores*, 29 March 2020 <www.hisutton.com/Narco%20Subs%20101.html>.

131 David Kushner, 'Drug-Sub Culture', *New York Times Magazine*, 23 April 2009 <www.nytimes.com/2009/04/26/magazine/26drugs-t.html>.

132 Jacome Jaramillo (n 125) 55. See also <www.geopoliticalmonitor.com/the-criminal-and-terrorist-threat-of-narco-submarine-technology/>.

the Soviet Union but were rebuffed.[133] Since that time, cartels have developed submarines of their own. The first known such vehicle was seized by Ecuadorian authorities in July 2010; it has been described as the 'true narco sub'.[134] An additional submarine was discovered near the Cucurrupi River in Colombia in 2020,[135] and, for the first time in 2022, a fully submersible narco-submarine was interdicted at sea (as opposed to during the process of construction) sailing on the Arauca River between Colombia and Venezuela.[136] In sum, these submarines are technically advanced and do not enjoy any sovereign immunity from seizure or prosecution because of their non-governmental status. Their international legal regulation falls within transnational criminal law, as well as potentially being subject to national laws seeking to prevent and deter illicit drug trafficking.

1.4.4.2 Submarines Operated by Rebels and Terrorist Groups

The development of submarines by cartels for drug smuggling purposes has led to commentary as to the potential possession of submarines by rebels and terrorist groups for other nefarious purposes, apart from drug smuggling. Stanislawski has observed, 'the discovery of a partially constructed Russian submarine by the Colombian police in 2000 . . . demonstrates the possibility for a terrorist organisation to acquire such a weapons platform to use in an attack'.[137] The 2005 Convention for the Suppression of Unlawful Acts against the Safety of Maritime Navigation (2005 SUA Convention) addresses 'a vessel of any type whatsoever not permanently attached to the sea-bed, including . . ., submersibles' and may thus include a submarine in its definition of 'vessel'.[138] This treaty identifies a range of

[133] Kushner (n 131).

[134] Nicholas B. Dial, 'At the Territorial Limit: Is the United States' Extraterritorial Response to Smuggling Submersibles on the High Seas Legitimate' (2013) 22 *Transnational Law and Contemporary Problems* 693, 697.

[135] H. I. Sutton, 'Rare Electric Narco Submarine Seized in Colombia', *USNI News*, 16 November 2020 <https://news.usni.org/2020/11/16/rare-electric-narco-submarine-seized-in-colombia>.

[136] H. I. Sutton, 'First Time Rare Fully-Submersible Narco Submarine Caught', *Covert Shores*, 2 May 2022 <www.hisutton.com/Fully-Submersible-Narco-Submarine-Apr-2022.html>. See further Chapter 14.

[137] Bartosz H. Stanislawski, 'Transnational Organized Crime, Terrorism and WMD' (2005) 7 *International Studies Review* 158, 159.

[138] The 2005 Convention for the Suppression of Unlawful Acts against the Safety of Maritime Navigation combines a 1998 Treaty and a 2005 Protocol (together, the '2005 SUA Convention'): Convention for the Suppression of Unlawful Acts against the Safety of Maritime Navigation, Rome, 10 March 1988, entered into force 1 March 1992, 1678

States operated a number of submersibles, most notably the *Alvin* and the *Deepsea Challenger*, in addition to UMAVS, which, with the assistance of a support ship, can dive to the deepest depths of the ocean. The People's Liberation Army Navy and various Chinese research institutes and universities operate submersibles.[150] The legal regulation of these submarines will depend on the nature and location of their activities.[151]

It has been suggested that government funding for oceanic research has been reduced in recent years; consequently '[i]nnovative creativity has emerged from private organizations, large and small, the most visible being wealthy patrons excited by the potential of ocean exploration and new deep sea research ... These efforts will expand and mature ... as various private/government partnership formulas are considered'.[152] The application of the law of the sea and its rules relating to marine scientific research will be the most apt for the regulation of these submarines. These activities are examined in Chapter 8.

1.4.4.4 Leisure Submarines

Since at least the 1980s, hobbyists and private researchers have constructed submersibles – highly diverse in nature – with the intention of satisfying curiosity, collecting data and exploring the oceans.[153] Advances in technology have made the production of submersibles for use by tourists and independent explorers, usually those of ultra-high net worth, more feasible. Separating these vehicles into their own category, independent from those vehicles used for research purposes, may be problematic as often their purposes are, at least to some extent, similar and intertwined. For instance, submersibles operated by individuals and organisations for private tourism and exploration purposes have resulted in public scientific discovery.[154] Indeed, is difficult to separate out the full

[150] Weicheng Cui, 'An Overview of Submersible Research and Development in China' (2018) 17 *Journal of Marine Science and Application* 459.

[151] See further Chapter 8, Section 8.3.2.

[152] William Kohnen, 'Review of Deep Ocean Manned Submersible Activity in 2013' (2013) 47(5) *Marine Technology Society Journal* 56, 56.

[153] Jennifer Saranow, 'For Sub Hobbyists, Smugglers' Craft Is Merely Subpar: A Drug Bust near Costa Rica Captivates Underworld of Garage Tinkerers', *The Wall Street Journal*, 30 November 2006, A1; William J Broad, 'Bubble Subs Arise, Opening Eyes to the Deep Sea', *New York Times*, 18 November 2019.

[154] For instance, the first footage of a giant squid was captured on a submersible owned by a mega wealthy American: William J Broad, 'Giant Squids Ready for Small-Screen Debut', *New York Times*, 14 January 2013 <www.nytimes.com/2013/01/15/science/elusive-giant-squids-are-set-to-make-small-screen-debut.html>. James Cameron's private trip to Challenger Deep resulted in the discovery of new deep sea life, including a new sea

range of private purposes from research purposes as the act of submersion can, in itself, contribute to research.[155] In addition, submarines otherwise in private use have been chartered for research purposes, including by States and State-affiliated institutions.[156] Government engagement may complicate any determination of whether the submarine is entitled to the sovereign immunity of the State.[157] In addition, the multiple purposes served by these vehicles may impact the jurisdiction of the coastal State in respect of the regulation of these submarines. While tourist journeys likely fall within the freedom of navigation, coastal States have the exclusive authority to conduct and regulate the conduct of marine scientific research within their EEZ.[158] The allocation of State authority over these different submarine activities in the EEZ is addressed in Chapter 8. International laws pertaining to navigational safety may also be apposite for leisure submarines and are discussed in Chapter 11.

The publicly available information concerning these submersibles is relatively scarce. Unlike submarines operated by States, there is comparatively less public exposure as to the specifications, ownership and operation of these private submersibles. Nearly all submarines within this class are made-to-order and are procured from private manufacturers, often with little governmental oversight or registration requirements due to the relative novelty of the private operation of submersibles; there is no reliable method to track the number of submersibles that may be in private operation. Kohnen estimates that, as at July 2020, seventy-eight crewed underwater vehicles had been constructed and thirty-eight were in operation, of which the majority were privately owned.[159] Another estimate, calculated in 2013, suggested there were ninety-six active submersibles, which included 'all submersibles involved in tourism,

cucumber and squid worm and single-celled amoebas: Jane J. Lee, 'Scientific Results from Challenger Deep', *National Geographic*, 6 December 2012 <www.nationalgeographic.com/travel/article/121204-challengerdeep-trenches-ocean-science>.

155 'Triton Submarines Reaches Milestone', *Florida Trend*, 25 October 2019 <www.floridatrend.com/article/28132/triton-submarines-reaches-milestone>.

156 See, e.g., Donald W. Stratsburg, Everet C. Jones and Robert T. B. Iversen, 'Use of a Small Submarine for Biological and Oceanographic Research' (1968) 31(3) *ICES Journal of Marine Science* 410.

157 Though if the submarine is privately owned, rather than State owned, the submarine may fall outside the scope of Article 96 of UNCLOS.

158 UNCLOS (n 20) art. 56(1)(b)(ii).

159 William Kohnen, 'Global Submersible MUV Database – 2020', 20 July 2020 <www.tinyurl.com/muvdatabase2020>.

research, commercial work, security, and leisure'.[160] A 2022 report observed that well-established Dutch recreational submersible manufacturer, U-Boat Worx, had sold forty submersibles with an additional fifteen on order, with a cost of US$2.5 million to US$3.5 million.[161] The capable depth of these submersibles ranges from just below the ocean's surface to the Challenger Deep.[162] There are substantial differences in the number of crew they are able to accommodate, their technical capacity, design and endurance.

1.4.4.5 Underwater Maritime Autonomous Vehicles

Non-State actors have begun using UMAVs for smuggling purposes and these underwater craft may further be deployed to support transnational criminal activity or terrorism.[163] Further, remotely operated UMAVs (ROVs) are used extensively by offshore oil, gas and renewables industries 'for observation, control and maintenance of infrastructure in locations otherwise unavailable to marine scientists';[164] often industry assists the academy by providing data obtained from its more extensive collection of UMAVs for use in scientific research.[165] As at 2014, the International Marine Contractors Association estimated that there were some 550 work class ROVs in operation in industry.[166] These UMAVs for private research would not be protected by sovereign immunity and hence UMAVs fall under both limbs of our legal taxonomy set out above in Figure 1.1.

1.5 International Laws Regulating Submarines

In this chapter, we have so far highlighted the diversity in the types of submarines in contemporary use; their purposes, functions, owners and *modus operandi*. In devising the legal taxonomy above, we come to a better understanding of how defining the submarine is a relatively vexed topic, and how changes in one element of the submarine (e.g., its

160 Kohnen (n 152) 57. Note that not all of these submarines are privately owned.

161 Kevin Koenig, 'A Personal Submarine for Every Orthodontist', *New York Times*, 22 August 2022 <www.nytimes.com/2022/08/22/style/submarines-affordable.html>.

162 The Challenger Deep, located in the Mariana Trench, is the deepest known seabed of the oceans.

163 Klein et al., 'Maritime Autonomous Vehicles: New Frontiers in the Law of the Sea' (n 40) 720. See also McLaughlin and Klein (n 125).

164 Dianne L. McLean et al., 'Enhancing the Scientific Value of Industry Remotely Operated Vehicles (ROVs) in Our Oceans' (2020) 7(220) *Frontiers in Marine Science* 1, 1–2.

165 Ibid, 2.

166 Ibid.

owner, mode of propulsion, purpose) can implicate the operation of distinct, and not always complementary, legal regimes, with different consequences and obligations. Yet there are situations when the relevant international law is decidedly unclear. Accordingly, both submarines and the legal regime governing their operation are of significant contemporary relevance and are a topic worthy of sustained academic study. This section briefly introduces the different international legal regimes that may be applicable to submarines, and which are discussed in greater detail in later chapters.

1.5.1 *International Legal Framework for Submarines*

As noted at the outset, the key starting point for discussing submarines in international law is UNCLOS, which has 171 parties and is often described as a 'constitution for the oceans'.[167] This treaty, which was opened for signature on 10 December 1982, establishes a comprehensive legal regime for the use of the ocean, inclusive of the water column, the suprajacent airspace and the seabed and subsoil. Its provisions regulate the activities of vessels in ocean spaces and are applicable to, inter alia, vessels operated by States Parties, as well as commercial vessels flagged to those States. Among other things, UNCLOS sets out the regimes applicable to the maritime zones of the coastal State, including the continental shelf and EEZ, and the rights and obligations of States therein,[168] the rights of passage of vessels through the territorial sea, archipelagic waters and straits used for international navigation,[169] the immunities of warships and ships on government service,[170] the freedom of the high seas and the qualifications thereto,[171] obligations to protect and preserve the marine environment,[172] how marine scientific research is to be conducted[173]

[167] See Elisabeth Mann Borgese, 'A Constitution for the Oceans' in Elisabeth Mann Borgese and David Krieger (eds.), *The Tides of Change: Peace, Pollution and the Potential of the Oceans* (Mason/Charter, 1975) 340. See also Alan Boyle, 'Further Development of the Law of the Sea Convention: Mechanisms for Change' (2005) 54(3) *International and Comparative Law Quarterly* 563, 566.

[168] UNCLOS (n 20) pts. II (territorial sea and contiguous zone), IV (archipelagic States), V (exclusive economic zone), VI (continental shelf).

[169] See, e.g., ibid, arts. 17–26, 32–45.

[170] Ibid, arts. 29–32.

[171] Ibid, pt. VII.

[172] Ibid, pt. XII.

[173] Ibid, pt. XIII.

and establishes a compulsory dispute settlement system.[174] Core constitutional aspects of UNCLOS, such as the establishment of the different maritime zones and the allocation of rights and duties within those zones, are accepted as customary international law.[175] Out of its 320 provisions and nine Annexes, only one article refers explicitly to submarines.[176] Nonetheless, UNCLOS provides the general framework for the regulation of submarines and is the most important piece of international law governing their use and activities.

In addition to UNCLOS, a range of other international laws regulate maritime activities and potentially apply to the use of submarines. Key international instruments related to navigational safety include the Convention on the International Regulations for Preventing Collisions at Sea (COLREGs),[177] and the International Convention for the Safety of Life at Sea (SOLAS Convention).[178] The safety of navigation, especially in the context of nuclear submarines, also prompts consideration of international nuclear law, including the NPT and other instruments of the international legal regime relating to nuclear disarmament as well as nuclear liability. If submarines do sink then regard may be had to international instruments relating to shipwrecks, such as the Nairobi International Convention on the Removal of Wrecks,[179] as well as those relating to the preservation of underwater cultural heritage, such as the Convention on the Protection of Underwater Cultural Heritage.[180] Further of interest in the regulation of submarines are rules seeking to protect the marine environment and are drawn from international environmental law.[181]

The roles of military submarines during times of peace as well as during armed conflicts require consideration of international instruments relating to the law on the use of force and international

[174] Ibid, pt. XV.

[175] See, e.g., *Alleged Violations of Sovereign Rights and Maritime Spaces in the Caribbean Sea* (Nicaragua v. Colombia) (Judgment of 21 April 2022) [2022] ICJ Rep 226, paras. 56 and 57.

[176] UNCLOS (n 20) art. 20.

[177] Convention on the International Regulations for Preventing Collisions at Sea, London, 20 October 1972, entered into force 15 July 1977, 1050 UNTS 16.

[178] International Convention for the Safety of Life at Sea, London, 1 November 1974, entered into force 25 May 1980, 1184 UNTS 1.

[179] Nairobi Convention on the Removal of Wrecks, Nairobi, 18 May 2007, entered into force 14 April 2015, 3283 UNTS 34.

[180] Convention on the Protection of the Underwater Cultural Heritage, Paris, 2 November 2001, entered into force 2 January 2009, 2562 UNTS 3.

[181] See Chapter 12, Section 12.2.

humanitarian law, such as the London Protocol on Submarine Warfare,[182] the Geneva Conventions[183] and the Hague Conventions of 1899 and 1907,[184] and manuals addressing the law of naval warfare.[185] For submarines implicated in criminal activity, we can have regard to instruments such as the 2005 SUA Convention;[186] and the 1988 Vienna Drugs Convention.[187] Other than formal international instruments, the use of submarines implicates different rules of customary international law. These laws include, for instance, rules on State responsibility, jurisdiction and sovereign immunities.

From this discussion, it becomes readily apparent that the use of submarines is regulated by a wide variety of different international laws. Yet these laws are most typically silent as to the exact roles, responsibilities and obligations attaching to the use of submarines. Determining what instruments are applicable, and which to obey and in what circumstances, is not always evident. As set out earlier in this chapter, a primary purpose of this book to draw together these disparate and sometimes ambiguous international legal regimes to clarify the international law applicable to submarines or otherwise identify what gaps in the law may need to be resolved.

1.5.2 Outline of the Book and Scope

This book is divided in two parts. In the first Part, we take a historico-legal approach to the study of submarines, highlighting the relevance of legal history to the development and current understandings of the modern legal regime. Understanding the historical context of our contemporary laws provides us with an opportunity to assess how we

[182] Procès-Verbal relating to the Rules of Submarine Warfare set forth in Part IV of the Treaty for the Limitation and Reduction of Naval Armament of 22 April 1930, London, 6 November 1936, entered into force 6 November 1936, 173 LNTS 353, [1936] ATS 14.

[183] See, e.g., Geneva Convention (II) for the Amelioration of the Condition of Wounded, Sick and Shipwrecked Members of Armed Forces at Sea, Geneva, 12 August 1949, 21 October 1950, 75 UNTS 85.

[184] See Natalino Ronzitti (ed.), *The Law of Naval Warfare: A Collection of Agreements and Documents with Commentaries* (Martinus Nijhoff, 1988).

[185] See Chapter 10, Section 10.2.1.

[186] 2005 SUA Convention (n 138).

[187] United Nations Convention against Illicit Traffic in Narcotic Drugs and Psychotropic Substances, Vienna, 20 December 1988, entered into force 11 November 1990, 1582 UNTS 95.

might move forward.[188] Materna, for example, has relied on approaches to the early regulation of submarines as a rationale for allowing legal change in defining warships with the development of maritime autonomous vehicles.[189] Moreover, the historical lens facilitates 'reflection as to the origins, aims and objectives of international law' of submarines,[190] enabling a better understanding of how to read contemporary laws that commonly fail to explicitly acknowledge submarines as an object of regulation. Our approach is thus not only to narrate the historical evolution of international law as it relates to submarines, but also to set out the legal outputs of these developments.[191] The focus of Part I is on international law concerning submarines and its sources, but inevitably the political, technological, cultural and strategic dimensions inform the legal positions and developments. We are by no means comprehensive in engaging with these differing contexts but seek to acknowledge in Part I that the legal developments must be situated within broader societal dynamics existing at various times. Consistent with the overarching aim of the book, we are endeavouring to highlight what international law has said, implicitly or explicitly, about the regulation of submarines.

Considering the role and development of submarines since WWI to the present day, we investigate in Part I how submarine developments contributed to the development of international laws regulating their maritime operations. Chapter 2 examines the role of submarines in WWI and the individual and collective efforts of States to ban, limit, or regulate their use, and the extent to which early international legal instruments relating to neutrality and maritime warfare regulated the new technologies and strategies of submarines adequately or at all. Chapter 3 traces developments relating to the legal regulation of submarines from the post-war settlement at Versailles to the Codification Conference at the Hague in 1930. While the Conference failed to adopt a treaty on the territorial sea, it did produce a set of draft articles that would significantly influence the subsequent

[188] Matthew Craven, 'Introduction: International Law and Its Histories', in Matthew Craven, Malgosia Fitzmaurice and Maria Vogiatzi (eds.), *Time, History and International Law* (Brill, 2007) 1, 5; Valentina Vadi, 'International Law and Its Histories: Methodological Risks and Opportunities' (2017) 58(2) *Harvard International Law Journal* 311, 320.

[189] See generally Malgorzata Materna, 'Adjusting the Aperture: The International Law Case for Unmanned Vessels Qualifying as Warships' (2023) 100 *International Law Studies* 452.

[190] Vadi (n 188) 317.

[191] Ibid, 318.

development of both the 1958 treaties on the law of the sea,[192] and, by way of these instruments, UNCLOS. Chapter 4 examines developments in the use and regulation of submarines during the second Sino-Japanese War and WWII, considering how States understood and sought to respond to developments in the use of submarines – as blockade runners, intelligence gatherers and as the subject of anti-submarine warfare – both in their practice and through the law at this time. Chapter 5 examines the post–WWII settlements, the 1958 conventions on the law of the sea and the Cold War nuclear deterrence era. During this period, nuclear submarines were developed and made operational, the acquisition and technical development of submarines increased rapidly and the modern submarine as we now know it came into existence. This chapter traces the influence of all these developments on the 1958 law of the sea conventions. Chapter 6 concludes Part I, situating the negotiation of UNCLOS in historical context. It considers how the contemporary usages of submarines factored into the development of international law concerning the passage of warships, intelligence gathering and nuclear proliferation. Part I concludes by linking the historical discussion to the contemporary setting that introduced the book, situating the reader for the analysis of current international law in relation to submarines that follows in Part II.

With an awareness of the historical development of the international law of submarines and the role of submarines in developing international law, Part II focuses in on submarines in modern international law. In this Part, we clarify the legal regime presently applying to submarines and further consider how the diverse usages, operators and *modus operandi* of submarines are impacted by different international laws. Chapter 7 examines the laws applying to the passage of submarines in the territorial sea, international straits and archipelagic waters. Chapter 8 considers the international laws governing activities of submarines in the EEZ, clarifying the scope of navigational rights in this maritime zone, particularly in relation to military exercises and intelligence gathering. Chapter 9 is concerned with determining when submarine operations may violate the international law prohibition on the threat or use of force and what consequences may emerge in relation to the law on the use of force (*jus ad bellum*). Chapter 10 addresses the current international laws governing submarine warfare, focusing on the modern law of neutrality and

[192] See Convention on the High Seas (n 29); Convention on the Continental Shelf, Geneva, 29 April 1958, entered into force 10 June 1964, 199 UNTS 311; Convention on the Territorial Sea and Contiguous Zone, Geneva, 29 April 1958, entered into force 10 September 1964, 516 UNTS 205.

relevant rules of international humanitarian law. Chapter 11 draws out the relevant international laws that may be applicable in light of accidents or collisions involving submarines, including the law of salvage and underwater cultural heritage law that may apply in relation to sunken submarines. Chapter 12 assesses how international environmental law applies in relation to submarines, most particularly with regards to implications arising from the deployment of nuclear submarines and questions concerning noise pollution. Chapter 13 considers the use of submersibles and submarines by private actors to perpetrate different crimes, predominantly smuggling offences. 'Narco-submarines' are a particular focus of this Chapter. Chapter 14 addresses the legal implications of UMAVs, focusing on the legal differences that emerge when a craft operates underwater and is uncrewed. As Chapter 14 examines the international laws concerned with the most recent submarine technology, this chapter also concludes Part II by taking stock of future directions for the international law of submarines. The book thus ends with issues for decision-makers to consider in the future, including in relation to adjustments to national operational rules and changes to State practice, and potential amendments or additions needed in international law.

This book does not focus on the strategic significance of submarines, although their role is critical in international relations more broadly and more specifically in security strategies,[193] and nuclear deterrence.[194] Instead, we are foremost concerned with the elucidation of the international laws that apply to submarine operations. The military importance of submarines has no doubt influenced the way that different laws have developed, as is especially apparent in our discussion in Part I, and the strategic significance of submarines colours the policy choices that may be needed in deciding on the interpretation and application of international law. That significance should not, however, exclude submarines from explicit regulation under international law.

Given the strategic significance and predominant military character of submarines, State efforts to counter submarines through anti-submarine warfare and in enhancing ocean transparency are also notable developments in ocean governance. We have occasionally referred to the impact of anti-submarine warfare (ASW) on international law, and it is clear that developments in ASW will also hold implications for international law

193 See, e.g., Michael D. Wallace and Charles A. Meconis, 'Submarine Proliferation and Regional Conflict' (1995) 32(1) *Journal of Peace Research* 79.

194 On their role in nuclear deterrence, see, e.g., James R. Holmes, 'Sea Changes: The Future of Nuclear Deterrence' (2016) 72(4) *Bulletin of the Atomic Scientists* 228–233.

regimes. For example, States foresee deploying 'subullites' across the ocean floor, which will then provide monitoring of vessels, including other submarines, passing above.[195] That prompts questions as to what the deployment of these subullites would mean for the regime of the continental shelf or the deep seabed, exclusive coastal State jurisdiction over artificial structures and installations in the EEZ, and for the protection of the marine environment. ASW tactics during armed conflict will also be governed by international humanitarian law. Nonetheless, to contain the book within a manageable scope, we have largely placed ASW beyond our consideration of the international law of submarines.

1.5.3 *Aims of the Book*

As noted above, a central purpose of this book is to bring together all the international law rules that apply to the operation of different types of submarines. In doing so, we are dealing with an object that by its nature seeks to avoid detection. The very secrecy of submarines, because of their submerged operations, not only increases their military utility but also the perceived threat that they may pose in different settings. Yet law generally is interested in detecting problems, elucidating the issues and regulating to reduce perceived risks. Like the submarines themselves, the international law of submarines is submerged across a broad field of international law and it is therefore necessary to look below the surface to elicit the relevant rules. The chapters in Part II especially seek to articulate what laws currently apply to submarines, as well as show where there are areas of disagreement and where it may be legally problematic that there is not more attention applied to the specific situation of submarines.

While we have thus sought to bring to light specific areas of international law pertaining to submarine operations (such as international humanitarian law or the law of the sea), there are some rules of international law that cut across all these areas. Notably, and as discussed in an early section in this chapter, rules concerning sovereign immunity hold consequences for how some rules are applied and certainly for how they may (or may not be) enforced. Equally, the characterisation of some submarines as 'nuclear submarines', because they are nuclear-powered or armed with nuclear weapons, cuts across a number of different legal regimes. There are consequences for nuclear disarmament and

[195] Ibid, 230.

proliferation, as well as for nuclear safeguards and liability regimes. We have addressed these dimensions across different chapters rather than in one chapter. While we have sought to show in various instances that there are specific rules applicable to nuclear submarines, it remains important to grasp that this source of power or weaponry does not preclude the ongoing application of other (non-nuclear) rules of international law.

The predominant function of the submarine as a military machine as well as its role in geopolitical strategy have undoubtedly facilitated the obfuscation of international laws addressing submarines. As one of the authors has previously commented, '[a] hallmark of the law of the sea has been the preference to treat security concerns implicitly rather than explicitly'.[196] Yet there should be a valid position that international law is better served when there is an explicit articulation of rules, and greater stability and accountability are achieved when there is a clear and shared understanding of what rights and responsibilities exist in any given scenario. A more precise account of submarines in international law should thereby promote greater transparency in inter-State relations as well as enhance peaceful coexistence. Kraska has acknowledged in relation to the legal regime governing military operations that 'some of the concepts and provisions in the regime are aging; others are rather opaque'.[197] He continues: 'Uncertainty in the regime and inconsistency in its application push the door ajar to disagreement and heightened tension'.[198] So much holds true in relation to submarines in particular.

Without a more singular focus on submarines in international law, the international legal system perpetuates so-called grey-zone tactics and fosters international disputes through both deliberate ambiguity and legal avoidance. Our book is intended as a clarion call to fix the legal ambiguities, fill gaps in the law and better articulate what international laws apply in the operations of submarines. There is an undoubted place for a precise articulation of rules, and it is then the policy decision as to whether those rules will be followed or not, or whether actions to change or develop the law should otherwise be pursued.

[196] Natalie Klein, 'Maritime Security' in Donald R. Rothwell et al. (eds.), *The Oxford Handbook on the Law of the Sea* (Oxford University Press, 2015) 582, 597.

[197] James Kraska, 'Military Operations' in Donald R. Rothwell et al. (eds.), *The Oxford Handbook on the Law of the Sea* (Oxford University Press, 2015) 867, 867.

[198] Ibid.

Beyond the articulation of international laws regulating submarine operations, the examination in the book reflects more broadly the greater challenge for the discipline in setting out rules that may ostensibly restrict policy choices that otherwise promote strategic and security interests. The questions that need to be asked ultimately reflect larger concerns about the interface between law and security, what priority is accorded to power in managing inter-State relations, as well as the role of the rule of law in the international legal system and in governing international relations. In seeking to articulate further and better what international laws regulate submarines, our contribution also aims to shift inter-State dialogue further towards not just a 'rules-based order' but a law-based order in ocean governance.

PART I

A Legal History of Submarines

2

The Rise of the Submarine: Belligerency, Neutrality and Emerging Laws of Passage in World War I

2.1 Introduction

Early submarines were short-range vessels subject to numerous mechanical problems. Up until the late nineteenth and early twentieth centuries, the successful construction of submarines and their use for government purposes – particularly military operations – were limited to isolated and mostly short-lived experiments.[1] It was nevertheless anticipated that with further improvements these vessels might play a role in coastal defence, especially in countries lacking strong navies.[2] As submarine construction improved, international law developed as well.

By 1899, the advances in submarine technology and its more widespread adoption by State navies – Germany in particular – prompted Russia to propose a ban on 'the use in naval battles of submarine or diving torpedo-boats or of other engines of destruction of the same nature' at the first Hague Peace Conference.[3] Though the United Kingdom and Germany indicated that they would agree to such a prohibition on the basis of unanimity,[4] the proposal was rejected with a number of States emphasising the submarine's utility for coastal

1 The chief example being the use of submarines in the American Civil War (1861–1865), during which the Confederate submarine *HL Hunley* sunk the Union vessel *Housatonic*. See Howard Levie, 'Submarine Warfare: With Emphasis on the 1936 London Protocol' (1998) 70 *Naval War College International Law Studies* 291; Michael Wilson, 'Early Submarines' in Robert Gardiner (ed.), *Steam, Steel and Shellfire: The Steam Warship 1815–1905* (Naval Institute Press, 1993) 148–52. See also Chapter 1, Section 1.1.

2 Levie (n 1) 295.

3 'Russian Circular January 11, 1899' in James Brown Scott, *The Hague Peace Conferences of 1899 and 1907: A Series of Lectures Delivered before the Johns Hopkins University in the Year 1908* (John Hopkins Press, 1909) vol. 2 <https://avalon.law.yale.edu/19th_century/hag99-02.asp>; Levie (n 1) 294–295.

4 Richard Dean-Burns, 'Regulating Submarine Warfare, 1921–41: A Case Study in Arms Control and Limited War' (1971) 35 (2) *Military Affairs* 56, 57.

defence and its character as 'a weapon of the weak'.[5] No further efforts were made to ban or specifically regulate the use of submarines prior to the outbreak of World War I (WWI) in 1914. However, there were a number of international efforts to clarify and progressively develop the laws on maritime neutrality and the conduct of hostilities at sea, all of which took into account or had implications for the advent of submarines. Key instruments included the Hague Convention (III) on Maritime Warfare of 1899,[6] Hague Conventions (VI) to (XIII) of 1907 (Hague Convention (X) of 1907 replacing Hague Convention (III) of 1899),[7] the 1909 London Declaration concerning the Laws of Naval War[8] (which was influential, though it lacked treaty status) and the 1913 Oxford Manual of the Laws of Naval War.[9] Though it had limited impact on the Hague Conventions, the work of two learned academies, the Institut de Droit International (IDI)[10] and the International Law

[5] James Brown Scott (ed.), *The Proceedings of the Hague Peace Conferences: The Conference of 1899* (Martinus Nijhoff, 1907) 367–368; Levie (n 1) 295.

[6] Hague Convention (III) for the Adaptation to Maritime Warfare of the Principles of the Geneva Convention of 22 August 1864, The Hague, 29 July 1899, entered into force 4 August 1900, 187 CTS 443.

[7] Hague Convention (VI) relative to the Legal Position of Enemy Merchant Ships at the Start of Hostilities, The Hague, 18 October 1907; Hague Convention (VII) relative to the Conversion of Merchant Ships into War-ships, The Hague, 18 October 1907, entered into force 26 January 1910, 205 CTS 319; Hague Convention (VIII) relative to the Laying of Automatic Submarine Contact Mines, The Hague, 18 October 1907, entered into force 18 October 1907, 205 CTS 331; Hague Convention (IX) concerning Bombardment by Naval Forces in Time of War, The Hague, 18 October 1907, entered into force 26 January 1910, 205 CTS 345; Hague Convention (X) for the Adaptation to Maritime Warfare of the Principles of the Geneva Convention, The Hague, entered into force 26 January 1910, 18 October 1907, 205 CTS 359; Hague Convention (XI) relative to Certain Restrictions with regard to the Exercise of the Right of Capture in Naval War, The Hague, 18 October 1907, entered into force 26 January 1910, 205 CTS 367; Hague Convention (XII) relative to the Establishment of an International Prize Court, The Hague, 18 October 1907, 205 CTS 381; Hague Convention (XIII) concerning the Rights and Duties of Neutral Powers in Naval War, The Hague, 18 October 1907, entered into force 26 January 1910, 205 CTS 395.

[8] Declaration concerning the Laws of Naval Warfare, London, 26 February 1909, (1914) 8 (S2) *American Journal of International Law* 88 ('1909 London Declaration').

[9] 'The Laws of Naval War Governing the Relations between Belligerents: Manual Adopted by the Institute of International Law (Oxford Manual of Naval War) at Oxford, 9 August 1913' in Dietrich Schindler and Jirí Toman (eds.), *The Laws of Armed Conflicts: A Collection of Conventions, Resolutions and Other Documents*, 4th ed. (Brill Nijhoff, 1988) 1123 ('1913 Oxford Manual').

[10] The IDI, also known as the Institute of International Law, was established in Ghent in 1873 as a private scholarly association working to progressively develop international law. See further Peter Macalister-Smith, 'Institut de Droit International' in Anne Peters and

Association (ILA),[11] developed in anticipation of the 1899 and 1907 Hague Conferences as well as a third Peace Conference planned for 1914 (which did not take place due to the outbreak of war) remains significant.

Yet it must be acknowledged that prior to the outbreak of war in 1914, submarines were not given a great deal of specific attention in debates within these institutions regarding the laws of neutrality and naval warfare. Nonetheless, both the IDI and the ILA considered the question of whether a coastal State had the right to prevent or regulate the passage of foreign (war)ships through its territorial waters, including straits. The deliberations of these academic institutions serve as a record of contemporary views (including points of agreement and disagreement) regarding what the law was or should be. The framing of the debate at this time – if not the specific conclusions drawn by the IDI and ILA – left its mark on the subsequent evolution of the law. Notably, the IDI and ILA asked whether any right to prevent or regulate passage in territorial waters flowed from neutrality or the sovereignty of the coastal State under general international law – a distinction of relevance to an account of the rights of the coastal State in its territorial waters during times of peace.

The importance of this question – which was not answered in the Hague Conventions – became increasingly apparent throughout WWI, as a number of neutral States asserted a right to preclude or regulate the passage of belligerent warships through territorial waters and straits, whether by decree or the laying of mines. State practice in this regard both responded to and impacted upon the activities of submarines during WWI. The capacity of submarines to avoid detection and their mobilisation against both neutral and belligerent merchant shipping meant that coastal States were particularly concerned with their presence in territorial waters. Efforts to regulate the activities of belligerent submarines in neutral waters and with respect to neutral shipping at this time informed the subsequent development of the law relating to neutrality and the

Rüdiger Wolfrum (eds.), *The Max Planck Encyclopedia of Public International Law* (Oxford University Press, February 2011).

[11] The International Law Association was founded just a month after the IDI at a meeting in Brussels in 1873. Like the IDI, the ILA is a private body concerned with the 'study, clarification and development of public and private international law': see further Torsten Stein, 'International Law Association' in Anne Peters and Rüdiger Wolfrum (eds.), *The Max Planck Encyclopedia of Public International Law* (Oxford University Press, May 2019).

regulation of naval operations in armed conflict more broadly. This influence remains apparent in key aspects of contemporary international law relating to neutrality and armed conflict, which will be discussed in Chapter 10. State claims to a right to bar or regulate passage as a consequence of sovereignty rather than neutrality form an important part of the context for the subsequent development and codification of passage regimes in the territorial sea and international straits, discussed in Chapter 7.

This chapter examines the role of submarines prior to and during WWI and the individual and collective efforts of States to ban, limit or regulate their use. Section 2.2 considers the contemporaneous work of international institutions such as the IDI and the ILA, and the extent to which early international legal instruments, adopted at the Hague Peace Conferences relating to neutrality and maritime warfare, regulated the new technologies and strategies of submarines adequately or at all. This history shows how States came to view submarines – and foreign submarine warships in particular – as a special threat to coastal State security when present in the territorial sea, in large part due to their ability to avoid detection through submergence. It is important to recognise that there was not necessarily a bright line between concerns relating to submarines in the context of war and in time of peace – though some attempts to clarify and develop the applicable law made use of such a distinction. Section 2.3 discusses the use of submarines against merchant shipping in WWI, which prompted further calls to ban the submarine as a weapon of war or to regulate its use in this context. The operation of submarines during WWI also brought to the fore the issue of how readily laws relating to warships could be transposed onto submarines. Section 2.4 focuses on State practice relating to neutrality and passage during WWI. These early uses of the submarine and State responses thereto have shaped the laws that remain in operation today.

While this chapter largely addresses international laws relating to warships generally, this body of law underpinned the developing law relating to submarines. Legal developments specific to submarines are highlighted in the discussion that follows. In the period under consideration in this chapter, most States seemed to have readily accepted that the government-owned and operated submarines were warships and were subject to the law generally applicable to such vessels, though some suggested that the ability of submarines to submerge warranted special regulation. The discussions at the learned academies, during the Hague Conferences and then State actions during WWI are all informative of the earliest developments of international laws governing submarines. A better understanding of this history helps to both clarify the content of the existing law and inform an assessment of its adequacy in regulating contemporary and emerging submarine technologies and practices – the subject of Part II of this book.

2.2 Belligerency, Neutrality and Passage before World War I

Prior to WWI, international efforts sought to both clarify and progressively develop the laws on maritime neutrality. This section examines both *lex lata* and *lex ferenda*.[12] The 1856 Paris Declaration respecting Maritime Law drew on the experience of States in the Crimean War to protect neutral goods from capture, including enemy goods other than contraband under a neutral flag.[13] In 1875, one of the earliest actions of the IDI was concluding its resolution on the 'Treatment of Private Property in Naval Warfare' in which it was stated that this principle of neutrality 'must be considered from now on as having entered the domain of the positive Law of Nations'.[14] It was incorporated into the 1909 London Declaration and the 1913 Oxford Manual as part of the customary international law relating to maritime prizes; however, WWI saw significant departures from these rules.[15]

In 1875, the IDI also adopted a resolution on the 'International Duties of Neutral States' drafted by Bluntschli, which provided, inter alia, that 'the neutral State must neither permit nor suffer one of the belligerents to make its ports or its waters the base of naval operations against the other, or that military transport vessels make use of its ports'.[16] The rights and duties of neutral States with respect to the mere passage of belligerent

[12] *Lex lata* refers to the existing law, while *lex ferenda* refers to proposals regarding what ought to be (but is not at present) law. For discussion of these concepts, see Hugh Thirlway, 'Reflections on Lex Ferenda' (2001) 32 *Netherlands Yearbook of International Law* 3.

[13] Declaration Respecting Maritime Law, Paris, 16 April 1856, entered into force 16 April 1856, 61 BFSP 155.

[14] IDI Resolution on 'Traitement de la propriété privée dans la guerre maritime', The Hague, 31 August 1875.

[15] J. Ashley Roach, 'Neutrality in Maritime Warfare' (last updated) in Anne Peters and Rüdiger Wolfrum (eds.), *The Max Planck Encyclopedia of Public International Law* (Oxford University Press, March 2017); James Kraska, 'Prize Law' in Anne Peters and Rüdiger Wolfrum (eds.), *The Max Planck Encyclopedia of Public International Law* (Oxford University Press, December 2009).

[16] IDI Resolution on 'Devoirs internationaux des Etats neutres: Règles de Washington', The Hague, 30 August 1875.

warships, however, were not addressed until 1894, when the question arose in connection with the IDI's work on the 'Définition et régime de la mer territoriale'.[17]

As discussed in this section, both the IDI and the ILA grappled with the implications of neutrality in this context and questions of passage also arose in their work on neutrality, particularly in connection with the laying of submarine mines. These debates are marked by the absence of a clear distinction between rights due to neutrality and rights due to the sovereignty of the coastal State. This ambiguity remains apparent in the proceedings of the 1899 and 1907 Hague Conferences, which did not resolve the question of whether neutral States might restrict or regulate the passage of warships through their territorial sea or straits. Though this question was given further attention in the work of the IDI and the ILA towards an anticipated (and unrealised) third Hague Peace Conference, it remained unsettled at the outbreak of war in 1914. Yet the views expressed by members of these institutes and States participating in the Hague Conferences remain significant, reflecting a complex of concerns that would be challenged, reconfigured and in some respects sharpened by the facts of WWI and the role of submarines in this conflict. It is of particular interest that the existence or desirability of a legal distinction between regimes of passage through the territorial sea and regimes of passage through straits suggested by the IDI and ILA was not clearly established at this time.

2.2.1 *Passage through the Territorial Sea Prior to the Hague Conferences*

The potential difference between the territorial sea and a zone of neutrality in coastal waters was apparent in the IDI's 1894 'Règles sur la définition et le régime de la mer territoriale', which announced in its preamble that 'there is no reason to confound in a single zone the distance necessary for the exercise of sovereignty and for the protection of coastwise fishing and that which is necessary to guarantee the neutrality of non-belligerents in time of war'.[18]

[17] See IDI Resolution on 'Règles sur la définition et le régime de la mer territoriale', Paris, 31 March 1894. An English translation is available in James Brown Scott (ed.), *Resolutions of the Institute of International Law Dealing with the Law of Nations* (Oxford University Press, 1916) 113.

[18] IDI, 'Règles sur la définition et le régime de la mer territoriale' (n 17); Scott, *Resolutions of the Institute of International Law* (n 17) 113.

Yet the IDI did not set aside the case of neutrality, which was repeatedly raised as an essential aspect of, or constraint upon, any elaboration of rules of passage.

Article 5 of the IDI's 'Règles' provided that

> All ships without distinction have the right of innocent passage through the territorial sea, save the right of belligerents to regulate and, for the purpose of defence, to bar the passage in the said sea for every ship, and save the right of neutrals to regulate the passage in the said sea for warships of all nationalities.[19]

While most members of the IDI had supported a right of innocent passage through the territorial sea,[20] this principle seems to have been considered a corollary of freedom of trade and primarily a right due to merchant ships.[21] The reference to the rights of belligerents and neutrals was added in response to concerns that allowing the passage of foreign vessels through territorial waters may be dangerous in the context of war.

It was initially proposed that a right of passage through the territorial sea should only be recognised 'in time of peace', with an express stipulation that this right would not apply to belligerent warships.[22] The reference to 'time of peace' was adopted by a majority,[23] before being removed on the basis that it was insufficiently precise.[24] While Barclay proposed 'd'accorder en tout temps à tous les navires sans distinction le droit de passage inoffensif par la mer territoriale', he also argued that the reference to 'passage inoffensif' (innocent passage) offered sufficient guarantees to counter the danger posed by the presence of foreign warships.[25] Other members considered it necessary to specifically provide for the right of belligerents and neutrals to limit the passage of foreign ships in territorial waters. A proposal to expressly recognise the right of belligerents and neutrals to bar belligerent warships in time of war was rephrased to refer to the right of belligerents to bar and regulate ships of all kinds, and the right of neutrals to regulate the passage of belligerent warships.

19 Scott, *Resolutions of the Institute of International Law* (n 17) 114; Thomas Barclay, Rapporteur, 'Règles sur la définition et le régime de la mer territoriale' (1894–1895) 13 *Annuaire de l'Institut de Droit International* 104, 311 ('1894 Rules').

20 See, however, the objections of Richard Kleen in Barclay, '1894 Rules' (n 19) 304.

21 Ibid, 303–311.

22 Ibid, 304.

23 Ibid, 305.

24 Ibid, 307–308.

25 Ibid, 309. The proposed text is translated as follows: 'to grant at all times to all ships without distinction the right of innocent passage through the territorial sea' (authors' translation).

While this formulation might suggest that the right of neutrals to interfere with passage was considered more limited than that of belligerents, debates in the plenary indicate that most members agreed that neutrals had a right to bar as well as regulate the passage of belligerent warships in the territorial sea.[26] Some members argued that neutral States could also exclude merchant ships from their waters in time of war.[27] As it was broadly agreed that the neutral State could regulate the passage of warships, this position was expressly stated. However, the provision was not considered to exhaust the possibilities for lawful action in respect of passage by neutral States or to specify all relevant limitations upon such action.

As well as recognising the neutral State's right to regulate passage, the IDI considered neutral States to have a right to establish neutrality zones extending beyond the limits of their territorial waters. While the IDI considered six nautical miles to be appropriate in the former case, Article 4 provided that '[i]n case of war a neutral littoral State has the right to fix, by declaration of neutrality or by special notification, its neutral zone beyond six miles up to the range of coast artillery'.[28] The IDI's 1894 Articles did not draw a clear line between *lex lata* and *lex ferenda*, though the Institute's goal was to influence both the codification and progressive development of the law.[29]

Barclay shared the IDI's Articles on the 'Définition et régime de la mer territoriale' with the ILA in 1895 (proposing minor amendments).[30] During those discussions, Barclay explained that Article 5 applied in the territorial sea rather than a neutrality zone that diverged from this area – suggesting, it appears, that the right to control passage followed from the sovereignty of the coastal State rather than any rights of neutrality.[31] It is important to differentiate the source of a State's right to control passage; if derived from neutrality, the right existed during times of war only, but if the right to control flowed more generally from the sovereignty of the coastal State, that right obtained during both times

26 Ibid, 304–311.

27 Ibid, 306.

28 Scott, *Resolutions of the Institute of International Law* (n 17) 114.

29 IDI, 'Statuts et règlements de l'Institut de Droit International' (1892–1894) 12 *Annuaire de l'Institut de Droit International* 1 (art. 1).

30 Thomas Barclay, 'Territorial Waters' (1895) 17 *International Law Association Reports of Conferences* 102, 102–107; Shigeru Oda, 'The Territorial Sea and Natural Resources' (1955) 4(3) *International and Comparative Law Quarterly* 415.

31 Barclay, 'Territorial Waters' (n 30) 110.

of peace and war. Article 5 as amended was adopted by the ILA without objection.[32]

In 1906, the IDI adopted several provisions on the 'Régime de la Neutralité', including Article 4 (originally Article 5), which provided that '[s]ont interdits l'entrée des forces de terre ou de mer des belligérants dans les territoires neutres et l'usage de ceux-ci dans des buts de guerre'.[33] Neutral territory was understood to include the territorial sea, though the IDI also understood the right to forbid the entry of belligerents to extend into 'neutral waters' (defined by the range of cannon-shot) beyond the territorial sea (defined by distance from the coast).[34]

The ILA also considered both laws of neutrality and the regulation of submarine mines in 1906.[35] However, no formal decisions were taken by the ILA on these provisions.[36] While the work of the IDI and ILA at this time was by no means conclusive as to either the *lex lata* or *lex ferenda*, the weight of their learned opinion seems to have favoured the right of neutral States to prohibit the passage of belligerent warships through their territorial waters, and allowed the use of submarine mines to this end.[37]

2.2.2 *Passage through Straits Prior to the Hague Conferences*

The question of the legal status of straits and the possibility of restricting passage through them was discussed by both the IDI and the ILA prior to the outbreak of WWI. In the IDI's 1894 articles on the 'Définition et régime de la mer territoriale', Article 10 had recognised that straits could be included in the territorial waters of coastal States, but further provided

[32] Ibid, 111.

[33] Richard Kleen, 'Régime de la Neutralité' (1906) 21 *Annuaire de l'Institut de Droit International* 100. Forbidden in this clause is the entry of the land or sea forces of the belligerents into neutral territories and the use of these territories for war purposes.

[34] Ibid, 101, 123–124, 142.

[35] ILA, 'Propositions concernant les lois de la neutralité' (1907) 24 *International Law Association Reports of Conferences* 251, 251–257.

[36] Erik Brüel, *International Straits: A Treatise on International Law* (Sweet & Maxwell, 1947) vol. 1, 79–80.

[37] ILA, 'Propositions concernant les lois de la neutralité' (n 37) 253, 257; Roland Vaughan Williams, 'The Use of Submarines in Maritime Warfare' (1906) 23 *International Law Association Reports of Conferences* 74, 74–79; M-S Kebedgy, Rapporteur, 'Réglementation internationale de l'usage des mines sons-marines et des torpilles automatiques' (1906) 21 *Annuaire de l'Institut de Droit International* 88, 99; Kleen, 'Régime de la Neutralité' (n 33) 168–171, 340–342.

that '[s]traits which serve as a passage from one open sea to another open sea can never be closed'.[38] Westlake, who had proposed the inclusion of an article to this effect, claimed that 'c'est un droit inscrit dans l'histoire, et qui a été exercé en particulier dans la guerre de la Franco et de l'Angleterre contre la Russie, et dans la guerre franco-allemande'.[39] While it was held that this rule ordinarily applied to 'straits whose breadth does not exceed twelve miles', Article 10 also provided that straits between States should be treated as territorial waters up to 'the middle line' and that '[s]traits whose shores belong to the same State and which are indispensable to maritime communication between two or more States other than the littoral State always form part of the territorial sea of such State, whatever the distance between the coasts'.[40] Article 11 noted that '[t]he regime of straits actually governed by special conventions or usages remains reserved'.[41]

In 1895, the ILA expressed its general support for the IDI's conclusions regarding straits,[42] though Barclay proposed that the territorial sea should only include straits more than twelve miles wide where they were twelve miles or less at their entrances.[43] Yet the straits question would ultimately be considered again by both institutions in 1906 in connection with the barring of passage by the laying of submarine mines.

2.2.3 The Hague Conferences of 1899 and 1907

The conclusions of the IDI and ILA regarding neutral State control over passage were not taken up in the text of the Conventions adopted at the Hague Peace Conferences of 1899 and 1907. Nonetheless the record of negotiations shows that States were similarly concerned with the question of the coastal State's right to exclude or regulate the passage of warships through its territorial waters and a majority seem to have

[38] Scott, *Resolutions of the Institute of International Law* (n 17) 115; Barclay, '1894 Rules' (n 19), 321; Brüel, *International Straits* (n 36) 71.

[39] Barclay, '1894 Rules' (n 19), 308. Translated as: 'It is a right enshrined in history, and which was exercised in particular in the war between France and England against Russia, and in the Franco-German war' (authors' translation).

[40] Scott, *Resolutions of the Institute of International Law* (n 17) 115; Barclay, '1894 Rules' (n 19) 321.

[41] Ibid.

[42] Barclay, 'Territorial Waters' (n 30) 113–114.

[43] Ibid, 113. The extension of the territorial sea to encompass straits exceeding this width at some points was considered necessary to prevent the enclaving of areas classified as high seas.

supported such a right. The idea that straits were a special case where such a right could not be exercised (a position advanced in the work of the IDI and ILA) was more hotly contested. Ultimately, the question of whether the passage of warships through the territorial sea and straits could be prohibited was deliberately left outside the ambit of the Hague Conventions. Interestingly, the rationale for this decision was the notion that certain measures taken to safeguard neutrality were justified by the sovereignty of the coastal State in its territorial waters rather than its neutral status. Thus, at the 1907 Conference it was held that the elaboration of rights derived from sovereignty and unaffected by neutrality was beyond the purview of Hague Convention (XIII) of 1907.[44] The focus was rather on rights and obligations flowing from neutrality in the event of war – though it was recognised that 'neutrals cannot exercise their liberty as in times of peace; they ought not to ignore the existence of war'.[45]

As already noted, a Russian proposal to entirely ban the use of submarines was rejected at the 1899 Conference.[46] The position of submarines was otherwise considered as part of the discussions on warships. Hague Convention (XIII) on the 'Rights and Duties of Neutral Powers in Naval War' did not expressly affirm or deny the right of a neutral State to bar or regulate the passage of belligerent warships through its territorial waters. Instead, Article 10 provided that '[t]he neutrality of a Power is not affected by the mere passage through its territorial waters of war-ships or prizes belonging to belligerents'. The drafting history shows that a British proposal that would have specifically protected a right of 'mere passage through neutral waters in time of war of a war-ship or auxiliary ship of a belligerent' was rejected by Sweden, Denmark, Norway, Turkey (as it was then known) and the United States, which did not support an 'unlimited right of mere passage' for warships.[47] Indeed, the US delegate, Admiral Sperry, continued to object to Article 10 as finally formulated,

[44] See e.g., James Brown Scott (ed.), *Reports to the Hague Conferences of 1899 & 1907* (Oxford University Press, 1917) 846–848: 'There is no question here of recognizing by treaty the rights of a neutral State that are derived from sovereignty and pre-exist war. The only element that war introduces is the obligation to treat the two belligerents in the same way'.

[45] Ibid, 840.

[46] Levie (n 1) 295.

[47] See 'Draft Convention on Rights and Duties of Neutral States in Naval and Aerial War with Commentaries' (1939) 33(S1) *American Journal of International Law* 175; James Brown Scott (ed.), *The Proceedings of the Hague Peace Conferences: Conference of 1907* (Oxford University Press, 1920) vol. 1, 297–298; Scott, *Reports to the Hague Conferences* (n 44) 847–848.

stating that 'he could not accept this article by reason of the political considerations involved in the question of passage through territorial waters'.[48]

While questions of passage through straits were not addressed directly, a report to the Hague Conference noted, '[f]rom the opinions there expressed [in discussions] it seems that a neutral State may forbid even innocent passage through limited parts of its territorial waters so far as that seems to it necessary to maintain its neutrality, but that this prohibition cannot extend to straits uniting two open seas'.[49] Sweden and Denmark had claimed that passage through straits could never be restricted in the course of their objections to an unlimited right of warships to 'mere passage' through the territorial sea.[50] Turkey and Japan lodged declarations responding to the Committee's observation regarding straits, noting that they 'undertook no engagement' to limit their right to bar or regulate passage in straits within their waters.[51] In any event, Hague Convention (XIII) did not recognise or refuse a right of passage on the part of warships in either territorial waters or straits. Nor, indeed, did it recognise a general right of neutral States to prohibit and prevent such passage. Instead, these questions were 'left under the empire of the general law of nations'.[52]

The question of passage through straits was also considered in connection with the laying of automatic submarine contact mines. Significantly, States agreed that neutral States were entitled to lay submarine mines off their coasts. Article 4 of Hague Convention (VIII) provided that '[n]eutral Powers which lay automatic contact mines off their coasts must observe the same rules and take the same precautions as are imposed on belligerents' as well as 'inform ship owners, by a notice issued in advance, where automatic contact mines have been laid'.[53]

The idea that States should be precluded from barring passage through straits was met with many objections – some 'drawn from rights of territorial sovereignty' and others 'from conventional stipulations existing on the subject of certain straits'.[54] A number of States argued that

[48] Scott, *Reports to the Hague Conferences* (n 44) 848. The United States initially abstained from voting on Hague Convention (XIII) but acceded in 1909: see Scott, *Conference of 1907* (n 47) vol. 1, 278–279.
[49] Scott, *Reports to the Hague Conferences* (n 44) 847.
[50] Ibid.
[51] Ibid, 848. See also Scott, *Conference of 1907* (n 47) vol. 1, 278.
[52] Scott, *Conference of 1907* (n 47) vol. 1, 298.
[53] See also ibid, vol. 3, 403.
[54] Ibid, vol. 3, 408.

express reservations would have to be made for cases where both sides of a strait belonged to a single State or a specific treaty regime applied.[55] Japan, for example, observed that while the rule could 'perhaps be adapted to the geographical conditions of continental States' it would not always be appropriate 'to those of insular Powers'.[56] It concluded that '[b]y reason of the particular configuration of Japan, of the great number of straits separating the islands (straits which are an integral part of its territory, but which, nevertheless, would fall within the definition as written in the said amendment), the Japanese delegation could not adhere to this provision'.[57] Japan subsequently noted that it would accept a provision recognising '[i]t is desirable that communication between two open seas be not entirely barred by automatic mines', but that '[n]evertheless, passage may be subjected to conditions to be decreed by the competent authorities'.[58]

The Hague Conferences of 1899 and 1907 and the resulting Conventions did not ultimately resolve the question of whether warships had a right of passage through the territorial sea or straits of another State in time of peace or war. The United Kingdom, unsurprisingly given its contemporary naval supremacy and imperial interests, appeared as the leading proponent of a general right of 'mere' passage for warships. The record of debates nevertheless indicates that such a right was not at this time generally recognised as part of the existing law. It is also apparent that many States considered such a right to be undesirable as a matter of *lex ferenda*. The priority of State sovereignty in matters of defence was widely referenced in this regard. The possibility of distinguishing between passage through the territorial sea and passage through straits, however, would be given further attention by international institutions anticipating a third Peace Conference.

2.2.4 *Towards a Third Hague Peace Conference*

The specific regulation of submarines was not revisited immediately after the two Hague Conferences. Instead, questions relating to warships' rights of passage continued to garner attention. In 1910, the IDI considered the question of straits in the context of 'Le Régime de Neutralité', having previously collected State views on 'first, whether the neutral state

[55] Ibid, vol. 3, 408–409.
[56] Ibid, vol. 3, 663.
[57] Ibid, vol. 3, 662.
[58] Ibid, vol. 3, 409.

has the right to forbid war ships of belligerent powers through its territorial waters, and secondly, if so, whether this right also extends to "les détroits unissant deux mers libres"'.[59] It also considered a new text on the use of submarine mines prepared by Rolin, which adapted Kleen's earlier draft in response to Hague Convention (VIII) of 1907.[60]

With respect to 'Le Régime de Neutralité', the prevailing response was that the neutral State was not 'obliged' to prevent the passage of belligerent warships through the territorial sea or straits.[61] Of course, this position did not answer the question of whether there was a right to forbid such passage; accordingly, the final report by Dupuis neither affirmed nor denied a right of passage for warships through straits within neutral waters.[62] Instead, Dupuis noted that the coastal State may only have a right to restrict such passage outside maritime routes necessary for navigation and 'ought' to allow it in international straits.

Brüel has drawn attention to the debates of the Inter-Parliamentary Union on the question of international straits between 1910 and 1914, where rules designed to preserve the free navigation of straits for commerce during war were debated and proposals made for a general convention on straits.[63] Article 1 of the Draft Convention provided that '[e]quality of treatment and the right of free passage in all straits connecting two non-inland seas, and in inter-oceanic canals properly speaking, are recognized and ensured to all ships without distinction of flag, either in time of peace or in time of war'. Yet it was also provided that 'the special regime for warships in maritime straits and canals governed by special treaties remains reserved', and (in Article 2) that '[t]he vessels of belligerent States shall remain subject to the special rules of the conventions and usages of war'.[64] While there was clearly a concern to protect the passage of neutral merchant ships through straits, there was still no

[59] Charles Dupuis, Rapporteur, 'Régime de la Neutralité' (1910) 23 *Annuaire de l'Institut de Droit International* 231; Brüel, *International Straits* (n 36) 73. Translated as 'straits uniting two open seas' (authors' translation).

[60] Edouard Rolin, Rapporteur, 'Mines sous-marines' (1910) 23 *Annuaire de l'Institut de Droit International* 177.

[61] Brüel, *International Straits* (n 36) 73.

[62] Ibid, 73–74. Lapradelle, who disagreed with Dupuis, presented a separate report supporting a general right of passage for belligerent warships in the territorial sea subject to regulations concerning the number of ships present at any time and reserving a right to close remote parts of the territorial sea: ibid.

[63] Brüel, *International Straits* (n 36) 81–88.

[64] Ibid, Appendix I (translated from French).

clear agreement on how warships and belligerent merchant vessels should be treated.

The work of the ILA and IDI at this time was directed towards the Third Hague Peace Conference planned for 1914, postponed until 1915, then deferred indefinitely with the outbreak of WWI.[65] In 1913, the IDI succeeded in adopting the Oxford Manual on Naval War, which prohibited the laying of mines in the high seas and regulated mine-laying by belligerents; however, the question of straits was not revisited.[66] During WWI, neutral States were for the first time seriously confronted with the threat posed by belligerent submarines in neutral waters and straits relied upon by merchant shipping. This scenario informed the subsequent evolution of neutral State practice regarding passage. As the military significance of submarines in the conflict also became apparent, belligerent strategies evolved – as did defensive measures taken in the name of neutrality or the sovereignty of the coastal State.

2.3 Submarines in World War I

By 1914, a number of European navies, including those of Austria-Hungary, France, Italy, Germany, Russia and the United Kingdom, possessed an operational submarine arm, as did the US Navy.[67] Although new designs were continually being developed, submarines had both a significantly enhanced range and capacity for armed attack at the outbreak of WWI.[68] Rather than being limited to short-range defensive operations within the territorial waters of a coastal State (as anticipated only twenty years earlier), these vessels were clearly capable of operations on the high seas and in the territorial waters of other States.[69]

Most States involved in WWI seem to have assumed, not surprisingly, that submarines were warships and governed by the rules applicable to

65 IDI, 'Rapport fait à l'Institut de Droit International au nom de la Commission spéciale constituée en vue de la prochaine conférence de la paix' (1912) 25 *Annuaire de l'Institut de Droit International* 23.

66 Harburger suggested the question of mine-laying in straits might be considered the following year, however, events intervened: 'Délibérations diverses en séance plénière' (1913) 26 *Annuaire de l'Institut de Droit International* 686, 687.

67 Lawrence Sondhaus, *Naval Warfare 1815–1914* (Routledge, 2001), 197–224; Spencer C. Tucker, *World War I: The Essential Reference Guide* (Bloomsbury, 2016), 222–229; Paul G. Halpern, *A Naval History of World War I* (Naval Institute Press, 1994), 1–20.

68 Norman Friedman, *Submarine Design and Development* (Naval Institute Press, 1984), 27–29.

69 Ibid.

the latter, though there was no express provision to this effect in the existing treaties on the laws of naval warfare. Levie draws attention to a German communication to the US government in which it claimed that the submarine was 'a new weapon, the use of which had not yet been regulated by international law'.[70] Germany claimed that its policy in using this weapon 'could not and did not violate any existing rules but only took into account the peculiarity of this new weapon, the submarine boat'.[71] This argument, however, was made in connection with the characterisation of German U-boat attacks against merchant ships as reprisals.[72]

Germany seems to have accepted at various times that submarines would be subject to a general requirement to give warning and ensure the security of a ship's papers and the safety of those on board before sinking an enemy or neutral merchant ship[73] – an obligation understood to be incumbent upon all warships.[74] It became apparent, however, that for a submarine to surface and give the requisite warning, the practice exposed the submarine to attack. When Germany dispensed with these measures in its operations against both enemy and neutral commerce, it alleged a right to do so on the basis that the Allies were breaching international law in their blockade of the Central Powers, the misuse of neutral flags to protect Allied vessels, and the arming of merchant ships.[75]

Levie also notes that, 'strange to relate', the British Secretary of State for Foreign Affairs, Sir Edward Grey, suggested in a 1916 communication to the British Ambassador to the United States that 'international law

[70] 'Memorandum from the German Embassy' (1916) 10 (Special Supplement) *American Journal of International Law* 178, 179; Levie (n 1) 297.

[71] Ibid.

[72] Ibid.

[73] See 'Correspondence with Germany regarding Submarine Interferences with Commercial Vessels' (1916) 10(S5) *American Journal of International Law* 161–344.

[74] This requirement is reflected in Article 50 of the Declaration of London, which applies to 'neutral prizes'. Article 50 refers specifically to the obligation to take persons and papers 'on board the warship'. The same requirement applies to 'enemy merchant ships' under Hague Convention (VI) (n 7) art. 3.

[75] 'Memorial of the Imperial German Government Respecting Retaliatory Measures Rendered Necessary by the Means Employed by England Contrary to International Law in Intercepting Neutral Maritime Trade with Germany' (1915) 9(S5) *American Journal of International Law* 83, 83–85; 'The German Minister for Foreign Affairs to Ambassador General' (1915) 9(S5) *American Journal of International Law* 90, 92–96. See also 'The Secretary of State to the German Ambassador (Bernstorff)' in Joseph V. Fuller (ed.), *Papers Relating to the Foreign Relations of the United States: 1917, Supplement 1, The World War* (United States Government Printing Office, 1931) 106 (File No. 763.72/3179) ('Paper from the Secretary of State').

ought not to transfer without modification to submarines, rules and regulations which work fairly well as regards surface vessels'.[76] Yet this claim appears less 'strange' in the context of British policy once it is understood that the argument being made was that a submarine could not be treated as a merchant ship even if it carried only cargo and no armaments. Grey's view was that submarines should *always* be classified as warships insofar as 'nine-tenths of work required to convert her into a completely equipped ship of war of most formidable type has already been put into her and cannot be removed'.[77] Specifically, the British Secretary of State considered the 'most formidable part' of a submarine to be 'its submersibility [*sic*]', and as 'one of its inseparable attributes'.[78]

The significant role of German submarines or U-boats in WWI is well known.[79] While there were a number of attacks by German submarines on Allied warships and vice versa, German U-boats were also mobilised against the merchant and, in some cases, passenger ships of both the Allies and neutral States. Germany's campaign famously resulted in the sinking of the British passenger liner RMS *Lusitania* in May 1915 by the torpedo of the German *U20* submarine.[80] This incident has been described as a 'milestone in the history of the submarine'.[81] The then-neutral United States objected strongly to the German practice of unrestricted submarine warfare, with the US Secretary of State writing in a note to the Imperial Minister of Foreign Affairs that the German submarine campaign constituted 'methods of retaliation which go much beyond the ordinary methods of warfare'.[82] This targeting was a significant factor prompting the entry of the United States into the conflict in December 1917.[83]

76 'The British Secretary of State for Foreign Affairs (Grey) to the British Ambassador at Washington (Spring Rice)' in Joseph V. Fuller (ed.), *Papers Relating to the Foreign Relations of the United States: 1916, Supplement, The World War* (United States Government Printing Office, 1929) 769 (File No. 763.72111D48/26) ('British Paper'); Levie (n 1) 297.

77 'British Paper' (n 76).

78 Ibid.

79 See, e.g., Halpern (n 67).

80 See Cameron Moore, '*RMS Lusitania*' in David Letts and Rob McLaughlin (eds.), *Maritime Operations Law in Practice: Key Cases and Incidents* (Routledge, 2023) 151, 152.

81 Antony Preston, *Submarine Warfare* (Brown Books, 1998) 31.

82 'The Secretary of State to the Ambassador in Germany (Gerard)' in Joseph V. Fuller (ed.), *Papers Relating to the Foreign Relations of the United States: 1915, Supplement, The World War* (United States Government Printing Office, 1929) 575 (File No. 763.72/1764a). See also Lawrence Sondhaus, *The Great War at Sea: A Naval History of the First World War* (Cambridge University Press, 2014) 149–157.

83 'Paper from the Secretary of State' (n 75); 'President Wilson's Address of January 22, 1917' (1917) 11(S5) *American Journal of International Law* 318; 'The Secretary of State to the

The German U-boat campaign against commerce was a response to the British-led blockade of the Central Powers. Technological developments in the form of naval mines, torpedo boats, and submarines meant that the traditional technique of 'close blockade' – preventing supply ships from entering and exiting an enemy port by close guard – was no longer feasible.[84] Instead the Allies' policy of 'long range blockade' proceeded through the regular patrolling of the high seas by the British fleet in order to capture vessels carrying contraband to Germany and other enemy States.[85] In 1914, the United Kingdom declared the entire North Sea a naval 'war zone' in which blockade patrols would take place.[86] The Allies also expanded the definition of contraband substantially beyond the lists traditionally set out in friendship, commerce and navigation treaties and reflected in the 1909 London Declaration.[87]

In early 1915, Germany responded to the Allies' long-range blockade by deploying U-boats to sink Allied and neutral merchant ships in the waters around the United Kingdom, which Germany declared a 'war zone'.[88] After a hiatus following the sinking of the RMS *Lusitania*, Germany resumed a policy of 'unrestricted submarine warfare' against

Diplomatic Representatives in All Countries except Russia' in Joseph V. Fuller (ed.), *Papers Relating to the Foreign Relations of the United States: 1917, Supplement 2, The World War* (United States Government Printing Office, 1932) vol. 1, 10 (File No. 763.72/3697a).

84 See Stephen C. Neff, 'Disrupting a Delicate Balance: The Allied Blockade Policy and the Law of Maritime Neutrality during the Great War' (2018) 29(2) *European Journal of International Law* 459.

85 Ibid, 463.

86 'The British Ambassador (Spring Rice) to the Secretary of State' in Joseph V. Fuller (ed.), *Papers Relating to the Foreign Relations of the United States: 1914, Supplement, The World War* (United States Government Printing Office, 1928) 463, 464 (File No. 763.72/1171).

87 Neff (n 84) 465. Though it did not formally enter into force as a treaty, the 1909 London Declaration purported to 'correspond in substance with the generally recognized principles of international law': 1909 London Declaration (n 8) Preliminary Provision. The Declaration was partly adopted by belligerents as a statement of rules applicable in the WWI conflict, though in some cases only provisionally. Germany, for instance, advised the US Secretary of State that it 'will apply the Declaration of London, provided its provisions are not disregarded by other belligerents'. The United Kingdom specified 'certain modifications and additions' relating to contraband and blockade. See 'Declaration of London' (1915) *International Law Studies* 93, 93–100.

88 'The Ambassador in Germany (Gerard) to the US Secretary of State' in Joseph V. Fuller (ed.), *Papers Relating to the Foreign Relations of the United States: 1915, Supplement, The World War* (United States Government Printing Office, 1928) 463 (File No. 763.72/1434).

neutral ships carrying supplies to the Allies in 1917.[89] This policy dispensed with a pre-existing customary international law requirement to give warning and ensure the safety of passengers and crew before sinking merchant ships.[90] The United Kingdom in turn amended its blockade policy to provide that 'a vessel which is encountered at sea on her way to or from a port in any neutral country afforded means of access to the enemy territory without calling at a port in British or allied territory shall until the contrary is established be deemed to be carrying goods with an enemy destination or of enemy origin'.[91] It sought to characterise this measure as a lawful reprisal – a move which did not go unchallenged.[92] The Allies also imposed quotas on goods to be imported into neutral States, applying a presumption that 'all further cargoes would . . . be ultimately destined for the enemy'.[93]

The impact of these policies on neutral States during WWI was considerable. The laws of neutrality in force during WWI had included an absolute prohibition on '[a]ny act of hostility, including capture and the exercise of the right of search, committed by belligerent war-ships in the territorial waters of a neutral Power'.[94] In the post-war period, governments and individuals expressed concern that the existing laws of neutrality had proved ineffective in constraining belligerent States; though it was also pointed out that 'the law of neutrality, while disregarded at times from the belligerent point of view, had never been more

[89] 'The German Ambassador to the Secretary of State' (1917) 11(S5) *American Journal of International Law* 330, 333. See also Dirk Steffen, 'The Holtzendorff Memorandum of 22 December 1916 and Germany's Declaration of Unrestricted U-boat Warfare' (2004) 68 *Journal of Military History* 215–224. In a further incident following the sinking of *Lusitania* (May 1915), a German U-boat sunk the SS *Arabic* (August 1915), killing forty-four passengers and crew, including three Americans. Germany, however, had already issued secret orders requiring submarine commanders to give notice and make provision for the safety of passengers before sinking merchant ships and was no longer pursuing a policy of unrestricted submarine warfare. New orders to this effect were reissued and conveyed to the United States following the incident with SS *Arabic*.

[90] Levie (n 1) 299. This customary obligation is reflected in Article 50 of the 1909 London Declaration (n 8) in relation to neutral ships.

[91] 'Consul General Skinner to the Secretary of State' (1917) 11(S5) *American Journal of International Law* 50, 51.

[92] Ibid; Neff (n 84) 469–470.

[93] Neff (n 84) 467–468.

[94] Hague Convention (XIII) (n 7) arts. 1, 2, 5. See also Article 1 of the 1913 Oxford Manual (n 9), which provides under the heading 'On Localities where Hostilities May Take Place' that '[r]ules peculiar to naval warfare are applicable only on the high seas and in the territorial waters of the belligerents'. The territorial waters of neutral States are excluded as a location for hostilities.

faithfully fulfilled by the neutral states and governments within the compass of their jurisdiction and with the means at their disposal'.[95] Significantly, one of the measures taken by a number of neutral States during the conflict was the exercise of an alleged right to exclude warships – and submarines in particular – from passage through their territorial waters. State practice in this regard would prove significant not only in the context of the further elaboration and evolution of laws of neutrality but in connection with the development of peacetime laws of passage. This influence is elaborated in the following chapter, which also describes how the role of submarines in WWI prompted post-war proposals to put a cap on fleets and to ban submarines as well as to restrict their tonnage and capacity and regulate their use in armed conflict.

2.4 Neutrality and Passage in State Practice

As discussed above, it was not clear at the outbreak of WWI whether neutral States could lawfully exclude belligerent warships from their territorial waters, straits or 'neutrality zones' at sea. While there is evidence that a number of scholars and States endorsed this position, no general rule to this effect had been recognised in conventional law and the unresolved debates suggest that customary law was not clearly established on this point. In this context, the practice of States during WWI is of particular significance, both for its potential contribution to the development of customary international law and its influence on subsequent efforts to formally develop the law in this regard. The sheer scale of WWI saw an unprecedented number of States proclaim neutrality and specify laws corresponding with this status. The ways in which these rules address or respond to the particular threat posed by submarines is of special interest. The laws developed to protect neutrality during times of armed conflict ultimately influenced the right of innocent passage for warships during times of peace.

Both prior to and during WWI, a number of States addressed the question of innocent passage in the context of laws and regulations relating to neutrality. Prior to WWI, Switzerland, Belgium and Luxembourg were recognized as having permanently neutral status – a status violated by the German invasion and occupation of Belgium and

[95] Malbone W. Graham Jr, 'Neutrality and the World War' (1923) 17 *American Journal of International Law* 704, 706.

Luxembourg in WWI.[96] Belgium, the only coastal State with permanently neutral status at the time,[97] had issued a Royal Decree in 1901 that sought to restrict and regulate the passage of belligerent warships through its territorial waters.[98] Article 8 of this Royal Decree limited the time belligerent warships could spend in Belgian territorial waters and ports (no more than twenty-four hours) and how many times the same vessel could enter (not twice within three months). Article 20 reserved the government's right to modify these provisions to allow 'measures which the strict observance of neutrality would render expedient or necessary'. Article 10 of the Decree provided that warships conveying prizes or, significantly, any *armed* warship, whether or not accompanying a prize, was forbidden access to the ports and territorial waters of Belgium in the North Sea.

In August 1914, following the commencement of war between Austria-Hungary and Serbia, Belgium advised the States parties to the 1839 Treaty of London, which guaranteed Belgium's independence and neutrality, that the Belgian army had been mobilised and 'the Forts of Antwerp and on the Meuse . . . put in a state of defence' to 'ensure respect of Belgian neutrality'.[99] Belgium also sought assurances from France and Germany that they would respect its neutrality, which were received from France alone.[100] Germany shortly thereafter issued its ultimatum requesting entry into Belgian territory to 'anticipate' an attack allegedly planned by France to proceed through Belgium and advising that refusal would result in Belgium being considered an enemy.[101] During its occupation of Belgium following the latter's refusal to comply, Germany made use of Belgian territorial waters to conduct or support the conduct of

96 This status was imposed on Belgium rather than assumed voluntarily: Albert Geouffre de Lapradelle, 'The Neutrality of Belgium' (1914) 200(709) *The North American Review* 849–850.

97 Permanent neutrality was proposed in 1831 as an element of a peace treaty relating to Belgium's separation from the Netherlands, incorporated by Belgium into its domestic law in the same year, and recognised in the 1839 Treaty of London establishing Belgium's independence: Royal Decree Regulating the Admission of Foreign Warships of Belgian Waters and Harbors, 18 February 1901 in Francis Deak and Phillip C. Jessup, *A Collection of Neutrality Laws, Regulations and Treaties of Various Countries* (Carnegie, 1939), vol. 1, 50–52; Treaty between Belgium and the Netherlands relative to the Separation of their Respective Territories, London, 19 April 1839, 88 CTS 427.

98 Ibid, 54–56.

99 Frank Lord Warrin Jr, *The Neutrality of Belgium* (United States Government Printing Office, 1918) 71.

100 Ibid, 72–73.

101 Ibid, 75–76.

hostilities at sea, including the positioning of the Flanders U-boat flotilla at the port of Bruges.[102] Belgium's coast and offshore waters were a site for numerous engagements between the Central Powers and the Allies throughout the war.[103]

The invasion of Serbia by Austria-Hungary and the expectation of a broader European war prompted a number of States to formally declare their neutrality with respect to the widening conflict and draw attention to existing and new regulations pertaining to their neutrality in domestic law – including limitations on passage through their territorial waters.[104] As observed by Harvard Research in the commentary to its 1939 Draft Convention on Rights and Duties of Neutral States in Naval and Aerial War, some of these regulations 'are not framed with sufficient precision to make it possible to say whether they apply to cases of mere passage through territorial waters as contrasted with entry into ports and other waters'.[105] Greece and Brazil (neutral at the outbreak of war) merely reproduced Article 10 of the 1907 Hague Convention, which, as discussed, provided only that neutrality was not affected by the passage of belligerent warships through a neutral State's territorial waters.[106] Other States, however, clearly prohibited the passage of warships through the territorial sea. Significantly, a number of these prohibitions were directed implicitly or explicitly towards submarines.

2.4.1 The Netherlands

The Netherlands' Neutrality Proclamation of 1914 prohibited 'the passage of belligerent warships or vessels converted into warships through Netherland waters situated within the territorial waters' and noted its intention to prevent such vessels from leaving the territory before the end of the war.[107] Exceptions were noted for warships in distress, warships

102 Germany occupied the majority of the Belgian coast after 'the race to the sea' of 1914, positioning submarine and surface raiders at the ports of Ostend, Zeebrugge and Bruges: Halpern (n 67) 162.

103 Julian S. Corbett, *History of the Great War: Naval Operations* (Longmans Green & Co, 1920), vol. 1, chs. 6, 8, 13, 15, 16; vol. 2, chs. 1, 3, 6.

104 Maartje Abbenhuis and Ismee Tames, *Global War, Global Catastrophe: Neutrals, Belligerents and the Transformation of the First World War* (Bloomsbury, 2021) 29.

105 'Draft Convention on Rights and Duties of Neutral States in Naval and Aerial War with Commentaries' (n 47) 423.

106 Ibid.

107 Proclamation of Neutrality in the World War, 4 August 1914 in Deak and Jessup (n 97) vol. 2, 802.

'used exclusively for a religious, scientific, or philanthropic mission', and warships refuelling or provisioning in the ports and roadsteads of 'colonies or possessions in other continents'.[108]

The 1914 Proclamation appears to be the first occasion that the Netherlands sought to exclude belligerent warships from passage through its territorial waters. Its 1911 Proclamation of Neutrality in the Italo-Turkish War had outlined a range of restrictions on the passage of such vessels to ensure Dutch neutrality but had not denied 'mere passage'.[109] In 1914, the Netherlands also issued a 'Decree Rendering Temporarily Inoperative the Royal Decree of October 30, 1909, respecting the Admission of Warships of Foreign Powers into Netherland Territorial Waters'.[110] The new Decree provided that while the 1909 Decree was inoperative 'it shall not be permissible for warships and vessels converted into warships belonging to foreign powers to proceed from the sea into Netherlands territorial waters and the Netherlands water-domain situated within those territorial waters, or to stay there'.[111] Exceptions were noted for cases of distress and foreign warships 'destined exclusively for religious, scientific or humanitarian purposes'.[112] The Decree also stated that

> Warships or vessels converted into warships belonging to foreign powers which, contrary to the provisions of this Decree, proceed into Netherlands territorial waters or into the Netherlands water-domain situated within those territorial waters, or stay there, and do not withdraw on receipt of the first notice to do so, will expose themselves to such measures of force as the Netherlands Government shall consider right to employ.[113]

The Dutch policy of non-admission of warships to its territorial waters was protested by Germany on several occasions during WWI. The Netherlands interned German submarines found within its territorial waters on at least three occasions, and dealt similarly with several surface vessels.[114] In 1915, the first Dutch internment of a German submarine found within its territorial waters prompted protest from Germany, which argued that warships

108 Proclamation of Neutrality in the Italo-Turkish War, 3 October 1911 in Deak and Jessup (n 97) vol. 2, 803.

109 Decree Rendering Temporarily Inoperative the Royal Decree of October 30, 1909 Respecting the Admission of Warships of Foreign Powers into Netherland Territorial Waters, 30 July 1914 in Deak and Jessup (n 97), vol. 2, 799–802.

110 Ibid, 806.

111 Ibid.

112 Ibid.

113 Ibid, 807.

114 Amry Vandenbosch, *The Neutrality of The Netherlands During the World War* (WB Eerdmans, 1927) 88–100.

have a right of passage through the territorial waters of neutral States under international law.[115] The Netherlands disagreed, arguing that '[n]owhere is the neutral prohibited from denying the right to belligerent warships of passage through its territorial waters .... The neutral is free to make such restrictions as it sees fit'.[116] Interestingly, it also seems to have suggested that a prohibition on passage would be unlawful if applied to 'ordinary navigation', though it is not clear what was meant by this term – presumably it could not have meant that warships in fact had a right of passage through territorial waters, as this right was expressly denied.[117] Germany reiterated its claim that warships possessed a right of passage through neutral territorial waters in a subsequent case involving the seizure of a German submarine; however, it also argued in a number of cases (with limited success) that the entry into Dutch waters was due to error (but not neglect), seeking the release of its vessels on this basis.[118] The Netherlands applied its policy regarding the passage of warships through its territorial waters equally to Allied vessels, and interned a British submarine and several British surface vessels.[119]

2.4.2 The Allied Memoranda of 1916

In August 1916, as the German U-boat campaign took an increasing toll on the Allies, France, the United Kingdom, Russia and Japan issued identical memoranda urging neutral States 'to take efficacious measures tending to prevent belligerent submarines, regardless of their use, to avail themselves of neutral waters, roadsteads, and harbors'.[120] The memoranda argued that

> In the case of submarines the application of the principles of international law offers features that are as peculiar as they are novel, by reason, on the one hand, of the facility possessed by such craft to navigate and sojourn in

[115] Ibid, 88–89; 'Draft Convention on Rights and Duties of Neutral States in Naval and Aerial War with Commentaries' (n 47) 424.

[116] Vandenbosch (n 114) 89.

[117] Ibid. See also Harvard Research, 'Draft Convention on Rights and Duties of Neutral States in Naval and Aerial War with Commentaries' (n 47) 424.

[118] Vandenbosch (n 114) 88–92. Claims of technical errors and navigational mistakes also abound in later cases where the entry of submerged foreign submarines into territorial waters has been detected by the coastal State. This position reflects an understanding that intentional submerged passage is not permitted by law.

[119] Ibid, 93, 97.

[120] 'Memorandum from the French Embassy' (1916) 10(S5) *American Journal of International Law* 342, 342.

> the seas while submerged and thus escape any supervision or surveillance, and, on the other hand, of the impossibility to identify them and determine their national character, whether neutral or belligerent, combatant or innocent, and to put out of consideration the power to do injury that is inherent in their very nature.[121]

On this basis, the Allies claimed that '[s]ubmarine vessels must be excluded from the benefit of the rules heretofore accepted in international law regarding the admission and sojourn of war and merchant vessels in the neutral waters, roadsteads, and harbors; any submarine of the belligerents that once enters a neutral harbor must be held there'.[122]

The Netherlands' response to the Allies' memoranda was critical of the theory that submarines warranted special regulation: it pointed out that current international law, including Hague Convention (XIII), did not provide for the special treatment of belligerent submarines, and that '[n]eutrals have, therefore, the same rights and duties with respect to belligerent submarines that they have with respect to other belligerent warships'.[123] It noted that all warships (including submarines) were already prohibited from entering its territorial waters, and that those that did would be interned.[124]

2.4.3 *Spain*

Spain seems to have been more amenable to the argument expressed in the Allies' memoranda about submarines being in a special category. In 1917, Spain issued a Decree prohibiting '[a]ll submarine vessels of any kind whatsoever, of belligerent powers' from Spanish waters and ports, and advising that any such vessels 'entering Spanish jurisdictional waters for any cause whatsoever shall be interned until the end of the war'.[125] The Decree also provided that '[n]eutral submarines entering Spanish waters shall do so navigating on the surface and displaying conspicuously their national flag'.[126]

In an explanatory memorandum accompanying the Decree, the Prime Minister, Eduardo Dato,[127] expressed the view that 'the rules set forth in

[121] Ibid.
[122] Ibid.
[123] Vandenbosch (n 114) 93.
[124] Ibid.
[125] Royal Decree regarding the Treatment of Submarines in Spanish Territorial Waters, 29 June 1917 in Deak and Jessup (n 97) vol. 2, 939–940.
[126] Ibid.
[127] Dato was also a member of the Permanent Court of Arbitration and the IDI.

XIII Hague Convention of 1907, relative to the rights and duties of neutral powers in case of maritime war … do not fully answer any more the purpose which inspired them, due to the evolution – more rapid in point of fact than in point of law – of the military elements used by the belligerent powers'.[128] Spain echoed the 1916 memoranda in that the submarine was identified as warranting special regulation departing from the Hague Convention. Dato observed that

> [t]he means at the disposal of these vessels, and their use in destructive operations, to an extent and with a range which could not be foreseen by those legislators – a use which has been the subject of express reservations and protests of neutral nations, among them Spain – have changed, in the opinion of Your Majesty's Government, the legal bases on which some of the provisions of the Hague Convention found their existence.[129]

Spain issued a parallel Decree prohibiting the navigation of '[a]ll submarine vessels of any kind whatsoever, of the belligerent nations' in the 'jurisdictional waters of the Spanish Zone in Morocco', again noting that any such vessels would be interned and specifying that neutral submarines must navigate on the surface and display their flag conspicuously.[130]

2.4.4 The United States

In response to the 1916 Memoranda, the United States

> [expressed] its surprise that there appears to be an endeavor of the Allied Powers to determine the rule of action governing what they regard as a 'novel situation' in respect to the use of submarines in time of war and to enforce acceptance of that rule, at least in part, by warning neutral powers of the great danger to their submarines in waters that may be visited by belligerent submarines.[131]

The United States denied that there were 'any circumstances, concerning the use of war or merchant submarines which would render the existing rules of international law inapplicable to them'.[132]

[128] Royal Decree regarding the Treatment of Neutral and Belligerent Submarines in the Territorial Waters of Spanish Morocco, 18 July 1917 in Deak and Jessup (n 97) vol. 2, 939–940.
[129] Ibid.
[130] Ibid, 940–941.
[131] 'Memorandum from the French Embassy' (n 120) 342–343.
[132] Ibid, 343.

The United States, however, did not at this time consider warships to have an unlimited right of mere passage in the territorial sea.[133] While its position was not elaborated upon at the 1907 Hague Conference, it is interesting to note that in proceedings leading to the 1910 Award of the Permanent Court of Arbitration in the *North Atlantic Coast Fisheries Case*, Elihu Root, as counsel for the United States, had expressed the view that '[w]arships may not pass without consent into [the territorial sea of another State], because they threaten. Merchant-ships may pass and repass because they do not threaten'.[134] It should also be noted that Root's comments related to navigation in territorial waters in time of peace.

During its period of neutrality in WWI, the United States allowed the passage of both the warships and merchant vessels of belligerents through its territorial sea but applied time limits and reserved the right to expel foreign vessels in the event of any breach of neutrality.[135] The United States also permitted the passage of belligerent warships through the Panama Canal, which was subject to its control under the Hay-Bunau-Varilla Treaty of 1903.[136] Submarines were not singled out from warships generally. There is no indication, however, that the United States considered itself legally bound to permit such passage or without the right to bar it should it see fit.

2.4.5 Norway, Sweden and Denmark

Norway, Sweden and Denmark, also neutral in WWI, had in 1912 enacted identical regulations regarding their neutrality in case of war between foreign powers.[137] These regulations provided inter alia that '[w]ar vessels of belligerent powers may enter . . . harbors and roadsteads as well as other . . . territorial waters with exceptions' for named harbours, roadsteads and 'inner territorial waters'.[138] The definition of 'inner territorial waters' included 'not only harbors, entrances to harbors,

[133] See the US position at the 1907 Hague Conference, discussed in Section 2.2.3.

[134] 'The Law of Territorial Waters' (1929) 23(S5) *American Journal of International Law* 241, 296; *North Atlantic Coast Fisheries Case* (Great Britain v. United States) (Award of 7 September 1910) (1910) 11 RIAA 167.

[135] Proclamation of Neutrality in The World War, 4 August 1914 in Deak and Jessup (n 97) vol. 2, 1201–1204.

[136] Proclamation relating to the Neutrality of the Panama Canal Zone, 13 November 1914 in Deak and Jessup (n 97) vol. 2, 1205–1207.

[137] Deak and Jessup (n 97) vol. 1, 476.

[138] Ibid.

roadsteads and bays, but also the sea territory between and inside islands, small islands, and reefs which are not continually submerged'.[139] However, 'natural routes of communication' between high seas areas were expressly excluded.[140] The regulations also stipulated a twenty-four-hour time limit on the presence of belligerent warships in harbours, roadsteads or territorial waters, with exceptions noted for cases of distress and warships used as 'floating hospitals' or 'exclusively intended for religious, scientific, or humane purposes'.[141] Belligerent warships were prohibited from entering harbours, roadsteads or territorial waters 'in order to renew or increase their military equipment or ammunition supplies or to increase their crew', and limits were imposed on refuelling and provisioning.[142]

In October 1916, Norway responded to the Allies' memoranda regarding belligerent submarines by varying these general rules mentioned above. It issued a Royal Decree providing that '[s]ubmarines, equipped for purposes of war and belonging to a belligerent nation, must not pass through or remain in Norwegian territorial waters' and that '[i]f they violate this prohibition they are subject with warning to seizure by armed force'.[143] Exception was made for cases of distress, in relation to which it was specified that 'within Norwegian waters the vessel shall remain above surface, keep hoisted its national flag and the international signal for the occasion of its visit'.[144] In a formulation intended to cover submarines used for commercial purposes, the Decree further provided that '[n]either can other submarines than those mentioned enter or traverse Norwegian territorial waters, unless this takes place in daylight in visible weather and above surface with the national flag hoisted'.[145]

Germany objected strenuously to the 1916 Decree, which it argued was in breach of Norway's neutrality as being 'to the detriment of one belligerent ... since it is obviously aimed at German submarine boats alone and openly admitted to be a counter measure against their legitimate cruiser warfare'.[146] Norway's attempt to regulate merchant submarines was

[139] Ibid.
[140] Ibid.
[141] Ibid, 477.
[142] Ibid, 477–478.
[143] Royal Resolution regarding Belligerent Submarines in Norwegian Waters, 13 October 1916 in Deak and Jessup (n 97) vol. 2, 842.
[144] Ibid.
[145] Ibid.
[146] 'The Minister in Norway (Schmedeman) to the Secretary of State' in Joseph V. Fuller (ed.), *Papers Relating to the Foreign Relations of the United States: 1916, Supplement, The*

taken to be exclusively aimed at Germany as the only State possessing such vessels[147] – Germany having equipped a number of submarines as cargo carriers to evade the Allied blockade. Norway denied this allegation of partiality, arguing that '[t]he object of the regulations concerning merchant submarines is exclusively to render the control of belligerent war submarines more effective'.[148] It refused to annul the Decree as requested by Germany, and in January 1917, amended it to provide that belligerent submarines violating the prohibition on navigation through the territorial sea will be 'liable to attack by armed force *without* previous warning'.[149]

In August 1914, Sweden took its position forward from the 1912 regulation noted above by issuing a 'Proclamation concerning Prohibition against Entry of Foreign War Vessels into Certain Inner Territorial Waters'.[150] It further 'supplemented' the 1912 regulations by a Decree of November 1915 providing that '[s]ubmarines of belligerent powers are forbidden to navigate or to sojourn in Swedish territorial waters within three marine miles (5,556 meters) from land or from the extreme outlying reefs which are not continually submerged'. Minor exceptions were made for specific fjords and cases of distress.[151]

In July 1916, Sweden issued another Decree noting that (subject to the same exceptions specified in the 1912 regulations), '[s]ubmarines belonging to foreign powers and equipped for use in warfare may not navigate or lie in Swedish territorial waters within 3 nautical minutes (5,556 meters) from land or from extreme outlying skerries, which are not continuously washed over by the sea, *under peril of being attacked by armed force without previous warning*'.[152] Notably, while Sweden

World War (United States Government Printing Office, 1929) 782 (File No. 763.72111/4180) ('28 October Norwegian Paper'). See also 'Zimmermann Calls Norway Unneutral', *New York Times*, 24 October 1916, 2.

[147] '28 October Norwegian Paper' (n 146).

[148] 'The Minister in Norway (Schmedeman) to the Secretary of State' in Joseph V. Fuller (ed.), *Papers Relating to the Foreign Relations of the United States: 1916, Supplement, The World War* (United States Government Printing Office, 1929) 783 (File No. 763.72111/4232).

[149] Royal Ordinance regarding Belligerent Submarines in Norwegian Waters, 30 January 1917 in Deak and Jessup (n 97) vol. 2, 843 (emphasis added).

[150] Proclamation concerning Prohibition against Entry of Foreign War Vessels into Certain Inner Territorial Waters, 6 August 1914 in Deak and Jessup (n 97) vol. 2, 974.

[151] Royal Decree supplementing the Royal Proclamation of December 20 1912, with regard to the Sojourn of Belligerent Submarines in Swedish Waters, 29 November 1915 in Deak and Jessup (n 97) vol. 2, 963.

[152] Royal Decree relating to the Entry and Sojourn of Armed Submarines in Swedish Territorial Waters, 19 July 1916 in Deak and Jessup (n 97) vol. 2, 964 (emphasis added).

officially allowed the passage of warships – including submarines – through Swedish channels in the Sound, it had in 1915 agreed to a German demand to switch off its lighthouses and remove markers in the Øresund to hamper the passage of the British Navy.[153] In 1916, again in response to German pressure, Sweden mined the Kogrundsrännan Channel in the Øresund Straits, limiting passage to Swedish vessels only – a move attracting Allied criticism on the basis that it unfairly disadvantaged the British Navy.[154]

It is important to note that the Swedish decrees regarding submarine passage were *not* a response to the Allies' memorandum regarding submarines, which they predated; indeed, they appear to have been primarily directed against Allied operations. Belligerent submarines had been used to sink a number of vessels in Swedish territorial waters during the summer of 1916 and the new policy was both a protest of this breach of neutrality and a response to the severe impact of the Allies' blockade on Swedish commerce.[155] The 1916 amendment also restricted the application of the Decree to belligerent submarines 'equipped for use in warfare'. The Allies objected to this policy, accusing Sweden of partiality in '[preventing] sub-marine navigation of her territorial waters, except for German submarines, which implies commercial pretext'.[156] The objection here was that the Swedish decree would continue to permit the passage of submarines used for merchant shipping, which were exclusively German.

Notably, the United States also admitted German merchant submarines to its waters and ports prior to its entry into WWI, facilitating breaches of the Allies' blockade. In July 1916, the Allies protested the United States' reception of the German merchant submarine *Deutschland*; however, the US position was that this commercial vessel was to be treated like any other.[157] This stance may have bolstered the position of Sweden and Norway in continuing to admit merchant

153 Halpern (n 67) 276.

154 Ibid, 308.

155 Eli F. Heckscher et al., *Sweden, Norway, Denmark and Iceland in the World War* (Yale University Press, 1930) 94–98.

156 'Sweden and the War: Partiality for the Germans: Protest by the Allies', *Hobart Mercury*, 19 September 1916, 5.

157 'The Department of State to the French Embassy' in Joseph V. Fuller (ed.), *Papers Relating to the Foreign Relations of the United States: 1916, Supplement, The World War* (United States Government Printing Office, 1929) 770 (Document No. 1008). See also 'Draft Convention on Rights and Duties of Neutral States in Naval and Aerial War with Commentaries' (n 47) 432.

submarines. The practice of the United States and Sweden was an important prompt for the Allies' memorandum of August 1916, which urged neutral States to 'prevent belligerent submarines, *regardless of their use*, to avail themselves of neutral waters, roadsteads, and harbors'.[158]

Denmark's response to the Allies' memorandum had been to reiterate the application of 'its law of December 20, 1912, the substance of which is that war submarines shall be treated as other war vessels'.[159] It made the same point in response to a circular telegram from the United States to Sweden, Norway, Denmark, the Netherlands and Spain in October 1916 seeking 'information as to what restrictions, if any, have been imposed upon use of neutral ports and waters by belligerent submarines, either before or since the Entente note of August last respecting treatment of submarines by neutral powers'.[160] Denmark clarified that it had 'issued no decrees or decisions concerning war submarines except as contained in its law of December 20, 1912, the substance of which is that war submarines shall be treated as other war vessels'.[161] It advised the United States that '[t]he question of merchant submarines has not arisen and the Government is not willing to give a decision until that question shall arise'.[162]

As noted above, the identical 1912 regulations of Norway, Sweden and Denmark had limited the access of warships to certain 'inner territorial waters' but otherwise allowed for their innocent passage. Denmark did, however, prohibit belligerent warships from straits ordinarily used for passage in the Great Belt, the Danish Channel in the south of Little Belt and the three Danish belts in the Sound.[163] The United Kingdom

158 'The Department of State to the French Embassy' (n 157) (emphasis added).

159 'The Minister in Denmark (Egan) to the Secretary of State' in Joseph V. Fuller (ed.), *Papers Relating to the Foreign Relations of the United States: 1916, Supplement, The World War* (United States Government Printing Office, 1929) 775 (File No. 763.72111/4127) ('Danish Paper').

160 'The Acting Secretary of State to Diplomatic Officers in Sweden, Norway, Denmark, the Netherlands and Spain' in Joseph V. Fuller (ed.), *Papers Relating to the Foreign Relations of the United States: 1916, Supplement, The World War* (United States Government Printing Office, 1929) 772 (File No. 763.72111/4121a).

161 'Danish Paper' (n 159).

162 Ibid.

163 For discussion, see Deak and Jessup (n 97) vol. 1 526–527; Brüel, *International Straits* (n 36) 119–120; Hugo Caminos and Vincent P. Cogliati-Bantz, *The Legal Regime of Straits: Contemporary Challenges and Solutions* (Cambridge University Press, 2014) 32; Richard R. Baxter, 'Passage of Ships through International Waterways in Time of War' (1954) 31 *British Yearbook of International Law* 187, 193–194; Ian O. Johnson, 'Strategy on the Wintry Sea: The Russo-British Submarine Flotilla in the Baltic, 1914–1918' (2020) *International Journal of Military History and Historiography* 187, 193.

nevertheless sent submarines through Danish waters in the Øresund from October 1914, and by 1915, a substantial Russo-British submarine flotilla was based in Reval (now Tallinn) under Russian command.[164] The successful operations of British submarines against both German warships and merchant shipping in 1915 (a strategic objective being to prevent the import of iron ore from Sweden to Germany),[165] coupled with an incident in which a British submarine stranded in the Danish Sound was attacked and destroyed by a German torpedo boat, prompted Denmark to take further action – in tacit cooperation with Germany – to prevent submarine passage through the Sound.[166] No protests seem to have been received and, apart from the northern part of Little Belt, which was kept open to allow continued use of the German Channel (Aaroesound), the Danish straits remained closed throughout the war.[167]

2.4.6 *Turkey and the Straits*

During WWI, the Ottoman Empire controlled the Bosphorus and Dardanelles Straits linking the Black Sea to the Mediterranean. The Ottoman Empire had long claimed the right to close the Turkish Straits to foreign warships, which was described as the 'ancient rule of the Ottoman Empire'.[168] In September 1914, the Ottoman Empire had issued 'Neutrality Regulations' providing that '[e]ntry to Turkish ports, roadsteads, and territorial waters, is forbidden to warships belonging to belligerent powers, except in the case of damage, or by reason of the state of the sea'.[169] These regulations post-dated a secret alliance with Germany of August 1914 and were shortly followed by the Ottoman Empire's entry into the war on the side of Germany and the Central Powers in October.[170] They provided that belligerent warships could still

164 Johnson (n 163) 193–201.

165 Ibid, 199–210.

166 See Michael H. Clemmesen, 'Military and Strategy (Denmark)', *International Encyclopedia of the First World War* <https://encyclopedia.1914-1918-online.net/article/military_and_strategy_denmark>.

167 Brüel, *International Straits* (n 36) 120.

168 Nilufer Oral, 'Black Sea Security under the 1936 Montreux Treaty' in Carlos Espósito et al. (eds.), *Ocean Law and Policy: Twenty Years of Development under the UNCLOS Regime* (Brill, 2016) 266, 267–268. See further Alexander L. MacFie, 'The Straits Question in the First World War, 1914–18' (1983) 19(1) *Middle Eastern Studies* 43, 46.

169 Neutrality Regulations in the World War, 28 September 1914 in Deak and Jessup (n 97) vol. 2, 1065.

170 Ulrich Trumpener, 'Turkey's Entry into WWI: An Assessment of Responsibilities' (1962) 34(4) *The Journal of Modern History* 369.

request permission to enter a port or roadstead 'for the purposes of refueling or revictualing', which might be specifically authorised (though access to the ports of Smyrna and Beirut was expressly prohibited).[171] It was also noted that '[t]he ... provisions in no way supersede the regulations governing the Straits, which remain as established by international treaty'.[172]

During WWI, Turkey exercised its right to close the Bosphorus and Dardanelles Straits to foreign warships, including Russian vessels, but admitted German warships; initially claiming that it had bought these vessels, and later sending out both Turkish and German warships from the Straits to attack Russian ports and shipping.[173] Among the Allied Powers, Russia protested this action most vehemently.[174]

The strategic importance of the Turkish Straits is clearly reflected in the 1918 Armistice Agreement of Mudros between the Ottoman Empire and Great Britain (representing the Allies).[175] Though several of the Allies had broader ambitions regarding parts of the Ottoman Empire, control of the Straits and access to the Black Sea was their foremost concern at this time – Russia having already officially exited the war upon signing a peace treaty with Germany in March 1918.[176] Yet the Mudros Armistice also anticipated the persistence of competing interests in both the Straits and Turkish land territory by providing for an Allied right to 'occupy any strategic points in the event of a situation arising which threatens the security of the allies'.[177] The question of access was thus at the forefront of this agreement, and submarines were not singled out for treatment.

2.4.7 *Italy and the Strait of Messina*

At the outbreak of WWI, Italy generally allowed the passage of warships through its territorial waters in time of peace, though it reserved a right to refuse permission 'in the interests of national defence, to

171 Deak and Jessup (n 97) vol. 2, 1065.
172 Ibid, 1067.
173 MacFie (n 168) 46–50.
174 Ibid, 50–53.
175 Armistice of Mudros, Mudros, 30 October 1918, 224 CTS 169. See Gwynne Dyer, 'The Turkish Armistice of 1918: A Lost Opportunity: The Armistice Negotiations of Moudros' (1972) 8(3) *Middle Eastern Studies* 313. See further the discussion on the Turkish Straits in Chapter 5.
176 Dyer (n 175), 317, 321.
177 Ibid, 338–339.

foreign war-ships to pass through or stop in such parts of the territorial waters that may from time to time be designated'.[178] Its Law of 16 June 1912 remains in force, though Italy is also party to both the 1958 law of the sea conventions and the United Nations Convention on the Law of the Sea (UNCLOS). This 1912 law provided that the passage and stay of national and foreign merchant ships may be prohibited at any time anywhere in the territorial sea or internal waters for reasons of national defence.[179]

Italy is often reported to have closed the Strait of Messina (encompassed by its then claim to a six nautical mile territorial sea) to foreign warships during its period of neutrality in WWI.[180] In fact, it appears that warships were not entirely excluded from the Strait, though Italy considered itself entitled to impose such an exclusion. Italy's laws at the time prohibited hostilities between belligerent warships in its territorial waters, including the pursuit and capture of prizes, but not mere passage.[181] It also limited the stay of warships to twenty-four hours, and may have considered the same time limit to apply to passage (the

178 Decree 243 of the King of Italy Laying Down Regulations in Time of Peace for the Arrival and Sojourn of Foreign War-Ships in the Harbours and the Coasts of the Kingdom, 24 May 1906 in (1909–1910) 103 *British and Foreign State Papers* 988.

179 Law No. 612 of 16 June 1912 [1912] 151 *Official Gazette of the Italian Republic* (27 June 1912).

180 Brüel, *International Straits* (n 36) 114; Baxter (n 163) 194; Caminos and Cogliati-Bantz (n 163) 32. This claim seems to have been first made by Brüel, who cites an Italian Decree of 1915 as authority – the same claim and authority being reiterated by later authors reviewing the history of the law relating to straits. However, the Decree in question (issued after Italy declared war with Austria-Hungary, though it remained neutral with respect to Germany) merely prohibited navigation at night and provided that:

> while maintaining the regulations in force with regard to warships, torpedo boats and submarines of the Allied national navies, or all Allied or neutral national merchant ships are ordered to wait for authorization before crossing the strait for ships coming from the north, by keeping on the meridian of forte apuria, at least 3 miles away and exchanging signals with this semaphore; for them coming from the south keeping on the meridian of Cape Dell Armi and observing the same prescriptions.

The regulations in force regarding warships allowed passage, though limits were placed on the number of ships admitted at any time and the length of their stay. See 'Avis aux navigateurs' (1915) 146 *Journal officiel de la République française* 3518, 3518–3519 (1 June 1915); 'Italy' in Deak and Jessup (n 97) vol. 1, 711.

181 Decree No. 243 (n 180); Merchant Marine Code, 24 October 1877 in Deak and Jessup (n 97) vol. 1, 719–720.

scope of the law in this regard is unclear).[182] A Decree of 1915 further prohibited passage at night and required 'torpedo boats and submarines of the Allied national navies, or all Allied or neutral national merchant ships' to wait for authorisation before crossing the strait during the day.[183] Passage as such was not prohibited.[184]

2.4.8 *South America*

Although the belligerent warships operating in South American waters were mostly cruisers, Germany's unrestricted submarine warfare had a substantial impact on South American merchant ships, particularly in the North Atlantic. While German merchant submarines used as 'blockade runners' travelled to North America from 1916, it was not until 1918 that large German U-cruiser submarines were deployed to attack shipping off the coast of the United States and in the vicinity of the Azores and the African coast.[185]

Chile claimed the entire Magellan Straits as territorial waters for the purposes of neutrality in a 1914 Decree,[186] but left the Straits and other territorial waters open to the passage of both the merchant ships and warships of belligerents.[187] Access to Chile reflected the importance of Chilean exports of nitrate-rich caliche used in the manufacture of explosives (though Chile's importance in this regard was reduced after Germany went on to develop synthetic nitrate during the war).[188]

Brazil, neutral at the start of WWI, joined the conflict on the side of the Allies in 1917 both in solidarity with the United States and 'to take measures for the defence of our navigation abroad'.[189] While neutral, it continued to permit the passage of belligerent merchant ships and

[182] Merchant Marine Code, 24 October 1877 in Deak and Jessup (n 97) vol. 1, 719–720.

[183] 'Avis aux navigateurs' (n 180).

[184] The understanding that the strait was closed to warships seems to have been prompted by circumstances surrounding the British pursuit of the German ships *Goeben* and *Breslau* in 1915. For discussion, see Halpern (n 67) 86, 90–92.

[185] Halpern (n 67) 610–617; Carroll Storrs Alden, 'American Submarine Operations in the War' (1920) 46/7/208 *US Naval Institute Proceedings* 811–850.

[186] Decree concerning Jurisdictional Waters, especially in the Straits of Magellan, 15 December 1914 in Deak and Jessup (n 97) vol. 1, 354–355.

[187] This is consistent with Article 5 of the Boundary Treaty between Chile and Argentina, Buenos Aires, 23 July 1881, 159 CTS 45, which provided that '[t]he Straits of Magellan shall be neutralized for ever, and free navigation assured to the flags of all nations'.

[188] David A. Gross, 'Caliche: The Conflict Mineral that Fuelled the First World War', *The Guardian*, 2 June 2014.

[189] See Decree No. 3266, 1 June 1917 in Deak and Jessup (n 97) vol. 1, 84–85.

warships through its territorial waters, though it imposed limits on the length of stay, refuelling and provisioning. Upon revoking its neutrality, Brazil requisitioned all German merchant ships anchored in Brazilian ports and added them to the Brazilian registry.[190] The Brazilian Navy did not deploy submarines but engaged in anti-submarine operations in the Atlantic.

Several other South American States broke off diplomatic relations with Germany in solidarity with the entry of the United States and then Brazil into WWI, but did not enter into the conflict.[191] Argentina was among those States maintaining (neutral) relations with Germany. This position was encouraged by Germany's exceptional agreement, following diplomatic incidents relating to German attacks on Argentinian merchant ships, to allow Argentine passage through its submarine blockade.[192]

2.4.9 *Japan*

Japan, already allied with the United Kingdom under a 1901 Agreement, was the only notable naval force in East Asia during WWI. Japan declared war on Germany in August 1914 following a communique from the British Foreign Secretary, Grey, requesting the assistance of the Japanese Imperial Navy to 'hunt out and destroy German armed merchant cruisers in East Asian waters'.[193] Japan's naval fleet participated in the seizure of German territories in the Pacific, the protection of convoys

190 Decree No. 11038 Ordering that Complete Neutrality be Observed during the War of the German Empire against the French Republic and the Empire of Russia, 4 August 1914 in Deak and Jessup (n 98) vol. 1, 83–85; Decree No. 11037 General Rules of Neutrality, 4 August 1914 in Deak and Jessup (n 97) 85–89.

191 Michael Streeter, *South America and the Treaty of Versailles: The Peace Conferences of 1919–23 and Their Aftermath* (Haus, 2011) 53–79. Streeter notes that Mexico, Chile, Argentina, Venezuela and Colombia did not break off relations with Germany: Ibid, 58. See also 'Relations of Latin-American Countries with the United States and with European Belligerent Countries as Affected by the War in General and by the German Submarine Warfare' in Joseph V. Fuller (ed.), *Papers Relating to the Foreign Relations of the United States: 1917, Supplement 1, The World War* (United States Government Printing Office, 1931) 219–400.

192 Phillip Dehne, 'How Important Was Latin America to the First World War?' (2014) 14(53) *Iberoamericana* 151, 154. President Irigoyen maintained neutrality against the wishes of the Argentinian Parliament, which voted twice to sever relations with Germany.

193 J. Charles Schencking, 'The Imperial Japanese Navy and the First World War' in Tosh Minohara, Tze-ki Hon and Evan Dawley (eds.), *The Decade of the Great War: Japan and the Wider World in the 1910s* (Brill, 2014) 83, 88.

of Australian and New Zealand troops through the Indian Ocean and Malacca Straits, and in 1917, Allied operations against German submarines in the Mediterranean.[194]

Japan had previously kept its own straits closed to all foreign ships before the United Kingdom, France, the Netherlands and the United States in 1863 and 1864 forced the opening of the Shimonoseki Strait to allow the passage of merchant ships.[195] In the 1904–1905 Russo-Japanese War, the Tsugaru Strait had been left open for neutral merchant shipping.[196] Upon its entry into WWI, Japan demanded that Germany withdraw its warships from Japanese and Chinese waters and quickly gained control of the German naval base at Tsingtao and Germany's colonies in the Pacific.[197] Japan's military success severely limited the activities of the German East-Asia squad in the Pacific. Japan's naval strength in the Pacific also allowed the US Navy to focus its energies on anti-submarine operations in the Atlantic.[198] Japanese submarines do not seem to have played a significant role in these operations.[199]

Japan had acquired its first submarines during its war with Russia in 1904; however, these vessels, purchased from an American company, were too primitive to be deployed in the conflict. In 1913, the naval minister, Saitō, supported by Prime Minister Yamamoto, introduced a plan for naval expansion that would have added ten submarines to the fleet by 1921.[200] This plan was denied finance by Japan's upper house of parliament in early 1914 (leading to Yamamoto's resignation).[201] Nevertheless, at the outbreak of WWI, Japan had enough submarines to establish a squad at Kure Naval District in the Seto Inland Sea. It expanded this fleet in 1917 and further at the end of WWI, when it received a number of German U-boats as reparations.[202]

194 Timothy D. Saxon, 'Anglo-Japanese Naval Cooperation, 1914–1918' (2000) 53(1) *Naval War College Review* 62–92.

195 Brüel, *International Straits* (n 36) 105.

196 Pirjo Kleemola-Juntunen, *The Åland Strait* (Brill Nijhoff, 2019) 150.

197 Saxon (n 194) 64.

198 Ibid, 79.

199 Ibid, 62–92.

200 Schencking (n 193) 84–87.

201 Ibid.

202 Peter J. Hooker, 'In the Shadow of the Fleet: The Development of Japan's Submarine Force, 1917–1941' (2018) 30(3) *International Journal of Maritime History* 458, 460–461.

2.4.10 The Significance of State Practice

State practice as a whole during WWI suggests that both belligerents and neutral States considered themselves entitled to prohibit the passage of warships through their territorial waters and, in some cases, international straits. Protests against these measures were largely based on claims that they unfairly disadvantaged certain belligerents, breaching the neutral duty of impartiality. Indeed, the key ground for objections to the closure of straits concerned breaches of neutrality. Claims to a right of innocent passage for warships were not insisted upon during WWI. Accordingly, it cannot be said that such a right was recognised in customary international law at this time. However, as we shall see, State practice during WWI informed further developments in both customary and conventional law after the conflict even for times of peace. The special threat posed by submarines due to their capacity for covert action and the experience of unrestricted submarine warfare would also leave their mark on both future conflict and future law, including regimes of passage and other regulations applying to submarines qua submarines or as warships in times of both peace and war.

2.5 Conclusion

This chapter has shown that while the right to exclude belligerent warships, including submarines, from territorial waters might be understood as a consequence of neutrality, many States considered it to follow instead from their sovereignty in coastal waters – and to be compatible with neutrality rather than contingent upon it. At the 1907 Hague Conference, the United States insisted that the measures taken by a State to ensure its neutrality were 'done in virtue of its own rights' as 'sovereign within its own jurisdiction'.[203] This view prompted 'earnest discussion' during which it was agreed that the only relevant obligation flowing from neutrality in time of war was 'the obligation to treat the two belligerents in the same way and to apply to them impartially the conditions, restrictions or prohibitions that it has pleased the neutral Government to make'.[204] The right to impose such 'conditions, restrictions or prohibitions' was 'derived from its sovereignty and pre-exist[ed] war'.[205] It was on this basis that Hague Convention (XIII) of 1907

[203] Scott, *Reports to the Hague Conferences* (n 44) 846.
[204] Ibid.
[205] Ibid.

omitted any mention of rights or obligations on the part of neutral States relating to passage through their territorial waters. Instead, Article 10 provided simply that a State's neutrality would not be impugned if they allowed the 'mere passage' of belligerent warships or prizes through its territorial waters. This approach suggests that a right on the part of the coastal State to bar the passage of warships through its territorial waters was not necessarily considered to be limited to time of war. At the very least, it indicates there was no generally recognised right of innocent passage through the territorial sea for warships at this time.

The effort of many States to exclude submarines in particular from both territorial waters and straits was part of a broader Allied strategy to disrupt Germany's U-boat campaign or, conversely, an Axis strategy to prevent British submarine forces from entering the Baltic. While these motives evidently underpinned, respectively, the Allied Memoranda of 1916 and the pressure placed by Germany on Sweden and Denmark with regard to their belts and sounds, neutral States also appear to have been concerned with particular features of submarines – their capacity to avoid detection and launch surprise attacks – as enhancing their threat. Several States that either permitted the passage of submarines through their waters as a general rule or noted an exception for such passage in cases of distress specified that these vessels should navigate on the surface and display their national flag.[206] These conditions are now familiar as a feature of the provisions of the 1958 Territorial Sea Convention and UNCLOS relating to passage through the territorial sea,[207] as discussed in Chapter 7.

State practice, the proceedings of the IDI and ILA, and negotiations at the Hague Conferences suggest that the right to take measures to bar or regulate the passage of submarines was widely understood to be a consequence of sovereignty rather than neutrality. This predicate has relevance for determining the basis of laws of peacetime, rather than limiting these early legal developments to the law of naval warfare. At the same time, it is evident that these measures were taken in response to the threat represented by belligerent submarines in the context of armed conflict. Yet the existence of such a threat or the presence of an armed

[206] See e.g., the regulations of Spain, Norway and Sweden discussed in Sections 2.4.3 and 2.4.5 above.

[207] Convention on the Territorial Sea and the Contiguous Zone, Geneva, 29 April 1958, entered into force 22 November 1964, 516 UNTS 205, art. 14; United Nations Convention on the Law of the Sea, Montego Bay, 10 December 1982, entered into force 16 November 1994, 1833 UNTS 397, art. 20

conflict does not seem to have been considered a legal precondition for limiting or regulating passage at this time. Subsequent developments would see certain aspects of this historical context evolve into conditions informing the concept of innocent passage and the capacity of the coastal State to limit or regulate passage through its territorial waters, including straits, during times of peace.

3

Regulating Submarines in the Inter-war Period from Versailles (1919) to The Hague (1930)

3.1 Introduction

The inter-war period was characterised by tensions between a push for naval disarmament and the concern of many States to build their naval forces and secure strategic advantages. Both interests were driven in significant part by the critical role naval warfare – and submarine warfare in particular – had played in World War I (WWI). The inter-war period was also characterised by renewed efforts to codify and progressively develop the legal regime of the territorial sea, including laws relating to passage. Some of these efforts sought to distinguish the rules generally applicable to the territorial sea in times of peace from those applicable in times of war, most notably in relation to the rights and obligations of neutral States. Yet experiences in WWI continued to inform the treatment of questions of passage, including the passage of submarines.

In the context of arms limitation talks, proposals to ban the submarine altogether were again raised and again failed. Further efforts were made to both limit the tonnage of submarines and regulate their engagements with merchant vessels in the context of naval war. The heavy toll exacted by German U-boats in WWI, including their rupture of past strategies and norms of naval warfare, was a significant stimulus for these efforts. However, States were also concerned to protect and advance a variety of national interests through manipulations of the balance of naval power. The post-war distribution of German U-boats as reparations and the allocation of former German territorial possessions as mandates played into power politics in the Pacific, raising tensions between Japan and the United States. Both States anticipated that submarines would play a critical role in any future conflict in this region. A view shared by the United Kingdom. This consideration played into both arms limitation negotiations and the project to codify the regime of the territorial sea.

The treatment of warships (including submarines) under the succession of treaty regimes developed with respect to the Turkish Straits in the post-war period was also an important part of the context for these legal projects. The content of these treaties and their successes and failures in application influenced the broader approach to passage through straits. At the same time, the Turkish Straits came to be identified as the preeminent example of a special treaty regime excluded from the application of any general rules.

The strategic positioning of States in the context of the post-war settlement and the evolving situation in the Pacific played into the preparatory work for the 1930 Hague Codification Conference and negotiations at the 1930 Conference itself. While the 1930 Conference failed to adopt a treaty on the territorial sea, it did produce a set of Draft Articles that would significantly influence the subsequent development of both the 1958 law of the sea conventions and, by way of these instruments, the UN Convention on the Law of the Sea (UNCLOS).

This chapter traces developments relating to the legal regulation of submarines from the post-war settlement at Versailles to the Codification Conference at the Hague in 1930. Section 3.2 focuses on specific implications of the Treaty of Versailles for naval strategy and Section 3.3 highlights issues arising from the treaties concerned with the regulation of the Turkish Straits, especially in terms of passage rights for warships and their foundational importance for subsequent rules relating to international straits. Section 3.4 shifts focus away from Eurasia to the Pacific, and Japan's growing sphere of influence. Notable for present purposes was Japan's expanding submarine fleet and the concomitant concerns of the United States and the United Kingdom to keep this development in check. This discussion is vital background for one of the only submarine-specific treaties to have been adopted and was accompanied by other agreements concerned with arms reduction. These international laws are examined in Section 3.5. Section 3.6 sets out the critical discussions of the Hague Codification Conference that considered rights of passage for submarines specifically and warships generally in the territorial sea. The chapter shows how the naval capacity and concerns of States altered with the redistribution of the warships and former colonies of the Central Powers after WWI as well as the demilitarisation of certain States and areas under the WWI peace treaties. These developments influenced State views regarding both the strategic value and threat of submarines, informing international efforts to limit arms and codify the law relating to the territorial sea. The perspectives articulated during these historic events have resounded in contemporary laws concerning the passage of submarines in the territorial sea and in internationals traits.

3.2 Naval Strategy and the Treaty of Versailles

An Armistice Agreement between Germany and the Allied and Associated Powers was signed on 11 November 1918. The 'Naval Conditions' set out in the agreement provided that neutrals were to be notified 'that freedom of navigation in all territorial waters is given to the navies and mercantile marines of the allied and associated powers, all questions of neutrality being waived'.[1] Germany was also required '[t]o surrender at the ports specified by the Allies and the United States all submarines at present in existence (including all submarine cruisers and mine layers), with armament and equipment complete'.[2] '[T]hose that can not put to sea' were to 'be deprived of armament and equipment and ... remain under the supervision of the Allies and the United States'.[3] The surrender of submarines was to be completed within fourteen days of signing the armistice.[4]

At the 1919 Paris Peace Conference, the 'Council of Four' – the United Kingdom, the United States, France and Italy – dominated the negotiation of the terms of the peace settlement, with Japan joining the proceedings to represent its interests with respect to a number of key issues (the 'Council of Five').[5] The 1919 Treaty between Germany and the Allied and Associated Powers redrew Germany's boundaries and provided for inter alia its renunciation of all former colonies.[6] Under the mandate system elaborated in Article 22, Japan was granted the 'South Seas Mandate', including the Caroline, Marshall and Mariana Islands (except for Guam), which were former German territories occupied by Japan during the war. As discussed in Section 3.4, naval strategy seems to

[1] Armistice between Germany and the Allied Powers, Compiègne, 11 November 1918, entered into force 11 November 1918, 224 CTS 286, art. 20.

[2] Ibid, art. 22.

[3] Ibid.

[4] Ibid.

[5] Frank Schorkopf, 'Versailles Peace Treaty (1919)' in Anne Peters and Rüdiger Wolfrum (eds.), *The Max Planck Encyclopedia of Public International Law* (Oxford University Press, October 2010).

[6] Treaty of Peace between the Allied and Associated Powers and Germany, Versailles, 28 June 1919, entered into force 10 January 1920, [1919] UKTS 4, pt. IV ('Treaty of Versailles').

have been particularly important in connection with Japan's mandates in the Pacific.[7]

Part V of the Treaty of Versailles effected an extensive disarmament of Germany, severely limiting the number of vessels the German naval forces could have in commission and entirely prohibiting the commission of submarines.[8] Article 191 provided that '[t]he construction or acquisition of any submarine, even for commercial purposes, shall be forbidden in Germany'. German vessels outside German harbours as well as an extensive list of warships within Germany were surrendered, and the provisions on reparations provided for the further transfer of German ships to Allied and Associated Powers.[9]

A broader programme of disarmament was reflected in the establishment of the League of Nations as an international organisation 'to promote international co-operation and to achieve international peace and security'.[10] It is interesting to note that the American legal adviser, David Hunter Miller (who worked with Cecil Hurst to produce the draft used as the basis for the meetings of the League Commission) had suggested to then US President Wilson that his draft be amended to provide that 'The Contracting Parties agree never to make use of armed submarines in naval operations, and further agree that they will hereafter build no submarines armed or capable of being armed and further agree that all submarines now in existence or under construction shall be dismantled and rendered incapable of being armed or shall be destroyed.'[11]

While this clause was not adopted in any of the draft plans for the League or the final Covenant, the project of reducing armaments continued to be advanced through naval treaties concluded in the inter-war period. These developments influenced the treatment of warships, including submarines, in discussions regarding the regime of the territorial sea at the 1930 Hague Codification Conference.

The 1919 Peace Treaty also included several provisions relating to passage. The Allied and Associated Powers insisted on 'freedom of transit' through German territories 'on the routes most convenient for

[7] See discussion in Section 3.4 below.

[8] Treaty of Versailles (n 6) art. 181.

[9] Ibid, arts. 130, 184, 185 and pt. VII.

[10] Ibid, preamble to pt. I.

[11] Howard Levie, 'Submarine Warfare: With Emphasis on the 1936 London Protocol' (1998) 70 *Naval War College International Law Studies* 291, 306–307; David Hunter Miller, *The Drafting of the Covenant* (GP Putnam's Sons, 1928) vol. 2, 73–74.

international transit, either by rail, navigable waterway, or canal, to persons, goods, vessels, carriages, wagons and mails coming from or going to the territories of any of the Allied and Associated Powers (whether contiguous or not)', specifying that 'for this purpose the crossing of territorial waters shall be allowed'.[12] Article 327 provided for a right of free navigation in German territorial waters, German ports, and 'inland navigation routes' on a basis of equality with German nationals, vessels and property.[13]

Article 195 of the Treaty of Versailles provided for the removal of fortifications and armaments to ensure 'free passage into the Baltic to all nations', and Germany was required to provide 'all hydrographical information now in its possession concerning the channels and adjoining waters between the Baltic and the North Sea'. Article 380 provided that '[t]he Kiel Canal and its approaches shall be maintained free and open to the vessels of commerce and of war of all nations at peace with Germany on terms of entire equality'. The Treaty also temporarily granted the Allied and Associated Powers freedom of passage and landing for aircraft over German land territory and territorial waters.[14] Article 271 provided that '[a]s regards sea fishing, maritime coasting trade, and maritime towage, vessels of the Allied and Associated Powers shall enjoy, in German territorial waters, the treatment accorded to vessels of the most favoured nation'.

The above provisions drastically reduced Germany's naval power, while allowing the Allies and Associated Powers to build their own naval resources (with German ships) and make strategic use of the territorial waters of Germany and its former possessions. While the Treaty of Versailles was only partly executed before its suspension at the outbreak of World War II (WWII) (and was not re-established), the terms of the peace settlement informed both the subsequent strategic use of submarines and attempts to legally regulate them. The tension between provisions aimed at disarmament and the interest of the Allied and Associated Powers in securing both commercial and military advantages is also apparent in the separate peace treaties concluded by a number of States with Germany – including the

[12] Treaty of Versailles (n 6) art. 321.

[13] Similarly, under Article 89, Poland was also required to 'accord freedom of transit to persons, goods, vessels, carriages, wagons and mails in transit between East Prussia and the rest of Germany over Polish territory, including territorial waters'.

[14] Treaty of Versailles (n 6) pt. XI.

United States, which did not ratify the 1919 Treaty of Versailles – as well as the peace treaties with other Central Powers.

3.3 The Turkish Straits: The Treaties of Sèvres (1920) and Lausanne (1923)

Of particular note among the separate peace treaties concluded with the Central Powers is the Treaty of Sèvres signed by the Allied and Associated Powers and Turkey (as it was then known) in 1920 (though never ratified).[15] This Treaty was heavily influenced by the British interest in control over the strategically important Dardanelles Straits with a view to both blocking Russian access to the Mediterranean and maintaining a channel for British naval access to Russia and the Black Sea.[16] The United Kingdom, France and the United States were also concerned by Italy's interest in expansion and thus supported Greece's occupation of Smyrna as a means of thwarting Italy; though a Commission set up under the auspices of the Peace Conference shortly thereafter declared that the occupation was 'not justifiable'.[17]

The Greek incursions galvanised the opposition of the Turkish National Movement to the Treaty of Sèvres. Led by Mustafa Kemal (Atatürk), the Movement rehabilitated what was left of the Ottoman army and mobilised it against the Greek occupation. The United Kingdom was concerned to oppose this move in the name of preserving the neutral, demilitarised Straits Zone established by the Treaty of Sèvres to support freedom of commerce through the Straits.[18] Yet faced with the prospect of war with Turkey over control of the Straits, France and Italy withdrew their forces,[19] and the United Kingdom ultimately accepted Turkey's demands, leading to a new settlement in the 1923 Treaty of Lausanne.[20] Each of these treaties and their relevance for the legal regulation of submarines are discussed in this Section.

[15] Treaty of Peace Between the Allied and Associated Powers and Turkey, Sèvres, 10 August 1920, never entered into force, 113 BFSP 652 ('Treaty of Sèvres').

[16] Theo Karvounarakis, 'End of an Empire: Great Britain, Turkey and Greece from the Treaty of Sevres to the Treaty of Lausanne' (2000) 41(1) *Balkan Studies* 171, 172.

[17] Peter M. Buzanski, 'The Interallied Investigation of the Greek Invasion of Smyrna' (1963) 25(3) *The Historian* 325, 333.

[18] Erik Brüel, *International Straits: A Treatise on International Law* (Sweet & Maxwell, 1947) vol. 1, 121–122.

[19] Ibid.

[20] Treaty of Peace with Turkey, Lausanne, 24 July 1923, entered into force 6 August 1923, 28 LNTS 11 ('Treaty of Lausanne').

3.3.1 *The Treaty of Sèvres*

The Treaty of Sèvres was designed to dismantle the Ottoman Empire, reducing Turkish territory to Central Anatolia. Article 37 provided that '[t]he navigation of the Straits, including the Dardanelles, the Sea of Marmora and the Bosphorus, shall in future be open, both in peace and war, to every vessel of commerce or of war and to military and commercial aircraft, without distinction of flag'. It also stated that '[t]hese waters shall not be subject to blockade, nor shall any belligerent right be exercised, nor any act of hostility be committed within them, unless in pursuance of a decision of the Council of the League of Nations'.

In the name of ensuring freedom of navigation in the Straits, Article 38 assigned control of the Dardanelles Strait to an international commission dominated by the United Kingdom and France.[21] Article 39 provided that 'the authority of the Commission will extend to all the waters between the Mediterranean mouth of the Dardanelles and the Black Sea mouth of the Bosphorus, and to the waters within three miles of each of these mouths', noting that '[t]his authority may be exercised on shore to such extent as may be necessary for the execution of the provisions of this Section'.

According to Article 56, '[s]hips of war in transit through the waters specified in Article 39' were to 'conform in all respects to the regulations issued by the Commission for the observance of the ordinary rules of navigation and of sanitary requirements'. Article 57 specified further regulations for belligerent warships, restricting revictualling and repairs to those determined by the Straits Commission to be 'strictly' or 'absolutely' necessary and requiring passage to be effected 'with the least possible delay, and without any other interruption than that resulting from the necessities of the service'. The stay of warships in ports was limited to twenty-four hours except in cases of distress, and it was noted that '[a]ny further regulations affecting in time of war the waters under the control of the Commission, and relating in particular to the passage of war material and contraband destined for the enemies of Turkey, or revictualling, taking in stores or carrying out repairs in the said waters, will be laid down by the League of Nations'. Article 58 applied the same conditions to prizes, while Article 59 provided that '[n]o belligerent shall embark or disembark troops, munitions of war or warlike materials in the waters under the control of the Commission, except in case of accidental

[21] See also Treaty of Sèvres (n 15) art. 40.

hindrance of the passage, and in such cases the passage shall be resumed with all possible despatch'. Article 60 clarified that '[n]othing in Articles 57, 58 or 59 shall be deemed to limit the powers of a belligerent or belligerents acting in pursuance of a decision by the Council of the League of Nations'.

As well as effectively usurping Turkish control of the Straits, the Treaty of Sèvres sought to destroy Turkey's naval forces. Under Article 181, Turkey was required to surrender all warships interned in Turkish ports since the Armistice to the Principal Allied Powers. Article 184 provided for the breaking up of '[a]ll warships, including submarines, now under construction in Turkey . . . with the exception of such surface vessels as can be completed for commercial purposes'. A number of Ottoman warships were scrapped immediately while others were moved to areas under Allied control (such as the Princes' Islands and Golden Horn).[22] Turkey had just one operational submarine during WWI that it had captured from France in 1915 but never commissioned.[23] This submarine was returned to France and scrapped in 1919.[24] Article 186 further provided that '[t]he construction or acquisition of any submarine, even for commercial purposes, shall be forbidden in Turkey'.

3.3.2 *The Treaty of Lausanne and the Straits Convention*

Following the defeat of Greek occupying forces in Smyrna by the Turkish army and Turkish troops' confrontation of the Allied forces in the Dardanelles area (the Chanak Crisis), the United Kingdom agreed to negotiate a new peace settlement with Turkey.[25] Under the 1922 Mudanya Armistice, a number of warships flagged for destruction under the Treaty of Sèvres were returned to Turkey, which would be permitted to maintain a small defensive fleet under the Treaty of Lausanne.[26]

The 1923 Treaty of Lausanne amended the legal regime governing the Turkish Straits.[27] The regime was subsequently altered by the Montreux

[22] See 'World War I at Sea: Turkish or Ottoman Navy', 8 November 2013 <www.naval-history.net/WW1Navy-Turkish_Navy_WW1.htm>.

[23] See 'List of French Submarines, 1863–Present' <www.worldnavalships.com/submarines2.htm>.

[24] Ibid.

[25] Karvounarakis (n 16) 175–181.

[26] Armistice of Mudanya between Turkey, Italy, France and Great Britain, Mudanya, 11 October 1922. See 'Turkish Ottoman Navy' <https://naval-encyclopedia.com/ww1/turkish-navy.php>.

[27] Treaty of Lausanne (n 20); Convention regarding the Regime of the Straits, Lausanne, 24 July 1923, 137 LNTS 213; [1924] ATS 10 ('Straits Convention').

Straits Convention of 1936,[28] which remains in force today. As will be discussed in Chapter 7, Article 35(c) of UNCLOS excludes 'the legal regime in straits in which passage is regulated in whole or in part by long-standing international conventions in force specifically relating to such straits' from the provisions of Part III of UNCLOS on international straits. This exception was formulated with the case of the Turkish Straits in mind. Nevertheless, the evolution of the rules generally applicable to straits have been influenced by these treaty regimes and the issues involved in their conclusion and application. The discussion below focuses on the 1923 Treaty of Lausanne and the accompanying Straits Convention, highlighting provisions that were forerunners to the regulations in place today.

While Russia had argued that the Straits should be closed to all warships and supported Turkey's unfettered sovereign right to defend the Straits against aggression, it was the British proposal to secure freedom of navigation through the Straits by means of their demilitarisation and internationalisation that won the support of other participants, including Turkey.[29] Article 23 of the Treaty of Lausanne provided that '[t]he High Contracting Parties are agreed to recognise and declare the principle of freedom of transit and of navigation, by sea and by air, in time of peace as in time of war, in the strait of the Dardanelles, the Sea of Marmora and the Bosphorus, as prescribed in the separate Convention signed this day, regarding the regime of the Straits'. The Straits Convention, held to have 'equal force and effect . . . as if it formed part of the present Treaty',[30] guaranteed freedom of passage through the Straits for both merchant ships and warships in time of peace.[31] There were, however, limitations on such passage.

The Straits Convention restricted 'the maximum force which any one Power may send through the Straits into the Black Sea', specifying that this amount 'is not to be greater than that of the most powerful fleet of the littoral Powers of the Black Sea existing in that sea at the time of passage'.[32] To facilitate such an assessment, it was provided that

[28] Convention Regarding the Regime of Straits, Montreux, 20 July 1936, entered into force 9 November 1936, 173 LNTS 213.

[29] Russia itself signed the Lausanne Treaty, but did not ratify it: Anthony R. Deluca, *Great Power Rivalry at the Turkish Straits: The Montreux Conference and Convention of 1936* (Columbia University Press, 1981) 8–9.

[30] Treaty of Lausanne (n 20) art. 24.

[31] Straits Convention (n 27) arts. 1, 2.

[32] Ibid, art. 2 annex(2)(a).

a Straits Commission (established by Article 10) would 'enquire of each Black Sea littoral Power the number of each of the following classes of vessel which such Power possesses in the Black Sea: Battle-ships, battle-cruisers, aircraft-carriers, cruisers, destroyers, submarines, or other types of vessels as well as naval aircraft' in commission and 'inform the Powers concerned' of the number and composition of 'the strongest naval force in the Black Sea' at a given time.[33] A proviso added that 'the Powers reserve to themselves the right to send into the Black Sea, at all times and under all circumstances, a force of not more than three ships, of which no individual ship shall exceed 10,000 tons'.[34]

In time of war, the Straits Convention provided for the passage of all merchant vessels and warships (including those of a belligerent State) through the Straits in the case of Turkish neutrality – warships being subject to the same limitations on number and tonnage. It was specified, however, that, notwithstanding Turkish neutrality, 'these limitations will not be applicable to any belligerent Power to the prejudice of its belligerent rights in the Black Sea'.[35] Warships were 'forbidden to make any capture, to exercise the right of visit and search, or to carry out any other hostile act in the Straits' and Hague Convention (XIII) of 1907 was held to apply '[a]s regards revictualling and carrying out repairs'.[36]

The Straits Convention also provided for 'freedom of navigation' of neutral merchant vessels and neutral warships in the case of Turkish belligerency, though this freedom would only apply if the ship in question 'does not assist the enemy, particularly by carrying contraband, troops or enemy nationals', and Turkey was recognised as having 'the right to visit and search such vessels'.[37] While Turkey could prevent enemy vessels from using the straits, such measures were not to prevent the free passage of neutral vessels (unless they were found to be 'assist[ing] the enemy').[38] It was nevertheless provided that 'warships in transit through the Straits' should not 'remain therein beyond the time which is necessary for them to effect their passage', though an exception was noted 'in the event of damage or peril of the sea'.[39] Significantly, it was also provided that

[33] Ibid.
[34] Ibid.
[35] Ibid, art. 2 annex(2)(b).
[36] Ibid.
[37] Ibid, art. 2 annex(1)(c).
[38] Ibid.
[39] Ibid, art. 2 annex(4).

'[t]he passage of the Straits by submarines of Powers at peace with Turkey must be made on the surface'.[40]

There was also a notification requirement for foreign warships: 'the officer in command of a foreign naval force, whether coming from the Mediterranean or the Black Sea' being required to 'communicate, without being compelled to stop, . . . , the number and the names of vessels under his orders which are entering the Straits'.[41] While the Straits Convention specified the regulations that would apply to passage through the straits, it recognised that Turkey had a right 'to make such regulations as she may consider necessary regarding the number of men-of-war and military aircraft of any one Power which may visit Turkish ports or aerodromes at one time, and the duration of their stay'.[42]

Under the Straits Convention, the shores of the Dardanelles and Bosphorus, as well as specified islands including Imbros and Tenedos, were to be demilitarised.[43] It was, however, provided that 'submarine vessels' (but no other 'submarine engines of war') could remain in the demilitarised zones and their territorial waters, as well as the sea of Marmora.[44] This allowance appears to have been a concession to the concern of the Turkish General Staff to put some form of coastal defence in place against the threat of an Italian attack from the west – submarines being preferred partly because of their relative affordability.[45] The Turkish fleet also retained the right to anchor in territorial waters within this 'Straits Zone', and a naval base was permitted at Constantinople.[46] While the Straits Convention seems to have anticipated that Turkey or Greece might 'in pursuance of their belligerent rights . . . modify . . . the provisions of demilitarisation' (which were to be reinstated upon the conclusion of peace), the security of the demilitarised zone was to be guaranteed by 'the High Contracting Parties, and in any case France, Great Britain, Italy, and Japan, acting in conjunction', which committed to 'meet[ing] such violation, attack, or other act of war or threat of war, by all the means that the Council of the League of Nations may decide for this purpose'.[47] Yet Turkey's ability to directly regulate passage through

[40] Ibid, art. 2 annex(2)(a).
[41] Ibid, art. 2 annex(2)(b).
[42] Ibid, art. 2 annex(5)(a).
[43] Ibid, art. 4.
[44] Ibid, arts. 6, 7.
[45] Serhat Guvenc, 'Building a Republican Navy in Turkey: 1924–1939' (2002) 1(1) *International Journal of Naval History* 1, 3.
[46] Straits Convention (n 27) art. 8.
[47] Ibid, art. 18.

the Straits was significantly hampered. It was ultimately the International Straits Commission that would 'see that the provisions relating to the passage of warships and military aircraft are carried out'.[48]

Even though Turkey lacked complete control over passage through the Straits, it is important to recognise that the Treaties of Sèvres and Lausanne had not guaranteed an unfettered right of passage through these waters for all States and all vessels. These treaties at most suggest the parties' support for the free passage of commercial vessels through straits and such passage could be restricted and regulated in a variety of ways. Under the Treaties of Sèvres and Lausanne, considerable restrictions were also applied to the passage of warships, including submarines. The requirement that submarines travel on the surface and the notification requirement for the passage of foreign warships are of particular note in connection with the subsequent development of the law relating to passage through straits.

3.4 The New Mandates: Pacific Interests

Following their defeat in WWI, Germany and the Ottoman Empire had been compelled to give up their colonial territories, and the 1918 Peace Treaty of Brest-Litovsk under which Russia had ceded certain territories to Germany was annulled.[49] Driven by the desirability of self-governance in former colonies, coupled with concern about continuing rivalry between existing and would-be colonial powers,[50] a mandate system was established with the creation of the League of Nations. In that system, 'advanced nations' were appointed as 'mandatories' responsible for the administration of the former colonies on behalf, and subject to the supervision, of the League of Nations.[51]

In categories of Class C and Class B mandates, the administering State was to '[prevent] . . . the establishment of fortifications or military and naval bases and of military training of the natives for other than police purposes and the defence of territory' and to 'secure equal opportunities for the trade and commerce of other Members of the League'.[52] It was

48 Ibid, art. 14.

49 Treaty of Peace between Austria-Hungary, Bulgaria, Germany and Turkey, and Russia, Brest-Litovsk, 3 March 1918, 223 CTS 80.

50 See Nele Matz, 'Civilization and the Mandate System under the League of Nations' (2005) 9 *Max Planck United Nations Yearbook* 47, 53.

51 Treaty of Versailles (n 6) art. 22 (being the Covenant of the League of Nations).

52 Ibid.

widely understood at the time that States seeking to administer territories under the mandate system were interested in securing strategic military and trade advantages. In practice, there was little effective constraint on the pursuit of these interests, particularly in the case of Class C mandates. In the Pacific, the distribution of former German territories among Japan and the United States played into power politics between the two States and increased the importance placed upon the submarine as an element of their naval forces. Japan's interest in closing the waters of the mandates to foreign vessels and the United States' interest in accessing them became a key point of contention.

Japan was given the mandate for 'German possessions in the Pacific Ocean lying North of the Equator' but had already occupied these territories during WWI and, among other things, had prohibited the access of foreign vessels to their waters. This restriction on access continued after being awarded the mandate by the League of Nations in 1920. The United Kingdom had secretly agreed to support Japan's claim to these territories during the war in return for naval assistance responding to Germany's submarine campaign.[53] The US Navy seems to have developed a special interest in the North Pacific islands following their occupation by Japan. In 1918, the US Navy's General Board issued a report noting that the Marshall and Caroline Islands would serve as an excellent base for submarines and destroyers and expressed concern that Japanese control of the Marianas could threaten Guam and prevent the defence of the Philippines in the event of war.[54] The General Board recommended US acquisition of the Islands or their control by a neutral power.[55] However, the United States did not ultimately play a role in the allocation of mandates, having already determined not to join the League of Nations or ratify the Treaty of Versailles. From 1919, however, it commenced work on the construction of a submarine base at Pearl Harbor in Hawaii[56] and the US Navy continued to push for the development of substantial bases in Guam and the Philippines.[57]

[53] E. T. Williams, 'Japan's Mandate in the Pacific' (1933) 27(3) *American Journal of International Law* 428, 431.

[54] Sumitra Rattan, 'The Yap Controversy and Its Significance' (1972) 7 *The Journal of Pacific History* 124, 125.

[55] Ibid.

[56] Naval History and Heritage Command, 'Pearl Harbor Submarine Base: 1918–1945' <www.history.navy.mil/>.

[57] Buel W. Patch, 'American Naval and Air Bases' (CQ Researcher Report, 1939).

The terms of the 'C mandates' confirmed by the League of Nations in 1920, including the South Seas Mandate awarded to Japan, were identical: in each case prohibiting inter alia 'the military training of the natives, otherwise than for purposes of internal police and the local defence of the territory' as well as 'the erection of fortifications' and the establishment of military or naval bases.[58] In 1921, the United States protested the award of the mandates, arguing that this action was invalid due to the absence of US consent.[59] Increasingly concerned that Japan might use the Pacific territories included in the South Seas Mandate as aviation and submarine bases, the United States also began negotiations for a separate bilateral treaty regarding Yap.[60] The General Board of the US Navy subsequently sought to extend the terms of this Treaty to cover the islands under Japan's mandate more generally.[61] Though an initial goal had been to secure continued access to communication cables in the Pacific via Yap, the General Board was now concerned to secure free access to the ports and waters of the islands for American warships and commercial vessels and to confirm the extension of existing treaties providing 'most favoured nation' trading rights to the mandates.[62] Japan ultimately agreed to these conditions; the resulting Treaty between the United States and Japan of 1922 referring also to the obligation not to militarise the islands under the terms of the mandate.[63]

A draft of the American Japanese Agreement on Yap and other Pacific Islands had been presented to the principal Allied powers and the Netherlands for their approval at the Washington Naval Conference convened between 1921 and 1922. The Conference had been initiated by the United States, which was concerned to limit what it considered to be a naval arms race and ensure its security in the Pacific in particular. The new and evolving Pacific balance of power informed developments

58 Green Haywood Hackworth, *Digest of International Law* (United States Government Printing Office, 1940) vol. 1, 124.

59 The US protests were issued to the Council of the League of Nations as well as the United Kingdom, France, Japan and Italy: see George H. Blakeslee, 'The Mandates of the Pacific' (1922) 1(1) *Foreign Affairs* 98, 100–101.

60 Rattan (n 54) 127–132. The Yap Islands were an archipelago in the Caroline Islands and are now within the Federated States of Micronesia.

61 Ibid, 133.

62 Ibid.

63 Treaty between the United States of America and Japan concerning the Yap Island and the Other Islands under Mandate Situated in the Pacific North of the Equator, Washington, 11 February 1922, 12 LNTS 202.

in submarine technology and strategy as well as proposals to ban submarines or otherwise limit their use.

3.5 Limiting Arms: the 1922 Washington Naval Treaty and the 1930 London Naval Treaty

Following WWI, arms reduction was identified as a measure contributing to the prevention of future wars in both Wilson's Fourteen Points (Point Four) and Article 8 of the Covenant of the League of Nations.[64] Yet tensions in the Pacific informed international efforts to secure a reduction in naval arms through multilateral treaties. British and US concern with Japan's expanding power in the region and Japan's interest in parity of arms or at least a more favourable ratio relative to these two States played into debates regarding the abolition or restriction of submarine forces in particular. France's insistence on the value of the submarine as a defensive weapon was also influential and hampered efforts to control the number, capacity and activities of such vessels.

3.5.1 The Washington Conference and the 1922 Submarine Treaty

In 1921, nine States were invited by US Secretary of State Charles Evans Hughes to discuss both disarmament (in the case of the United Kingdom, Japan, France and Italy, together with the United States, known as the 'Five Powers') and the situation in East Asia, where Japan's expanding power appeared to threaten American and European trading interests. When the Five Powers came to discuss submarines, the United Kingdom proposed that 'what was required was not merely restrictions on submarines, but their total and final abolition'.[65]

The United States had privately considered a proposal by US Navy Captain F. H. Schofield to the same effect in their work to develop a policy position prior to the Washington Conference; it was otherwise proposed to prohibit the construction of new submarines except to replace vessels with twelve years of service and to limit submarine tonnage – with the United States and the United Kingdom having a higher tonnage on the basis of parity than Japan, France and Italy.[66] Assistant Secretary of the Navy, Theodore Roosevelt, Jr, was concerned

[64] Treaty of Versailles (n 6) art. 8.
[65] Levie (n 11) 307.
[66] Lawrence H. Douglas, 'The Submarine and the Washington Conference of 1921' (1974) 26(4) *Naval War College Review* 86, 87.

that the United States should 'not be permitted to have our hands tied as regards the submarines', which he considered of particular value in any future conflict 'against the two island empires, Great Britain and Japan'; Japan being the immediate threat in the Pacific.[67] The latter approach was endorsed at the Washington Conference. The United States replaced its previous support for the abolition of the submarine with a policy of stabilising submarine tonnage at present levels and regulating submarine warfare (though US support for the abolition of the submarine was revived in 1932).[68]

France, Italy and Japan were also opposed to the abolition of the submarine, with France insisting on the importance of the submarine as a defensive weapon for 'a nation scantily clad with capital ships'.[69] France also argued that 'every method of warfare may or may not be employed in conformity with the laws of war, and that the inhuman and barbarous use made of the submarine by a belligerent in the late war is a reason for condemning that belligerent, but not for condemning the submarine'.[70]

The US proposal to limit submarines (and other warships) by tonnage was accepted, although the limits and ratios between the participating States were debated. The United Kingdom proposed a reduction on the tonnage limits proposed by the United States. US Captain Sinclair Canon (a member of Roosevelt Jr's staff) objected to this move, suggesting that the reduction or abolition of submarines would simply facilitate the free movement of the British Navy in offensive operations.[71] Canon also insisted that a reduction of US submarine tonnage would jeopardise the security of US possessions in the Pacific, arguing that 'the presence of submarines with our fleet would be of vital importance' in the event of conflict in the region.[72]

Japan was more broadly unhappy with the 5:5:3 ratio between the United States, the United Kingdom and Japan, proposing a ratio of 10:10:7 instead. The United States vehemently opposed this change as a threat to its interests in the Pacific. Japan's agreement to the 5:5:3 ratio was eventually obtained when Japan, the United Kingdom and France

[67] Ibid.
[68] Ibid, 91–92.
[69] Richard Dean Burns, 'Regulating Submarine Warfare, 1921–41: A Case Study in Arms Control and Limited War' (1971) 35(2) *Military Affairs* 56, 57, 91.
[70] Levie (n 11) 307.
[71] Douglas (n 66) 89.
[72] Ibid.

agreed that 'with respect to fortifications and naval bases in the Pacific region ... the status quo shall be maintained, that is, there shall be no increase in these fortifications and naval bases'; a clause referring to mandates and colonies rather than 'the islands composing Japan proper'.[73] In a 'Four Power Treaty' signed in December 1921, Japan, the United Kingdom, France and the United States agreed 'between themselves to respect their rights in relation to their insular possessions and insular dominions in the region of the Pacific Ocean' (though the United States declared that the agreement did not amount to an assent to Japan's South Seas Mandate) and to consult in the event of hostilities.[74] The Yap Treaty between the United States and Japan, discussed in Section 3.4, was also concluded at the Washington Conference.

In the Washington Naval Treaty (or Five Power Treaty) of 1922, France and Italy were granted a smaller tonnage at 1.67 to Japan's three and the United States and United Kingdom's five.[75] While Italy insisted on parity with France, France refused to accept the application of the limitation to auxiliary vessels and submarines, arguing that the latter were purely defensive.[76] Citing a limit of 90,000 tonnes as a minimum for submarines – well above its present capacity and the limits accepted by the United States, the United Kingdom and France – French intransigence on the point prevented the specification of any limit on either the size or overall tonnage of submarines in the final agreement.[77] It was, however, agreed that '[n]o vessel of war exceeding 10,000 tons (10,160 metric tons) standard displacement, other than a capital ship or aircraft carrier, shall be acquired by, or constructed by, for, or within the jurisdiction of, any of the Contracting Powers' – a restriction which did apply to submarines.[78]

The United Kingdom, France, Italy, Japan and the United States also adopted a separate Treaty Relating to the Use of Submarines and Noxious

[73] 'Conference on the Limitation of Armament' (1922) 10 *Senate Documents* 252 (US Congressional Serial Set No. 7976).

[74] Treaty between the British Empire, France, Japan and the United States of America relating to their Insular Possessions and Insular Dominions in the Pacific Ocean, Washington, 13 December 1921, entered into force 17 August 1923, 24 LNTS 193, [1923] ATS 7, art. I.

[75] Treaty between the British Empire, the United States of America, France, Italy and Japan for the Limitation of Naval Armaments, Washington, 6 February 1922, entered into force 17 August 1923, 25 LNTS 202, art. IV ('Washington Naval Treaty of 1922').

[76] Douglas (n 66) 89–90.

[77] Ibid, 96.

[78] Washington Naval Treaty of 1922 (n 75) art. XI.

Gases in Warfare (1922), which proposed to regulate submarine warfare.[79] The regulations were based on proposals presented to the Washington Conference by America's Elihu Root and responded to the U-boat strategies of WWI.[80] The treaty as adopted expressly recognised that the existing international law requirement to ascertain the character of a merchant vessel through search and visit prior to seizure and to ensure the safety of the crew and passengers before destroying such a vessel applied to belligerent submarines. If a belligerent submarine could not comply with these requirements, 'the existing law of nations requires it to desist from attack and from seizure and to permit the merchant vessel to proceed unmolested'.[81] It was also agreed between the parties, though not recognised as a matter of existing international law, that a violation of these laws could be prosecuted by and in any State as a matter of universal jurisdiction akin to piracy.[82] Finally, it was agreed between the parties that the use of submarines as commerce destroyers should be entirely prohibited; a prohibition that, again, was understood to develop rather than codify existing law, and to which 'all other nations' were invited to adhere.[83]

Though France joined the United Kingdom, Italy, Japan and the United States in adopting the Submarine Treaty in 1922, it did not ratify the agreement and the Submarine Treaty never entered into force. While a number of neutrality agreements and declarations prior to and at the outbreak of WWII expressly noted that submarines were bound by the general requirement to ensure the safety of passengers and crew before destroying a merchant ship,[84] which was still accepted as an existing rule of international law despite being flouted by Germany in WWI, submarine attacks against merchant shipping re-emerged as a key strategy in hostilities during WWII.

3.5.2 The Geneva Conference, the London Conference and the 1930 London Naval Treaty

Following the conclusion of the Washington Conference, the United States remained concerned with naval growth in the categories of vessels

[79] Treaty Relating to the Use of Submarines and Noxious Gases in Warfare, Washington, 6 February 1922, never entered into force, in Dietrich Schindler and Jirí Toman (eds.), *The Laws of Armed Conflicts* (Martinus Nijhoff, 1988) 877 ('Submarine Treaty of 1922').

[80] Levie (n 11) 307–309.

[81] Submarine Treaty of 1922, art. 1.

[82] Ibid, art. 3.

[83] Ibid, art. 4; Levie (n 11) 308–309.

[84] See, e.g., Inter-American Convention on Maritime Neutrality, Havana, 20 February 1928, entered unto force 21 January 1931, 135 LNTS 187.

unrestricted by the Five Power Treaty. In 1927, US President Coolidge invited the United Kingdom, France, Italy and Japan to a Conference in Geneva aspiring to secure agreement on limitations for cruisers, destroyers and submarines.[85] Italy and France declined the invitation, referring to the League of Nations preparatory work for a general conference on disarmament, which they considered the appropriate forum for a discussion of naval disarmament.[86] The United Kingdom, Japan and the United States discussed the possibility of a total tonnage limit for these categories of ship, but were unable to reach agreement due to differences regarding the appropriate restrictions on cruisers and a possible distinction between heavy cruisers, which the United States and Japan valued, and light cruisers, which the United Kingdom valued to protect its shipping trade. Towards the end of the Geneva Conference, the United Kingdom proposed a simple restatement of the 10,000 tonne limit for individual submarines, cruisers and destroyers that had been agreed upon at the Washington Conference. However, the United States rejected this proposal on the basis that the cruiser question had not been settled.[87]

The United States was perturbed by the increasing number of submarines acquired by the United Kingdom, France, Italy and Japan. According to Burns, 'between 1922 and 1929 Japan had laid down 35 submarines, France 42, Italy 28, and Great Britain 14, while the United States had begun but three'.[88] At the London Naval Conference of 1930, the United Kingdom again proposed the abolition of the submarine.[89] The United States (now under President Hoover) fully supported this proposal, though it suggested in the alternative the regulation of the use of submarines as a weapon of war by application of the rules governing surface craft.[90] France, Italy and Japan again refused to contemplate prohibition. Nonetheless, France similarly proposed that submarines should be '[forbidden to] ... act towards merchant ships otherwise than in strict conformity with the rules, either present or future, to be observed by surface warships'.[91]

[85] Richard E. J. Galilee, 'The Breakdown of Naval Limitation in the Far East 1932–1936' (Thesis Submitted to the University of Canterbury, 1975) 29.

[86] Ibid.

[87] Krystian Maciej Szudarek, 'The British Government and the Naval Disarmament Conference in Geneva (1927)' (2014) 27(1) *Studia Maritima* 87, 140.

[88] Burns (n 69) 58.

[89] Levie (n 11) 311.

[90] Ibid. On the new US policy on disarmament, see Galilee (n 85) 36–37.

[91] Levie (n 11) 311.

A rule to this effect was adopted as Article 22 of the 1930 London Naval Treaty.[92] As well as providing that '[i]n their action with regard to merchant ships, submarines must conform to the rules of International Law to which surface vessels are subject', it was specified that this included a requirement to '[place] the passengers, crew, and ship's papers in a place of safety'. Significantly, it was also specified that this provision would apply 'without limitation of time' in contrast to the rest of the Treaty, which would expire in December 1936 (or in some cases up until the expiry of the Submarine Treaty of 1922).[93]

In view of the lack of support for abolition at this time, tonnage limits for submarines were also discussed. Japan generally sought a 10:10:7 ratio, even though the existing tonnage of Japanese submarines already exceeded that ratio relative to the American figures used as a reference.[94] Japan instead suggested a reduction in its light cruiser or destroyer tonnage to allow the higher tonnage for submarines, but the United States rejected this proposal.[95] An extensive Japanese submarine fleet 'would necessitate counter-building on the part of America' to protect its Pacific interests.[96] The United States subsequently proposed that Japan should have parity with itself and the United Kingdom in the case of submarines and a 10:10:7 ratio in surface vessels.[97] This apparent concession in fact entailed a reduction of Japan's current armaments, while limiting the expense of the necessary increases in US naval forces. Parity in submarines would be at 52,729 tonnes, substantially less than Japan's existing 78,000 tonnes of submarines that had either been built or planned for construction.[98] While the Japanese government ultimately agreed to this limit, it did so against strenuous opposition from the Imperial Japanese Navy leaving 'a rift between the Cabinet and the Privy Council and between the Cabinet and the Naval General Staff'.[99] Some members of the US Navy were also unhappy with the change, sharing the view of Admiral Reeves that

> [t]his increase in the ratio with Japan imperils our interests in the Pacific and the Far East. With the sacrifice of the defense of our possessions in the

[92] Treaty for the Limitation and Reduction of Naval Armament, London, 22 April 1930, entered into force 31 December 1930, 112 LNTS 65 ('London Naval Treaty').

[93] Ibid, art. 23; Levie (n 11) 311.

[94] Galilee (n 85) 38–39.

[95] Ibid.

[96] Ibid.

[97] Ibid, 41–42.

[98] Ibid.

[99] Ibid, 42–44.

> Far East our ratio should be 10:5, or two to one. The ratio 5:3 gives us a bare chance of success.[100]

Ultimately, the 1930 London Naval Treaty did not bring about any real reduction in the submarine forces of the participating States. While the tonnage limits would allow the United States and the United Kingdom to construct new submarines, the continued public opposition of Japan's Navy to this Treaty stood in the way of any straightforward implementation of Japan's obligation to reduce its planned and existing submarine forces.[101]

When States met at the Hague for the 1930 Codification Conference it was still hoped that the three powers participating in the London Conference would achieve a certain kind of 'equilibrium' by constraining future increases in naval armaments if not reducing existing stock.[102] At the same time, it was clear that more radical disarmament measures (such as the abolition of the submarine) would not be endorsed, meaning that warships, including submarines, would continue to be constructed, maintained and used by States in time of peace as well as war. The evolving situation in the Pacific meant that a number of States were interested in stationing or mobilising warships in the region to protect or advance imperial and trade interests. Naval strategising, including the conduct of naval exercises, patrols and other shows of power, formed part of the context in which States sought to clarify and codify the law relating to territorial waters.

3.6 The 1930 Hague Codification Conference

While the aforementioned powers were in London to discuss naval disarmament, the League of Nations Codification Conference took place in the Hague. Among the topics determined to be 'sufficiently ripe' for codification was the question of 'territorial waters' and 'in particular ... [the question of] the rights of jurisdiction of a State over foreign commercial ships within its territorial waters or in its ports'.[103]

100 *Abstract of Testimony on Certain Salient Questions of the London Naval Treaty given before the Committee on Naval Affairs of the Senate* (United States Government Printing Office, 1930) 36 (Congressional Serial Set No. 9220).

101 Galilee (n 85) 41–49.

102 See J. Ramsay MacDonald, 'The London Naval Conference, 1930' (1930) 9(4) *Journal of the Royal Institute of International Affairs* 49.

103 'Report to the Council of the League of Nations on the Questions which Appear Ripe for International Regulation' in Shabtai Rosenne (ed.), *League of Nations Committee of*

The Committee of Experts tasked with preparing an initial report on this topic sought to distinguish between (a) 'the rights of belligerents and neutrals in time of war' and (b) the general rules applying to territorial waters in time of peace.[104] Yet while the codification project was chiefly concerned with peacetime rules, debates regarding the rights and duties of both merchant vessels and foreign warships in the territorial sea continued to be influenced by the wartime experience.

State views on the rights and duties of neutral States in relation to such vessels, and submarines in particular, remained relevant to debates regarding the rules applicable to passage in time of peace. As discussed in Chapter 2, a number of neutral States had declared neutrality zones in which the passage and presence of foreign warships was precluded or strictly regulated. These declarations did not always make clear whether the alleged right to impose such rules and restrictions flowed from neutrality or the sovereignty of the coastal State in the territorial sea. However, the decision to leave any positive statement of the rights and obligations of neutral States with respect to passage out of Hague Convention (XIII) of 1907 seems to have been based on the understanding that such rights were a consequence of coastal State sovereignty, with any relevant obligations governed by general international law. As discussed in Chapter 2, this understanding was also apparent in the work of the Institut de Droit International (IDI) and International Law Association (ILA).

In the preparatory work for the Hague Codification Conference and debates at the Conference itself, State practice in the context of neutrality was understood to illuminate the rights and duties of the coastal State in the territorial sea.[105] It was also taken to bear upon the vexed question of the extent of the territorial sea.[106] During WWI, a number of neutral States described the area in which the prohibition and regulation of the passage of foreign vessels would apply in terms of distance from the coast. In some cases, this area was identified as the territorial sea. In other cases, States declared a 'neutrality zone' extending beyond the limits of their

Experts for the Progressive Codification of International Law (1925–1928) (Oceana Publications, 1972) vol. 2, 55 ('*League of Nations 1925–1928*').

104 'Work of the Committee of Experts for the Progressive Codification of International Law During Its First Session' (1925) 6 *League of Nations Official Journal* 842, 843; Rosenne (n 103) vol. 2, 69.

105 See e.g., 'Memorandum by M Schücking in Report of the Sub-Committee on Territorial Waters (1926)' in Rosenne, *League of Nations 1925–1928* (n 103) vol. 2, 69–71 ('Schücking Memorandum').

106 See e.g., ibid, 59–64.

territorial seas without purporting to suggest the legal basis for the extension of their rights in this zone to flow from neutrality rather than sovereignty.[107]

Identifying a fixed limit of the territorial sea and clarifying the rights and duties of the coastal State in relation to foreign vessels therein were identified as key tasks for the League of Nations' codification project. Notwithstanding efforts to limit or reduce naval armaments through multilateral treaties in the post-war period, it was clear that State navies would continue to be a significant presence on the oceans in times of peace as well as war. The special threat presented by submarines due to their capacity to evade detection was identified as a concern beyond the wartime context.[108] Germany's use of submarines as blockade runners in WWI had also suggested to States that these vessels might not only be used as warships but also as merchant ships. Submarines were accordingly considered in connection with rules relating to merchant ships and rules relating to warships. Although the anticipated use of submarines for merchant shipping has not come to pass, this approach has left its legacy in the 1958 law of the sea conventions and UNCLOS as both specify conditions applying to submarines both as merchant ships and warships. The extent to which this facilitates the application of the existing law to novel contemporary uses of submarines (such as for tourism) is discussed in Part II of the book.

3.6.1 *The League of Nations Committee of Experts*

The passage of submarines through territorial waters was among the issues considered by the League of Nations Committee of Experts for the Progressive Codification of International Law between 1925 and 1928. In 1926, the Committee of Experts presented governments with a report prepared by a three-member Sub-Committee on Territorial Waters, which included a draft Convention prepared by the Rapporteur, Walther Schücking, and amended in response to the Sub-Committee's discussions.[109] This draft affirmed a right of 'free passage' through the territorial sea in the case of 'pacific passage'.[110]

[107] This practice is discussed in Chapter 2, Section 2.2.1.

[108] 'Schücking Memorandum' (n 105) 71.

[109] 'Draft Convention amended by M Schücking in Consequence of the Discussion in the Committee of Experts' in Rosenne, *League of Nations 1925–1928* (n 103) vol. 2, 98 ('Draft Convention').

[110] Ibid, 98 (art. 7).

In his Memorandum, Schücking had emphasised that this general legal principle should apply to 'all vessels without distinction', though he noted the view that 'a right of free passage for warships can only be presumed and that the riparian State may arbitrarily prohibit the passage of warships through its territorial sea by the same right as it forbids access to its ports and internal waters'.[111] Schücking's opinion, however, was that 'even warships possess a right of common user in respect of foreign territorial waters which cannot be restricted arbitrarily', though the passage of warships might be restricted 'for reasons of national self-preservation'.[112] Schücking also noted that a right of free 'pacific' passage 'should even be extended to submarines, though in their case it has often been disputed when occasion has arisen'.[113]

Schücking noted with approval Giulio Diena's proposed solution at the 1925 meeting of the IDI, which was a requirement that 'submarines … pass through territorial waters on the surface'.[114] While this requirement had not been included in the Draft Articles adopted by the Institut in 1928,[115] Schücking took the view that '[w]ithout this safeguard, the riparian State could not be certain whether the passage was really pacific'.[116] Article 7 of his Draft Convention, understood to apply to warships as well as merchant vessels, provided inter alia that

> All vessels, without distinction, shall have the right of pacific passage through the territorial sea. In the case of submarine vessels, this right shall be subject to the condition of passage on the surface.

As noted above, the requirement that submarines travel on the surface was already a feature of the Straits Convention forming part of the 1923 Treaty of Lausanne, as well as the neutrality laws of a number of States during WWI.[117] Schücking's formulation of this requirement as a condition on the right of pacific passage suggests that a submarine that does not comply – that is, a submerged submarine – is not merely in breach of a regulation applying to passage but does not have a right to passage through the territorial sea at all.

[111] 'Schücking Memorandum' (n 105) 70.
[112] Ibid, 69–71.
[113] Ibid, 71.
[114] Ibid.
[115] IDI Resolution on 'Projet de règlement relatif à la mer territoriale en temps de paix', Stockholm, 28 August 1928.
[116] 'Schücking Memorandum' (n 105) 71.
[117] See Chapter 2, Section 2.4.

The passage of warships was also dealt with separately in Draft Article 12, which recognised a right to not only request but, if necessary, compel a warship committing a 'serious and continued offence' to leave the territorial sea. Draft Article 10 provided more generally that 'the riparian State shall have full powers of legislation and administration in all domains of public activity, subject to the restrictions imposed by the present Convention, and may employ *all measures of constraint necessary* to ensure respect for its jurisdiction so as to permit it to deal with offences'.[118] These discussions resonate with the contemporary rules relating to the passage of submarines through another State's territorial sea and potential coastal State responses, which are assessed in Chapter 7.

The other members of the Sub-Committee on Territorial Waters did not raise any objections to Draft Articles 7 and 12. They did, however, understand the right of innocent passage to be a right of common user; indeed, Schücking described it as the most important of these rights.[119] This view would be challenged by States in later proceedings. The Sub-Committee did not consider how the right of passage might be 'restricted by the rights of belligerents and neutrals' in time of war.[120]

3.6.2 *The Preparatory Committee*

The Preparatory Committee for the Codification Conference was tasked with drawing up 'Bases of Discussion' by reference to the work of the Committee of Experts and State replies to questionnaires.[121] It began by elaborating a schedule of 'points which were suitable for being examined with a view to reaching agreement thereon'.[122] States were asked to provide information on these points referring to '(a) the state of their positive law . . ., (b) information derived from their practice at home and abroad; and (c) their view regarding possible additions to the rules in force, and the manner of making good existing deficiencies in international law'.[123]

With respect to the 'innocent passage of foreign ships through territorial waters' (Point IX), the Preparatory Committee requested that

[118] 'Draft Convention' (n 109) 99 (emphasis added).
[119] 'Schücking Memorandum' (n 105) 69.
[120] Rosenne, *League of Nations 1925–1928* (n 103) 69.
[121] Shabtai Rosenne, *League of Nations Conference for the Codification of International Law (1930)* (Oceana Publications, 1975) vol. 1, xvi, xx, xxi ('*League of Nations 1930*').
[122] Ibid, vol. 1, xvi, xx.
[123] Ibid, xvi, xx.

governments provide information on inter alia '[r]ights of passage: (a) of merchant ships; (b) of warships; (c) of submarines'.[124] The responses to this questionnaire prompted a further request for information on '[r]regulation of the passage and the anchoring in territorial waters of foreign warships' and '[p]enalties for non-observance of the local laws and regulations. Right to require the ship to depart' (Point X).[125]

Those States submitting replies agreed that merchant ships should have a right of innocent passage in the territorial sea, though several also suggested that this right might be suspended for security reasons.[126] A majority of States also recognised that submarines would have a right of innocent passage through territorial water provided they navigate on the surface.[127] A number of States further insisted, however, on notification and authorisation in the case of the passage of warships, including submarines.[128] Of particular note here is the US reply, which quoted Elihu Root's statement in the *North Atlantic Coast Fisheries Case* that '[w]arships may not pass without consent into this zone, because they threaten', while '[m]erchantmen may pass and repass because they do not threaten'.[129] The United States considered that 'statements made with respect to warships should be applicable to submarines', but did not comment directly on whether submarines should be required to navigate on the surface.[130]

Governments replying to Point X on the passage of warships seem to have broadly agreed that such passage should be permitted in time of peace, though not all States considered this allowance a 'right' as opposed to a concession by the coastal State.[131] The replies also indicated that most States agreed that the coastal State could 'require' a warship to leave if it failed to comply with the coastal State's regulations or threatened the security of the State.[132] The United States and the Netherlands asserted a right to forcibly compel a warship to leave in these circumstances.[133] Several States also reiterated that the passage of warships must be

[124] Ibid, vol. 2, 283.
[125] Ibid, 290.
[126] Ibid, 283–289.
[127] Ibid, 283–293.
[128] Ibid.
[129] Ibid, 284; *North Atlantic Coast Fisheries Case* (Great Britain v. United States) (Award of 7 September 1910) (1910) 11 RIAA 167.
[130] Rosenne, *League of Nations 1930* (n 121) vol. 2, 284.
[131] Ibid, 290–293.
[132] Ibid.
[133] Ibid, 291, 292.

authorised by the coastal State; Belgium, Bulgaria, Latvia, Romania and the United States expressing this view in their responses to either or both Points IX and X.[134]

For its part, the Preparatory Committee was unconcerned by 'divergences of view on points of detail', which it considered to be 'of little importance'.[135] It considered the replies to indicate that 'the right of innocent passage for warships and the right of the coastal State to regulate the conditions of such passage and the conditions in which they may anchor in its territorial waters' was 'accepted without difficulty'.[136] 'Basis of Discussion No 20' was formulated as follows:

A coastal State should recognise the right of innocent passage through its territorial waters of foreign warships, including submarines navigating on the surface.

A coastal State is entitled to make rules regulating the conditions of such passage without, however, having the right to require a previous authorisation.

A coastal State is entitled to make rules governing the anchoring of foreign warships in its territorial waters, but it may not forbid anchoring in case of damage to the ship or distress.[137]

What is most notable about this formulation is its denial of 'the right to require a previous authorisation'. This provision is clearly at odds with the previously expressed government views, even though those views had not incited objections from other governments.

It is possible that the Preparatory Committee misinterpreted an aspect of Schücking's memorandum in which he discussed the American Institute of International Law's inclusion of a clause providing that: 'Neither warships nor merchant vessels can sojourn in the territorial sea without the authorization of the said Republics'.[138] Schücking considered such a rule to be unnecessary 'in so far as the vessels are sojourning in the territorial sea with the intention of proceeding further'.[139] To conclude that there should be no general rule requiring such authorisation for such a sojourn *during passage*, however, is not to say that individual States would not be entitled to require previous authorisation

134 Ibid, 283–293.
135 Ibid, 293.
136 Ibid.
137 Ibid.
138 'Schücking Memorandum' (n 105) 71.
139 Ibid.

for passage as a whole. The Preparatory Committee did not see fit to include any specific reference to freedom of passage in its three Bases of Discussion on straits.[140] As such, the rules of passage generally applicable in the territorial sea would also apply in straits.

3.6.3 The IDI, ILA and Harvard Research

At the time the Committee of Experts and Preparatory Committee were completing their work, several academic institutions had also prepared or were in the process of finalising drafts on the topic of the territorial sea. The IDI's earlier Draft Articles of 1925 had specified that the 'right of pacific passage through the territorial sea' would, in the case of submarines, be 'subject to the condition of passage on the surface'. This rule would apply to submarines classified as warships as well as those categorised as merchant ships. While no such provision was included in the 1928 Draft Articles, this consequence seems to emerge from the decision to provide more generally for the coastal State's right to apply regulations to the passage of both warships and merchant ships, including submarines, in the territorial sea. Under the 1928 Draft Articles, it remained open to the coastal State to require that submarines navigate on the surface in regulating passage within the territorial sea.

The ILA's 1926 Draft Convention on Maritime Jurisdiction in Time of Peace provided in Article 12 that '[t]he ships of all countries, public as well as private, have the right to pass freely through territorial waters, but are subject to the regulations enacted by the State through whose territorial waters they pass, provided that such regulations do not infringe any of the provisions contained in this Convention'.[141] The Draft Convention did not specify limitations on the type of regulations that might be applied. Like the IDI's 1928 Draft Articles, the ILA's Draft Convention does not specifically require the passage of submarines on the surface but leaves room for the coastal State to impose such a requirement.

In 1926, the Japanese branch of the ILA also adopted a Draft Code providing that '[a]ll ships without distinction shall enjoy the right of inoffensive passage through littoral waters, conforming themselves to any rules which may be laid down by the adjacent State for the security of

[140] Basis of Discussion No. 17, however, provided that '[w]here a strait is merely a channel of communication with an inland sea, the rules regarding bays apply to such strait and sea': Rosenne, *League of Nations 1930* (n 121) vol. 2, 278.

[141] ILA, 'Report of the Neutrality Committee' (1926) 34 *International Law Association Reports of Conferences* 40, 44.

navigation, for the police of the seas, or for the defence and security of its own territory'.[142] It further specified that '[a] man-of-war may enter the ports, harbours, roadsteads and littoral waters of every foreign State, in so far as her access thereto is in no way prohibited or restricted by the littoral State'.[143] This provision anticipates the right of the littoral State to 'prohibit or restrict' the passage of warships. There is again clearly scope under these rules for the coastal State to require the passage of submarines on the surface whether they are classified as merchant ships or warships, although no general rule to this effect is provided.

The Harvard Research Draft Articles on the Territorial Sea, adopted in 1929, provided in Draft Article 14 that '[a] state must permit innocent passage through its marginal seas by the vessels of other states, but it may prescribe reasonable regulations for such passage'.[144] The term 'vessels' here, however, was explicitly restricted to 'vessels which are privately owned and privately operated and to vessels the legal status of which is assimilated to that of such vessels'.[145] The Commentary explicitly states that '[t]his excludes vessels of war from exercising the right of innocent passage'.[146] In the view of the authors (eminent American jurists working under the chairmanship of Wickersham of the League of Nations Committee of Experts, and the directorship of Manley Hudson, who served as a member of the Drafting Committee at the 1930 Conference),[147]

> [t]he sovereignty of the littoral state is restricted by the right of innocent passage because of a recognition of the freedom of the seas for the commerce of all states. There is, therefore, no reason for freedom of innocent passage of vessels of war.[148]

Notably, a different conclusion was reached in respect of straits: Draft Article 10 providing that '[a] strait connecting high seas shall remain

[142] Sanford D. Cole, 'Draft Code of International Law Adopted by the Japanese Branch of the International Law Association and the Kokusaiho Gakkwai (International Law Association of Japan)' (1926) 34 *International Law Association Reports of Conferences* 378, 389 (pt. IV, art. 6).

[143] Ibid, 389 (pt. V, art. 3).

[144] Harvard Research, 'Territorial Waters' (1929) 23(S5) *American Journal of International Law* 243.

[145] Ibid, 295 (Commentary to Draft Article 14), 362 (Commentary to Draft Article 22).

[146] Ibid, 295.

[147] James T. Kenny, 'Manley O. Hudson and the Harvard Research in International Law 1927–1940' (1977) 11(2) *The International Lawyer* 31.

[148] Harvard Research (n 144) 295.

open to navigation by the private and public vessels of all states, including vessels of war'.[149]

The Commentary to Harvard Research's Draft Article 14 also concluded that '[e]ven for vessels entitled to exercise the right of innocent passage it is obviously necessary that each state should be permitted to make reasonable regulations governing that passage, subject only to the restriction that these regulations be uniform for all states'.[150] It added that '[s]uch regulations may, of course, distinguish between different kinds of vessels', noting as an example that 'a littoral state might require all submarine vessels of other states to navigate upon the surface in order that shipping in the marginal sea may not be subjected to unknown risks'.[151]

The work of Harvard Research was particularly influential in negotiations at the Hague Codification Conference. The Secretary General of the League of Nations praised the organisation and provided copies of its work to participating States.[152] Although States failed to conclude a treaty on territorial waters in 1930, the record of negotiations shows that many agreed with Harvard Research that the coastal State was under no obligation to allow the passage of warships through the territorial sea. This widely held view was not, however, reflected in the Draft Articles appended to the Final Report of the Territorial Sea Committee. While these articles were not adopted, their influence on the later work of the International Law Commission (ILC) in advance of the 1958 Conference on the Law of the Sea was significant. As discussed in Chapter 5, the importance placed on them in this context was arguably unjustified given that they failed to reflect agreements between States on the issues concerned.

3.6.4 *Discussions at and Final Output of the 1930 Hague Codification Conference*

The Hague Conference was attended by forty-seven States and one observer, the Soviet Union. Negotiations at the Hague Conference proceeded in three Committees composed of delegates from participating States. J. P. A. François was appointed Rapporteur for the Second Committee on Territorial Waters.[153] It is worth noting that Schücking,

[149] Ibid, 281.
[150] Ibid, 295–296.
[151] Ibid, 296.
[152] Kenny (n 147) 322–323.
[153] Rosenne, *League of Nations 1930* (n 121) vol. 4, 1213.

who had prepared the Draft Convention on Territorial Waters for the Committee of Experts, served as a delegate for Germany, while members of Harvard Research, David Miller and Manley Hudson, were listed as delegate and substitute delegate respectively for the United States.[154]

The Territorial Sea Committee opened proceedings with a general discussion of the Bases of Discussion drawn up by the Preparatory Committee.[155] It went on to establish two Sub-Committees, allocating certain Bases of Discussion to consider in greater detail. The issue of passage through the territorial sea was allocated to the First Sub-Committee, which had twelve members comprising delegates from Belgium, Cuba, Finland, France, Germany, Italy, Japan, Norway, Portugal, the United Kingdom and the United States, and François acting as rapporteur.[156]

In the initial discussions of the Territorial Sea Committee as a whole, the US delegate David Miller introduced the topic of 'Foreign Ships passing through Territorial Waters' with the argument that 'the value of [the right of innocent passage] has been considerably exaggerated', claiming that 'there are very large parts of the coast throughout the world where the right of innocent passage is never employed by merchant ships'.[157] He also suggested that 'in most cases, the deviation in the course of a ship is very slight if it is required to go outside [the limits of the territorial sea]'.[158] It is important to bear in mind in this regard that the United States supported a territorial sea of three nautical miles at this time.[159] Notably, however, the United States also strongly supported Basis of Discussion 5, which provided that '[o]n the high seas adjacent to its territorial waters, the coastal State may exercise the control necessary to prevent, within its territory or territorial waters, the infringement of its customs or sanitary regulations or interference with its security by foreign ships'.[160] The rights available to the coastal State in precursor to the contiguous zone were evidently more expansive than the regulations later agreed upon in the 1958 Territorial Sea Convention, and Basis of Discussion 5 suggested that these rights could be exercised up to twelve miles from the coast.

[154] Ibid, 1210, 1212.
[155] Ibid, 1212–1277.
[156] Ibid, 1277.
[157] Ibid, 1260.
[158] Ibid.
[159] Ibid, 1220.
[160] Rosenne, *League of Nations 1930* (n 121) vol. 2, 252, vol. 4, 1220.

The United States' insistence on the priority of coastal State sovereignty in the territorial sea over the passage of foreign vessels was made even more apparent in connection with Basis of Discussion 19, which provided that

> A coastal State is bound to allow foreign merchant ships a right of innocent passage through its territorial waters; any police or navigation regulations with which such ships may be required to comply must be applied in such a manner as to respect the right of passage and without discrimination.
>
> The right of innocent passage covers persons and goods.
>
> The right of passage comprises the right of anchoring so far as is necessary for purposes of navigation.[161]

The United States proposed to insert the words '[s]ubject to the rights of the coastal State to the use of territorial waters or the subsoil for its national purposes' at the beginning of this text.[162] The US delegate, Miller, explained that '[o]ur desire is to emphasise what we consider in this connection to be the superior right of the coastal State'.[163] The United States also proposed the suppression of the second and third lines of Basis 19 concerning the innocent passage of foreign merchant ships on the grounds that they failed to properly reflect the right of the coastal State to interfere in some cases with the innocent passage of persons and goods and to regulate anchoring.[164]

With respect to Basis of Discussion 20, the United States stated clearly that in its view 'the right of innocent passage as a matter of right does not extend to warships'; that is, 'the right of innocent passage for warships does not exist' in the territorial sea.[165] Though denying a right of innocent passage, the United States accepted that warships might be granted passage on the basis of comity, proposing an amendment to Basis 20 providing that 'A coastal State should ordinarily, as a matter of comity, permit innocent passage through its territorial waters of foreign warships, including submarines navigating on the surface only and not submerged or half-awash.'[166]

The United States also expressed its support for the coastal State's right to require previous authorisation for the passage of warships. It

161 Ibid, vol. 2, 289.
162 Ibid, vol. 4, 1260.
163 Ibid.
164 Ibid, 1260–1261.
165 Ibid, 1261.
166 Ibid.

accordingly requested that the words 'without, however, having the right to require a previous authorisation' be struck out.[167]

Romania agreed with the US position on the passage of foreign vessels other than warships, but took the even stronger view that authorisation was required for a warship to pass through territorial waters, observing that '[i]n any case, notification of the presence of the warship is absolutely indispensable'.[168] The Romanian delegate, Meitani, explained that '[t]he passage of a foreign warship through the territorial waters of a State, if not notified to it, may constitute a source of danger'.[169] He considered it relatively easy for a warship to pass through the high seas beyond a territorial sea of three or even six nautical miles, suggesting that 'if it passes through the territorial waters of a State, some ulterior motive may be suspected'.[170] Romania was especially concerned that '[t]he warship may carry out unfriendly acts, such as taking soundings and charting'.[171] These activities seem to have been considered to constitute impermissible intelligence gathering.

France proposed to amend Basis of Discussion 19 to provide that '[a] coastal State is bound to allow foreign ships, other than ships belonging to naval forces, a right of innocent passage'.[172] This proposal clearly removed warships from the scope of this provision, and replaced the term 'merchant ships' with 'foreign ships' in order 'to prevent any ambiguity in regard to the right of passage through territorial waters of certain foreign vessels which are not, strictly speaking, merchant ships, such as vessels used for certain public services or pleasure craft'.[173] The French delegate, Gidel, also proposed that Basis 19 refer specifically to the case of submarines, providing that 'commercial submarines will not be entitled to make use of this right of passage except on the surface'.[174] Noting that submarines had only been mentioned in Basis 20 on warships, Gidel suggested that 'it might perhaps be advisable . . . to provide for the possibility – by no means chimerical – of submarines being used for commercial purposes'.[175]

[167] Ibid.
[168] Ibid.
[169] Ibid.
[170] Ibid.
[171] Ibid.
[172] Ibid, 1263.
[173] Ibid.
[174] Ibid.
[175] Ibid.

Portugal also thought it advisable to provide that the right of innocent passage belonged to 'foreign ships other than warships' and supported a reference to commercial submarines.[176] Yugoslavia too supported the French proposal to include a requirement for the surface navigation of commercial submarines in Basis 19.[177] As noted at the outset of Section 3.6, Germany's use of submarines as blockade runners in WWI had suggested that the commercial use of such vessels may become more widespread in times of peace. As discussed below, a parallel provision requiring that submarines navigate on the surface was included in Draft Article 12 on warships as formulated by the First Sub-Committee.[178]

The United Kingdom, along with a number of other States, criticised the absence of a definition of the right of innocent passage in the Bases of Discussion.[179] The British delegate, Gwyer, proposed a new Basis of Discussion to remedy this gap, specifying inter alia that 'passage is not innocent if the ship makes use of the territorial waters of the coastal State for any purpose prejudicial to the safety, good order or revenues of the coastal State'.[180] The United Kingdom also sought further clarification of 'the rights of the coastal State over or in respect of the ships which are exercising that right of passage', arguing that 'it is not to be assumed for one moment that a ship which is exercising the right of innocent passage is outside the jurisdiction of the coastal State for all purposes'.[181] It proposed the inclusion of specific references to the right to regulate passage for '(a) ... safety of traffic and of traffic channels, (b) ... the protection of the waters of the coastal State from oil and ships' refuse; (c) ... the protection of any exclusive fishing rights which the coastal State possesses', and more broadly '(c), for such other matters as, in accordance with international usage and passage, a coastal State may regulate in the case of foreign ships exercising the right of innocent passage'.[182] States were divided on whether the kind of regulations that may be applied by the coastal State should be specified in this manner, some preferring a general reference to the right to regulate passage and the duty to do so without discrimination between States. As Gidel

[176] Ibid, 1263–1264.
[177] Ibid, 1276.
[178] Rosenne, *League of Nations 1930* (n 121) vol. 3, 832.
[179] Ibid, vol. 4, 1264. See e.g., 1266 (Cuba), 1267 (Netherlands), 1272 (Norway), 1273 (Greece), 1276 (France).
[180] Ibid.
[181] Ibid.
[182] Ibid, 1265.

observed, '[n]o one question[ed] the right of the coastal State to prescribe regulations'.[183]

Spain strongly supported a right of passage on the part of foreign vessels other than warships, going so far as to suggest that the term 'innocent' be removed as an unnecessary limitation on the right.[184] Yet the Spanish delegate, Goicoeehea, 'very much question[ed] whether such a right exists in regard to warships'.[185] On this basis, he did not accept the first paragraph of Basis 20 and suggested that 'it would be better to say that the coastal State may authorize the innocent passage through its territorial waters of foreign warships', noting that '[i]n this case, the use of the word "innocent" is justified'.[186] Spain agreed with Romania and the United States that 'the words, "without, however, having the right to require a previous authorisation" … be omitted', arguing that '[e]ach State must choose between the systems of prevention and punishment as regards the treatment of foreign warships'.[187] Denmark also proposed that these words be omitted or, in the alternative, be replaced with a formulation recognising a right to require authorisation in 'certain limited areas' of the territorial sea.[188]

At the Seventh Meeting of the Committee on Territorial Waters, it was agreed that the question of warships should be set aside in order to focus on the right of passage of foreign merchant vessels.[189] Basis of Discussion 20 was thereafter left to debates in the First Sub-Committee, which had been established in the same meeting.[190]

There is no record of the discussions of the Sub-Committees, only the Draft Articles adopted by them together with accompanying observations. This absence is unfortunate, as on at least one point – the question of prior authorisation or notification for the passage of warships – there was, if not a discrepancy then clearly a difference of emphasis between the views expressed by (a) the majority of States in their replies to the Preparatory Committee and submissions in the general debates of the Territorial Sea Committee at the Hague Conference, and (b) the Draft Articles prepared by the Sub-Committee. The Territorial Sea Committee

183 Ibid, 1276.
184 Ibid, 1267.
185 Ibid, 1268.
186 Ibid.
187 Ibid. See also the Spanish proposal at 1396.
188 Ibid, 1385 (emphasis added).
189 Ibid, 1268.
190 Ibid, 1277, 1279.

as a whole had very limited time to consider the Draft Articles prepared by the Sub-Committee; the provisions were merely read, with delegates given an opportunity to comment on them.[191] While some of these comments prompted the Sub-Committee to make minor amendments to its draft, the Report of the Sub-Committee and its Draft Articles were ultimately adopted by the Sub-Committee alone. The Committee on Territorial Waters considered it inappropriate to adopt Draft Articles it had not had time to properly review.[192]

The Draft Report of the First Sub-Committee circulated to the Committee on Territorial Waters provided in Article 4, under the heading 'Vessels other than Warships' that

> A coastal State may not hinder the innocent passage of foreign vessels in the territorial sea.
>
> Submarine vessels shall navigate on the surface.[193]

The 'Observations' clarified that '[t]he expression "vessels other than warships" [in the heading] includes not only merchant vessels, but all other vessels not registered in the navy list of a State at the time of passage'. In the final version, Draft Article 4 was slightly rephrased to provide that the coastal State 'may put no obstacles in the way of' innocent passage.[194] The origin of this amendment is not clear, as draft Article 4 was not fully discussed by the Committee on Territorial Waters. In response to a British proposal, the Observation was rephrased to give examples of 'vessels not belonging to the naval forces at the time of passage'.[195]

Draft Articles 5 and 6 were dealt with very briefly by the Committee, with a short comment added to the Observations under Article 6 on the initiative of Portugal. The Sub-Committee's final version of Draft Article 5 provided that

> The right of passage does not prevent the coastal State from taking all necessary steps to protect itself in the territorial sea against any act prejudicial to the security, public policy or fiscal interests of the State, and, in the case of vessels proceeding to inland waters, against any breach of the conditions to which admission of those vessels is subject.

[191] Ibid, 1368–1370.

[192] Ibid. Some amendments to Draft Article 1 and the accompanying Observations were, however, adopted by the Committee as a whole before this decision was made.

[193] Ibid, 1405.

[194] Ibid, 1415.

[195] Ibid, 1416, 1368.

The Observations noted the coastal State's 'right to verify, if necessary, the innocent character of the passage of a vessel' but stated that 'in order to avoid unnecessary hindrances to navigation, the coastal State is bound to act with great discretion in exercising this right'.[196] Draft Article 6 provided that '[f]oreign vessels exercising the right of innocent passage shall comply with the laws and regulations enacted in conformity with international usage by the coastal State', referring in particular to laws and regulations ensuring navigational safety, protection from vessel source pollution, protection of the products of the sea, and 'rights of fishing, shooting and analogous rights belonging to the coastal State'.[197] The text indicates that regulations beyond those listed – provided they were 'in conformity with international usage' – could also apply to foreign vessels exercising a right of passage.

Of most significance for present purposes, the final version of Draft Article 12 provided (under the heading 'Warships') that

> As a general rule, a coastal State will not forbid the passage of foreign warships in its territorial sea and will not require a previous authorisation or notification.
>
> The coastal State has the right to regulate the conditions of such passage.
>
> Submarines shall navigate on the surface.

The Sub-Committee stated in its Observations that '[t]o state that a coastal State will not forbid the innocent passage of foreign warships through its territorial sea is but to recognize existing practice'. It went on to clarify, however, that '[t]hat practice also, without laying down any strict and absolute rule, leaves to the State the power, in exceptional cases, to prohibit the passage of foreign warships through its territorial sea'.[198] The Observation also stated that while '[t]he coastal State may regulate the conditions of passage, particularly as regards the number of foreign units passing simultaneously through its territorial sea . . . as a general rule, no previous authorisation or even notification will be required'.[199] The Observation – though not the text of Draft Article 12 – also stated that '[u]nder no pretext, however, may there be any interference with the passage of warships through straits constituting a route for international maritime traffic between two parts of the high sea'. Draft Article 13

[196] Ibid, 1416.
[197] Ibid, 1405.
[198] Ibid, 1418.
[199] Ibid, 1419.

provided that 'If a foreign warship passing through the territorial sea does not comply with the regulations of the coastal State and disregards any request or compliance which may be brought to its notice, the coastal State may require the warship to leave the territorial sea.'

Significantly, objections to the treatment of 'previous authorisation or notification' in Draft Article 12 were raised upon its reading by the Committee on Territorial Waters as a whole. Romania, which had already made its support for a right to require previous authorisation or notification very clear, drew attention to its previous observations on this point and stated that these views were fully maintained.[200] Denmark stated that it

> [assumed] that the words 'as a general rule' refer not only to the beginning of the first paragraph but to the end of that paragraph. Special cases may arise where previous notification is required for reasons of safety.[201]

The Special Rapporteur did not indicate that Denmark's assumption was incorrect, and a right to require previous authorisation or notification remains consistent with the phrase '[a]s a general rule' – albeit possibly in more limited circumstances than supported by many States. The Observation further supports Denmark's reading, clarifying that the expression 'as a general rule' does indeed apply to the provision that 'no previous authorisation or even notification will be required'.[202] The shift in emphasis from a general right to require prior authorisation or notification to a more exceptional right to do so is not accounted for by the available records. As we shall see in Chapter 7, subsequent comments by François suggest that he may have incorrectly assumed that the Preparatory Committee's formulation of Basis of Discussion 20, which denied 'the right to require a previous authorisation', reflected State views on the matter. This was not the case.

In any event, the Committee on Territorial Waters declined to adopt the Draft Articles prepared by the First Sub-Committee, instead attaching them as an Appendix to the Committee's Report. Though the first thirteen Draft Articles were described in that Report (drafted by Special Rapporteur François) as being 'provisionally approved' (as compared with the Draft Articles prepared by the Second Sub-Committee, which were not), the Committee stressed that it had not had the opportunity to fully consider these provisions and had not approved them in accordance

200 Ibid, 1373.
201 Ibid.
202 Ibid, 1419 (emphasis added).

with the Rules of Procedure.[203] This status was reflected in their characterisation as an annex – understood to be 'a sufficiently good way of drawing attention to our work', which was, however, 'no more than material prepared for a subsequent conference'.[204]

The Report of the Second Committee on Territorial Waters was considered in the Eighth Plenary Meeting on the final day of the Conference.[205] François explained that the Committee was unable to present the Conference with a convention for adoption due to continuing disagreement on the breadth of the territorial sea.[206] He claimed that significant agreement had nevertheless been reached on the two groups of articles drafted by the Second Committee and expressed 'hope that these articles may subsequently be revived'.[207] François himself would be chiefly responsible for their revival in his work with the International Law Commission in advance of the 1958 Conference on the Law of the Sea.[208]

3.7 Conclusion

The inter-war period from Versailles in 1919 to the Hague in 1930 saw significant shifts in the balance of power between States in both Europe and the Pacific. The post-war peace settlement involved the demilitarisation of the defeated Central Powers after WWI and the distribution of both ships and territory among the Allied and Associated Powers. Submarines were destroyed or transferred to victorious powers. Germany's unrestricted submarine warfare in WWI also encouraged the United Kingdom to advocate for the submarine's abolition as part of international efforts to secure a reduction in naval arms through multilateral treaties. Yet the strategic value of this type of vessel also became apparent for Japan and its chief rival, the United States, with Japan's expansionism in the Pacific.

The United Kingdom's proposals to abolish the submarine were not successful, though the United States expressed support for this policy at various times. Arms reduction treaties also failed to restrict the tonnage or capacity of submarines up until the conclusion of the London Naval Treaty in 1930. The limits agreed upon at this time in fact allowed most

[203] Ibid, 1378.
[204] Ibid.
[205] Rosenne, *League of Nations 1930* (n 121) vol. 3, 752.
[206] Ibid.
[207] Ibid.
[208] See Chapter 5.

parties, except Japan, to increase their existing and planned submarine forces. As discussed in Chapter 4, the opposition of Japan's Imperial Navy to the 1930 Treaty led to Japan's withdrawal from the international arms limitation project altogether. Japan nevertheless continued to support the regulation of submarine attacks on merchant shipping that had been recognised in Article 22 of the London Naval Treaty – at least up until WWII.

Article 22 of the London Naval Treaty provided that 'in their action with regard to merchant ships, submarines must conform to the rules of International Law to which surface vessels are subject' and, more specifically, that 'a warship, whether surface vessel or submarine, may not sink or render incapable of navigation a merchant vessel without having first placed passengers, crew and ship's papers in a place of safety'.[209] This rule had also been recognised in the Treaty Relating to the Use of Submarines and Noxious Gases in Warfare (1922), though this agreement did not enter into force.[210] The core requirement was widely understood to form part of customary international law – a conclusion that Germany's repeated breach of the rule in WWI does not impugn insofar as it characterised its actions as an exception to the rule.[211] The following chapter discusses the reiteration of this rule in the 1936 Submarine Protocol and its relationship with State practice in WWII.[212]

Questions relating to the passage of warships and merchant ships, including submarines in both categories, were considered in a number of international fora in the post-war period. In the Turkish Straits, the 1920 Treaty of Sèvres and the 1923 Treaty of Lausanne formalised the interest of the Allies and the United Kingdom especially in preventing the Straits being closed to merchant vessels generally and their own warships in particular. While Brüel has suggested that the Treaty of Lausanne recognised freedom of navigation in Straits as a broader principle rather than a specific regime established by agreement for the Turkish Straits, this view is not supported by the treaty text.[213] Article 23 provides that

[209] London Naval Treaty (n 92) art. 22.

[210] Submarine Treaty of 1922 (n 75).

[211] See Chapter 2, Section 2.3.

[212] Procès-Verbal relating to the Rules of Submarine Warfare set forth in Part IV of the Treaty for the Limitation and Reduction of Naval Armament of 22 April 1930, London, 6 November 1936, entered into force 6 November 1936, 173 LNTS 353, [1936] ATS 14.

[213] Erik Brüel, 'The Turkish Straits (Part 3)' (1943) 14 *Nordisk Tidsskrift for International Ret* 131, 133–134.

> [t]he High Contracting Parties are agreed to recognise and declare the principle of freedom of transit and of navigation, by sea and by air, in time of peace as in time of war, in the strait of the Dardanelles, the Sea of Marmora and the Bosphorus, *as prescribed in the separate Convention signed this day, regarding the regime of the Straits.*[214]

The requirement that submarines travel on the surface and the notification requirement for the passage of foreign warships are of particular note in connection with debates regarding the laws of passage leading up to the 1930 Hague Conference.

In the post-WWI period, submarines were understood to be classifiable as either merchant ships or warships because of their role as blockade runners, as well as their offensive role in WWI. These roles of submarines then informed debates at the 1930 Hague Codification Conference regarding the content of rules applying more broadly to merchant ships and warships during passage in the territorial sea. As we have seen, the Draft Articles annexed to the Final Report of the Territorial Sea Committee presented at the Hague Conference did not necessarily reflect the agreement of States. At best, these provisions reflect the views of some States and incomplete attempts to compromise with others. Reading the Draft Articles without attending to the record of proceedings leading up to and at the Hague Conference or, indeed, to the status of the Draft Articles as unapproved, leaves the reader with an inaccurate picture of State views on the regime of the territorial sea at this time.

The record of proceedings shows that a majority of States did not accept a right of passage for foreign warships in the territorial sea at the Hague Conference but considered such passage to depend upon the consent of the coastal State. A number of States claimed a right to require prior notification and authorisation for the passage of warships. It was widely accepted that States had the right to deny the passage of warships altogether. While there was greater support for a right of innocent passage for foreign merchant ships, this right was understood to remain subject to coastal State regulation. Moreover, even under the First Sub-Committee's Draft Articles, it seems to have been recognised that the coastal State retained a right to suspend such passage altogether for security reasons.

With respect to straits, the stipulation in the Observations to Draft Article 13 that '[u]nder no pretext . . . may there be any interference with

[214] Emphasis added. See further Section 3.3.2 above.

the passage of warships through straits constituting a route for international maritime traffic between two parts of the high sea' is noteworthy but again at odds with the views of many States at this time. Most States appear to have been satisfied with the application in straits of the regime of passage otherwise obtaining in the territorial sea – a regime understood to allow considerable interference with passage by the coastal State. This understanding is perhaps indirectly recognised by the location of the statement in the Observation to the Draft Article rather than in the proposed text.

The position of States in the post-WWI period regarding the regulation of submarines both as merchant ships and warships is of continuing interest in connection with claims regarding both treaty law and custom today. The efforts of learned societies and the work of the Hague Codification Conference indicate some support for the requirement of submarines to surface while in the territorial sea. Of course, the failure of States to adopt a convention on territorial waters meant that these views were not codified as law in 1930. State positions continued to shift in response to both domestic and international developments, as seen in the following chapters.

4

The Impact of the Second Sino-Japanese War and World War II

4.1 Introduction

The 1930s saw tensions develop into hostilities in both Europe and the Pacific. Japan and Germany withdrew from the League of Nations in 1933. Western States with interests in the Pacific were presented with the prospect of fighting two wars simultaneously, facing new challenges in relation to questions of armament, security policies, and military (including naval) strategies. This chapter begins (in Section 4.2) with important geopolitical context for international law developments at this time. The naval strategies pursued, especially in the Pacific, had flow on consequences for multilateral negotiations on matters of international law. The role of the submarine in this context was a key issue, and States continued to grapple with the question of whether submarines should be outlawed or limited by number and/or tonnage. These issues were considered in treaty negotiations relating to general disarmament and the particular regime governing the Turkish Straits.

States were also concerned to regulate the use of submarines against merchant shipping. As discussed in Section 4.3 of this chapter, the 1936 London Protocol on Submarine Warfare reiterated earlier (post–World War I (WWI)) statements of the obligation to '[place] passengers, crew and ship's papers in a place of safety' before sinking or incapacitating a merchant vessel.[1] Although thirty-seven States had signed up to the Protocol prior to World War II (WWII), it proved unable to constrain submarine operations against merchant shipping during that conflict.

Section 4.4 examines the negotiations for adoption of the 1936 Montreux Convention, which governs the Turkish Straits to this day.

[1] Procès-Verbal relating to the Rules of Submarine Warfare set forth in Part IV of the Treaty for the Limitation and Reduction of Naval Armament of 22 April 1930, London, 6 November 1936, entered into force 6 November 1936, 173 LNTS 353, [1936] ATS 14 ('London Protocol of 1936').

While the negotiations were highly flavoured by the geopolitical and security imperatives of the day, the issues addressed in relation to this body of water found reflection in contemporaneous legal developments as well as during and after WWII. In Section 4.5, we explore how submarines were deployed during WWII and highlight how international law regulated (or failed to regulate) their use during that conflict. Consistent with State practice and experiences set out in the two previous Chapters, the evolving threat of the submarine was addressed in neutrality laws, which were developed prior to and during WWII, with an increasing number of States moving to entirely prohibit the passage of belligerent submarines through their territorial seas. Section 4.6 explores this issue. Again, where 'mere passage' was permitted pursuant to Hague Convention (XIII) of 1907,[2] it was frequently specified that submarines must travel on the surface. As discussed in the following chapter, State practice in this regard played into negotiations at the 1958 Conference on the Law of the Sea and the resulting treaties – aspects of which are reproduced in the United Nations Convention on the Law of the Sea (UNCLOS).[3]

What this time period demonstrates are different responses in international law as submarines became more widespread among naval powers. International law was initially relied upon as a tool to limit submarine acquisitions as part of arms reduction efforts. International law was also drawn upon to respond to the most threatening aspects of submarines: their ability to be undetected in waters close to shore and the potential high destruction of merchant shipping, again because of their increasing elusiveness. Rules developed at this time banning submarines from certain maritime areas, seeking to align standards of submarine use to surface warships, and increasing requirements allowing for their detection have all contributed to the current legal framework of submarines in international law.

4.2 Conflict and Competition in the Pacific

In 1931, the Japanese military staged a false flag incident as a pretext for invading Manchuria.[4] China appealed to the League of Nations to consider the matter under Article 11 of the Covenant as a threat to peace, but

[2] Hague Convention (XIII) concerning the Rights and Duties of Neutral Powers in Naval War, The Hague, 18 October 1907, entered into force 26 January 1910, 205 CTS 395, art. 10.

[3] United Nations Convention on the Law of the Sea, Montego Bay, 10 December 1982, entered into force 16 November 1994, 1833 UNTS 397.

[4] 'Manchukuo' in Ian C. B. Dear and Michael R. D. Foot (eds.), *The Oxford Companion to World War II* (Oxford University Press, 2014).

Japan vetoed a resolution seeking its partial withdrawal from the region.[5] The United States, which was particularly concerned that Japan's expansionism might threaten its own interests in the Pacific region, issued the Stimson Doctrine – named after the US Secretary of State – indicating its refusal to recognise 'any situation, treaty, or agreement which may be brought about by means contrary to the covenants and obligations of the Pact of Paris of August 27, 1928, to which treaty both China and Japan, as well as the United States, are parties'.[6] In 1932, Japan commenced its attack on Shanghai, in breach of the 'Nine-Power Treaty' securing the territorial integrity of China, which was agreed at the 1921 Washington Conference.[7] Stimson suggested that Japan's violation of the 'Nine-Power Treaty' threatened the basis on which all participating States had undertaken to limit their naval armaments, noting that

> The willingness of the American government to surrender its then commanding lead in battleship construction and to leave its positions at Guam and in the Philippines without further fortification, was predicated upon, among other things, the self-denying covenants contained in the Nine Power Treaty, which assured the nations of the world not only of equal opportunity for their Eastern trade but also against the military aggrandizement of any other power at the expense of China.[8]

Stimson also stationed the US battlefleet off Hawai'i, though at the time it was clear that neither the United States nor British navies could match the strength of the Imperial Japanese Navy in the Pacific.[9]

[5] Ian Nish, *Japan's Struggle with Internationalism: Japan, China and the League of Nations, 1931–1933* (Routledge, 2009) 32–39; Treaty of Peace between the Allied and Associated Powers and Germany, Versailles, 28 June 1919, entered into force 10 January 1920, [1919] UKTS 4, art. 11 ('Treaty of Versailles').

[6] 'Identic Notes from the United States Secretary of State to the Chinese and Japanese Governments, January 8, 1932', in John W. Wheeler-Bennett (ed.), *Documents on International Affairs 1932* (Oxford University Press, 1933) 262; General Treaty for the Renunciation of the War as an Instrument of National Policy, Paris, 27 August 1928, 94 LNTS 57 (also known as the Kellogg-Briand Pact).

[7] See Chapter 3, Section 3.5.1. Treaty relating to Principles and Policies to be Followed in Matters concerning China, Washington, 5 February 1922, entered into force 5 August 1925, 38 LNTS 277, [1925] ATS 12.

[8] 'The Secretary of State to the Consul General at Shanghai (Cunningham)' in Joseph V. Fuller (ed.), *Papers Relating to the Foreign Relations of the United States: Japan, 1931–1941* (United States Government Printing Office, 1943) vol. 1, 83, 85–86 (File No. 793.94/4291).

[9] Richard E. J. Galilee, 'The Breakdown of Naval Limitation in the Far East 1932–1936' (Thesis Submitted to the University of Canterbury, 1975) 72.

Stimson's veiled threats regarding naval armament appear to have been a significant prompt for Japan's request for an increase of its ratio of allowable weapons under the 1930 London Naval Treaty at the 1932 General Disarmament Conference in Geneva.[10] The United Kingdom and the United States again proposed that the submarine should be entirely abolished as an unacceptable offensive weapon, while Japan (along with France) argued that the submarine was used for defensive purposes and should not be outlawed.[11] The United States shifted its position during negotiations to propose limitations on the tonnage of submarines rather than their prohibition.[12] However, States failed to reach agreement on new qualitative or quantitative limitations on naval arms. The 'Macdonald Plan' eventually agreed to in 1933 as the basis for a future convention merely noted the continued application of the 1922 Washington Naval Treaty and the 1930 London Naval Treaty pending their expiry in 1936.[13]

Japan had invested substantially in the development of submarine forces following WWI.[14] At the outbreak of the second Sino-Japanese War, Japan's submarine fleet was considerable and included large ocean-going submarines based on the German U-Kreuzer of 1917–18.[15] In the years following Japan's withdrawal from the League of Nations, both the United States and Japan greatly invested in their naval forces, which had not yet reached the upper limits imposed by the naval arms limitation treaties.[16] Japan invested significantly in submarine technology, developing both midget attack submarines (an efficient use of limited tonnage) and large ocean-going submarines capable of carrying reconnaissance seaplanes and launching catapults.[17] At the same time, negotiations were underway for an Anglo-Japanese non-aggression pact. The United

[10] Ibid, 70–74. See Chapter 3, Section 3.5.2 in relation to the limits established by the Treaty for the Limitation and Reduction of Naval Armament, London, 22 April 1930, entered into force 31 December 1930, 112 LNTS 65 ('London Naval Treaty of 1930').

[11] Galilee (n 9) 80–82.

[12] Ibid, 84–85.

[13] Ibid, 92–94. Treaty between the British Empire, the United States of America, France, Italy and Japan for the Limitation of Naval Armaments, Washington, 6 February 1922, entered into force 17 August 1923, 25 LNTS 202, art. XXIII ('Washington Naval Treaty of 1922'); London Naval Treaty of 1930 (n 10) art. XXII.

[14] Norman Friedman, *Submarine Design and Development* (Naval Institute Press, 1984) 39–42.

[15] Ibid.

[16] Galilee (n 9) 96–127.

[17] Ibid, 120; Friedman (n 14) 40.

Kingdom hoped that such an agreement might encourage Japan to give up on its demand for parity in a new naval arms limitation treaty.[18]

When the Second London Naval Disarmament Conference opened in 1935, it was clear that Japan would not agree to the continued application of the limits in the Washington and London Treaties or any new agreement that did not accord to Japan the same ratios as the United Kingdom and the United States.[19] Japan withdrew from the Conference on 15 January 1936, continuing both its programme to increase naval arms and its expansionist operations in China.[20] The United States also believed that Japan was fortifying its Pacific mandates in violation of the Washington and London Treaties, though it is not established that Japan did so before the expiry of those agreements.[21] In 1935, US President Roosevelt approved both a Naval Supply Bill financing the construction of twenty-four new vessels (including six submarines) and Pan-American Airways' development of an air base with the potential for military use at Guam.[22] The coincidence of these developments with US naval manoeuvres as part of 'Problem XVI' in the Pacific exacerbated tensions with Japan, prompting the latter to claim that the United States was unlawfully fortifying its Pacific possessions and conduct counter-manoeuvres showcasing its clearly competitive naval forces.[23]

As tensions between the United States and Japan increased, so too did the conflict between Japan and China. In 1937, the Marco Polo bridge incident saw Chinese resistance to Japanese expansionism escalate into full-scale war. While this war was largely fought on land, Japan reinforced its naval superiority in the region by destroying Chinese ships (the Chinese Navy already having suffered severe losses during the first Sino-Japanese War)[24] from air and sea.[25]

Motivated by imperialist aspirations that were at times expressed as an ideology of 'Pan-Asianism' – the alliance of Asia against western

[18] Galilee (n 9) 147–154; Chihiro Hosoya, 'The 1934 Anglo-Japanese Non-Aggression Pact' (1981) 25(3) *International Studies Quarterly* 491.

[19] 'Naval Limitation and Pacific Problems, 1921–1936' (CQ Researcher Report, 1934); Galilee (n 9) 108–121.

[20] SCM Paine, *The Wars for Asia 1911–1949* (Cambridge University Press, 2014) 77–106.

[21] Dorothy Borg, *The United States and the Far Eastern Crisis* (Harvard University Press, 1964) 237–239; Richard Dean Burns, 'Inspection of the Mandates, 1919–1941' (1968) 37(4) *Pacific Historical Review* 445, 458.

[22] Galilee (n 9) 188–190.

[23] Ibid, 190–192.

[24] Simon P. MacKenzie, 'Sino-Japanese War (1894–1895)' in Gordon Martel (ed.), *The Encyclopedia of War* (Blackwell, 2011).

[25] See 'Chinese Navy 1930–45', *Naval Encyclopedia Online* <https://naval-encyclopedia.com/ww2/chinese-navy-1930-45.php>. On the first Sino-Japanese War, see Andrew Rhodes,

domination[26] – and freed from the constraints of the Washington and London Treaties, Japan continued to build its naval forces.

New additions to its fleet of long-range cruiser submarines were tweaked to achieve faster surface speeds and from 1933 scouting aircraft and catapults became a standard feature.[27] Japan later fitted out several submarines to carry attack aircraft for special missions.[28] Other submarines were designed to carry and launch midget submarines carrying torpedoes.[29] Surface ships were also designed to carry midget submarines; Japan initially developed midget submarines to attack fast warships from carrier ships.[30] The use of larger submarines to carry midget submarines to attack enemy ships within harbours was a strategy developed during WWII.[31] From the late 1930s, Japan developed very fast midget submarines to defend naval bases on outlying islands.[32] Submarine tenders were designed to carry fuel, arms and provisions to seaplanes.[33] During the conflict, Japan also developed submarines to carry troops.[34]

Naval development was also proceeding elsewhere, with especially substantial investments in submarine technology by the United States, the Soviet Union, and Germany (contrary to the terms of the Treaty of Versailles).[35] The United Kingdom was also concerned with the development of its submarine fleet to defend its colonies and trade in the 'Far East' and experimented with a number of models for use as 'Overseas Patrol Submarines'.[36] Yet it struggled to balance the need for both substantial range and speed in this context with its commitment to limitations on submarine sizes under arms reduction treaties.[37] France invested in smaller submarines for use in the North Sea and Mediterranean as well as a number of longer range vessels.[38] As discussed

'Same Water, Different Dreams Salient Lessons of the Sino-Japanese War for Future Naval Warfare' (2020) 11(2) *Journal of Advanced Military Studies* 35, 36–40.

26 Eri Hotta, *Pan-Asianism and Japan's War 1931–1945* (Palgrave Macmillan, 2007).

27 Friedman (n 14) 40.

28 Ibid.

29 Ibid, 41.

30 Ibid.

31 Ibid.

32 Ibid, 41–42.

33 Ibid, 42.

34 Ibid.

35 Galilee (n 9) 96–97; Friedman (n 14) 37–48, 93–94.

36 Friedman (n 14) 37–39.

37 Ibid.

38 Ibid, 43.

in Section 4.5, France also constructed a large ocean-going submarine cruiser, the *Surcouf*, which was designed with a view to commerce raiding (attacks upon merchant ships).[39] Italy too built a number of submarines for use as commerce raiders, anticipating their use against French merchant shipping in the Atlantic.[40]

Investment in military aircraft and the development of radar enhancing the capacity for submarine detection drove further developments in submarine technology and strategy. While submarines in WWI had travelled on the surface, submerging just prior to attack, the improved ability to detect submarines from the air necessitated increased periods of submersion.[41] Improvements in the capacity for lengthy submergence were a factor influencing neutrality laws developed leading up to and during WWII as well as post-war efforts to regulate the passage of submarines in times of peace. The negotiation of international treaties to limit naval arms and regulate their use also played into State investment in submarines leading up to WWII.

4.3 The 1936 London Naval Treaty and the Submarine Protocol

The Second Naval Disarmament Conference opened in London in December 1935. Preliminary conversations had already made apparent key differences between the United States, which proposed either a 20 per cent reduction on existing limits or their retention; the United Kingdom, which sought arms reduction through qualitative rather than quantitative limits (namely, size and gun calibre) but an increase in cruisers; and Japan, which pursued parity with the United Kingdom and the United States.[42] Japan had already abrogated the 1922 Washington Naval Treaty in December 1934 and was adamant that it would not agree to an unequal ratio like that of the earlier agreement.[43] Japan also distinguished between 'offensive' and 'defensive' armaments, arguing that while the former (including, in Japan's assessment, aircraft carriers, capital ships and heavy cruisers)[44] should be 'reduced to the

[39] Ibid.
[40] Ibid.
[41] Ibid, 33–34.
[42] Merze Tate, *The United States and Armaments* (Harvard University Press, 1948) 185–198; Galilee (n 9) 140–161.
[43] Galilee (n 9) 185–188.
[44] As Galilee notes, the question of which armaments were offensive and which were defensive differed between States. The United Kingdom, for example, considered both the capital ship and aircraft carrier essential for defence: ibid, 164.

minimum or abolished altogether', submarines as well as light cruisers and destroyers fell into the latter category and 'should be merged into a single category with complete liberty for each power to build as it chooses'.[45] The United States responded by pointing to the role of submarines in destroying commerce, which was clearly offensive.[46] Japan in turn suggested that this offensive use of submarines could be addressed by making the provisions on submarines in the London Naval Treaty of 1930 'effective and universal'.[47]

The United Kingdom had again come to the Conference with a preference for the abolition of submarines but observed in its opening remarks that '[i]f it proves impossible to obtain agreement for the abolition of submarines, it is of vital importance to reach an agreement which will prevent their misuse'.[48] It indicated that preliminary talks had established support for incorporating the rules relating to the treatment of merchant ships by submarines in Part IV of the London Naval Treaty of 1930 ('already in force between the United States, Japan and the members of the British Commonwealth of Nations') in a new and separate instrument.[49] Italy and France had indicated they would 'definitely' accept such an instrument, which the United Kingdom 'hope[d] . . . will be the signal for the acceptance of these rules by all the maritime Powers of the world'.[50]

The opposition of the United Kingdom and the United States to Japan's demand for parity, as well as Japan's refusal to countenance qualitative limits without quantitative limits, led to Japan's withdrawal from proceedings in January 1936.[51] In March 1936, the Second London Naval Treaty was signed by the United Kingdom, France, the United States, India, Australia, Canada and New Zealand.[52] Italy, which was subject to League of Nations sanctions over its invasion of Abyssinia (Ethiopia), refused to sign the agreement, as did South Africa and the Irish Free State (the latter having no navy).[53]

45 Ibid, 163.
46 Ibid.
47 Ibid.
48 Howard Levie, 'Submarine Warfare: With Emphasis on the 1936 London Protocol' (1998) 70 *Naval War College International Law Studies* 291, 312.
49 Ibid.
50 Ibid.
51 Galilee (n 9) 205.
52 Treaty for the Limitation of Naval Armament, London, 25 March 1936, entered into force 29 July 1937, 184 LNTS 115 ('London Naval Treaty of 1936').
53 Galilee (n 9) 230–231.

The Second London Naval Treaty described qualitative limits for the various categories of ship: submarines being limited to 2,000 tonnes displacement with a maximum gun calibre of 5.1 inches.[54] Instead of quantitative restrictions, it was agreed that the parties would exchange information annually, giving advance notice of the warships to be built by or for them and would thereafter be prohibited from building or acquiring warships not indicated in this programme.[55] Design modifications would also have to be notified to the other parties at least four months before being implemented.[56]

Significantly, the Second London Naval Treaty included a number of clauses admitting departures from these restrictions in the interests of national security.[57] Most notably, Article 25 provided that in the case of a power not party to the Treaty authorising, constructing, or acquiring 'any vessel not in conformity with the limitations and restrictions as to standard displacement and armament prescribed ... by the present treaty ... each High Contracting Party reserves the right to depart, and to the extent to which, he considers such departures necessary in order to meet the requirements of his national security'.[58] Article 26 provided that parties could depart from a declared building plan if 'a change of circumstances' affected their security.[59] As Galilee notes, these provisions were intended to ensure States party to the Second London Naval Treaty had adequate means of protecting their security if States not party to the agreement – namely, Italy and Japan – were to increase armaments beyond the specified limits.[60]

Germany had not been invited to the 1935–1936 Conference on Naval Disarmament at France's behest. Instead, as part of a policy of appeasement, the United Kingdom concluded a bilateral agreement with Germany in June 1935 establishing that 'the future strength of the German Navy in relation to the aggregate naval strength of the Members of the British Commonwealth of Nations should be in the proportion of 35:100', and that this should be a 'permanent relationship'.[61] This agreement effectively accepted Germany's violation of the Treaty of Versailles by

[54] London Naval Treaty of 1936 (n 52) art. 7.
[55] Ibid, pt. III.
[56] Ibid, art. 16. See also Galilee (n 9) 225–226, 232.
[57] London Naval Treaty of 1936 (n 52) pt. IV. See also Galilee (n 9) 233.
[58] London Naval Treaty of 1936 (n 52) art. 25.
[59] Ibid, art. 26(1).
[60] Galilee (n 9) 232.
[61] Exchange of Notes between His Majesty's Government in the United Kingdom of Great Britain and Northern Ireland and the Government of the German Reich regarding the

rearmament.[62] Significantly, while Germany had accepted that the 35 per cent ratio should apply to 'the tonnage of each category of vessel to be maintained',[63] the agreement also provided that

> In the matter of submarines . . . Germany, while not exceeding the ratio of 35:100 in respect of total tonnage, shall have the right to possess a submarine tonnage equal to the total submarine tonnage possessed by the Members of the British Commonwealth of Nations. The German Government, however, undertake that, except in the circumstances indicated in the immediately following sentence, Germany's submarine tonnage shall not exceed 45 per cent. of the total of that possessed by the Members of the British Commonwealth of Nations. The German Government reserve the right, in the event of a situation arising, which in their opinion, makes it necessary for Germany to avail herself of her right to a percentage of submarine tonnage exceeding the 45 per cent. above mentioned, to give notice [to] this effect to His Majesty's Government in the United Kingdom, and agree that the matter shall be the subject of friendly discussion before the German Government exercise that right.[64]

The conclusion of a separate agreement regulating the actions of submarines against merchant ships was signed by the United Kingdom and the Commonwealth nations, the United States, France and, despite their non-participation in the Second London Naval Treaty, Italy and Japan. The 1936 London Protocol on Submarine Warfare was formulated as a 'Procès-verbal relating to the Rules of Submarine Warfare set forth in Part IV of the Treaty of London of 22 April 1930'.[65] It restated the rules set out in Article 22 of the 1930 London Naval Treaty, providing that '[i]n their action with regard to merchant ships, submarines must conform to the rules of international law to which surface vessels are subject'[66] and the obligation 'except in the case of persistent refusal to stop on being duly summoned, or of active resistance to visit or search' to '[place] passengers, crew and ship's papers in a place of safety' before sinking or incapacitating a merchant vessel.[67] While Article 22 of the 1930 London Naval Treaty remained in force 'without

Limitation of Naval Armaments, London, 18 June 1935, entered into force 18 June 1935, [1935] ATS 7, art. 2(a) ('UK-Germany Exchange of Notes').

62 Treaty of Versailles (n 5).

63 UK-Germany Exchange of Notes (n 61) art. 2(d).

64 Ibid, art. 2(f).

65 London Protocol of 1936 (n 1).

66 Ibid, art. 1.

67 Ibid, art. 2.

limit of time', the Protocol allowed a number of States not party to that agreement to register their acceptance of these rules. At the outbreak of WWII, thirty-seven more States – including Germany and Japan – had acceded to the 1936 Submarine Protocol.[68]

In 1937, the United Kingdom signed another bilateral agreement on Naval Arms Limitation with Germany and a parallel agreement with the Soviet Union extending the qualitative limits set out in the 1936 London Naval Treaty to these non-signatory States.[69] According to Maiolo, the Soviet Union's agreement with the United Kingdom was premised on its interest in accessing quality British naval technology to build up substantial ocean-going forces to serve its interests in both defending its coasts and projecting force in support of communist revolution through naval operations in the Arctic and Pacific Oceans and the Baltic and Black Seas.[70] While agreeing to qualitative limitations, the Soviet Union managed to convince the United Kingdom to accept an 'Eastern reservation' preserving 'the Soviet Union's right to build warships for the Pacific outside of qualitative limits and to conceal the details of that construction from the other signatories until Japan signed the 1936 London Naval Treaty'.[71]

While Italy acceded to the Second London Naval Treaty in 1938, Japan never did. The inability of this instrument together with other interwar efforts to secure peace through arms limitation agreements, as well as the failure of the Submarine Protocol to constrain belligerent actions against merchant shipping, became clearly apparent in WWII.

68 Levie (n 48) 313. See also '11C. 1936 London Procès-Verbal Relating to the Rules of Submarine Warfare Set Forth in Part IV of the Treaty of London of 22 April 1930' in Edwin I. Nwogugu (ed.), *The Law of Naval Warfare: A Collection of Agreements and Documents with Commentaries* (Brill, 1988) 349.

69 D. C. Watt, 'Anglo-German Negotiations on the Eve of the Second World War – I' (1985) 103(610) *Journal of the Royal United Services 201*; Joseph A. Maiolo, 'Anglo-Soviet Naval Armaments Diplomacy before the Second World War (2008) 123(501) *English Historical Review* 351, 372; Agreement between His Majesty's Government in the United Kingdom and the German Government providing for the Limitation of Naval Armament and the Exchange of Information concerning Naval Construction, London, 17 July 1937, [1938] UKTS 2; Agreement between His Majesty's Government in the United Kingdom and the Government of the Union of Soviet Socialist Republics providing for the Limitation of Naval Armament and the Exchange of Information concerning Naval Construction, London, 17 July 1937, [1938] UKTS 17.

70 Maiolo (n 69) 256–372.

71 Ibid, 363–364.

4.4 The 1936 Montreux Convention on the Turkish Straits

Mussolini's invasion of Abyssinia (Ethiopia) in 1935 and Hitler's announcement in the same year of the rearmament of Germany (followed in March 1936 by the remilitarisation of the Rhineland) prompted unease in Turkey (as it was then known) regarding the demilitarised and internationalised status of the Straits.[72] Turkey had already argued that the military clauses of the 1923 Treaty of Lausanne were 'incompatible with the legitimate right of self-defence' at the failed 1933 Geneva Disarmament Conference.[73] In February 1936, Turkey informally notified the British Foreign Office of its interest in renegotiating the terms of the Treaty of Lausanne: a proposal met with some sympathy, though the United Kingdom insisted that the process must be multilateral.[74]

Turkey issued a note to the parties and signatories to the Treaty of Lausanne and the Secretary of the League of Nations in April 1936 arguing that the trend towards disarmament apparent in 1923 that would have assured Turkish security despite the demilitarisation of the Straits had been reversed.[75] While Turkey suggested that this situation amounted to a fundamental change of circumstances, it also indicated that it sought the development of a new agreement revising the terms of the Treaty of Lausanne rather than unilateral withdrawal or termination.[76]

A Conference was convened in Montreux, Switzerland, in June, attended by all signatories to the Treaty of Lausanne bar Italy, which declined to engage in the process due to its continued subjection to League of Nations sanctions and its objection to the United Kingdom's mutual assistance agreements in the Eastern Mediterranean.[77] Soviet Russia, which had never ratified the Treaty of Lausanne, was particularly supportive of the prospect of a new agreement that might better protect its interests in the Black Sea.[78]

[72] Philip Towle, 'The Montreux Convention as a Regional Arms Control Treaty – Negotiation and Practice' (1981) 45(3) *Military Affairs* 121, 122. See further Chapter 3, Section 3.3.

[73] Harry N. Howard, 'The Straits after the Montreux Conference' (1936) 15(1) *Foreign Affairs* 199.

[74] Towle (n 72) 122.

[75] Ibid.

[76] Ibid.

[77] Howard (n 73).

[78] Mensur Akgün, 'Great Powers and the Straits: From Lausanne to Montreux (1994) 24 *Turkish Yearbook of International Relations* 57, 68.

At the Conference, Turkey opened proceedings with a proposal to abolish the Straits Commission and reinstate Turkish sovereign and military control over the Straits for reasons of self-defence. Under the terms of this proposal, Turkey would be entitled to remilitarise the Straits and to close them entirely in the event of a general or specific threat of war – the presence of which was to be determined by Turkey rather than the League of Nations.[79] When the Straits were open (including in the case of Turkish neutrality), the passage of foreign warships would be limited to 14,000 tonnes at any one time (half of the tonnage of the existing Turkish fleet) and 25,000 tonnes in the case of littoral States subject to certain conditions.[80] If Turkey was a belligerent, the passage of the warships of any power would be forbidden unless specifically authorised by Turkey.[81] Turkey also argued that it should be able to limit the number of warships passing through the Straits where it was neither neutral nor belligerent but bound by its obligations as a member of the League of Nations to impose sanctions.[82] Significantly, submarines as well as civil and military aircraft were to be prohibited in the Straits at all times.[83]

The Turkish proposal met with a number of objections from the United Kingdom in particular. While it was prepared to support Turkey's remilitarisation of the Straits, the United Kingdom was also concerned to ensure its own continued ability to deploy naval units in the Black Sea.[84] It accordingly sought to increase the tonnage limit for non-littoral States to 45,000 tonnes and provide for the pursuit of enemy warships through the Straits into the Black Sea.[85] The United Kingdom also thought that Turkey's right to close the Straits should be contingent upon the support of at least two thirds of the League Council, to be established by a vote.[86] Finally, it proposed that a Straits Commission should be retained.[87]

Russia was far more supportive of the Turkish proposal. Yet it sought explicit recognition of 'full liberty of passage' through the Straits for the

[79] Ibid, 69.
[80] Ibid.
[81] Ibid.
[82] Anthony R. Deluca, *Great Power Rivalry at the Turkish Straits: The Montreux Conference and Convention of 1936* (Columbia University Press, 1981) 46.
[83] Howard (n 73) 201.
[84] Deluca (n 82) 45.
[85] Howard (n 73) 201.
[86] Ibid.
[87] Ibid.

warships of Black Sea States.[88] While its chief interest was in facilitating the movement of fleets between members of the Soviet Union, Russia presented this proposal as necessary to ensure collective security under the League system.[89] Russia also argued that the passage of the warships of non-Black Sea States should be limited by reference to the purpose of their entry into this 'closed sea'.[90] While Turkey had proposed that warships could pass through the Straits (subject to tonnage and time restrictions) in both peacetime and in the event of Turkish neutrality, Russia sought to deny the entry of the warships of non-Black Sea States into the Black Sea if no riverain States were at war and where any Black Sea State was a belligerent.[91] An exception was noted for the passage of warships operating within the framework of the Covenant; an implicit reference to the Franco-Soviet Mutual Assistance Pact that would ensure the continued passage of French and Soviet warships through the Straits.[92] Russia further proposed that the prohibition on the passage of submarines in the Turkish draft be extended to aircraft carriers – though in its view Soviet submarines and aircraft carriers, as warships of a Black Sea State, should not be subject to this prohibition in times of peace.[93]

Russia's proposals were enthusiastically supported by France (which sought to strengthen its alliance with the Soviet Union) and Bulgaria.[94] The United Kingdom objected strenuously to the even greater disadvantage of non-riverain States in the Russian text. It was particularly concerned with the proposal to prevent the entry of warships into the Black Sea where a Black Sea State other than Turkey was a belligerent, which 'would have closed the Straits and transformed the Black Sea into a "secure and inaccessible refuge for the Soviet fleet"'.[95] The United Kingdom's proposed solution was to remove all restrictions on the passage of belligerent warships.[96] While it recognised that Turkey might still have a right to 'veto' such passage for security reasons, it stressed that, when neutral, any such veto would have to be applied impartially.[97] Later in proceedings, the United Kingdom accepted that

[88] Deluca (n 82) 55.
[89] Ibid, 55–56.
[90] Ibid, 55–57.
[91] Ibid, 57.
[92] Ibid, 57, 60.
[93] Ibid, 57, 79.
[94] Ibid, 57–58.
[95] Deluca (n 82) 60.
[96] Ibid, 60–61.
[97] Ibid, 60–62, 75, 87.

the Straits should be closed to all belligerents in the event of a conflict in which no Black Sea State was participating.[98] The United Kingdom also objected to any special (and so discriminatory) allowance for free passage in pursuance of pacts of mutual assistance.[99] Significantly, it agreed that the passage of submarines should be prohibited in the Straits in peacetime albeit arguing that this restriction should apply equally to Black Sea States.[100]

For its part, Turkey was also keen to avoid a situation where it would be required to open the Straits to some warships and not others, risking its neutral status in the event of war. Its priority remained sovereign control over the Straits to ensure its security. It was also concerned to prevent Russia from 'unduly augmenting' its Black Sea fleet and using Turkey as 'door-keeper' for 'a Russian lake'.[101] Turkey's interests were well served by the Montreux Convention as adopted.[102] While a general affirmation of 'the principle of freedom of transit and navigation by sea in the Straits' was included at the United Kingdom's behest and provision was made for the 'complete freedom of transit and navigation in the Straits' by merchant ships in time of peace and in the case of Turkish neutrality 'without any formalities' beyond sanitary controls,[103] the Montreux Convention recognised a Turkish right to regulate, restrict and even prohibit passage in many circumstances. Notably, Articles 6 and 21 of the Convention specifically recognise these rights not only in the case of Turkish belligerency but in cases where 'Turkey consider[s] herself to be threatened with imminent danger of war'.[104] As this formulation makes clear, the existence of such a threat is to be determined by Turkey itself, though the Convention also provides for the review of such a determination by the Council of the League of Nations. The dissolution of the League in 1946 has left it unclear whether its review function in this regard can or should be taken over by the United Nations.[105] Türkiye's 2022 decision to close the Straits to warships in response to the Russian

98 Ibid, 87.
99 Ibid, 86–87.
100 Ibid, 79.
101 Ibid, 62.
102 Convention Regarding the Regime of Straits, Montreux, 20 July 1936, entered into force 9 November 1936, 173 LNTS 213 ('Montreux Convention').
103 Ibid, arts 1–4. *See Actes de la Conférence de Montreux concernant le régime des Détroits: Compte rendu des séances plénières et procès-verbal des débats du comité technique* (A Pedone, 1936) 278–288.
104 Montreux Convention (n 102) arts. 6, 21.
105 Nihan Ünlü, *The Legal Regime of the Turkish Straits* (Martinus Nijhoff, 2002) 101–104.

war on Ukraine was not first referred to the United Nations, though it should also be noted that Türkiye did not explicitly invoke Article 21 of the Montreux Convention in support of this move.[106]

The Montreux Convention substantially limits the passage of warships in times of peace and in the case of Turkish neutrality. While Article 10 provides that 'light surface vessels, minor war vessels and auxiliary vessels, whether belonging to Black Sea or non-Black Sea Powers, and whatever their flag, shall enjoy freedom of transit through the Straits without any taxes or charges whatever, provided that such transit is begun during daylight', other types of vessels – including submarines – are not as a rule permitted to pass through the Straits. Limited exceptions are made for submarines belonging to a Black Sea State. To this end, Article 12 provides that

> Black Sea Powers shall have the right to send through the Straits, for the purpose of rejoining their base, submarines constructed or purchased outside the Black Sea, provided that adequate notice of the laying down or purchase of such submarines shall have been given to Turkey.
>
> Submarines belonging to the said Powers shall also be entitled to pass through the Straits to be repaired in dockyards outside the Black Sea on condition that detailed information on the matter is given to Turkey.
>
> In either case, the said submarines must travel by day and on the surface, and must pass through the Straits singly.

This provision, together with the general prohibition on the passage of submarines through the Straits in time of peace or Turkish neutrality, was a response to the interests of the Soviet Union and Romania in building their own submarine forces while keeping foreign submarines out of the Black Sea.[107] The *belligerent* submarines of any State, however, would not be permitted to pass through the Straits. Article 19 provides that

> [v]essels of war belonging to belligerent Powers shall not ... pass through the Straits except in cases arising out of the application of Article 25 of the present Convention, and in cases of assistance rendered to a State victim of aggression in virtue of a treaty of mutual assistance

[106] See Tayfun Ozberk, 'Turkey Closes the Dardanelles and Bosphorus to Warships', *Naval News*, 28 February 2022 <www.navalnews.com/naval-news/2022/02/turkey-closes-the-dardanelles-and-bosphorus-to-warships/>; Raul (Pete) Pedrozo, 'Closing the Turkish Straits in Times of War', *Leiber Institute*, 3 March 2022 <https://lieber.westpoint.edu/closing-turkish-straits-war/>.

[107] Deluca (n 82) 79.

> binding Turkey, concluded within the framework of the Covenant of the League of Nations.

According to Article 25, '[n]othing in the present Convention shall prejudice the rights and obligations of Turkey, or of any of the other High Contracting Parties members of the League of Nations, arising out of the Covenant of the League of Nations'.

The Montreux Convention sets out further conditions that apply to the passage of warships through the Straits in the limited circumstances where this is permitted. Warships of all types are required to give prior notification in advance of passage: eight days in advance for Black Sea States and fifteen days for non-Black Sea States.[108] Article 13 further provides that '[w]hen effecting transit, the commander of the naval force shall, without being under any obligation to stop, communicate to a signal station at the entrance to the Dardanelles or the Bosphorus the exact composition of the force under his orders'. Limits on the tonnage and number of foreign warships transiting the Straits or present in the Black Sea, as well as conditions regarding the length of stay, are also specified in the Montreux Convention.[109]

The Montreux Convention clearly constrains the passage of warships through the Turkish Straits and recognises the Turkish government as having considerable discretion to prohibit such passage altogether.[110] Submarines belonging to States other than Turkey are effectively prohibited in the Straits, though Black Sea States are afforded passage through the Straits to add to or repair their submarine forces in time of peace and Turkish neutrality. Turkey is to be notified prior to the passage of any such submarines, which must also 'travel by day and on the surface, and must pass through the Straits singly'.[111] While the general rule is that belligerent submarines are entirely excluded from the Straits, there remains scope for such vessels to pass through the Straits 'in cases of assistance rendered to a State victim of aggression in virtue of a treaty of mutual assistance binding Turkey, concluded within the framework of the Covenant of the League of Nations', or otherwise in connection with rights and obligations under the Covenant. In view of the specific

[108] Montreux Convention (n 102) art. 13.

[109] Ibid, arts. 11, 14, 18.

[110] Article 24 of the Montreux Convention transfers the functions of the Straits Commission under the Lausanne Government to the Turkish government, including supervision of 'the execution of all the provisions of the present Convention relating to the passage of vessels of war through the Straits': art. 24. See Ünlü (n 105) 101–104.

[111] Montreux Convention (n 102) art. 12.

references to the Covenant of the League of Nations here, it appears that this clause cannot cover mutual security agreements under other frameworks.[112]

The Montreux Convention presents an interesting snapshot of State views regarding the passage of both merchant vessels and warships through Straits at this time, and the passage of submarines in particular. Though the specific geopolitical context of the Turkish Straits undoubtedly influenced State positions, the negotiations indicated general agreement on the right of a coastal State to both *regulate* the passage of warships through straits within its territorial waters – for example, by requiring prior notification and restricting their size, type and number – and to *prohibit* their passage entirely for security reasons. Indeed, the Montreux Convention also recognises the right of Turkey to regulate the passage of merchant ships, by requiring passage by day following designated routes with compulsory pilotage, in cases where 'Turkey consider[s] herself to be threatened with imminent danger of war'.[113] The general prohibition on the passage of submarines through the Straits together with the conditions applying to their passage where it is exceptionally permitted (i.e., a requirement to travel by day, on the surface, and singly) reflects the parties' appreciation of the special threat posed by submarines due to their ability to evade detection. These views remain of relevance in connection with the subsequent development of rules of passage in the territorial sea and straits.

Australia, Bulgaria, France, Greece, Japan, Romania, Turkey, the Soviet Union, the United Kingdom and Yugoslavia signed the Montreux Convention in 1936. Japan and Romania lodged reservations, with Japan stating that since it was not a member of the League of Nations it 'conserved all freedom of appreciation' in relation to the Covenant and treaties of mutual assistance concluded under it.[114] While all of the other signatories ratified the Convention in 1936, Japan's ratification was delayed until 1937.[115] Although it did not play a central role in negotiations, Japan had made several (unsuccessful) interventions proposing equal treatment for Black Sea States and non-Black Sea States – a strategy apparently intended to limit the ability of the Soviet Fleet to exit the Black Sea and enter the Pacific in the event of a Soviet-Japanese war.[116] The

112 Ünlü (n 105) 105.
113 Montreux Convention (n 102) art. 6.
114 Deluca (n 82) 111.
115 Howard (n 73) 201.
116 Deluca (n 82) 178–179.

prospect of such a conflict was increased by the 1936 Anti-Comintern (Communist International) Pact between Japan and Germany.[117]

Italy joined the Anti-Comintern Pact in 1937.[118] In 1938, it also formalised its acceptance of the Montreux Convention; however, like Japan, it lodged a reservation reserving its 'full liberty of appreciation' in relation to mutual assistance pacts under the League Covenant.[119] Between 1937 and 1939, Germany and Turkey also discussed several possibilities for formalising German adherence to the Montreux Convention, though no agreement was reached before the outbreak of WWII.[120]

4.5 Submarine Warfare in World War II

On 3 September 1939, following Germany's invasion of Poland, the United Kingdom and France declared war on Germany. On the same day, the British passenger liner *Athenia* was sunk by a German U-boat in the Atlantic Ocean (the Western Approaches) – although not, at this time, as part of an active policy of unrestricted submarine warfare.[121] Turkey remained neutral in the escalating conflict until August 1945, seeking to manage pressures from both the Allied and Axis powers through treaties of friendship and other diplomatic manoeuvring. This position included a somewhat uneven and shifting policy regarding passage through the Turkish Straits.[122] However, submarines were effectively excluded from these Straits throughout the war.[123]

In WWII, Germany again made use of submarines as commerce destroyers, adopting a policy of unrestricted submarine warfare from

[117] Tajima Nobuo, 'The Berlin-Tokyo Axis Reconsidered: From the Anti-Comintern Pact to the Plot to Assassinate Stalin' in Christian W. Spang and Rolf-Harald Wippich (eds.), *Japanese-German Relations, 1895–1945: War, Diplomacy and Public Opinion* (Taylor & Francis, 2006) 161, 165–166; Agreement between Germany and Japan Against the Communist International (Komintern), Berlin, 25 November 1936, entered into force 25 November 1936, 140 BFSP 529.

[118] Peter Krüger, 'From the Paris Peace Treaties to the End of the Second World War' in Bardo Fassbender and Anne Peters (eds.), *The Oxford Handbook of the History of International Law* (Oxford University Press, 2012) 679, 693.

[119] Deluca (n 82) 138.

[120] Ibid, 138–139.

[121] Michael Gunton, *Submarines at War: A History of Undersea Warfare from the American Revolution to the Cold War* (Carroll & Graf, 2003) 39.

[122] This policy is discussed in connection with Turkish neutrality in the following Section.

[123] Süleyman Seydi and Steven Morewood, 'Turkey's Application of the Montreux Convention in the Second World War' (2005) 41 (1) *Middle Eastern Studies* 79–101.

October 1939.[124] From 1940, German U-boats made use of a 'pack tactic' whereby a group of submarines simultaneously attacked an enemy convoy.[125] Italian submarines also operated in the Mediterranean and Atlantic from 1940, engaging British warships and merchant shipping as well as laying mines.[126] In the same year, British submarines were deployed to Norway in anticipation of Germany's invasion and ordered to sink 'all German ships by day and all ships by night . . . as opportunity served' in the Skagerrak between Denmark and Norway.[127] This policy was evidently a departure from the requirement in the 1936 Submarine Protocol to '[place] passengers, crew and ship's papers in a place of safety' before sinking or incapacitating a merchant vessel.[128] Yet the United Kingdom suggested that the departure from the Submarine Protocol was justified as a reprisal against Germany's assault on merchant shipping.[129] Germany's position was that by arming merchant ships, ordering them to report information regarding the location of enemy submarines, and requiring their passage in convoys protected by warships, the United Kingdom had effectively removed such vessels from the scope of the Submarine Protocol, meaning that they would no longer be protected by its terms.[130]

The Armistice Agreement accompanying France's surrender to Germany in June 1940 included a promise by the latter that the French fleet would not be used 'for its own purposes in the war'.[131] In July 1940, Germany demanded the return of all French ships to France. The United Kingdom, sceptical that Germany would honour its promise to refrain from commandeering the fleet, led an operation to destroy or immobilise French warships and sunk a number of French submarines by the end of 1942.[132] Following Germany's breach of the terms of the Armistice Agreement with the invasion of the Vichy region in 1942, several

124 Gunton (n 121) 42.

125 Wolff Heintschel von Heinegg, 'Submarine Operations and International Law' in Ola Engdahl and Pål Wrange (eds.), *Law at War: The Law as it Was and the Law as it Should Be* (Brill, 2008) 141, 142; Marc Milner, 'Battle of the Atlantic' in Ian C. B. Dear and Michael R. D. Foot (eds.), *The Oxford Companion to World War II* (Oxford University Press, 2014).

126 Gunton (n 121) 138–143, 152, 160–162.

127 Levie (n 48) 315.

128 London Protocol of 1936 (n 1) art. 2.

129 Levie (n 48) 315.

130 Ibid. The legality of this policy is considered in greater detail in Chapter 5, Section 5.4.1.

131 Gunton (n 121) 131; Armistice Agreement between the German High Command of the Armed Forces and French Plenipotentiaries, Compiègne, 22 June 1940, art. 8.

132 Gunton (n 121) 132–136.

French submarine commanders joined the Allied side – scuttling their vessels to prevent their seizure by Germany and in some cases escaping to join the Allied fleet.[133]

Of particular note among the French submarines was the *Surcouf*, which had been constructed to facilitate compliance with the rules governing submarine engagement with merchant vessels. As Friedman points out, the United Kingdom had also designed a submarine intended to facilitate compliance with the rules governing submarine engagement with merchant vessels in the interwar period, though the British model was not very successful.[134] The French *Surcouf* was a large gun-armed submarine cruiser that had the capacity to stop submarines and to take on the crew of a merchant vessel.[135] The fact that only one such vessel was so equipped points to the discrepancy between the rules set out in the 1936 Submarine Protocol and standard submarine designs at this time.[136] Yet the overall failure of the 1936 Submarine Protocol to regulate submarine attacks on merchant shipping during WWII was a consequence of naval policy rather than technology. *Surcouf* was seized by the British Navy in July 1940 and deployed in the North Atlantic before being sunk in 1942 in an accidental collision with a US freighter.[137] The submarine does not appear to have been used against merchant shipping and it is unknown whether the United Kingdom would have made use of its facilities for observance of the Submarine Protocol if it had.

In 1941, German submarines took a heavy toll on merchant shipping from North America to Europe across the Atlantic.[138] Canada, the United Kingdom, and the United States combined forces to protect Atlantic merchant shipping in 1941 and the operations of German U-boats shifted to the Mediterranean and Arctic with the declaration of war between Germany and Russia. In 1942, US naval forces moved to the Caribbean and to the new Pacific theatre of war ignited by Japan's 1941 invasion of Thailand and attacks on British Malaya, Singapore, and Hong Kong and US bases in Hawai'i (Pearl Harbor), the

133 Ibid, 135–137.

134 Friedman (n 14) 43.

135 Ibid.

136 Note that the French *Surcouf* and a similar design by the United Kingdom were developed prior to conclusion of the Submarine Protocol in 1936 but responded to the understanding that the same rules were part of customary international law as well as earlier efforts to enshrine them in an international treaty, e.g., the 1922 Submarine Treaty discussed in Chapter 3, Section 3.5.1.

137 Gunton (n 121) 210–211.

138 Milner (n 125).

Philippines, Guam and Wake Island. Taking advantage of this deployment, German U-boats were mobilised against merchant shipping off the east coast of the United States, exacting heavy losses until Canada stepped up its support for convoys. German U-boats were also deployed in South Atlantic shipping lanes to Asia and the Middle East. Yet the use of radar (though limited to the identification of surfaced submarines during daylight hours),[139] together with the United Kingdom's success in cracking the German Enigma code used in radio messaging to U-boats to advise planned targets and meetings with supply ships, allowed the Allies to respond increasingly effectively to U-boat operations.[140] As von Heinegg notes, '[w]hile the 1,171 German submarines commissioned between 1935 and 1945 sank 14 million tons, German submarine losses totalled 784'.[141] As well as attacking German U-boats from the air and surface vessels, British submarines engaged German submarines directly in the Mediterranean. Allied submarines were deployed against surface vessels and Italian merchant shipping in the Mediterranean.

In the Pacific, submarines were used by both Japan and the Allies; most notably, the United States. Prior to the outbreak of WWII, tensions with Japan had led the United States, the United Kingdom and the Netherlands to station submarine fleets in the Pacific. In response to Japan's attack on Pearl Harbor, the Commander-in-Chief of the US Pacific Fleet was issued a secret directive to 'execute against Japan unrestricted air and submarine warfare'.[142] As US Admiral Nimitz explained in his replies to an 'interrogatory' of the Nuremberg Tribunal in 1946, this order was held to apply against all Japanese 'merchantmen' – a term taken to cover all noncombatant vessels, including fishing vessels.[143] Nimitz also testified that

> On general principles, the US submarines did not rescue enemy survivors if undue additional hazard to the submarine resulted or the submarine would thereby be prevented from accomplishing its further mission. US submarines were limited in rescue measures by small passenger carrying facilities combined with the known desperate and suicidal character of the enemy. Therefore, it was unsafe to pick up many survivors. Frequently

139 Ibid.

140 Heintschel von Heinegg (n 125) 143.

141 Ibid.

142 Sally V. Mallison and Thomas W. Mallison, 'The Naval Practices of Belligerents in WWII: Legal Criteria and Developments' (1993) 65 *International Law Studies* 87, 91.

143 *Trial of German Major War Criminals: Proceedings of the International Military Tribunal Sitting at Nuremberg, Part 18, 2nd July, 1946 to 15th July, 1946* (His Majesty's Stationery Office, 1948) 26–27.

> survivors were given rubber boats and/or provisions. Almost invariably survivors did not come aboard the submarine voluntarily, and it was necessary to take them prisoner by force.[144]

US submarines took a particularly heavy toll on Japanese merchant shipping in 1943 and 1944 – largely due to the adoption of 'wolfpack tactics' against Japanese convoys.[145] They also sunk a number of Japanese warships during the course of the war, including twenty-five submarines.[146] Technical flaws in the torpedoes used by the United States in the first years of the war, which had resulted in them frequently missing targets and failing to detonate, were rectified late in 1943.[147]

Japan seems to have underestimated the importance of anti-submarine warfare both prior to and during WWII. Although it possessed sonar technology and equipped many of its warships with depth charges, Japan's radar capacity was lacking, and its depth charges were often too shallow to damage or sink US submarines.[148] Its focus on fleet-to-fleet combat over the defence of merchant shipping left the latter vulnerable to Allied submarines.[149]

Japan itself made use of a diverse array of submarines during WWII, including high-speed attack submarines, underwater aircraft carriers, cargo/transport submarines, midget submarines and 'Kaiten', which were crewed-torpedoes for suicide missions.[150] In the first years of the war, Japan primarily deployed its submarine fleet for reconnaissance and direct combat alongside the surface fleet.[151] At Pearl Harbor, the concerted aerial attack of 7 December 1941 was supported by three submarine flotillas located outside Oahu with directions to intercept fleeing and counter-attacking ships, though they did not take any casualties.[152] According to the Japanese plan, five midget submarines were also to be

144 Ibid, 27.

145 Gunton (n 121) 119, 126.

146 Ibid, 119.

147 Ibid, 44–46.

148 US Navy Department Bureau of Ships, *War Damage Report No 58: Submarine Report* (US Hydrographic Office, 1949) s. III <www.history.navy.mil/research/library/online-reading-room/title-list-alphabetically/w/war-damage-reports/submarine-report-vol1-war-damage-report-no58.html>.

149 Atsushi Ōi, 'Why Japan's Anti-Submarine Warfare Failed' (1952) 78(6) *US Naval Institute Proceedings* 592.

150 Dorr Carpenter and Norman Polmar, *Submarines of the Imperial Japanese Navy* (Conway Maritime Press, 1986) preface.

151 Ibid.

152 'Attack on Pearl Harbour' in Ian C. B. Dear and Michael R. D. Foot (eds.), *The Oxford Companion to World War II* (Oxford University Press, 2014).

sent into Pearl Harbor itself to launch torpedoes and contribute to general mayhem. However, just one midget submarine made it into the harbour where it was sunk by a patrolling destroyer. Three of the remaining midget submarines were sunk outside the harbour, while the fourth was captured together with a surviving crew member after washing ashore the following day.[153] The failure of the submarine fleet to contribute to the assault on Pearl Harbor is considered by some commentators to have resulted in 'a loss of prestige [within the Japanese Navy] from which it never wholly recovered'.[154] Submarines were also deployed to support Japan's attack on Wake Island but again took no casualties, though they played an important role in reconnaissance both here and in Japan's 1941 Malayan campaign.[155] It appears that a Japanese submarine may have sunk a Dutch submarine off the Malayan coast.[156]

After Pearl Harbor, Japanese submarines continued operations off the Hawai'ian Islands and the West Coast of the United States, sinking some merchant ships but no warships.[157] In 1942, submarines were also deployed in mine-laying operations around Darwin, Australia and in the Torres Strait.[158] Three Japanese midget submarines each armed with two torpedoes were sent into Sydney Harbour on 31 May 1942, though the first was detonated by its own crew after being entangled in anti-submarine nets.[159] The two remaining midget submarines were destroyed after sinking just one vessel that was not the intended target – the Sydney Harbour ferry *Kuttabul* that was being used as an Australian Navy depot ship.[160]

Between April 1942 and August 1945, Japan shifted its tactics to deploy submarines against merchant shipping.[161] It also used submarines to carry supplies to island garrisons and to transport the sick and wounded as well as troops off the islands.[162] In the last years of the war leading up

[153] Carpenter and Polmar (n 150) 14–17.

[154] See e.g., 'Attack on Pearl Harbour' in Ian C. B. Dear and Michael R. D. Foot (eds.), *The Oxford Companion to World War II* (Oxford University Press, 2014).

[155] Carpenter and Polmar (n 150) 17–18.

[156] Ibid, 18.

[157] Ibid.

[158] Ibid, 19.

[159] J Perryman, 'Japanese Midget Submarine Attack on Sydney Harbour', *Sea Power Centre of Australia* <www.navy.gov.au/history/feature-histories/japanese-midget-submarine-attack-sydney-harbour>.

[160] Ibid.

[161] Carpenter and Polmar (n 150) 11, 22.

[162] Ibid, 29–30.

to Japan's surrender in August 1945, Kaiten were used against warships at anchor and in the open sea.[163] Yet Japan's use of submarines in WWII contributed relatively little to its offensive and defensive operations.[164] Japan lost 132 submarines to the United States' 52,[165] and US submarines are reported to have sunk more than five million tonnes of Japanese naval and merchant vessels during WWII.[166]

Submarine warfare during WWII was marked above all by the widespread targeting of merchant shipping and non-observance of the rules set out in the 1936 Submarine Protocol and understood to form part of customary international law. As Levie argues, the customary status of these rules is not necessarily undermined by their non-observance during WWII as 'this was frequently excused by the particular belligerent, not on the basis that they were no longer a part of the law of war at sea, but on the basis of reprisals against illegal actions on the part of the enemy . . . in itself a recognition of the continuing validity of those provisions'.[167] The continuing relevance of the 1936 Submarine Protocol and the customary law it reflects will be discussed in Chapter 10, which considers the contemporary law governing the conduct of submarine warfare. For present purposes, it is interesting to consider how the threat that submarines posed to merchant shipping that first became apparent in WWI and increased dramatically in WWII may have played into the approach taken to the passage of submarines in neutrality laws prior to and during WWII. The following chapter will reflect inter alia on how these neutrality laws and the practices they respond to may have influenced the development of the law of the sea as it relates to the passage of submarine warships, warships more broadly and merchant vessels – including merchant submarines.

4.6 Neutrality in World War II: New Rules for Submarines

The evolving threat of the submarine was addressed in neutrality laws developed prior to and during WWII. Both prohibitions on the passage of submarines and a requirement to navigate on the surface where 'mere passage' was permitted were a feature of these laws.

163 Ibid, 11.
164 Ibid, 65.
165 Ibid.
166 US Joint Army-Navy Assessment Committee, *Japanese Naval and Merchant Shipping Losses During World War II by All Causes* (United States Government Printing Office, 1947) vi.
167 Levie (n 48) 325.

The targeting of merchant ships by belligerent submarines during WWI had already prompted special treatment of these vessels in neutrality laws prior to the outbreak of WWII. The 1928 Havana Convention on Maritime Neutrality largely reproduced the provisions in Hague Convention (XIII) of 1907,[168] but responded to the wartime experience (and the 1922 Submarine Treaty, though it never entered into force)[169] by providing that belligerent warships could not render a merchant ship 'incapable of navigation before the crew and passengers have been placed in safety' and, specifically, that

> Belligerent submarines are subject to the foregoing rules. If the submarine cannot capture the ship while observing these rules, it shall not have the right to continue to attack or to destroy the ship.[170]

The Havana Convention also specified that a belligerent warship's right to stop and search a merchant ship could only take place 'on the high seas and in territorial waters *that are not neutral*'.[171] This requirement expressly recognised that the stopping and searching of merchant vessels by belligerent warships should be treated similarly to the conduct of hostilities, which was clearly prohibited in neutral waters. Article 3 of the Havana Convention reiterated this customary rule, providing that '[b]elligerent states are obligated to refrain from performing acts of war in neutral waters or other acts which may constitute on the part of the state that tolerates them, a violation of neutrality'.

Interestingly, the Havana Convention recognised a right on the part of belligerent warships to enter and sojourn in neutral ports and waters as well as make repairs and take on supplies. This right was subject to restrictions on the time spent in neutral waters (no more than twenty-four hours in most cases),[172] the number of warships present in a neutral port at any one time (no more than three),[173] and the period between instances of refuelling (not less than three months).[174] Submarines were

[168] Inter-American Convention on Maritime Neutrality, Havana, 20 February 1928, entered unto force 21 January 1931, 135 LNTS 187 ('Havana Convention'); Hague Convention (XIII) concerning the Rights and Duties of Neutral Powers in Naval War, The Hague, 18 October 1907, entered into force 26 January 1910, 205 CTS 395.

[169] Treaty Relating to the Use of Submarines and Noxious Gases in Warfare, Washington, 6 February 1922, never entered into force, in Dietrich Schindler and Jirí Toman (eds.), *The Laws of Armed Conflicts* (Martinus Nijhoff, 1988) 877.

[170] Havana Convention (n 168) art. 1(2).

[171] Ibid, art. 1 (emphasis added).

[172] Ibid, art. 5.

[173] Ibid, art. 6.

[174] Ibid, art. 11.

not mentioned expressly in this connection but were apparently covered by the provisions as warships or under other identified categories.[175] Notably, allowing warships including submarines to make use of neutral ports for repairs and resupplying represents a departure from the project of the American Institute of International Law on Maritime Neutrality (1926) on which the Havana Convention was substantially based.[176] Instead, that project more closely reflected neutral practice in WWI by removing any reference to a right of belligerent warships to enter neutral waters or ports other than in cases of *force majeure*.[177]

The prospect of another war in the late 1930s led a number of States to amend their existing neutrality laws. In 1927, Italy's neutrality laws had provided that '[a]s a rule, the mere passage through the territorial waters of the State and dependent territories of the warships and prizes of the belligerents is tolerated; but submersible vessels must navigate on the surface'.[178] In 1938, however, it was provided that '[b]y royal decree even the innocent passage in the territorial waters of belligerent warships and of ships captured by them may be prohibited. Submarines must in every case navigate on the surface'.[179] The 1912 neutrality laws agreed upon by Sweden, Norway, and Denmark (amended by individual States during WWI) were also replaced in 1938 by rules agreed upon between Denmark, Finland, Iceland, Norway and Sweden.[180] The new rules stated a general prohibition on belligerent submarines in the territorial sea.

Although the United States was party to the 1928 Havana Convention on Neutrality, its own Neutrality Act of 1939 provided in Section 11 that

> Whenever, during any war in which the United States is neutral, the President shall find that special restrictions placed on the use of the ports and territorial waters of the United States by the submarines or armed merchant vessels of a foreign state will serve to maintain peace between the United States and foreign states, or to protect the commercial

175 See James W. Garner, 'The Pan American Convention on Maritime Neutrality' (1932) 26(3) *American Journal of International Law* 574, 577.

176 American Institute of International Law, 'Project No 26 on Maritime Neutrality' (1926) 20(S5) *American Journal of International Law* 361; Havana Convention (n 168).

177 American Institute of International Law (n 176) 362, art. 7; Garner (n 175) 577–578; Quincy Wright, 'Project of the American Institute of International Law on Maritime Neutrality' (1927) 21(1) *American Journal of International Law* 127, 134.

178 Rules of Law of Maritime War, July 1927 in Francis Deak and Phillip C. Jessup (eds.), *A Collection of Neutrality Laws, Regulations and Treaties of Various Countries* (Carnegie, 1939) vol. 1, 722, 723, art. 127.

179 Law of Neutrality, 8 July 1938 in Deak and Jessup (n 178) vol. 1, 725, 727, art. 13.

180 See, e.g., Royal Order No. 293 concerning the Neutrality of Denmark in Case of War between Foreign Powers, 20 December 1912 in Deak and Jessup (n 178), vol. 1, 478.

> interests of the United States and its citizens, or to promote the security of the United States, and shall make proclamation thereof, it shall thereafter be unlawful for any such submarine or armed merchant vessel to enter a port or the territorial waters of the United States or to depart therefrom, except under such conditions and subject to such limitations as the President may prescribe.[181]

This law was accompanied by a Proclamation on the 'Use of Ports or Territorial Waters of the United States by Submarines of Foreign Belligerent States', which applied the special restrictions in question to the ports and waters of the United States (other than the [Panama] Canal Zone).[182] Significantly, the Proclamation further specified that 'in such cases of *force majeure*', submarines could only enter US ports or territorial waters 'while running on the surface with conning tower and superstructure above water and flying the flags of the foreign belligerent states of which they are vessels'.[183] The same conditions were held to apply to the departure of such submarines from US ports or territorial waters.[184]

In 1939, the United States joined the other American Republics in the Declaration of Panama, which asserted that

> As a measure of continental self-protection, the American Republics, so long as they maintain their neutrality, are as of inherent right entitled to have those waters adjacent to the American continent, which they regard as of primary concern and direct utility in their relations, free from the commission of any hostile act by any non-American belligerent nation, whether such hostile act be attempted or made from land, sea or air.[185]

To this end, the signatory States proposed to establish a Pan-American Security Zone encompassing 300 nautical mile zones off the coasts of all twenty-one States and their island possessions and additional areas produced by the delineation of the Zone using straight lines measured from turning points located on the most seaward point of these 300 nautical mile limits.[186] This Zone was to be patrolled individually and jointly by the American Republics, with the United States explaining that

[181] Neutrality Act of 1939, Joint Res. 4 November 1939, ch. 2, §11, 54 Stat. 12.

[182] Use of Ports or Territorial Waters of the United States by Submarines of Foreign Belligerent States, Presidential Proclamation of 4 November 1939, 54 Stat. 2764 (1939).

[183] Ibid.

[184] Ibid.

[185] Declaration of Panama, Panama City, 3 October 1939 in Matilda F. Axton et al. (eds.), *Foreign Relations of the United States: Diplomatic Papers, 1939, The American Republics* (United States Government Printing Office, 1957) vol. 5, 36, 36–37 (File No. 740.0011 A.R./508).

[186] Ibid.

in the case of joint patrols '[t]he primary purpose . . . would be to prevent establishment of submarine bases and to assure that unneutral use of these coasts was not made by any belligerent'.[187]

At the same meeting in Panama, the American Republics adopted a General Declaration of Neutrality providing inter alia that, while it remained for each State to 'regulate in their individual and sovereign capacities the manner in which they are to give [their neutral status] concrete application', 'there exist certain standards recognized by the American Republics applicable in these circumstances'.[188] It was here noted that the American Republics 'may exclude belligerent submarines from the waters adjacent to their territories or admit them under the condition that they conform to the regulations which each country may prescribe'.[189] Consistently with this provision, the United States (as discussed above), Brazil, Mexico, Venezuela, the Dominican Republic, Panama and Honduras all adopted laws prohibiting or limiting the entry of belligerent submarines into their territorial waters in 1939.[190]

In 1940, the Inter-American Committee on Neutrality established pursuant to the General Declaration of Neutrality also discussed a proposal by Uruguay to recommend that all neutral American Republics exclude belligerent submarines from their ports and waters 'because of the difficulty of watching their movements in order to prevent violations of neutrality'.[191] According to the Committee's Report and the recommendation finally adopted, 'a majority of the Committee favored exclusion'; however, in view of Chile and Argentina's objection to the complete exclusion of belligerent submarines from territorial waters 'the compromise finally agreed upon was to recommend the alternative of complete exclusion, subject to conditions of *force majeure*, or of admission, subject to consent being obtained in each particular case of admission to ports and harbors'.[192] Notably, where belligerent submarines

187 'The Secretary of State to the American Delegate (Welles)' in Axton et al. (n 185) 32, 32.

188 General Declaration of Neutrality of the American Republics, Panama City, 3 October 1939 in (1939) 1 *Department of State Bulletin* 326, 327.

189 Ibid.

190 'The Secretary of State to Diplomatic Missions in the American Republics' in Axton et al. (n 185) 40.

191 'The Inter-American Neutrality Committee: Report Submitted by Mr. C. G. Fenwick, Covering January 15 to February 3, 1940' in Victor J. Farrar et al. (eds.), *Foreign Relations of the United States: Diplomatic Papers, 1940, The American Republics* (United States Government Printing Office, 1961) vol. 5, 282, 283.

192 Ibid, 284.

were exceptionally admitted due to *force majeure*, the Committee recommended that

> in such cases the neutral require that the submarines shall run on the surface with their superstructure clearly visible and the national flag flying and give the international signal indicative of the cause which forces them to enter into the port or navigate in territorial waters, and also require them to follow the routes and channels of navigation, where such exist, indicated by the local government.[193]

In the case of States deciding to admit belligerent submarines as a general rule, the Committee similarly recommended that 'they shall do so under the following conditions':

> (1) Submarines shall run on the surface with their superstructure clearly visible and the national flag flying; and they shall follow the routes or channels of navigation, where there are such, indicated by the local government;
> (2) In the case of entrance into ports or harbors, special permission must be obtained from the neutral government in each particular instance.[194]

Significantly, the Committee also recommended '[t]hat territorial waters in which an international freedom of passage has been granted by customary or by conventional law be excluded from the prohibition of access of submarines'.[195] Despite the general terminology, this language seems to have been primarily intended to cover the case of the Straits of Magellan, which, though recognised as Chilean territory, were declared to be 'neutralized for ever' with 'free navigation ... guaranteed to the flags of all nations' under Article V of the 1881 Boundary Treaty between Chile and Argentina.[196] It should also be noted that the Committee's recommendations regarding submarines were expressly directed towards 'submarines which have the character of warships or which are equipped for war purposes' not submarines in general.[197]

193 'Inter-American Neutrality Committee: Recommendation relative to the Entry of Submarines into the Ports and Territorial Waters of the American Republics' (1940) 34(S2) *American Journal of International Law* 78, 79.

194 Ibid, 80.

195 Ibid.

196 See María Teresa Infante, 'Straits in Latin America: The Case of the Strait of Magellan' (1995) 26 *Ocean Development and International Law* 175–187; Boundary Treaty between Chile and Argentina, Buenos Aires, 23 July 1881, 159 CTS 45.

197 'Recommendation relative to the Entry of Submarines into the Ports and Territorial Waters of the American Republics' (n 193) 79.

The Turkish Straits were, of course, another region subject to a special treaty regime. When Italy declared war on the Allies in June 1940, Turkey declined a request from the United Kingdom and France (just prior to France's surrender to Germany) to break off relations with Italy, close the Straits to Axis vessels and grant the Allies naval and air bases in the region.[198] Instead, Turkey opted to remain neutral and closed the Straits to the warships of all belligerents. While Turkey seems to have successfully enforced the prohibition on the passage of submarines through the Straits, it provoked protests from the United Kingdom for allowing the passage of Italian naval auxiliaries in 1941 and the passage of German merchant vessels equipped for conversion to naval auxiliaries or warships in 1944.[199] Allied and Axis interests in the Straits were not always coherent and shifted during the war. German and Russian cooperation in 1939 supported both States' expansionist interests as well as a mutual concern to prevent British and French operations in the Black Sea region.[200] MacFie observes that these concerns 'were in fact fully justified . . . Already in October Churchill was agitating for the dispatch of submarines into the Black Sea, in order that they might cut off Russian oil supplies by that route to Germany; and again in March 1940 the French considered such an operation'.[201]

On 18 June 1941, Turkey concluded a Treaty of Friendship with Germany,[202] which was followed by the German invasion of the Soviet Union on 22 June 1941.[203] Both the Axis and Allied Powers placed pressure on Turkey in support of their evolving strategies regarding the Straits. In 1941, the Axis powers sought passage through the Straits to the Black Sea in order to continue their assault on the Soviet Union, but also considered it advantageous to contain the Soviet fleet in the Black Sea. While the Allies and the Soviet Union first insisted on Turkey's strict prohibition of the passage of belligerent warships through the Straits under the Montreux Convention, the United Kingdom also recognised the value of having the Soviet Black Sea fleet support its operations in 'the Far East'.[204] Given the Soviet Union's status as a belligerent, this proposal was clearly at odds with

198 Deluca (n 82) 142.
199 Seydi and Morewood (n 123) 80–83.
200 A. L. Macfie, 'The Turkish Straits in the Second World War, 1939–45' (1989) 25(2) *Middle Eastern Studies* 238, 240.
201 Ibid.
202 German-Turkish Treaty of Friendship, Ankara, 18 June 1941.
203 Seydi and Morewood (n 123) 81.
204 Ibid, 83.

the Montreux Convention. Turkey continued to formally deny belligerent warships passage, though in 1941, following a secret request from the United Kingdom, it facilitated the movement of a number of Soviet tankers out of the Black Sea with a view to their use in Allied war operations elsewhere.[205] Germany, on the other hand, benefited considerably from the guarantees regarding the passage of merchant ships under the Montreux Convention as it sent both supplies for its military forces, and vessels classified as merchant ships under the Convention but capable of conversion into naval auxiliaries or warships through the Straits.[206]

This practice was brought to an end in 1944, when a subsequent inspection indicated that Germany's vessels were fitted out for use as warships.[207] This development encouraged Turkey to effectively block all Axis shipping from the Straits in the last years of the war.[208] Turkey also indicated that it would be amenable to the passage of Soviet motor launches (submarine chasers) purchased from the United States and defensively armed merchant vessels belonging to the Allies through the Straits.[209] This approach evidently strained both the terms of the Montreux Convention and Turkish neutrality. Turkey broke off relations with Germany in August 1944 and entered the war in August 1945.[210]

The neutrality of many of the States discussed above did not survive the war. The United States entered into the conflict in 1941, as did many of the other American Republics. It is nevertheless clear that the laws and practices of neutral States during WWII with respect to the passage of submarines was a response to both (1) the particular threat posed by belligerent submarines under policies of unrestricted warfare and the widespread targeting of merchant shipping, and (2) a broader concern that submarines may threaten coastal State security in view of their capacity to travel undetected. Many neutral States prohibited belligerent submarines in their territorial waters and ports altogether. Yet where submarines were admitted, it was also frequently required that they should travel on the surface and show their flag. A number of regulations also required notification and coastal State permission for the entry of submarines into territorial waters and ports, and some required warships generally or submarines specifically to follow routes designated by the coastal State.

205 Ibid, 85.
206 Ibid, 83.
207 Ibid, 94.
208 Ibid.
209 Ibid, 96–97.
210 Harry N. Howard, 'The Entry of Turkey into World War II' (1967) 31 *Belleten* 221, 223.

The regime governing the Turkish Straits during its period of neutrality in WWII is largely consistent with this approach, though its legal basis was the Montreux Convention rather than general international law. Chile's objection to the prohibition of belligerent submarines in the Magellan Strait also refers to the guarantee of free navigation under the 1881 Boundary Treaty rather than any customary right of passage through international straits. As such, State practice during WWII does not suggest that the passage of submarines through straits was considered to be subject to different considerations than the passage of submarines through territorial waters in the case of neutrality – except where the strait in question was governed by a specific treaty regime. Instead, the bulk of State practice supports the understanding that a neutral State was entitled to close its territorial waters to belligerent submarines or, if it admitted them, to regulate their passage by requiring notification and coastal State consent, passage on the surface, display of flags and passage through routes designated by the coastal State. As with earlier neutrality laws, it is unclear whether the States imposing these conditions considered their right to do so to depend upon their status as neutrals or to flow directly from their sovereignty in the territorial sea. The significance of this practice in connection with the formulation of laws relating to passage in the 1958 Convention on the Territorial Sea and the Contiguous Zone will be discussed in the following Chapter.[211]

4.7 Conclusion

The 1930s saw proposals to abolish the submarine as a 'weapon of war' raised once more by the United Kingdom, although somewhat half-heartedly in view of the clear preference of a majority of States for regulation of its use against merchant vessels. A number of States also argued that submarines should be subject to mutually agreed limits on their number, tonnage and arms capacity. While the 1936 London Naval Treaty succeeded in restricting submarines to 2,000 tonnes displacement with a maximum gun calibre of 5.1 inches, no quantitative restrictions could be agreed upon. There were also notable exceptions to the list of State parties to the 1936 Treaty – the United Kingdom, France, the United States, India, Australia, Canada and New Zealand were

[211] Convention on the Territorial Sea and the Contiguous Zone, Geneva, 29 April 1958, entered into force 10 September 1964, 516 UNTS 205 ('1958 Territorial Sea Convention').

signatories, but Japan and Italy refused to sign the agreement (though Italy acceded to the Treaty in 1938) while Germany and the Soviet Union had not participated at all.

A separate agreement concluded between the United Kingdom and Germany in 1935 had established a ratio of 35:100 between the German Navy and the 'aggregate naval strength of the Members of the British Commonwealth of Nations'. However, it was also provided that Germany could within this overall tonnage 'possess a submarine tonnage equal to the total submarine tonnage possessed by the Members of the British Commonwealth of Nations'.[212] The agreement also recognised that Germany reserved the right to exceed this submarine tonnage if it considered necessary, though notice must be given to the United Kingdom and the matter discussed before the right was exercised.[213] In practice, Germany had already been investing in its submarine technology through commercial collaborations between a consortium of German shipyards based in The Hague and in Finnish shipyards.[214] Immediately after concluding the 1935 Naval Agreement with the United Kingdom, Germany embarked on its own national submarine construction programme using plans developed through this collaboration with Finland.[215]

The United Kingdom concluded a separate naval arms limitation agreement with the Soviet Union in 1937 in which it accepted, among other things, the Soviet Union's 'Far Eastern reservation' regarding 'the Soviet Union's right to build warships for the Pacific outside of qualitative limits and to conceal the details of that construction from the other signatories until Japan signed the 1936 London Naval Treaty'.[216] In practice, the Soviet Union's fleet building programme of 1937 went beyond the agreed limits, with the head of the navy recommending that 'the figures for number, speed and weapons sent to London should be "significantly lower" than the real ones, especially for cruisers, destroyers and submarines'.[217] New additions included a large number of 1,500 tonne K-class cruiser submarines, which the Soviet Navy sought to conceal from the United Kingdom.[218]

212 UK-Germany Exchange of Notes (n 61) art. 2(f).

213 Ibid, art. 2(f).

214 Jason Lavery, 'Finnish-German Submarine Cooperation 1923–35' (1999) 71(4) *Scandinavian Studies* 393, 395–397.

215 Ibid, 414–415.

216 Maiolo (n 69) 372.

217 Ibid, 374–375.

218 Ibid, 374.

The London Protocol on Submarine Warfare appeared to be a significant achievement upon its conclusion in 1936 by France, the United Kingdom and the Commonwealth nations, Italy, Japan and the United States. As noted above, thirty-seven more States had acceded to the Treaty by 1939.[219] The Submarine Protocol reiterated the rule contained in Article 22 of the 1930 London Naval Treaty requiring that '[i]n their action with regard to merchant ships, submarines must conform to the rules of international law to which surface vessels are subject'. It provided more specifically that 'except in the case of persistent refusal to stop on being duly summoned, or of active resistance to visit or search', submarines must '[place] passengers, crew and ship's papers in a place of safety' before sinking or incapacitating a merchant vessel. In WWII, however, submarine warfare against merchant shipping became a key strategy on both sides and in both the European and Pacific theatres of war, and these rules were rarely respected.

Notably, as Levie observes, States departing from these rules also argued that such departures were justified on the basis that the merchant ships in question were no longer protected by the Submarine Protocol because they were armed, sending intelligence reports to belligerents, or travelling with armed convoys.[220] Submarine attacks upon merchant shipping were frequently justified as reprisals or counter-reprisals to the unlawful activities of the enemy.[221] This practice suggests that while the Submarine Protocol failed to restrain the actions of belligerent submarines against merchant shipping in WWII, the rules it contained continued to be recognised as part of conventional and, it seems, customary international law.[222]

WWII also saw the more widespread imposition of restrictions on the passage of submarines through territorial waters, including straits. While the 1936 Montreux Convention recognises and affirms 'the principle of freedom of transit and navigation by sea' in the Turkish Straits, there is a tendency in some subsequent scholarly literature to overstate the significance of this fact.[223] As discussed above, the Montreux Convention in fact recognises Turkey's sovereign right to regulate and restrict the passage of merchant vessels and especially warships. Indeed, it prohibits the passage of foreign submarines through the Straits at all times, with a limited

219 Levie (n 48) 313.

220 Ibid, 325.

221 Ibid.

222 Ibid.

223 See e.g., Erik Brüel, *International Straits: A Treatise on International Law* (Sweet & Maxwell, 1947) vol. 1, 195–198.

exception in time of peace or in the case of Turkish neutrality for 'Black Sea Powers . . . to send through the Straits, for the purpose of rejoining their base, submarines constructed or purchased outside the Black Sea, provided that adequate notice of the laying down or purchase of such submarines shall have been given to Turkey'.[224] Article 12 further provides that '[s]ubmarines belonging to the said Powers shall also be entitled to pass through the Straits to be repaired in dockyards outside the Black Sea on condition that detailed information on the matter is given to Turkey'. Yet it also specifies that '[i]n either case, the said submarines must travel by day and on the surface, and must pass through the Straits singly'.[225] This exceptional right of passage for the submarines of Black Sea States through the Straits does not apply in time of war where Turkey is a belligerent.

While the Montreux Convention now appears as *lex specialis* regarding passage through international straits, it has much in common with the neutrality laws developed by a number of States prior to and during WWII. As discussed above, it seems to have been widely accepted that neutral States were entitled to close their territorial waters to belligerent submarines or to regulate their passage by requiring prior notification and authorisation, passage on the surface, the display of the ship's flag, and passage along routes designated by the coastal State. It is not always clear whether the States in question understood these measures with respect to passage to follow from their neutral status or simply their sovereignty as the coastal State (or some conjunction of the two). Yet the text and context of the instruments establishing such rules and restrictions suggest that (a) States considered themselves entitled to take measures to preclude or regulate passage in coastal waters to protect their own security, and (b) the passage of submarines and, in particular, the passage of submarines without the coastal State's knowledge (such as without prior notification, submerged, unflagged) was a threat to State security warranting such measures. The following chapter will examine the persistence and evolution of these views during the early years of the Cold War, tracing their influence on the legal regulation of the submarine in the context of arms control initiatives and the articulation of the right of innocent passage in the 1958 Convention on the Territorial Sea and the Contiguous Zone.[226]

224 Montreux Convention (n 102) art. 12.

225 Ibid.

226 1958 Territorial Sea Convention (n 211).

5

The Post-war Settlement, the Early Cold War and the 1958 Law of the Sea Conventions

5.1 Introduction

The peace settlement process that followed World War II (WWII) saw the disarmament and demilitarisation of defeated powers, the redistribution of submarines and other warships among the Allies and the extension of US power in the Pacific. Breaches of the 1936 Submarine Protocol during WWII were considered in criminal trials at Nuremberg and Tokyo.[1] However, while the relevant judgments upheld the validity and applicability of these rules, they left room for uncertainty regarding the circumstances in which merchant vessels may be removed from their protection or when breaches may be justified as reprisals.

State military uses of submarines burgeoned after WWII as tensions between the United States and the Soviet Union escalated into the Cold War. This dynamic encouraged competing military alliances under the North Atlantic Treaty,[2] which is implemented by the North Atlantic Treaty Organization (NATO), and the Warsaw Pact.[3] As well as playing a minor role in the Korean War, submarines were used extensively for Cold War espionage and 'nuclear deterrence' operations. These practices as well as projections regarding the future use of submarines played into developments in international law.

The United States' deployment of atomic bombs in WWII prompted both international efforts to prohibit nuclear weapons and defensive investment in their development. The US-Soviet nuclear arms race saw

[1] Procès-Verbal relating to the Rules of Submarine Warfare set forth in Part IV of the Treaty for the Limitation and Reduction of Naval Armament of 22 April 1930, London, 6 November 1936, entered into force 6 November 1936, 173 LNTS 353, [1936] ATS 14.

[2] North Atlantic Treaty, Washington, 4 April 1949, entered into force 24 August 1949, 34 UNTS 243.

[3] Treaty of Friendship, Cooperation and Mutual Assistance, Warsaw, 14 May 1955, entered into force 6 June 1955, 219 UNTS 3 ('Warsaw Pact').

the development of nuclear-powered submarines armed with ballistic missiles carrying nuclear warheads (SSBNs)[4] – an innovation realising 'second-strike capability'.[5] By the late 1950s, both the United States/NATO and the Soviet Union considered nuclear weapons to be key to their military strategy and were keenly aware of the advantages of submarines as a means of delivery.[6] Anti-submarine warfare (ASW) was also a concern on both sides. State interests in the detection of submarines and their exclusion from certain sea areas as well as State interests in accessing sea areas sufficiently proximate to the coasts of their enemies for intelligence gathering and nuclear deterrence informed negotiations at the 1958 Conference on the Law of the Sea.

This chapter shows how the redistribution of naval power after WWII and into the Cold War had both geographical and technological dimensions informed by developments in the capabilities and use of submarines. From initial post-war efforts to destroy and redistribute German U-boats to the strategic control of islands well-situated for naval bases as well as the new role of the submarine as a nuclear deterrent, international law was called upon to both facilitate and regulate State military uses of submarines. Section 5.2 explains how efforts at arms control were one aspect of the legal responses to submarines, beginning with the peace treaties concluding WWII through to the debates regarding nuclear tests and nuclear weapons in the 1950s. Section 5.3 focuses on issues for submarines during the Korean War and the onset of the Cold War, especially in relation to ASW. Section 5.4 reflects on the implications of the unrestricted submarine warfare during WWII and consequences for the law of naval warfare. However, the 1949 Geneva Conventions adopted to regulate armed conflict did not directly clarify the laws relating to naval warfare.[7] Future warfare also had to address the advent

[4] See Chapter 1, Section 1.4.1.2.

[5] The ability to respond to a nuclear attack with an equally or more powerful nuclear strike.

[6] NATO Military Committee, 'Overall Strategic Concept for the Defense of the North Atlantic Treaty Organization Area' (NATO Doc. MC 14/2 (Revised), 23 May 1957); Richard L. Kugler, *Laying the Foundations: The Evolution of NATO in the 1950s* (RAND Corporation, 1990) 86–89.

[7] Geneva Convention (I) for the Amelioration of the Condition of the Wounded and Sick in Armed Forces in the Field, Geneva, 12 August 1949, entered into force 21 October 1950, 75 UNTS 31; Geneva Convention (II) for the Amelioration of the Condition of Wounded, Sick and Shipwrecked Members of Armed Forces at Sea, Geneva, 12 August 1949, entered into force 21 October 1950, 75 UNTS 85; Geneva Convention (III) relative to the Treatment of Prisoners of War, Geneva, 12 August 1949, entered into force 21 October 1950, 75 UNTS 135 ('Geneva Convention (III) of 1949'); Geneva

and development of nuclear-powered and nuclear-armed submarines. Initial efforts at regulation may be seen through the creation of the International Atomic Energy Agency (IAEA) and the United Nations Disarmament Commission, as well as efforts to control nuclear weapons tests. Section 5.5 considers how the continuing development and deployment of submarines by the Soviet Union and the United States, with its NATO allies, during the early Cold War played into debates at the 1958 Conference on the Law of the Sea regarding the breadth of the territorial sea as well as the lawfulness of military operations and nuclear tests on the high seas. The Chapter thus highlights how government policies and strategies with regards to submarines influenced the regulatory framework for submarines following WWII; this discussion further underlines how a legal historical frame on the international law of submarines furnishes a multilayered understanding of the current legal regime, which is explored in Part II of the book.

5.2 Submarines in the Post-War Settlement

The post-war settlement from 1945 commenced with a series of separate treaties between the Allied powers establishing their agreement on the principles and policies to be pursued in peace treaties with the defeated States. Disarmament and demilitarisation were among these policies, and submarines were identified as a special threat warranting strict measures regarding both the existing and future navies of the defeated powers. The United Kingdom secured US and Soviet support for the destruction of the majority of Axis submarines with just a small number retained for redistribution among the Allied powers, and most of the peace treaties specifically prohibited the possession of submarines by the defeated State. Yet, as we consider in Section 5.4, State military uses of submarines burgeoned after WWII as tensions between the United States and Soviet Union escalated into the Cold War.

The destruction and redistribution of Axis submarines after WWII was a key feature of the peace treaties negotiated pursuant to the post-war settlement agreements at the Yalta and Potsdam Conferences. Most of the defeated powers were also prohibited from acquiring, constructing or experimenting with submarines. Other international law developments of note in the post-war settlement include the Soviet Union's (failed)

Convention (IV) relative to the Protection of Civilian Persons in Time of War, Geneva, 12 August 1949, entered into force 21 October 1950, 75 UNTS 287.

attempt to revisit the Montreux Convention to allow both the passage of Russian warships (including submarines) through the Turkish Straits and the construction of Soviet military bases in range of the Bosporus. US President Truman's attempt to fold the Soviet's proposal into his own suggestion for 'Free and Unrestricted Navigation of International Inland Waterways' – the Danube and the Rhine in particular – is also notable, though again for the lack of support for such a principle among interested States. Each of the key political developments arising from the settlements following WWII had implications not only for the military uses of submarines, but also the international laws that would be developed to regulate those uses.

5.2.1 *Yalta, San Francisco and Potsdam Conferences of 1945*

Anticipating Germany's imminent surrender but less certain of a proximate end to the Pacific War, the heads of state of the United States, the United Kingdom and the Soviet Union (Roosevelt, Churchill and Stalin) and accompanying officials met in Yalta in February 1945. Significant among the agreements reached at this time was the Soviet Union's commitment to participate in a new international organisation under development – the United Nations. The Soviet Union made further use of the Yalta Conference to advance its interest in renegotiating the Montreux Convention governing the Turkish Straits. Stalin sought to revise the Montreux Convention to allow Russian warships passage through the Straits in all circumstances and had already received indications that Churchill would support such a move.[8] The Yalta Conference resulted in the Yalta Protocol,[9] in which the Soviet Union secured a clause providing that 'at the next meeting of the three Foreign Secretaries to be held in London, they should consider proposals which it was understood the Soviet Government would put forward in relation to the Montreux Convention, and report to their Governments', and that '[t]he Turkish Government should be informed at the appropriate moment'.[10]

[8] Herbert Feis, *Between War and Peace: The Potsdam Conference* (Princeton University Press, 1960) 291; Convention Regarding the Regime of Straits, Montreux, 20 July 1936, 173 LNTS 213.

[9] Protocol of the Proceedings of the Crimea (Yalta) Conference, Yalta, 24 March 1947, entered into force 24 March 1947, 148 BFSP 80.

[10] Ibid, art. XIV.

The Charter of the United Nations was drafted and signed by fifty States at the San Francisco Conference in June 1945.[11] The new Polish government became the fifty-first original member State in October of the same year.[12] The Charter's prohibition on the use of force in Article 2(4) and recognition in Article 51 of an 'inherent right of individual or collective self-defence' in the event of 'armed attack' as an exception to this prohibition have since shaped the legal landscape relating to the use of force. As discussed in Chapter 9, this body of law bears upon the use of armed submarines as well as the use of force against foreign submarines.

Following Germany's surrender and the conclusion of the Charter, in July 1945 the American, British and Soviet heads of state (Truman, Churchill and Attlee and Stalin)[13] met at Potsdam for further discussions regarding the post-war settlement. The Potsdam Conference resulted in a Communique that was published immediately and a Protocol that was made public in 1946.[14] A 'Proclamation calling for the Unconditional Surrender of Japan' was also issued by the Conference on 26 July 1945.[15]

The Potsdam agreements provided for the 'complete disarmament and demilitarization of Germany and the elimination or control of all German industry that could be used for military production'.[16] '[A]rrangements for the use and disposal of the surrendered German Fleet and merchant ships' were elaborated in the Potsdam Protocol.[17] Under these arrangements, '[n]ot more than thirty submarines' were to

11 Charter of the United Nations, San Francisco, 26 June 1945, entered into force 24 October 1945, 1 UNTS 16.

12 See Christoph Vedder, 'Article 110' in Bruno Simma et al. (eds.), *The Charter of the United Nations: A Commentary* (4th ed., Oxford University Press, 2024) para. 13.

13 Truman replaced Roosevelt following the latter's death on 12 April 1945. Churchill was initially the representative of the United Kingdom at the Conference, but was replaced by Attlee on 28 July 1945 after the result of the 1945 election became known.

14 Protocol of the Proceedings of the Berlin (Potsdam) Conference, Berlin, 1 August 1945, art. II(A)(3) in Richardson Dougall (ed.), *Foreign Relations of the United States: Diplomatic Papers, The Conference of Berlin (The Potsdam Conference), 1945* (United States Government Printing Office, 1967) vol. 2, 1478 ('Potsdam Protocol'); 'Report on the Tripartite Conference of Berlin', Berlin, 2 August 1945 in Richardson Dougall (ed.), *Foreign Relations of the United States: Diplomatic Papers, The Conference of Berlin (The Potsdam Conference), 1945* (United States Government Printing Office, 1967) vol. 2, 1499 ('Potsdam Communique').

15 Jochen A. Frowein, 'Potsdam Conference (1945)' in Anne Peters and Rüdiger Wolfrum (eds.), *The Max Planck Encyclopedia of Public International Law* (Oxford University Press, April 2009).

16 Potsdam Protocol (n 14) art. II(A)(3).

17 Potsdam Communique (n 14) 1507.

be 'preserved and divided equally between the USSR, UK, and US for experimental and technical purposes', with the remainder to be sunk.[18]

The United Kingdom was particularly concerned to ensure the destruction of most if not all German submarines, arguing that these 'were in a different class from other ships, since they had only limited legal use'.[19] While the Soviet Union would have preferred to retain a larger number of submarines, it agreed to the retention of just thirty boats since, as a member of the 'Big Three', it would also have an equal share in other categories of German warships, which were to be transferred immediately.[20] The distribution of the German Merchant Marine between the United Kingdom, the United States and the Soviet Union (which were to pass on some of these vessels to allies suffering heavy losses of their merchant fleets 'in the common cause against Germany') was deferred until the end of the war with Japan.[21] It was also provided that 'German inland and coastal ships determined to be necessary to the maintenance of the basic German peace economy by the Allied Control Council of Germany shall not be included in the shipping pool thus divided among the Three Powers'.[22] The disposal of the German Navy and Merchant Marine was one of the few elements of the Protocol to be implemented as specified.[23]

As anticipated in the Yalta Protocol, the Soviet Union raised the issue of the revision of the Montreux Convention at Potsdam.[24] In the lead-up to the Conference, however, it became apparent that the Soviet Union's claims would go beyond those touched upon at Yalta.[25] Among other things, the Soviet Foreign Minister Molotov sought the return of territories ceded to Turkey, as it was then known, in 1921 and Turkish consent to 'Soviet military bases on Turkish territory in range of the Bosporus'.[26] Turkey unsurprisingly refused to countenance such concessions and sought to ensure British and US support for its position in their negotiations with the Soviet Union at Potsdam – though only the United Kingdom clearly affirmed that it would support the Turkish stance.[27]

[18] Potsdam Protocol (n 14) art. IV(A)(3).
[19] Feis (n 8) 334.
[20] Potsdam Protocol (n 14) arts. IV(A)(1), IV(A)(6).
[21] Ibid, art. IV(B)(1).
[22] Ibid, art. IV(B)(4).
[23] Frowein (n 15)
[24] Feis (n 8) 291–292.
[25] Ibid.
[26] Feis (n 8) 292.
[27] Ibid, 293–295.

At Potsdam, Stalin made three requests with respect to the Turkish Straits:

> first, that the Montreux Convention would be terminated as no longer corresponding to current conditions; second, that the determination of the governance of the Straits – the only sea passage from the Black Sea – should fall within the province of Turkey and the Soviet Union as the states chiefly concerned; and third, that the new arrangements should provide that Turkey and the Soviet Union would both have military bases in the Straits in order to defend them against any enemy of the Black Sea powers.[28]

While Churchill openly opposed these claims in the name of Turkish sovereignty and security, he expressed support for a subsequent proposal by Truman for 'Free and Unrestricted Navigation of International Inland Waterways'.[29]

Truman's particular interest (and Churchill's) was in the Danube and the Rhine, which Truman proposed should be regulated by 'international authorities' including 'the United States, the United Kingdom, the U.S.S.R., France, and the sovereign riparian states recognized by these Governments'. With Churchill's backing, Truman attempted to win Stalin's support for this proposal by identifying the 'Straits of the Dardanelles, the Sea of Marmora and the Bosphorus' as an inland waterway in which there should be 'free and unrestricted navigation ... assured by international agreement' – though it was not proposed that such an agreement could be made at Potsdam.[30] Stalin, however, was unmoved by the suggestion that free navigation and international control of the Straits would serve the Soviet Union's interests and continued to insist upon Soviet rights in and control over the Turkish Straits.[31] In view of this difference of opinion, he recommended that discussion of the Straits question be postponed, which was a result that the United States and the United Kingdom were forced to accept.[32] Truman's proposals regarding the Rhine and the Danube at Potsdam were thus unsuccessful. Notably, when the United Kingdom advised Turkey of these

[28] Ibid, 295–296.

[29] Ibid, 298–300; 'Proposal by the United States Delegation, Berlin Conference, July 23, 1945' in Dougall (n 14) 654 (Doc. No. 755); 'Proposal by the United States Delegation, Berlin Conference, July 25, 1945' in Dougall (n 14) 656 (Doc. No. 656).

[30] Feis (n 8) 298–300.

[31] Ibid, 299–300.

[32] Ibid.

developments, the Turkish government also indicated that it did not support the US proposal for the Straits.[33]

5.2.2 *Post-War Peace Agreements*

At Potsdam, it was agreed that a Council composed of the foreign ministers of the United Kingdom, the Soviet Union, China, France and the United States would be established to draw up peace treaties and 'propose settlements of territorial questions outstanding on the termination of the war in Europe'.[34] The Paris Peace Treaties of 1947 between the Allies and each of Italy, Romania, Bulgaria, Hungary and Finland were adopted at the Paris Peace Conference of 1947. The Treaty with Italy required inter alia that the latter scuttle all of its submarines other than those specifically identified for transfer to Allied States.[35] The Treaty also provided that '[n]o aircraft carrier, submarine or other submersible craft, motor torpedo boat or specialised types of assault craft shall be constructed, acquired, employed or experimented with by Italy'.[36] The Treaty with Finland imposed limits on the total tonnage and personnel of the Finnish Navy, restricting its capacity to that considered necessary for 'meeting tasks of an internal character and local defence of frontiers'.[37] Similar restrictions were placed on Romania and Bulgaria, which together with Hungary were further prohibited from

> possess[ing], construct[ing] or experiment[ing] with any atomic weapon, any self-propelled or guided missiles or apparatus connected with their discharge (other than torpedoes and torpedo-launching gear comprising the normal armament of naval vessels permitted by the present Treaty), sea mines or torpedoes of non-contact types actuated by influence mechanisms, torpedoes capable of being manned, submarine or other submersible craft, motor torpedo boats, or specialised types of assault craft.[38]

[33] Ibid, 300.

[34] Potsdam Protocol (n 14) art. I(3)(i).

[35] Treaty of Peace between the Allied and Associated Powers and Italy, Paris, 10 February 1947, entered into force 15 September 1947, 49 UNTS 3, art. 58.

[36] Ibid, art. 59.

[37] Treaty of Peace between the Allied and Associated Powers and Finland, Paris, 10 February 1947, entered into force 15 September 1947, 48 UNTS 203, art. 13.

[38] Treaty of Peace between the Allied and Associated Powers and Romania, Paris, 10 February 1947, entered into force 15 September 1947, 42 UNTS 3, arts. 11, 14; Treaty of Peace between the Allied and Associated Powers and Bulgaria, Paris, 10 February 1947, entered into force 15 September 1947, 41 UNTS 21, arts. 9, 13; Treaty of Peace between the Allied and Associated Powers and Hungary, Paris, 10 February 1947, entered into force 15 September 1947, 41 UNTS 135, art. 14.

The Paris Peace Treaties of 1947 were intended to provide a model for subsequent peace treaties to be concluded with Germany and Japan.[39] Following Japan's surrender in 1945, the Supreme Command of Allied Powers led by US General Douglas Macarthur occupied Japan and embarked on a programme to both demilitarise and politically reform the State. A Treaty of Peace with Japan was signed at San Francisco in 1951 and entered into force the following year (the San Francisco Treaty).[40] Japan and the United States signed a separate Security Treaty at San Francisco in 1951.[41] These agreements were said to mark 'the emergence of a new Pacific maritime order', which 'differed from those of the past in that one power, the US, became the dominant naval force in the Pacific'.[42]

Tensions between the United States and the Soviet Union were clearly apparent during the peace settlement process and the 1951 San Francisco Conference; both powers recognising the strategic importance of the islands and waters of Japan in the event of wider conflict in this region (the Korean War having begun in 1950).[43] The Soviet Union failed to win support for the participation of its new ally, the People's Republic of China, in the Conference and (together with Poland and Czechoslovakia) did not sign the 1951 treaty, which it decried as inter alia '[providing] for the participation of Japan in an aggressive military alliance with the United States'.[44] Notably, the Peace Treaty of 1951 did not impose a requirement of demilitarisation upon Japan and hence no scuttling of or reductions to Japan's remaining submarine fleet.

39 Ellinor von Puttkamer, 'Peace Treaties (1947)' in Anne Peters and Rüdiger Wolfrum (eds.), *The Max Planck Encyclopedia of Public International Law* (Oxford University Press, 1982).

40 Treaty of Peace with Japan, San Francisco, 8 September 1951, entered into force 28 April 1952, 136 UNTS 45.

41 Security Treaty between the United States and Japan, San Francisco, 8 September 1951, entered into force 28 April 1952, 136 UNTS 211, art. 1.

42 Roger Dingman, 'Anchor for Peace: The United States Navy in the Shaping of the Japanese Peace Settlement' (2003) 15(3) *Japan Forum* 365, 366.

43 Frederick Sherwood Dunn, *Peace-Making and the Settlement with Japan* (Princeton University Press, 1963) 172–186.

44 Ibid; 'Statement of the First Deputy Minister of Foreign Affairs of the USSR, A.A. Gromyko, at the Conference in San Francisco (1951)' in Hiroshi Kimura and Mark Ealey, *The Kurillian Knot: A History of Japanese-Russian Border Negotiations* (Stanford University Press, 2008) 185–187.

5.2.3 *The Settlement with Germany*

While two German governments were formed in 1949 – the Federal Republic of Germany (FRG) in the combined occupation zones of the United Kingdom, France and the United States, and the German Democratic Republic (GDR) in the Soviet Zone – the FRG insisted that unification was a precondition for the conclusion of any peace settlement. The 'Two Plus Four Treaty' of 1990 (between the two German governments and the four occupying powers) provided for the unification of Germany together with a peace settlement emphasising Germany's commitments to renounce 'the manufacture and possession of and control over nuclear, chemical and biological weapons' and to reduce its armed forces under other agreements.[45]

The rearmament of West Germany had already been facilitated by the Paris Agreements of 1954, which terminated the occupation and brought West Germany into a reconfigured Western European Union (WEU) and NATO.[46] By bringing West Germany into the WEU and NATO, the existing members of these organisations sought to both contain West Germany's military aspirations and strengthen the collective security alliance countering the Soviet Union.[47] While France in particular had opposed first any post-WWII German Navy and then the inclusion of destroyers and submarines in any such force, the constraints imposed by WEU membership seem to have alleviated these concerns.[48]

[45] Treaty on the Final Settlement with Respect to Germany, Moscow, 12 September 1990, entered into force 15 March 1991, 1969 UNTS 115, art. 3(1). See also Treaty on the Non-Proliferation of Nuclear Weapons, Moscow, London and Washington, 1 July 1968, entered into force 15 March 1970, 729 UNTS 161, which is discussed in the following chapter.

[46] The Bonn Agreements of 1952 had also sought the rearmament of West Germany and its contribution to collective European defence but failed to come into force after France declined to ratify the European Defence Treaty forming part of these agreements. See generally Protocol Modifying and Completing the Treaty for Collaboration in Economic, Social and Cultural Matters and for Collective Self Defence, Paris, 23 October 1954, entered into force 6 May 1955, 211 UNTS 342; Frank Schorkopf, 'Bonn and Paris Agreements on Germany (1952 and 1954)' in Anne Peters and Rüdiger Wolfrum (eds.), *The Max Planck Encyclopedia of Public International Law* (Oxford University Press, May 2019).

[47] Thilo Marauhn, 'North Atlantic Treaty Organization (NATO)' in Anne Peters and Rüdiger Wolfrum (eds.), *The Max Planck Encyclopedia of Public International Law* (Oxford University Press, July 2016).

[48] David R Snyder, 'Arming the *Bundesmarine*: The United States and the Build-up of the German Federal Navy 1950–1960' (2002) 66(2) *The Journal of Military History* 477, 482–484, 488–489.

The Bundesmarine (West German Navy) was established in 1956 with the build-up of its fleet largely financed by the United States, which had worked towards the rearmament of West Germany and its contribution to collective defence from as early as 1949.[49] The Treaty of Brussels, which founded the WEU, restricted West German submarines to 350 tonnes (a limit subsequently increased in line with NATO requirements),[50] with the US Navy prioritising the provision of destroyers to facilitate reconnaissance and ASW in the Baltic in the face of increases in 'the number and capabilities of Soviet submarines' as well as the potential for 'submarine-launched missile attacks on North America'.[51] The Soviet Union's response to the accession of West Germany to NATO was to conclude a treaty of alliance, the Warsaw Pact, with Albania, Bulgaria, Czechoslovakia, the GDR, Hungary, Poland and Romania (most of which already had bilateral treaties of alliance with the Soviet Union).[52]

While the Soviet Union had implemented a new twenty-year programme to build up its naval defence forces in 1945, the 1950s saw both NATO and Warsaw Pact members focus increasingly upon nuclear strike capabilities.[53] Aircraft carriers became a key asset in this context, as did submarines capable of launching nuclear missiles.[54] Submarines were also increasingly valued as a tool for intelligence gathering and both anti-carrier warfare and ASW.[55] In 1959, NATO members established the SACLANT ASW Research Centre (still operational as the NATO Undersea Research Centre) 'to provide scientific and technical advice and assistance to the Supreme Allied Commander Atlantic in the field of antisubmarine warfare and to respond to the requirements of NATO naval forces in the field'.[56] The post-WWII settlement thus saw that

[49] Ibid.

[50] Protocol III on the Control of Armaments, Paris, 23 October 1954, 211 UNTS 364, annex. IV, art. V(b); Norman Friedman, *Submarine Design and Development* (Naval Institute Press, 1984) 90–91.

[51] Snyder (n 48) 500.

[52] Warsaw Pact (n 3).

[53] Michael MccGwire, 'The Background to Soviet Naval Developments' (1971) 27(3) *The World Today* 93, 94–96.

[54] Ibid, 94–96.

[55] Norman Polmar and K. J. Moore, *Cold War Submarines: The Design & Construction of US and Soviet Submarines* (Potomac Books, 2004) 172; ibid 96–97.

[56] Donald Ross, 'Twenty Years of Research at the SACLANT ASW Research Centre 1959-1979' (NATO STO Centre for Maritime Research and Experimentation (CMRE) Special Report M-93, 1980); Peter Ranelli, 'A Little History of the NATO Undersea Research Centre' (2008) 21(2) *Oceanography* 16–17.

submarines were not banned as weapons, as had been contemplated following World War I, but instrumentalised in the new geopolitical arena given their important position in nuclear policies.

5.3 Submarines in the Korean War and Early Nuclear Submarines

Following WWII, the United States initially sought to modify its existing submarine fleet by reference to the technologies used in German U-boats, increasing their capacity for prolonged and rapid underwater travel and manoeuvres. It also modified a number of submarines with a view to their role in specific missions, developing 'a fleet oiler (SSO), a picket-RADAR submarine (SSR), a guided-missile submarine (SSG), and the troop transport (SSP)'.[57] The United States was also increasingly concerned to develop submarine-based ASW capable of responding to Soviet developments, making use of advances in listening range through sonar technology.[58] Effective ASW also required submarines that made minimal noise, to which end the United States developed a new class of ASW diesel-electric submarines known as the 'SSK', which traded speed for greater silence.[59] While other NATO members were also concerned with ASW, only France followed the United States in building specialised submarines for this role.[60]

When the Korean War broke out in 1950, US submarines already located in the Western Pacific for ASW training purposes were called to the Yokosuka Naval Base in Japan, which had been occupied by the United States since 1945.[61] Several other Japanese ports were used by United Nations Forces under United States command 'to assist the Republic of Korea in defending itself against armed attack and thus to restore international peace and security in the area'.[62] During the Korean

[57] Nathaniel Patch, 'Silently. Quickly. By Sea, in Darkness: How US Submarines Helped Special Troops Destroy Enemy Supply Lines in the Korean War' (2016) 48(4) *Prologue* 1.

[58] Friedman (n 50) 67; ibid 6–17.

[59] Friedman (n 50) 67–70.

[60] Ibid, 70.

[61] Sean R. Filipowski, 'US Submarine Operations during the Korean War' (October 1994) *The Submarine Review* 77.

[62] United Nations Security Council Resolution 82 (1950), 25 June 1950 (UN Doc. S/RES/82(1950)); United Nations Security Council Resolution 83 (1950), 27 June 1950 (UN Doc. S/RES/83(1950)); United Nations Security Council Resolution 84 (1950), 7 July 1950 (UN Doc. S/RES/84(1950)); Yasuzo Ishimaru, 'The Korean War and Japanese Ports: Support for the UN Forces and Its Influences' (2007) 8 *NIDS Security Reports* 50, 55–70.

War (1950–1953), the United States made use of submarines as troop carriers, operating as 'undersea raiders', in reconnaissance missions and to patrol the Formosa (Taiwan) Straits and the Sea of Okhotsk.[63] Prompted by the belief that Soviet submarines were likely to become involved in the war, the United States also devoted submarines to ASW training.[64]

While the Korean War was largely land-based, US Lieutenant Commander Gregory Billy has argued that 'Korean War operational reconnaissance set the stage for submarine operations throughout the Cold War'.[65] US submariners gained experience in covert reconnaissance patrols close to Soviet territory and continued such operations following the armistice with Korea; two additional submarines were allocated to this task.[66] These operations were understood to remain necessary in light of the expansion of the Soviet submarine force.[67]

In 1949, the Soviet Union's successful detonation of their first atomic bomb led to speculation in the United States that the submarine would be the most likely carrier for such a weapon – a suspicion based in part on the United States' own experiments to that end.[68] During the 1950s, US intelligence confirmed that the Soviet Union was undertaking similar experiments, though the latter did not deploy submarines armed with nuclear weapons until the early 1960s.[69] In the early 1950s, the United States had also embarked on a project to develop a nuclear-powered submarine, with the first operational vessel completed in 1955.[70] USS *Nautilus* (SSN-571) was developed with a view to evading the ASW systems of other States; however, the US Navy also developed their own ASW in response to the nuclear-powered submarine's capabilities, anticipating the development of nuclear-powered submarines by the Soviet Union and others.[71] A key point of difference from the diesel-electric submarine was the constant and significant noise emitted by the nuclear

63 Patch (n 57) 6–17.

64 Filipowski (n 61) 77–85.

65 Gregory M. Billy, *Operational Analysis of US Submarine Employment in the Korean War* (Paper Submitted to the Faculty of the Naval War College, 1994) ii.

66 Ibid, 17–18.

67 Ibid.

68 Owen R. Cote Jr, *The Third Battle: Innovation in the US Navy's Silent Cold War Struggle with Submarines* (Naval War College, Newport Papers No. 16, 2003) 20.

69 Ibid.

70 Ibid, 21.

71 Ibid.

submarine – at least early models.[72] This recommended passive acoustic technologies as a key feature of ASW and prompted the United States' development of SOSUS (SOund SUrveillance System).[73]

SOSUS was based on the scientific discovery of what the United States would call the SOFAR channel (SOund Fixing And Ranging) at the end of WWII.[74] This channel was a naturally occurring layer of the ocean along which low-frequency soundwaves could travel great distances.[75] SOSUS tapped into this channel with hydrophone arrays placed on the seabed, which were linked to onshore processing centres by underwater cables. Low Frequency Analysis and Recording (LOFAR) instruments in the processing centres could analyse the sound information provided by the hydrophone array to detect submarines based on their distinctive sound signature. This system was understood to be particularly valuable in connection with the development of nuclear-powered submarines, which were capable of both higher speeds and longer periods of submersion compared to diesel-electric types but more consistently produced low-frequency noise.[76] In the early Cold War, SOSUS line arrays were installed at the outer edge of the continental shelf along the length of the US East Coast, with similar arrays being installed along the west coast and the coast of Hawai'i in 1954.[77]

The first nuclear-powered ballistic missile submarines (SSBNs) were launched in 1959 by both the Soviet Union (designated 'Hotel I' class submarines by NATO) and the United States (George Washington-class SSBNs).[78] Stalin's successor, Khrushchev, had set out a new defence plan in 1957 that would both 'emphasize cruise and ballistic missiles over conventional air, ground, and naval forces' and 'convert our navy primarily to submarines', especially nuclear-powered submarines.[79] While the Soviet Union lagged behind the United States in efforts to upgrade its submarine fleet with both nuclear propulsion and nuclear arms, it responded to US achievements in this field by shifting its ASW strategy from a narrower focus on coastal defence by diesel-electric submarines to

72 Ibid, 21–22.

73 Ibid.

74 Edward C. Whitman, 'SOSUS: The "Secret Weapon" of Undersea Surveillance' (2005) 7(2) *Undersea Warfare* 7.

75 US National Oceanic and Atmospheric Administration, 'What Is SOFAR?' <https://oceanservice.noaa.gov/facts/sofar.html>.

76 See further Chapter 1, Sections 1.4.1.1 and 1.4.1.2.

77 Cote (n 68) 25.

78 Ibid, 112, 120–121.

79 Ibid, 83.

include open ocean ASW where submarines and aircraft were to detect and destroy SSBNs. Conversely, it was not until the Soviet Union's launch of the Yankee-class SSBN in 1967 that the United States moved to adjust its own ASW strategy to respond to the prospect of continuous SSBN patrols at sea.[80]

Throughout these developments, international law was also slow and uncertain in its response. The role for international law was moderated by the application of the law of armed conflict during WWII and an unwillingness to engage in the law of naval warfare in subsequent codification efforts. The advent of nuclear technology, and especially nuclear weapons, further challenged the reach of international law. These issues are discussed immediately below.

5.4 Submarines, Naval Warfare and Arms Control in the Post–World War II Period

The immediate focus in terms of submarines after WWII was the issue of submarine attacks on merchant shipping, which was not addressed entirely satisfactorily in either the trial of war criminals in Nuremburg or Tokyo, or the 1949 Geneva Conventions on the law of armed conflict. While States were clearly concerned with the threat posed by nuclear weapons following the US bombing of Hiroshima and Nagasaki, efforts to restrict their development, testing and use during the 1940s and 1950s had limited success and did little to hamper a US-Soviet nuclear arms race.[81] Instead, the development of nuclear-powered submarines added complexity to legal questions related not only to disarmament and the law of armed conflict, but also in relation to core principles of the law of the sea relating to navigation in the territorial sea and uses of the high seas.

5.4.1 Post-War Assessments of Submarines in the Law of Armed Conflict

As discussed in the previous Chapter, unrestricted submarine warfare was widely used in WWII even though this practice contravened the 1936 Submarine Protocol.[82] As discussed in this section, this breach by

[80] Ibid, 172.

[81] See Section 5.6 below and Chapter 6, Sections 6.3.2, 6.4.2 and 6.4.3.

[82] See Chapter 4, Section 4.5.

German U-boat Commander Admiral Karl Dönitz was not taken into account in the assessment of Dönitz's sentence at the Nuremberg trial, apparently in view of the widespread application of the same policy by the Allied Forces.[83]

In 1946, General MacArthur announced the establishment of an International Military Tribunal for the Far East with trials to be held in Tokyo.[84] The judgment of the Tribunal on 4 November 1948 condemned inter alia the murder of 'passengers and crews of torpedoed ships' by both surface vessels and submarines as 'inhuman, illegal warfare at sea'.[85] It referred specifically to an order from the Commander of the First Submarine Force at Truk in 1943 commanding that:

> All submarines shall act together in order to concentrate their attacks against enemy convoys and shall totally destroy them. Do not stop with the sinking of enemy ships and cargoes; at the same time, you will carry out the complete destruction of the crews of the enemy's ships; if possible, seize part of the crew and endeavor to secure information about the enemy.[86]

This order was found to have been followed by Japanese submarine commanders, as the Tokyo Tribunal determined that:

> Between 13 December 1943 and 29 October 1944, Japanese submarines, after sinking eight British, American and Dutch merchant vessels in the Indian Ocean and one American vessel in the Pacific Ocean, surfaced after firing their torpedoes attempted to or did take on board the master of the ship and then proceeded to destroy the life-boats and murder the survivors.[87]

The practice of submarines on both sides during WWII focused attention on the question of lawful targets for submarine attacks. While the 1936 London Protocol remained (and remains) applicable and in force, States frequently argued that the arming of merchant ships, their travel in convoys with armed guards, and their use for passing intelligence to

[83] Judgment of the International Military Tribunal for the Trial of German Major War Criminals in *Trial of German Major War Criminals: Proceedings of the International Military Tribunal Sitting at Nuremberg, Part 22, 22nd August 1946 to 1st October 1946* (His Majesty's Stationery Office, 1950) 509 ('Nuremberg Judgment').

[84] Judgment of the International Military Tribunal for the Far East in R. John Pritchard and Sonia Magbanua Zaide (eds.), *The Tokyo War Crimes Trial* (Garland, 1981) vol. 22, paras. 48418–48419.

[85] Ibid, paras. 48415–48216.

[86] Ibid, para. 49682.

[87] Ibid, para. 49682.

belligerent forces removed such vessels from the protection of this treaty.[88] When the German U-boat Commander Admiral Karl Dönitz was tried at the International Military Tribunal in Nuremberg for, among other things, the conduct of unrestricted submarine warfare in contravention of the terms of the 1936 Submarine Protocol, the Tribunal appears to have accepted arguments regarding the removal of British merchant ships from the scope of the Protocol's protection – further noting that in 1939 the United Kingdom had ordered its merchant ships to ram enemy submarines where possible.[89] The Tribunal in the *Dönitz* case further determined that the practice of unrestricted submarine warfare in 'operational zones' was in breach of the Protocol, which 'made no exception' for such a practice.[90] Yet it cited the British policy of unrestricted submarine warfare in the Skagarrak in 1940 as well as the statement of the US Admiral Nimitz that 'unrestricted submarine warfare was carried on in the Pacific Ocean by the United States from the first day that nation entered the war' as grounds for not assessing Dönitz's sentence by reference to these 'breaches of the international law of submarine warfare'.[91]

Setting aside the broader question of the legality of 'operational' or 'war zones',[92] it is clear that, as Kraska and Pedrozo conclude, 'protected ships and aircraft, such as merchant ships, do not lose their protection merely because they operate inside the zone. An exclusion zone may not become a "free fire" zone'.[93] As Kraska and Pedrozo also note, '[t]he most basic rule of [the law of armed conflict] for submarines is that they must be able to distinguish between lawful military objectives and civilian or protected vessels'.[94]

[88] Howard Levie, 'Submarine Warfare: With Emphasis on the 1936 London Protocol' (1998) 70 *Naval War College International Law Studies* 291, 325.

[89] Nuremberg Judgment (n 83) 508.

[90] Ibid.

[91] Ibid.

[92] See further Wolff Heintschel von Heinegg, 'War Zones' in Anne Peters and Rüdiger Wolfrum (eds.), *The Max Planck Encyclopedia of Public International Law* (Oxford University Press, October 2015).

[93] James Kraska and Raul Pedrozo, *Disruptive Technology and the Law of Naval Warfare* (Oxford University Press, 2022) 160.

[94] Ibid, 141. This rule applies as a matter of customary law. It is worth noting that Article 49 of Protocol I to the 1949 Geneva Conventions states that its provisions apply to 'attacks from the sea or from the air against objectives *on land* but do not otherwise affect the rules of international law applicable in armed conflict at sea or in the air': Protocol Additional to the Geneva Conventions of 12 August 1949 relating to the Protection of Victims of

In the post-WWII period, this principle of distinction became a key factor bearing upon the lawfulness or otherwise of belligerent operations in the context of armed conflict. However, there was less clarity in the context of naval warfare as compared to war on land. The Third Geneva Convention of 1949 responded to the fact that 'the merchant marine was considered necessary for maintaining national supplies, they were armed and were often the subject of attack' by providing that merchant marines 'who do not benefit by more favourable treatment under any other provisions of international law' should have the status and protections of prisoners of war.[95] Yet the 1949 Geneva Conventions did not resolve the question of when a merchant vessel might be lawfully targeted by belligerent warships, including submarines.

5.4.2 *Efforts to Regulate Nuclear Technology and Nuclear Weapons*

The development of nuclear capabilities following WWII increased the threat represented by the submarine, both as a result of nuclear propulsion, which facilitated long periods of submersion and faster speeds, and the utility of such vessels as a platform for launching nuclear weapons. The United States developed its first cruise missile (Regulus) in the early 1950s.[96] Specialised submarines were built to carry this large weapon, which could only be launched from the surface and had to be guided by accompanying attack submarines when in operation.[97] The Soviet Union began to develop nuclear-armed torpedoes from 1949 to 1950 – constructing a larger model (T-15) to be launched from a nuclear-propelled submarine and intended as a 'strategic attack weapon' against the United States, and a smaller model (T-5) to be launched by diesel-electric submarines in an anti-shipping campaign.[98] In the early 1950s, the Soviet Union also developed a submarine-launched cruise missile that could be armed with either a conventional or nuclear warhead (P-5 Pyatyorka/

International Armed Conflicts, Geneva, 8 June 1977, 1125 UNTS 3 (emphasis added). See further Chapter 10.

95 Geneva Convention (III) of 1949 (n 7), arts. 4(A), 5; International Committee of the Red Cross, *Commentary to the Third Geneva Convention* (Cambridge University Press, 2021) paras. 1052–1053.

96 Friedman (n 50) 76; Norman Polmar and John O'Connell, *Strike from the Sea: The Development and Deployment of Strategic Cruise Missiles since 1934* (Naval Institute Press, 2020) ch. 3.

97 Polmar and O'Connell (n 96) 33, ch. 4.

98 Ibid, 106.

NATO Codename SS-N-3 Shaddock).[99] Like the Regulus missile, Shaddock had to be launched from the surface.[100]

In 1955, the United States launched the first nuclear-powered submarine (USS *Nautilus*). In 1959, it launched both a nuclear-propelled Regulus missile submarine, the USS *Halibut* (SSGN-587), and the nuclear-propelled USS *George Washington* (SSBN-598),[101] which in 1960 test-ran the first nuclear-armed ballistic missile developed under the US Polaris project.[102] While the Soviet Union was responsible for the first launch of a ballistic missile (R-11FM) from a submarine (Project 611/Zulu Class) in 1955, the USS *George Washington* was the first submarine to launch a ballistic missile from a submerged position.[103] The Soviet Union launched its first nuclear-powered submarine in 1957: the Project 627/November-class attack submarine. In 1960, the Soviet Union launched the nuclear-powered Project 659/Echo-class 1 designed to carry Shaddock nuclear cruise missiles and torpedoes.[104] Diesel-powered Project 629/Golf-class submarines and nuclear-powered Project 658/Hotel-class submarines capable of launching ballistic missiles were also developed by the Soviet Union in the late 1950s.[105]

While the United States indicated its willingness to give up its atomic weapons if a system of international control preventing and punishing the development and use of atomic weapons was established, its (failed) efforts towards this goal in the 1940s were replaced by a strategy of 'massive retaliation' in the 1950s.[106] The establishment of the IAEA in 1957 was partly a response to concern regarding the military uses of nuclear power as well as enthusiasm about its non-military applications. The IAEA was tasked with inter alia implementing safeguards to ensure that nuclear materials and technologies 'made available by the Agency or

[99] Ibid, 107.

[100] Ibid, 111–115.

[101] Ibid, 41–42.

[102] Graham Spinardi, *From Polaris to Trident: The Development of US Fleet Ballistic Missile Technology* (Cambridge University Press, 1994) 57–60.

[103] US Naval History and Heritage Command, 'USS George Washington (SSBN 598)', 20 September 2024, <www.history.navy.mil/browse-by-topic/ships/submarines/george-washington-ssbn-598.html>.

[104] Polmar and O'Connell (n 96) 115.

[105] Ibid, 107–113.

[106] David W. Kearn Jr, 'The Baruch Plan and the Quest for Atomic Disarmament' (2010) 21(1) *Diplomacy & Statecraft* 41; Stefan Kadelbach, 'Nuclear Weapons and Warfare' in Anne Peters and Rüdiger Wolfrum (eds.), *The Max Planck Encyclopedia of Public International Law* (Oxford University Press, May 2019); Milton Leitenberg, 'Disarmament and Arms Control Since 1945' (1977) 27(2) *Cross Currents* 130, 131.

at its request or under its supervision or control' would not be used for military purposes.[107] During negotiations, a number of non-nuclear States pointed out these safeguards would have little impact on existing nuclear powers, which 'owing to their advanced stage of development, they would never have to request the assistance of the new agency'.[108] The Agency could also 'apply safeguards, at the request of the parties, to any bilateral or multilateral arrangement, or at the request of a State, to any of that State's activities in the field of atomic energy'.[109]

The development of both nuclear-powered submarines and submarine-launched nuclear-armed ballistic missiles in the 1950s played into debates regarding the control of nuclear weapons as well as restrictions on nuclear testing. Partial rather than comprehensive nuclear testing bans were negotiated through a variety of instruments.[110] In 1958, the United Kingdom, the United States and the Soviet Union agreed to a one-year moratorium on nuclear testing, though only after the United Kingdom had both completed thermonuclear testing and secured the United States agreement to the exchange of nuclear materials, technology and information under a Mutual Defence Agreement.[111] Continuing negotiations resulted in the United States, the United Kingdom and the Soviet Union signing a Partial Test Ban Treaty in 1963, which prohibited nuclear weapon tests in the atmosphere, in outer space and underwater (i.e., limiting tests to those underground within the territory of the testing State).[112] This Treaty was then opened up for signature by other States.

While the United States had originally conceived of submarine-launched nuclear weapons as a counterbalance to the Soviet Union's greater conventional power, the Soviet Union's development of similar

[107] Statute of the International Atomic Energy Agency, New York, 26 October 1956, entered into force 29 July 1957, 276 UNTS 3, art. II ('IAEA Statute').

[108] Bertrand Goldschmidt, 'The Origins of the International Atomic Energy Agency' (1977) 19(4) *IAEA Bulletin* 1, 18.

[109] IAEA Statute (n 107) art. III(5).

[110] Some of these agreements were limited by area though more comprehensive in terms of the materials and activities banned. For example, the 1959 Antarctic Treaty prohibited weapons testing and the explosion of nuclear devices and disposal of radioactive waste specifically in Antarctica: Antarctic Treaty, Washington, 1 December 1959, entered into force 23 June 1961, 402 UNTS 71, art. V.

[111] John R. Walker, *British Nuclear Weapons and the Test Ban 1954–1973* (Ashgate, 2013) ch. 3; Agreement for Co-operation on the Uses of Atomic Energy for Mutual Defense Purposes, Washington, 3 July 1958, entered into force 27 July 1959, 326 UNTS 3.

[112] Treaty Banning Nuclear Weapon Tests in the Atmosphere, in Outer Space and Under Water, Moscow, 5 August 1963, entered into force 10 October 1963, 480 UNTS 43.

capacity prompted a shift in focus to deterrence through second strike capability.[113] As Friedman explains,

> submarines would be maintained continuously on patrol in missile-launch areas, ready to attack on command. They are valued for their survivability: even were the Soviets to destroy the carriers and the weapons based in the United States, they would be unable to avoid retaliation from under the sea.[114]

SSBNs were a key element of the US policy of 'strategic deterrence' in the Cold War. In 1957, the Soviet Union 'made a decision to convert our navy primarily to submarines', specifically 'nuclear-powered submarines'.[115] For the Soviet Union, 'submarines represented an effective defensive capability as well as a reliable means of launching a missile counter-attack'.[116]

5.5 The 1958 Conference and Treaties on the Law of the Sea

The International Law Commission (ILC) identified the regime of territorial waters and the regime of the high seas as topics 'ripe for codification' at its first session in 1949. J. P. A. François, who had served as Rapporteur for the Second Committee considering Territorial Waters at the 1930 Hague Conference[117] was appointed Special Rapporteur for both topics, commencing work on the high seas in 1950 and territorial waters in 1951. In his first report on territorial waters in 1952, François drew heavily on the earlier work on this topic at the 1930 Hague Conference, most notably the thirteen draft articles and report of Subcommittee II. In doing so, his mandate was only to identify and, if necessary, further develop the laws applicable in time of peace.[118] The Special Rapporteur noted, however, that while the ILC would not deal with the rights of belligerents and neutrals, the decisions made on matters such as the breadth of the territorial sea would be equally relevant in times of war.[119]

[113] Friedman (n 50) 75–76.
[114] Ibid.
[115] Polmar and Moore (n 55) 83.
[116] Ibid.
[117] See Chapter 3, Section 3.6.4.
[118] J. P. A. François, Special Rapporteur, 'Regime of the Territorial Sea' (1952) 2 *Yearbook of the International Law Commission* 26.
[119] Ibid.

The ILC was unable to recommend a specific limit on the breadth of the territorial sea though it expressed the view that 'international law does not permit an extension of the territorial sea beyond twelve miles'.[120] At the 1958 Conference, several States pointed to the potential wartime implications of various solutions regarding the breadth of the territorial sea – though their concerns and conclusions also varied. The United States, for example, which initially supported a three nautical mile limit and later in proceedings, a six nautical mile limit, argued that 'in time of war, a neutral State would have greater difficulty in safeguarding the broader belt of territorial waters against the incursions of ships of Belligerents'.[121] Saudi Arabia, which had already proclaimed a twelve nautical mile territorial sea, argued that 'the concept of the coastal State's dominion over its territorial sea had been founded on the rule of self-defence' but that '[s]ecurity requirements were . . . bound to change with the times, as was the criterion of delimitation'.[122] New technologies and new threats to coastal State security were understood to support a wider territorial sea. The USSR proposed that 'each State shall determine the breadth of its territorial waters in accordance with established practice within the limits, as a rule, of three to twelve miles, having regard to historical and geographical conditions, economic interests, the interests of the security of the coastal State and the interests of international navigation'.[123]

Ultimately, the question of the breadth of the territorial sea could not be resolved at the 1958 Conference and the Territorial Sea Convention did not define its maximum extent.[124] Nor did the Territorial Sea Convention address the interplay between the regime of the territorial sea and the rights of belligerents and neutrals in the context of armed conflict. Although the question of rights of passage in the territorial sea was closely tied to the question of its breadth, the Territorial Sea Convention was more successful in specifying rules of passage, recognising that warships had a right of innocent passage in the territorial sea and that submarines must navigate on the surface and show their flag. As

[120] Ibid, 265–266.

[121] 'Consideration of the Draft Articles Adopted by the International Law Commission at its Eight Session' (UN Doc. A/3159) in United Nations Conference on the Law of the Sea, *Official Records*, vol. 3 (UN Doc. A/CONF.13/39) 26 ('*Official Records*, vol. 3').

[122] Ibid, 36.

[123] 'Union of Soviet Socialist Republics: Proposal' (UN Doc. A/CONF.13/C.1/L.80) in *Official Records*, vol. 3 (n 121) 233.

[124] Convention on the Territorial Sea and Contiguous Zone, Geneva, 29 April 1958, entered into force 10 September 1964, 516 UNTS 205.

discussed in Chapter 7, the question of whether prior notification or authorisation for such passage could be required was not resolved.[125] Notably, the USSR 'could not agree with the contention that foreign warships could pass through the territorial sea without the consent of the coastal State, because that could entail a security risk for the latter and had in practice given rise to abuse'.[126] The United States, on the other hand, objected to a requirement of prior authorisation but not, at this time, prior notification. Despite its claims to the contrary, this position was new for the United States, which had previously objected to the presence of warships in the territorial sea at all.[127]

The respective positions of the United States and the Soviet Union on navigational freedoms at the 1958 Conference on the Law of the Sea were no doubt informed by Cold War tensions. Beyond the territorial sea, which it sought to limit, the United States emphasised the freedom of the high seas for military manoeuvres.[128] The Soviet Union, on the other hand, argued that 'certain states were violating the principle of the freedom of the high seas by taking over large areas for naval and air force manoeuvres'.[129] It specifically objected to the practice of the United States in using 'areas in the southern part of the Sea of Japan, including the Korean Straits, in the north-west Pacific, south and east of Japan, and in the Yellow Sea and Caribbean Sea for such purposes', as well as the practice of the United Kingdom, which 'at the end of 1957 . . . had taken over for submarine manoeuvres large areas of the English Channel which were situated on international shipping routes'.[130] These issues were significant for warships generally, and not just submarines.

On the question of the lawfulness of military manoeuvres on the high seas, the Soviet Union argued that

> [w]ith a view to developing friendly relations between states, it would be fitting that the Conference should adopt, on the basis of the principle of the freedom of the high seas, a decision prohibiting the establishment of military manoeuvre areas on the high seas near foreign shores and on international shipping routes, for such manoeuvre areas restricted the

[125] See Chapter 7, Section 7.2.4.

[126] 'Consideration of the Draft Articles Adopted by the International Law Commission at its Eight Session (Articles 1 to 25 and 66)' in *Official Records*, vol. 3 (n 121) 32.

[127] See Chapter 3, Section 3.6.4.

[128] 'Consideration of the Draft Articles Adopted by the International Law Commission at its Eighth Session' (UN Doc. A/3159) in United Nations Conference on the Law of the Sea, *Official Records*, vol. 4 (UN Doc. A/CONF.13/39) 16 ('*Official Records*, vol. 4').

[129] Ibid, 10.

[130] Ibid.

> freedom of navigation and created a threat to the security of other states.[131]

The United States replied that it

> could not understand the U.S.S.R. representative's reference to the illegality of establishing military exercise areas on the high seas. The use of the high seas for such exercises was recognized in international law, and the navies of all nations used the high seas for those purposes.[132]

The United States further pointed out that '[i]n September 1957, the Soviet Union itself had conducted surface and air manoeuvres in the Kara Sea and Barents Sea, and had established a danger area of approximately 760,000 square miles, apparently the largest danger area ever recorded'.[133]

At the 1958 Conference, the United States also defended nuclear testing as consistent with freedoms of the high seas and, together with the United Kingdom, sidestepped further discussions by characterising the key issue as one of disarmament.[134] The 1958 Conference ultimately adopted a resolution proposed by India '[r]ecognizing that there is a serious and genuine apprehension on the part of many States that nuclear explosions constitute an infringement of the freedom of the seas' but 'refer[ring] this matter to the General Assembly for appropriate action'.[135] The 1958 Conference did not adopt any provision directly addressing the lawfulness of military manoeuvres on the high seas either, rejecting a proposal by Albania, Bulgaria and the Soviet Union providing that '[n]o naval or air ranges or other combat training areas limiting freedom of navigation may be designated on the high seas near foreign coasts or on international sea routes'.[136]

A number of States sought to indirectly regulate military activities by incorporating part of the ILC's commentary on Article 27 on the 'Freedom of the high seas' into the Convention text: specifically, the principle that 'States are bound to refrain from any acts which might adversely affect the use of the high seas by nationals of other States'.[137]

131 Ibid.
132 Ibid, 16.
133 Ibid.
134 Ibid, 5–23, 43–44.
135 Ibid, 52, 134.
136 'Albania, Bulgaria, Union of Soviet Socialist Republics: Proposal' (UN Doc. A/CONF.13/C.2/L.32) in *Official Records*, vol. 4 (n 128) 124.
137 International Law Commission, 'Commentary to Articles concerning the Law of the Sea' (1956) 2 *Yearbook of the International Law Commission* 265, 278. See, e.g., 'Poland: Proposal' (UN Doc. A/CONF.13/C.2/L.29) in *Official Records*, vol. 4 (n 128) 123.

While the ILC did not 'make any express pronouncement on the freedom to undertake nuclear weapon tests on the high seas', it had observed that '[i]n this connexion the general principle enunciated in the third sentence of paragraph 1 of this commentary is applicable'.[138] Interestingly, its stated reason for not addressing the issue directly was that it 'did not . . . wish to prejudge the findings of the Scientific Committee set up under General Assembly resolution 913 (X) of 3 December 1955 to study the effects of atomic radiation', suggesting that further evidence of its ill effects 'upon man and his environment' would clarify the issue.[139] Romania and Bulgaria linked the notion of 'adverse effects' to naval manoeuvres on shipping routes or near the coasts of other States.[140] Even Canada, which considered 'the freedom to conduct nuclear tests and naval exercises' to have 'hitherto been regarded as permissible', recognised that an obligation to 'to refrain from any acts which might adversely affect the use of the high seas by nationals of other states' would affect such alleged freedoms.[141]

Unsurprisingly, the United Kingdom and the United States were opposed to the inclusion of any such text in the 1958 High Seas Convention.[142] The United States argued that '[t]hat wording was . . . an unacceptable version of the phrase submitted for consideration to the International Law Commission by its rapporteur, Mr. François (Netherlands), since it rejected the test of reasonableness that had since time immemorial been used to determine whether the high seas were being used legally or illegally'.[143] Endorsing this reasoning, the United Kingdom proposed an alternative text providing that: 'These freedoms, and others which are recognized by the general principles of international law, shall be exercised by all states with reasonable regard to the interests of other states in their exercise of the freedom of the high seas'.[144] This text was adopted as the final paragraph of Article 2 of the

[138] International Law Commission (n 137) 278.

[139] Ibid.

[140] 'Consideration of the Draft Articles Adopted by the International Law Commission at its Eighth Session' (UN Doc. A/3159) in *Official Records*, vol. 4 (n 128) 16, 19.

[141] Ibid.

[142] Convention on the High Seas, Geneva, 29 April 1958, entered into force 30 September 1962, 450 UNTS 11.

[143] 'Consideration of the Draft Articles Adopted by the International Law Commission at its Eighth Session' (UN Doc. A/3159) in *Official Records*, vol. 4 (n 128) 41.

[144] Ibid; 'United Kingdom of Great Britain and Northern Ireland: Proposal' (UN Doc. A/CONF.13/C.2/L.68) in *Official Records*, vol. 4 (n 128) 134.

1958 High Seas Convention.[145] As was perhaps the intention, the capacity of this formulation to restrain States engaged in nuclear testing or military exercises on the high seas remained unclear. It holds relevance for military submarines by implication, as submarines were not otherwise a specific point of focus in discussions on the high seas. What the negotiations and resulting 1958 Conventions did make clear, however, was the increasing influence of ideological and strategic tensions between State 'freedoms' at sea and rights facilitating more traditional coastal defence on the evolution of the law of the sea. This tension subsequently resounded in the drafting process of the 1982 United Nations Convention on the Law of the Sea (UNCLOS).[146]

5.6 Conclusion

By the late 1950s, Cold War strategising was a key consideration in the technological development of submarines and their tactical deployment. The United States remained concerned that the Soviet Union would deploy attack submarines in anti-shipping campaigns akin to those waged in WWII and developed its ASW capabilities, which included anti-submarine submarines, with this strategy in mind. Yet like the United States, the Soviet Union had recognised the value of submarines for their combination of stealth and firepower as launchpads for cruise and ballistic missiles.

From the mid-1950s, the Soviet Union shifted from a post-war focus on countering air bombardment through the use of intercepting aircraft and surface-to-air missiles to increasing investment in defensive missile systems intended to counter ballistic missile attacks from the sea.[147] The Soviet Union also worked to develop submarines capable of launching missile attacks against land-based targets.[148] Both the United States and the Soviet Union invested in research and development programmes to facilitate the detection of enemy submarines and enhance the capacity of their own submarines to avoid detection. Yet differences between the military strategies of the Cold War powers also appear to be reflected in

[145] Convention on the High Seas (n 145) art. 2.

[146] United Nations Convention on the Law of the Sea, Montego Bay, 10 December 1982, entered into force 16 November 1994, 1833 UNTS 397.

[147] Bruce Parrott, *The Soviet Union and Ballistic Missile Defense* (Westview Press/FPI, 1987) 25.

[148] Norman Polmar and Edward Whitman, *Hunters and Killers* (Naval Institute Press, 2016) vol. 2, 141; Friedman (n 50) 103.

their positions in negotiations at the 1958 Conference: the Soviet Union privileging coastal defence, while the United States sought to maximise its capacity to patrol and undertake military exercises in sea areas far beyond its own shores in pursuit of a new strategy of nuclear deterrence. The United States deployed submarines in nuclear deterrence patrols from 1959 and had forty-one 'for freedom' SSBNs on continuous patrol by the early 1960s.[149]

While nuclear deterrence was a major focus for submarines in the early Cold War, the value of these vessels for intelligence gathering was also being explored. In WWII, intelligence gathering by submarines primarily took the form of reconnaissance of landing beaches. In the early Cold War, the United States began to equip and deploy submarines for a number of intelligence gathering operations including capturing telemetry from missile tests, photographing new Soviet warships, including submarines, and more broadly tracking Soviet vessels and providing information about their operations.[150] The first of these vessels was USS *Cochino*, which was deployed to the Norwegian Sea in 1949 to capture Soviet telemetry from missile tests but sank after a series of battery explosions.[151] In 1952, the British Navy deployed HMS *Alcide* to Arctic waters to monitor the concentration of Russian naval vessels in the high north.[152]

Notably, these activities frequently required intelligence gathering submarines to travel close to the coast, within the twelve nautical mile territorial sea claimed by the Soviet Union. In 1957, the diesel-electric submarine USS *Gudgeon* was detected by the Soviet Union and forced to surface as a result of both Soviet ASW tactics including the use of depth charges as well as a lack of battery power and fouling air within the boat.[153] While the submarine was permitted to leave, the incident seems to have encouraged the United States to prioritise the development and deployment of nuclear-propelled submarines for near coast operations.

149 US Naval History and Heritage Command, 'Strategic Deterrence', 24 June 2024 <www.history.navy.mil/browse-by-topic/wars-conflicts-and-operations/cold-war/strategic-deterrence.html>.

150 Roger Lane-Nott, 'Submarine Intelligence and the Cold War' in Michael R. Fitzgerald and Allen Packwood (eds.), *Out of the Cold: The Cold War and Its Legacy* (Bloomsbury, 2013) 111; Sherry Sontag, Christopher Drew and Annette Lawrence Drew, *Blind Man's Buff: The Untold Story of American Submarine Espionage* (Public Affairs, 1998).

151 Sontag, Drew and Lawrence Drew (n 150) ch. 1.

152 Andrew Ward, 'Has The Cold War Started Yet? Evidence from the Royal Navy's *Monthly Intelligence Report* 1946–52' (2023) 22(3) *Journal of Intelligence History* 356, 360.

153 Sontag, Drew and Lawrence Drew (n 150) ch. 2.

The issue of submerged submarine incursions into territorial waters has persisted through and beyond the Cold War, as has the question of the lawfulness of intelligence gathering and military operations by submarines beyond the territorial sea. The following chapter traces further developments in technology and practice involving submarines in the period leading up to and including the negotiation of UNCLOS. It elaborates on the relationship between these developments and efforts to enforce and evolve international law as it relates to submarines.

6

To UNCLOS and Beyond: Strategic Domination in Submarine Regulation

6.1 Introduction

Chapter 5 reflected the shift from post–World War II peace settlements to geopolitical competition as a hallmark of the Cold War and discussed the concomitant implications for international laws relating to submarines. In particular, the role of nuclear submarines became a critical feature of defence and security policies during the Cold War, but international laws developed at the time only weakly responded to the advent of this technology. The response was weak because submarines were typically not explicitly regulated so as to reduce possible impediments to military interests. Rules established under the 1958 Territorial Sea Convention and 1958 High Seas Convention held some significance for confirming or establishing legal parameters for the conduct of warships.[1] These decisions necessarily had implications for military submarines and were important precursors for the legal developments that followed with the two subsequent law of the sea conferences. More notably, the growth in number and capabilities of nuclear submarines contributed to developments in international laws relating to arms reduction and nuclear proliferation. These legal developments are analysed in this chapter, which canvases the time during which the UN Convention on the Law of the Sea (UNCLOS)[2] was negotiated as well as considering the

[1] Convention on the Territorial Sea and Contiguous Zone, Geneva, 29 April 1958, entered into force 10 September 1964, 516 UNTS 205, art. 14 ('Territorial Sea Convention'); Convention on the High Seas, Geneva, 29 April 1958, entered into force 30 September 1962, 450 UNTS 11, art. 2 ('High Seas Convention').

Article 14 of the Territorial Sea Convention referred explicitly to the requirement of submarines to surface during passage through the territorial sea. As discussed in Chapter 5, the High Seas Convention established an obligation of reasonable regard for activities on the high seas in response to concerns about nuclear weapons test. See also Chapter 5, Section 5.5.

[2] United Nations Convention on the Law of the Sea, Montego Bay, 10 December 1982, entered into force 16 November 1994, 1833 UNTS 397 ('UNCLOS').

contemporary setting that subsequently emerged and continues to inform the modern international law of submarines.

This chapter first outlines in Section 6.2 the failed efforts of the Second Conference on the Law of the Sea, highlighting the military and security interests at play at the time. Section 6.3 situates the negotiation of UNCLOS in its historical context, focusing on the continuing Cold War and superpower rivalry as key factors influencing the development of laws relating to the passage of warships, including submarines. This discussion sets the scene for the 'deep dive' into the laws concerning submarine passage through the territorial sea, international straits and archipelagic waters in Chapter 7. The current chapter also examines the increasing peacetime use of submarines for intelligence gathering and military operations other than war and a corresponding increase in the peacetime use of anti-submarine warfare (ASW). In doing so, we are well-placed to assess the extent to which submarine activities were considered in the development of the provisions recognising and regulating coastal State rights in the exclusive economic zone (EEZ). This analysis foregrounds the discussion on submarine regulations in the EEZ in Chapter 8.

Accounting as always for the dominant position of military submarines, we also explore in this chapter the significance of ballistic missile submarines (SSBNs) in connection with negotiations regarding nuclear weapons, including the conclusion of the Treaty on the Non-Proliferation of Nuclear Weapons in 1968,[3] and its extension in 1995.[4] Sections 6.3 and 6.4 address international developments regarding nuclear disarmament and non-proliferation as they relate to submarines, which resonated both during UNCLOS negotiations and subsequent to the adoption of UNCLOS.

The chapter concludes, in Section 6.5, in explaining the current security setting of submarines. Section 6.6 then brings Part I to a close by linking the historical discussion to the contemporary setting that introduced the book, situating the reader for the analysis of current international law in relation to submarines in Part II. As submarine technologies and their concomitant uses have improved and diversified, States have considered how existing international law could apply to submarines and also what new rules were needed. Frequently, the

[3] Treaty on the Non-Proliferation of Nuclear Weapons, Moscow, London and Washington, 1 July 1968, entered into force 5 March 1970, 729 UNTS 161 ('NPT').

[4] 'Decision: Extension of the Treaty on the Non-Proliferation of Nuclear Weapons', 11 May 1995 (UN Doc. NPT/CONF.1995/32/DEC.3).

strategic benefits of submarines have prevented firm commitment to rules that were perceived as hampering these security interests. The conclusion to this chapter indicates the emerging strands of submarine regulation in different areas of international law. The legal history of submarines set out in Part I of the book reflects the core problem facing lawyers and policymakers: what specific international law rules govern the use of submarines today? Part II of the book seeks to answer this question.

6.2 The Second Conference on the Law of the Sea

The failure of the 1958 Conference on the Law of the Sea to reach a conclusion on the breadth of the territorial sea and fishery limits led to the convening of a Second Conference in 1960 to specifically address these questions. As Bowett has pointed out, security issues were discussed even 'more frequently and openly' at the Second Conference than the first.[5] Again, the United States supported a narrow (six nautical mile) territorial sea. Writing in the *American Journal of International Law* in 1960, the Chairman of the United States delegation, Arthur Dean, characterised the US position as 'a fight for the freedom of the seas'.[6] The freedom of warships and submarines in particular was clearly at the forefront of Dean's mind; he opened the piece by proclaiming that 'The opening of the Northwest Passage between the Atlantic and the Pacific Oceans under the Arctic ice by the atomic submarines U.S.S. Seadragon and USS Nautilus heralds the conquest of hitherto impenetrable undersea depths.'[7]

In 1958, USS *Nautilus* had become the first submarine to pass submerged under the North Pole.[8] USS *Seadragon* completed the first submerged transit of the Northwest Passage in 1960.[9] Reporting to the Foreign Affairs Committee of the US Senate in the same year, Dean explained that

> Our navy would like to see as narrow a territorial sea as possible in order to preserve the maximum possibility of deployment, transit and

[5] Derek Bowett, 'The Second United Nations Conference on the Law of the Sea' (1960) 9 (3) *International and Comparative Law Quarterly* 415, 416.

[6] Arthur H. Dean, 'The Second United Nations Conference on the Law of the Sea: The Fight for Freedom of the Seas' (1960) 54 (4) *American Journal of International Law* 751–789.

[7] Ibid, 751.

[8] Marion D Williams, *Submarines Under Ice: The US Navy's Polar Operations* (Naval Institute Press, 1998) ch. 11.

[9] Ibid, ch. 15.

> manoeuvrability on and over the high seas. . . . The primary danger to the continuance of the ability of our warships and supporting aircraft to move, unhampered, to wherever they may be needed to support American foreign policy presents itself in the great international straits of the world – the narrows which lie athwart the sea routes which connect us and our widely scattered friends and allies and admit us to the strategic materials we do not ourselves possess.[10]

While the Second Conference on the Law of the Sea was in progress, the United States' nuclear-powered submarine USS *Triton* completed a circumnavigation of the globe, deliberately '[passing] submerged through waters within the Indonesian and Philippine archipelagos'.[11] At the 1960 Conference, Indonesia and the Philippines reiterated their claims to exclusive sovereignty over the waters within their archipelagos, including a right to restrict navigation for security reasons.[12] This aspect of their claims was emphasised by Dean as the chief reason for the United States' objection thereto,[13] though neither State formally proposed principles or rules specifically relating to archipelagic States at this time. Instead, they argued that their exceptional character meant that they may properly be subject to an exception from any general rule regarding the breadth of the territorial sea.[14]

The implications of 'security' for the question of the breadth of the territorial sea were disputed at the Second Conference. In a statement representative of the view of many States supporting a breadth of twelve nautical miles, the Saudi Arabian delegate argued that

> A wider territorial sea is a wider zone of international security and safety. The territorial sea is a belt of peace in time of war. The reason is obvious. Belligerent States cannot conduct any military operations within the territorial seas of other States – neither the battleships on the surface, the submarine beneath, nor the jet fighters above. In time of war the high seas are the battlefield of military operations. Thus a twelve-mile limitation expands the area of peace and contracts the area of war, while a six-mile limitation expands the area of war and contracts the area of peace.[15]

[10] Bowett (n 5) 417.

[11] Dean (n 6) 753.

[12] 'Statements Made in the General Debate in the Committee of the Whole' in Second United Nations Conference on the Law of the Sea, *Official Records*, vol. 2 (UN Doc. A/CONF.19/9) 70–77 (Philippines), 266–268 (Indonesia) ('UNCLOS 2, *Official Records*, vol. 2').

[13] Dean (n 6) 753.

[14] UNCLOS 2, *Official Records*, vol. 2 (n 12) 70–77 (Philippines), 266–268 (Indonesia).

[15] Ibid, 399–400 (Saudi Arabia).

The United Kingdom alternatively suggested that

> A wide belt of waters round our shores is not in fact a suit of armour that will isolate us from danger. We all know this. On the contrary, in the conditions of modern warfare a wide territorial limit gives no added protection from attack. Such a limit is difficult and costly to police and control. It becomes hard to fix precisely the position of ships at sea. This can only increase the likelihood of incidents and so jeopardize the safety of coastal States.[16]

Notwithstanding this riposte to arguments based on security, the United Kingdom's preference for a narrow territorial sea was chiefly based on its interests as a distant water fishing nation.[17] On this basis, it supported a 'compromise' proposal by the United States – also a distant water fishing nation – to recognise a six nautical mile territorial sea together with a further six nautical mile fishery zone in which foreign States with existing fishing practices would retain rights.[18] Statements by Dean, however, suggest that 'the security of the free world' remained the chief concern underpinning the United States' views on the breadth of the territorial sea.[19] Naval force projection and nuclear deterrence had become central pillars of the Cold War strategies of the United States and the North Atlantic Treaty Organization (NATO) from the 1960s, with submarines playing a key role on both fronts.

For its part, the Soviet Union, asserting a general right to a twelve nautical mile territorial sea, emphasised above all the security of the coastal State.[20] It further noted that

> Il arrive souvent que, même en temps de paix, certains Etats envoient leurs navires de guerre vers les côtes d'autres Etats, organisent des démonstrations de force, ainsi que des manœuvres faisant intervenir d'importantes formations navales et aériennes, pour exercer une pression sur l'Etat riverain et sur le peuple de cet Etat. Au large des côtes, ils organisent des missions de reconnaissance et cherchent à contrôler la navigation en faisant survoler les navires de commerce par des appareils militaires, etc. Les eaux côtières sont englobées dans les zones d'opérations assignées à la marine de guerre de blocs militaires agressifs.[21]

[16] Ibid, 95 (United Kingdom).
[17] Ibid, 96–100.
[18] Ibid (United States).
[19] Dean (n 6) 754.
[20] UNCLOS 2, *Official Records*, vol. 2 (n 12) 16 (USSR).
[21] Ibid. Authors' translation: 'It often happens that, even in peacetime, certain states send their warships towards the coasts of other States, organize shows of force, and conduct

In the Soviet Union's view, objections to a twelve nautical mile territorial sea based on such military and strategic considerations were at odds with maintaining peace and developing international cooperation.[22] The Byelorussian Soviet Socialist Republic argued even more bluntly that '[t]he main objective of the champions of the six-mile limit was to obtain for their naval forces unconditional, so-called legitimate, access to foreign waters close to coasts in which they were interested for strategic or political reasons'.[23]

Writing in 1960, Bowett suggested that '[t]he security implications of any decision on the breadth of the territorial sea were not generally appreciated outside those circles actively concerned with the Conference', noting that 'in the United Kingdom, certainly, Press comment has concentrated almost entirely on the fisheries question'.[24] Yet security concerns were indeed at play and the Cold War context significantly influenced negotiations on the breadth of the territorial sea and the ultimate failure of the 1960 Conference to reach agreement on this point. As Bowett argued, it was from the standpoint of

> the apprehension of the use of the fleet as an instrument of foreign policy, that the objections by certain States to a six-mile limit are to be understood: the presence of the U.S. Sixth fleet in the Mediterranean, of the Seventh off China, and of the Fifth in the Indian Ocean created what the delegation of Iran termed 'a highly important psychological factor'.[25]

Bowett also opined that

> It is without doubt that memories of the use of the British fleet in the Persian Gulf in 1950 and of the United States fleet off Lebanon in 1958 conditioned the thinking of many States. For them, therefore, it was not enough to point out that the advent of the ballistic missile had made a wide territorial sea useless as a means of security; they thought in terms of pressure and political coercion in circumstances falling far short of an atomic war.[26]

maneuvers involving large naval and air forces to exert pressure on the coastal State and the people of this State. Off the coast, they organize reconnaissance missions and seek to control shipping by having military aircraft fly over merchant vessels, etc. Coastal waters are encompassed in the operational zones assigned to the navies of aggressive military blocs.'

22 Ibid, 17.

23 Ibid, 323 (Byelorussian Soviet Socialist Republic), trans. in Bowett (n 5) 416–417.

24 Bowett (n 5) 416.

25 Ibid, 417.

26 Ibid.

Following the failure of the Second Conference to reach any resolution of this issue, State interests in applying or resisting 'pressure and political coercion' continued to inform negotiations on many issues, including questions of the breadth of the territorial sea, entitlement to archipelagic waters and the emerging concept of the EEZ. Each of the latter issues, which featured in UNCLOS negotiations, carried implications for the use of military submarines and the political and defence strategies associated with submarines.

6.3 Superpower Dynamics and UNCLOS Negotiations

In terms of security, a period of détente in relations between the Soviet Union and the United States from 1969 to 1979, underpinned by arms control talks, did not alleviate other States' apprehension about strategies of 'forward deployment' now embraced by both superpowers. While the Soviet Union remained concerned about the security of its own extensive coastlines (especially in the north), the expansion of both its fleet and distant water activities meant that it shared the United States' interest in naval mobility.[27] This coalescence of interests resulted in novel cooperation between the two superpowers during UNCLOS negotiations in support of measures securing freedom of navigation for warships in international straits and throughout the EEZ. It also allowed for agreement to be reached on the outstanding question of the breadth of the territorial sea and the navigational rights of warships through this maritime zone.

6.3.1 Navigational Rights of Warships

At the Third Conference on the Law of the Sea (1973–1982), both the Soviet Union and the United States supported a twelve nautical mile territorial sea subject to a right of innocent passage for not only merchant ships but warships (the Soviet Union insisted, however, upon prior notification and authorisation for such passage in its domestic legislation).[28] Both powers also supported a less restrictive regime of

[27] Anthony P. Allison, 'The Soviet Union and UNCLOS III: Pragmatism and Policy Evolution' (1986) 16(2) *Ocean Development & International Law* 109, 111–113; Pierre Thévenin, 'A Liberal Maritime Power as Any Other? The Soviet Union during the Negotiations of the Law of the Sea Convention' (2021) 52(2) *Ocean Development and International Law* 193–223.

[28] Allison (n 27) 115–121; Thévenin (n 27) 211–215.

passage for warships through international straits – though the Soviet Union manoeuvred to exempt particular straits and sea areas from these regimes.[29] The Soviet Union and the United States were also in accord in their efforts to characterise coastal State rights in the 200 nautical mile EEZ recognised at the Conference as 'preferential' rights in an area otherwise subject to continuing high seas freedoms.[30]

China, galvanised by its recent split with the Soviet Union to further its alignment with developing States, was particularly vehement in its criticism of this approach and suggested that a Soviet interest in the 'economic zones' of other States was linked to espionage and military objectives.[31] Albania also decried 'efforts by the United States and the Soviet Union to internationalise the exclusive economic zone and to substitute a pitifully reduced regime of competences for the sovereign rights and exclusive national jurisdiction of coastal States'.[32] Yet even when it became clear that the rights of the coastal State in the EEZ would be recognised as 'sovereign' and 'exclusive' rather than merely preferential, both the United States and Soviet Union insisted that other 'high seas freedoms' would be retained in this zone.[33] This objective was achieved in Article 58 of UNCLOS.[34] Somewhat ironically, the superpowers' agreement on this point stemmed in large part from their mutual interest in using these sea areas for force projection and other strategic military purposes with a view to countering one another's power.

From the early 1970s, the Soviet Union had in service SSBNs capable of reaching targets in the United States from a submerged position in the Barents Sea and the Sea of Okhotsk.[35] The Polaris missile system had

[29] Allison (n 27) 115–121; Thévenin (n 27) 211–215.

[30] See e.g., 'Bulgaria, Byelorussian Soviet Socialist Republic, German Democratic Republic, Poland, Ukrainian Soviet Socialist Republic, and Union of Soviet Socialist Republics: Draft Articles on the Economic Zone', 5 August 1974 (UN Doc. A/CONF.62/C.2/L.38) in Third United Nations Conference on the Law of the Sea, *Official Records*, vol. 3, 214–216 ('UNCLOS 3, *Official Records*') ('Soviet Proposal'); Renate Platzöder, *Third United Nations Conference on the Law of the Sea: Documents*, 15 vols. (Oceana Publications, 1987) vol. 11, 574.

[31] 'Coastal State Preferential rights or Other Non-Exclusive Jurisdiction over Resources Beyond the Territorial Sea' (UN Doc. A/CONF.62/C.2/SR.30) in UNCLOS 3, *Official Records* (n 31) vol. 2, 226, 228 (China).

[32] 'Exclusive Economic Zone beyond the Territorial Sea' (UN Doc. A/CONF.62/C.2/SR.26) in UNCLOS 3, *Official Records* (n 31) vol. 2, 202, 206–207 (Albania).

[33] 'Soviet Proposal' in UNCLOS 3, *Official Records* (n 31) 214–216; Platzöder (n 31) vol. 11, 574.

[34] Discussed further in Chapter 8, Section 8.2.

[35] Milan Vego, 'Submarines in Soviet ASW Doctrine and Tactics' (1983) 36(2) *Naval War College Review* 2, 3.

a similar range, as did the otherwise more accurate and powerful new Poseidon missile system deployed by the United States in 1971, which replaced Polaris on thirty-one of its '41 for Freedom' submarines.[36] Both the United States and the Soviet Union continued to work on submarine-launched ballistic missile systems with greater range to better avoid ASW – the former deploying 'Trident' in 1979. While greater missile ranges would mean that SSBNs could be positioned closer to their bases, their presence within striking distance of foreign shores remained a key element of the Cold War strategy of both sides. Submarines also played a role in intelligence gathering (especially for the United States), though the covert nature of such operations, which are known to have included submerged activities in the territorial sea of foreign States,[37] meant the States concerned did not seek to defend their lawfulness in connection with the law of the sea. Notably, the Soviet submarine fleet was a key target of these intelligence gathering operations.[38] This use of submarines is discussed further in Section 6.4, below.

6.3.2 *Demilitarisation and Nuclear Proliferation*

Beyond navigational rights, the concept of 'peaceful uses of the ocean' was frequently invoked as a guide and constraint in UNCLOS negotiations. The concept was linked to concerns about demilitarisation and further aligned to efforts to prevent nuclear proliferation. These priorities were predicated on broad concern that a rapidly increasing number of countries could join the nuclear arms race. The 1960s saw the United Kingdom acquire the Polaris missile system from the United States in accordance with the 1958 US-UK Mutual Defence Agreement.[39] China and France developed SSBN capability independently during the 1970s.[40]

Prior to UNCLOS negotiations, States had sought to reduce the nuclear imprint across the globe through different multilateral treaties.

[36] Graham Spinardi, *From Polaris to Trident: The Development of US Ballistic Missile Technology* (Cambridge University Press, 1994) 86–112.

[37] Jeffrey T. Richelson, *The US Intelligence Community* (Taylor & Francis, 2015) 252–253.

[38] Ibid, 253.

[39] Agreement for Co-operation on the Uses of Atomic Energy for Mutual Defense Purposes, Washington, 3 July 1958, entered into force 27 July 1959, 326 UNTS 3; Polaris Sales Agreement between the Government of the United Kingdom and the United States of America, Washington, 6 April 1963, entered into force 6 April 1963, [1963] UKTS 59.

[40] Norman Polmar and K. J. Moore, *Cold War Submarines: The Design & Construction of US and Soviet Submarines* (Potomac Books, 2004) 172.

The 1971 Seabed Treaty,[41] like the earlier Antarctic Treaty[42] and the Outer Space Treaty,[43] prohibited nuclear weapons in a specific area (the seabed), while the 1968 Treaty on the Non-Proliferation of Nuclear Weapons (NPT) sought to balance the interests of 'nuclear-weapon States' (NWS) and 'non-nuclear-weapon States' (NNWS).[44] Under the NPT, the NNWS agreed not to receive or manufacture nuclear weapons in return for the 'exchange of equipment, materials and scientific and technological information for the peaceful uses of nuclear energy' from NWS, and accepted safeguards to ensure that the use of nuclear energy was indeed peaceful.[45] The identified NWS (China, France, the Soviet Union, the United Kingdom, and the United States)[46] undertook 'not to transfer to any recipient whatsoever nuclear weapons or other nuclear explosive devices or control over such weapons or explosive devices directly, or indirectly; and not in any way to assist, encourage, or induce any non-nuclear-weapon State to manufacture or otherwise acquire nuclear weapons or other nuclear explosive devices, or control over such weapons or explosive devices'.[47] The parties to the NPT also undertook 'to pursue negotiations in good faith on effective measures relating to cessation of the nuclear arms race at an early date and to nuclear disarmament, and on a treaty on general and complete disarmament under strict and effective international control'.[48]

The United States and the Soviet Union were chiefly responsible for drafting the NPT, and the text reflects inter alia their compromise on nuclear-sharing arrangements in NATO. The Soviet Union at this time dropped its former objections to the presence of 'nuclear weapons under US command and control on the soil of otherwise non-nuclear NATO allies' in exchange for the United States' commitment not to assist any NNWS (including NATO members) in acquiring

[41] Treaty on the Prohibition of the Emplacement of Nuclear Weapons and Other Weapons of Mass Destruction on the Sea-Bed and the Ocean Floor and in the Subsoil thereof, Washington, Moscow and London, 11 February 1971, 955 UNTS 115.

[42] Antarctic Treaty, Washington, 1 December 1959, entered into force 23 June 1961, 402 UNTS 71.

[43] Treaty on Principles Governing the Activities of States in the Exploration and Use of Outer Space, including the Moon and Other Celestial Bodies, Washington, Moscow and London, 27 January 1967, entered into force 10 October 1967, 610 UNTS 205.

[44] NPT (n 3).

[45] Ibid, arts. II, III.

[46] NWS were defined as those States that had 'manufactured and exploded a nuclear weapon or other nuclear explosive device prior to 1 January, 1967': ibid, art. IX(3).

[47] Ibid, art. I.

[48] Ibid, art. VI.

nuclear weapons.[49] From the mid-1960s, the Soviet Union, like the United States, maintained a strategy of nuclear deterrence (though a policy of pre-emption was not entirely abandoned).[50] By the end of the decade, the two superpowers had reached 'strategic parity'.[51] This context allowed for the superpower détente of the 1970s, during which the United States and Soviet Union engaged in a series of strategic arms limitation talks (SALT) with varying results.[52]

SALT I, concluded in 1972, consisted of two separate treaties: the Anti-Ballistic Missile (ABM) Treaty, which limited the ABM defence systems of both powers to just two sites to defend (a) the national capital, and (b) an intercontinental ballistic missile field;[53] and an Interim Agreement on Strategic Offensive Arms, which froze the number of land-based Intercontinental Ballistic Missiles (ICBM) launchers as well as 'submarine-launched ballistic missile (SLBM) launchers and modern ballistic missile submarines' to their current numbers.[54] At the time, the Soviet Union had a greater number of both ICBMs and SLBMs whereas the United States had an advantage in the form of Multiple Independently Targetable Re-entry Vehicles (MIRVs), which permitted 'a single missile to deliver multiple nuclear warheads to different targets' and were not regulated by SALT I.[55] As MIRVs could be used with both land-based ICBMs and SLBMs, this technology became a new focus in the continuing arms race between the United States and the Soviet Union. The latter soon followed the former in deploying both ICBMs and SLBMs using MIRV technology.

[49] Andrew J. Grotto, 'Non-Proliferation Treaty (1968)' in Anne Peters and Rüdiger Wolfrum (eds.), *The Max Planck Encyclopedia of Public International Law* (Oxford University Press, February 2009).

[50] William Burr and David Rosenberg, 'Nuclear Competition in an Era of Stalemate, 1963–1975' in Melven P. Leffler and Odd Arne Westad (eds.), *The Cambridge History of the Cold War*, vol. 2 (Cambridge University Press, 2010) 88.

[51] Ibid.

[52] Ibid, 88–111; Robert J. McMahon, *The Cold War* (Oxford University Press, 2021) 120–139.

[53] Treaty between the United States of America and the Union of Soviet Socialist Republics on the Limitation of Anti-Ballistic Missile Systems, Moscow, 26 May 1972, entered into force 3 October 1972, 944 UNTS 13. A 1977 Protocol further provided that ABM systems could only be deployed at one site at a time: Protocol to the Treaty between the United States of America and the Union of Socialist Soviet Republics on the Limitation of Anti-Ballistic Missile Systems, Moscow, 26 May 1972, entered into force 26 May 1972, 1042 UNTS 424.

[54] Interim Agreement between the United States of America and the Union of Soviet Socialist Republics on Certain Measures with respect to the Limitation of Strategic Offensive Arms, Moscow, 26 May 1972, 944 UNTS 3.

[55] McMahon (n 52) 125–126.

In 1979, the earlier interim agreement was replaced by SALT II, which placed numerical limits on MIRVs as well as ICBM launchers, SLBM launchers, heavy bombers and ASBMs.[56] SALT II was not ratified by the United States and the Soviet Union's invasion of Afghanistan in December 1979 conclusively marked the end of the era of détente; however, both States nevertheless complied with its terms for some time on the basis of reciprocity.[57]

During UNCLOS negotiations, multilateral and bilateral negotiations regarding the limitation of arms and nuclear weapons in particular were referenced by States seeking a commitment to a demilitarised and denuclearised ocean in the new law of the sea treaty, while other States considered military patrols carrying nuclear weapons and other military exercises a key element of the freedom of the seas.[58] While the former group of States considered demilitarisation and denuclearisation to be consistent with and to further advance broader developments in disarmament, the latter (including the two superpowers) argued that the issue was beyond the scope of the Third Conference.[59] The United States and the Soviet Union both claimed that military uses of the ocean were compatible with the concepts of 'peaceful uses' and 'peaceful purposes'.[60] China countered that '[t]he obstacles to the peaceful uses of ocean space came mainly from the two super-Powers', which 'were competing with each other in building up huge naval forces and installing naval bases everywhere, each trying to overwhelm the other' and 'had made a show of force to intimidate and threaten other countries in all parts of the world'.[61]

UNCLOS did ultimately include provisions on the peaceful uses of the oceans. However, as a 'package deal' it reflects, but does not entirely resolve, the tensions between States concerned to limit military mobility at sea and States concerned to enhance it. UNCLOS expressly restricts uses of the high seas and the Area to those for peaceful purposes, while Article 301 of UNCLOS generally provides that '[i]n exercising their

[56] Treaty Between the United States of America and The Union of Soviet Socialist Republics on the Limitation of Strategic Offensive Arms (SALT II), Vienna, 18 June 1979, never entered into force (1979) 18 ILM 1138.

[57] McMahon (n 52) 138–139.

[58] See, e.g., 'Peaceful Uses of Ocean Space: Zones of Peace and Security' (UN Docs. A/CONF.62/SR.66, A/CONF.62/SR.67, A/CONF.62/SR.68) in UNCLOS 3, *Official Records* (n 31) vol. 5, 54–69.

[59] See ibid.

[60] Ibid, 58–59 (Soviet Union), 62 (United States).

[61] Ibid, 59 (China).

rights and performing their duties under this Convention, States Parties shall refrain from any threat or use of force against the territorial integrity or political independence of any State, or in any other manner inconsistent with the principles of international law embodied in the Charter of the United Nations'.[62] The combined effect of these provisions, coupled with the widespread State practice of military uses of the oceans, suggests that meeting an obligation of peacefully using the ocean only requires that States not violate the *jus cogens* prohibition on the threat or use of force.[63]

As discussed in detail in Chapter 7, UNCLOS ultimately included only one provision (Article 20) that explicitly references submarines, requiring surface navigation and flying their flag while in the territorial sea.[64] Military and security issues are infrequently addressed in UNCLOS, though warships are singled out in relation to the rights and duties of passage in the territorial sea.[65] UNCLOS contains only two provisions directly relating to 'nuclear-powered ships and ships carrying nuclear … materials': Article 22(2), which provides that such vessels 'may be required [by the coastal State] to confine their passage to … sea lanes' in the territorial sea and Article 23, which provides that such vessels 'shall, when exercising the right of innocent passage through the territorial sea, carry documents and observe special precautionary measures established for such ships by international agreements'.[66] Warships' rights of visit[67] and of hot pursuit,[68] as well as their sovereign immunity are also set out in UNCLOS.[69] Protections for military activities are afforded by disclosure of information restrictions,[70] and by the possible exclusion of military activities from the scope of compulsory dispute settlement procedures.[71] While UNCLOS thus has critical bearing for the regulation of submarines in international law, as evident in the discussions in Chapters 7 and 8, the

62 UNCLOS (n 2) arts. 88, 141, 301. See also preamble and the use of force as rendering passage non-innocent: art. 19.

63 The parameters of the prohibition on the threat or use of force in relation to submarines is addressed in Chapter 9. Chapter 8 discusses the regulation of military activities in the EEZ. See Chapter 8, Section 8.3.1.

64 UNCLOS (n 2) art. 20.

65 Ibid, arts. 29–32.

66 See further Chapters 7, Section 7.2.2; UNCLOS (n 2), arts. 22(2), 23.

67 UNCLOS (n 2) art. 110.

68 Ibid, art. 111.

69 Ibid, art. 95.

70 Ibid, art. 302.

71 Ibid, art. 298(1)(b).

limited treatment underlines the need to look to other legal regimes as well as general principles of international law.

6.4 Beyond the Adoption of UNCLOS

When UNCLOS was adopted in 1982, States were well aware of the capacity of submarines to launch nuclear missiles (key to their significance in force projection) as well as their role in intelligence gathering and (alongside bathyscape-style submersibles) scientific research. However, as noted above, explicit regulation of these vessels is not found in UNCLOS beyond Article 20. Rather, the relevant legal framework instead depends on their characterisation as warships or other government vessels operated on non-commercial service or must be drawn from the regulation of the specific activities in which the submarine is engaged. Yet questions continued to arise regarding the interpretation, application and adequacy of UNCLOS and other existing instruments of international law in connection with the continually evolving capabilities and practices of submarines.

6.4.1 Increased Intelligence Gathering, Surveillance and Reconnaissance

One of the central questions concerning the legal regulation of submarines concerns the rights and duties under international law for the conduct of intelligence gathering, surveillance and reconnaissance (ISR) by submarines. These legal questions are examined in Chapters 7 and 8 of Part II. Those questions must be set against State experiences of submarines being used for this activity both while UNCLOS was being negotiated and to the present day. These experiences are outlined here as a background to the legal debates explored in Part II.

US submarines played a role in the Vietnam War from the mid-1960s, but chiefly for beach reconnaissance and other intelligence gathering as well as enforcing the United States' blockade of North Viet Nam by interfering with merchant ships from the USSR and China.[72] These vessels were part of the US Seventh Fleet based at Subic Bay in the Philippines.[73]

[72] Edward J. Marolda, *US Seventh Fleet, Vietnam 1964–75: American Naval Power in Southeast Asia 1964–75* (Osprey, 2023) 16, 33.
[73] Ibid, 4.

As the Cold War continued into the 1970s, the United States deployed submarines in signals, signature and imagery intelligence operations, at times within the territorial sea of the Soviet Union and other States, including Viet Nam and China.[74] In 1975, 'Holystone' operations 'apparently provided vital information on the Soviet submarine fleet, including its configuration, capabilities, noise patterns, missiles and missile-firing capabilities'.[75] Submarines also played a role in US Operation 'Ivy Bells', which, in 1972, succeeded in tapping an undersea military communications cable in the Sea of Okhotsk that connected a Soviet submarine base at Petropavlovsk with the mainland.[76] 'Ivy Bells' became an ongoing operation until 1981, and the intelligence gathered ostensibly played a critical role in the negotiation of SALT II.[77]

British submarines were also involved in ISR during the Cold War. In the 1960s, the Royal Navy's Submarine Service was engaged in the surveillance of Soviet fleet exercises and special intelligence gathering operations in northern waters close to Soviet territorial seas.[78] In the late 1960s and early 1970s, the United States and the United Kingdom worked together to track forward deployed Soviet submarines in the 'GIUK' gap – an area of the northern Atlantic Ocean that Soviet Hotel-class and Yankee-class SSBNs had to cross to come within range of their north American targets.[79] A sound surveillance system (SOSUS) was used to identify the approximate location of Soviet SSBNs with US and British submarines pinpointing and tracking the vessels (on occasion so closely as to result in collisions).[80] France also put its first SSBNs into service between 1971 and 1980 as an independent deterrent to Soviet aggression (France having withdrawn from NATO's integrated military command structure in 1966).[81]

74 Richelson (n 37) 227–228.
75 Ibid, 227.
76 Ibid, 229.
77 Caitlin Morris, 'Operation IVY BELLS: Lessons Learned from an "Intelligence Success"' (2012) 20(3) *Journal of the Australian Institute of Professional Intelligence Officers* 17.
78 James Jinks and Peter Hennessy, *The Silent Deep: The Royal Navy Submarine Service Since 1945* (Penguin, 2016) 274–285.
79 Austin Long and Brendan Ritterhouse Green, 'Stalking the Secure Second Strike: Intelligence, Counterforce, and Nuclear Strategy' (2015) 38(1–2) *Journal of Strategic Studies* 38, 47–49.
80 Ibid, 48–49. On the development of SOSUS, see Chapter 5, Section 5.3.
81 David S. Yost, 'France's Nuclear Deterrence Strategy: Concepts and Operational Implementation' in Henry D. Sokolski (ed.), *Getting MAD: Nuclear Mutual Assured Destruction, its Origins and Practice* (Strategic Studies Institute, 2004) 197, 200, 224.

The 1970's saw the development of new systems to collate and analyse an increased quality and variety of intelligence – initially for the benefit of navy commanders who could be provided 'with an integrated, "God's-eye view" of their operating environment'.[82] By 1980, such operational intelligence also 'provided Navy operational commanders and strategic planners with an unprecedented picture of the capabilities and disposition of current Soviet maritime force', which together with more highly classified signals and human intelligence penetrations, revealed a clearer picture of Soviet naval operations and intentions.[83]

Following the Cold War and the end of the Warsaw Pact,[84] the United States shifted its focus from 'a central, agreed-upon threat' (the Soviet Union) to a more diverse array of challenges including '[d]rives for regional hegemony, resurgent nationalism, ethnic and religious rivalries, drug trafficking and terrorism'.[85] Since the adoption of UNCLOS, the military submarines of the major naval powers have become increasingly quieter and harder to detect.[86] Yet ASW and knowledge about military submarines' presence and operations remain critical concerns for coastal States in ensuring their own maritime security and achieving strategic objectives. The international laws regulating navigational rights and limiting the resort to threats or use of force play into this dynamic.

6.4.2 *Submarines and Arms Reduction Agreements*

During the time that UNCLOS was being negotiated and after its adoption, both the United Kingdom and the United States continued to

[82] Christopher A. Ford and David A. Rosenberg, 'The Naval Intelligence Underpinnings of Reagan's Maritime Strategy' (2005) 28(2) *Journal of Strategic Studies* 379, 381.

[83] David A. Rosenberg, 'American Naval Strategy in the Era of the Third World War: An Inquiry into the Structure and Process of General War at Sea, 1945–9' in N. A. M. Rodger (ed.), *Naval Power in the Twentieth Century* (US Naval Institute Press, 1996), 249; Ford and Rosenberg (n 83) 381.

[84] Treaty of Friendship, Cooperation and Mutual Assistance, Warsaw, 14 May 1955, entered into force 4 June 1955, 219 UNTS 3.

[85] Amund Lundesgaard, 'US Navy Strategy and Force Structure After the Cold War' (2011) *The Norwegian Institute for Defence Insights* 7–8.

[86] See Norman Friedman, 'Strategic Submarines and Strategic Stability: Looking Towards the 2030s' in Rory Medcalf et al. (eds.), *The Future of the Undersea Deterrent: A Global Survey* (ANU, 2019) 69. See also Roger Bradbury et al., *Transparent Oceans? The Coming SSBN Counter-Detection Task May be Insuperable* (ANU, 2020); Sydney J. Freedberg Jr, 'Transparent Sea: AUKUS Looks to AI, Quantum in Hunt for Chinese Submarines', *Breaking Defense* (29 January 2024) <https://breakingdefense.com/2024/01/transparent-sea-aukus-looks-to-ai-quantum-in-hunt-for-chinese-submarines>; Polmar and Moore (n 40) 290.

deploy SSBNs in deterrence patrols.[87] While the majority of Soviet SSBNs stayed in northern waters, Soviet nuclear-powered attack submarines (SSNs) and the occasional SSBN were identified by US and British ships in the Atlantic and Pacific Oceans in the 1980s, apparently seeking 'to probe the West's anti-submarine capability, attempting to detect and compromise the Royal Navy and US Navy's SSBNs'.[88] The quiet Soviet Victor III-class SSNs were, however, challenging to track, and their submariners made use of tactics responding to intelligence on SOSUS and western ASW – avoiding SOSUS arrays and using 'disruptive steering' (periodic zigzagging) to break contact with trailing British and American submarines.[89]

In 1987, China's first SSBN entered into service.[90] Though China had been developing this technology for some time and its first (Xia-class) submarine was slow, noisy and rapidly replaced by a new generation (Jin-class),[91] the realisation of SSBN capacity followed a significant shift in naval policy. The focus of the People's Liberation Army (PLA) Navy following the Sino-Soviet split of the early 1960s[92] had been 'anti-Soviet coastal defence' – its capacity for which had been developed with prior Soviet assistance, including the supply of diesel-electric attack submarines (both completed Whiskey-class models and designs for the Romeo-class); China independently developed its first SSN, which was launched in 1970.[93] By the mid 1980s, however, the Soviet threat was considered sufficiently diminished to warrant a shift in the PLA Navy's focus to a strategy of 'Offshore Active Defence'.[94]

[87] Polmar and Moore (n 40) 191–193.

[88] Jinks and Hennessy (n 68) 564.

[89] Ibid, 568.

[90] Nuclear Threat Initiative, 'China Submarine Capabilities Fact Sheet', 13 August 2024 <www.nti.org/analysis/articles/china-submarine-capabilities/>.

[91] Ibid.

[92] See Sergey Radchenko, 'The Sino-Soviet Split' in Melvyn P. Leffler and Odd Arne Westad (eds.), *The Cambridge History of the Cold War*, vol. 2 (Cambridge University Press, 2010) 349; Lorenz M. Lüthi, *The Sino-Soviet Split: The Cold War in the Communist World* (Princeton University Press, 2008).

[93] John B. Hattendorf and Peter M. Swartz (eds.), *US Naval Strategy in the 1980s: Selected Documents* (Newport Paper 33, Naval War College Press, 2008) 6; Paul An-hao Huang, *Maritime Strategy of China in the Asia-Pacific: Origins, Development and Impact* (Edwin Mellen Press, 2010) 181; Christopher P. Carlson and Howard Wang, 'A Brief Technical History of PLAN Nuclear Submarines' (China Maritime Report No. 30, China Maritime Studies Institute, August 2023) 30.

[94] Hattendorf and Swartz (n 93) 6; Huang (n 93) 138–139.

Following the Cold War, the reduction of submarine forces was linked to bilateral treaties between the United States and the Soviet Union/Russian Federation on the Reduction and Limitation of Strategic Offensive Arms (START). The parties to START I (1991) were required to reduce inter alia SLBMs, SLBM warheads, and SLBM launchers (though the Soviet Union/Russian Federation was required to make deeper reductions than the United States).[95] START II signed in 1993 would have resulted in further cuts to these weapons, but never entered into force.[96] The Clinton Administration's 1994 Nuclear Posture Review nevertheless proposed reducing the number of Trident SSBNs from eighteen to fourteen – a reduction endorsed in the Bush administration's 2002 Nuclear Posture Review.[97] This goal was achieved by the conversion of four Trident submarines into guided cruise missile submarines (SSGNs), which entered into service between 2006 and 2007.[98]

START III, as anticipated by a Joint Statement on Parameters on Future Reduction in Nuclear Forces agreed upon by Presidents Clinton and Yeltsin at Helsinki in 1997, was projected to include 'measures relating to nuclear long-range sea-launched cruise missiles'; however, negotiations were dependent on the entry into force of START II, which did not eventuate.[99] Instead, Russia and the United States signed the Strategic Offensive Reductions Treaty (SORT) in 2002, committing to further reduce strategic nuclear warheads below START I levels (from 6,000 to below 2,200).[100]

95 Wolff Heintschel von Heinegg, 'Strategic Offensive Arms, Treaties on Reduction and Limitation (START)' in Anne Peters and Rüdiger Wolfrum (eds.), *The Max Planck Encyclopedia of Public International Law* (Oxford University Press, March 2021); Treaty between the United States of America and the Union of Soviet Socialist Republics on the Reduction and Limitation of Strategic Offensive Arms (START I Treaty), Moscow, 31 July 1991, entered into force 5 December 1994 (1992) 31 ILM 246.

96 Heintschel von Heinegg (n 95); Treaty between the United States of America and the Union of Soviet Socialist Republics on Further Reduction and Limitation of Strategic Offensive Arms (START II Treaty), Moscow, 3 January 1993, never entered into force.

97 Ronald O'Rourke, 'Navy Trident Submarine Conversion (SSGN) Program: Background and Issues for Congress' (Congressional Research Service Report for Congress, 2008) 1–2.

98 Ibid, 5.

99 US-Russia Joint Statement on Parameters on Future Reduction in Nuclear Forces, Helsinki, 21 March 1997.

100 Treaty between the Russian Federation and the United States of America on Strategic Offensive Reductions, Moscow, 24 May 2002, entered into force 1 June 2003, 2350 UNTS 415 ('SORT').

Notably, these limits were understood to apply only to deployed warheads and did not require the reduction or destruction of reserves.[101] Nor was any provision made for ensuring compliance.[102]

START I and SORT were superseded by New START (2010), which, following a five-year extension in 2021, remains in force.[103] New START limits the strategic offensive arms of the United States and Russia to no more than 700 deployed ICBMs, SLBMS and heavy bombers equipped for nuclear armaments; 1,550 nuclear warheads on deployed ICBMs, SLBMs, and heavy bombers equipped for nuclear armaments; and 800 deployed and non-deployed ICBM launchers, SLBM launchers and heavy bombers.[104] It remains for the parties to structure their forces within these limits, and New START provides for a range of verification measures, including on-site inspections and satellite imagery.[105] In the context of the Russia-Ukraine war, however, Russia first claimed a temporary exemption in August 2022, postponed a Bilateral Consultative Commission for more than the allowed period in November 2022, and in February 2023 announced that Russia would suspend its participation in New START.[106] The United States subsequently claimed the right to withhold data from Russia as a counter measure.[107]

6.4.3 *Nuclear Non-Proliferation Agreements*

As well as being targeted by regional arms control treaties, SLBMs, SSBNs and on some views even SSNs that are not armed with nuclear weapons (such as those being acquired by Australia under the AUKUS

101 Daryl G. Kimball, 'The Strategic Offensive Reductions Treaty (SORT) At a Glance', *Arms Control Association*, October 2022 <www.armscontrol.org/factsheets/sort-glance>.

102 Ibid.

103 Treaty between the United States of America and the Russian Federation on Measures for the Further Reduction and Limitation of Strategic Offensive Arms, Prague, 8 April 2010, entered into force 5 February 2011 (2011) 50 ILM 342 ('New START Treaty').

104 Bureau of Arms Control, Deterrence and Stability, 'New Start Treaty Aggregate Numbers of Strategic Offensive Arms', *US Department of State*, 12 May 2023 <www.state.gov/new-start-treaty-aggregate-numbers-of-strategic-offensive-arms-5/>.

105 Ibid.

106 See further 'United States Accuses Russia of Not Complying with New START Treaty and Russia Suspends Its Participation' (2023) 117(3) *American Journal of International Law* 522.

107 Ibid, 526–527.

Agreement)[108] may be subject to regulation under international agreements on the non-proliferation of nuclear weapons. As set out above, China, France, Russia, the United Kingdom and the United States are 'nuclear weapons States' under the NPT and possess both SSNs and SSBNs. India, which is not party to the NPT, began leasing nuclear-powered attack submarines from Russia in the late 1980s and commissioned its first SSBN in 2016.[109] North Korea, which unilaterally withdrew from the NPT in 2003 (the legal effectiveness of which is disputed), continues to conduct nuclear tests with a notable number conducted in 2022, including tests of SLBMs.[110] While the Comprehensive Test Ban Treaty concluded in 1996[111] was intended to expand on the 1963 Limited Test Ban Treaty[112] and complement the NPT and the safeguards system of the International Atomic Energy Agency by ending nuclear test explosions, it has not yet entered into force and awaits ratification by a number of key States including China, Egypt, India, Iran, Israel, North Korea, Pakistan, the United States and Russia (which withdrew its ratification in 2023).

Further efforts to restrict nuclear weapons include the five Nuclear-Weapon-Free-Zones established by regional treaties between 1967 and 2006,[113] as well as the 2017 United Nations Treaty on the Prohibition of Nuclear Weapons (TPNW), which entered into force in

[108] Agreement between the Government of Australia, the Government of the United Kingdom of Great Britain and Northern Ireland, and the Government of the United States of America for the Exchange of Naval Nuclear Propulsion Information, Canberra, 22 November 2021, entered into force 8 February 2022, [2022] ATS 4.

[109] Nuclear Threat Initiative, 'India Submarine Capabilities Fact Sheet', 25 March 2025 <www.nti.org/analysis/articles/india-submarine-capabilities/>.

[110] Arms Control Association, 'Arms Control and Proliferation Profile: North Korea', June 2024 <www.armscontrol.org/factsheets/northkoreaprofile>.

[111] Comprehensive Nuclear-Test-Ban Treaty, New York, 10 September 1996, not entered into force, UNGA Res. 50/245 (UN Doc. A/50/1027).

[112] Treaty Banning Nuclear Weapon Tests in the Atmosphere, in Outer Space and Under Water, Moscow, 5 August 1963, entered into force 10 October 1963, 480 UNTS 43.

[113] These are the Treaty for the Prohibition of Nuclear Weapons in Latin America (Treaty of Tlatelolco), Mexico City, 14 February 1967, entered into force 22 April 1968, 634 UNTS 281; South Pacific Nuclear Free Zone Treaty (Treaty of Rarotonga), Rarotonga, 6 August 1985, entered into force 11 December 1986, 1445 UNTS 177; Southeast Asia Nuclear Weapon-Free Zone Treaty (Treaty of Bangkok), Bangkok, 15 December 1995, entered into force 27 March 1997, 1981 UNTS 129; Africa Nuclear-Weapon-Free Zone Treaty (Treaty of Pelindaba), Cairo, 12 April 1996, entered into force 15 July 2009, 35 ILM 698; Central Asian Nuclear-Weapon-Free Zone Treaty (Treaty of Semipalatinsk in Central Asia), Semipalatinsk, 8 September 2006, entered into force 21 March 2009, 2970 UNTS 91. The United States has not ratified the three protocols to the Treaty of Rarotonga that would inter alia 'prohibit the manufacture, stationing, or testing of

January 2021.[114] While undoubtedly a significant contribution towards nuclear non-proliferation, the TPNW is not supported by those States that currently possess nuclear arms.[115] At the time of its adoption, France, the United Kingdom and the United States issued a joint statement asserting that they had not participated in the negotiation of the TPNW and did not intend to 'sign, ratify, or ever become party to it'.[116] This position was underpinned by their belief that '[t]his initiative clearly disregards the realities of the international security environment' and that '[a]ccession to the ban treaty is incompatible with the policy of nuclear deterrence, which has been essential to keeping the peace in Europe and North Asia for over 70 years'.[117] While there are undoubted limitations on the applicability of the TPNW as it concerned nuclear-armed submarines, other principles of international law remain relevant for these submarines, including as concerns the protection of the marine environment and in relation to navigational rights and safety. These aspects are explored further in Part II of the book.[118]

6.5 Contemporary Security Setting for Submarines

As discussed in Chapter 1, the Asia Pacific has become a particular site of concern in relation to the increasing acquisition and deployment of submarines.[119] Regional security has more recently been a key focus for the United States, and in 2017 the Quadrilateral Security Dialogue between Australia, India, Japan and the United States was reconfigured around the concept of a 'Free and Open Indo-Pacific'.[120] AUKUS, the

nuclear explosive devices in American Samoa or on Jarvis Island', preclude the use or threat to use 'any nuclear explosive device against Parties to the Treaty or against any territory within the zone for which a State Party to Protocol 1 is internationally responsible', and the testing of 'any nuclear explosive device anywhere within the zone': Protocol 1 to the South Pacific Nuclear Free Zone Treaty, Suva, 8 August 1986, 1971 UNTS 470; Protocol 2 to the South Pacific Nuclear Free Zone Treaty, Suva, 8 August 1986, 1971 UNTS 475; Protocol 3 to the South Pacific Nuclear Free Zone Treaty, Suva, 8 August 1986, 1971 UNTS 482. See further Chapter 12, Section 12.3.2.

114 Treaty on the Prohibition of Nuclear Weapons, New York, 7 July 2017, entered into force 22 January 2021, 3379 UNTS 36.

115 Stuart Casey-Maslen, *The Treaty on the Prohibition of Nuclear Weapons* (Oxford University Press, 2020) 52–53.

116 Ibid, 52–53.

117 Ibid.

118 See Chapters 7, 8, 11 and 12.

119 See Chapter 1, Section 1.1.

120 'Quad Leaders Vision Statement', *Prime Minister of Australia*, 20 May 2023 <www.pm.gov.au/media/quad-leaders-vision-statement-enduring-partners-indo-pacific>.

trilateral security partnership between Australia, the United Kingdom and the United States announced in 2021, also aims to 'uphold peace and stability in the Indo-Pacific and to deter and defend against rapidly evolving threats to the international order and system there'.[121] The first initiative of the partnership has been to facilitate Australia's acquisition of nuclear-powered submarines, which, according to the member States, 'will optimize the capability, commonality and interoperability of all three nations' SSN platforms'.[122] The AUKUS Submarine Rotational Force West (SRF-West) will involve the rotational presence of one British SSN and up to four US SSNs at HMAS Stirling, an Australian naval base in Western Australia, from 2027.[123]

China's claims in the South China Sea and broader projection of its military power in the region are a key context for these developments. China appears to have taken the conclusion of UNCLOS with its recognition of a twelve nautical mile territorial sea and EEZ to support its claims to '"haiyang guoto" (national maritime territory)'.[124] The objectives of the new policy were to 'safeguard China's territorial waters, coastal economy, sea lanes of communication, and the Exclusive Economic Zones', as well as to 'deter Taiwanese independence' and modernise China's naval forces.[125] China's control purported to extend into two zones: 'the first . . . [encompassing] the Yellow Sea opposite Japan and the Korean Peninsula; the western part of the East China Sea, including Taiwan; and the South China Sea', the second 'delineated by the "second island chain" . . . a north–south line which goes through the Kurile Islands and Japan, and then takes a more eastern course through the Bonin, Mariana and Caroline Islands'.[126] As Howarth observes, '[t]he control of this geographic zone . . . would secure for the PRC control of the whole of East Asia's oceanic area' and '[t]he achievement of this goal implicitly assumes the withdrawal of the United States' military presence from the region'.[127] China's continued investment in its submarine fleet

[121] 'AUKUS Joint Leaders Statement', *US Embassy Canberra*, 14 March 2023 <https://au.usembassy.gov/aukus-joint-leaders-statement/>.

[122] Ibid.

[123] Australian Submarine Agency, 'Submarine Rotational Force West', 2 October 2024 <www.asa.gov.au/aukus/submarine-rotational-force-west>.

[124] Huang (n 93) 194, 344; Alexander Chieh-cheng Huang, 'The Chinese Navy's Offshore Active Defense Strategy' (1994) 47(3) *Naval War College Review* 1, 16–25.

[125] Huang (n 93) 203–204.

[126] Peter Howarth, *China's Rising Sea Power: The PLA Navy's Submarine Challenge* (Routledge, 2006) 41–42.

[127] Ibid, 41–42.

and SSNs in particular is,[128] according to Howarth, chiefly directed towards preventing US access to its littoral waters or freedom of action in waters up to 200 miles off its coast and in the Taiwan Strait in particular.[129] PLA Navy submarines would also play a role in any future blockade of Taiwan.[130]

Other States possessing SSBNs also deploy these vessels in deterrence patrols. The British Navy keeps Vanguard-class submarines carrying the Trident missile system on patrol as a 'continuous at sea deterrent'.[131] France also keeps at least one Triomphant-class SSBN on patrol at all times.[132] India completed its first SSBN patrol in 2018 and now has two Arihant class SSBNs, with a further two planned for construction.[133] In 2023, China was reported as 'for the first time keeping at least one nuclear-armed ballistic missile submarine constantly at sea', with 'China's fleet of six Jin-class ballistic missile submarines ... operating "near-continuous" patrols from Hainan Island into the South China Sea'.[134] Russia conducts periodic rather than continuous deterrent patrols, though in the context of the Russo-Ukrainian War and following the accession of Finland and Sweden to NATO in 2023 and 2024 respectively, Norwegian intelligence reports suggest Russia is extending the patrols of SSBNs in its Northern Fleet as a regional deterrent.[135] Russia currently operates five Delta IV SSBNs and seven Borei SSBNs, which are divided between its Northern and Pacific Fleets.[136] Russia's Black Sea Fleet does not include SSBNs but does include small attack submarines

128 Nuclear Threat Initiative, 'China Submarine Capabilities Fact Sheet' (n 90).

129 Howarth (n 126) 97.

130 Ibid, 48–56.

131 UK Ministry of Defence, 'The UK's Nuclear Deterrent: What You Need to Know', 28 March 2024 <www.gov.uk/government/publications/uk-nuclear-deterrence-factsheet/uk-nuclear-deterrence-what-you-need-to-know>.

132 Xavier Vavasseur, 'France Launches Third Generation SSBN Program – SNLE 3G', *Naval News*, 21 February 2021 <www.navalnews.com/naval-news/2021/02/france-launches-third-generation-ssbn-program-snle-3g/>.

133 Nuclear Threat Initiative, 'India Submarine Capabilities Fact Sheet' (n 109).

134 Greg Torode and Eduardo Baptista 'China's Intensifying Nuclear-armed Submarine Patrols add Complexity for US Allies', *Reuters*, 4 April 2023 <www.reuters.com/world/chinas-intensifying-nuclear-armed-submarine-patrols-add-complexity-us-allies-2023-04-04/>.

135 Maxim Starchak, 'Russia to Lengthen Submarine Patrols, says Norwegian Intel Report', *DefenseNews*, 17 February 2023 <www.defensenews.com/global/europe/2023/02/16/russia-to-lengthen-submarine-patrols-says-norwegian-intel-report/>.

136 Hans M. Kirstensen et al., 'Russian Nuclear Weapons, 2024', *Bulletin of the Atomic Scientists*, 7 March 2024 <https://thebulletin.org/premium/2024-03/russian-nuclear-weapons-2024/>.

capable of launching long-range cruise missiles.[137] Notably, underwater maritime autonomous vehicles (UMAVs) carrying explosives have recently become an important element of Ukraine's response to Russia in the Black Sea.[138] Given these ongoing strategic uses and benefits of military submarines, the articulation of the legal framework within which they must operate becomes a more pressing question for resolution.

These contemporary security settings prompt a variety of questions for international law. For example, the United States' Freedom of Navigation Operations (FONOPS), while chiefly intended to 'operationally challenge' what the United States considers 'excessive maritime claims' including 'a variety of restrictions on the exercise of navigation and overflight rights and other freedoms and lawful uses of the seas', can also be understood to involve power projection.[139] These exercises have included the passage of submarines without prior notification or authorisation in the territorial sea and the submerged passage of submarines in waters considered subject to transit passage or archipelagic sea lane passage, as well as the conduct of military exercises involving submarines in the EEZ of another State.[140] The legal questions engaged by the latter exercise of navigational rights are discussed in Chapters 7 and 8 of this book. The deployment of nuclear-powered submarines and SSBNs in the maritime zones of another State may also raise questions regarding the threat of the use of force – an issue addressed in Chapter 9. The ongoing conduct of military exercises in the EEZ of another State is a particularly contentious issue, and the legality of such exercises during times of peace is discussed in Chapter 8.

The role of submarines in intelligence gathering did not end with the Cold War and again the legality of this activity in the EEZ of another State is a matter of contention that will be discussed in Chapter 8. Chapter 7 also considers the lawfulness of data collection by submarines transiting

[137] Igor Delanoë, 'Russia's Black Sea Fleet in the "Special Military Operation" in Ukraine' (Foreign Policy Research Institute Report, 2024) <www.fpri.org/article/2024/02/russias-black-sea-fleet-in-the-special-military-operation-in-ukraine/>.

[138] H. I. Sutton, 'Exclusive: New Ukrainian Underwater Drone Project to Dominate the Black Sea', *NavalNews*, 24 January 2024 <www.navalnews.com/naval-news/2024/01/exclusive-new-ukrainian-underwater-drone-project-to-dominate-the-black-sea/>. See further Chapter 14.

[139] US Department of Defense, 'DOD Releases Fiscal Year 2023 Freedom of Navigation Report' (Media Release, 8 May 2024) <www.defense.gov/News/Releases/Release/Article/3769479/dod-releases-fiscal-year-2023-freedom-of-navigation-report/>.

[140] See generally J. Ashley Roach and Robert W. Smith, *Excessive Maritime Claims* (3rd ed., Martinus Nijhoff, 2012).

straits. The capacity of submarines to tap submarine cables or lay cables for the purposes of underwater surveillance raises its own set of legal questions. While UNCLOS provides for the criminalisation of the 'breaking or injury' of a submarine cable 'wilfully or through culpable negligence' in the EEZ or high seas,[141] the legality of intelligence gathering by tapping undersea cables is only clearly prohibited in the territorial sea and not otherwise expressly regulated by the law of the sea.[142] Chapter 8 considers the legality of this activity, while Chapter 9 asks whether and when intelligence gathering might constitute an unlawful threat of the use of force.

The role of submarines in scientific research may be a complicating factor in cases involving allegations of covert intelligence gathering for military purposes, as these operations may coincide or overlap – oceanographic information may also have military applications.[143] Conversely, ASW technologies may be used for scientific research purposes. The SOSUS hydrophone array, which was built for tracking Soviet submarines 'under the cover of civilian oceanographic research',[144] is now used for seismic and marine mammal monitoring.[145] UMAVs are also used in scientific research – for example, to map the seafloor and record measurements and other observations.[146] These technologies may also be used in seabed mining operations.[147] The legal questions associated with these developments are discussed in Chapter 14. The role of UMAVs in military operations and in both perpetrating and responding to other maritime security threats such as terrorism and drug smuggling will also be discussed in Chapter 14.

The threat that submarines, particularly nuclear-powered and nuclear-armed submarines, pose to the environment is considered in Chapter 12. As Chapters 11 and 12 of this book elaborate, laws and regulations

141 UNCLOS (n 2) art. 113. Article 113 applies to the EEZ via Article 58(2): see Tara Davenport, 'Submarine Cables, Cybersecurity and International Law' (2015) 24(1) *Catholic University Journal of Law and Technology* 57, 77.

142 Davenport (n 142) 103–109.

143 See Chapter 8, Section 8.3.1.2.

144 UK Royal Navy, 'Listening to the Ocean: The Secretive Enablers in the Underwater Battle', *Navy Lookout*, 22 December 2017 <www.navylookout.com/listening-to-the-ocean-the-secretive-enablers-in-the-underwater-battle/>.

145 See US National Oceanic and Atmospheric Administration, 'SOund SUrveillance System (SOSUS) – Scientific Applications' <www.pmel.noaa.gov/acoustics/sosus_apps.html>.

146 William Stoichevski, 'Subsea Mining: The Next Big Thing for UUVs', *Marine Technology News*, April 2019 <www.marinetechnologynews.com/news/subsea-mining-thing-588211>.

147 See e.g., ibid.

relating to navigational safety are closely linked to the management of these risks. Sunken submarines may represent a navigational hazard and also engage laws of salvage and questions of underwater cultural heritage. Nuclear waste from Cold War submarines (including reactors) is known to have been dumped at sea and some of the vessels themselves were also sunk as a means of disposal or as a result of accidents.[148] The post–Cold War period has seen further accidents including collisions involving submarines, beginning with the 1992 collision of a US SSN and Russian SSN near the Russian port of Severomorsk.[149] As UMAVs increase in use, navigational safety rules may also need to be adapted to respond to the contemporary development of submarine technologies.

6.6 Conclusion to Part I

Part I of this book has demonstrated the interplay between the evolution of submarine technologies and activities and developments in international law bearing upon their regulation. This historical perspective is of more than antiquarian interest: past events and circumstances have left a significant mark on the current law, which in some cases retains rules formulated in response to technologies and practices that have since changed. From the chapters in this Part, efforts at regulation have been apparent in several specific domains. First, the passage of submarines in territorial waters, including in straits, was a concern for coastal States with these States seemingly relying on their sovereignty as the basis to impose conditions on passage of foreign warships, including (sometimes explicitly) submarines. These restrictions were initially focused on times of war but ultimately extended to times of peace. Second, the devastation wrought by submarine warfare prompted proposals to ban submarines, or reduce their number, or otherwise impose requirements on submarines comparable to those of warships on the surface. These efforts were mostly unsuccessful because of the strategic importance of submarines in States' naval forces. The push for disarmament and non-proliferation

[148] Paul Marks, 'How Do You Dismantle a Submarine?', *BBC News*, 30 March 2015 <www.bbc.com/future/article/20150330-where-nuclear-subs-go-to-die>; Alec Luhn, 'Russia's "Slow-motion Chernobyl" at Sea', *BBC News*, 2 September 2020 <www.bbc.com/future/article/20200901-the-radioactive-risk-of-sunken-nuclear-soviet-submarines>. See also Chapter 12, Section 12.1.

[149] Peter Suciu, 'Why A Russian Sierra-Class Nuclear Submarine and US Sub Collided in 1992', *National Interest*, 3 December 2023 <https://nationalinterest.org/blog/buzz/why-russian-sierra-class-nuclear-submarine-and-us-sub-collided-1992-207694>.

became more concerted with the advent of nuclear submarines but again has enjoyed only modest success. Finally, the deployment of submarines for covert operations and intelligence gathering has also served the strategic interests of naval powers, with the primary regulatory response to be insisting on submarines surfacing in territorial waters to protect the security interests of coastal States. While some of the early laws anticipated greater private ownership of submarines, submarines have predominantly had military applications and been regulated accordingly.

Our discussion of the legal history of submarines has demonstrated that critical questions thus arise about the capacity of the law to regulate contemporary submarine technologies and activities. It is important to bear in mind that the law of the sea together with other areas of law applying to submarines (for instance, laws relating to armed conflict and the use of force more broadly, or international environmental law) have been developed with an awareness of the fact that the technologies and practices they regulate are likely to evolve. While gaps may still emerge or existing forms of regulation may appear excessive or inappropriate in relation to new developments, both the adaptability of the law and its responses to new developments in practice are important features of the legal landscape (or seascape) as it relates to submarines. The historical positions of States with respect to the legal regulation of submarines either *qua* submarines or as warships or commercial vessels engaged in varied types of activities – and changes in these positions over time – are also of doctrinal interest insofar as they may bear upon contemporary claims regarding treaty interpretation, customary law or a State's status as a persistent objector.

In turning to the contemporary international laws governing the operations of submarines, it will be seen that relatively few rules and principles of international law explicitly address the use of submarines. The requirement in Article 20 of UNCLOS that foreign submarines travel on the surface and show their flag when passing through the territorial sea is a notable example, as are the various arms limitation treaties that have sought to restrict the number of submarines within the naval forces of participating States. Yet this minimal explicit regulation does not mean that submarine technologies and activities are unregulated or even under-regulated by international law. In the case of both the 1958 law of the sea treaties and UNCLOS, the intention to capture certain types and uses of submarines can be identified in the drafting history and shaped the resulting treaty text. The progress and use of submarines has influenced the development of international law to a much greater extent than the handful of direct references to these vessels might suggest.

While military submarines dominate strategic policies and legal assessments, the steady growth of private submarines also warrants attention. Most notably, submarines now play a significant role in scientific research, including that connected with the exploitation of marine and particularly seabed resources. There is also a niche market for submarine tourism, which gained wider notoriety after the loss of the *Titan* submersible with its crew and passengers in June 2023,[150] and the sinking of a tourist submarine in the Red Sea off Hurghada, Egypt in March 2025.[151] Many submarine applications, however, continue to capitalise on the distinctive capacity of submarines to avoid detection, not only for State military purposes but also private criminal purposes. The legality of submarine activities can thus vary considerably.

From an international law perspective, the twenty-first century seascape of SSBNs, SSNs, diesel-electric submarines and UMAVs, as well as the enhanced technologies and systems for detecting and in some cases destroying these vessels, may be difficult to traverse with rules and regulations developed with simpler submarine technologies and activities in view or, indeed, without reference to the particularities of submarines at all. Yet as the following chapters will elaborate, the existing law – while not without gaps or points of strain – continues to regulate the activities of modern submarines. It is the purpose of the remainder of this book to clarify the laws that govern submarines today as well as to illuminate areas of ambiguity or gaps in the law that may be addressed by developments in conventional law, customary law or other law-making initiatives.

[150] Discussed in Chapter 11, Sections 11.1 and 11.3.

[151] Raina Khaled and Lynsey Chutel, 'Tourist Submarine Sinks Off Egypt with 6 People Dead', *New York Times*, 27 March 2025 <www.nytimes.com/2025/03/27/world/middleeast/egypt-tourist-submarine-hurghada-red-sea.html>.

PART II

Contemporary International Law of Submarines

7

Regimes of Passage in the Territorial Sea, International Straits and Archipelagic Waters

7.1 Introduction

As evident in the legal developments discussed throughout Part I of the book, one of the most vexing issues relating to submarines concerns their navigational rights and duties through waters closest to land. While the territorial sea and archipelagic waters are subject to the sovereignty of the coastal State,[1] foreign-flagged vessels, including submarines, have rights of passage through these maritime areas. As will be discussed in this chapter, coastal State sovereignty is limited by the right of innocent passage, as well as the right of transit passage in certain international straits and the right of archipelagic sea lane passage through the waters of archipelagic States. Some straits are governed by their own specific passage regimes.[2] The critical issue for each passage regime is the balance between, on the one hand, the sovereignty of the coastal State and the many national interests flowing from that sovereignty and, on the other hand, the navigational interests of other States for any of its vessels (military, government or private).

A clear understanding of the existing international law, especially under the United Nations Convention on the Law of the Sea (UNCLOS),[3] applying to the passage of submarines is necessary in order to determine whether and how far practices or incidents involving submarines conform to or depart from the law. Such an analysis

[1] United Nations Convention on the Law of the Sea, Montego Bay, 10 December 1982, 1833 UNTS 397, arts. 2(1), 49(1) ('UNCLOS').

[2] The UNCLOS provisions relating to transit passage do not apply to straits 'in which passage is regulated in whole or in part by long-standing international conventions in force specifically relating to such straits': ibid art. 35(c). The legal regime established under the Montreux Convention and its relevance for submarines is discussed in Chapter 4, Section 4.4.

[3] UNCLOS (n 1).

nevertheless exposes regulatory difficulties. Moreover, while it is of critical importance to know whether certain practices are lawful, it might also be asked whether common departures from the law suggest a need to amend or further develop it – either to admit the activity in question or to better facilitate its suppression or regulation. These questions will be addressed in the discussion below. As we shall see, the laws of passage have been shaped in interesting ways by past submarine technologies and activities as well as by expectations regarding their future development; however, submarines are often covered by more broadly applicable rules – as merchant vessels or warships, and, increasingly, as '[f]oreign nuclear-powered ships and ships carrying nuclear or other inherently dangerous or noxious substances'.[4]

In order to analyse the existing laws relating to submarine passage through the territorial sea, international straits or archipelagic waters, the rules of treaty interpretation have especial importance given the detailed rules set out in UNCLOS on regimes of passage in the territorial sea, international straits and archipelagic waters. As the discussion in this chapter highlights, it is illuminating to refer to the 'preparatory work' of the law of the sea treaties and 'the circumstances of [their] conclusion', which may be drawn on as a 'supplementary means of [treaty] interpretation'.[5] More generally, the historical context in which the rules of passage were developed may bear upon an assessment of the adequacy of these rules in connection with new types of submarines and submarine activities today. 'Subsequent agreement between the parties regarding the interpretation of the treaty or the application of its provisions' and 'any subsequent practice in the application of the treaty which establishes the agreement of the parties regarding its interpretation' have even greater priority in an interpretation of the treaty law.[6] Regimes of passage may also be governed by customary international law, and State practice with respect to the passage of submarines will bear upon the question of whether customary rights or obligations claimed by States are in fact established.

The contemporary rules of passage reflect their historic antecedents, which were examined in detail in Part I of this book. The primary focus of

[4] See, e.g., ibid, arts. 22, 23. These submarines are referred to as 'nuclear submarines' in this Chapter unless the fact that the submarines are nuclear-powered or nuclear-armed warrants a distinction.

[5] Vienna Convention on the Law of Treaties, Vienna, 23 May 1969, entered into force 27 January 1980, 1155 UNTS 331, art. 32.

[6] Ibid, art. 31.

this chapter concerns the current rules of innocent passage in the territorial sea, as some of the issues concerning that passage provide contrast or remain applicable in relation to certain international straits or in archipelagic waters. In the case of the passage of foreign submarines in the territorial sea, Section 7.2 addresses requirements for innocent passage, the use of sea lanes for different types of submarine (such as nuclear-powered submarines), the issue of prior notification or authorisation, and permissible responses to a submarine's violation of passage rights. It is in passage through the territorial sea that submarines are singled out for specific regulation, in addition to being bound by rules that are equally applicable to warships and/or private vessels. Section 7.3 considers transit passage in international straits and Section 7.4 turns to passage in archipelagic waters and the requirements of archipelagic sea lane passage. Through this discussion, we seek to articulate – to the extent possible – the international law rules governing the passage of submarines through waters closest to coastal States.

7.2 Submarine Passage through the Territorial Sea

A coastal State's sovereignty over its territorial sea both entitles it to a variety of rights and entails certain obligations in relation to the passage of foreign-flagged submarines. As noted in Article 2(3) of UNCLOS, a coastal State's sovereignty over its territorial sea 'is exercised subject to' UNCLOS and 'to other rules of international law'. The scope of what may fall within the 'other rules of international law' has been a source of speculation before tribunals constituted under the UNCLOS dispute settlement regime.[7] Such 'other rules of international law' may potentially be relevant for submarine passage if a coastal State has entered into a defence agreement with another State that sets out specific rules and requirements.[8]

[7] See *Chagos Marine Protected Area Arbitration* (Mauritius v. United Kingdom) (Award of 18 March 2015) PCA Case No. 2011-03, paras. 515–517; *South China Sea Arbitration* (Philippines v. China) (Award of 12 July 2016) PCA Case No. 2013-19, para. 780. For discussion, see Natalie Klein and Kate Parlett, *Judging the Law of the Sea* (Oxford University Press, 2022) 147–156, 181–183.

[8] Defence agreements may provide for more extensive or restrictive passage rights for submarines. Notably, the US Visiting Forces Agreement with the Philippines provides in Article VIII that 'Vessels operated by or for the United States armed forces may enter the Philippines *upon approval of the Government of the Philippines*. The movement of vessels shall be in accordance with international custom and practice governing such vessels, and such agreed implementing arrangements as necessary' (emphasis added). As discussed

Part II of UNCLOS sets out a series of provisions that hold relevance for the passage of submarines through the territorial sea of another State. Under the modern law of the sea, it is well established that submarines, like other 'ships', 'enjoy the right of innocent passage through the territorial sea'.[9] While neither the 1958 Territorial Sea Convention nor UNCLOS expressly identify submarines as 'ships' – and, indeed, Article 20 of UNCLOS refers to 'submarines and other underwater *vehicles*' (emphasis added) – both instruments specify conditions for the passage of submarines through the territorial sea within a section addressing innocent passage through the territorial sea generally and a subsection titled 'Rules Applicable to All Ships'.[10]

As discussed in Chapter 1, submarines will also qualify as 'warships' where they meet the legal definition set out in Article 29 of UNCLOS.[11] The practice of States in armed conflict, including the enactment and enforcement of neutrality laws in World War I and World War II discussed in earlier chapters, shows that submarines belonging to a State's armed forces have been widely recognised as warships. Rules relating to submarines were originally located under the provisions on warships but were moved to the general provisions to make clear that they would apply equally to merchant submarines. Although submarines had not in fact played a significant role in merchant shipping beyond their historical use in blockade running, the general applicability of the requirement that submarines navigate on the surface and show their flag may prove useful if new types of submarine vessels are further developed for commercial purposes. Foreign submarines used for private purposes – such as research, leisure and tourism – would also be covered by the rules applicable to 'all ships' passing through the territorial sea.

below, the United States denies that prior authorisation can be required for the passage of submarines in the territorial sea, so presumably considers its consent to this arrangement to support an exception to the usual rule. The Philippines, however, requires prior notification and authorisation for the passage of warships in its territorial sea and archipelagic waters (though it has not specified this obligation in domestic laws or regulations): Anh Duc Ton, 'Innocent Passage of Warships: International Law and the Practice of East Asian Littoral States' (2016) 1 *Asia-Pacific Journal of Ocean Law and Policy* 210, 233.

9 UNCLOS (n 1) art. 17; Convention on the Territorial Sea and Contiguous Zone, Geneva, 29 April 1958, entered into force 10 September 1964, 516 UNTS 205, art. 14(1) ('1958 Territorial Sea Convention').

10 1958 Territorial Sea Convention (n 9) ss. A, art. 14; UNCLOS (n 1) pt. II, ss. A, arts. 17, 20.

11 Chapter 1, Section 1.3.

The section immediately below addresses the applicability of Part II of UNCLOS based on the classification of submarines as 'ships' or 'warships'. It further addresses the requirements for lawful passage, notably the requirements for innocent passage and to surface and show the flag. The designation of sea lanes also has relevance for surfaced submarines, especially nuclear submarines. The extent of coastal State control over the territorial sea and hence the passage of submarines therein further raises legal questions as to any conditions a coastal State may impose and what a coastal State may do in response to a violation of its laws, or a violation of the international law rights of passage. Any response must account for the sovereign immunity enjoyed by a military submarine as a warship or other government vessel operated on non-commercial service.

7.2.1 *Innocent Passage in the Territorial Sea*

Ships, including submarines, enjoy the right of innocent passage through the territorial sea of any State under Article 17 of UNCLOS. UNCLOS defines 'passage' as being 'for the purpose of':

> (a) traversing that sea without entering internal waters or calling at a roadstead or port facility outside internal waters; or
> (b) proceeding to or from internal waters or a call at such roadstead or port facility.[12]

In addition, passage must be 'continuous and expeditious', though it may include 'stopping and anchoring, but only in so far as the same are incidental to ordinary navigation or are rendered necessary by force majeure or distress or for the purpose of rendering assistance to persons, ships or aircraft in danger or distress'.[13]

For passage to be 'innocent', it must not be prejudicial to the 'peace, good order or security' of the coastal State.[14] To understand how a submarine's passage may not prejudice the peace, good order or security of the coastal State, it is important to have regard to the manner of passage[15] and the possible activities deemed as prejudicial under Article 19(2) of UNCLOS. Article 19(2) lists a number of activities, including:

[12] UNCLOS (n 1) art. 18(1).
[13] Ibid, art. 18(2).
[14] Ibid, art. 19(1).
[15] Natalie Klein, *Maritime Security and the Law of the Sea* (Oxford University Press, 2011) 31–32.

(a) any threat or use of force against the sovereignty, territorial integrity or political independence of the coastal State, or in any other manner in violation of the principles of international law embodied in the Charter of the United Nations;
(b) any exercise or practice with weapons of any kind;
(c) any act aimed at collecting information to the prejudice of the defence or security of the coastal State;
(d) any act of propaganda aimed at affecting the defence or security of the coastal State;
(e) the launching, landing or taking on board of any aircraft;
(f) the launching, landing or taking on board of any military device;
(g) the loading or unloading of any commodity, currency or person contrary to the customs, fiscal, immigration or sanitary laws and regulations of the coastal State;
(h) any act of wilful and serious pollution contrary to this Convention;
(i) any fishing activities;
(j) the carrying out of research or survey activities;
(k) any act aimed at interfering with any systems of communication or any other facilities or installations of the coastal State;
(l) any other activity not having a direct bearing on passage.

Many of these activities are clearly within the functional capabilities of submarines, which are commonly designed and equipped to engage in military exercises and intelligence-gathering and may also play a role in marine scientific research. It is evident that conducting these activities in a foreign State's territorial sea would render passage of that submarine non-innocent. Kraska has observed that the intelligence-gathering of submarines that prejudices a neighbouring State, rather than the coastal State, may not fall within non-innocent passage.[16] However, the intelligence-gathering may still be considered an activity not having a direct bearing on passage and thus non-innocent. The passage of privately owned submarines under the flag of a foreign State, including underwater maritime autonomous vehicles (UMAVs), would also be rendered non-innocent should they engage in any of the activities listed as 'prejudicial to the peace, good order or security of the coastal State'.

It is worth drawing particular attention to the final reference in Article 19(2) of UNCLOS to 'any other activity not having a direct bearing on passage'. Engaging in any activity not directly bearing on passage will be considered 'prejudicial to the peace, good order or

[16] James Kraska, 'Putting Your Head in the Tiger's Mouth: Submarine Espionage in Territorial Sea' (2015) 54 *Columbia Journal of Transnational Law* 164, 219.

security of the coastal State' – rendering passage non-innocent. This clause more broadly suggests that the list of 'prejudicial activities' in Article 19(2) is open-ended, and may be expanded upon to include new activities, including those associated with the development of new technologies – at least insofar as these technologies/activities do not have a direct bearing on passage. However, the United States and former Soviet Union signed a joint Declaration in 1989 stating inter alia that 'Article 19 of [UNCLOS] sets out in paragraph 2 an *exhaustive* list of activities that would render passage not innocent'.[17] Lowe suggests that this Declaration has given 'provisions that have already found their way into the legislation of states such as France a (probably decisive) push into customary law'.[18] More exactly, these provisions support the conclusion that customary law recognises the activities listed in Article 19(2) as rendering passage non-innocent. However, there remains scope for identifying further activities rendering passage 'non-innocent' under the heading of 'any other activity not having a direct bearing on passage'. Of course, activities that do have 'a direct bearing on passage' may also evolve with shipping technology – as Kaye observes '[n]ormal navigation will require some forms of data gathering to take place' though other data collection activities may compromise the innocence of passage.[19] Where that data gathering crosses the line into an activity that is prejudicial to peace, good order or security of the coastal State remains a core difficulty.[20]

17 United States of America-Union of Soviet Socialist Republics Joint Statement on the Uniform Interpretation of Rules of International Law Governing Innocent Passage, Wyoming, 23 September 1989, para. 3 (emphasis added) ('USA-USSR Joint Statement'). Interestingly, in 1958 the United States 'did not believe it was necessary to mention the kind of acts that rendered passage no longer innocent': United Nations Conference on the Law of the Sea, *Official Records*, vol. 3 (UN Doc. A/CONF.13/39) 76 ('UNCLOS I, *Official Records*'). While the International Chamber of Shipping and subsequently Germany had been critical of the open-ended character of Article 19(2)(l) during UNCLOS negotiations, there is no record of the United States expressing such a view and the open-ended provision was adopted. Though the United States did not go on to become a party to UNCLOS, it did express the view that the provisions on innocent passage 'codify existing rules of international law', which, as such, it would respect: Renate Platzöder, *Third United Nations Conference on the Law of the Sea: Documents*, 15 vols. (Oceana Publications, 1987) vol. 13, 42–43.

18 Vaughan Lowe, 'Uniform Interpretation of the Rules of International Law Governing Innocent Passage' (1991) 6(1) *Journal of Estuarine and Coastal Law* 73, 73.

19 Stuart Kaye, 'Freedom of Navigation, Surveillance and Security: Legal Issues Surrounding the Collection of Intelligence from Beyond the Littoral' (2005) 93 *Australian Yearbook of International Law* 93, 96.

20 Kraska (n 16) 222–223.

For submarines, their innocent passage must conform to other requirements set out in UNCLOS. Article 20 of UNCLOS (like Article 14(6) of the 1958 Territorial Sea Convention) provides that 'submarines and other underwater vehicles are required to navigate on the surface and to show their flag' when passing through the territorial sea.[21] A question arising in relation to the definition of innocent passage in the 1958 Territorial Sea Convention and UNCLOS is whether a failure to comply with the requirement that submarines 'navigate on the surface and ... show their flag' can itself render passage non-innocent. It is clear that the passage of a submarine that complies with the requirement to 'navigate on the surface and to show their flag' could still be non-innocent if it engages in any activity that is 'prejudicial to the peace, good order or security of the coastal State'. It is less clear whether the passage of a submarine that fails to comply with either or both the requirement to navigate on the surface and show its flag can be considered non-innocent for this reason alone.

To resolve this question, it may first be observed that the requirement to navigate on the surface and show the flag is located in Article 20, a separate provision following Article 19 on the '[m]eaning of innocent passage' and preceding Article 21 on '[l]aws and regulations of the coastal State relating to innocent passage'. Article 19(1) of UNCLOS provides in full that:

> Passage is innocent so long as it is not prejudicial to the peace, good order or security of the coastal State. *Such passage shall take place in conformity with this Convention and with other rules of international law.*[22]

Submerged passage is not listed as an activity rendering passage non-innocent under Article 19(2). Yet submerged passage is not merely one among other '[l]aws and regulations of the coastal State' that may apply to passage through the territorial sea. Rather, it is given independent status as a provision of the Convention with which innocent passage 'shall take place in conformity'.[23] Even if it is argued that passage through the territorial sea by a submarine that is either or both submerged and not displaying its flag does not render passage non-innocent, that passage is still in violation of international law because of the distinct requirements in Article 20.

[21] UNCLOS (n 1) art. 20; 1958 Territorial Sea Convention (n 10) art. 14(6).

[22] This wording reflects near identical text to Article 14(4) of the Territorial Sea Convention (n 10) (emphasis added).

[23] UNCLOS (n 1) art. 19(1).

To resolve any outstanding ambiguities as to whether a failure to meet the requirements of Article 20 constitutes non-innocent passage, regard may be had to the drafting history. In relation to Article 14(4) of the 1958 Territorial Sea Convention, which reflects the wording of Article 19(1) of UNCLOS, it appears that States intentionally drew a distinction between the requirements for innocent passage and the requirement to comply with other provisions in that Convention and 'other rules of international law'. The International Law Commission's (ILC) 1956 draft article 15 on the 'meaning of the right of innocent passage' had provided in paragraph 3 that '[p]assage is innocent so long as a ship does not use the territorial sea for committing any acts prejudicial to the security of the coastal State or contrary to the present rules, or other rules of international law'.[24] Paragraph 5 of the same article provided that '[s]ubmarines are required to navigate on the surface'. As Norway and Denmark observed, this formulation suggested that a failure to navigate on the surface would independently render the passage of a submarine non-innocent as 'contrary to the present rules'. At the 1958 Conference, however, the ILC's text was reformulated to provide in Article 14(4) of the 1958 Territorial Sea Convention that

> Passage is innocent so long as it is not prejudicial to the peace, good order or security of the coastal State. Such passage shall take place in conformity with these articles and with other rules of international law.

The separation of the ILC's text into two sentences was the result of revisions to a US proposal that further sought (unsuccessfully) to limit non-innocent passage to that 'prejudicial to the security of the coastal State' and remove the reference to 'other rules of international law'.[25] The United States had explained that '[i]t was the intention of the amendment to indicate that the sole test of the innocence of a passage was whether or not it was prejudicial to the security of the coastal State'. It also stated that '[t]he second sentence of the amendment was meant to indicate that a ship in innocent passage must conform to the laws and regulations of the coastal State. However, such laws and regulations could not prohibit innocent passage'.[26]

[24] International Law Commission, 'Commentary to Articles concerning the Law of the Sea' (1956) 2 *Yearbook of the International Law Commission* 265, 272.

[25] UNCLOS I, *Official Records* (n 17) vol. 3. 82–83, 216.

[26] Ibid, 82–83, 216. Notably, the United States and other States supporting the removal of the reference to 'other rules of international law' here did not deny that such rules applied;

The distinction between the 'the concept of innocence of passage and . . . the obligation of a vessel in passage to conform to the laws and regulations of the coastal State' was expressly endorsed by the United Kingdom, which considered that '[t]hose two aspects had not been clearly set out in the International Law Commission's draft'.[27] Israel also approved of 'the distinction drawn between the innocence of the passage and the conformity with rules',[28] as did Norway, observing that '[t]he paragraph dealt with two distinct questions: firstly, the conditions which had to be fulfilled by a ship in order that its passage should be innocent; and secondly, the extent of the jurisdiction of the coastal State'.[29] As these observations indicate, the chief concern seems to have been to prevent the coastal State imposing rules that would effectively undermine a right of innocent passage. Other States clearly considered a failure to comply with 'the present rules' or 'other rules of international law' to render passage non-innocent.[30]

When UNCLOS was negotiated, it was specifically proposed, first by the United Arab Emirates and then the Group of Arab States, that the provision on submarines should be amended to indicate that a failure to travel on the surface or show their flag would render passage non-innocent.[31] These proposals, however, were made in 1976 when an Informal Single Negotiating Text had already been prepared as the basis for negotiations and only informal amendments were admitted for consideration by the Chairman of the Second Committee, who 'would judge whether an amendment had majority support in the light of statements and consultations'.[32] There is no record of the informal meetings in which these proposals were made, nor of the reasoning underpinning the decision not to include the proposed amendments in the Revised Single Negotiating Text. It is thus likely that the Chairman did not consider the amendment to have majority support. Whether that support was lacking because the text was already considered to render 'such passage' as innocent when in conformity with Article 20 remains

rather they considered the text both vague and redundant as such rules would apply in any case if consistent with the Convention: Ibid, 75–76, 82–85, 216.

27 Ibid, 83.

28 Ibid.

29 Ibid, 84.

30 See proposals by Saudi Arabia and Burma, as well as a French proposal closer to the ILC text: Ibid, 85, 230.

31 Platzöder (n 17) vol. IV, 268, 270.

32 See Third United Nations Conference on the Law of the Sea, *Official Records*, vol. 5 (UN Doc. A/CONF.62/VOL.5) 99–100 ('UNCLOS III, *Official Records*') on this procedure.

a matter of speculation. Insofar as the text points to two distinct requirements imposed on submarines, submerged passage may still raise the suspicions of the coastal State that the vessel is not engaged in innocent passage.[33]

The question of whether submergence or a failure to show the flag would also render a submarine's passage non-innocent remains legally significant insofar as it bears upon the ability of the coastal State to respond to such violations. Article 25 of UNCLOS provides that '[t]he coastal State may take the necessary steps in its territorial sea to prevent passage *which is not innocent*'.[34] If a failure to comply with the conditions for passage set out in Article 20 of UNCLOS does render passage non-innocent, the coastal State has authority to take 'the necessary steps' in response. Coastal State responses are discussed further below in Section 7.2.4.

Kraska has argued that the current US position is that submarines may enter submerged into a territorial sea as a form of lawful non-innocent passage.[35] Interestingly, this position reflects an understanding that submergence is independently sufficient to render passage non-innocent. More controversially, it entails considering the right of innocent passage as 'a privilege that may be accepted or rejected'.[36] If rejected, Kraska has argued that there still exists other grounds for transiting another State's territorial sea, as rights accruing from force majeure may indicate.[37] Kraska posits that 'recognition of non-innocent passage simply means that the transit is not illegal, but it is also neither a right nor protected'.[38] A core difficulty with this position is its dissonance with State sovereignty. If the 'privilege' of innocent passage is not accepted, all that remains is the sovereignty of the coastal State over its territorial sea. In that situation of a rejected privilege, a foreign warship entering without the consent of the coastal State violates that sovereign territory. The grounds to enter a territorial sea because of a force majeure would constitute circumstances precluding the wrongfulness of what would

[33] Barnes writes that 'a better approach [than making surfaced passage a requirement of innocent passage] would be to permit coastal States to have regard to this factor as a means of determining the character of passage': Richard Barnes, 'Article 20' in Alexander Proelss (ed.), *The United Nations Convention on the Law of the Sea: A Commentary* (CH Beck; Hart; Nomos, 2017) 199, para. 8.

[34] Emphasis added.

[35] Kraska (n 16) 227–228.

[36] Ibid, 226.

[37] Ibid.

[38] Ibid.

otherwise be a violation of State sovereignty. Where a submarine undertakes intelligence-gathering submerged in the territorial sea of another State, that submarine is in violation of the right of innocent passage and the obligation to voyage on the surface in another State's territorial sea, as required under Article 20 of UNCLOS. It is also likely violating obligations of non-interference in the domestic affairs of a State.[39]

A remaining question is whether Article 20 of UNCLOS currently reflects customary international law. If not, States that are not parties to UNCLOS, like the United States, would have further reason for their submarines not to surface when engaged in passage through the territorial sea. The rule in Article 20 can be traced back to neutrality laws put in place during World War I. At that time, the submerged passage of belligerent submarines in neutral territorial waters was construed as a violation of coastal State laws regulating passage. For example, the Netherlands seized German submarines found in its territorial waters and Germany protested the seizure due to navigational errors rather than arguing that there was a right to submerged passage.[40] Noting the specific threats of submarines during World War I, Spain was one of first States to articulate the requirement of neutral submarines to navigate on the surface and 'conspicuously' display their national flag.[41] Similar requirements were adopted in neutrality laws and agreements in the context of World War II.[42] The requirement to surface in the territorial sea was not, however, purely considered a requirement during times of armed conflict. Early scholarly efforts at codification had encompassed the principle in their work,[43] and a provision reflected this obligation in the draft

39 Spying arguably violates this principle and State sovereignty. See Dieter Fleck, 'Individual and State Responsibility for Intelligence Gathering' (2007) 28(3) *Michigan Journal of International Law* 687, 692–693. Even Kraska confirms that this position is the 'conventional view' and that espionage in the territory of another State is 'illegal per se': Kraska (n 16) 181. An alternative perspective on spying under international law is considered in Asaf Lubin, 'The Liberty to Spy' (2020) 61(1) *Harvard International Law Journal* 185.

40 Amry Vandenbosch, *The Neutrality of The Netherlands During the World War* (WB Eerdmans, 1927) 88–92. See Chapter 2, Section 2.4.1.

41 Royal Decree Regarding the Treatment of Submarines in Spanish Territorial Waters, 29 June 1917 in Francis Deak and Phillip C. Jessup, *A Collection of Neutrality Laws, Regulations and Treaties of Various Countries* (Carnegie, 1939) vol. 2, 939–940. Norway also set out such a requirement: Royal Resolution regarding Belligerent Submarines in Norwegian Waters, 13 October 1916 in Deak and Jessup (n 41) vol. 2, 842. Other States at this time insisted on submarines being treated comparably to other warships. See Chapter 2, Sections 2.4.4 and 2.4.5.

42 See Chapter 4, Section 4.6.

43 As evident in the work of the Institut de Droit International and the Harvard Research project. See Chapter 3, Sections 3.6.1 and 3.6.3.

articles prepared at the 1930 Hague Codification Conference.[44] The rule was codified in the 1958 Territorial Sea Convention,[45] and was readily accepted during UNCLOS negotiations.[46] The requirement to navigate on the surface has been reflected in national military manuals,[47] and States have routinely protested instances where submarines have been detected submerged in the territorial sea during times of peace.[48] The insistence that submarines may stay submerged during transit passage, as discussed in Section 7.3.1, affirms the view that foreign-flagged submarines must otherwise be surfaced in maritime areas under the sovereignty of the coastal State. While the customary international law status of Article 20 has not been articulated in any judicial decision to date, the obligation appears very well-accepted among States. Indeed, it is arguably the clearest international law rule that exists with regards to submarines.

7.2.2 *Permissible Safety Measures for Innocent Passage*

Beyond requirements of innocent passage and the obligation to surface, nuclear-powered submarines and submarines carrying nuclear weapons or fissionable material ('nuclear submarines') must also comply with Article 23 of UNCLOS. Article 23 provides that '[f]oreign nuclear-powered ships and ships carrying nuclear or other inherently dangerous or noxious substances shall, when exercising the right of innocent passage through the territorial sea, carry documents and observe special precautionary measures established for such ships by international agreements'. Nuclear submarines thus potentially have two additional requirements for passage in the territorial sea by dint of Article 23. The 'special precautionary measures' are to be established 'by international agreements',

[44] See Chapter 3, Section 3.6.4.

[45] 1958 Territorial Sea Convention (n 10) art. 14(6).

[46] There were some proposals during UNCLOS negotiations to allow the coastal State to waive the requirement to navigate on the surface but these were ultimately not accommodated in the wording of Article 20 (and no discretion is admitted in other language versions of the text). Myron H. Nordquist (ed.), *United Nations Convention on the Law of the Sea 1982: A Commentary* (Brill, 1985–2011) vol. 2, 180–183.

[47] See, e.g., *Manual of Armed Forces Law* (2nd ed., New Zealand Defence Force, 2017) vol. 4, para. 10.3.8; Norwegian University Defence College and Norwegian Defence Command and Staff College, *Manual on the Law of Armed Conflict* (Norwegian Ministry of Defence, 2018) para. 10.13. See also James Kraska, Raul Pedrozo and Michael N. Schmitt, 'Annotated Supplement to the Commander's Handbook on the Law of Naval Operations' (2024) 102 *International Law Studies* 1, para. 2.5.2.1.

[48] Examples of this practice are discussed in Kraska (n 16). See also examples discussed in Section 7.2.4.

which ostensibly reduces the authority of the coastal State to impose additional conditions on nuclear submarines unilaterally. While international agreements on the transport of hazardous waste or the carriage of dangerous goods and other material by private vessels are generally relevant,[49] there is no 'international agreement' setting out special precautionary measures applicable to military submarines specifically.[50]

Under the Safety of Life at Sea (SOLAS) Convention, States are allowed to adopt routeing measures, or vessel traffic services, to enhance safety of navigation and/or protect the marine environment.[51] The International Maritime Organization (IMO) has sole responsibility for developing guidelines, criteria or regulations in relation to ship routeing measures, and any State party to the SOLAS Convention should submit specific ship routeing measures to the IMO for adoption.[52] However, there is no *requirement* that any such routeing measures are to be approved at the IMO prior to their implementation by a coastal State. Rather, States are to ensure that their actions, including enforcement actions, relating to ships' routeing are consistent with UNCLOS.[53] In this regard, it is worth recalling the immunity enjoyed by military submarines as well as the inapplicability of SOLAS Convention requirements relating to navigational safety to warships and other government ships operated on non-commercial service.[54]

Yet while the compliance of warships with Chapter V of the SOLAS Convention is only 'encouraged' and not obligatory, Article 21(4) of UNCLOS provides that '[f]oreign ships exercising the right of innocent passage through the territorial sea shall comply with all such laws and regulations [i.e. coastal State laws relating inter alia to 'safety of navigation and the regulation of maritime traffic'] and all generally accepted international regulations relating to the prevention of collisions at sea'. This provision applies to all ships, including military submarines and other warships. In the case of non-compliance, a military submarine

49 The IMO has identified a number of different agreements falling within the scope of Article 23. See Richard Barnes, 'Article 23' in Proelss (n 33) 216, para. 9.

50 See further Chapter 12, Section 12.3.2 (which discusses the limitations on treaties concerning nuclear safety applying to warships and other naval vessels).

51 International Convention for the Safety of Life at Sea, London, 1 November 1974, entered into force 25 May 1980, 1184 UNTS 2, ch. V, regs. 10, 12 ('SOLAS Convention').

52 Ibid, ch. V, regs. 10(b), 10(d).

53 Ibid, ch. V, reg. 10(i).

54 Ibid, ch. V, reg. 1(a)(i).

could be requested to leave the territorial sea in accordance with Article 30 of UNCLOS.

In 2021, China adopted a Maritime Traffic Safety Law that included new reporting rules for 'submersibles' as well as nuclear-powered vessels.[55] These rules apply in China's territorial sea, although there is ambiguity as to the geographic scope of application of these rules in light of China's ongoing and disputed claims in the South China Sea, East China Sea and Yellow Sea.[56] The information to be reported under China's legislation includes the ship's name, IMO number, last and next ports of call and onboard satellite phone number.[57] Other provisions purport to introduce a requirement of compulsory pilotage within the territorial sea for foreign-flagged vessels.[58] If China sought to impose a compulsory pilotage requirement throughout all its claimed territorial sea areas, in relation to all foreign-flagged vessels, the infringement on the right of innocent passage would be manifest as such a general rule would not appear to relate to 'the safety of navigation and the regulation of maritime traffic' or any other matter with respect to which the coastal State may adopt laws and regulations relating to innocent passage under Article 21 of UNCLOS. Any such laws and regulations must also be 'in conformity with the provisions of this Convention and other rules of international law', and in particular cannot 'hamper' innocent passage.[59] Pedrozo has questioned aspects of China's Maritime Traffic Safety Law, especially as to whether the requirements set out in the new legislation have the practical effect of impairing or hampering innocent passage in violation of Article 24 of UNCLOS.[60] A shipping industry commentator has observed, however, that the pilotage regime appears to be operating

[55] Maritime Traffic Safety Law, 1 September 2021 (China). Commentators have suggested that while ostensibly directed at navigational safety, political rhetoric around the new law indicated that the law also seeks to protect China's national sovereignty and security. See, e.g., John Feng, 'China Strengthens Claims Over Disputed Waters With New Maritime Law Against Foreign Ships', *Newsweek*, 31 August 2021 <www.newsweek.com/china-strengthens-claims-over-disputed-waters-new-maritime-law-against-foreign-ships-1624479>.

[56] Raul (Pete) Pedrozo, 'China's Revised Maritime Traffic Safety Law' (2021) 97 *International Law Studies* 956, 957.

[57] Maritime Traffic Safety Law (n 55) art. 3(1).

[58] Ibid, art. 30.

[59] UNCLOS (n 1) arts. 21(1), 24(1).

[60] Pedrozo (n 56) 965.

consistently with existing international standards.[61] Whether China seeks to establish 'pilotage zones' more extensively throughout its claimed maritime areas remains to be seen.

The ship routeing measures that have been most controversial in relation to military submarines (as well as other warships) concern the coastal State's authority to require foreign ships to use specific sea lanes and traffic separation schemes in accordance with Article 22 of UNCLOS. Coastal States may require nuclear submarines to confine their passage through the territorial sea to designated sea lanes given the safety issues associated with 'nuclear-powered ships and ships carrying nuclear or other inherently dangerous or noxious substances or materials'.[62] Sea lanes and traffic separation schemes must take into account '(a) the recommendations of the competent international organization; (b) any channels customarily used for international navigation; (c) the special characteristics of particular ships and channels; and (d) the density of traffic'.[63] The coastal State must 'clearly indicate such sea lanes and traffic separation schemes on charts to which due publicity shall be given'.[64]

The United States has objected to the restriction of the passage of warships to designated sea lanes in the territorial sea.[65] Its objections have been based on two key arguments: one suggesting that it is unlawful to single out certain types of vessels (namely warships) in order to restrict their passage to designated sea lanes,[66] the other insisting that restricting innocent passage to sea lanes is only warranted where necessary to ensure navigational safety.[67] With respect to the first argument, it should be

[61] Andrew Salmon and Jeff Pao, 'China flexes sea power with new foreign ship law' *Asia Times*, 1 September 2021 <https://asiatimes.com/2021/09/china-flexes-sea-power-with-new-foreign-ship-law/>.

[62] UNCLOS (n 1) arts. 22(1), 22(2).

[63] Ibid, art. 22(3).

[64] Ibid, art. 22(4).

[65] See the United States' response to Soviet Rules for Navigation and Sojourn of Foreign Warships in Waters (1983) and subsequent 'Joint Statement on the Uniform Interpretation of Rules of International Law Governing Innocent Passage' (1989) following an incident in 1988 in which Soviet vessels 'bumped' US navy vessels in the Soviet territorial sea: J. Ashley Roach, *Excessive Maritime Claims* (4th ed., Brill Nijhoff, 2021) 252–260. See also the US objection to Article 18 of the Maritime Code of Slovenia (2001), including operations under its Freedom of Navigation programme protesting this law in 2017 and 2018: Office of the Staff Judge Advocate, US Indo-Pacific Command, 'US Freedom of Navigation Program' (2021) 97 *International Law Studies* 70, 74; US Navy JAG Corps, 'Slovenia', *US Maritime Claims Reference Manual*, 2020 <www.jag.navy.mil/organization/code_10_mcrm.htm>.

[66] Roach (n 65) 256–260.

[67] USA-USSR Joint Statement (n 17) para. 5.

noted that Article 22(3) of UNCLOS expressly requires the coastal State to 'take into account . . . the special characteristics of particular ships and channels' in designating sea lanes and traffic separation schemes.[68] Article 22(2) also expressly provides that 'tankers, nuclear-powered ships and ships carrying nuclear or other inherently dangerous or noxious substances or materials may be required to confine their passage to such sea lanes'. These provisions suggest that particular types of vessels may indeed be singled out for regulation through the use of sea lanes. As such, it appears that a coastal State might lawfully 'take into account' the submergibility of submarines and their ability to avoid detection (and potentially lawful regulation) by designating sea lanes allowing appropriate monitoring to ensure compliant passage and/or minimise harm from non-compliant passage.

This conclusion, however, comes up against the United States' second line of reasoning with respect to sea lanes – that, in accordance with Article 22(1) of UNCLOS, they are only warranted 'where necessary having regard to the safety of navigation'. Restricting warships generally or submarines specifically to sea lanes would appear to respond to the coastal State's security concerns rather than what is necessary for navigational safety. This issue raises the question of whether sea lanes may be used for purposes other than safety of navigation. The authors of the Virginia Commentary conclude that the phrase 'where necessary having regard to the safety of navigation' indicates that 'the coastal State may not invoke other interests which it may have in limiting innocent passage' as a justification for restricting passage to designated sea lanes.[69] They also suggest that '[t]his conclusion is reinforced by paragraph 3, in which the factors to be taken into account by the coastal State are all related to the safety of navigation'.[70]

The drafting history shows that a number of States did, indeed, expressly advocate the use of sea lanes as a measure that could be used to manage security and environmental risks as well as navigational safety. Draft articles on navigation submitted to the Seabed Committee by Cyprus, Greece, Indonesia, Malaysia, Morocco, the Philippines, Spain and Yemen had provided that '[f]oreign warships exercising the right of innocent passage may be required to pass through certain sea lanes as may be designated for this purpose by

68 UNCLOS (n 1) art. 22(3).
69 Nordquist (n 46) vol. 2, 211–212.
70 Ibid.

the coastal State'.[71] These proposals were not accepted by all members of the Seabed Committee, and its Second Subcommittee's summary of work in 1973 indicates that there was disagreement on whether the coastal State had a 'right . . . to establish rules applicable to the passage of certain types of ships, including ships with special characteristics, as well as regulations for the protection of the marine environment and for marine pollution' – including the question of whether passage could be limited to designated channels.[72]

During the course of UNCLOS negotiations, the idea that submarines should be restricted to sea lanes seems to have been dropped in view of the requirement that such vessels travel on the surface and show their flag.[73] Nonetheless, the coastal State's right to restrict the passage of 'nuclear-powered ships and ships carrying nuclear . . . materials' to sea lanes was expressly recognised in Article 22(2) of UNCLOS. Article 22(1) appears to set out what is 'necessary having regard to safety of navigation' as a threshold test for the designation of sea lanes, with attention to 'the special characteristics of particular ships' only bearing upon their specification once this test has been passed. However, Article 22(2) disturbs this reading of the provision by identifying the restriction of 'tankers, nuclear-powered ships and ships carrying nuclear or other inherently dangerous or noxious substances or materials' to sea lanes as a 'particular' case of the exercise of the right identified in paragraph 1.

While navigational safety is a factor bearing upon such restriction, this provision is also clearly a response to the coastal State's concern to prevent marine pollution. The potential impact for warships, including military submarines, is limited, however. Article 211(1) of UNCLOS recognises the role of routeing systems in '[minimising] the threat of accidents which might cause pollution of the marine environment,

[71] *Report of the Committee on the Peaceful Uses of the Sea-bed and the Ocean Floor beyond the Limits of National Jurisdiction* (United Nations, 1973) vol. 3, 5 ('Seabed Committee Report'). Fiji had also envisioned a broader role for compulsory sea lanes passage in support of the security interests of the coastal State. 'Seabed Committee Report' (n 71) vol. 3, 91.

[72] 'Seabed Committee Report' (n 71) vol. 1, 50–51.

[73] In 1974, Fiji revised its proposal regarding submarines to provide that 'Submarines and other underwater vehicles may be required to navigate on the surface and to show their flag except in cases where they: (a) Have given prior notification of their passage to the coastal State; and (b) If so required by the coastal State, confine their passage to such sea lanes as may be designated for that purpose by the coastal State': UNCLOS III, *Official Records* (n 32) vol. 3, 197. This text suggests an understanding that prior notification of passage by submarines or their restriction does the same work as a requirement to travel on the surface.

including the coastline, and pollution damage to the related interests of coastal States'; as does SOLAS Chapter V, Regulation 10. As noted above, the latter is not directly binding on warships.[74] Moreover, if sea lanes are designated specifically for marine protection purposes, Article 236 of UNCLOS excludes the application of rules to protect and preserve the marine environment to warships and other sovereign-immune vessels.[75] Nuclear submarines travelling on the surface, showing their flag, may thus only be restricted to sea lanes within another State's territorial sea when necessary for navigational safety. If the sea lanes are only for the purposes of marine environmental protection, nuclear submarines should also adhere to the routeing requirements consistent with Article 236 of UNCLOS, namely so far as is reasonable and practicable and without impairing their operations or operational capabilities.

7.2.3 Prior Notification or Authorisation for Passage

An ongoing controversy regarding the passage of foreign warships through the territorial sea has concerned whether the coastal State has the right to insist on prior notification or authorisation. This issue is not specific to submarines but concerns the passage of warships more broadly through the territorial sea. Nevertheless, the case of submarines may cast additional light on this question – particularly through consideration of the requirement that such vessels navigate on the surface and show their flag. This issue reflects the coastal State's broader concern of being aware of foreign warships in its territorial waters, which is associated with the understanding that such vessels may threaten (or be perceived as threatening) the security of the coastal State.

UNCLOS does not *require* warships to give notice or seek authorisation for innocent passage in the territorial sea. Whether it nevertheless *allows* a coastal State to require such notification or authorisation remains the subject of debate. In the absence of clear wording, it is worth investigating the drafting history to elucidate the relevant rules in this ongoing debate. As discussed in Part I of this book, historically, concerns were voiced in different fora as to the threatening nature of warships generally and submarines particularly.[76] These early views

[74] SOLAS Convention (n 51) ch. V, reg. 1.
[75] See further Chapter 12.
[76] See discussion in Chapter 3, Section 3.6.

supported a right for coastal States to insist on prior notice or authority for the passage of warships through the territorial sea.

As discussed in Chapter 3, while most governments participating in the 1930 Codification Conference seem to have agreed that the passage of warships through the territorial sea should be permitted in time of peace, not all considered this passage a 'right' as opposed to a concession by the coastal State.[77] While government replies to the Preparatory Committee for the Hague Conference had either expressly asserted such a right or simply not commented on (or objected to) this practice, the Preparatory Committee nonetheless formulated 'Basis of Discussion No 20' for the 1930 Conference as follows:

> A coastal State should recognise the right of innocent passage through its territorial waters of foreign warships, including submarines navigating on the surface.
>
> A coastal State is entitled to make rules regulating the conditions of such passage *without, however, having the right to require a previous authorization.*
>
> A coastal State is entitled to make rules governing the anchoring of foreign warships in its territorial waters, but it may not forbid anchoring in case of damage to the ship or distress.[78]

It is unclear why this clause regarding prior authorisation was included when it was so patently at odds with the views of participating governments.[79]

Objections to the treatment of 'previous authorization or notification' in what became Draft Article 12 were raised upon its reading by the Committee on Territorial Waters as a whole. The shift in emphasis from a broad right to require prior authorisation or notification to a more exceptional right to do so is not accounted for by the available records. As we shall see, subsequent comments by François suggest that he may have taken for granted that the Preparatory Committee's formulation of Basis of Discussion 20, which denied 'the right to require a previous authorization', was a reflection of State views on the matter – an assumption not supported by the evidence.

François was responsible for reviving the 1930 draft articles in his work as the ILC's Special Rapporteur on the regime of territorial waters.[80] His

[77] Shabtai Rosenne (ed.), *League of Nations Conference for the Codification of International Law (1930)* (Oceana Publications, 1975) vol. 2, 290–293.

[78] Ibid, 293 (emphasis added).

[79] See also Chapter 3, Section 3.6.4 (discussing these developments).

[80] J. P. A. François, Special Rapporteur, 'Regime of the Territorial Sea' (UN Doc. A/CN.4/53) [1952] 2 *Yearbook of the International Law Commission* 25, 26.

initial reports provided inter alia that '1. En règle générale, l'Etat riverain n'empêchera pas le passage des navires de guerre étrangers dans sa mer territoriale et n'exigera pas une autorisation ou notification préalables'.[81] This text was not discussed until the ILC's sixth session in 1954,[82] where it attracted a number of objections from Commission members who considered the coastal State to have a right not only to require prior notification or authorisation but also to forbid the passage of warships through the territorial sea – an argument linked in some cases with the view that there was no *right* of innocent passage for warships in the territorial sea, only a concession to this effect on the part of the coastal State.[83] Responding to this view, François claimed that 'the Preparatory Committee of the 1930 Conference had received replies from governments which expressed the unanimous view that the right of passage of warships through territorial waters was generally recognized'[84] – a claim that was not supported by the records.[85] Most ILC members prioritised coastal State sovereignty over foreign warships within the territorial sea, some noting that this balance shifted in the case of international straits.[86]

In 1955, the Special Rapporteur proposed 'a new text to safeguard the right of coastal States to demand previous authorization or notification'.[87] The new text provided that

> 1. The coastal State may make the passage of warships through the territorial sea subject to previous authorization or notification. Normally it shall grant innocent passage subject to the observance of the provisions of articles 18 and 19.

[81] Ibid, 42 [Authors' translation: As a general rule, the coastal State will not prevent the passage of foreign warships through its territorial sea and will not require prior authorization or notification.]; J. P. A. François, Special Rapporteur, 'Regime of the Territorial Sea: Second Report of Special Rapporteur' (UN Doc. A/CN.4/61) [1953] 2 *Yearbook of the International Law Commission* 57, 74.

[82] J. P. A. François, Special Rapporteur, 'Regime of the Territorial Sea: Third Report of Special Rapporteur' (UN Doc. A/CN.4/77) [1954] 2 *Yearbook of the International Law Commission* 1, 6.

[83] '272nd Meeting: Regime of the Territorial Sea' [1954] 1 *Yearbook of the International Law Commission* 154, 158–160.

[84] Ibid, 159.

[85] See further Chapter 3, Section 3.6.4.

[86] '272nd Meeting: Regime of the Territorial Sea' (n 83) 158–160.

[87] '306th Meeting: Regime of the Territorial Sea' [1955] 1 *Yearbook of the International Law Commission* 139, 143.

Paragraph 2 of the same article provided that the coastal State 'may not interfere in any way with innocent passage through straits normally used for international navigation between two parts of the high seas'.

The latter text reflected the decision in the *Corfu Channel* case, where the International Court of Justice (ICJ) had held that '[i]t is . . . generally recognized and in accordance with international custom that States in time of peace have a right to send their warships through straits used for international navigation between two parts of the high seas without the previous authorization of a coastal State, provided that the passage is *innocent*'.[88] Thus, as the ILC recognised,[89] the *Corfu Channel* judgment did not comment on the issue of prior notification or authorisation in relation to passage through the territorial sea. Indeed, both parties to the dispute and the ICJ clearly considered the question of whether the United Kingdom had a right to send warships through the channel without Albania's prior authorisation to depend upon whether or not the channel was properly considered a strait.[90] Elaborating a legal definition of international straits and finding that the Corfu Channel met this definition, the ICJ clarified the peacetime rights of foreign warships in these waters.[91] It did not comment on whether a coastal State could insist upon prior authorisation for passage through the territorial sea more generally.

At the 1958 Conference on the Law of the Sea, the First Committee on the Territorial Sea and Contiguous Zone saw some disagreement between States on whether previous authorisation or notification for passage in the territorial sea was permitted. However, several proposals that would have 'denied any possibility of requiring previous authorization' were rejected and the ILC's Article 24 was adopted with minor amendments by fifty-four votes to five, with eight abstentions.[92] Immediately after the vote, Sir Gerald Fitzmaurice clarified that 'with the rejection of the amendments voted upon the Committee [on the Territorial Sea and Contiguous Zone] had endorsed the principle laid down in the Commission's text that the passage of warships must be

88 *Corfu Channel* (United Kingdom v. Albania) (Judgment of 9 April 1949) [1949] ICJ Rep 4, 28 (emphasis added).

89 See 'Commentary to the Articles concerning the Law of the Sea' [1956] 2 *Yearbook of the International Law Commission* 265, 277.

90 *Corfu Channel* (n 88) 27–28.

91 Ibid, 28–29.

92 UNCLOS I, *Official Records* (n 17) vol. 3, 131.

subject to previous authorization'.[93] In fact, the article adopted remained permissive, reiterating the ILC's formulation that

> The coastal State may make the passage of warships through the territorial sea subject to previous authorization or notification. Normally it shall grant innocent passage subject to the observance of the provisions of articles 17 and 18.

The sole amendment was the addition of a further paragraph providing (based on Yugoslavia's proposal) that '[d]uring passage warships have complete immunity from the jurisdiction of any State other than its flag State'.[94]

Despite the First Committee's endorsement of Article 24, the provision was not adopted as part of the 1958 Territorial Sea Convention. At the twentieth meeting of the Plenary, just hours before the 1958 Territorial Sea Convention would be adopted, Italy proposed that a separate vote be taken on the words 'authorization or' in Article 24(1).[95] While a number of States objected to such a vote, the motion was passed and the deletion of the words 'authorization or' was approved by forty-five votes to twenty-seven, with six abstentions.[96]

This result prompted a flurry of protests from States supporting not only prior notification but prior authorisation as a condition for the entry of warships into the territorial sea.[97] Many of these States indicated that this substantial amendment meant that they could no longer support the adoption of Article 24 at all, insofar as this change would be tantamount to giving up their right to require not only notification but authorisation for the passage of warships in their territorial waters.[98] This change shifted the balance of support in respect of Article 24, which then failed to reach the two thirds majority required for adoption by the Plenary (the result of the vote being forty-three in favour and twenty-four against, with twelve abstentions). The failure to adopt Article 24, as such, cannot be considered a rejection of the alleged right of the coastal State to require previous notification or authorisation for the passage of warships in the territorial sea. Instead, it reflects the continuing disagreement between States on precisely this issue. The drafting history on this point also offers

93 Ibid, 131.
94 Ibid, vol. 2, 122, 125.
95 Ibid, 67.
96 Ibid.
97 Ibid, 67–68.
98 Ibid.

evidence of the persistent objection of a number of States to efforts to either limit such a right to notification (implying the impermissibility of requirements for previous authorisation) or deny it altogether. It further indicates that several States objected to either or both prior notification or authorisation on principle at the time of the 1958 Conference. However, it is worth emphasising that, as in the case of the United States,[99] this position has not since been maintained, which may have consequences for claims to any customary rule to this effect or the status of such States as persistent objectors.

UNCLOS, like the 1958 Territorial Sea Convention, does not expressly refer to the issue of prior notice or authorisation for the innocent passage of warships. Yet a number of States, both during UNCLOS negotiations and since, have claimed that the coastal State is not precluded from requiring prior notice or authorisation for the innocent passage of warships.[100] The United States has drawn attention to the fact that

[99] The United States did not object to the coastal State's right to require prior notification or authorisation for passage through the territorial sea in its 1956 response to the ILC's proposed draft articles: 'United States of America' (UN Doc. A/CN.4/99/Add.1) [1956] 2 *Yearbook of the International Law Commission* 91, 94. It was not until the 1958 Conference that it proposed an amendment that would have done away with any obligation for foreign vessels engaged in innocent passage (including warships) to comply with a 'requirement of advance authorization': UNCLOS I, *Official Records* (n 17) vol. 3, 221. While this amendment was subsequently withdrawn, the US representative, Arthur H. Dean, again supported the removal of a reference to prior authorisation at the twentieth plenary meeting, arguing that '[t]he rights of coastal States were fully protected by [article 25, under which warships were called upon to comply with coastal regulations] in accordance with the customary provisions of international law': UNCLOS I, *Official Records* (n 17) vol. 2, 68. Dean further claimed that: '[t]he United States of America had never required prior authorization for warships entering its territorial waters'. In fact, until at least 1945 the United States had denied a right of innocent passage for foreign warships in the territorial sea, while accepting such passage would be allowed where authorised by the coastal State. It is also notable that while the United States voted for the removal of the reference to 'authorization' in 1958, it did not at this time object to a requirement of prior notification. Indeed, it was not until 1959 that regulations by the Office of the Chief of Naval Operations were amended to remove the rule that United States warships 'should not be navigated in or near [the territorial waters of other States] . . . without having obtained prior authorization from higher authority'. Marjorie Millace Whiteman, *Digest of International Law* (US Government Printing Office, 1965) vol. 4, 417.

[100] States expressly indicating their support of the coastal State's right to require prior notification or authorisation for warships during UNCLOS negotiations included Argentina, Cape Verde, China, Congo, Democratic People's Republic of Korea, Ecuador, Egypt, Guinea-Bissau, Libyan Arab Jamahiriya, Malta, Morocco, Oman, Pakistan, Panama, Papua New Guinea, Peru, Philippines, São Tomé and Príncipe, Somalia and Uruguay (sponsors of an amendment to this effect: Platzöder (n 17) vol.

a proposal expressly recognising 'the right to require prior authorization or notification for passage through the territorial sea'[101] was mooted during the negotiations of UNCLOS but subsequently withdrawn.[102] This withdrawal responded to an appeal by the President 'not to press for a vote' where an amendment 'did not lend itself to adoption by consensus', as this 'might well unravel the package so laboriously put together over so many years'.[103] However, a lack of consensus does not conclusively reflect a rejection of the right to require prior notification or authorisation. Instead, the sponsors of the amendment sought recognition of an existing right rather than the creation of a new one in the treaty. They emphasised that '[i]t must not be inferred that a new right would thereby be created, nor should it be assumed that such a right would have been excluded or voided under the draft convention', pointing out that '[d]ozens of national legislations already contained provisions for such prior notification or authorization in the case of foreign warships, in keeping with generally recognized rules of international customary law explicitly acknowledged in the draft convention as covering those matters not regulated by the convention itself'.[104] Upon withdrawing the proposed amendment, the sponsoring States '[reaffirmed] that their decision is without prejudice to the rights of coastal States to adopt measures to

V, 62); as well as Iran, Romania, UAE, Guyana, Bahrain, Suriname, Albania, Djibouti, Angola, Algeria, Nigeria, Gabon, Syrian Arab Republic, Sierra Leone, United Republic of Cameroon, Sudan, Qatar and Zaire: see Nordquist (n 46) vol. 2, 197, note 15. Algeria, Argentina, Bangladesh, Cape Verde, China, Croatia, Ecuador, Egypt, Finland, Iran, Malta, Montenegro, Pakistan, São Tomé and Príncipe, Serbia, Sudan, Sweden, Uruguay, Oman and Yemen expressly or implicitly (by reference to existing or prospective laws governing passage in the territorial sea) affirmed a right to require prior notification or authorisation for the passage of warships (and not only nuclear-powered vessels) in declarations upon signing, ratifying or acceding to UNCLOS: see United Nations Division for Ocean Affairs and the Law of the Sea, 'Declarations or Statements upon UNCLOS Ratification', 17 May 2024 <www.un.org/depts/los/convention_agreements/convention_declarations.htm>. Germany, Italy, the Netherlands and the United Kingdom have declared that they do not consider prior notification or authorisation requirements to be consistent with the Convention: ibid.

101 Platzöder (n 17) vol. V, 62, sponsored by 20 States (Argentina, Cape Verde, China, Congo, Democratic People's Republic of Korea, Ecuador, Egypt, Guinea-Bissau, Libyan Arab Jamahiriya, Malta, Morocco, Oman, Pakistan, Panama, Papua New Guinea, Peru, Philippines, São Tomé and Príncipe, Somalia and Uruguay).

102 See e.g., United States, 'Written Statement of 8 March 1983' in Platzöder (n 17) vol. XIII, 43–44.

103 UNCLOS III, *Official Records* (n 32) vol. 16, 129–130.

104 Ibid, 29.

safeguard their security interests, in accordance with article[s] 19 and 25 of the Convention'.[105]

States continuing to require prior authorisation or notification for the passage of warships in the territorial sea include Albania, Algeria, Antigua and Barbuda, Argentina, Bangladesh, Barbados, Burma, Chile (on the basis of reciprocity – 'In cases in which the State places restrictions on the right of innocent passage for foreign warships, the Republic of Chile reserves the right to apply similar restrictive measures'), China, Colombia, Croatia, Denmark (requires prior notification for passage of more than three warships in designated locations), Ecuador, Egypt, Estonia, Guyana, India, Iran, North Korea, South Korea, Latvia, Libya, Lithuania (on the basis of reciprocity where other States have such a requirement), Maldives, Malta, Mexico (on the basis of reciprocity where other States have such a requirement), Montenegro, Oman, Pakistan, Romania, Russia, Saint Vincent and the Grenadines, Seychelles, Sierra Leone, Slovenia, Somalia, Sri Lanka, Sudan, Sweden, Syria, United Arab Emirates, Vanuatu, Vietnam and Yemen. Some other States (Malaysia, Samoa, Saudia Arabia) require prior notification or authorisation for the passage of vessels, including warships, that are either or both nuclear-powered or carrying nuclear material only. Still other States have reserved the right to regulate the foreign passage of warships in unspecified ways, such as Poland and Ukraine.[106]

Stephens and Quadrio have argued that since the adoption of UNCLOS, while a minority of States retain a requirement of prior notification or authorisation in their national laws, they do not necessarily insist on such formalities in practice or apply the same standard in their own actions.[107] Moreover, they argue that what was already a minority in State practice is trending away from requirements of

105 Ibid, 132.

106 Information in this paragraph compiled from US Navy JAG Corps, *US Maritime Claims Reference Manual* <www.jag.navy.mil/organization/code_10_mcrm.htm>; United Nations Division for Ocean Affairs and the Law of the Sea, 'Maritime Space: Maritime Zones and Maritime Delimitation', 10 April 2024 <www.un.org/depts/los/LEGISLATIONANDTREATIES/regionslist.htm>. The Philippines in practice requires prior notification and authorisation for the passage of warships in its territorial sea and archipelagic waters although it has not specified this position in domestic laws or regulations: Ton (n 8) 233. It may be noted that lists as to States with these requirements have varied in different academic accounts.

107 For discussion, see Dale Stephens and Tim Quadrio, '"Do as I Do, Not as I Say": Navigational Freedom and the Law of the Sea Convention' in Donald R. Rothwell and David Letts (eds.), *Law of the Sea in South East Asia: Environmental, Navigational and Security Challenges* (Routledge, 2020) 163, 169–170; Klein (n 15) 38–39.

prior notice and authorisation.[108] Requiring prior notification or authorisation for the passage of warships in the territorial sea has overwhelmingly been figured as a right that *may* be exercised by the coastal State, not a general requirement that *must* be applied.[109] To take Stephens and Quadrio's example, the fact that Chinese warships have passed through the United States' territorial sea 'without obtaining prior permission or providing prior notification' is consistent with the fact that the United States does not require prior authorisation or notification for such passage. This practice does not mean that China would deny that the United States (or any other coastal State) is entitled to impose such requirements if it sees fit, nor does it in any way contradict China's decision to impose such requirements itself. These arguments will likely persist in relation to the passage of military submarines when they navigate through the territorial sea on the surface. Clarification of this rule is desirable, especially as the context arguably changed during UNCLOS negotiations when it was accepted that the territorial sea could extend up to twelve nautical miles in breadth.

It might be suggested that a requirement for prior notification or authorisation for the passage of warships in the territorial sea would in any case run counter to Article 24 of UNCLOS, which prohibits coastal States from adopting laws and regulations that 'have the practical effect of denying or impairing the right of innocent passage'. Contrary to this argument is the view that Article 24 is an elaboration on the duty not to hamper innocent passage already expressed in Article 15 of the 1958 Territorial Sea Convention. At the 1958 Conference and during UNCLOS negotiations, many States considered a right to require prior notification or authorisation to be entirely consistent with this duty.

It could nonetheless be suggested that a requirement of prior notification – rather than authorisation – is consistent with Article 24.[110] Where prior authorisation is required but never denied by the coastal State, it may in practice function as a form of notification while symbolically asserting the priority of the coastal State in the territorial sea. Notification would retain importance for coastal States that do not otherwise have the resources to surveille their seas for foreign vessels by other means. As with requiring

108 Stephens and Quadrio (n 107) 169–170.

109 The same laws may be considered *opinio juris*, reflecting a belief that the coastal State is lawfully entitled to require such prior notification or authorisation (not that prior notification or authorisation is universally required as a matter of law).

110 Stephens and Quadrio (n 107) 166. The authors conclude, however, that there is no entitlement to prior knowledge that may be implied either.

submarines to surface, the notification could be understood as enabling the coastal State to better monitor activities in its territorial sea. For the minority of States that continue to assert a right to require notice from foreign warships, a failure to provide such notice would be one factor among others that the coastal State will consider in assessing whether the passage is prejudicial to its peace, good order or security.[111] A mere failure to provide prior notice would not automatically violate the right of innocent passage. Moreover, a requirement of prior notice does not necessarily violate Article 24 of UNCLOS whereas prior authorisation more clearly does so.

7.2.4 Responses to Passage Violations in the Territorial Sea

If the coastal State considers that a submarine is in violation of its right of innocent passage, the permissible responses are set out, albeit not exclusively, in UNCLOS.[112] Article 25(1) of UNCLOS only provides that 'the coastal State may take the necessary steps in its territorial sea to prevent passage which is not innocent'. These steps may be taken based on the coastal State's characterisation of the passage as non-innocent, rather than any distinct violation of coastal State's laws. A coastal State also has 'the right to take the necessary steps to prevent any breach of the conditions' applying to admission to internal waters or a port facility outside internal waters. There is no separate reference in Article 25 to a right to respond to breaches of other laws and regulations of the coastal State relating to innocent passage, though Article 21 provides that foreign ships have a duty to comply with these laws and regulations. There remains scope to respond to such breaches in accordance with subsection B of Part II of UNCLOS on 'rules applicable to merchant ships and government ships operated for commercial purposes' and subsection C on 'rules applicable to warships and other government ships operated for non-commercial purposes'.

Yet in the case of a submarine that qualifies as a warship, the 'necessary steps' would appear to be limited to requests that the submarine (a) 'comply with the laws and regulations of the coastal State concerning

111 See further, Natalie Klein, 'The South China Sea Code of Conduct and the Freedom of Navigation: A Proposal in Honor of Ted L. McDorman' (2024) 55(4) *Ocean Development and International Law* 490, 493.

112 See further, Natalie Klein, 'Responding to Law of the Sea Violations' (2020) 27 *Australian International Law Journal* 1.

passage through the territorial sea'[113] and the requirement under UNCLOS to navigate on the surface and show its flag, and (b) leave the State's territorial sea. These responses are consistent with Article 30 of UNCLOS, which provides that '[i]f any warship does not comply with the laws and regulations of the coastal State concerning passage through the territorial sea and disregards any request for compliance therewith which is made to it, the coastal State may require it to leave the territorial sea immediately'.

The coastal State is restricted in its ability to respond to non-innocent passage or the breach of its laws or regulations relating to passage as a consequence of the immunity of warships, which are ordinarily exempt from the enforcement jurisdiction of the coastal State. For government vessels other than warships, sovereign immunity is limited to when those vessels are employed in non-commercial activities.[114] The fact that Article 30 of UNCLOS specifies that the coastal State may require a warship to leave its territorial waters reflects the impermissibility of the arrest and detention of such vessels by dint of its sovereign immunity. Japan protested the entry of a Soviet nuclear submarine into its territorial sea in an incident in 1980, after the submarine caught fire in waters outside Okinawa Island.[115] Japan expressed concerned that there were no assurances with regards to the risk of radioactive pollution, and that the passage was in violation of Japan's Three Non-Nuclear Principles.[116] The diplomatic protest was the primary response possible given the immunity enjoyed by the Soviet submarine. More recently, the 2004 submerged passage of a Chinese submarine through Japan's territorial sea prompted environmental concerns given that the submarine was nuclear-powered.[117] Again, the immunity enjoyed by the submarine limited the actions that Japan could take against the submarine for the purposes of

[113] UNCLOS (n 1) art. 30.

[114] Ted McDorman, 'Sovereign Immune Vessels: Immunities, Responsibilities and Exemptions' in Henrik Ringbom (ed.), *Jurisdiction Over Ships: Post-UNCLOS Developments in the Law of the Sea* (Brill, 2015) 82, 88–89. See further Chapter 1, Section 1.3.

[115] Kazuhiro Nakatani, 'Submarines' in Anne Peters and Rüdiger Wolfrum (eds.), *Max Planck Encyclopedia of Public International Law* (Oxford University Press, July 2008) para. 9.

[116] Ibid. The three principles prohibit the manufacture and possession of nuclear weapons, as well as forbidding nuclear weapons being brought into Japan's territory.

[117] For discussion, see Miyoshi Masahiro, 'The Submerged Passage of a Submarine Through the Territorial Sea: The Incident of a Chinese Atomic-Powered Submarine' (2006) 10 *Singapore Yearbook of International Law* 243.

marine environmental protection,[118] and a series of diplomatic démarches between the States ensued.

In practice, however, States have used low power depth charges to 'signal' to a submerged submarine that it has been identified. While higher powered depth charges are weapons used in anti-submarine warfare to destroy submerged submarines, it appears that low power depth charges cannot harm a submarine and have been widely used as a signalling measure. This practice suggests that they should not be considered either a prohibited use of force or a threat of the use of force.[119] However, as discussed further in Chapter 9, context matters in assessing the legality of any threat of use of force.[120]

If the submarine is a 'merchant ship' or 'government ship operated for commercial purposes' and the threatened action is simply the arrest of the vessel, this response may be a legitimate exercise of coastal State jurisdiction with regard to this category of ships, provided the required international law conditions are met.[121] In the case of commercial vessels, Article 25 of UNCLOS – located in Subsection A on 'Rules applicable to All Ships' – must be read in conjunction with 'Subsection B: 'Rules Applicable to Merchant Ships and Government Ships Operated for Commercial Purposes'. The 'necessary steps' that may be taken 'to prevent passage that is not innocent' or '[i]n the case of ships proceeding to internal waters or a call at a port facility outside internal waters . . . the necessary steps to prevent any breach of the conditions to which admission of those ships to internal waters or such a call is subject' are qualified and elaborated upon by Articles 27 and 28 on the criminal and civil jurisdiction of the coastal State. These provisions would allow the exercise of criminal or civil jurisdiction, including the arrest of the vessel, in cases of transnational crime – which may be prohibited by both international and domestic law – and in cases of espionage, including industrial espionage, if this offence is set out under domestic criminal or civil law. While actions may thus be taken against private submarines in line with Articles 27 and 28, it is important to underline that such jurisdiction

118 Ibid, 249.

119 See further Chapter 9. Sweden, for example, anticipates in its national laws and regulations that the 'force of arms' may be used albeit when there is a hostile intent on the part of the intruding submarine. Marie Jacobsson, 'Sweden and the Law of the Sea' in Laura Pineschi and Tullio Treves (eds.), *The Law of the Sea: The European Union and its Member States* (Martinus Nijhoff, 1997) 495, 514–515.

120 See further Chapter 9, Section 9.2.

121 See UNCLOS (n 1) arts. 25, 27, 28.

to enforce does not pertain to warships or government vessels operated on non-commercial service (i.e., military submarines).[122]

Rather than taking action against any specific submarine, a coastal State may decide to temporarily suspend innocent passage 'if such suspension is essential for the protection of its security'.[123] The lawful suspension of innocent passage must be given due publicity and must not discriminate in form or in fact among foreign ships.[124] There are thus four criteria to be met for a lawful suspension: temporary; to protect security; given due publicity; non-discriminatory. Barnes suggests that any such suspension may only last as long as may be necessary to respond to the security concern that prompted the suspension.[125]

While the coastal State has extensive authority to adopt laws and regulations relating to innocent passage in the territorial sea,[126] according to Article 24 of UNCLOS, '[t]he coastal State shall not hamper the innocent passage of foreign ships through the territorial sea except in accordance with this Convention'.[127] The coastal State's regulatory powers are thus tempered by consideration of other States' right of innocent passage.[128] Article 24 further provides that

> In particular, in the application of this Convention or of any laws or regulations adopted in conformity with this Convention, the coastal State shall not:
>
> (a) impose requirements on foreign ships which have the practical effect of denying or impairing the right of innocent passage; or
> (b) discriminate in form or in fact against the ships of any State or against ships carrying cargoes to, from or on behalf of any State.[129]

It is clear that discrimination in this context refers to discrimination between States ('any State') rather than between types of vessels. Actions that discriminate against the ships of a State under Article 24(b) are likely to also violate Article 24(a). What will matter the most is the extent of impact on the right of innocent passage in light of the balance to be

122 As evident in the decision of ITLOS in *ARA Libertad* (Argentina v. Ghana) (Order of 15 December 2012) [2012] ITLOS Rep 332.
123 UNCLOS (n 1) art. 25(3).
124 Ibid.
125 Richard Barnes, 'Article 25' in Proelss (n 33) 226, para. 14.
126 UNCLOS (n 1) art. 21.
127 Ibid, art. 24.
128 Richard Barnes, 'Article 24' in Proelss (n 33) 218, para. 1, 220, para. 6.
129 UNCLOS (n 1) art. 24.

achieved between coastal States and other States. The coastal State is also required to 'give appropriate publicity to any danger to navigation, of which it has knowledge, within its territorial sea'.[130] The standard of publicity is 'appropriate' rather than 'due' publicity, which may account for the extent of knowledge that a coastal State may have in relation to those dangers.[131] During times of peace, a coastal State thus does not have the option of denying innocent passage to the submarines of a specific State; any exclusion must be non-discriminatory as between States, suitably publicised, and any blanket prohibition on foreign submarines from specific areas must be temporary and for security reasons.

Overall, the rules setting out the navigational rights and duties of submarines in the territorial sea are the same as those rules that apply to warships or, if a submarine is not a warship or otherwise sovereign-immune, to private vessels. However, it is in the territorial sea that the key distinctive feature of submarines – their ability to submerge – is recognised explicitly in the applicable rules. The requirement to surface and display the flag is a distinct rule of conventional, and likely customary, international law. Beyond Article 20 of UNCLOS, the rules applying to submarines in the territorial sea are also important in relation to passage through some international straits and in archipelagic waters in areas not subject to the regime of archipelagic sea lane passage. These two passage regimes are next discussed.

7.3 Transit Passage in International Straits

For States operating military submarines, the critical questions for passage through straits relate to, first, the meaning of transit passage, and second, what straits are subject to the regime of transit passage. The passage of submarines, as well as other warships, through straits was a critical concern in the negotiations of UNCLOS in the context of coastal States extending the outer limit of their territorial sea to twelve nautical miles. The concern of States with large naval fleets was that international 'chokepoints' would be subject to greater coastal State control and defence interests thereby compromised.[132] The littoral States considered their own security at risk if the freedom of navigation,

[130] Ibid, art. 24(2). This inclusion reflects a finding of *Corfu Channel* (n 88).

[131] Richard Barnes, 'Article 24' in Proelss (n 33) 221, para. 11.

[132] In this regard, Kraska has observed that the major maritime powers at the time of UNCLOS negotiations (comprising the United States, the United Kingdom, the Soviet Union, Japan, France) 'were united in their advancement of transit passage through

rather than innocent passage, was allowed through these narrow maritime areas.[133] Coastal States were further concerned to both protect the marine environment in areas immediately adjacent to their coasts, as well as uphold maritime safety requirements.[134] The regime of transit passage through international straits was the compromise reached during UNCLOS negotiations and is set out in Part III of UNCLOS. The discussion in this Section examines how submarines may exercise their right of transit passage (Section 7.3.1), then sets out the characteristics of straits subject to the regime of transit passage (Section 7.3.2) and, finally, considers the rights and duties of coastal States that may impact submarines when regulating transit passage through international straits (Section 7.3.3).

7.3.1 *Exercise of the Right of Transit Passage*

Article 38(2) of UNCLOS provides, in part: 'Transit passage means the exercise in accordance with this Part of the *freedom of navigation* and overflight *solely for the purpose of continuous and expeditious transit of the strait* between one part of the high seas or an exclusive economic zone and another part of the high seas or an exclusive economic zone.'[135] The starting position is thus that submarines enjoy the freedom of navigation through international straits and that freedom of navigation includes submerged passage. The freedom is then subject to restrictions, which balance the interests of coastal States in maritime areas over which they exercise sovereignty.

The transit passage of submarines, as with other vessels, must be 'continuous and expeditious', which is the same requirement imposed on ships subject to the regime of innocent passage under Article 18 of UNCLOS. However, transit passage is not subject to the requirement that it must not prejudice the peace, good order or security of the coastal State. Rather, the duties are fewer, as set out under Article 39(1) of UNCLOS. These requirements on submarines in transit passage entail that they:

straits, which were regarded as the crown jewels of freedom of navigation and essential for submarine operations': Kraska (n 16) 221.

133 Karin M. Burke and Deborah A. DeLeo, 'Innocent Passage and Transit Passage in the United Nations Convention on the Law of the Sea' (1983) 9 *Yale Journal of World Public Order* 389, 401.

134 Bing Bing Jia, 'Article 38' in Proelss (n 33) 295, para. 6. See also Burke and DeLeo (n 133) 401.

135 UNCLOS (n 1) art. 38(2) (emphasis added).

(a) proceed without delay through or over the strait;
(b) refrain from any threat or use of force against the sovereignty, territorial integrity or political independence of States bordering the strait, or in any other manner in violation of the principles of international law embodied in the Charter of the United Nations;
(c) refrain from any activities other than those incident to their normal modes of continuous and expeditious transit unless rendered necessary by force majeure or by distress;
(d) comply with other relevant provisions of this Part.

Article 39 further stipulates compliance with 'generally accepted international regulations, procedures and practices' relating to safety at sea and for the prevention of marine pollution.

It could be argued that Article 39 adds little to the requirements on submarines in passage through international straits: there is already an obligation to proceed continuously and expeditiously under Article 38(2), which would seemingly equate with proceeding 'without delay'; States are already bound by the UN Charter prohibition on the threat or use of force;[136] and States are likely bound by treaties adopted under the auspices of the IMO, such as the International Regulations for Preventing Collisions at Sea (COLREGs),[137] and those protecting the marine environment.[138] Though importantly, if a State was not a party to those IMO treaties but a party to UNCLOS, the *renvoi* nature of Article 39(2) would effectively render the requirements of the IMO treaties binding by virtue of the UNCLOS obligations.[139]

Nonetheless, what likely matters the most for submarines in Article 39(1) of UNCLOS is the duty to 'refrain from any activities *other than those incident to their normal modes* of continuous and expeditious transit'.[140] The normal mode of submarines is submerged, and it is also anticipated that some data collection would be undertaken for the purposes of safe navigation through the strait.

136 An obligation also recognised under customary international law and indeed a *jus cogens* norm. See further Chapter 9, Section 9.3.

137 Convention on the International Regulations for Preventing Collisions at Sea, London, 20 October 1972, entered into force 15 July 1977, 1050 UNTS 16 ('COLREGs').

138 See e.g., International Convention for the Prevention of Pollution from Ships, London, 2 November 1973, entered into force 2 October 1983, 1340 UNTS 62 ('MARPOL Convention').

139 UNCLOS includes a number of rules of reference. For discussion see, e.g., Lan N. Nguyen, 'Expanding the Environmental Regulatory Scope of UNCLOS Through the Rule of Reference: Potentials and Limits' (2022) 52(4) *Ocean Development and International Law* 419.

140 UNCLOS (n 1) art. 39(1)(d) (emphasis added).

There is no equivalent provision to Article 20, which requires submarines to voyage on the surface in the territorial sea, in Part III of UNCLOS. What may be 'normal mode' may potentially be assessed by reference to the geographic characteristics of a strait, with Jia suggesting that normal mode may be on the surface for shallow straits.[141] The Virginia Commentary also suggests that what is normal mode will depend on 'the navigational and hydrographical characteristics of the strait'.[142]

While the 'normal mode' of a submarine may allow for the operation of its navigational and other equipment needed for continuous and expeditious passage, the activities must not extend to marine scientific research or a hydrographic survey.[143] This requirement may be especially relevant for small UMAVs that are classified as ships and seek to exercise rights of passage in international straits.[144] Where a line is drawn between research and surveys on the one hand, and equipment operated incidental to 'normal mode' on the other must be assessed by reference to specific submarines and the activities undertaken. The reality, however, may be that the coastal State has no practical opportunity to challenge the activities because illicit research or surveys may occur in settings where the precise activities of the submarines cannot be easily detected by that coastal State.

The status of the right of transit passage under customary international law has been asserted by a number of States, predominantly the major maritime powers, but disputed by Iran and some other States bordering straits.[145] The latter States have insisted on the right of transit passage applying as a treaty right between the contracting parties,[146] which excludes the United States as a non-party to UNCLOS. Contestations over the transit rights of surface ships have occurred in the Strait of Hormuz, particularly in 2019 and 2020 following tit-for-tat encounters between Iran, on the one hand, and the United States and the United

[141] Jia refers to part of the Strait of Malacca as an example: Bing Bing Jia, *The Regime of Straits in International Law* (Oxford University Press, 1998) 151–152.

[142] Nordquist (n 46) vol. 2, 343.

[143] UNCLOS (n 1) art. 40. See also UNCLOS (n 1) art. 245.

[144] See further Chapter 14, Section 14.3.

[145] Said Mahmoudi and Martin Ratcovich Leopardi, 'Transit Passage' in Anne Peters and Rüdiger Wolfrum (eds.), *Max Planck Encyclopedia of Public International Law* (Oxford University Press, January 2021) paras. 24–30.

[146] See, e.g., Iran's 'Interpretative declaration on the subject of straits' made upon signature of UNCLOS: United Nations Division for Ocean Affairs and the Law of the Sea (n 100). Iran has signed but not ratified UNCLOS.

Kingdom on the other.[147] The less obtrusive presence of submarines may render comparable encounters less likely but nonetheless indicate the occasionally polemic nature of the exercise of these rights. The more compelling position is that the right of transit passage was a trade-off for recognition of the extension of the breadth of the territorial sea to twelve nautical miles, and both may be considered general international law.[148]

7.3.2 *Straits Subject to the Regime of Transit Passage*

Not every strait joining two other bodies of water is considered a strait subject to the regime of transit passage, irrespective of the name of the maritime area. Determining where submarines may exercise their right of transit passage is critical given it is the difference between navigating on the surface or submerged. The United States has taken the position that transit passage also applies in the approaches to international straits, claiming that position in relation to the Strait of Hormuz, the Strait of Magellan and the Beagle Channel.[149] Pursuing this position may seem irrelevant at first blush on the basis that international straits fall between exclusive economic zone (EEZ) and/or high seas areas. It is said, though, to have implications for navigating through specific areas where submerged passage may be more easily accommodated even if there is no overlap of territorial sea.[150] This position does not appear to have been contested by other States.

The regime of transit passage applies in relation to straits that are 'used for international navigation between one part of the high seas or an exclusive economic zone and another part of the high seas or an exclusive economic zone'.[151] The definition thus has a geographic dimension, as it

[147] Farzin Nadimi, 'Risks of Maritime Escalation in the Strait of Hormuz' (Washington Institute, PolicyWatch 3762, 21 July 2023) <www.washingtoninstitute.org/policy-analysis/risks-maritime-escalation-strait-hormuz>.

[148] Mahmoudi and Leopardi (n 146) paras. 37–38. Other commentators have resisted concluding that the right of transit passage is recognised in customary international law. See, e.g., Robin Churchill, Vaughan Lowe and Amy Sander, *The Law of the Sea* (4th ed., Manchester University Press, 2022) 179–183 (presenting a considered view that it is difficult to establish a 'general right of transit passage through every strait used for international navigation' as customary international law); Yoshifumi Tanaka, *The International Law of the Sea* (4th ed., Cambridge University Press, 2023) 134.

[149] Roach (n 65) 301–302.

[150] Ibid.

[151] UNCLOS (n 1) art. 37.

is a body of water that links EEZs or high seas,[152] and a functional dimension given the reference to 'international navigation'.[153] What counts as 'used for international navigation' does not require reference to the volume of traffic in a strait, but the actuality of it connecting high seas and/or EEZs and it being used to voyage from one of these locations to the other.[154] Jia has suggested that the 'test for use for navigation is satisfied if only non-coastal States in the region have made use of the strait'.[155] A diversity of foreign-flagged vessels transiting the area will reflect a strait 'used for international navigation'. Rothwell has queried whether the submerged passage of submarines through Arctic waters may qualify as 'international navigation' and considers that 'nothing in principle . . . would bar' submarines' passage being considered in assessing whether a strait is used for international navigation.[156]

Straits that are *not* subject to the regime of transit passage include those where 'the legal regime in straits in which passage is regulated in whole or in part by long-standing international conventions in force

[152] Thereby excluding straits leading from the high seas or an EEZ to the territorial sea of a foreign State. These straits are addressed in UNCLOS (n 1) art. 45(1)(b).

[153] Donald R. Rothwell, 'International Straits' in Donald R. Rothwell et al. (eds.), *Oxford Handbook of the Law of the Sea* (Oxford University Press, 2015) 114, 119.

[154] *Corfu Channel* (n 88) 28.

[155] Jia (n 141) 42.

[156] Rothwell (n 153) 120. Notably, all regimes of passage in 'ice-covered areas', including transit passage, would be subject to the *lex specialis* of Article 234 of UNCLOS, which provides that:

> Coastal States have the right to adopt and enforce non-discriminatory laws and regulations for the prevention, reduction and control of marine pollution from vessels in ice-covered areas within the limits of the [EEZ], where particularly severe climatic conditions and the presence of ice covering such areas for most of the year create obstructions or exceptional hazards to navigation, and pollution of the marine environment could cause major harm to or irreversible disturbance of the ecological balance.

Nilufer Oral, 'The Regime of Straits: Safety, Security and Protection of the Marine Environment' in Harry N. Scheiber and Jin-Hyun Paik (eds.), *Regions, Institutions, and Law of the Sea* (Brill, 2013) 161, 177; see also Erik Jaap Molenaar, *Coastal State Jurisdiction over Vessel-Source Pollution* (Kluwer, 1998) 102–103. The drafting history indicates that the expression 'within the limits of the EEZ' was understood to include the territorial sea: Jan Jacub Solski, 'The Genesis of Article 234 of the UNCLOS' (2021) 52(1) *Ocean Development and International Law* 1, 12, 16.

specifically relating to such straits'.[157] This exclusion was primarily motivated by the treaty regime governing the Turkish Straits,[158] and had also been recognised in Article 25 of the 1958 Territorial Sea Convention. Other straits that have their own legal regimes include the Strait of Magellan, the Danish Belts and the Sound, as well as the Strait of Tiran and the Gulf of Aqaba.

Also excluded from the regime of transit passage are straits where 'there exists through the strait a route through the high seas or through an exclusive economic zone of similar convenience with respect to navigational and hydrographical characteristics'.[159] Straits that fall within this exception include the Florida Strait between the United States and Cuba.[160] In this situation, the expectation is that submarines will remain in the high seas or EEZ route exercising the freedom of navigation, or will otherwise be required to exercise the right of innocent passage in the territorial sea areas of the littoral States. There may, though, be debate as to whether the high seas or EEZ route is 'of similar convenience'. Presumably the burden would fall on the State purporting to exercise the right of transit passage in another State's strait to demonstrate that the high seas or EEZ route was not of similar convenience when regard is had to 'navigational and hydrographical characteristics'. The latter qualification at least prevents a State from claiming greater convenience for its submarines based on political interests, economic concerns or strategic considerations.

The right of transit passage for submarines is further precluded where a 'strait is formed by an island of a State bordering the strait and its mainland, ... if there exists seaward of the island a route through the high seas or through an exclusive economic zone of similar convenience with respect to navigational and hydrographical characteristics'.[161] Once again, consideration must be afforded to the geographical situation of a particular strait (between an island and the mainland) and the

[157] UNCLOS (n 1) art. 35(c).

[158] See Chapters 3, Section 3.3 and Chapter 4, Section 4.3.

[159] UNCLOS (n 1) art. 36.

[160] David L. Larson, 'Innocent, Transit, and Archipelagic Sea Lanes Passage' (1987) 18(4) *Ocean Development and International Law* 411, 415. For additional examples, see Lewis M. Alexander, 'Exceptions to the Transit Passage Regime: Straits with Routes of "Similar Convenience"' (1987) 18(4) *Ocean Development and International Law* 479.

[161] UNCLOS (n 1) art. 38(1).

alternative passage options, namely in the EEZ or on the high seas if the criteria of 'similar convenience' with regards to 'navigational and hydrographical characteristics' are met. Straits falling within this category are very limited in any event, but potentially include Sweden's Kalmar Sound,[162] Italy's Strait of Messina and Tanzania's Pemba Channel.[163] Within these straits a non-suspendable right of innocent passage applies.[164]

Where the regime of transit passage is inapplicable and a submarine is navigating within the territorial sea of a coastal State, the submarine has the right of innocent passage only and must pass through those waters on the surface, showing its flag. The requirement to surface under Article 20 remains applicable by virtue of Article 38(3) of UNCLOS, which reads: 'Any activity which is not an exercise of the right of transit passage through a strait remains subject to the other applicable provisions of this Convention'. A right of non-suspendable innocent passage – rather than transit passage – further applies to straits where, as a matter of geography, the strait falls between a part of the high seas or an EEZ and the territorial sea of a foreign State.[165]

7.3.3 *Rights and Duties of Strait States*

States bordering straits that are subject to the regime of transit passage are entitled to regulate passage within the international strait in relation to:

> (a) the safety of navigation and the regulation of maritime traffic, as provided in article 41;
> (b) the prevention, reduction and control of pollution, by giving effect to applicable international regulations regarding the discharge of oil, oily wastes and other noxious substances in the strait;
> (c) with respect to fishing vessels, the prevention of fishing, including the stowage of fishing gear;

[162] Jia (n 141) 142.

[163] Hugo Caminos, 'Categories of International Straits Excluded from the Transit Passage Reime under Part III of the United Nations Convention on the Law of the Sea' in Tafsir Malick Ndiaye and Rudiger Wolfrum (eds.), *Law of the Sea, Environmental Law and Settlement of Disputes: Liber Amicorum Judge Thomas A Mensah* (Martinus Nijhoff, 2007) 583, 591.

[164] UNCLOS (n 1) art. 45(1)(a).

[165] Ibid, art. 45(1)(b).

(d) the loading or unloading of any commodity, currency or person in contravention of the customs, fiscal, immigration or sanitary laws and regulations of States bordering straits.[166]

For submarines that are not entitled to sovereign immunity, the law enforcement powers of States bordering straits are not explicitly acknowledged in Part III of UNCLOS but would instead be drawn from the sovereignty of coastal States recognised in their territorial seas.[167]

Of possible significance for submarines will be coastal State requirements around the safety of navigation and regulation of maritime traffic, as well as environmental requirements. In regulating maritime traffic, strait States may designate sea lanes and traffic separation schemes pursuant to the processes and requirements in Article 41 of UNCLOS. The littoral States may also prescribe sea lanes or traffic separation schemes in the approaches to straits in the event that their territorial sea outside the strait is commonly used as an entry point to the strait rather than the EEZ or high seas area.[168] These schemes are most typically applicable in relation to ships transiting on the surface of the water and thus submarines that are submerged for transit passage could potentially disregard the traffic separation schemes if it is clear that they are exclusively concerned with surface vessels.[169] Traffic separation schemes are in place for Dover Strait, the Straits of Malacca and Singapore, as well as the Strait of Hormuz.[170]

The critical question for military submarines is whether their passage can be restricted to sea lanes when travelling submerged through international straits if the coastal State does purport to establish a scheme applicable for both surface and submerged vessels. On the one hand, Article 41(7) of UNCLOS provides that '[s]hips in transit passage shall respect applicable sea lanes and traffic separation schemes established in accordance with this article'. The latter formulation admits no distinction between sovereign-immune vessels and other ships. Moreover, Article 41 sets out rules regarding the designation of sea lanes and prescription of traffic separation schemes in 'conformity with this Part'.[171] Part III of UNCLOS does not draw distinctions

166 UNCLOS (n 1) art. 42(1).
167 Rothwell (n 153) 123. See further Churchill, Lowe and Sander (n 148) 177.
168 Churchill, Lowe and Sander (n 148) 171–172.
169 Jia (n 141) 159.
170 Donald R. Rothwell and Tim Stephens, *The International Law of the Sea* (3rd ed., Hart, 2023) 286.
171 UNCLOS (n 1) art. 41 (1).

between warships or merchant vessels unlike the different sections of Part II of UNCLOS. It could thus be argued that military submarines must comply with any traffic separation scheme or sea lane designation in an international strait.

On the other hand, Article 32 in Part II does explicitly preserve the immunity of warships and other sovereign-immune vessels in relation to 'the Convention'. The United States has claimed that '[w]arships, auxiliaries, and government ships operated on exclusive government non-commercial service (i.e., sovereign-immune vessels . . .) are not legally required to comply with . . . sea-lanes and traffic separation schemes while in transit passage' though they may do so voluntarily.[172] Whether sovereign immunity prevents the prescription of rules regulating navigation as well as their enforcement emerges as an issue in this situation. The duties of vessels in transit passage are reflected in Article 39(2) of UNCLOS as follows:

> Ships in transit passage shall:
>
> (a) comply with generally accepted international regulations, procedures and practices for safety at sea, including the International Regulations for Preventing Collisions at Sea;
> (b) comply with generally accepted international regulations, procedures and practices for the prevention, reduction and control of pollution from ships.

Each of the 'generally accepted international regulations' may allow in some instances that sovereign-immune vessels are excepted from their application,[173] but certainly not all. The United States, for example, recognises the ongoing applicability of international rules concerned with collision prevention.[174] However, as discussed further in Chapter 12, rules relating to marine environmental protection do not apply to warships and other sovereign-immune vessels.[175] The application of international standards to promote the safety of navigation remain important given that, as discussed in Chapter 11, there have been instances where US submarines have collided with other vessels in the Strait of Hormuz.[176] While

172 United States Navy, United States Marine Corps and United States Coast Guard, *The Commander's Handbook on the Law of Naval Operations* (Naval War College, March 2022) para. 2.5.3.2 ('*Commander's Handbook*').

173 See, e.g., SOLAS Convention (n 51) ch. V, reg. 1(a)(i).

174 *Commander's Handbook* (n 172) para. 2.5.3.2.

175 See Chapter 12, Sections 12.1 and 12.3.

176 See Chapter 11, Section 11.2.

compliance may be expected under Article 39(2), enforcing such requirements against military submarines would be contrary to their sovereign-immune status. Diplomatic démarches would instead need to be pursued. UNCLOS does no more than stipulate that the flag State in these instances 'shall bear international responsibility for any loss or damage which results to States bordering straits'.[177]

Duties imposed on the strait States include not hampering or suspending transit passage, as well as giving notice of navigational dangers of which they are aware.[178] In relation to the latter obligation, which is drawn from the *Corfu Channel* judgment,[179] hazards for submarines may include any anti-submarine devices or other seabed equipment, as well as submerged wrecks.[180] The strait States are also obligated not to adopt any laws or regulations that 'discriminate in form or in fact among foreign ships'.[181] Earlier drafts of this provision indicated that the negotiating States were concerned to prevent discrimination between *States* rather than between different types of vessels.[182]

Unlike innocent passage, there is no entitlement resting with the coastal State to take steps to prevent passage that is not consistent with the transit passage regime.[183] Equally, there is no explicit entitlement to ask warships (and hence military submarines) to leave.[184] A request to leave could instead be construed as an unlawful act of hampering transit passage.[185] A State bordering a strait that objected to the transit passage of a submarine would be required to communicate that view to the flag State of the submarine to resolve the issue diplomatically in first instance, with the possibility of an inter-State claim for any loss or damage.[186] If the strait State was to take action against a submarine to hamper passage that is considered inconsistent with the right of transit passage, that response could otherwise be construed

177 UNCLOS (n 1) art. 42(5).

178 Ibid, art. 44.

179 *Corfu Channel* (n 88).

180 Chapter 11, Section 11.4.2 discusses laws relating to the removal and treatment of wrecks.

181 UNCLOS (n 1) art. 42(2).

182 Norquist (n 46) vol. 2, 371, paras. 42.3–42.4 (art. 42).

183 As is allowed under Article 25 of UNCLOS in relation to innocent passage.

184 As is permitted under Article 30 of UNCLOS.

185 In violation of Article 44 of UNCLOS.

186 UNCLOS (n 1) art. 42(5).

as a lawful counter-measure, provided all criteria associated with counter-measures were met.[187]

It is worth reiterating that submarines without sovereign immunity (i.e., commercial or private vessels) may be subject to enforcement action in accordance with Article 233 of UNCLOS in the case of 'a violation of the laws and regulations referred to in article 42, paragraph 1(a) and (b), causing or threatening major damage to the marine environment of the straits'. In such a case, 'the States bordering the straits may take appropriate enforcement measures and if so shall respect *mutatis mutandis* the provisions of [section 7 (Safeguards)]'. Enforcement action is also permitted in the case of violations of 'non-discriminatory laws and regulations for the prevention, reduction and control of marine pollution from vessels in ice-covered areas'.[188] The scope of action allowed for straits States against private submarines is thus greater than in relation to military submarines.

7.4 Archipelagic Waters and Archipelagic Sea Lanes Passage

Beyond transit passage, one of the other signature creations during the negotiations of UNCLOS was the concept of the archipelagic State, which further incorporates archipelagic waters and archipelagic sea lanes passage. Part IV of UNCLOS sets out the criteria for a State to claim archipelagic State status and thereby enclose its outer islands with straight archipelagic baselines under the Convention.[189] Archipelagic baselines apply in relation to a State comprised entirely of islands, and not to an offshore archipelago under the sovereignty of a continental State.[190] There are twenty-two island States that have claimed status as archipelagic States and drawn straight archipelagic baselines.[191] The

[187] ILC, 'Responsibility of States for Internationally Wrongful Acts' (2001) 2 *Yearbook of the International Law Commission* 26, arts. 22, 49–54. See further Natalie Klein, 'Responses to Law of the Sea Violations' (2020) 27 *Australian International Law Journal* 1, 19–22.

[188] UNCLOS (n 1) art. 234.

[189] Ibid, art. 47.

[190] For discussion on the restricted use of archipelagic baselines to archipelagic States, see Catherine Redgwell and Antonios Tzanakopoulos, 'The Interaction of Treaty and Custom in the Concept of Offshore Archipelagos' (2023) 72(3) *International and Comparative Law Quarterly* 573.

[191] Antigua and Barbuda, Bahamas, Cabo Verde, Comoros, Fiji, Grenada, Indonesia, Jamaica, Kiribati, Maldives, Marshall Islands, Mauritius, Papua New Guinea, Philippines, Saint Vince and the Grenadines, São Tomé and Príncipe, Seychelles, Solomon Islands, Trinidad and Tobago, Tuvalu and Vanuatu. The Dominican Republic, which is not a party to UNCLOS, has also claimed the status of an archipelagic

archipelagic waters within those baselines are subject to the sovereignty of the archipelagic State, albeit bound by requirements set out in Part IV of UNCLOS.[192]

Prior to the adoption of UNCLOS, Indonesia and the Philippines were core proponents of recognising their rights as large archipelagos and had sought to introduce restrictions on passage within their waters.[193] For example, Indonesia had specifically provided for a right of innocent passage in the 1957 Djuanda Declaration asserting its claim to archipelagic waters; it reaffirmed this position in Act No. 4 of 1960.[194] However, the latter Act was accompanied by an 'Elucidation' describing innocent passage as a 'privilege' granted by Indonesia rather than a right of all States.[195] In 1962, Indonesia issued 'Government Regulation No. 8 on Innocent Passage of Foreign Vessels Through Indonesian Waters', which affirmed a suspendable right of innocent passage through archipelagic waters previously comprising high seas or territorial waters.[196] The regulation further required both submarine navigation on the surface and prior notification for the passage of foreign warships and government ships used for non-commercial purposes – though notification was not required if these vessels sailed through 'shipping lanes fixed by the Minister-Chief of Navy Staff'.[197] Kwiatkowska suggested that 'submarines are presumably allowed to navigate submerged in such shipping lanes',[198] but it is clear from the text of the regulation that submarines were in fact required to navigate on the surface in all circumstances.[199]

The Philippines had similarly taken a restrictive approach to passage through its archipelagic waters prior to the adoption of UNCLOS. In

State, but the United States and the United Kingdom have disputed the validity of the Dominican Republic's claim. Sean D. Murphy, 'International Law Relating to Islands' (2017) 386 *Recueil des cours de l'Académie de La Haye* 1, 148.

192 UNCLOS (n 1) arts. 49(1), 49(3).

193 Indonesia is comprised of over 18,000 islands whereas the Philippines consists of more than 7,000 islands. Tara Davenport, 'The Archipelagic Regime' in Donald R. Rothwell et al. (eds.), *Oxford Handbook on the Law of the Sea* (Oxford University Press, 2015) 134, 139.

194 Barbara Kwiatkowska, 'The Archipelagic Regime in Practice in Indonesia and the Philippines: Making or Breaking International Law?' (1991) 6(1) *International Journal of Estuarine and Coastal Law* 1, 16.

195 Ibid.

196 Government Regulation No. 8 on Innocent Passage of Foreign Vessels through Indonesian Waters, 25 July 1962, arts. 1, 4 (Indonesia).

197 Ibid, art. 7.

198 Kwiatkowska (n 194) 17.

199 Government Regulation No. 8 on Innocent Passage of Foreign Vessels through Indonesian Waters (n 196) art. 7.

notes verbales to the UN Secretary-General in 1955 and the ILC in 1956, it claimed inter alia that '[a]ll waters around, between and connecting different islands belonging to Philippine Archipelago ... are necessary appurtenances of its land territory, forming an integral part of the national or inland waters'.[200] While it defined other areas within the limits established by various treaties as 'territorial waters' in which 'friendly foreign vessels' could exercise 'the right of innocent passage', the Philippines did not recognise a right of innocent passage in the areas described as 'national or inland waters'.[201] In Acts of 1961 and 1968 defining the baselines and the territorial sea, the Philippines again described the waters within archipelagic baselines as 'inland or internal waters' and did not refer to a right of innocent passage through these waters.[202]

Yet consistent with the resistance to the recognition of twelve mile territorial sea limits, the major maritime powers also opposed the claims of archipelagic States. In an article published shortly after the conclusion of the Second UN Conference on the Law of the Sea in 1960, Arthur Dean, Chairman of the US delegation at the Conference, reported that on 31 March 1960 the US submarine *Triton* had 'passed submerged through the Surigao Strait, south of Luzon in the Philippines, across the Mindanao Sea; then through the Macassar Strait and South of Java into the Indian Ocean'.[203] 'Thus', he explained, 'the *Triton* passed submerged through waters within the Indonesian and Philippine archipelagos, which are claimed unilaterally by each of those nations as "internal waters", although they include vast high sea areas'.[204] Observing that such passage would not be permitted 'as of right' if these were indeed 'internal waters', Dean explained that '[i]t is for this reason that we do not recognize the validity of this extensive and unilateral archipelago theory'.[205] As noted previously, the United States also objected to the extension of the territorial sea to twelve nautical miles at the time of this

[200] 'Philippines' (UN Doc. A/CN.4/99) [1956] 2 *Yearbook of the International Law Commission* 69, 69–70.

[201] Ibid. Cf. Kwiatkowska (n 195), who overlooked this important distinction between inland and territorial waters in the notes verbales: at 5.

[202] Republic Act No. 3046, 17 June 1961 (Philippines); Republic Act No. 5446, 18 September 1968 (Philippines).

[203] Arthur H. Dean, 'The Second Geneva Conference on the Law of the Sea: The Fight for Freedom of the Seas' (1960) 54(4) *American Journal of International Law* 751, 753. See also Chapter 6, Section 6.2.

[204] Dean (n 203) 753.

[205] Ibid.

Conference, citing among other reasons a concern that this change would restrict naval movements.[206] In his 1960 article, Dean further suggested that 'the territorial seas of neutral nations, if extended to 12 miles, could offer a safe haven from which enemy submarines might operate submerged and undetected by the coastal state, although in violation of international law'.[207] The acceptance of the concept of archipelagic waters thus had clear implications for the operations of submarines.

As with the establishment of the right of transit passage in international straits concomitant with the acceptance of a twelve mile territorial sea limit, any legal recognition of archipelagic States would necessitate balancing other States' interests in maintaining navigational rights within these waters.[208] For submarine passage, it is important to note that two rights of passage exist within archipelagic waters: the right of innocent passage and the right of archipelagic sea lanes passage. Each is discussed in this section.

7.4.1 *Innocent Passage in Archipelagic Waters*

Article 52 of UNCLOS sets out a suspendable right of innocent passage through archipelagic waters, with several qualifications. First, archipelagic States are not precluded from designating internal waters within its archipelagic waters and where closing lines are drawn for this purpose,[209] no right of innocent passage applies within those internal waters.[210] Second, the right of innocent passage must be exercised 'in accordance with Part II, section 3' of the Convention.[211] Section 3 of Part II includes the requirements discussed above in Section 7.2 as to what will constitute innocent passage,[212] that submarines must navigate on the surface[213] and the rights of the coastal State to put in place precautionary measures for

206 Chapter 6, Section 6.2.

207 Dean (n 203) 756.

208 The United States has referred to archipelagic sea lanes passage as 'an indispensable [right] which is a necessary concomitant to an archipelagic state juridical regime'. US Department of State Diplomatic Note No. 34, March 1987, cited in Kevin Baumert and Brian Melchior, 'The Practice of Archipelagic States: A Study of Studies' (2015) 46(1) *Ocean Development and International Law* 60, 71–72.

209 The closing lines must be drawn consistently with the requirements of Articles 9, 10 and 11 of UNCLOS for this purpose. UNCLOS (n 1) art. 50.

210 UNCLOS (n 1) art. 52(1) (noting that the right of innocent passage is 'without prejudice to article 50').

211 Ibid, art. 52(1).

212 Ibid, arts. 18, 19.

213 Ibid, art. 20.

foreign nuclear submarines[214] or adopt other laws and regulations.[215] Even though the right of innocent passage in archipelagic waters thus appears entirely comparable to the right of innocent passage in the territorial sea, commentators have suggested that because the underlying sovereignty is in archipelagic waters, which 'is a sui generis regime, wherein the waters are considered to be an "integral part of the territory of the ocean State"', this status may influence what a coastal State perceives to be prejudicial to its peace, good order or security.[216]

A third qualification on the right of innocent passage is that the archipelagic State may only suspend innocent passage if essential to protect its security and must do so temporarily, within a limited area of the archipelagic waters, and without discrimination 'in form or in fact among foreign ships'.[217] The latter phrasing is intended to ensure that there is no explicit discrimination, nor should there be any actions that have the effect of discriminating between certain foreign vessels.[218] The suspension must only commence after its terms have been duly published.[219]

A final qualification on the right of innocent passage in archipelagic waters is that it is subject to Article 53, which provides for the right of archipelagic sea lanes passage for 'all ships'.[220] Whether an autonomous submersible constitutes a 'ship' entitled to this right of passage is a question addressed in Chapter 14. In any event, it may be further noted that the sovereign immunity of military submarines continues to

214 Ibid, art. 23.
215 Ibid, art. 21.
216 Richard Barnes and Carmino Massarella, 'Article 52' in Proelss (n 33) 392, para. 7.
217 UNCLOS (n 1) art. 52(2). The inclusion of this provision may have been redundant given that Article 52(1) already cross-referred to Article 25(3), which is almost identical in terms. Article 25(3) references 'weapons exercises' as an activity essential for the protection of the coastal State's security but no such description is included within Article 52(2). It may therefore be arguable that weapons exercises are not considered essential for security within archipelagic waters and the inclusion of a separate provision that provides slightly differently for the suspension of innocent passage seeks to underline that the conditions are indeed distinct. But see Barnes and Massarella, 'Article 52' (n 216) 393, para. 10 (arguing that weapons exercises should still be included within the broader category of actions essential for security).
218 Nordquist (n 46) vol. 2, 462.
219 UNCLOS (n 1) art. 52(2).
220 Ibid, art. 52(1). Article 53(2) provides that 'all ships' enjoy the right of archipelagic sea lanes passage, and as such this right accrues for submarines, whether military, nuclear or private. See further Richard Barnes and Carmino Massarella, 'Article 53' in Proelss (n 33) 399, para. 11.

apply in undertaking innocent passage in archipelagic waters.[221] The archipelagic State thus continues to be limited in the responses it may take vis-à-vis foreign military submarines in the event that State considers such a submarine is in violation of the right of innocent passage.

7.4.2 *Archipelagic Sea Lanes Passage*

Submarines have the right of archipelagic sea lanes passage where the archipelagic State has designated sea lanes for this purpose or, if not designated, in 'the routes normally used for international navigation'.[222] Similar to transit passage through international straits, the key questions in relation to archipelagic sea lanes passage are where it applies within archipelagic waters, and what is permissible during this type of passage. Both aspects are addressed immediately below.

Article 53 of UNCLOS sets out the process and requirements for archipelagic States to utilise in designating sea lanes, which includes consideration of 'generally accepted international regulations'[223] and adoption within the IMO (as the 'competent international organization').[224] Moreover, the sea lanes 'shall include all normal passage routes used as routes for international navigation'.[225] These requirements associated with the designation of archipelagic sea lanes may be considered as internationalising the decisions of archipelagic States; such a task is not purely dependent on the subjective choices of the archipelagic State. An archipelagic State is not required to designate archipelagic sea lanes, however.[226]

In the Philippines, a number of bills were introduced proposing to designate archipelagic sea lanes and elaborated the obligations of foreign ships and aircraft when exercising 'the right of archipelagic sea lanes passage'. In House Bill 8018 of 2020, the Philippine Department of Foreign Affairs argued that 'not designating ASLs (Archipelagic Sea Lanes) would allow foreign countries [to] exercise archipelagic sea lanes passage in whatever route they consider or insist as routes normally used for international navigation'.[227] The move was apparently

221 Article 32, recognising this immunity, is also within Part II, Section 3 of UNCLOS.
222 UNCLOS (n 1) art. 53(12).
223 Ibid, art. 53(8).
224 Ibid, art. 53(9).
225 Ibid, art. 53(4).
226 Ibid, art. 53(1). In the absence of so doing, Article 53(12) of UNCLOS applies.
227 'DFA Urges Forming "Archipelagic Sea Lanes" within Philippine Waters', *ABS-CBN News*, 19 March 2021 <www.abs-cbn.com/news/03/19/21/dfa-urges-forming-archipelagic-sea-lanes-within-philippine-waters>.

a response to ongoing concerns about the passage of Chinese warships through archipelagic waters.[228] In November 2024, the Philippines adopted the Philippine Archipelagic Sea Lanes Act and the Philippine Maritime Zones Act, with the former Act setting out three general routes (and excluding other routes that may have been considered straits).[229] As at time of writing, the designation of these sea lanes must still be formalised at the IMO.

Disputes have arisen where designated archipelagic sea lanes depart from 'channels customarily used for international navigation'. Notably Indonesia's effort to designate only three channels that ran north-south rather than any channels running east–west was met with resistance from the United States and Australia at the IMO.[230] The result was a 'partial' designation of archipelagic sea lanes at the IMO and Indonesian legislation purporting to deny the existence of any other sea lanes, despite the ongoing existence of 'routes normally used for international navigation' even if not formally designated.[231] Following a proposal from Indonesia in 2019, the IMO also approved a traffic separation scheme in the Lombok Strait and Sunda Strait.[232] Archipelagic States may institute traffic separation schemes in their archipelagic sea lanes in accordance with Article 53(6) of UNCLOS.

As for the type of permissible passage in archipelagic sea lanes, it must be 'continuous and expeditious'.[233] Article 53(3) describes the required passage as 'unobstructed transit between one part of the high seas or an

[228] 'Philippine Lawmakers Want to Designate Inter-island Sea Lanes amid Chinese Incursions', *Radio Free Asia*, 28 October 2022 <www.rfa.org/english/news/southchinasea/sealanes-10282022175504.html>.

[229] For discussion, see Alex P. Dela Cruz, 'Why the Philippines Made a Dramatic Turnaround on the Question of Archipelagos in the Law of the Sea', *Lowy Interpreter*, 19 November 2024 <www.lowyinstitute.org/the-interpreter/why-philippines-made-dramatic-turnaround-question-archipelagos-law-sea>; Liu Xiaobo, 'The Influence of the Philippine Archipelagic Sea Lanes Act on Navigation Rights', *Asia Maritime Transparency Initiative*, 14 November 2024 <https://amti.csis.org/the-influence-of-the-philippine-archipelagic-sea-lanes-act-on-navigation-rights/>.

[230] For discussion, see Robin Warner, 'Implementing the Archipelagic Regime in the International Maritime Organization' in Donald R. Rothwell and Sam Bateman (eds.), *Navigational Rights and Freedoms and the New Law of the Sea* (Brill Nijhoff, 2000) 170.

[231] For discussion, see Chris Forward, 'Archipelagic Sea Lanes in Indonesia: Their Legality in International Law' (2009) 23 *Australian and New Zealand Maritime Law Journal* 143, 151–154.

[232] 'Routeing Measures other than Traffic Separation Schemes', 14 June 2019 (IMO Doc. SN.1/Circ.337); 'New Traffic Separation Schemes', 14 June 2019 (IMO Doc. COLREG.2/Circ.74).

[233] UNCLOS (n 1) art. 53(1).

exclusive economic zone and another part of the high seas or an exclusive economic zone'. As with the other passage regimes under UNCLOS discussed in this chapter, the intention is to allow submarines to navigate through sovereign waters and not loiter or undertake any activities other than continuous and expeditious navigation.

Archipelagic sea lanes passage otherwise aligns with requirements for transit passage.[234] Submarines are thus required to proceed without delay, refrain from any violation of Article 2(4) of the UN Charter, and 'refrain from any activities other than those incident to their normal modes of continuous and expeditious transit'.[235] As with transit passage, submarines may engage in submerged passage within archipelagic sea lanes, consistent with their 'normal mode'.[236] No research or survey activities are permissible during archipelagic sea lanes passage.[237] Archipelagic States have explicit parameters in relation to the laws and regulations that may be permissibly adopted in relation to archipelagic sea lanes passage,[238] including that the right of archipelagic sea lanes passage is non-suspendable.[239]

Commentators have observed that some archipelagic States have adopted requirements of prior notification or permission for warships to pass through archipelagic waters, but these requirements seem to relate to innocent passage through archipelagic waters rather than archipelagic sea lanes passage.[240] Other States, most notably the United States, have objected to this practice. Singling out warships for such regulation is not necessarily problematic; as discussed above, the coastal State is not to discriminate between States in its regulation of transit passage, but this non-discrimination clause does not preclude laws pertaining to particular types of vessels. In the case of innocent passage, the

234 Article 54 of UNCLOS provides that Articles 39, 40, 42 and 44 all apply *mutatis mutandis* to archipelagic sea lanes passage.

235 UNCLOS (n 1) art. 39(1).

236 This possibility was viewed as 'the biggest concession' by archipelagic States during UNCLOS negotiations: Davenport (n 149) fn 115.

237 As set out in Article 40 and applied to Part IV of UNCLOS by virtue of Article 54.

238 UNCLOS (n 1) art. 42.

239 Ibid, art. 44.

240 See, e.g., Barnes and Massarella, 'Article 53' (n 220) 400, para. 13. Such States include the Philippines, Indonesia, Antigua and Barbuda, Maldives, Seychelles, Saint Vincent and the Grenadines and Vanuatu. Baumert and Melchior also claim that some archipelagic States have unlawfully sought to restrict the movement of foreign nuclear or other inherently dangerous vessels: Kevin Baumert and Brian Melchior, 'The Practice of Archipelagic States: A Study of Studies' (2015) 46(1) *Ocean Development and International Law* 60, 73.

considerations concerning prior notification or authorisation discussed in Section 7.2.4 above obtain. In the case of archipelagic sea lanes passage, the freedom of navigation applies. Indonesia, which is the only State so far to have designated archipelagic sea lanes, does not appear to require prior notification or authorisation for archipelagic sea lanes.[241] Any such requirement or notice or authorisation would likely run counter to archipelagic sea lane passage given its emphasis on the freedom of navigation and the reduced limitations applying to this passage as compared to innocent passage.

In connection with archipelagic sea lanes passage, two further points are worth noting. The first is that Article 41 of UNCLOS, which governs sea lanes and traffic separation schemes in straits used for international navigation, is *not* among the provisions held to apply 'mutatis mutandis' to archipelagic sea lanes passage under Article 54. While Article 41 might appear to link the use of sea lanes in international straits to navigational safety, the right of the coastal State to restrict the passage of foreign vessels in its archipelagic waters to archipelagic sea lanes responds chiefly to the security concerns of archipelagic States.[242] This point of distinction means that at a general level the right to designate archipelagic sea lanes recognised under UNCLOS is not restricted by an interest to ensure navigational safety.

The second point of relevance is that Article 42 of UNCLOS does apply to passage through archipelagic sea lanes and would appear to restrict the coastal State's right to make laws and regulation in respect of such passage to those concerning

> (a) the safety of navigation and the regulation of maritime traffic, as provided in article 41;
> (b) the prevention, reduction and control of pollution, by giving effect to applicable international regulations regarding the discharge of oil, oily wastes and other noxious substances in the strait;
> (c) with respect to fishing vessels, the prevention of fishing, including the stowage of fishing gear;
> (d) the loading or unloading of any commodity, currency or person in contravention of the customs, fiscal, immigration or sanitary laws and regulations of States bordering straits.

[241] Government Regulation No. 37 on the Rights and Obligations of Foreign Ships and Aircraft Exercising the Right of Archipelagic Sea Lanes Passage through Designated Archipelagic Sea Lanes, 28 June 2002 (Indonesia).

[242] See United Nations, *Law of the Sea: Archipelagic States: Legislative History of Part IV of the United Nations Convention on the Law of the Sea* (United Nations Publications, 1990) 23, 29, 59, 62, 110.

This provision underlines that any requirements for prior notice or authorisation are not consonant with archipelagic sea lanes passage.

In this context, it is interesting to consider the possibility that restricting passage to archipelagic sea lanes does some of the work that prior notification/authorisation and the requirement that submarines show their flag and travel on the surface may do in the case of innocent passage – that is to say, giving the coastal State some knowledge of where foreign vessels, including warships, are located within its waters. While this advantage is somewhat diminished in the case of submarines, which may travel submerged in archipelagic sea lanes, it is a regime that nevertheless limits the paths by which such vessels may lawfully transit archipelagic waters submerged and may allow a focus for monitoring activities by the archipelagic State. The designation of archipelagic sea lanes represents a compromise between the interests of maritime States in navigation and the security interests of archipelagic States.

7.5 Conclusion

It is important to have a strong grasp of the requirements for submarines traversing the territorial sea of another State, including because the rules of innocent passage continue to have relevance in certain straits and in archipelagic waters. Submarine passage in the territorial sea of another State must meet a number of criteria associated with characterising innocent passage, plus must be on the surface and displaying the flag of the State. Failures to meet these requirements mean an international law violation has occurred. Additional requirements exist for nuclear-powered submarines; they may be required to use sea lanes and other ship routeing measures for navigational safety reasons. States may seek to challenge the validity of sea lane and routeing requirements if they are not considered to be applicable for navigational safety.

In each instance, it is apparent that there is a constant balance of rights and duties that exist in relation to the exercise of the right of innocent passage in another State's territorial sea. The coastal State view is likely to be favoured because of its sovereignty over this maritime territory but the existence of the right of innocent passage does mean that the coastal State view is not an entirely subjective assessment. Referring to existing international standards will assist in ensuring that coastal State decisions are consistent with international law.

A central conflict persists on the question of prior notification or authorisation for warships to traverse the territorial sea of another

State. The issue is not explicitly addressed in UNCLOS. A consideration of the drafting history back to the 1930 Hague Codification Conference indicates a view that many States have considered that a *right* to impose such a requirement rests with the coastal State. The current position reflects conflicting views among States with the right of coastal States to require prior notification or authorisation cast as the minority position. In view of the lack of an explicit position in UNCLOS and conflicting State practice, the better point of reference on this issue is Article 24 of UNCLOS, which prevents States from hampering innocent passage. A coastal State right to insist on prior authorisation for the passage of foreign-flagged warships through its territorial sea clearly falls foul of Article 24 of UNCLOS. Prior notification does not necessarily hamper passage. A failure of a warship to notify a coastal State of its impending passage may ultimately be another factor that a coastal State then considers in its determination as to whether the passage is prejudicial to its peace, good order and security.

For submarines, there is uniformity in the view that submerged passage is allowed as an exercise of the right of transit passage. Debates may continue as to what maritime areas are subject to the right of transit passage (which may include questions regarding the approaches to international straits) and what precise rights and duties associated with transit passage may be exercised. The status of each international strait and the maritime conditions of the available passage must be considered to determine what right of passage applies and how it may be exercised. Moreover, the relevance of coastal States' laws and regulations for military submarines will be largely limited to maritime safety concerns. Enforcement actions on the part of the coastal State will be limited by the requirement of strait States not to deny, hamper, impair or suspend transit passage, as well as the sovereign immunity of military submarines. The critical importance of straits for international navigation may, and should, favour a balance of rights and duties that allows for unimpeded passage of foreign warships.

In archipelagic waters, the regime of innocent passage applies apart from passage in archipelagic sea lanes. Archipelagic sea lanes are either those established by the archipelagic State through an international process at the IMO or are those considered 'routes normally used for international navigation'.[243] The exercise of archipelagic sea lane passage is generally aligned with the regime of transit passage. For military

[243] UNCLOS (n 1) art. 53(12).

submarines, it allows the possibility of traversing these waters submerged; but outside the archipelagic sea lanes, submarines must surface and act consistently with the requirements of innocent passage. Ensuring that submerged passage is undertaken only in archipelagic sea lanes is critical given the emphasis on the security interests of archipelagic States. As seems to have been the case with the Philippines recently, security considerations should serve as a motivation to formally designate archipelagic sea lanes, as it may also serve as a de facto traffic separation scheme within archipelagic waters. Archipelagic States remain limited in the actions that can be taken against submarines during archipelagic sea lane passage, both because of the navigational rights granted for this type of passage and because of the sovereign immunity enjoyed by military submarines, which will be the submarines most commonly traversing these waters.[244]

[244] Though there may be an increase in the deployment of UMAVs in archipelagic waters. See, e.g., Jeoffrey Maitem, 'Armed Forces of the Philippines Investigate Chinese Submarine Drone', *Naval News*, 3 January 2025 <www.navalnews.com/naval-news/2025/01/armed-forces-of-the-philippines-investigate-chinese-submarine-drone/>. For the regulation of these vehicles, see Chapter 14.

8

Military Activities, Intelligence Gathering and Other Submarine Activities in the Exclusive Economic Zone

8.1 Introduction

This chapter examines the international laws governing the activities of submarines in the exclusive economic zone (EEZ) with a focus on foreign-flagged submarines operating in the EEZs of coastal States.[1] The discussion below indicates that the scope of navigational rights in this maritime zone has been a long-standing debate, which existed at the point that the EEZ was created during negotiations of the UN Convention on the Law of the Sea (UNCLOS)[2] and has since persisted. This difficulty emerges because of the *sui generis* status of the EEZ, as discussed in Section 8.2; a maritime zone where there is an allocation of exclusive authority to the coastal State in relation to specific matters and ongoing recognition of rights of other States intended to coexist with the coastal State's rights. A key question in relation to the scope of navigational rights for foreign-flagged military submarines is whether intelligence gathering and other military activities can be considered as exercises of freedom of navigation within the EEZ or whether any of those activities are regulated by the coastal State. This debate has been well ventilated in relation to warships generally and is considered in this chapter in terms of whether the interpretation or application of international law changes at all when the warships in question are submarines.

Foreign-flagged submarines may operate in the EEZ of a coastal State for a diversity of reasons: for military purposes, scientific research, supporting commercial endeavours such as oil exploration and exploitation and in laying submarine cables, and for tourism. The core international law rules relating to these submarine activities are also addressed

[1] That is, the situation where a submarine is flagged to a State other than the coastal State and is operating in the EEZ of the latter State.

[2] United Nations Convention on the Law of the Sea, Montego Bay, 10 December 1982, entered into force 16 November 1994, 1833 UNTS 397 ('UNCLOS').

in Section 8.3, partly as a foundation for more detailed discussion of rules that further implicate their use, especially navigational safety and marine environmental protection in later chapters.

While there is a strong argument that most foreign-flagged submarine activities fall within the scope of navigational freedom 'and other internationally lawful uses related to these freedoms',[3] any assessment of the lawfulness of such activities must account for the obligation of 'due regard', which applies both in EEZs[4] and on the high seas.[5] We further ask in Section 8.4 whether these activities could constitute an abuse of rights under UNCLOS.[6] These restrictions apply in relation to all activities in the EEZ (as well as on the high seas).[7] Other sources of regulation, such as rules relating to navigational safety, the use of force and marine environmental protection, are explored in subsequent chapters. Coastal State responses to submarine activities must also be assessed for their consistency with international law, as they must also show due regard,[8] not abuse rights, nor unjustifiably interfere with navigational rights over the continental shelf.[9] The question of whether and when submarine activities (or coastal State measures responding to such activities) may constitute an unlawful threat or use of force is considered in the following chapter.

8.2 Allocation of Rights and Duties in the EEZ

The EEZ was one of the most notable developments emerging with the adoption of UNCLOS. Indeed, even prior to the conclusion of negotiations, the International Court of Justice (ICJ) recognised that the EEZ had emerged within customary international law.[10] Prior to and during the negotiations of UNCLOS, some developing States sought to extend their full sovereignty up to 200 nautical miles from their baselines but the major maritime States refused to accept such wholesale 'territorialisation' of these maritime areas.[11] While the zone itself as a legal construct over

[3] Ibid, art. 58(1).
[4] Ibid, art. 58(3).
[5] Ibid, art. 87(2).
[6] Ibid, art. 300.
[7] Ibid, art. 87(2).
[8] Ibid, art. 56(2)
[9] Ibid, art. 78(2).
[10] *Continental Shelf* (Libya v. Malta) (Judgment of 3 June 1985) [1985] ICJ Rep 13, para. 34.
[11] Sam Bateman, 'The Regime of the Exclusive Economic Zone: Military Activities and the Need for Compromise?' in Tafsir Malick Ndiaye and Rüdiger Wolfrum (eds.), *Law of the*

which the coastal State may exercise sovereign rights up to 200 nautical miles from its baselines has been widely accepted as customary international law,[12] the precise understandings of the nature of the EEZ and the scope of the rights and duties allocated to States therein have been ongoing matters of discussion.[13]

On the nature of the EEZ, many States and commentators have argued that the EEZ is *sui generis*[14] and any interpretation of the allocations of rights and duties within the EEZ should therefore account for the new status of the zone rather than importing other understandings of maritime zones into the EEZ. Other States and commentators, notably the United States, have held the view that the EEZ is the high seas with coastal States being accorded specific rights within that zone.[15] In this conception, the underlying status of the EEZ as high seas would then influence what activities were allowed and how they could be conducted within the EEZ. Bateman, for example, observed:

> The United States believes that the coastal State cannot unduly restrict or impede the freedoms of navigation in and overflight of the EEZ, and its

Sea, Environmental Law and Settlement of Disputes: Liber Amicorum Judge Thomas A Mensah (Brill, 2007) 569, 570. See also George V. Galdorisi and Alan G. Kaufman, 'Military Activities in the Exclusive Economic Zone: Preventing Uncertainty and Defusing Conflict' (2002) 32(2) *California Western International Law Journal* 253, 265–267; Francesco Francioni, 'Peacetime Use of Force, Military Activities, and the New Law of the Sea' (1985) 18(2) *Cornell International Law Journal* 203, 214.

12 *Alleged Violations of Sovereign Rights and Maritime Spaces in the Caribbean Sea* (Nicaragua v. Colombia) (Judgment of 21 April 2022) [2022] ICJ Rep 266, paras. 56–57.

13 These debates are tracked in both early and more recent accounts of the EEZ. See generally, e.g., Barbara Kwiatkowska, *The 200 Mile Exclusive Economic Zone in the New Law of the Sea* (Brill, 1989); Francisco Orrego Vicuña, *The Exclusive Economic Zone: Regime and Legal Nature under International Law* (Cambridge University Press, 1989); Zhen Sun, *Finding a Balance in the Exclusive Economic Zone: Conflict and Stability in the Law of the Sea* (Cambridge University Press, 2025) 13–36.

14 Francioni calls it an 'amphibious' status: Francioni (n 11) 216. On the *sui generis* status see, e.g., Robin Churchill, Vaughan Lowe and Amy Sander, *The Law of the Sea* (4th ed., Manchester University Press, 2022) 262; Gemma Andreone, 'The Exclusive Economic Zone' in Donald R. Rothwell et al. (eds.), *The Oxford Handbook on the Law of the Sea* (Oxford University Press, 2015) 159, 162.

15 See, e.g., Cameron Moore, *Freedom of Navigation and the Law of the Sea: Warships, States and the Use of Force* (Routledge, 2021) 97–98. Proelss has bridged these perspectives in commenting 'in terms of territory, the EEZ is a no man's land (and thus high seas), whereas in terms of function (i.e., usage and protection rights) the EEZ is a sui generis zone subject to a "specific legal regime" (Article 55 of [UNCLOS]), located quasi "between" the maritime territory of a coastal state and the high seas'. Alexander Proelss, 'The Law on the Exclusive Economic Zone in Perspective: Legal Status and Resolution of User Conflicts Revisited' (2012) 26 *Ocean Yearbook* 87, 89.

> naval commanders are advised that 'the existence of an exclusive economic zone need not, of itself, be of operational concern'. At the other extreme, China appears to interpret 'due regard' as requiring foreign users of its EEZ to refrain from activities that endanger its sovereignty, security and national interests. This is an unsatisfactory division of views.[16]

These different perspectives on the nature of the EEZ could potentially influence the interpretation of the key provisions in UNCLOS that set out the respective rights and duties of States within the EEZ and that have implications for the operation of submarines.

Article 56 of UNCLOS first articulates the sovereign rights and exclusive jurisdiction enjoyed by coastal States in the EEZ. Most notable for present purposes is that Article 56 accords rights to the coastal State in relation to the conservation and management, exploration and exploitation of the natural resources of this maritime zone.[17] In addition, the coastal State has exclusive jurisdiction in relation to the protection and preservation of the marine environment, marine scientific research and artificial islands, structures and installations.[18] In terms of duties, coastal States must have due regard to 'the rights and duties of other States'.[19] Further, exploration and exploitation activities in relation to the natural resources of the continental shelf 'must not infringe or result in any unjustifiable interference with navigation and other rights and freedoms of other States as provided for in the Convention'.[20] Coastal States will thus have authority to regulate submarines that are engaged in marine scientific research, as that regime is understood in UNCLOS,[21] when submarines are used in relation to the exploitation of marine resources,[22] and where the operation of submarines may potentially impinge on the duty to protect and preserve the marine environment.[23] Any activities of the coastal State in the EEZ are also constrained by duties intended to

[16] Bateman (n 11) 571 (citation omitted). See also Hugh Williamson, 'Intelligence Gathering and Espionage in the Exclusive Economic Zone: Peaceful or Not?' in Dirk Werle et al. (eds.), *The Future of Ocean Governance and Capacity Development: Essays in Honor of Elisabeth Mann Borgese (1918–2002)* (Brill, 2018) 416, 418.

[17] UNCLOS (n 1) art. 56(1).

[18] Ibid, art. 56(1).

[19] Ibid, art. 56(2).

[20] Ibid, art. 78(2).

[21] The debate over military research and marine scientific research for public purposes is discussed in Section 8.3.1.2.

[22] Discussed in Section 8.3.3.1.

[23] This latter duty is subject to the sovereign immunities enjoyed by military submarines, as set out in Article 236 of UNCLOS and discussed further in Chapter 12.

protect navigational freedoms enjoyed by other States, such as due regard and non-abuse of rights.[24]

Pursuant to Article 58 of UNCLOS, all States (including the coastal State) continue to enjoy 'the freedoms referred to in article 87 of navigation . . ., and other internationally lawful uses of the sea related to these freedoms, such as those associated with the operation of ships, air craft and submarine cables and pipelines, and compatible with the other provisions of this Convention'.[25] Most critical for submarines is the freedom of navigation and other internationally lawful uses of the sea related to this freedom.[26] One immediate constraint on the rights enjoyed by all other States within the EEZ is that those States are to accord the coastal State due regard in the exercise of its sovereign rights and exclusive jurisdiction.[27] States exercising the freedom of navigation must also comply with the laws and regulations adopted by the coastal State in accordance with UNCLOS and other rules of international law.[28] While the navigational rights enjoyed by foreign-flagged submarines in the EEZ are clearly greater than those exercised in international straits or within the territorial sea,[29] the extent that these navigational rights are entirely comparable to the freedom enjoyed on the high seas is a debate that has emerged between States in the claims and counter-claims as to lawful activities by foreign-flagged warships, including submarines, in the coastal State's EEZ.[30]

Articles 56 and 58 of UNCLOS provide the fundamental allocation of rights between States in the EEZ and the ICJ has noted that these

[24] Discussed in Section 8.4.

[25] UNCLOS (n 1) art. 58(1).

[26] In Australia, the entire EEZ 'is a permanently established Australian submarine exercise area': Australian Hydrographic Office, 'Information Concerning Submarines' (Notice to Mariners 612/2014) para. 3.

[27] UNCLOS (n 1) art. 58(3).

[28] Ibid, art. 58(3). Other rules of international law would include, for example, duties relating to navigational safety. The coastal State's laws and regulations with which other States must comply are only those coastal State laws and regulations that are consistent with UNCLOS. Hence, if a coastal State adopted a law going beyond the scope of its authority under UNCLOS, a State would not be required to comply with that law.

[29] A proposal that military activities other than navigation in the EEZ would be subject to coastal State consent was rejected during UNCLOS negotiations. Francioni (n 11) 215.

[30] This debate is often described in the literature. See, e.g., Albert Hoffman, 'Freedom of Navigation' in Anne Peters and Rüdiger Wolfrum (eds.), *Max Planck Encyclopedia of Public International Law* (Oxford University Press, April 2011) para. 18; Francioni (n 11) 214–216.

provisions reflect customary international law.[31] Yet in drafting UNCLOS, there was some anticipation by the negotiators that not every activity or use of the oceans could be foreseen and hence a provision was needed in anticipation of disputes regarding activities over which there was not a clear allocation of authority. Article 59 of UNCLOS thus reads:

> In cases where this Convention does not attribute rights or jurisdiction to the coastal State or to other States within the exclusive economic zone, and a conflict arises between the interests of the coastal State and any other State or States, the conflict should be resolved on the basis of equity and in the light of all the relevant circumstances, taking into account the respective importance of the interests involved to the parties as well as to the international community as a whole.[32]

Article 59 is occasionally raised in the literature as a potential point of reference for resolving contests within the EEZ.[33] However, it appears that no State has relied on Article 59 to assert rights in the EEZ, and it has not yet been the source of discussion in any case arising under the dispute settlement procedures set out in Part XV of UNCLOS.

While it is apparent that there is a split allocation of rights and duties between the coastal State and other States in the EEZ, the existing legal framework relies heavily on the characterisation of activities being undertaken as well as on the interpretation and application of the relevant standards (especially 'due regard'). The discussion that follows first considers in Section 8.3 the different activities in which submarines may be engaged in the EEZ and the international law requirements associated with those activities and then turns in Section 8.4 to the over-arching duties either restraining submarine activities or coastal State responses to submarine activities.

8.3 International Laws Regulating Foreign-Flagged Submarine Activities in the EEZ

Submarine activities in the EEZ range between military exercises, naval patrols and intelligence gathering, which are all conducted by warships,

[31] *Alleged Violations of Sovereign Rights and Maritime Spaces in the Caribbean Sea* (n 12) para. 57.

[32] UNCLOS (n 1) art. 59.

[33] See, e.g., Sienho Yee, 'Agora: Military Activities in the EEZ Sketching the Debate on Military Activities in the EEZ: An Editorial Comment' (2010) 9 *Chinese Journal of International Law* 1, 3–4; Sun (n 13) 199–361.

to marine scientific research in pursuit of economic objectives, for scientific projects and for other commercial activities (such as tourism). This section first considers the actions of foreign-flagged warship submarines and then assesses the international legal regime for the operation of private submarines in the EEZ for commercial and scientific activities. A core difficulty to acknowledge is that warship submarines may engage in activities that are also important for scientific endeavours and that private submarine activities may hold relevance for military planning; one activity may have more than one purpose or hold more than one use. Equally, the mission of a submarine may encompass a variety of activities. For example, USS *Dolphin*, which was an experimental US Navy submarine with a displacement of some 860 long tons and with a complement of 27 crew, was involved in surveying and mapping, submarine technology testing and other activities.[34] The United States also operated *NR-1*, the now decommissioned nuclear-powered research submarine, which was slightly larger than the midget submarines of today and capable of carrying thirteen persons for twenty-five days at depths of about 900 metres. Its purpose was to undertake seabed research and oceanographic mapping, as well as to recover items from wrecks.[35] Thus in one mission, a submarine may undertake activities that potentially require coastal State consent and other actions that are permissible as part of the submarine's freedom of navigation. The applicable legal regime may depend on whether the submarine is a warship or not or whether the submarine is privately owned or operated for commercial purposes. For military submarines, the sovereign immunity enjoyed will limit the actions a coastal State may take against a submarine in response to a possible violation of its rights; however, that immunity will not necessarily preclude a diplomatic protest emanating from, and potential dispute with, the coastal State concerned.

Section 8.3.1 discusses the international law applying to military activities of foreign-flagged submarines in a coastal State's EEZ, including an examination of intelligence gathering and military data collection. We also assess in Section 8.3.2 the requirements associated with marine scientific research, which will apply most commonly to privately owned submarines or submersibles engaged in research that leads to publicly

[34] Paul Stillwell, 'The Last Diesel Boat' (2008) 22(1) *Naval History* 2; G. Verd and G. Hunsaker, 'Dolphin: Flexibility for Submarine Research and Development' (Oceans '77 Conference Record, 17–19 October 2022, Los Angeles).

[35] See generally, Frank W. Lacroix et al., *A Concept of Operations for a New Deep-Diving Submarine* (RAND Corporation, 2002).

shared outputs. Private submarines are also used for certain commercial activities in the EEZ, discussed in Section 8.3.3, including being used as part of the exploration and exploitation of the natural resources, the laying and repair of submarine cables, and for tourism, especially the exploration of wrecks.

8.3.1 *Legality of Military Activities in the EEZ*

As indicated in the introduction to this chapter, an ongoing source of debate between States has been the legality of military activities by foreign-flagged vessels within the EEZ of a coastal State and whether the coastal State may lawfully prevent such activities,[36] as some States have purported to do in their national legislation.[37] Military activities have traditionally been considered as a freedom of the high seas even if not explicitly denoted as such in either the 1958 High Seas Convention[38] or in Article 87(1) of UNCLOS.[39] Yet different viewpoints have emerged over the precise scope of these freedoms in the EEZ and the extent that a coastal State may limit those freedoms. The arguments have been articulated in the literature over the last twenty years at least.[40] The debate is usefully encapsulated in the competing pieces of Pedrozo and Zhang in the *Chinese Journal of International Law*.[41] Pedrozo argues inter alia that States may undertake military activities in foreign EEZs without the need for prior consent or notice,[42] and that State practice,

[36] Writing in 1985, Francioni remarked that the 'majority of authors . . . believe that military uses of the seas remain unaffected by the establishment of the EEZ'. Francioni (n 11) 214.

[37] See n 48 below.

[38] Convention on the High Seas, Geneva, 29 April 1958, entered into force 30 September 1962, 450 UNTS 11, art. 2 ('1958 High Seas Convention').

[39] Hoffman (n 30) para 5.

[40] The issues as of 2005 are captured in a volume of *Marine Policy*. The discussions between commentators at that time led to a proposal for a set of guidelines addressing military activities in the EEZ, but those guidelines have not been pursued by States: Hasjim Djalal, Alexander Yankov and Anthony Bergin, 'Draft Guidelines for Military and Intelligence Gathering Activities in the EEZ and their Means and Manner of Implementation and Enforcement' (2005) 29 *Marine Policy* 175. For a more recent account and proposal for ways forward, see Sun (n 13) 201–270.

[41] Raul (Pete) Pedrozo, 'Preserving Navigational Rights and Freedoms: The Right to Conduct Military Activities in China's Exclusive Economic Zone' (2010) 9 *Chinese Journal of International Law* 9; Haiwen Zhang, 'Is It Safeguarding the Freedom of Navigation or Maritime Hegemony of the United States? Comments on Raul (Pete) Pedrozo's Article on Military Activities in the EEZ' (2010) 9 *Chinese Journal of International Law* 31.

[42] Pedrozo, 'Preserving Navigational Rights and Freedoms' (n 41) 13.

including China's practice,[43] strongly supports such a position given the continued freedom of navigation in the EEZ. Zhang instead posits that the establishment of the EEZ fundamentally changed the pre-existing freedom of navigation as enjoyed on the high seas,[44] and highlights the lack of agreement during UNCLOS negotiations with a position that explicitly allowed the continuation of military activities as practiced previously on the high seas.[45] Contemporary writing continues to assess what seem to be irreconcilable positions.[46]

At its broadest, Pedrozo has described lawful military activities as including:

> intelligence, surveillance and reconnaissance (ISR) operations; military marine data collection and naval oceanographic surveys; war games and military exercises; bunkering and underway replenishment; testing and use of weapons; aircraft carrier flight operations and submarine operations; acoustic and sonar operations; naval control and protection of shipping; establishment and maintenance of military-related artificial installations; ballistic missile defence operations and ballistic missile test support; maritime interdiction operations (e.g., visit, board, search and seizure); conventional and ballistic missile testing; belligerent rights in naval warfare (e.g., right of visit and search); strategic arms control verification; maritime security operations (e.g., counter-terrorism and counter-proliferation); and sea control.[47]

From this perspective, all 'submarine operations' are within the scope of military activities and part of the 'other internationally lawful uses of the sea' related to the freedom of navigation. This interpretation makes sense in relation to submarines that are classed as warships but would not encompass private or commercially operated submarines.

[43] Ibid, 16–18. Zhang disputes Pedrozo's account of State practice, highlighting the difficulty in knowing the relevant maritime zones at issue when there are various incidences of disputed territorial sovereignty, which implicates the claimed maritime zones: Zhang (n 41) 40–41.

[44] Zhang (n 41) 31, 33, 37.

[45] Ibid, 47.

[46] See, e.g., Frederik Rogiers, 'A New Cold War at Sea: Fishing Rights vs. The Proliferation of Military Activities in the EEZ' (2024) 163 *Marine Policy* 106077. Klein has sought to propose a middle ground: Natalie Klein, 'The South China Sea Code of Conduct and the Freedom of Navigation: A Proposal in honor of Ted L. McDorman' (2024) 55(4) *Ocean Development and International Law* 490.

[47] Raul 'Pete' Pedrozo, 'Military Activities in the Exclusive Economic Zone: East Asia Focus' (2014) 90 *International Law Studies* 514, 517.

It is arguably the case that the reference to the freedom of navigation and other related uses is indeed wide enough to cover the variety of peaceful activities undertaken by military submarines. National legislation seeking to limit military activities has referenced 'military exercises or manoeuvres, in particular those that imply the use of weapons or explosives',[48] but has been protested by other States.[49] China has particularly taken issue with military marine data collection being classed as military research or military activities and thereby excluded from the marine scientific research legal regime.[50] Koh considered that a compromise position was needed on this question and that UNCLOS sought to encapsulate that 'middle ground' of not specifically including military activities in the text but that they were generally understood as included in the rights enjoyed under Article 58.[51] Both the language of UNCLOS and State practice, especially in relation to military submarine operations, indicate that such activity is lawful in a coastal State's EEZ albeit subject to general restrictions (not including coastal State consent) that are discussed in Section 8.4 below.[52] Nonetheless, in light of the controversy regarding this issue, the questions of intelligence gathering and military research are examined more closely as critical aspects of military submarines' operations in other States' EEZ.

[48] See, e.g., Declaration of the Brazilian Government made upon Ratification of the Convention, 22 December 1988. Kaye compiled data on States either restricting or potentially restricting military activities in the EEZ in relation to Cabo Verde, El Salvador, India, Indonesia, Iran, Malaysia, Maldives, Mauritania, Mauritius, Myanmar, North Korea, Pakistan, Peru, Philippines, Portugal, Senegal, Uruguay, Venezuela: Stuart Kaye, 'Freedom of Navigation in a Post 9/11 World: Security and Creeping Jurisdiction' in David Freestone, Richard Barnes and David Ong (eds.) *The Law of the Sea: Progress and Prospects* (Oxford University Press, 2006) 347, 354–356. More recently, Pedrozo has noted 30 States seek to regulate foreign military activities in the EEZ (or beyond the lawful limit of the territorial sea): Pedrozo, 'Military Activities in the Exclusive Economic Zone' (n 47) 521–522. Similarly, see Sun (n 13) 225–229, 230.

[49] See, e.g., Declaration of Italy made upon Ratification of the Convention, 13 January 1995.

[50] Zhang (n 41) 35–36, 38, 42–43.

[51] Tommy T. B. Koh, 'Remarks on the Legal Status of the Exclusive Economic Zone' in Myron H. Nordquist, Tommy T. B. Koh and John Norton Moore (eds.), *Freedom of Seas, Passage Rights and the 1982 Law of the Sea Convention* (Martinus Nijhoff Publishers, 2009) 53–54.

[52] Other restrictions are canvassed in chapters that follow, especially in relation to the use of force.

8.3.1.1 Legality of Intelligence Gathering in the EEZ

Williamson identifies five types of information-gathering in the EEZ: 'academic scientific research, natural resource research, hydrographic research, military related research, and intelligence gathering'.[53] States deploy submarines for the purpose of ISR missions.[54] The US Navy's surveillance ships conduct underwater surveillance and gather data to detect threats to underwater platforms, enhance navigational safety of submarines and improve technology for undersea warfare.[55]

Submarines gather intelligence 'to inform military operations and the conduct of statecraft',[56] and 'to inform civilian leaders and military commanders of the strength, location, and intentions of the adversary'.[57] Submersibles may also facilitate surveillance on submarine cables, which are discussed in Section 8.3.3.2 below, through the placement of recording devices on cables or by allowing collection of data that passes through the cable. It has been reported that Russia has deployed host nuclear-powered submarines that hold mini-submarines able to 'lay taps (even on fiber optic cables), make inspections or cut the cables in hard to fix places'.[58] The United States has engaged in this form of espionage since the 1970s and has deployed submarines for this

[53] Williamson (n 16) 416, 418.

[54] Reconnaissance involves information-gathering in relation to a specific question whereas surveillance refers to ongoing monitoring of a target; intelligence is the product derived from reconnaissance and surveillance, in conjunction with other information. See Andrew Torelli, 'US Intelligence, Surveillance and Reconnaissance Challenges in the Asia-Pacific' (Royal Australian Air Force Air Power Development Centre, Working Paper 37, 2013) (referring to definitions provided by the US Joint Chiefs of Staff dictionary of military terms).

[55] Pedrozo, 'Military Activities in the Exclusive Economic Zone' (n 47) 529.

[56] James Kraska, 'Intelligence Collection and the International Law of the Sea' (2022) 99 *International Law Studies* 602, 603.

[57] Ibid, 604.

[58] H. I. Sutton, 'How Russian Spy Submarines Can Interfere with Undersea Internet Cables', *Forbes*, 19 August 2020 <www.forbes.com/sites/hisutton/2020/08/19/how-russian-spy-submarines-can-interfere-with-undersea-internet-cables/>. Hinck refers to similar Russian practice from 2015: 'Russian ships and submarines near cable routes around the world caused concern within the U.S. intelligence community that Russia was attempting to tap or cut critical internet communications lines. A Cold War-style drama played out between the Russian subs following cable lines and the American ships, subs and spy satellites tracking them': Garrett Hinck, 'Cutting the Cord: The Legal Regime Protecting Undersea Cables', *Lawfare*, 21 November 2017 <www.lawfaremedia.org/article/cutting-cord-legal-regime-protecting-undersea-cables>.

purpose.[59] China's Navy also uses its submarines for surveys and reconnaissance.[60]

While there are limitations on intelligence gathering within the territorial sea of another State in light of the requirements of the right of innocent passage,[61] those limitations do not adhere within the EEZ.[62] Instead, it is anticipated that State actors will be gathering information, which is essential to conduct necessary policing activities, such as detecting and suppressing different criminal offences.[63] Moreover, ISR have been consistent activities of navies in State practice.[64] Intelligence gathering further enables the pursuit of information from the sea that may benefit a State's national security, and may be critical in supporting maritime domain awareness.[65]

Kraska rightly argues that intelligence gathering is a freedom of the high seas in light of State practice that includes reports of intelligence agencies of States and the very design and construction of State vessels for this purpose.[66] He considers that this freedom applies within the EEZ by virtue of Article 58 of UNCLOS, albeit subject to a requirement of due regard and peaceful purposes, which relates back to the prohibition on

[59] Olga Khazan, 'The Creepy, Long-Standing Practice of Undersea Cable Tapping', *The Atlantic*, 16 July 2013 <www.theatlantic.com/international/archive/2013/07/the-creepy-long-standing-practice-of-undersea-cable-tapping/277855/>. While acknowledging its uncommonness, Davenport has noted:

> [I]n 2005, it was reported that the submarine USS Jimmy Carter was equipped with the ability to tap undersea cables and eavesdrop on the communications passing through them. Such an operation involves the submarine lifting the cable from the seabed and onto the submarine into a special chamber where crew would extract data either by bending the fiber or by splicing a second fiber to each of the fibers.

Tara Davenport, 'Submarine Cables, Cybersecurity and International Law: An Intersectional Analysis' (2015) 24(1) *Catholic University Journal of Law and Technology* 57, 104.

[60] Pedrozo, 'Preserving Navigational Rights and Freedoms' (n 41) 16–18.

[61] UNCLOS (n 1) art. 19(2)(c). See further Chapter 7, Section 7.2.1.

[62] Douglas Guilfoyle, 'Maritime Security' in Jill Barrett and Richard Barnes (eds.), *Law of the Sea: UNCLOS as a Living Treaty* (British Institute of International and Comparative Law, 2016) 329, 356.

[63] See further Chapter 13, Section 13.3.

[64] Pedrozo, 'Military Activities in the Exclusive Economic Zone' (n 47) 528. See also Sun (n 13) 239.

[65] Natalie Klein, *Maritime Security and the Law of the Sea* (OUP, 2011) 211 and 214–215.

[66] Kraska (n 56) 605–606.

the threat or use of force under the UN Charter,[67] and the specific rights of the coastal State.[68] While States may entertain long-held objections to other States spying on them, Lubin has persuasively argued in favour of a sovereign's prerogative to engage in peacetime espionage.[69] Lubin argues against using a territorial frame as a helpful way to assess the legality of intelligence gathering,[70] and emphasises the articulation of legal limits to constrain the practice. In this regard, Lubin relies on the principle of abuse of rights as one such limit, which is discussed below in Section 8.4 of this chapter in light of the inclusion of this limitation in Article 300 of UNCLOS.

8.3.1.2 Undertaking Military Research or Marine Scientific Research

Submarines provide unique opportunities for oceanic data collection. They were first deployed by Dutch scientists in the 1920s to take gravity measurements at sea.[71] Scientific research involving submarines was subsequently limited due to the predominant warship status and operations of submarines and any data collected was primarily used to support those military missions.[72] Military research may include 'the collection of hydrographic, oceanographic, marine geological, geophysical, chemical, biological, and acoustic data'.[73] States such as China and India have protested military research undertaken by US and British vessels.[74] Military surveys are usually considered essential for submarine operations as well as for anti-submarine warfare (ASW).[75] It is, however, also apparent that the data collected may have relevance for other studies

[67] Ibid, 606–609.

[68] Ibid, 610.

[69] See Asaf Lubin, 'The Liberty to Spy' (2020) 61(1) *Harvard International Law Journal* 185.

[70] Ibid, 205–206 (referring to the EEZ in this context but the reasoning would seemingly apply equally in relation to the territorial sea).

[71] Margo H. Edwards and Bernard J. Coakley, 'SCICEX Investigations of the Arctic Ocean System' (2003) 63(4) *Geochemistry* 281, 312. For the development of submarines for research purposes, see William Kohnen, 'Human Exploration of the Deep Seas: Fifty Years and the Inspiration Continues' (2009) 43(5) *Marine Technology Society Journal* 42.

[72] The broader relevance of any data, especially for environmental studies, was largely ancillary: Edwards and Coakley (n 71) 283.

[73] Williamson (n 16) 416, 419.

[74] Christopher Whomersley, 'What Is and What Is Not Covered by Part XIII of UNCLOS?' in Anastasia Telesetsky and Keyuan Zou (eds.), *Marine Scientific Research, New Marine Technologies and the Law of the Sea* (Brill, 2021) 27, 38.

[75] To this end, Whomersley argues 'the right to collect data is inextricably linked to the right of freedom of navigation in the EEZ enjoyed by military vessels, especially submarines, since without such data it would be impossible for the right to be exercised safely': ibid, 38.

and the distinction between military research and marine scientific research may be obscure in light of the multiple potential uses of the data and other information collected.

Compounding this difficulty, there are instances of scientists collaborating with naval forces on submarines to advance their respective goals.[76] Such cooperative efforts may permit research into deeper ocean waters, as well as access to more inhospitable ocean environments. One prominent example of a collaborative research programme between military submarine operations and scientific researchers is reflected in the SCience ICe EXercise (SCICEX) programme in the Arctic Ocean, which commenced in 1993.[77] This programme involved science-dedicated deployments of nuclear-powered submarines with civilian scientists aboard and the data collected was published and disseminated in the public domain upon completion of the missions.[78] The significance of this collaboration was described by Edwards and Coakley as follows:

> Data collected by the SCICEX submarines have been and are being used by dozens of scientists to investigate regions ranging from above the ice canopy to below the seafloor of the Arctic Ocean, from the continental shelves to the deep interior basins and ridges. SCICEX-derived publications have contributed to almost every field of marine science, providing important, novel observations as well as testable hypotheses and an increased understanding of both arctic and global processes.[79]

The programme was varied from 1999 following the rapid decommissioning of the Sturgeon-class submarines.[80] Instead of science-dedicated missions, the US Navy has instead facilitated so-called Science Accommodation Missions, which 'would allow time to be set aside for the collection of unclassified data during otherwise classified submarine exercises, but did not include civilian scientists to embark'.[81] The

[76] For example, an academic sailed with the British Royal Navy to study sea-ice thickness across thirty years: Toni Feder, 'Submarines Afford a View from below the Arctic' (2021) 74(8) *Physics Today* 24.

[77] Edwards and Coakley (n 71) 283–284.

[78] Ibid. See also Richard Hollingham, 'The Record-breaking Dive under the Arctic Ice', *BBC News*, 4 May 2022 <www.bbc.com/future/article/20220503-the-record-breaking-dive-under-the-arctic-ice>. Hollingham notes that the programme was continuing as of 2022.

[79] Edwards and Coakley (n 71) 284.

[80] Ann Windnagel and Jackie Richter-Menge, 'Teaching an Old Submarine Data Collection Program New Tricks', *ARCUS: Witness the Arctic*, February 2015 <www.arcus.org/witness-the-arctic/2015/2/article/23163>.

[81] National Snow and Ice Data Center, 'SCICEX: Submarine Arctic Science Program' <https://nsidc.org/scicex>. The Phase II Memorandum of Agreement sets out the distinction more fully: see Memorandum of Agreement between the US Submarine Force,

Memorandum of Agreement emphasises that all scientific and other data collected is evaluated for security purposes in first instance and then potentially declassified and made publicly available.[82] From an international law perspective, the SCICEX programme brings into sharp relief the distinction drawn between military research and marine scientific research.

Beyond the United States, other historical and current examples of scientific submarine work include the French *Nautile*,[83] the Japanese *Shinkai 6500*,[84] the Chinese *Jiaolong*, *Shenhai Yongshi* and *Fendouzhe*[85] and the Russian *Mir-1* and *Mir-2*. The operation of *Mir-1* and *Mir-2*, which had a working depth of 6000 metres, allowed Russia and the former Soviet Union to make scientific discoveries in the deep sea over hundreds of submersions.[86] More recently, Russia has taken possession of a special-purpose nuclear-powered submarine *Belgorod*, one of the largest submarines in existence, which Russia claims to be a research vessel.[87] It is to 'be used principally as a mother ship for mini submarines and unmanned underwater vehicles'.[88] That vessel was fitted to carry the *Losharik*, a nuclear-powered deep-diving submarine, which suffered a fatal fire and which Russia again claimed was a research vessel.[89] The

Chief of Naval Research and National Science Foundation: Submarine Arctic Science Program – Phase 2, 12 June 2000 <https://nsidc.org/sites/default/files/scicex_moa_2000.pdfhttps://nsidc.org/sites/default/files/scicex_moa_2000.pdf> ('Phase 2 MOU').

82 Phase 2 MOU (n 81) paras. 5(3)(c), 6.

83 French National Institute for Ocean Science and Technology, 'Exploration of the Abysses: A Second Life for the Nautile', 3 September 2024 <https://en.ifremer.fr/Latest-news/Exploration-of-the-abysses-a-second-life-for-the-Nautile>.

84 JAMSTEC (Japan Agency for Marine-Earth Science and Technology), 'Deep Submergence Research Vehicle: Shinkai 6500' <www.jamstec.go.jp/e/about/equipment/ships/shinkai6500.html>.

85 Zhang Kaiwei and Liang Jun, 'China's 3 Deep-sea Manned Submersibles Conduct over 1,100 Dives', *People's Daily Online*, 5 March 2024 <http://en.people.cn/n3/2024/0305/c90000-20140758.html>.

86 A. M. Sagalevitch, '25th Anniversary of the Deep Manned Submersibles *Mir-1* and *Mir-2*'(2012) 52(6) *Oceanology* 817.

87 'Russian Navy Takes Delivery of Special-Purpose Submarine *Belgorod*', *Naval Technology*, 11 July 2002 <www.naval-technology.com/news/russian-special-purpose-submarine-belgorod/>.

88 Kate Tringham and Manash Pratim Boruah, 'Russian Navy Takes Delivery of Belgorod Special-Mission Submarine', *Janes*, 14 July 2022.

89 Sam Lagrone, '14 Sailors Die on Secretive Russian Nuclear Submarine; Putin Calls Incident "Great Loss"', *USNI News*, 2 July 2019 <https://news.usni.org/2019/07/02/14-sailors-die-on-secretive-russian-nuclear-submarine>; 'Fourteen Sailors Die in Submersible Vehicle in Russian Waters on July 1', *Tass*, 2 July 2019 <https://tass.com/emergencies/1066739>. At the time it was said that the submarine was 'carrying out

extent to which these vessels are true research submarines, as opposed to submarines used for military purposes or for other special operations such as reconnaissance tasks, is contested.[90] Such activities underline how the definition of 'research' is not always uniform.

Ocean research has been described by reference to a variety of terms in UNCLOS, including marine scientific research, military surveys and hydrographic surveys. However, none of these terms are formally defined in UNCLOS.[91] The ICJ eschewed the opportunity to define 'scientific research' in the *Whaling in the Antarctic* case.[92] Bateman noted that there is a general tendency to refer to all forms of data collection in ocean space as marine scientific research and that it can be difficult to distinguish between different types of research in practice, including in the type of output from the research.[93] Yet the distinction matters under international law, as different legal regimes are in place depending on the classification of the research and the location in which it occurs.

The issue has been contested in relation to the EEZ because the rules are less clear than in relation to maritime areas under national jurisdiction. In the territorial sea of coastal States, vessels exercising the right of innocent passage may not conduct 'research or survey activities'.[94] Further, in international straits, 'marine scientific research and hydrographic survey ships' engaged in transit passage 'may not carry out any research or survey activities' without the prior authorisation of the strait States.[95] While there are explicit references

bathymetric measurements in Russian territorial waters': Ridzwan Rahmat, 'Russia Launches Probe into Research Submariners' Death', *Jane's Navy International*, 3 July 2019.

90 James Glanz and Thomas Nilsen, 'A Deep-Diving Sub. A Deadly Fire. And Russia's Secret Undersea Agenda', *New York Times*, 20 April 2020 <www.nytimes.com/2020/04/20/world/europe/russian-submarine-fire-losharik.html>.

91 For discussion of the different terminology, see Churchill, Lowe and Sander (n 14) 783–790.

92 *Whaling in the Antarctic* (Australia v. Japan: New Zealand Intervening) (Judgment of 31 March 2014) [2014] ICJ Rep 226, para. 86.

93 Sam Bateman, 'Hydrographic Surveying in the EEZ: Differences and Overlaps with Marine Scientific Research' (2005) 29 *Marine Policy* 163, 164. Bateman illustrates the latter point in noting '[b]athymetric charts providing a description of seabed topography are an example of multi-purpose data collection. These charts are a routine output of hydrographic surveys but are also a basic tool of resource exploration and exploitation': Bateman, 'The Regime of the Exclusive Economic Zone (n 11) 576.

94 UNCLOS (n 1) art. 19(2)(j).

95 Ibid, art. 40. The same restrictions apply in relation to archipelagic waters. See ibid, arts. 52 (in relation to archipelagic sea lane passage) and 54 (innocent passage in archipelagic waters).

to survey activities and hydrographic research in relation to maritime areas subject to the sovereignty of the coastal State, no such references occur in relation to the coastal State's exclusive jurisdiction over marine scientific research in the EEZ. It is thus argued that coastal State's powers in the EEZ are limited to activities constituting marine scientific research, which is distinct to hydrographic surveys and military data collection.[96] By contrast, Zhang has argued that no distinction should be drawn between different types of research, whether pure or applied or military or not; instead, the pursuit of scientific discovery in the oceans falls within the realm of marine scientific research and is regulated as such under UNCLOS.[97]

As made apparent in relation to the SCICEX programme, the central difference between marine scientific research and military research is that the latter is for military purposes and hence not attributed with commercial value nor released to the public whereas the former is research of the ocean environment intended to add to the scientific knowledge of the world.[98] The SCICEX programme further highlights possible distinctions between data that is collected by civilian scientists as opposed to military personnel as well as data that is collected for specific experiments or as general baseline data. However, the latter could have dual purposes (civilian and military). These characteristics or personnel and types of experiment are thus not necessarily decisive. The use of the information appears more determinative. The critical legal distinction between these two types of research is thus to place military research outside the consent regime that would otherwise apply within the EEZ of a coastal State, denying the coastal State this form of control over military activities undertaken within its EEZ.

[96] Pedrozo, 'Military Activities in the Exclusive Economic Zone' (n 47) 526. Rothwell and Stephens posit that 'military-related survey activities in the EEZ are consistent with the [UNCLOS] and general international law'. Donald R. Rothwell and Tim Stephens, *The International Law of the Sea* (3rd ed., Hart, 2023) 326.

[97] Haiwen Zhang, 'The Conflict Between Jurisdiction of Coastal States on MSR in EEZ and Military Survey' in Myron Nordquist, John Norton Moore and Kuen-Chen Fu (eds.), *Recent Developments in the Law of the Sea and China* (Brill, 2005) 317, 328.

[98] To this end, Papastravidis has commented that 'the distinction between [marine scientific research] and [military data gathering] [lying] in the application of the data, and not in the process of the data gathering itself, appears to be on a firm legal ground': Efthymios Papastravidis, 'Intelligence Gathering in the Exclusive Economic Zone' (2017) 93 *International Law Studies* 446, 452. Zhang has, however, argued that the purpose of the research or the use of the data makes no difference: Zhang (n 41) 38.

8.3.2 Regulating Marine Scientific Research by Submarines

Marine scientific research incorporates at least two forms of information-gathering from Williamson's five categories mentioned above: academic scientific research and natural resource research, with both forms of research subject to the consent of the coastal State when undertaken within the EEZ.[99] During the negotiations of UNCLOS, a primary concern in discussions on marine scientific research was the potential commercial or industrial research that would implicate the exploitation of ocean resources.[100] Assuming that a submarine, or most likely a submersible,[101] is in fact engaged in marine scientific research then it is important to understand the parameters for conducting such research in the EEZ of another State. Submarines used for scientific purposes may be crewed by scientists, remotely operated and typically tethered to a surface vessel (as remotely operated vehicles (ROVs)), or operate autonomously.[102] Research submarines have many different scientific applications; depending on the purpose of the research, the submarines may operate video or other recording equipment and may have tools to take water samples or measurements of different ocean conditions.[103]

While all States, and competent international organisations, have the right to conduct marine scientific research, that right is subject to a variety of limitations.[104] Notably, the research must be conducted exclusively for peaceful purposes, in accordance with appropriate

[99] Williamson (n 16) 419. There is some debate as to whether hydrographic surveys fall within the regime of marine scientific research or whether they should be considered as military research. See ibid; Sam Bateman, 'Hydrographic Surveying in Exclusive Economic Zones: Jurisdictional Issues' (2004) 5(1) *International Hydrographic Review* 24.

[100] See UN Office for Ocean Affairs and the Law of the Sea, *A Revised Guide to the Implementation of the Relevant Provisions of the United Nations Convention on the Law of the Sea* (United Nations, 2010) 4–6.

[101] As discussed in Chapter 1, a submersible typically refers to smaller underwater vehicles, such as bathyscapes, which are not generally capable of travelling long distances or otherwise undertaking autonomous activity independent of a support vessel. Chapter 1, Section 1.2.

[102] Underwater maritime autonomous vehicles are analysed in Chapter 14.

[103] NOAA, 'Observation Platforms: Submersibles' <https://oceanexplorer.noaa.gov/technology/subs/subs.html>.

[104] For marine scientific research in areas beyond the EEZ, there may be other treaties governing the conduct of research with one notable example being the Antarctic treaty regime. See, e.g., René Lefeber, 'Marine Scientific Research in the Antarctic Treaty System' in Erik J. Molenaar, Alex G. Oude Elferink and Donald R. Rothwell (eds.), *The Law of the Sea and the Polar Regions: Interactions between Global and Regional Regimes* (Martinus Nijhoff, 2013) 323.

scientific methods and align with obligations to protect and preserve the marine environment.[105] Most significantly, for marine scientific research by foreign-flagged submarines in a coastal State's EEZ, the right to conduct that research is subject to the exclusive jurisdiction of that coastal State,[106] and must not 'unjustifiably interfere with other legitimate uses of the sea'.[107] The coastal State has authority to 'regulate, authorize and conduct' marine scientific research in its EEZ[108] and may order the suspension, or cessation, of marine scientific research.[109] The consent of the coastal State for marine scientific research is required and will normally be given apart from specific research activities, such as those of direct significance for the exploration and exploitation of natural resources in the EEZ.[110]

The scope of coastal State authority over marine scientific research in its EEZ is broad, consistent with the exclusive jurisdiction held by that State, and may allow for a significant number of conditions to be imposed on any marine scientific research undertaken in the EEZ.[111] If any submersible or ROV are considered 'equipment', their deployment is still subject to the same conditions for marine scientific research that are set out in UNCLOS.[112] The deployment of scientific equipment is not to 'constitute an obstacle to established international shipping routes',[113] and must have identification markings as well as warning signals to meet navigational safety requirements.[114] There are also a suite of conditions that a coastal State may impose at the completion of marine scientific research in its EEZ, including requirements to share data collected,

105 UNCLOS (n 1) art. 240.

106 Ibid, art. 56(1)(b)(ii).

107 Ibid, art. 240(c).

108 Ibid, art. 246(1).

109 Ibid, art. 253. Harrison has observed that although the language of Article 246 does not reference enforcement powers they are nonetheless implied, especially when regard is had to the possible exclusion of law enforcement disputes under Article 298(1)(b) from the scope of compulsory dispute settlement proceedings: James Harrison, 'Safeguards against Excessive Enforcement Measures in the Exclusive Economic Zone: Law and Practice' in Henrik Ringbom (ed.), *Jurisdiction over Ships: Post-UNCLOS Developments in the Law of the Sea* (Brill, 2015) 217, 227.

110 UNCLOS (n 1) art. 246(5)(a). Rothwell and Stephens indicate the difficulty in determining what research is of 'direct significance' when considering advances in biotechnology and difficulties in categorising bioprospecting within the consent regime. See Rothwell and Stephens (n 96) 387–388.

111 See UNCLOS (n 1) art. 249.

112 Ibid, art. 258.

113 Ibid, art. 261.

114 Ibid, art. 262.

providing assessments of the data, samples and research results and removing any equipment.[115] Requirements relating to the deployment of floats and gliders for research purposes are considered in Chapter 14 in relation to underwater maritime autonomous vehicles.

8.3.3 *Regulating Commercial Activities of Submarines in the EEZ*

Commercial uses of submarines within the EEZ or on the continental shelf most typically relate to the use of submersibles, including ROVs, in connection with: (1) activities to explore and exploit the natural resources of the continental shelf, including in connection with the laying and maintenance of pipelines; (2) the laying and maintenance or repair of submarine cables; and (3) tourism, especially for visiting underwater wrecks. This section considers the legal rules that would have a bearing on the deployment of submersibles for these purposes. While acknowledging the complexities of the legal regimes relating to the exploration and exploitation of the continental shelf, as well as submarine cables, the intention is to highlight rules that would be most relevant in instances where submersibles will be deployed.

As an initial matter, there may be a need to consider whether all submersibles are to be regulated as 'ships' under UNCLOS or whether their small size and limited function warrant a designation as equipment, gear or devices.[116] While all of these terms have been used in UNCLOS, none of them are defined therein. This debate has become especially acute in relation to underwater maritime autonomous vehicles.[117] A draft Convention on the Legal Status of Ocean Data Acquisition Systems, Aids, and Devices (ODAS) defines ODAS as a 'structure, platform, installation, buoy or other device, not being a ship, together with its appurtenant equipment deployed at sea for non-military purposes essentially for the purpose of collecting, storing or transmitting samples and data relating to the marine environment or the atmosphere or the uses thereof'.[118] While this definition may be indicative of characteristics of submersibles that

[115] Ibid, art. 259.

[116] This distinction is considered in Daiana Seabra Venancio, 'Law of the Sea and the Titan Incident: The Legal Loophole for Underwater Vehicles', *EJIL Talk!*, 14 July 2023 <www.ejiltalk.org/law-of-the-sea-and-the-titan-incident-the-legal-loophole-for-underwater-vehicles/>.

[117] Discussed in Chapter 14.

[118] Draft Convention on the Legal Status of Ocean Data Acquisition Systems, Aids, and Devices, 21 January 1993, 2nd rev. (UNESCO Doc. SC.93/CONF.209/LD/13) art. I(2), cited in Venancio (n 116).

are not ships, the treaty has not been adopted.[119] In any event, it is difficult to use a definition that deploys one of the terms that it seeks to define. If submersibles are considered 'equipment' as opposed to 'ships', there may be some legal relevance for rules of navigational safety.[120] However, as noted above in relation to the marine scientific research regime, the use of equipment for marine scientific research is subject to the same requirements under UNCLOS as ships conducting such research.[121]

Another preliminary matter concerns the deployment of submersibles that operate both in the water column and on the seabed outside the territorial sea. The EEZ intersects with the legal regime of the continental shelf as the allocation of authority granted to States under Articles 56(1) and 58(1) of UNCLOS refers to the seabed and subsoil and Part V of UNCLOS addresses activities that occur on the seabed and subsoil (such as exploiting natural resources of the seabed, laying submarine cables and pipelines and constructing artificial islands, installations and structures that typically sit on the seabed). Article 56(3) of UNCLOS does, however, provide that the coastal State's rights in the EEZ are to be exercised in accordance with Part VI of the Convention, which sets out the rights and duties relating to the continental shelf. As a consequence, it is necessary to have regard to rules relating to both the EEZ and the continental shelf when considering the regulation of submarine activities that implicate activities on or in the seabed and subsoil of the ocean.

8.3.3.1 Submersibles for Seabed Resource Exploitation

Research submarines and submersibles have long been used in the exploration and exploitation of the natural resources of the seabed.[122] For example, small, privately owned submarines (holding two to four people) were deployed in the late 1960s to explore seabed resources in the Gulf of Mexico and Gulf of Alaska.[123] The modern oil and gas industry extensively relies on a variety of robotics to enhance operations, which includes ROVs or potentially underwater maritime autonomous

[119] The efforts to adopt this convention were abandoned in the mid-1990s and the draft annexes were adopted as guidelines instead: Churchill, Lowe and Sander (n 14) 805.

[120] These rules concerning registration requirements and collision avoidance are addressed in Chapter 11.

[121] See above Section 8.3.2.

[122] Early research submarines built in Japan were developed to study fishing grounds: Kohnen (n 71) 50.

[123] R. W. Bybee, 'Use of a Submarine in Offshore Petroleum Exploration' (Paper Presented at the Offshore Technology Conference, Houston, Texas, April 1971).

vehicles.[124] There is an industry-organised classification and certification process related to ROVs, which is intended to promote safe and efficient operations.[125] This private industry engagement occurs across the oil and gas industry in developing safety and environmental standards.[126]

Private actors engaged in the exploration and exploitation of seabed resources are subject to coastal State authority when operating in that State's EEZ or on its continental shelf. As noted previously, the coastal State has sovereign rights over these resources, as well as exclusive jurisdiction for marine scientific research.[127] While the coastal State must normally consent to research in its EEZ, as discussed in Section 8.3.2, that consent may be withheld for research 'of direct significance for the exploration and exploitation of natural resources' and for 'drilling into the continental shelf'.[128]

Where submersibles, or ROVs, are deployed for seabed resource exploration and exploitation within a coastal State's EEZ, those activities must adhere to the laws and regulations of that coastal State. Coastal State's rights to the resources of the continental shelf are exclusive and no formal claim is required for those rights to accrue.[129] That entitlement includes 'all rights necessary for or connected with the exploration of the continental shelf and the exploitation of its natural resources'.[130] The coastal State also has powers to enforce its laws regulating seabed exploration and exploitation.[131] National standards concerned with safety and environmental protection will typically be included in leases, licences,

[124] See, e.g., Amit Shukla and Hamad Karki, 'Application of Robotics in Offshore Oil and Gas Industry: A Review Part II' (2016) 75(B) *Robotics and Autonomous Systems* 508; Dianne McLeod et al., 'Enhancing the Scientific Value of Industry Remotely Operated Vehicles (ROVs) in Our Oceans' (2020) 7 *Frontiers in Marine Science* 1.

[125] See International Marine Contractors Association, 'Remote Systems and ROV' <www.imca-int.com/committees/divisional/remote-systems-rov/>.

[126] See Seline Trevisanut, 'Unconventional Lawmaking in the Offshore Energy Sector: Flexibilities and Weaknesses of the International Legal Framework' in Natalie Klein (ed.) *Unconventional Lawmaking in the Law of the Sea* (Oxford University Press, 2022) 163, 178–179.

[127] UNCLOS (n 1) art. 56(1).

[128] Ibid, arts. 246(5)(a)–(b). The coastal State has an exclusive right to authorise and regulate all drilling on its continental shelf: ibid, art. 81.

[129] Ibid, arts. 77(2)–(3).

[130] *Dispute concerning Delimitation of the Maritime Boundary between Ghana and Côte d'Ivoire in the Atlantic Ocean* (Ghana/ Côte d'Ivoire) (Order of 25 April 2015) [2015] ITLOS Rep 146, para. 61.

[131] *Arctic Sunrise* (Netherlands v. Russia) (Award on the Merits of 14 August 2015) PCA Case No. 2014-02, paras. 281–282.

permits or concessions issued by the coastal State granting operators permission to explore and exploit the seabed resources.

8.3.3.2 Laying and Repair of Submarine Cables

Submarine cables are vital to the global economy as 99 per cent of internet traffic, including the world's financial transactions, depend on submarine fibre optic cables for data transmission.[132] Additionally, submarine cables are deployed to transmit electricity.[133] UNCLOS anticipates that States enjoy a freedom to lay submarine cables and pipelines on the high seas and in the EEZs and on continental shelves of coastal States.[134] The right to lay submarine cables is not subject to the consent of the coastal State, nor may the coastal State require taxes or fees, and the right is only subject to the general restrictions for balancing competing rights in this maritime area.[135] The freedom to lay these cables extends to their survey, repair and maintenance.[136] Even if the freedom was not construed this broadly, repair would fall within the other internationally lawful uses associated with submarine cables that is anticipated under Article 58(1) of UNCLOS.[137]

While the freedom to lay submarine cables is one enjoyed by States, the current reality is that submarine cables are predominantly owned and maintained by private actors.[138] The process of laying submarine cables involves surveying the seabed to determine the optimal route for the cable, laying the cable and potentially burying it in the seabed, and then maintaining and repairing the cable as needed.[139] ROVs may be 'used to inspect, bury or exhume cables', are typically fitted with cameras and any required tools, and are controlled from surface vessels.[140] Limitations on

[132] Andrew Boyd, 'The Security of Subsea Cables: An Enduring Naval Challenge', *Maritime Foundation*, 1 December 2022 <www.maritimefoundation.uk/publications/maritime-2023/the-security-of-subsea-cables-an-enduring-naval-challenge/>.

[133] Yoshifumi Tanaka, *The International Law of the Sea* (4th ed., Cambridge University Press, 2023) 190.

[134] UNCLOS (n 1) arts. 87(1)(c), 79, 58(1).

[135] Keith Ford-Ramsden and Tara Davenport, 'The Manufacture and Laying of Submarine Cables' in Douglas R. Burnett, Robert Beckman and Tara Davenport (eds.), *Submarine Cables: The Handbook of Law and Policy* (Brill, 2014) 123, 148–149. Coastal State duties are discussed below, nn 202–204 and accompanying text.

[136] Davenport, 'Submarine Cables, Cybersecurity and International Law' (n 59) 70, 73.

[137] Tanaka (n 133) 191–192.

[138] Hinck (n 158).

[139] Davenport, 'Submarine Cables, Cybersecurity and International Law' (n 59) 68–69.

[140] Lionel Carter et al., *Submarine Cables and the Oceans – Connecting the World* (ICPC/UNEP/UNEP-WCMC, 2009) 57. See also ibid, 23–24, 32 (referring to use of ROVs to

the laying of cables are discussed in Section 8.4.2 below. Beyond the installation phase, ROVs may also be used to retrieve damaged submarine cables that are on and below the seabed.[141] Repairing submarine cables does not require the consent of the coastal State given that this activity falls under Article 58(1) of UNCLOS.[142] One commentator has instead argued that coastal States are obliged not to impede the maintenance of cables on the continental shelf.[143]

Given the critical importance of this seabed infrastructure, States must anticipate the possibility of criminal interference in addition to State espionage and accidental damage. Intentional damage to submarine cables was initially addressed in the 1884 Submarine Cable Convention.[144] This treaty required States to criminalise in national legislation 'the breaking or injury of a submarine cable, done willfully or through culpable negligence'.[145] UNCLOS similarly anticipates that States adopt laws and regulations over ships and persons within their jurisdiction for wilfully, or through culpable negligence, breaking or damaging submarine cables or pipelines.[146] Intentional damage may occur by a surface ship dragging its anchor on the seafloor and severing the cable,[147] or potentially through the deployment of

bury cable). The primary role for laying submarine cables rests with surface cable ships, however. See Ford-Ramsden and Davenport (n 135).

141 Carter et al. (n 140) 34. See also Keith Ford-Ramsden and Douglas R. Burnett, 'Submarine Cable Repair and Maintenance' in Douglas R. Burnett, Robert Beckman and Tara Davenport (eds.), *Submarine Cables: The Handbook of Law and Policy* (Brill, 2014) 155, 165–166.

142 States in Southeast Asia have, however, adopted guidelines requiring the prior authorisation of the coastal State or payment of fees to this end: see Hai Dang Vu, 'ASEAN Guidelines for Strengthening Resilience and Repair of Submarine Cables' (2021) 36 *International Journal of Marine and Coastal Law* 180. China and India have also imposed permitting requirements on repair: Ford-Ramsden and Burnett (n 141) 173–176. See also Stephany Aw, 'Coastal State Duties in the Repair of Submarine Cables' (2024) 39 *International Journal of Marine and Coastal Law* 132, 137–138.

143 Aw (n 142) 145.

144 1884 Convention on the Protection of Submarine Cables, Paris, 14 March 1884, 163 CTS 391.

145 Ibid, art. 2.

146 UNCLOS (n 1) art. 113. The 1958 High Seas Convention had also provided similarly: 1958 High Seas Convention (n 38) art. 27.

147 As occurred in December 2024 when the Cook Island-flagged *Eagle S*, which is considered part of Russia's 'shadow fleet', sailed across an undersea power cable connecting Finland and Estonia. See Rebecca Rosman, 'What to Know about Finland, Russia's "Shadow Fleet" and a Severed Undersea Cable', *NPR*, 31 December 2024 <www.npr.org/2024/12/31/nx-s1-5243302/finland-russia-severed-undersea-cable-shadow-fleet>. This action followed earlier claims of sabotage of cables in the Baltic Sea. See, e.g.,

submersibles.[148] The latter activity may constitute terrorism (private or State-sponsored) or a cyber-attack.[149] While international law anticipates that States will criminalise intentional damage to submarine cables within national legislature, considerable concern exists that such steps have not been taken or the penalties are insufficient to address the importance of submarine cables in modern society.[150] Various studies are currently underway to determine what law reform may be needed to improve the legal protection of submarine cables from intentional damage by both State and non-State actors.[151] It remains to be seen if the clandestine use of submersibles for these malicious acts are captured by any proposals for new or revised laws.

8.3.3.3 Submersibles for Tourism and Leisure Use

Beyond scientific endeavours, submarines have been used to explore deep sea areas (which may or may not be in a coastal State's EEZ), partly to satisfy human curiosity about the marine environment and, more recently, as a commercial enterprise within the tourism industry. Some tourism operations will operate close to shore and fall within the territorial sea, or internal waters, of a coastal State and be subject to the laws and regulations of the coastal State by virtue of the sovereignty exercised over those maritime areas.[152] This section is concerned with tourism and

Freddie Clayton, 'US Allies Warn of "Hybrid Warfare" After Two Undersea Cables Are Cut in Baltic Sea', *NBC News*, 19 November 2024 <www.nbcnews.com/news/world/undersea-cables-cut-baltic-sea-hybrid-warfare-russia-germany-finland-rcna180742>.

148 Sun notes 'the military could use a purpose-built submarine or unmanned underwater vehicle to physically tap communication cables in order to collect, alter or jam any traffic transmitted through them, particularly in relation to cyber operations': Sun (n 13) 255.

149 'A cyber-attack consists of any action taken to undermine the functions of a computer network for a political or national security purpose': Oona A. Hathaway et al., 'The Law of Cyber-Attack' (2012) 100 *California Law Review* 817, 826.

150 Robert Beckman, 'Protecting Submarine Cables from Intentional Damage: The Security Gap' in Douglas R. Burnett, Robert Beckman and Tara Davenport (eds.), *Submarine Cables: The Handbook of Law and Policy* (Brill, 2014) 281, 287–288.

151 See, e.g., ILA Committee on Submarine Cables and Pipelines under International Law, *[Third] Interim Report* (2024).

152 For example, the Bahamas has issued a marine notice that applies to crewed submersibles operating for commercial purposes in Bahamian waters or launched, recovered, operated or supported from a Bahamian ship: Bahamas Maritime Authority, 'Manned Submersible Craft', Marine Notice 74, 17 May 2021 <www.bahamasmaritime.com/wp-content/uploads/2021/05/MN074-Manned-Submersible-Craft.pdf>. Viet Nam is also amending Decree 58 of 2017 to regulate tourism submersibles based on their operation areas. See 'In the Pipeline: Tourist Submersibles to be under Stricter Management', *Vietnam Law and Legal Forum*, 14 July 2024 <https://vietnamlawmagazine.vn/tourist-submersibles-to-be-under-stricter-management-72139.html>.

recreational uses that occur within the EEZ. The exploration of some deep sea areas, including different trenches or abysses, may fall within 200 nautical miles of a coastal State or will otherwise be part of the high seas (in relation to the water column) or the Area, defined in UNCLOS as the seabed and ocean floor beyond the limits of national jurisdiction.[153] Without specifying the precise location, it has been determined that the total number of submersible dives performed each year for civilian use, including research, commercial, and tourism operations, increased dramatically (approximately tenfold) from the 1960s through to 2005 reaching over 50,000 crewed submersible dives.[154] The introduction of tourism submersibles is credited with being the key driver for this increase.[155]

While cruise ships that voyage through an EEZ to reach various destinations are enjoying navigational rights, a query may be raised as to whether tourism or private, recreational submersibles are similarly enjoying navigational rights in the EEZ. In most instances, where the tourism or recreational experience is centred around the underwater voyage itself,[156] then the submarine in question is exercising navigational rights subject to the requirements that apply to any other foreign-flagged private vessel in the EEZ. Coastal States may, however, have restrictions on commercial or tourist operations in parts of their EEZ that are subject to area-based management tools, including marine parks or marine protected areas, in line with their exclusive jurisdiction to protect and preserve the marine environment in their EEZ.[157] Australia, for example, has a licensing system in place for commercial tourism operators in areas declared as marine parks in Australia's maritime zones.[158]

Where tourism submersibles are visiting wrecks, rules relating to underwater cultural heritage (UCH) may be applicable. According to

[153] UNCLOS (n 1) art. 1(1).
[154] Kohnen (n 71) 61.
[155] Ibid.
[156] As is the case, for example, with the 'Lover's Deep Submarine', which is no longer available but was centred on providing a 'quirky destination' for travel experiences: 'Lovers Deep Submarine: Oliver's Travels Brings You Love Beneath the Waterline', *Oliver's Travels*, 5 February 2014 <www.oliverstravels.com/blog/the-mile-low-club-olivers-travels-announces-its-most-exclusive-property-yet/>.
[157] UNCLOS (n 1) art. 56(1).
[158] Australian Marine Parks, 'Tourism Operators', *Parks Australia* <https://australianmarineparks.gov.au/access-use/commercial-approvals/tourism-operators/>. 'Nature-watching tourism' is allowed in Australian marine parks, apart from designated sanctuary zones: ibid.

the Convention for the Protection of the Underwater Cultural Heritage (2001 UNESCO Convention), UCH refers to 'all traces of human existence having a cultural, historical or archaeological character' that have been submerged for at least 100 years.[159] The 2001 UNESCO Convention entered into force in 2009 and has seventy-eight parties at time of writing.[160] The 2001 UNESCO Convention is to be interpreted and applied in the context of and in a manner consistent with UNCLOS.[161] For UCH located in the EEZ or on the continental shelf of a coastal State, a State Party must require its nationals or the master of a ship flagged to that State to report to it a discovery or activity directed at UCH[162] and the State Party must communicate that report to the coastal State and other State parties.[163] This requirement should be included in any national laws and regulations directed at private or commercial submersibles engaged in these activities.[164]

Where there is a discovery or activity directed at UCH, a State party to the 2001 UNESCO Convention must consult with all other State parties that have an interest in protecting that cultural heritage.[165] The coastal State may serve, if it wishes, as a Coordinating State to consult all interested States in efforts to protect the UCH.[166] An interested State is one that holds a verifiable cultural, historical or archaeological link to the property concerned.[167] Under Article 10 of the 2001 UNESCO Convention, the Coordinating State then 'may take all practicable measures, and/or issue any necessary authorizations . . . to prevent any immediate danger to the underwater cultural heritage, . . . including looting'.[168] The actions of the Coordinating State are not to be undertaken in its own interest but the Coordinating State must act on behalf of the State Parties

159 Convention on the Protection of the Underwater Cultural Heritage, Paris, 2 November 2001, entered into force 2 January 2009, 2562 UNTS 3, art. 1(a) ('2001 UNESCO Convention').

160 UNESCO, 'States Parties to the 2001 Convention' <www.unesco.org/en/underwater-heritage/states-parties>.

161 2001 UNESCO Convention (n 159) art. 3.

162 This term is defined as 'activities having underwater cultural heritage as their primary object and which may, directly or indirectly, physically disturb or otherwise damage underwater cultural heritage': ibid, art. 1(6).

163 Ibid, arts. 9(1)(a)–(b).

164 Nothing in the 2001 UNESCO Convention is intended to modify the sovereign immunity enjoyed by military submarines, however: ibid, art. 2(8). See also ibid, art. 13.

165 Ibid, art. 9(5).

166 Ibid, art. 10(3).

167 Ibid, art. 9(5).

168 Ibid, art. 10(4).

as a whole.[169] Such consideration of the community interest is required in light of the requirement imposed on all State Parties to preserve UCH for the benefit of humanity and to cooperate in its protection.[170]

At the time that the 2001 UNESCO Convention was adopted, some States were opposed to increasing coastal State authority in the EEZ and considered that the terms of Article 10 were incompatible with UNCLOS.[171] Tanaka suggests that the 2001 UNESCO Convention prevails over UNCLOS if there is any inconsistency between the two treaties on the basis that 2001 UNESCO Convention is *lex specialis* and hence the more specific agreement prevails over the general agreement.[172] Churchill, Lowe and Sander observe that even though the 2001 UNESCO Convention is not to prejudice the rights, jurisdiction and duties of States under UNCLOS, the grant of rights to coastal States in this context may be justified on the basis of Article 59 of UNCLOS, which addresses unattributed rights and duties in the EEZ.[173] The 2001 UNESCO Convention is thus a key point of reference for assessing what international laws apply in searching for and visiting wrecks by submersibles.

In practice, submersibles are used to visit existing wrecks, as well as searching for new wrecks.[174] The Russian *Mir* submersibles have been deployed to visit the wrecks of the *Titanic* (famously supporting James Cameron's film about this ship) and the *Bismarck*, as well as the wreck of the sunken Japanese submarine *I-52*.[175] The 2001 UNESCO Convention does, however, prohibit commercial exploitation of UCH.[176] Commercial exploitation does not seemingly include tourist visits to sites of UCH, but is primarily concerned with the UCH being traded, sold, bought or bartered as commercial goods.[177] Instead, Rule 7 provides: 'Public access to in situ underwater cultural heritage shall be promoted, except where such access is incompatible with protection and management.'[178] As indicated by the example of the *Mir* submersibles, both sunken ships and submarines may

169 Ibid, art. 10(6).
170 Ibid, arts. 2(2), 2(3). Article 303(1) of UNCLOS (n 1) provides similarly.
171 Churchill, Lowe and Sander (n 14) 275.
172 Tanaka (n 133) 198.
173 See above notes 31–33 and accompanying text.
174 Churchill, Lowe and Sander note the view that *searching* for wrecks may be considered as marine scientific research and subject to UNCLOS provisions addressing marine scientific research: Churchill, Lowe and Sander (n 14) 788–789.
175 Kohnen (n 71) 61.
176 2001 UNESCO Convention (n 159) art. 2(7).
177 Ibid, annex, r. 2.
178 Ibid, r. 7.

warrant classification as UCH, if meeting the age criterion in the 2001 UNESCO Convention. Other legal issues associated with sunken submarines are discussed further in Chapter 11.

8.4 Legal Limitations on Activities of Foreign-Flagged Submarines in Another State's EEZ

Having discussed the different bases under international law for foreign-flagged submarines to operate within the EEZ of a coastal State, the exercise of those rights is limited in different ways under UNCLOS and general international law.[179] Thus it is not the conduct itself that is unlawful but more so the conditions associated with the conduct. Most particularly, the EEZ is a zone in which all States enjoy rights and hold a duty of due regard.[180] Further restrictions may be drawn from both the text of UNCLOS, with reference to the non-abuse of rights[181] and the reservation of the high seas for peaceful purposes,[182] as well as general international law, which has an obligation of non-interference as well as an obligation of cooperation.

In relation to the obligation to cooperate, Beckman has posited that States should notify or consult a coastal State when planning to undertake military surveys in that coastal State's EEZ.[183] However, any requirement to notify or consult may be construed as granting too many powers to the coastal State in relation to activities that do not otherwise fall within its exclusive authority. Such steps may otherwise be indicative of whether a State has acted with due regard,[184] or is not abusing their rights rather than potentially establishing a distinct claim for cooperation in pursuit of military activities.

[179] Contrary to Pedrozo's view that there is an absolute right for States to conduct military activities in the EEZs of other States: Pedrozo, 'Military Activities in the Exclusive Economic Zone' (n 47) 515.

[180] UNCLOS (n 1) arts. 56(2), 58(3).

[181] Ibid, art. 300.

[182] Ibid, art. 88.

[183] Robert Beckman, 'Military Activities in the Exclusive Economic Zone: Towards a Common Understanding' in Yang Razali Kassim (ed.), *Strategic Currents, Singapore: Institute of Defence and Strategic Studies* (Nanyang Technological University, 2006), 42, 42–43, cited in Bateman, 'The Regime of the Exclusive Economic Zone (n 11) 580.

[184] Prezas has discussed the importance of prior notice or consultation as part of a procedural aspect to the due regard obligation. See Ioannis Prezas, 'Foreign Military Activities in the Exclusive Economic Zone: Remarks on the Applicability and Scope of the Reciprocal "Due Regard" Duties of Coastal and Third States' (2019) 34(1) *International Journal of Marine and Coastal Law* 97, 106–110.

This Section thus focuses on the potential parameters of due regard and non-abuse of rights as key limitations on submarines, particularly when they are undertaking military activities in another State's EEZ. The reservation of the high seas for peaceful purposes under Article 88 of UNCLOS, which is imported into the EEZ by virtue of Article 58, does not limit military activities unless those activities constitute a violation of the prohibition on the threat or use of force.[185] The regulation of submarines in relation to international law on the use of force is addressed in Chapter 9. It should also be borne in mind that submarine operations may violate other international law norms,[186] including the protection of the marine environment, which is discussed in Chapter 12, or navigational safety obligations, which are detailed in Chapter 11. The discussion below is concerned with the over-arching limitations that apply to foreign-flagged submarines operating in the EEZ of the coastal State.

8.4.1 Due Regard

As an initial matter, the obligation of due regard is found in a variety of international instruments as a means of regulating State conduct at sea (and elsewhere). The obligation is not only applicable during times of peace but may also apply in times of armed conflict.[187] Navigational safety requires that the master of a ship show due regard so as to avoid collisions,[188] and the possible strictures entailed in showing due regard in

185 The potential use of Article 88 to limit military activities in the EEZ has been considered in the literature, but the weight of State practice in using the EEZ for diverse military activities short of the threat or use of force clearly supports a narrow interpretation of the limit in Article 88: see Douglas Guilfoyle, 'Article 88' in Alexander Proelss (ed.), *The United Nations Convention on the Law of the Sea: A Commentary* (CH Beck; Hart; Nomos, 2017) paras. 5–6; Sun (n 13) 212–214. The earlier debate is set out in Francioni (n 11) 221–225; Boleslaw A. Boczek, 'Peaceful Purposes Provisions of the United Nations Convention on the Law of the Sea' (1989) 20 *Ocean Development and International Law* 359. Kraska argues that peaceful purposes 'encompasses normal maritime diplomacy and activities of warships and routine operations, exercises, and engagement' and that the UN Charter, particularly Articles 2(4) and 51, determine if an operation is peaceful or not: James Kraska, 'Military Operations' in Donald R. Rothwell et al. (eds.), *The Oxford Handbook on the Law of the Sea* (Oxford University Press, 2015) 866, 869.

186 Williamson (n 16) 420.

187 As anticipated in relation to the law of naval warfare: see Louise Doswald-Beck (ed.), *San Remo Manual on International Law Applicable to Armed Conflicts at Sea* (Cambridge University Press, 1995), paras. 12, 34, 37, 44. See further Chapter 10 for discussion on this body of law as it relates to submarines.

188 Convention on the International Regulations for Preventing Collisions at Sea, London, 20 October 1972, entered into force 15 July 1977, 1050 UNTS 16, r. 2(b).

exercising navigational rights have been further articulated in different legally non-binding instruments.[189] This Section contemplates the requirement of due regard as encapsulated in Articles 56(2) and 58(3) of UNCLOS in the context of foreign-flagged submarine operations in a coastal State's EEZ.

While the requirement of due regard as a benchmark for assessing the legality of foreign-flagged submarines' activities is firmly established in UNCLOS, how this standard may work as an operational matter holds challenges.[190] Prezas has argued that the obligation of due regard is only applicable in a situation where States are seeking to exercise different rights within the EEZ and there is a conflict between those rights (rather than a situation where both the coastal State and other States are exercising the same right to conduct military activities).[191] Rogiers has recounted an example of competing interests from 2022 when Russia relocated planned military exercises in Ireland's EEZ when Irish fishers protested that the activities would interfere with key fishing grounds and activities, as well as noting that this sort of contest between fishers and navies is far from an isolated example.[192]

How to balance the competing rights by reference to due regard is the crucial issue. The arbitral tribunal constituted for the *Chagos Marine Protected Area* (*Chagos MPA*) arbitration sought to describe the due regard requirement that the United Kingdom owed to Mauritius in the following terms: 'the extent of the regard required by the Convention will depend upon the nature of the rights held by Mauritius, their importance, the extent of the anticipated impairment, the nature and importance of the activities contemplated by the United Kingdom, and the availability of alternative approaches'.[193]

This formulation provides a set of considerations for decision-makers and while States may well differ as to the significance of any particular factor, the process of assessing an activity against a set of criteria may

[189] See Natalie Klein, 'The Use of Informal Agreements to Enhance Navigational Safety' in Natalie Klein (ed.), *Unconventional Lawmaking in the Law of the Sea* (Oxford University Press, 2022) 137, 148, 152–153.

[190] Bateman, 'The Regime of the Exclusive Economic Zone (n 11) 572.

[191] Prezas (n 184) 105.

[192] Rogiers (n 46) 1–2.

[193] *Chagos Marine Protected Area Arbitration* (Mauritius v. United Kingdom) (Award of 18 March 2015) PCA Case No. 2011–03, para. 519. In the earlier *Icelandic Fisheries* case, the ICJ suggested that in showing reasonable (or due) regard, there was 'an obligation to take full account of each other's rights': *Fisheries Jurisdiction* (United Kingdom v. Iceland) (Judgment of 25 July 1974) [1974] ICJ Rep 3, para. 72.

prompt a modification in initial plans;[194] active consideration of these different interests should reflect that 'due regard' has been accorded. There is thus a clear procedural element to the requirement to show due regard.[195] While not mandating what a State must do to respect another State's rights in the EEZ, the application of the principle indicates that some restraint may be necessitated. Criteria of reasonableness, necessity and proportionality may all be brought to bear.[196]

Showing due regard does not necessarily prevent an activity from proceeding. In the *South China Sea* arbitration, in assessing China's conduct in preventing its fishers from violating the Philippines' rights as coastal State, the Tribunal commented that a standard of due diligence was essential to meet a requirement of due regard.[197] In light of this holding, Papastravidis has suggested that showing due regard is an obligation of conduct and not one of result.[198] Further, the tribunal in the *Enrica Lexie* arbitration noted that due regard 'does not contemplate priority for one activity over another', but a balance is to be achieved.[199] The intention is 'to find an accommodation allowing both [coastal and other] states to exercise their rights'.[200] Tanaka further suggests that the balance of rights is not only between coastal and other States but is also 'relevant when harmonising community interests and State interests in the EEZ'.[201]

As with the freedom of navigation, the freedom to lay submarine cables and pipelines is not unrestricted but subject to due regard

194 Klein, 'The South China Sea Code of Conduct' (n 46) 497.

195 Mathias Forteau, 'The Legal Nature and Content of "Due Regard" Obligations in Recent International Case Law' (2019) 34 *International Journal of Marine and Coastal Law* 25, 32. Proelss confirms that 'the mutual obligation to have due regard must thus be considered as being of a procedural nature': Alexander Proelss, 'Article 56' in Proelss (n 185) 418, 431.

196 *Arctic Sunrise* (n 131) para. 326. See further Yurika Ishii, 'The "Due Regard" Obligation and the Peaceful and Economic Uses of the EEZ other than Fisheries' (2019) 34 *International Journal of Marine and Coastal Law* 73, 78–80.

197 *South China Sea Arbitration* (Philippines v. China) (Award of 12 July 2016) PCA Case No. 2013–19, para. 744.

198 Papastravidis (n 98) 458 (though noting this standard in relation to the coastal State having 'regard for the potential interference with the other States' rights and to attempt to mitigate such interference'). See also Rolf Einar Fife, 'Obligations of "Due Regard" in the Exclusive Economic Zone: Their Context, Purpose and State Practice' (2019) 34 *International Journal of Marine and Coastal Law* 43, 45.

199 *The Enrica Lexie Incident* (Italy v. India) (Award of 21 May 2020) PCA Case No. 2015–28, paras. 973, 975.

200 Rothwell and Stephens (n 96) 95 (referring to *Enrica Lexie*). See also Sun (n 13) 219.

201 Tanaka (n 133) 167.

requirements. Those due regard requirements include taking into account cables or pipelines that are already in position and not prejudicing the repair of existing cables or pipelines.[202] Moreover, under Article 79(2) of UNCLOS, the coastal State may not impede the laying or maintenance of cables or pipelines. Though what amounts to impeding the laying or maintenance of cables or pipelines is subject to the 'reasonable measures' that the coastal State may take for the exploration and exploitation of its natural resources and for marine environmental protection.[203] Moreover, the coastal State may establish conditions for any cable or pipeline entering its territory or territorial sea and also maintains exclusive jurisdiction in relation to cables and pipelines constructed or used in connection with continental shelf exploration and exploitation.[204] This allocation of authority is relevant for operations that deploy submersibles for laying or repair of different types of cables and pipelines.

While the literature has placed some emphasis on consultation and/or notification to meet due regard requirements, there is equally recognition that any assessment of due regard is context-specific. The critical requirement is that the obligation of due regard be fulfilled: that a State actively consider the interests of other State(s) and account for factors, such as those referenced in *Chagos MPA* and a standard of reasonableness, before proceeding with its particular conduct. Merely noting another State's rights is not sufficient. The greater the anticipated impairment of another State's rights, the more likely it will become that a State must notify or consult with the potentially impaired State. Kaye has posited that surveillance 'in the ordinary course of events' would not be without due regard to other ships.[205] The anticipated impairment would likely be low in this setting so the need for notification is not apparent. Military exercises or manoeuvres that may disrupt fishing activities or harm marine mammals will more likely prompt a requirement of notification or consultation to meet an obligation of due regard. The planned deployment and operation

[202] UNCLOS (n 1) art. 79(5).

[203] UNCLOS (n 1) art. 79(2). This provision refers to pollution from pipelines specifically but the narrower consideration in this instance would not likely undermine the general requirements to prevent, reduce and control pollution that are set out in Part XII of the Convention.

[204] UNCLOS (n 1) art. 79(4).

[205] Stuart Kaye, 'Freedom of Navigation, Surveillance and Security: Legal Issues Surrounding the Collection of Intelligence from beyond the Littoral' (2005) 24 *Australian Yearbook of International Law* 93, 101.

of submarines should thus include a procedure that deliberately accounts for the rights of other States so as to meet the obligation of due regard.

8.4.2 *Non-Abuse of Rights*

An abuse of right refers to 'the prohibition of the exercise of a right for an end different from that for which the right was created, to the injury of another person or the community'.[206] This possibility emerged in the *Corfu Channel* case,[207] where the United Kingdom sought to respond to Albania's denial of its navigational rights to transit the Corfu Channel. While the ICJ endorsed the United Kingdom's initial actions in sending its warships through the Corfu Channel,[208] Judge Alvarez observed in his separate opinion that States should not misuse their rights.[209] This position reflected an early judicial articulation of the abuse of rights doctrine.[210]

An act does not typically have to be illegal to be an abuse of right.[211] In another separate opinion, Judge Alvarez suggested that a State may abuse its lawful right of passage if it collected information about natural

[206] B. O. Iluyomade, 'Scope and Content of a Complaint of Abuse of Right in International Law' (1975) 16 *Harvard International Law Journal* 47, 48. Some of the content in this section is drawn from Natalie Klein, 'Responses to Law of the Sea Violations' (2020) 27 *Australian International Law Journal* 1.

[207] *Corfu Channel* (United Kingdom v. Albania) (Judgment of 9 April 1949) [1949] ICJ Rep 4.

[208] Ibid, 30.

[209] Ibid, 47 (Judge Alvarez).

[210] The doctrine was also discussed before the Permanent Court of International Justice. See *Case of the Free Zones of Upper Savoy and the District of Gex* (France v. Switzerland) (Judgment of 7 June 1932) PCIJ Rep Series A/B No. 46, 167; *Certain German Interests in Polish Upper Silesia* (Germany v. Poland) (Merits) (Judgment of 25 May 1926) PCIJ Rep Series A No. 7, 30. This jurisprudence is assessed in Iluyomade (n 206) 61–62; Alexandre Kiss, 'Abuse of Rights' in Anne Peters and Rüdiger Wolfrum (eds.), *Max Planck Encyclopedia of Public International Law* (Oxford University Press, December 2006) para. 12.

[211] Kaikobad writes: 'an act must, in formal terms, be a lawful act: it is when a lawful act constitutes an exercise of a right or power which is an abuse of such a right or power, that it becomes an unlawful act, not in formal terms but in terms of essential validity': Kaiyan Homi Kaikobad, 'Non Consensual Aerial Surveillance in the Airspace over the Exclusive Economic Zone for Military and Defence Purposes' in Kaiyan Homi Kaikobad and Michael Bohlander (eds.), *International Law and Power: Perspectives on Legal Order and Justice* (Martinus Nijhoff Publishers, 2009) 513, 556. Similarly, Triggs has observed, '[t]he concept of an abuse of right assumes that a State has a legal right to act; the relevant inquiry being whether this right has been abused': Gillian Triggs, 'Japanese Scientific Whaling: An Abuse of Right or Optimum Utilisation' (2000) 5(1) *Asia Pacific Journal of Environmental Law* 33, 53.

resources or strategic bases during that passage.[212] In this vein, Papastravidis has argued, 'intelligence gathering ... may still result in abusive conduct, such as when it is conducted arbitrarily or unaligned with a purpose associated with the *jus communicationis*'.[213] Aceves has similarly suggested 'a state which engages in conduct that is confrontational in nature and uses military force to assert its rights when nonviolent forms of dispute resolution are available would appear to violate the abuse of rights doctrine'.[214] A State alleging an abuse of rights has the burden of establishing the abuse and showing that it was injured by the actions in question.[215]

Article 300 of UNCLOS requires that parties to the Convention exercise their rights, jurisdiction and freedoms 'in a manner which would not constitute an abuse of right'.[216] The International Tribunal for the Law of the Sea (ITLOS) has interpreted Article 300 to mean that any State claiming that another State has abused its rights must demonstrate that the abuse has occurred in connection with the violation of another provision of UNCLOS.[217] In *M/V Norstar,* ITLOS stipulated that:

> a State Party claiming a breach of article 300 must first identify 'the obligations assumed under this Convention' that are not fulfilled in good faith or 'the rights, jurisdiction and freedoms recognized in this Convention' that are exercised in an abusive manner. The State Party then has to establish a link between its claim under article 300 and 'the obligations assumed under this Convention' or 'the rights, jurisdiction and freedoms recognized in this Convention'.[218]

212 *Competence of the General Assembly Regarding Admission to the United Nations* (Advisory Opinion) [1950] ICJ Rep 4, 15 cited in Kaiyan Homi Kaikobad and Michael Bohlander (eds.), *International Law and Power: Perspectives on Legal Order and Justice* (Martinus Nijhoff Publishers, 2009) 513, 561.

213 Papastravidis (n 98) 474.

214 William J. Aceves, 'The Freedom of Navigation Program: A Study of the Relationship Between Law and Politics' (1996) 19(2) *Hastings International and Comparative Law Review* 259, 323.

215 Kiss (n 210) para. 31. These requirements are also discussed in Hyun Jung Kim and Anne Thida Norodom, 'An Appraisal of Article 300 of the United Nations Convention on the Law of the Sea' (2022) 53(2–3) *Ocean Development and International Law* 214, 226 and 228.

216 UNCLOS, art. 300.

217 See *M/V 'Louisa'* (Saint Vincent and the Grenadines v. Spain) (Judgment of 28 May 2013) [2013] ITLOS Rep 4, para. 137; *'Virginia G'* (Panama/Guinea-Bissau) (Judgment of 14 April 2014) [2014] ITLOS Rep 4, paras. 396, 398.

218 *M/V 'Norstar'* (Panama v. Italy) (Judgement of 10 April 2019) [2019] ITLOS Rep 10, para. 241.

ITLOS then considered if a violation of an UNCLOS provision was established before it would decide whether there was a further basis to establish a breach of Article 300. The *Chagos MPA* tribunal determined that the United Kingdom had violated provisions of UNCLOS, but did not consider that the United Kingdom had done so with 'an ulterior motive or improper purpose'.[219] Hence, Article 300 of UNCLOS was not violated.[220] If the approach of ITLOS is to establish a violation of UNCLOS and then consider if the rights, jurisdiction and freedoms were exercised abusively,[221] the obligation under Article 300 is arguably narrower than the general obligation not to abuse rights in international law.[222] This perspective appears different to a position where a State exercises a lawful right, such as the freedom of navigation, but exercises the right in an abusive way.[223]

In a commentary to Article 300 of UNCLOS, it has instead been proposed that what might constitute an abuse of right includes situations where a State's exercise of its rights hinders the exercise of another State's rights, or where a right is exercised for a purpose other than the right was intended, or an arbitrary exercise of rights resulting in an injury to another State even if that State's rights are not violated.[224] This listing does not look to a violation of UNCLOS occurring in an abusive way but to any conduct generally and aligns more closely with the position under general international law. On this interpretation, what is potentially helpful is that the prohibition on abuse of rights thus endeavours to 'draw[] the line where other lines do not exist'.[225] This task will be most feasible where the existing legal requirements have some existing clarity, such as the obligation of submarines to surface while navigating through another State's territorial sea.

219 *Chagos Marine Protected Area Arbitration* (n 193) para. 543.

220 Ibid.

221 This approach was also followed in *Enrica Lexie* (n 199) paras. 729–730. For an alternative interpretation of the jurisprudence, see Kim and Norodom (n 215) 221.

222 Aw (n 142) 140–141. Aw does go on to note that Article 300 should be read consistently with general international law albeit not as a 'free-standing source of obligation': ibid, 141, citing Mathias Forteau, 'Regulating the Competition between International Courts and Tribunals' (2016) 15 *The Law and Practice of International Courts and Tribunals* 190, 199.

223 To this end, Iluyomade observed, '[r]esponsibility is not for a lawful act (the exercise of a right) but for an unlawful act (the abusive exercise of a right)': Iluyomade (n 206) 74.

224 Killian O'Brien, 'Article 300' in Proelss (n 185) 1937, para. 13. This approach adopts the meanings according to abuse of rights by Kiss (n 210) paras. 4–6.

225 O'Brien (n 224) 1937, para. 13.

Ultimately where the line is drawn in any assessment of conduct amounting to an abusive exercise of rights remains unarticulated and possibly inarticulable in relation to the EEZ. At a minimum, more extreme interpretations of existing rights and duties should be eliminated by reference to the requirement not to abuse rights. Lubin's use of the abuse of rights doctrine to constrain spying considers four instances of where spying is unlawful; namely when it is a means to: advance personal interests; commit an internationally wrongful act; advance corporate interests; and to exploit post-colonial relations.[226] The most pertinent for the present discussion would be the intelligence gathering by submarines with the intention to commit a violation of Article 2(4) of the UN Charter. Yet separating out ISR missions as being for defensive or aggressive purposes may not be readily apparent – at least not until the actual violation of the prohibition on the use of force occurs. Moreover, even contemplating potential examples in relation to submarine operations in the EEZ remains especially difficult when any exercise of rights necessarily entails consideration of other States' rights because of the attribution of different rights and duties to States in this maritime zone. Where a State has engaged in conduct that could fall foul of Article 300, it is highly likely that the conduct also violates the requirement of due regard or other rules of international law that circumscribe State conduct in this maritime zone and are discussed in the chapters that follow.

8.5 Conclusion

This chapter has focused on the different allocations of authority to coastal States and other States when operating submarines and submersibles within 200 nautical miles of the baselines of a State.[227] Critical to understanding what laws regulate submarine activities within the EEZ of a coastal State is the determination of what a submarine is doing and whether it is a military submarine or one operated for commercial, scientific or other private purposes. The latter submarines (and submersibles) will be subject to coastal

[226] Lubin (n 69) 237–242.

[227] This chapter has focused on the competing rights of coastal States and other States in the EEZ. There may also be a contest between two different non-coastal States when operating in a coastal State's EEZ. In this instance, the due regard requirement under Article 87(2) would apply in relation to accommodating the uses of each State. For discussion on this perspective, see Geneviève Bastid Burdeau, 'The Respect of Other States' Rights (Freedom of Navigation and Other Rights and Freedoms Set Out in the LOSC) as a Limitation to the Military Uses of the EEZ by Third States' (2019) 34 *International Journal of Marine and Coastal Law* 117.

State authority for the exploration and exploitation of natural resources and for marine scientific research. Submarines engaged in navigation 'and other internationally lawful uses of the sea related to these freedoms' are entitled to engage in these activities in another State's EEZ.[228] These freedoms may, though, be qualified by coastal State authority in the EEZ,[229] albeit not subject to coastal State consent.

It is the parameters of each State's rights within the EEZ that causes friction between States. As discussed above, continued engagement of foreign-flagged submarines in military activities, including intelligence gathering, in a coastal State's EEZ was anticipated during the negotiations of UNCLOS and has been pursued in State practice since the Convention was adopted. Military activities, including intelligence gathering, are permissible by a foreign-flagged submarine in another State's EEZ. However, these operations are subject to limitations and no 'absolute' freedom is enjoyed within the EEZ; the foreign-flagged submarine must not abuse its rights, must show due regard to the coastal State's rights and duties, comply with its laws and regulations, as well as not violate the prohibition on the threat or use of force under Article 2(4) of the UN Charter and Article 301 of UNCLOS. There are also requirements imposed in relation to environmental protection and navigational safety. The operating environment of a submarine in the EEZ thus entails a complex regulatory framework and must be accounted for in planning and deployment of submarines.

Coastal States have greater authority to regulate private submarines, unless those vessels are simply exercising navigational rights (to voyage to a particular destination beyond the coastal State's EEZ, for example, or for leisure purposes). A coastal State is limited in the action it can take directly against a military submarine because of the sovereign immunity enjoyed by that submarine. There would, however, remain scope for a coastal State to follow diplomatic channels to protest the submarine's actions and potentially resort to third-party dispute settlement procedures where available.[230] Coastal States do, however, have rights to regulate marine scientific research where that research concerns the ocean

[228] UNCLOS, art. 58(1).

[229] Tanaka (n 133) 170.

[230] While UNCLOS anticipates the use of arbitration or adjudication to resolve disputes relating to the interpretation or application of that Convention under Part XV of UNCLOS, its availability is limited to States party to that treaty (and hence excludes the United States) as well as potentially excludes 'military activities' from the scope of subject matter jurisdiction of any court or tribunal constituted under UNCLOS in line with Article 298(1)(b).

environment and is intended to add to the scientific knowledge of the world. Equally, submersibles deployed in the course of commercial activities for the exploitation of natural resources fall within the scope of coastal State authority.

In sum, submarine operations in the EEZ are highly regulated under existing international law when they are categorised with other maritime activities and their submerged operations do not necessarily prompt new considerations in relation to the core international law framework regulating the EEZ. Rather, concerns about some activities are more acute – such as military activities and ISR – because they may be less detectable when conducted by submerged vessels. These factors instead influence the balance of rights and duties that is inherent to assessments of the legality of conduct in the EEZ. The legality of submarine activities in the EEZ will thus be highly contextual, depending on what the submarine is doing and what other activities or interests are implicated by the submarine's operations. There are also additional international laws at play in relation to different submarine activities beyond the core framework established in UNCLOS and these rules are addressed in the following chapters.

9

Submarines, Threats or Uses of Force and the Right of Self-Defence

9.1 Introduction

The operation of military submarines[1] may have implications for international law extending beyond the law of the sea and warrant consideration in relation to the law of armed conflict. Most particularly, attention must be accorded to the question of when the actions of military submarines may constitute either a prohibited threat or a prohibited use of force, as set out in Article 2(4) of the UN Charter and Article 301 of the UN Convention on the Law of the Sea (UNCLOS).[2] This question further holds relevance in negating rights of innocent,[3] transit[4] and archipelagic sea lanes passage.[5] The passage regimes were discussed in Chapter 7, whereas the present chapter is concerned with determining when submarine operations may violate the international law prohibition on the threat or use of force and what consequences may emerge in relation to the law on the use of force (*jus ad bellum*).

As always, context is everything and it may be necessary to differentiate as between the simple passage of a submarine as it voyages to different locations; the weaponry aboard a submarine during passage; passage that involves intelligence-gathering in particular locations, or the deployment of submarines to operate at full capacity during military exercises. The previous two chapters considered the legality of these different

[1] This chapter is focused on military submarines, i.e. warships and other government vessels on non-commercial service and subject to sovereign immunity, as discussed in Chapter 1. As the experience of the Tamil Tigers demonstrates, insurgents may deploy submarines and these craft will not be considered as 'warships' under the definition in Article 29 of the United Nations Convention on the Law of the Sea, Montego Bay, 10 December 1982, entered into force 16 November 1994, 1833 UNTS 397 ('UNCLOS').

[2] Ibid, art. 301; Charter of the United Nations, San Francisco, 26 June 1945, entered into force 24 October 1945, XV UNCIO 335.

[3] UNCLOS (n 1) art. 19(2)(a).

[4] Ibid, art. 39(1)(b).

[5] Ibid, art. 54 (incorporating *mutatis mutandis* Article 39).

submarine activities in the territorial sea, international straits, archipelagic sea lanes and in the Exclusive Economic Zone (EEZ) during times of peace. This chapter focuses on these activities to ask whether (or when) they may constitute a violation of the prohibition on the threat or use of force and/or may trigger the right of self-defence. The operation of military submarines during an armed conflict is addressed in Chapter 10 on the law of naval warfare (*jus in bello*). This chapter is concerned with the threshold questions of when the use of submarines may constitute a threat or use of force, when their use constitutes an armed attack and when submarines may be utilised in exercise of the right of self-defence. Once the threshold is reached and an armed conflict begins, the law of naval warfare is applicable.[6]

The general prohibition on the use of force is articulated in Article 2(4) of the UN Charter as follows: 'All Members shall refrain in their international relations from the threat or use of force against the territorial integrity or political independence of any state, or in any other manner inconsistent with the Purposes of the United Nations.'[7]

This prohibition is not only considered part of customary international law,[8] but also a *jus cogens* (peremptory) norm.[9] The prohibition is not limited to land territory but also applies in ocean space, as reflected in Article 301 of UNCLOS: 'In exercising their rights and performing their duties under this Convention, States Parties shall refrain from any threat or use of force against the territorial integrity or political independence of any State, or in any other manner inconsistent with the principles of international law embodied in the Charter of the United Nations.'

There has been tremendous debate as to what constitutes a prohibited *use* of force, with less attention on what will separately count as

[6] The rules of naval warfare apply 'whenever there is a resort to armed force between States' or there is 'hostile resort to armed force involving two or more States': James Kraska et al., 'The Newport Manual on the Law of Naval Warfare' (2023) 101 *International Law Studies* 1, para 2.1.2.1, citing Prosecutor v. Tadić (Decision on Defence Motion for Interlocutory Appeal on Jurisdiction, 2 October 1995) International Criminal Tribunal for the Former Yugoslavia Case No. IT-94–1, para. 70; International Committee of the Red Cross, Commentary on the Second Geneva Convention: Convention (II) for the Amelioration of the Condition of the Wounded, Sick and Ship-Wrecked Members of Armed Forces at Sea (Cambridge University Press, 2017) para. 241. See further Chapter 10, Section 10.5.

[7] Charter of the United Nations (n 2) art. 2(4).

[8] *Military and Paramilitary Activities in and against Nicaragua* (Nicaragua v. United States) (Judgment of 27 June 1986) [1986] ICJ Rep 14, paras. 188–190.

[9] Christine Gray, *International Law and the Use of Force* (4th ed., Oxford University Press, 2018) 32.

a prohibited *threat* of force. Of relevance for present purposes is when different uses of military submarines may violate these norms. The answer will depend on where a submarine is located and what it is doing.

Maritime law enforcement operations may involve the use of force in different settings as warships or other government vessels on non-commercial service seek to arrest and detain privately-owned vessels and their crew for violations of laws applying in the different maritime zones. According to the judgment in *Guyana v. Suriname*, there may be instances where law enforcement tactics amount to a violation of the prohibition on the threat or use of force, even when directed against private actors rather than another State.[10] No clear threshold has been established as to when the violence associated with maritime law enforcement will violate the prohibition on the threat or use of force. The parameters for violating the prohibition on the threat or use of force are considered in this chapter in the context of the operation of military submarines.

9.2 Submarines as Unlawful Threats of Force

When military submarines were initially deployed as part of States' navies, it will be recalled that the very fact that submarines were submerged vehicles was a key concern,[11] even prompting a suggestion that submarines should be considered as a weapon.[12] As discussed in Part I, the covert characteristic of submarines was an early consideration in identifying rights and duties of passage in territorial waters.[13] The discussion immediately below first addresses what factors have been considered in assessing whether acts are a prohibited threat of the use of force and subsequently suggests when submarine operations may violate this prohibition.

[10] *Maritime Boundary* (Guyana v. Suriname) (Award of 17 September 2007) PCA Case No. 2004–04, [2007] 30 RIAA 1, 143. In the *Spanish-Canadian Fisheries Jurisdiction* case, Spain invoked article 2(4) of the UN Charter in regard to the coerced interception of its fishing boats by Canadian patrol vessels: *Fisheries Jurisdiction* (Spain v. Canada) ICJ General List No. 96. However, this case did not progress to the merits for resolution of this claim.

[11] See Chapter 2, Section 2.3 (noting the comments of the British Secretary of State on the 'submersibility' of submarines being one of the 'most formidable' aspects of submarines).

[12] As discussed in Chapters 2 and 3, several initiatives sought to limit not only the use but also the very existence of submarines. See especially, Chapter 3, Section 3.5.

[13] See, e.g., Chapter 2, Section 2.4 (discussing laws adopted on neutrality during World War I).

9.2.1 *Prohibited Threats of Force under International Law*

The prohibition on the threat of force is distinct to the prohibition on the use of force, though the duties are frequently coupled together.[14] The International Court of Justice (ICJ) has observed that a threat of force is unlawful when the actual use of force would be unlawful in the situation at hand.[15] To this end, the ICJ stated in its *Nuclear Weapons Advisory Opinion*:

> In order to lessen or eliminate the risk of unlawful attack, States sometimes signal that they possess certain weapons to use in self-defence against any State violating their territorial integrity or political independence. Whether a signalled intention to use force if certain events occur is or is not a 'threat' within Article 2, paragraph 4, of the Charter depends upon various factors. If the envisaged use of force is itself unlawful, the stated readiness to use it would be a threat prohibited under Article 2, paragraph 4. Thus it would be unlawful for a State to threaten force to secure territory from another State, or to cause it to follow or not to follow certain political or economic paths. The notions of 'threat' and 'use' of force under Article 2, paragraph 4, of the Charter stand together in the sense that if the use of force itself in a given case is illegal – for whatever reason – the threat to use such force will likewise be illegal. In short, if it is to be lawful, the declared readiness of a State to use force must be a use of force that is in conformity with the Charter. For the rest, no State – whether or not it defended the policy of deterrence – suggested to the Court that it would be lawful to threaten to use force if the use of force contemplated would be illegal.[16]

This view suggests that if what falls within the 'use of force' is broadly construed, threats of the use of force may also involve casting a wide net over a range of potentially illicit activities.

What constitutes a threat of force has been subject to academic commentary, primarily relying on the available State practice.[17] Brownlie used the following definition in 1963:

[14] As evident in Article 2(4) of the Charter of the United Nations (n 2).

[15] *Legality of the Threat or Use of Nuclear Weapons* (Advisory Opinion) [1996] ICJ Rep 226.

[16] Ibid, para. 47.

[17] Wood has noted a lack of relevant case law and practice. Michael Wood, 'Use of Force, Prohibition of Threat' in Anne Peters and Rüdiger Wolfrum (eds.), *Max Planck Encyclopedia of International Law* (Oxford University Press, June 2013) para. 2. Roscini, however, considers that such practice does exist: Marco Roscini, 'Threats of Armed Force and Contemporary International Law' (2007) 54(2) *Netherlands International Law Review* 229, 243–250.

> A threat of force consists in an express or implied promise by a government of a resort to force conditional on non-acceptance of certain demands of that government. If the promise is to resort to force in conditions in which no justification for the use of force exists, the threat itself is illegal.[18]

This definition largely still holds good to this day,[19] although the literature on the topic has varied in the interpretations of Article 2(4) and in the treatment of the threat of force in the small amount of case law and its use in State practice.[20] The simple possession of conventional weapons is not a prohibited threat of force,[21] nor is general preparation for the use of force.[22] These activities cannot in their own right constitute unlawful threats of the use of force. While it may be possible to indicate what is *not* a threat of force, it prompts the question as to what is such a threat? If the actions of a military submarine do not constitute a prohibited threat of force, other norms of international law may still be violated.

Several key elements for establishing an unlawful threat of force may be discerned from the literature. First, would the actual use of force be unlawful in the same circumstances? This question arises because of the close linkage in the prohibition of a 'threat or use of force' and the view of the ICJ, set out above, that 'the declared readiness of a State to use force must be a use of force that is in conformity with the Charter'.[23] The lawful uses of force, particularly in relation to military submarines, is addressed further below.[24]

Second, a threat of force will typically involve coercion,[25] as a demand is being placed on the threatened government. The form of coercion may

[18] Ian Brownlie, *International Law and the Use of Force by States* (Oxford University Press, 1963) 364.

[19] Nicholas Tsagourias, 'The Prohibition of Threats of Force' in Nigel D. White and Christian Henderson (eds.), *Research Handbook on International Conflict and Security Law: Jus Ad Bellum, Just in Bello and Jus Post Bellum* (Edward Elgar, 2013) 67, 76 (describing it as the 'classic definition').

[20] See, e.g., Francis Grimal, *Threats of Force: International Law and Strategy* (Routledge, 2012) 38–48 (considering some of the different views).

[21] *Military and Paramilitary Activities* (n 8) para. 269.

[22] *Legality of the Threat or Use of Nuclear Weapons* (n 15). See also Roscini (n 17) 230.

[23] *Legality of the Threat or Use of Nuclear Weapons* (n 15) para. 47.

[24] See Section 9.3.

[25] Referring to coercion as the 'defining ingredient': Nikolas Stürchler, *The Threat of Force in International Law* (Cambridge University Press, 2007) 57. See also Anne Lagerwall and François Dubuisson, 'The Threat of the Use of Force and Ultimata' in Marc Weller (ed.), *The Oxford Handbook of the Use of Force in International Law* (Oxford University Press, 2015) 924; Romana Sadurska, 'Threats of Force' (1988) 82(2) *American Journal of International Law* 239, 241.

be communicated through the actions of a State as well as through official statements. What is being demanded and what the consequence is if the demand is not met requires clarity in the communications between States. Lagerwell and Dubuisson suggest that a 'signalled intention' to use force if certain events occur must be manifested rather than relying on any implicit communication.[26] For present purposes, it is the use of submarines in certain maritime areas – such as close proximity to naval bases or other military infrastructure – or in certain ways – potentially involving a form of electronic warfare[27] – that may communicate the seriousness of a State's intentions in wanting its demands met. What amount of signalling is needed remains obscure, but at least reduces the instances where actions could be cast as unlawful threats of force. In the absence of the necessary signalled intent to use force, any military activities may instead be considered as a lawful naval demonstration to communicate disagreement on an issue or to influence the development of the law.[28] Without the signalled intent to use force, the actions in question may thus instead be cast as a lawful warning.[29]

Third, an unlawful threat of force is associated with a sense of imminence to the use of force.[30] This third element may also be linked to the idea of the credibility of the threat.[31] Stürchler suggests '[a] threat is credible when it appears rational to implement it, when there is a sufficiently serious commitment to run the risk of armed encounter'.[32] A State's lack of capability or proximity in relation to threatening force may render the possible use of force less imminent or reduce the likelihood that force will result. A State with powerful weapons that would reach the threatened State may present a more credible or

[26] Lagerwall and Dubuisson (n 25) 915. This view cuts against the earlier formulations of a threat of force. See Sadurska (n 25) 242.

[27] An example may be breaking a submarine cable to disrupt telecommunications, though at present this damage is more commonly inflicted by surface vessels or natural disasters: see, e.g., Henri Astier and Paul Kirby, 'Germany Suspects Sabotage Behind Severed Undersea Cables', *BBC News*, 20 November 2024 <www.bbc.com/news/articles/c9dl4vxw501o>.

[28] Dale Stephens and Tristan Skousgaard, 'Naval Demonstrations and Manoeuvres' in Anne Peters and Rüdiger Wolfrum (eds.), *Max Planck Encyclopedia of International Law* (Oxford University Press, May 2009) para. 2.

[29] Roscini (n 17) 235 (referring to the 'threatener's will').

[30] Stürchler (n 25) 55–57 (concluding that imminence of actual force may be an indicator of rather than a precondition for establishing an unlawful threat of force). See also Roscini (n 17) 254.

[31] Tsagourias (n 19) 77; Sadurska (n 25) 245.

[32] Stürchler (n 25) 259.

more imminent use of force; the hostile intent in the military demonstrations may thus be more apparent.[33]

The standard utilised in the *Corfu Channel* case arguably set a high threshold for a 'threat of force' to be reached. The ICJ rejected Albania's view that the United Kingdom's mine-sweeping operation was 'a demonstration of force for the purpose of exercising political pressure on Albania'.[34] Moreover, sending warships through the Corfu Channel in combat formation to test Albania's resolve was still considered innocent passage and hence not construed as a threat of force. Equally, continuous military and naval manoeuvres by the United States beyond Nicaragua's borders with the purpose of pressuring the Nicaraguan government was not determined by the ICJ to be an unlawful threat of force given surrounding circumstances.[35]

However, in *Guyana v. Suriname*, a declaration by the Surinamese Navy that failure of a mining operation to leave a disputed maritime area or 'the consequences will be yours' was determined to reflect an unlawful threat of force.[36] The alternative view would have been that the interaction was part of staged uses of force in the course of maritime law enforcement. The finding of the violation of the prohibition of the threat of force in *Guyana v. Suriname* has been strongly criticised,[37] including because the threat was directed against private actors rather than another State.[38] While commentators have doubted the finding of the Tribunal on the basis that the exchange of the officials indicated an initial phase of law enforcement, Kwast has highlighted the following circumstances as pointing more to an unlawful threat of force:

> these include the close involvement of the President – including his demand to the Guyanese President to order the *C.E. Thornton* leave or otherwise face action by Suriname to defend its territory – and the highest ranking officers of the armed forces, the primary purpose of taking action as being the prevention by the military of an 'imminent threat to the

[33] As Stürchler suggests is critical: ibid, 273.

[34] *Corfu Channel* (United Kingdom v. Albania) (Judgment of 9 April 1949) [1948] ICJ Rep 4, 35.

[35] *Military and Paramilitary Activities* (n 8) para. 118.

[36] *Maritime Boundary* (Guyana v. Suriname) (n 10).

[37] James Crawford, *Brownlie's Principles of Public International Law* (9th ed., Oxford University Press, 2019) 720, fn 22; Wood (n 17) para. 7; Lagerwall and Dubuisson (n 25) 921–922.

[38] Lagerwall and Dubuisson (n 25) 921.

> sovereignty of Suriname' from materialising, and the awareness that the action carried a real threat of escalation of the dispute into armed hostilities.[39]

As such, Kwast considered that there was not a low-level situation of law enforcement but engagement at the highest reaches of government with a signalled intention of the forceful means that could be used to prevent sovereignty violations.[40]

Much may depend on the circumstances in every instance. In this regard, Tsagourias has suggested that the determination of whether an action is a threat of force is largely a self-judging exercise because of the difficulty of applying objective criteria in any assessment;[41] the 'existence of a threat is subjective and contextual'.[42] The deployment of the military may not have an express purpose, or what may be the stated purpose is understood differently by the target State because of the relationship of the actors and/or the conditions prevailing between them at the time.[43] However, some commentators suggest that there is high tolerance for threats of force: threats of use of force 'play the role of a ritualized substitute for the use of force and, as such, may help to speed up the peaceful settlement of disputes'.[44] This tolerance for threats of force may indicate there must be a level of objectivity in the assessment of the situation to establish the imminence or credibility of any potential use of force. As such, not every threat that emerges in the diplomatic relations between States necessarily entails a violation of the prohibition of threats of force.[45]

39 Patricia Jimenez Kwast, 'Maritime Law Enforcement and the Use of Force: Reflections on the Categorization of Forcible Action at Sea in the Light of the Guyana/Suriname Award' (2008) 13 *Journal of Conflict and Security Law* 49, 81–82.

40 Corten writes that the 'essential point is to test whether the threshold between a police measure and the use of force in international relations has or has not been crossed. Only if it has will the UN Charter be enforced rather than the provisions of [UNCLOS] on simple police measures of coercion': Olivier Corten, *The Law Against War* (Hart Publishing, 2010) 68.

41 Nicholas Tsagourias, 'The Prohibition of Threats of Force' in Nigel D. White and Christian Henderson (eds.), *Research Handbook on International Conflict and Security Law: Jus Ad Bellum, Just in Bello and Jus Post Bellum* (Edward Elgar, 2013) 67, 77.

42 Ibid, 69.

43 Oscar Schachter, 'The Right of States to Use Armed Force' (1984) 82 *Michigan Law Review* 1620, 1625, cited in Sadurska (n 25) 240.

44 Oliver Dörr and Albrecht Randelzhofer, 'Article 2(4)' in Bruno Simma et al. (eds.), *The Charter of the United Nations: A Commentary* (3rd ed., Oxford University Press, 2012) vol. 1, 200, 217, para. 43; Sadurska (n 25) 246.

45 Francis Grimal, *Threats of Force: International Law and Strategy* (Routledge, 2012) 48; Sadurska (n 25) 239–240.

States have alleged violations of the prohibition on the threat of force in different ICJ cases involving competing maritime claims. Allegations of threats of force were made in relation to the Cod Wars, and in pleadings in the *Icelandic Fisheries* case between Iceland and the United Kingdom, but ultimately there were insufficient facts or other details for this issue to be resolved by the ICJ.[46] Iran pointed to 'a threatening and provocative position vis-à-vis Iran with the deployment of substantial naval and air forces just off the shores of the Islamic Republic' in *Oil Platforms*,[47] but did not pursue a specific claim of an unlawful threat of force. More recently, in *Alleged Violations of Sovereign Rights* Nicaragua claimed that Colombia's actions 'in instructing Nicaraguan vessels to leave the area or face the consequences, and in dispatching its own vessels to chase those of Nicaragua out of the area', Colombia was in violation of the prohibition of the threat or use of force enshrined in Article 2(4) of the UN Charter.[48] This submission was ultimately determined to be outside the jurisdiction of the Court,[49] and not resolved.

In sum, the factual predicate for establishing an unlawful threat of force necessitates that a State issues a clear demand of another State and that resort to force is a consequence if the threatened State does not conform to the demand. Further, the possible use of force in this scenario must be imminent and credible; while these factors may indicate subjectivity, the apparent tolerance for naval demonstrations in international relations and the lack of third-party condemnations of unlawful threats of force suggest an objective assessment of imminence and credibility can and should be undertaken. Naval demonstrations may be perceived as a form of communication between States and while such demonstrations may violate the law of the sea, the same actions do not necessarily also violate the prohibition on the threat of the use of force. Finally, there must be an examination as to whether the actual use of force would be permissible in the prevailing circumstances. If the use of force would be unlawful then threatening that force is also unlawful. This legal assessment may be determinative as to the violation of the

46 *Fisheries Jurisdiction* (United Kingdom v. Iceland) (Judgment of 2 February 1973) [1973] ICJ Rep 3, para. 24.

47 *Oil Platforms* (Iran v. United States) (Application Instituting Proceedings) General List No. 90, cited in Stürchler (n 25) 67.

48 *Alleged Violations of Sovereign Rights and Maritime Spaces in the Caribbean Sea* (Nicaragua v. Colombia) (Memorial of Nicaragua of 3 October 2014) para. 3.39. Nicaragua did not distinguish between 'threat' and 'use of force' in its Memorial.

49 *Alleged Violations of Sovereign Rights and Maritime Spaces in the Caribbean Sea* (Nicaragua v. Colombia) (Judgment of 21 April 2022) [2022] ICJ Rep 266, para. 78.

prohibition on the threat of force, even if there is some ambiguity as to coercion, credibility or imminence.

9.2.2 *Submarines as Threats of Use of Force*

As noted at the outset, determining if the activities of submarines constitute a prohibited threat or use of force will depend on where the submarine is located and what it is doing. Article 19 of UNCLOS recognises that a vessel is in violation of the right of innocent passage if its activities constitute a threat or use of force.[50] Any intelligence-gathering, weapons activities, communications interference or surveying, which are all activities that could be undertaken by submarines, are also violations of the right of innocent passage.[51] The question of interest for present purposes is whether these activities are also violations of the prohibition on the threat of force? Given that these activities are listed as separate examples of those violating innocent passage in addition to a prohibited threat or use of force, this distinct listing already suggests that they are not considered within the same category. Moreover, if the actions are done clandestinely, there is arguably no coercion and no imminent use of force about to occur. As such, no unlawful threat of force occurs.

It could be argued that covert, submerged, passage through the territorial sea to gather information about coastal defences and to test electronics or locate vulnerable positions as a precursor to the use of force in the future should be condemned as an unlawful threat to the coastal State concerned. The suggestion in this instance is that the mere fact of being submerged and in proximity to the coast is enough to demonstrate a prohibited threat of force. Yet without any element of coercion, immediacy or signalled intention, on the part of the State sending the submerged submarine into another State's territorial sea, it is difficult to establish that there is a violation of the international prohibition on the threat of force. There have been numerous allegations of unlawful submerged passage in the territorial sea of coastal States. States that have claimed that Russian (or previously Soviet) submarines have unlawfully entered their territorial sea include Norway, Finland, Sweden, Italy and Chile.[52] These intrusions appear to have more typically been considered as acts of espionage rather than an unlawful threat of the use of force.

50 UNCLOS (n 1) art. 19(2)(a).

51 Ibid, art. 19(2). See further Chapter 7, Section 7.2.1.

52 James Kraska, 'Putting Your Head in the Tiger's Mouth: Submarine Espionage in Territorial Sea' (2015) 54 *Columbia Journal of Transnational Law* 164, 193–201.

Similarly, the incursion of US submarines into waters of Russia, China, Canada and Cuba have prompted protests on occasions.[53] China has labelled these incidents as 'provocations'[54] and Russia has observed the violation of its territorial sea.[55] Other international laws are clearly violated, including the requirement that submarines only traverse the territorial sea on the surface,[56] as well as the right of innocent passage.[57] However, it is much less likely that a coastal State could claim that there has been an unlawful threat of force when foreign submarines are submerged in its territorial sea.

When a submarine navigates through an international strait in exercise of its right of transit passage or in archipelagic sea lanes pursuant to the right of archipelagic sea lanes passage, it is allowed to do so in normal mode.[58] As discussed in Chapter 7, the 'normal mode' anticipated for submarines under UNCLOS is submerged passage.[59] These rights of passage are violated when there is 'any threat or use of force against the sovereignty, territorial integrity or political independence of States bordering the strait'.[60] One implication from this regime is that submerged, continuous passage (i.e., normal mode) is permissible in an international strait or archipelagic sea lane and not viewed as a threat of force. This position reinforces the above-stated view that submerged passage in the territorial sea, without more, is a violation of Article 20 of UNCLOS but not necessarily violate the prohibition on the threat of force. If a submarine does more than continuous and expeditious passage through an international strait or archipelagic sea lane, it will be in violation of its passage rights. Whether it constitutes a threat of force would depend on additional factors, such as the communications between the States at the time, which may indicate there is a demand being made and a hostile intent in relation to what the submarine is doing and where it is going (such as approaching a naval base).

When submarines are navigating through the EEZ of another State or are voyaging on the high seas, this exercise of the freedom of navigation is a lawful activity and so does not constitute a threat of the use of force,

[53] Ibid, 201–207.
[54] Ibid, 203.
[55] Ibid, 204, 206.
[56] UNCLOS (n 1) art. 20.
[57] See further Chapter 7, Section 7.2.1.
[58] UNCLOS (n 1) arts. 39(1)(c), 53(3).
[59] See Chapter 7, Sections 3.1 and 4.2.
[60] UNCLOS (n 1) arts. 39(1)(a), 54.

even for a submarine carrying significant weaponry (such as nuclear missiles). Even where a submarine is engaged in intelligence, surveillance or reconnaissance, or conducting military exercises, those activities are not coercive in their own right nor necessarily indicative that an unlawful use of force is imminent. These routine submarine operations in the EEZ or on the high seas are not an unlawful threat of force and it is unlikely their use would violate the prohibition on the threat of force. It would only be situations where submarines are being deployed, most likely in conjunction with other naval vessels, as if an armed attack was in preparation and imminent, and accompanied by communications from the State concerned against another State (signalling intention to use force if demands are not met) that it may be plausible to contemplate a violation of the prohibition on the threat of use of force through the deployment of submarines in these maritime areas.

9.3 Unlawful Uses of Force at Sea

What actions will be considered as a violation of the prohibition on the use of force is a controversial question in international law, especially in light of the varied practice of States.[61] An initial point is that this prohibition is concerned with armed (military) force, rather than economic or political coercion.[62] Force entails physical violence.[63] As armed warships, the operation of military submarines during times of peace may thus fall within this prohibition, but in what circumstances? At one end of the spectrum, it has been argued that any force will be considered as a violation of Article 2(4) of the UN Charter,[64] whereas other commentators have acknowledged that force is permissible in some contexts outside of armed conflicts, such as for law enforcement purposes.[65] For

[61] Gray (n 9) 33–39.

[62] Dörr and Randelzhofer (n 44) para. 16.

[63] As physical force is anticipated, a cyber attack is considered a use of force when kinetic results follow. The Tallinn Manual looks to eight criteria: severity, immediacy, invasiveness, directness, military character, presumptive legality, State involvement, measurability of effects, as well as scale and effect: Michael N. Schmitt (ed.), *Tallinn Manual 2.0 on the International Law Applicable to Cyber Operations* (Cambridge University Press, 2017) 328–356 (Rule 69).

[64] See, e.g., Tom Ruys, 'The Meaning of "Force" and the Boundaries of the Jus ad Bellum: Are "Minimal" Uses of Force Excluded from UN Charter Article 2(4)?' (2014) 108(2) *American Journal of International Law* 159, 164. See below nn 73–80 and accompanying text.

[65] See below Section 9.4.

the purposes of this chapter, our focus is on the question as to when submarine activities may be characterised as an unlawful use of force.

In *Military and Paramilitary Activities*, the ICJ distinguished between less grave and grave uses of force, stating: 'It is necessary to distinguish the most grave forms of the use of force (those constituting an armed attack) from other less grave forms.'[66] This distinction was necessary because a State subject to an armed attack may be entitled to the right of self-defence under Article 51 of the UN Charter.[67] However, on this reasoning, a less grave use of force would not entitle a State to respond in self-defence. In *Military and Paramilitary Activities*, the ICJ had regard to the 'scale and effects' of the use of force in making such an assessment.[68] The distinction was subsequently affirmed in *Oil Platforms*,[69] and by the Eritrea Ethiopia Claims Commission.[70] Commentators have been critical of any policy that would allow for the continuance of low-level violence between States (seemingly without regard to the view that these actions would still be in violation of Article 2(4) of the UN Charter), given that there was no 'armed attack' triggering a right of self-defence.[71] Yet recognising that a variety of acts could constitute an unlawful use of force as a Charter violation, and as a violation of different UNCLOS provisions, is not without significance, both legally and politically.

In relation to submarines, the initial question is whether the intrusion of a military submarine into the maritime territory (internal waters, territorial sea, or EEZ) of another State is an unlawful use of force. Given the navigational rights that exist in the EEZ, military submarines may be present in another State's EEZ without necessarily infringing on the sovereign rights and jurisdiction enjoyed by the coastal State. Yet is the presence of a military submarine, including weapons and its armed

[66] *Military and Paramilitary Activities* (n 8) para. 191.

[67] See further below, Section 9.6.

[68] *Military and Paramilitary Activities* (n 8) 103. This position was reaffirmed in *Armed Activities on the Territory of the Congo* (Democratic Republic of the Congo v. Uganda) (Judgment of 19 December 2005) [2005] ICJ Rep 168, 222–223. The Court did not, however, characterise Uganda's conduct as aggression.

[69] *Oil Platforms* (Iran v. United States) (Judgment of 6 November 2003) [2003] ICJ Rep 161.

[70] Eritrea Ethiopia Claims Commission, Partial Award: Jus Ad Bellum: Ethiopia's Claims 1–8, 19 December 2005 in (2006) 45 *International Legal Materials* 430.

[71] See, e.g., W. Michael Reisman, 'Allocating Competences to use Coercion in the Post Cold-War World, Practises, Conditions, and Prospects', in Lori Fishler Damrosch and David J. Scheffer (eds.), *Law and Force in the New International Order* (Westview Press, 1991) 26, 39–40.

forces on board that submarine, within a maritime area subject to another State's sovereignty analogous to the presence of land forces entering the territory of another State as a forcible incursion? A coastal State may not be able to readily discern if the intrusion is a navigational error[72] or distress, or a deliberate and forceful incursion.

Ruys has argued that the scope of Article 2(4) of the UN Charter should be understood broadly.[73] He suggests, 'whenever state A deliberately uses lethal force – even within its own territory – against the military or police units of state B, such actions come within the scope of Article 2(4)'.[74] Ruys also contemplates whether 'small-scale intrusions' may be an unlawful use of force and posits 'the key is to determine whether they reflect a hostile intent'.[75] Without hostile (or forcible) intent, there is less reason for the 'victim' State to respond with like force.[76] Instead, a gradual response is necessitated whereby the reactions to the response may reveal a hostile intent or otherwise.[77] Ruys considers that hostile intent may be demonstrated by the following factors: general geopolitical and security context, repeated nature of incursions, location of the intrusion, nature of the intruding units and specific indications, such as preparedness to use weapons.[78] Where there is a hostile intent, Ruys accepts that it is permissible for the victim State to resort to 'on-the-spot reactions in self-defense in the context of such localized hostile encounters (again, subject to a particularly strict application of the necessity and proportionality criteria)'.[79] Thus even on a broad understanding of what falls within a prohibited use of force, the mere entry of a military submarine into the territorial sea of another State, without any physical violence, would not be a prohibited use of force.[80] Instead, repeated incursions with a communicated hostile intent may be more

[72] As was the situation in 1990 when a German submarine entered Swedish internal waters and for which Germany apologised: Said Mahmoudi, 'Use of Armed Force against Suspected Foreign Submarines in the Swedish Internal Waters and Territorial Sea' (2018) 33 *International Journal of Marine and Coastal Law* 585, 586.

[73] Ruys (n 64) 164.

[74] Ibid, 171.

[75] Ibid, 172.

[76] Ibid, 173.

[77] Ibid, 173.

[78] Ibid, 175–176.

[79] Ibid, 182. A view that aligns with the concept of unit self-defence, which is discussed further below in Section 9.6.

[80] Whether it could constitute a prohibited threat of force is addressed above in Section 9.2.1 of this chapter.

likely to trigger an arguable position that there has been an unlawful use of force.

Rather than a broad understanding of the prohibition under Article 2(4), other commentators have posited that not every use of armed force necessarily violates Article 2(4) of the UN Charter. For example, O'Connell has argued that 'Article 2(4) prohibits any use of armed force or armed force equivalent by a state against another state when the force involved is more than *de minimis*'.[81] On this basis, what might be prohibited armed force would exclude 'unconsented presence of official vessels or vehicles within another state's jurisdiction'.[82] Corten considers that establishing what falls within the prohibition on the use of force is a question of gravity that may be assessed through consideration of the extent of damage sustained, the location (as to whether it was within a State's jurisdiction or not) and the context surrounding the incident.[83] He further points to considerations as to the target of the operation, the authorisation for the action, and the scope of resources deployed in the action.[84]

Several examples of State practice may be considered to test these perspectives on the use of force in relation to submarine operations. The so-called 'Whiskey on the Rocks' incident, in relation to the presence of Soviet submarines in the Swedish territorial sea provides one such example. This incident concerned a Soviet Whiskey-class submarine that ran aground in Swedish internal waters, near a military base, in 1981.[85] Sweden determined that 'the submarine had intentionally violated Swedish territory to gather intelligence'.[86] The Soviet response was that there had been a navigational error (a point clearly demonstrable on the facts) and asserted the sovereign immunity of the submarine.[87] There was seemingly no contemplation that the entry of the Soviet submarine

[81] Mary Ellen O'Connell, 'The Prohibition on the Use of Force' in Nigel D. White and Christian Henderson (eds.), *Research Handbook on International Conflict and Security Law* (Edward Elgar, 2013) 89, 99.

[82] Ibid, 101.

[83] Corten (n 40) 82.

[84] Ibid, 90.

[85] For discussion of the incident, see Cameron Moore, 'The "Whiskey on the Rocks" Incident' in David Letts and Rob McLaughlin (eds.), *Maritime Operations Law in Practice* (Routledge, 2022) 136.

[86] Cited in David Froman, 'Uncharted Waters: Non-Innocent Passage of Warships in the Territorial Sea' (1984) 21 *San Diego Law Review* 625, 626–627.

[87] Cameron Moore, *Freedom of Navigation and the Law of the Sea: Warships, States and the Use of Force* (Routledge, 2021) 77.

violated the prohibition on the threat or use of force. A more recent example concerned the entry of a Chinese submarine into Japan's territorial sea in 2004, which China alleged was due to a technical error.[88] Japan's protest referenced a violation of international law, without specifically identifying what international law norms were violated.[89] As discussed in relation to potential threats of the use of force, the mere presence of a submerged submarine in another State's territorial sea will not, without more, constitute a violation of the prohibition on the use of force.

More problematic has been North Korean submarine incursions into South Korean waters. North Korea has deployed submarines into South Korean territorial seas so as to land commandos to infiltrate South Korea.[90] In 2010, a North Korean submarine fired upon and sank the *Cheonan*, a South Korean warship,[91] causing the deaths of forty-six persons on board.[92] The cause of the explosion was initially unknown, but there were suspicions of an attack by a North Korean submarine or collision with an underwater mine.[93] Those suspicions were later confirmed through an inquiry conducted by an international Joint Investigation Group,[94] which determined that there was 'no other plausible explanation' for the *Cheonan*'s demise than attack by a North Korean submarine armed with an indigenously-produced CHT-02D torpedo.[95]

[88] Miyoshi Masahiro, 'The Submerged Passage of a Submarine Through the Territorial Sea – The Incident of a Chinese Atomic-Powered Submarine' (2006) 10 *Singapore Yearbook of International Law* 243, 249.

[89] Kraska (n 52) 211.

[90] Ibid (n 52) 207–208.

[91] Reuters, 'North Korean Torpedo Sank Cheonan, South Korea Military Source Claims', *The Guardian*, 22 April 2010 <www.theguardian.com/world/2010/apr/22/north-korea-cheonan-sinking-torpedo>.

[92] Tania Branigan and Caroline Davies, 'South Korean Naval Ship Sinks in Disputed Area After "Explosion"', *The Guardian*, 27 March 2010 <www.theguardian.com/world/2010/mar/26/south-korea-navy-ship-attack>.

[93] 'The Koreans Have That Similar Sinking Feeling', *Jane's Intelligence Weekly*, 12 April 2010.

[94] Comprised of experts from Australia, South Korea, Sweden, the United Kingdom and the United States.

[95] Republic of Korea Ministry of Defence, *Joint Investigation Report on the Attack Against ROK Ship Cheonan* (September 2010) 33. See also 'Seoul Reacts to North Korean Cheonan Attack', *Jane's Intelligence Weekly*, 24 May 2010; Bruce E. Bechtol Jr, 'The Implications of the Cheonan Sinking: A Security Studies Perspective' (2010) 19(2) *International Journal of Korean Unification Studies* 1, 2, 18 (noting that the finding that the attack was conducted by Yeoneo-class submarine was revealed in a question and answer session following the release of the JIC Report). See also Mi-yeon Hur, 'Revisiting the Cheonan

South Korea imposed sanctions against the North, which denied (and continues to deny) any involvement in the sinking of the *Cheonan*.[96] North Korea's actions clearly constituted an unlawful use of force, and was characterised as an armed attack by the United States in the UN Security Council.[97] The UN Security Council did not, however, name North Korea as the perpetrator of the attack on the *Cheonan* in light of its denial of involvement.[98] Instead, the Presidential Statement 'underscore[d] the importance of preventing further such attacks or hostilities against the Republic of Korea or in the region'.[99]

Actions that do not violate the prohibition on the use of force may nonetheless count as violations of another State's sovereignty or a breach of the principle of non-intervention.[100] The Declaration on Friendly Relations elaborates on the duty of non-intervention in the following terms:

> No State or group of States has the right to intervene, directly or indirectly, for any reason whatever, in the internal or external affairs of any other State. Consequently, armed intervention and all other forms of interference or attempted threats against the personality of the State or against its political, economic and cultural elements, are in violation of international law.[101]

The inclusive wording would indicate that there is scope for this principle to be violated when foreign submarines enter another State's territorial sea, submerged and for surveillance or like purposes. This violation of international law still entails State responsibility and a duty to make

Sinking in the Yellow Sea' (2017) 30(3) *Pacific Review* 348, 352ff (noting some criticisms as to the JIC's conclusions).

96 'South Korea Shoots at North Korean Vessel', *Jane's Country Risk Daily Report*, 5 November 2010; 'North Korea: "No Apology" for S Korea Cheonan Sinking', *BBC News*, 24 March 2015 <www.bbc.com/news/world-asia-32013750>; Bechtol (n 95) 19–22; Hur (n 95) 355.

97 'UN Security Council Condemns "Cheonan" Sinking', *VOA News*, 8 July 2010 <www.voanews.com/a/un-council-draft-condemns-sinking-of-south-korean-ship-98097064/121396.html>.

98 United Nations, 'Security Council Condemns Attack on Republic of Korea Naval Ship "Cheonan", Stresses Need to Prevent Further Attacks, Other Hostilities in Region' (Media Release, 9 July 2010, UN Doc. SC/9975).

99 Ibid (setting out the text of the statement).

100 O'Connell (n 81) 101.

101 Declaration on the Principles of International Law concerning Friendly Relations and Cooperation among States in accordance with the Charter of the United Nations, 24 October 1970, UNGA Res. 2625(XXV) (UN Doc. A/RES/2625(XXV)).

reparations by the intruding State and is in addition to violations of the law of the sea in relation to innocent passage.

9.4 Prohibition on Force in Relation to Maritime Law Enforcement

During times of peace, warships and other government vessels on non-commercial service, including submarines, may deploy varying degrees of force during law enforcement operations. This situation prompts the question as to the legal justification of such force in light of the general prohibition on the threat or use of force. One possibility is that the UNCLOS provisions permitting States to take steps to enforce their laws operate as exceptions to the prohibition on the threat or use of force.[102] On this basis, force is not only permissible in self-defence or pursuant to Security Council authorisation (as discussed in Section 9.6) but also where a State wishes to enforce its laws against vessels under the law of the sea.

Rather, it may be the case that the use of force against private actors is distinguishable to the use of force against a State actor. On this basis, UNCLOS allows for the right of the coastal State to 'take the necessary steps in its territorial sea to prevent passage which is not innocent',[103] or, in the case of commercial vessels, its right 'to take any steps authorized by its [criminal] laws for the purpose of an arrest or investigation on board a foreign ship passing through the territorial sea after leaving internal waters'[104] or 'levy execution against or arrest the ship for the purpose of any civil proceedings ... in respect of obligations or liabilities assumed or incurred by the ship itself in the course or for the purpose of its voyage through the waters of the coastal State'.[105] The exercise of law enforcement jurisdiction is also envisaged beyond the territorial sea and does not necessarily infringe the prohibition on the use of force as set out in Article 301 of UNCLOS.[106] Maritime law enforcement does not bring the prohibition on the use of force into

[102] O'Connell has argued that force in the context of law enforcement falls outside the prohibition on the use of force under Article 2(4) of the UN Charter: O'Connell (n 81) 102.

[103] UNCLOS (n 1) art. 25.

[104] Ibid, art. 27.

[105] Ibid, art. 28.

[106] *The Enrica Lexie Incident* (Italy v. India) (Award of 21 May 2020) PCA Case No. 2015-28, paras. 1073–1074.

play, seemingly because the force is not against 'the territorial integrity or political independence of the State'.[107]

Yet while force may be used against private actors for law enforcement purposes, two situations must be considered. First, there are limits on the amount of force used in the context of law enforcement. These limits have been articulated in jurisprudence, notably in the *M/V Saiga (No. 2)* in which the International Tribunal for the Law of the Sea (ITLOS) noted that force was to be avoided and if used, 'must not go beyond what is reasonable and necessary in the circumstances'.[108] Similarly, in the Award in *Guyana v. Suriname*, the arbitral tribunal took the view that 'force may be used in law enforcement activities provided that such force is unavoidable, reasonable and necessary'.[109] The Tribunal in *M/V Saiga (No. 2)* further recognised that 'considerations of humanity apply at sea as they do on land'.[110] More precisely, a State may owe human rights obligations to those on board a vessel against which the State is taking law enforcement measures.[111] Even if a State does not have a valid basis for exercising law enforcement jurisdiction, the conduct may still be assessed against these limits and does not automatically constitute an unlawful use of force.[112]

Second, there are situations where actions against private vessels may still be an unlawful use of force. In *Oil Platforms,* the ICJ was concerned with action during an armed conflict between Iran and Iraq and efforts by the United States and other neutral States to ensure the safety of ships transporting oil out of the Persian Gulf through the use of military escorts. The United States alleged that Iran was attacking neutral shipping and laying naval mines in the Gulf, which damaged a Kuwaiti-flagged tanker and USS *Samuel B Roberts*. The United States responded, claiming that it was acting in self-defence, by attacking and

[107] As stipulated in Charter of the United Nations (n 2) art. 2(4) and UNCLOS (n 1) art. 301.

[108] *M/V 'Saiga' (No. 2)* (Saint Vincent and the Grenadines v. Guinea) (Judgment of 1 July 1999) [1999] ITLOS Rep 10, para. 155.

[109] *Maritime Boundary* (Guyana v. Suriname) (n 10) para. 445.

[110] *M/V 'Saiga' (No. 2)* (n 108) para. 155.

[111] States will potentially be held to account for human rights violations in situations where they exercise effective control over a vessel or when a vessel is within its territorial sea or internal waters and hence subject to the State's sovereignty. See Natalie Klein, 'Geneva Declaration on Human Rights at Sea: An Endeavor to Connect Law of the Sea and International Human Rights Law' (2022) 53(2–3) *Ocean Development and International Law* 232, 237.

[112] Kwast (n 39) 88–89.

destroying three Iranian oil production platforms. In assessing the US actions under customary international law on the use of force, the judgment implies that the use of force by one State against a commercial vessel flagged to another State could be subject to the general prohibition on the use of force in international law – that is, its commercial character is no obstacle to the application of the law on the use of force.[113] While there are certain conditions that must be met – including the deliberate targeting of the flagged vessel – the Court seems to have considered the fact that a commercial vessel is flying a State's flag is sufficient to treat the use of force against it as being directed towards the flag State.

It should also be noted that in *Guyana v. Suriname*, the Tribunal found that Suriname's naval gunboat's orders that an oil rig and drill ship operating under a Guyanese concession in a disputed area of the continental shelf leave or face unspecified consequence 'seemed more akin to a threat of military action rather than a mere law enforcement activity . . . [and] therefore constituted a threat of the use of force in contravention of the Convention, the UN Charter and general international law'.[114] As discussed in Section 8.2.1, this conclusion was reached even though the threat was against a private operator rather than a State entity.[115] In this instance, the private operator was acting on the basis of a licence issued by Guyana and could not be viewed as entirely disconnected from the State. Also, as noted above, the issue was seemingly a proxy for a more serious contest between the two States over sovereignty at the time.[116] Thus, the simple fact of a private vessel being targeted in forcible actions does not necessarily negate an assessment under the laws on use of force in favour of an assessment on law enforcement.

For submarines to be deployed for law enforcement purposes against private vessels, it must be expected that they will either be classified as a warship or otherwise be 'clearly marked and identifiable as on government service' and authorised to conduct law enforcement.[117] The most likely scenario in which a submarine is deployed for law enforcement purposes would be in the context of the exercise of the right of hot pursuit, provided the submarine gives the suspect vessel the necessary

113 *Oil Platforms* (n 69) paras. 50–61, 78.
114 *Maritime Boundary* (Guyana v. Suriname) (n 10) 147, para. 445.
115 Commentators have doubted the reliability of this determination as a result. See above nn 37–38 and accompanying text.
116 See above nn 39–40 and accompanying text.
117 UNCLOS (n 1) arts. 110(5), 111(5).

signal to stop and meets the criteria for lawful hot pursuit.[118] Whether the right of visit and effecting an arrest by a submarine could occur would depend either on the capabilities of the submarine or whether a surface vessel could lawfully continue a hot pursuit commenced by a submarine, as is permissible in relation to aircraft.[119] Submarine engagement in law enforcement would otherwise be anticipated in the context of maritime domain awareness, and may also be undertaken by uncrewed submarines. The latter scenarios are considered further in Chapters 13 and 14.

While force may be permitted in the course of law enforcement against private actors, the situation is different in relation to law enforcement against warships or other government vessels operated on non-commercial service. In this situation, the targeted ships are subject to sovereign immunity.[120] In this regard, Oxman has observed '[a]n attempt to exercise law enforcement jurisdiction against a foreign warship is in fact an attempt to threaten or use force against a sovereign instrumentality of a foreign State'.[121] As discussed in Chapter 7,[122] as well as further below,[123] a variety of steps may be taken in asking a foreign warship to leave an area subject to the coastal State's sovereignty, but seizing or detaining a warship for law enforcement purposes violates its sovereign immunity.

9.5 Submarines and Armed Attack

Another element of the *jus ad bellum* to consider in the operation of submarines is when their use may constitute a prohibited 'armed attack' that triggers the right of self-defence.[124] Frequently, whether there has been an armed attack or not is very much a question of fact.[125] Fleck has observed, 'mere threats to use force, wrongful harm to the State's subjective rights not yet resulting in imminent attacks, and political pressure not involving recourse to arms cannot be considered as justifying self-defence'.[126] It is,

[118] See ibid, art. 111. The conditions listed therein are cumulative.

[119] Ibid, art. 111(6).

[120] Ibid, arts. 32, 95, 96. See also, Chapter 1, Section 1.3.

[121] Bernard H. Oxman, 'The Regime of Warships Under the United Nations Convention on the Law of the Sea' (1984) 24 *Virginia Journal of International Law* 809, 815.

[122] See Chapter 7, Section 7.2.4.

[123] See Section 9.6 below.

[124] Article 51 of the UN Charter refers to the inherent right of self-defence 'if an armed attack occurs': Charter of the United Nations (n 2) art. 51.

[125] Gray (n 9) 121.

[126] Dieter Fleck, 'Rules of Engagement of Maritime Forces and the Limitation of the Use of Force Under the UN Charter' (1988) 31 *German Yearbook of International Law* 165, 176.

though, generally accepted that an attack on the armed forces of a State, including its sea forces, when outside their State constitutes an armed attack.[127] Acts of espionage, even when intruding on the territorial sea of another State, do not rise to the level of an 'armed attack',[128] even if still potentially in violation of international law. This section considers the legal parameters of an 'armed attack' to assess submarine operations.

In *Military and Paramilitary Activities*, the ICJ determined the legality of US mining in Nicaraguan waters, which damaged a dozen private vessels.[129] Despite the damage to vessels and the loss of lives, as well as human injury, the Court did not consider these actions to amount to an 'armed attack' against Nicaragua.[130] Instead, the mining was an infringement of navigational rights,[131] and consequently a less grave form of conduct. Mining of waters, which could target both submarines and surface vessels, could thus be construed as a violation of the prohibition on the use of force albeit not an 'armed attack'. It is arguable as to whether other examples of excessive or high levels of interference with navigational rights, including equipment that prejudices the operation of submarines (such as the use of anti-submarine booms) may similarly be construed as unlawful uses of force. It may be suggested that a loss of life or human injuries as a result of this interference, or the extent of violence involved, may colour these determinations and warrant consideration as to whether an armed attack has occurred.

Also debated is whether a series of events could amount to an 'armed attack', which may become relevant in the maritime context when taking into account the so-called 'grey zone' tactics of some States.[132]

[127] Georg Nolte and Albrecht Randelzhofer, 'Article 51' in Simma et al. (n 44) vol. 2, 1411.

[128] Fleck (n 126) 180.

[129] *Military and Paramilitary Activities* (n 8) para. 76.

[130] Ibid, 117.

[131] Ibid, 101–102.

[132] While there are different definitions of the grey zone, Morris et al. explain the term as follows:

> The gray zone is an operational space between peace and war, involving coercive actions to change the status quo below a threshold that, in most cases, would prompt a conventional military response, often by blurring the line between military and nonmilitary actions and the attribution for events.

Lyle J. Morris et al., *Gaining Competitive Advantage in the Gray Zone: Response Options for Coercive Aggression Below the Threshold of Major War* (RAND Corporation, 2017) 8.

A scenario that could be contemplated in this instance would be repeated incursions of submarines, despite protests from the targeted State and possible harm to coastal State interests. Further, in *Oil Platforms*, the Court said that it 'does not exclude the possibility that the mining of a single military vessel might be sufficient to bring into play the inherent right of self-defence'.[133] A cumulation of incidents is thus not essential when a single military vessel is targeted,[134] but may be considered in relation to a series of attacks on merchant vessels. In *Oil Platforms*, as well as concluding that the United States had not established Iranian responsibility for the missile attacks or mine-laying damaging US-owned or flagged ships, the Court found that it had not established that these actions were 'specifically aimed at the US'.[135] In the case of missiles and mines that did hit US-flagged vessels, it was not established that these vessels were a specific target – rather, such measures seem to have been aimed at any vessel in Kuwaiti waters. A specific requirement of intention in an armed attack thus emerges from the Court's reasoning.[136] Yet, the Court concluded on the basis of the facts before it, that 'these incidents do not seem to the Court to constitute an armed attack on the United States, of the kind that the Court, in the case concerning *Military and Paramilitary Activities*, qualified as a "most grave" form of the use of force'.[137]

Beyond the physical violence by armed forces that are associated with armed attacks and uses of force, the UN Charter also references 'threats to the peace, breaches of the peace and acts of aggression', which may warrant reaction by the UN Security Council.[138] An act of aggression, if sufficiently grave, may constitute an 'armed attack', or at least constitute a violation of the prohibition on the use of force. From a maritime perspective, it must be noted that the UN General Assembly's

133 *Oil Platforms* (n 69) para. 72.

134 An attack on a merchant vessel, however flagged, must be treated differently to an attack on a military vessel in the law on the use of force. The Court noted in *Oil Platforms* that 'the Texaco Caribbean, whatever its ownership, was not flying a United States flag', thus concluding that 'an attack on the vessel is not in itself to be equated with an attack on that State': *Oil Platforms* (n 69) 191.

135 Ibid, 191–192.

136 Though criticised by the US Legal Adviser. See William H. Taft IV, 'Self Defense and the Oil Platforms Decision' (2004) 29 *Yale Journal of International Law* 295.

137 *Oil Platforms* (n 69) 192.

138 Article 39 refers to a threat to the peace, breach of the peace or an act of aggression as the bases upon which the UN Security Council can take action, including authorising forcible action, under Chapter VII of the UN Charter.

'Definition of Aggression' includes blockades of ports and coasts,[139] as well as an attack by the armed forces of a State on maritime forces of another State to constitute 'aggression'.[140] Submarines could be deployed for either of these purposes and, within the law of naval warfare once an armed conflict has begun, such operations reflect the exercise of belligerent rights.[141] To determine if the acts of aggression may also constitute an 'armed attack', the critical element remains a question of whether those actions are of 'sufficient gravity'.[142] There remains scope for uncertainty about the relevant threshold[143] and as such, the interpretative assistance of this General Assembly resolution may be limited and perhaps holds greatest relevance in establishing the Security Council's authority to take decisions under Chapter VII of the UN Charter.[144] An attack on a submarine will seemingly constitute an armed attack only when the submarine is specifically targeted and it is targeted because it is flagged to a specific State, plus there is a high level of damage as well as human injury or losses.

9.6 Submarines and the Right of Self-Defence

The right of self-defence as an exception to the prohibition on the use of force is reflected in Article 51 of the UN Charter,[145] which provides:

> Nothing in the present Charter shall impair the inherent right of individual or collective self-defence if an armed attack occurs against a member of the United Nations, until the Security Council has taken measures necessary to maintain international peace and security. Measures taken by Members in the exercise of the right of self-defence shall be immediately reported to the Security Council and shall not in any way affect the

139 Definition of Aggression, 14 December 1974, UNGA Res. 3314(XXIX) (UN Doc A/RES/3314(XXIX)), art. 2(c).

140 Ibid, art 2(d).

141 See, e.g., United States Navy, United States Marine Corps and United States Coast Guard, *The Commander's Handbook on the Law of Naval Operations* (Naval War College, March 2022) para. 2.2.1.1. See further Chapter 10.

142 Definition of Aggression (n 139) art. 1.

143 Kraska has argued that the mere presence of a submarine in the territorial sea, even if spying, does not reach the 'gravity' threshold warranting a forceful response. Further indicia of threats or use of force are needed: Kraska (n 52) 236.

144 See Fleck (n 126) 175–176.

145 Another exception to the prohibition on the use of force emerges when the UN Security Council acts under Chapter VII of the UN Charter to authorise enforcement actions when there has been a threat to the peace, a breach of the peace or an act of aggression, as envisaged under Article 39 of the UN Charter.

> authority and responsibility of the Security Council under the present Charter to take at any time such action as it deems necessary to maintain or restore international peace and security.[146]

Gray has observed that there are, in essence, two competing interpretations of the right of self-defence as set out in Article 51 of the UN Charter.[147] One interpretation allows for an emphasis on the 'inherent' right of self-defence to reflect a broader right beyond a response to an armed attack and potentially allow for its use to protect nationals abroad or in anticipation of an armed attack. This understanding of the right of self-defence allows for a pre-existing customary international law right that permits the invocation of this right in circumstances other than those set out in the UN Charter. The second interpretation, which Gray describes, considers that Article 51 and its reference to an 'armed attack' should be understood strictly to give the treaty provision full effect and limit the opportunities for States to use force in self-defence.[148] This latter view considers that the customary international law right of self-defence is narrow and should not go beyond the UN Charter provisions. Which perspective is preferred is relevant in the context of submarines because it implicates any assessments on the legality of 'unit self-defence' that may apply at sea.

Article 51 of the UN Charter anticipates that any resort to the right of self-defence follows an 'armed attack'. While an 'imminent' armed attack may also justify resorting to self-defence,[149] where there is a latent threat of such an attack, a collective response through the UN Security Council should be sought rather than individual action.[150] Gray has argued that State practice does not support a right of anticipatory self-defence, as States more commonly rely on differing views as to whether an armed attack has occurred or not.[151] An alternative perspective is that what counts as an armed attack may be varied so that advance planning of an attack would be considered the start of an armed attack whereas the same

[146] Charter of the United Nations (n 2) art. 51.

[147] Gray (n 9) 124–125.

[148] Ibid, 124.

[149] High-Level Panel on Threats, Challenges and Change, *A More Secure World: Our Shared Responsibility*, 2 December 2004 (UN Doc. A/59/565) para. 124. This view has been criticised as not reflecting State practice, however. See Gray (n 9) 173.

[150] Franklin Berman, 'The UN Charter and the Use of Force' (2006) 10 *Singapore Yearbook of International Law* 9, 13.

[151] Gray (n 9) 170–173.

situation could be described as an 'imminent' attack.[152] The debate may have relevance for submarines given the inability of coastal States to assess objectively whether a foreign military submarine is in its waters for the purposes of attack or by navigational accident.[153] Communication will be essential in the latter scenario to avoid a misunderstanding and loss of life.

Article 51 requires States to report to the Security Council, which is a duty that has occasionally been used as a frame of reference for assessing the legality of the resort to the right of self-defence.[154] Security Council responses to uses of force have been inconsistent and the role of the Security Council, despite explicit instructions in Article 51, has been erratic.[155] Much depends on the specific use of force that has occurred, and the States involved. The Security Council responded with a Presidential Statement following the 1996 grounding of a North Korean submarine in South Korea, but this statement did not classify the incident as an armed attack or self-defence; instead, both countries were called upon to observe their Armistice Agreement and not take action that would undermine peace and security in the region.[156] Even after the armed attack on the *Cheonan*, a South Korean warship, South Korea did not resort to any force in self-defence against North Korean submarines.[157]

Two important conditions to be fulfilled for the lawful exercise of the right of self-defence concern necessity and proportionality. These conditions are typically drawn from the 1837 *Caroline* incident, which concerned the sinking of a steamer, the *Caroline*, as the United States sought to preserve its neutrality during a Canadian insurrection.[158] Correspondence

[152] Elizabeth Wilmshurst, 'The Chatham House Principles of International Law on the Use of Force in Self-Defence' (2006) 55 *International and Comparative Law Quarterly* 963, 965.

[153] Especially as States criticised for unlawful incursions of submerged submarines into another State's territorial sea will frequently claim navigation or technical errors as the reason for this passage. See examples discussed in Kraska (n 52) 195, 208, 211.

[154] *Armed Activities on the Territory of the Congo* (n 68) para. 145; Eritrea Ethiopia Claims Commission (n 70) para. 11.

[155] Gray (n 9) 127–128.

[156] Statement by the President of the Security Council, 15 October 1996 (UN Doc. S/PRST/1996/42).

[157] South Korea did engage in naval war games with the United States, however. See Kraska (n 52) 208–209. South Korea also suspended aid programmes to and trade with North Korea in response: 'North Korea: "No Apology" for S Korea Cheonan Sinking', *BBC News*, 24 March 2015 <www.bbc.com/news/world-asia-32013750>.

[158] Moore (n 87) 16.

ensued between the United States and the United Kingdom in which differing views were expressed as to the necessity of the actions taken.[159] Moore notes that the attack on the Caroline was 'in response to a serious, *but not immediate*, threat'.[160]

Understanding what is 'necessary' and 'proportionate' will undoubtedly vary. Necessity suggests that a State has no other option to a forcible response whereas the response must be proportionate as to size, duration and target.[161] In *Oil Platforms*,[162] the ICJ was asked to pronounce on the legality of armed attacks by US naval warships on Iranian oil installations in the Persian Gulf under the 1955 Treaty of Amity between the United States and Iran, which in Article X provided for 'freedom of commerce and navigation' between the territories of the two States.[163] At the time of its attacks, the United States claimed its actions were justified as an exercise of the right to self-defence in response to alleged attacks by Iran on US-owned or -flagged vessels, including merchant vessels. In assessing the US attacks in *Oil Platforms*, the Court confirmed its earlier view in the *Military and Paramilitary Activities* that 'the criteria of necessity and proportionality must be observed if a measure is to be qualified as self-defence', concluding that the attacks on the oil platforms – which were not in use – were neither necessary nor proportionate.[164]

The most critical requirements for a lawful resort to self-defence in the present day remain that the response must be necessary and proportionate.[165] These requirements are frequently dependent on the facts of any incident and States may rely on these elements to condemn a use of force without dealing with the preceding question of whether an armed attack has occurred or not.[166] In such an assessment, it is worth recalling the approach of the ICJ in *Oil Platforms*, which observed, 'the requirement of international law that measures taken avowedly in self-defence must have

[159] Hunter Miller (ed.), *Treaties and Other International Acts of the United States of America* (US Government Printing Office, 1934) vol. 4, 1836–1846.

[160] Moore (n 87) 17 (emphasis in original).

[161] Crawford (n 37) 722.

[162] *Oil Platforms* (n 69).

[163] Treaty of Amity, Economic Relations, and Consular Rights, Tehran, 15 August 1955, entered into force 16 June 1957, 284 UNTS 93.

[164] *Oil Platforms* (n 69) 183.

[165] *Armed Activities on the Territory of the Congo* (n 68) para 147. See further Gray (n 9) 163, who observes 'in state practice these factors of necessity and proportionality are often the only factors relied on in deciding the legality of particular actions'.

[166] Gray (n 9) 163.

been necessary for the purpose is strict and objective, leaving no room for any "measure of discretion"'.[167]

The illegal entry of a foreign submarine into the territorial sea of another State would not normally give rise to a right of self-defence for the coastal State. Following the possible intrusion of an Indian submarine, a

> spokesperson from Pakistan's Navy announced, 'The submarine could have been easily engaged and destroyed had it not been Pakistan's policy to exercise restraint in the face of Indian aggression and to give peace a chance to prevail. However, the submarine is being kept under watch along with monitoring of other Indian navy units. The detected submarine is one of the latest submarines of Indian navy'.[168]

The destruction of the Indian submarine for entering Pakistan's territorial sea would not have been lawful self-defence, nor even a proportionate or necessary response in the absence of any hostile or forcible action by the submarine.

A scenario that should be contemplated in relation to submarines may be a one-off incident targeting a submarine. For example, where depth charges are dropped on a submarine, can the submarine respond in self-defence? Moore has argued that there is a separate right of 'unit self-defence', which would allow recourse to force where neither the initial force amounts to an armed attack nor the responding amount of force could be so great as to represent an armed attack.[169] He describes it as follows: 'The essence of unit self-defence is that a warship or task group that is defending itself as a unit may only use force against those targets which immediately threaten that unit, whether they be opposing vessels, aircraft or shore installations.'[170]

Moore points in this regard to the views of Judge Simma in *Oil Platforms*, who noted that certain hostile actions could 'have been countered immediately by "proportionate counter-measures" also of a military nature, consisting of defensive measures designed to eliminate the specific source of the threat or harm to affected ships in, and at the

[167] *Oil Platforms* (n 69) 196.

[168] Zia Mian, M. V. Ramana and Abdul Hameed Nayyara, 'Nuclear Submarines in South Asia: New Risks and Dangers' (2019) 2(1) *Journal for Peace and Nuclear Disarmament* 184, 194.

[169] Cameron Moore (n 87) 32–38. In a similar vein, Fleck has observed: 'Imminent peril of death of soldiers is a case for self-defence even in situations in which the territorial integrity or political independence of the State are not involved': Fleck (n 126) 178.

[170] Moore (n 87) 33.

time of, the specific incidents'.[171] Unit self-defence may allow a military submarine to use force against a surface vessel that had fired upon it and remained a threat to its safety and those on board. The response must be directed at the source of the immediate threat to the submarine, rather than any other military target.

The concept of unit self-defence may be reflected in national rules of engagement. Rules of engagement 'reflect political, operational, legal, and diplomatic factors relevant for the use of armed forces in peacetime and in times of crisis'.[172] For example, in the so-called Cod Wars of 1959, 'British ships had to wait until force had been used and then seek to fend it off by every means short of gunfire, which could only be resorted to when all other means were unavailing, and even then at the lowest level of use'.[173] Yet even where a State (or individual submarine) might have a right of self-defence, there may be principled, political or practical reasons not to exercise that right.[174]

If there is no armed attack and the right to self-defence does not apply, there are other lawful responses available if a State considers that the presence or activities of a foreign submarine constitutes an unlawful threat or use of force against its territorial integrity or political independence. Sweden's responses to Soviet or Russian submarines included prevention methods, such as increased patrols, military training exercises to search for submarines, mining and electronic monitoring, as well as deterrent tactics through the use of depth charges,[175] including legislating to allow such responses. A State may argue that dropping depth charges on its submarine constitutes an unlawful countermeasure, or a violation of sovereign immunity.[176] However, the lack of protest against the Swedish legislation has been considered indicative of international acceptance of such a step in response to submerged passage of submarines in the territorial sea.[177] It may thus

[171] *Oil Platforms* (n 69) 333 (Separate Opinion of Judge Simma).

[172] Fleck (n 126) 165.

[173] Ibid, 169.

[174] Wilmshurst (n 152) 964. As occurred in relation to the attack on South Korea's warship by a North Korean submarine. See above nn 90–99 and accompanying text.

[175] Mahmoudi (n 72) 587.

[176] Mahmoudi has observed that Article 30 of UNCLOS 'may cause some doubts about the viability of the argument for the use of force directly against an unauthorized submarine submerged in the territorial sea': ibid 590.

[177] See Romana Sadurska, 'Foreign Submarines in Swedish Waters: The Erosion of an International Norm' (1984) 10 *Yale Journal of International Law* 34.

be argued that the use of low-power depth charges is akin to warning shots against a surfaced vessel.[178]

Where submarine operations are unlawful, the permissible responses would still need to account for the sovereign immunity of any military submarine that is classed as a warship or other government vessel on non-commercial service. As such, a State could not seize or otherwise detain the submarine. The targeted State may be justified in applying countermeasures (which cannot include the use of force)[179] or seek reparations for the wrongful act.[180] Arguably, dropping low-power depth charges may be a means of signalling a request for a submarine to leave the territorial sea. The types of charges used and the likelihood of serious damage to the submarine and/or harm to those on board may indicate whether a coastal State has abused its rights in responding to the warship's actions in this regard.[181] States must, in any event, deploy peaceful means of dispute settlement.[182] The requirement to settle disputes by peaceful means is 'inseparable' to the requirement to refrain from the threat or use of force.[183] Any State responding excessively to perceived illegal action by a foreign submarine may potentially constitute an unlawful threat or use of force in its own right.

9.7 Conclusion

Both distinct and connected questions arise in relation to the prohibition on the threat or use of force in the law of the sea when submarines are in operation. On the one hand, threats or use of force are prohibited at sea as they are on land, and such actions will constitute violations of the rights of passage allowed in the territorial sea, international straits and in archipelagic sea lanes. On the other hand, submarine activities must be assessed to determine not only if they violate requirements under the law of the sea (such as illicit submerged passage, showing due regard, unjustifiable interference with coastal State economic rights) but if they also violate the *jus ad bellum*. To establish an unlawful threat of force, what

178 Kraska (n 52) 199.

179 ILC, 'Responsibility of States for Internationally Wrongful Acts' [2001] 2 *Yearbook of the International Law Commission* 26, arts. 22, 49–54.

180 Ibid, art. 31.

181 The doctrine of abuse of rights is discussed in Chapter 8, Section 8.4.2.

182 Charter of the United Nations (n 2) art. 2(3).

183 Declaration on the Enhancement of the Effectiveness of the Principle of Refraining from the Threat or Use of Force in International Relations, 18 November 1987, UNGA Res. 42/22 (UN Doc. A/RES/42/22) para. 16.

matters in this regard is that the deployment of the submarine and its activities show some element of coercion and that they foreshadow an imminent use of force where that force itself would be unlawful. The use of force by a submarine will be unlawful if it involves physical force against the armed forces of another State; espionage activities of a submarine, without some violent act or the imminent threat of a violent act, will not violate the prohibition on the use of force.

Lawful action in self-defence is allowed if an armed attack has occurred, provided that the action in self-defence is necessary and proportionate. Military submarines may be deployed by a State when exercising its right of self-defence. The concept of 'unit self-defence' may allow a specific submarine to take necessary and proportionate forceful measures against the immediate threat of or attack. If a foreign military submarine has acted unlawfully, the sovereign immunity of that warship precludes it from being arrested or detained by another State, even if that State purports to be exercising its authority for maritime law enforcement purposes. Instead, as also discussed in Chapter 7, a coastal State may take different steps against a foreign military submarine that is in violation of its navigational rights, short of arrest and detention. The steps taken by a coastal State include shadowing the submarine or possibly dropping low-power depth charges as a form of signalling for a submerged submarine to surface or leave the territorial sea. Criteria of necessity, proportionality and considerations of humanity remain applicable so as to not imperil the lives of those onboard the submarine.

10

Submarine Warfare under International Law

10.1 Introduction

The previous chapter considered the laws concerned with States' resort to the threat or use of force. This chapter considers the international legal regime applicable to the conduct of submarine warfare once there is an armed conflict. In the context of an international armed conflict, submarines can be used in several capacities and for different strategic objectives: to hunt other submarines, to strike surface vessels (warships, naval auxiliaries and merchant vessels), to lay mines, to attack land targets and, in the case of nuclear weapon States, to provide second strike capability as part of the nuclear triad.[1] These objectives can broadly fall within the two categories of submarine warfare and anti-submarine warfare. The former generally refers to the offensive use of a submarine, such as to destroy a surface vessel or land target, whereas the latter refers to defensive actions designed to interfere with the efficacy of an enemy submarine.[2] The focus in this chapter is on submarine warfare rather than anti-submarine warfare.[3]

[1] The term 'nuclear triad' refers to the three methods of delivery of nuclear weapons: by land, by air and by sea. See generally Chapter 1, Section 1.4.1.2 and Chapter 6, Section 6.3.2.

[2] Anti-submarine warfare involves a coordinated effort across several domains: submarines, warships, fixed-wing military aircraft and helicopters, land platforms (such as acoustic detection systems installed on the seabed or on shore) and other strategies like communications and decryption intelligence, which inform the appropriate countermeasures: Leona Alleslev, 'NATO Anti-Submarine Warfare: Rebuilding Capability, Preparing for the Future' (Special Report, NATO Parliamentary Assembly Science and Technology Committee, 13 October 2019) 11; Romney B. Duffey, 'Submarine Warfare and Intelligence in the Atlantic and Pacific in the Second World War: Comparisons and Lessons Learned for Two Opponents' (2017) 19(2) *Journal for Maritime Research* 143, 144 (regarding communications and decryption intelligence).

[3] As discussed in Chapter 1, Section 1.5.2, anti-submarine warfare is largely outside the scope of the book, but we note it is also governed by international humanitarian law.

The sections that follow consider three interdependent bodies of international law that regulate or impact the conduct of submarine warfare. First, the law of the sea largely regulates peaceful uses of the oceans but many of its principles also structure the broader environment in which an international armed conflict at sea occurs. Second, the modern law of neutrality regulates interactions between 'belligerents', which are States that are engaged in the international armed conflict, and 'neutrals', a term broadly defined as 'any State not party to the conflict'.[4] Third, the law of armed conflict or international humanitarian law regulates the activities of warships and naval auxiliaries during an international armed conflict. As discussed in earlier chapters, it is generally accepted that submarines fall within the established definition of 'warship'.[5] Consequently, submarines engaged in armed conflict are both entitled to the immunity of warships,[6] and have belligerent rights allowing them to take an active role in hostilities at sea.[7] This chapter is not concerned with other government or private submarines. The use of submarines in non-international armed conflict has not featured significantly in practice to date and is not addressed as a distinct issue in this chapter.[8]

[4] Louise Doswald-Beck, 'San Remo Manual on International Law Applicable to Armed Conflicts at Sea' (1995) 35(309) *International Review of the Red Cross* 583, para. 13(d) ('San Remo Manual').

[5] James Kraska et al., 'The Newport Manual on the Law of Naval Warfare' (2023) 101 *International Law Studies* 1, para. 3.2.1 ('Newport Manual'); Wolff Heintschel von Heinegg, 'Warships' in Anne Peters and Rüdiger Wolfrum (eds.), *Max Planck Encyclopedia of Public International Law* (Oxford University Press, October 2015) paras. 7–8; Heintschel von Heinegg, 'Submarine Operations and International Law' (n 5) 149; Wolff Heintschel von Heinegg, 'The Law of Military Operations at Sea' in Terry D. Gill and Dieter Fleck (eds.), *The Handbook of the International Law of Military Operations* (Oxford University Press, 2016) 375, para. 20.07.2.

[6] United Nations Convention on the Law of the Sea, Montego Bay, 10 December 1982, entered into force 16 November 1994, 1833 UNTS 397, arts. 32, 95, 236 ('UNCLOS'); Newport Manual (n 5) para. 3.2.1; United States Navy, United States Marine Corps and United States Coast Guard, *The Commander's Handbook on the Law of Naval Operations* (Naval War College, March 2022) para. 2.1.1 ('Commander's Handbook').

[7] Heintschel von Heinegg, 'Submarine Operations and International Law' (n 5) 149; Wolff Heintschel von Heinegg, 'The Development of the Law of Naval Warfare from the Nineteenth to the Twenty-First Century: Some Select Issues' (2014) 17 *Yearbook of International Humanitarian Law* 69, 72.

[8] While Tamil Tigers used submarines as part of their conflict against the Sri Lankan government, this deployment of submarines is considered in the book as terrorist activity (without engaging in the characterisation of that conflict) and addressed in Chapter 13. The deployment of submarines by the Tamil Tigers could otherwise be considered in the frame of international law applicable in non-international armed

Submarines have been used to conduct hostilities since the late eighteenth century. During the American Revolutionary War, *Turtle*, a one-man submersible, carried out the first known act of submarine warfare when it unsuccessfully attempted to lay explosive charges on HMS *Eagle*, a Royal Navy ship.[9] It was not until nearly a century later, during the American Civil War, that the submarine became a successful instrument of warfare. On the evening of 17 February 1864, *Hunley*, a submarine of the Confederate States of America, was on patrol off Charlestown Harbour, which had been blockaded by Union forces. Attached to its bow was a spar torpedo – a charge at the end of a long pole. Not only was *Hunley* successful in sinking its target, USS *Housatonic*, but it too met its demise during the encounter.[10] *Housatonic* was the 'first vessel destroyed by a contrivance of this character'.[11] With that distinction, the era of submarine warfare was born.

It was not until the outbreak of World War I (WWI) that the conduct of submarine warfare resumed and the 'military significance [of submarines] as warships was recognized'.[12] In what was undeniably the 'first submarine war',[13] submarines attempted to execute a naval attrition role during WWI, including in attempts to engage enemy battle fleets, though not to great effect.[14] Submarines were used for the purpose of commerce raiding in both WWI and World War II (WWII), a conflict in which 'unrestricted submarine warfare and the sinking of merchant vessels became the rule rather than the exception'.[15] The legal developments influenced by this practice were discussed in Chapters 2 and 3. In WWII, a key milestone in the use of submarine warfare in the Atlantic theatre

conflict. Much more commonly, submarine warfare is considered in the context of international armed conflict.

[9] See generally Antony Preston, *Submarine Warfare* (Brown Books, 1998) 8; Frank Uhlig Jr, 'The Submarine, 1776–1918' (2004) 57(2) *Naval War College Review* 146, 147.

[10] The sinking of the *Hunley* has puzzled historians and underwater archaeologists alike. See generally Rachel M. Lance, Henry Warder and Cameron R. Bass, 'Did a "Lucky Shot" Sink the Submarine *H.L. Hunley*?' (2017) 270 *Forensic Science International* 103; Mark K. Ragan, *Submarine Warfare in the Civil War* (Da Capo Press, 2002) 196–198; Uhlig (n 9) 148.

[11] 'The Loss of the Housatonic' (1864) 28(1) *Army and Navy Journal* 465, 467.

[12] William T. Mallison Jr, 'Submarine Warfare and International Law' (1966) 58 *International Law Studies* 1, 2.

[13] Norman Friedman, *British Submarines in Two World Wars* (Pen and Sword, 2019) 218.

[14] Karl Lautenschläger, 'The Submarine in Naval Warfare, 1901–2001' (1986–1987) 11(3) *International Security* 94, 105–106.

[15] Diana Panke and Ulriche Petersohn, 'Why International Norms Disappear Sometimes' (2012) 18(4) *European Journal of International Relations* 719, 721.

was the 1945 sinking of the German *U-864* by the British HMS *Venturer* in the North Sea. The *U-864* remains the only known submarine sunk in submerged submarine-to-submarine combat.[16] The conclusion of WWII brought with it the end of any sustained practice of naval and submarine warfare. This period is discussed in Chapter 5. Armed conflicts with naval dimensions since 1945 have all 'been markedly limited in their naval scope, with none having strategic naval influence beyond the immediate region of the core conflict'.[17]

Contemporary practice suggests that there has been a significant redevelopment in the purpose and role of submarines as an instrument of modern warfare. Submarines no longer 'exist simply to fight at sea with other navies',[18] and some commentators predict that they are unlikely to play a significant role in economic warfare in the future.[19] Instead, advancements in submarine technology have 'affected the nature and role assignments of the submarine more than any other preexisting war machine'.[20] These new roles include, for instance, the Cold War-era second strike nuclear deterrent role played by submarines armed with nuclear weapons as the 'most survivable leg of the … nuclear triad',[21] which has been described as 'arguably the most critical military capability available to the modern state'.[22] The development of propulsion technology (including nuclear propulsion) has improved the maximum

[16] There have, however, been several instances of surfaced submarine-to-submarine combat.

[17] Haines suggests that there have been a dozen or so such conflicts, including the Arab-Israeli Wars (1948–present), the Korean War (1950–1953), the Vietnam War (1955–1975), the Indo-Pakistan War (1971), the Battle of the Paracels (1974), the Iran-Iraq War (1980–1988), the Falklands/Malvinas War (1982), the Sri Lankan Civil War (1983–2009), the Gulf of Sidra Action (1986) and the Gulf Wars (1990–1991, 2003): Steven Haines, 'War at Sea: Nineteenth-century Laws for Twenty-first Century Wars?' (2016) 98(2) *International Review of the Red Cross* 419, 426–428.

[18] Ibid, 421.

[19] Lautenschläger (n 14) 134; Haines (n 17) 419, 428, 438; Heintschel von Heinegg, 'Submarine Operations and International Law' (n 5) 143; Martin Fink, 'The Ever-Existing "Crisis" of the Law of Naval Warfare' (2022) 104 *International Review of the Red Cross* 1971, 1978.

[20] Jon L Jacobson, 'The Law of Submarine Warfare Today' (1991) 64 *International Law Studies* 205, 206.

[21] Anya L. Fink, 'Defense Primer: Strategic Nuclear Forces' (Congressional Research Service Report No. IF10519, 18 November 2024). See further Chapter 6, Section 6.4.

[22] Isaac Jenkins, 'Producing Second Strike' in Mark Cancian (ed.), *Project on Nuclear Issues: A Collection of Papers from the 2017 Conference Series and Nuclear Scholars Initiative* (Center for Strategic and International Studies, 2018) 121, 121. See also Preston (n 9) 71ff; Austin Long and Brendan Rittenhouse Green, 'Stalking the Secure Second Strike: Intelligence, Counterforce, and Nuclear Strategy' (2015) 38(1–2) *Journal of Strategic*

underwater speed for submarines, which has allowed the underwater platforms to more effectively engage surface fleets.[23]

Perhaps the most significant development in contemporary submarine warfare has been the arming of submarines with cruise missiles.[24] This development has allowed undersea platforms to strike inland targets and therefore play a fundamental role in onshore power projection.[25] It is this role that has been the primary conduit for contemporary submarine warfare. While the first surface-to-surface cruise missile was launched by a submarine in 1947,[26] it was not until the 1991 Gulf War that submarine-launched Tomahawk cruise missiles were used in the context of armed conflict.[27] Submarine-launched missiles have been used to strike land targets in several other conflicts, including during Operation Desert Strike (1996),[28] Operation Infinite Reach (1998),[29] the NATO bombing of Yugoslavia (1999), Operation Odyssey Dawn (2011)[30] and more recently to strike targets in Syria in April 2018[31] and Houthi-controlled

Studies 38, 38–40. The strategic importance of submarines following the Cold War is discussed in Chapter 6, Section 6.4.5.

23 Lautenschläger (n 14) 127–128.

24 A cruise missile is propelled by a jet engine. It flies at a low altitude, in a relatively straight line and may rely on GPS technology to strike its target. Cruise missiles can be compared with ballistic missiles, which are generally capable of leaving the Earth's atmosphere and rely on the speed of its launch and gravity to guide the missile to its target: The Center for Arms Control and Non-Proliferation, 'Fact Sheet: Ballistic vs. Cruise Missiles', 2017 <https://armscontrolcenter.org/wp-content/uploads/2017/04/Ballistic-vs.-Cruise-Missiles-Fact-Sheet.pdf>.

25 Lautenschläger (n 14) 124.

26 Preston (n 9) 67.

27 'Tomahawk Missiles Brought Power to the Punch During Operation Enduring Freedom', *The Sextant*, 7 October 2014 <https://usnhistory.navylive.dodlive.mil/recent/article-view/article/2686540/tomahawk-missiles-brought-power-to-the-punch-during-operation-enduring-freedom/>. See also Ross R. Hatch, Joseph L. Luber and James H. Walker, 'Fifty Years of Strike Warfare Research at the Applied Physics Laboratory' (1992) 13(1) *Johns Hopkins APL Technical Digest*, 113 (observing that the response to the Gulf War 'for the first time brought into play the use of ship- and submarine-launched cruise missile as a complement to air strikes').

28 Strikes performed against targets in Southern Iraq.

29 Strikes performed against al-Qaeda targets in Afghanistan and Sudan.

30 Strikes performed against targets in Libya. See Gregory Bereiter, 'The US Navy in Operation Enduring Freedom, 2001–2002', *Naval History and Heritage Command*, 2016 <www.history.navy.mil/research/library/online-reading-room/title-list-alphabetically/u/us-navy-operation-enduring-freedom-2001-2002.html>.

31 Ben Werner, 'USS John Warner Is First Virginia-Class Attack Sub to Fire Missiles in Anger', *USNI News*, 16 April 2018 <https://news.usni.org/2018/04/16/32965>.

targets in Yemen in 2024.[32] Other examples include the use of British submarine-launched cruise missiles in the Kosovo War, Iraq War and the conflicts in Afghanistan and Libya.[33] Israeli forces fired submarine-launched missiles to attack targets in Syria in 2013.[34] Russia fired cruise missiles from the *Rostov-on-Don* in December 2015, at the request of the Assad government, to strike alleged Islamic State targets in Syria.[35] The *Rostov-on-Don* was sunk by a Ukrainian long-range missile in August 2024 at the port of Sevastopol in the disputed Crimean Peninsula.[36] The incident is the first combat loss of a Russian or Soviet submarine, and one of, if not the only, known sinking of a submarine in an armed conflict since the end of WWII.[37] In July 2022, Russian submarine-launched *Kabir* cruise

[32] Associated Press, 'US Military Launches Another Barrage of Missiles against Houthi Sites in Yemen', *NPR*, 17 January 2014 <www.npr.org/2024/01/17/1225294463/houthis-yemen-us-airstrikes-red-sea-israel-hamas>.

[33] Richard Norton-Taylor, 'Missiles Fired from British Subs', *The Guardian*, 9 October 2001 <www.theguardian.com/world/2001/oct/08/september11.afghanistan>; 'UK's Last Trafalgar Submarine Makes Final Voyage', *BBC News*, 13 December 2024 <www.bbc.com/news/articles/c938gwvxg2no>.

[34] 'Report: Israeli Submarine Strike Hit Syrian Arms Depot', *The Jerusalem Post*, 14 July 2013 <www.jpost.com/Middle-East/Report-Israeli-submarine-strike-hit-Syrian-arms-depot-319756>.

[35] 'Russia Hits Targets in Syria from Mediterranean Submarine', *BBC News*, 8 December 2015 <www.bbc.com/news/world-middle-east-35041656>.

[36] Warren Murray, 'Ukraine War Briefing: Ukrainians Sink Russian Submarine and Blow Up Airbase – Officials', *The Guardian*, 5 August 2024 <www.theguardian.com/world/article/2024/aug/05/ukraine-war-briefing-ukrainians-sink-russian-submarine-and-blow-up-airbase-officials>; Matt Murphy, 'Ukraine Says It Sank Russian Submarine in Crimea', *BBC News*, 4 August 2024 <www.bbc.com/news/articles/c4nggvg1yggo>; Samya Kullab, 'Ukraine Intensifies its Long-range Strikes, Sinking a Russian Submarine and Striking an Airfield', *Associated Press*, 4 August 2024 <https://apnews.com/article/russia-ukraine-submarine-8183f3a952b4d81893677e1b272c23fb>.

[37] Nicholas Aucott, 'Russia's Illegal War Continues to Be a Military Disaster: UK Statement to the OSCE' (Speech, 18 September 2024) <www.gov.uk/government/speeches/russias-illegal-war-continues-to-be-a-military-disaster-uk-statement-to-the-osce>; David Axe, 'After Months of Work, a Damaged Russian Submarine was Repaired. So the Ukrainians Hit it Again', *The Telegraph*, 10 August 2024 <www.telegraph.co.uk/news/2024/08/10/russia-submarine-rostov-on-don-ukraine-missile-strike/>. The only other incident that could possibly be characterised as the sinking of a submarine during armed conflict following the end of WWII is the British attack on the Argentine ARA *Santa Fe* during the Falklands/Malvinas War (1982). The *Santa Fe* was badly damaged (but not sunk) following an attack by British warships; it later sunk at port because of the damage: Lawrence Freedman, *The Official History of the Falklands Campaign* (Routledge, 2005) vol. 2, 208–217. The last sinking of a submarine in armed conflict is likely the sinking of USS *Bullhead*, a US Navy submarine thought to have been sunk by Japanese aircraft on the same day as the bombings of Hiroshima and Nagasaki.

missiles were used to strike the Ukrainian city of Vinnytsia as part of the Russo-Ukrainian War, causing the deaths of twenty-three civilians.[38]

Part I of this Book has explained how submarine operations during WWI and WWII influenced legal developments following those armed conflicts and prompted consideration of the laws of neutrality and the standards to which submarines should be held as warships engaged in armed conflict. This chapter builds on aspects of that earlier work. Section 10.2 provides an initial examination of the sources of law relating to submarine warfare, in light of the intersecting bodies of law across the law of the sea, international humanitarian law and the law of neutrality. Section 10.3 explains how international law applies in different maritime zones recognised in the law of the sea during times of armed conflict. Section 10.4 examines the law of neutrality and Section 10.5 brings together the law of armed conflict as it applies to submarines. As noted at the outset, anti-submarine warfare is not considered as a discrete topic but should instead be considered as governed by the rules set out in each section. It will be seen that although the international law regulating submarine warfare is largely derived from eras that pre-date the modern submarine, the articulated rules on the law of naval warfare remain applicable today given their reflection in current national manuals, as well as expert-produced manuals,[39] even if not set out in a widely agreed multilateral treaty.

10.2 Sources of Law Concerned with Submarine Warfare

As set out in the Introduction, there are three primary bodies of international law concerned with submarine warfare: the law of the sea, the law of maritime neutrality, and the law of armed conflict (including the law of prize).[40] The law of armed conflict is sometimes referred to as international humanitarian law; these expressions 'are synonymous, and the choice between them is simply lexical'.[41] There may also be further sources of law applicable to certain aspects of armed conflict. For

[38] 'Russia Defends Submarine Missile Attack that Killed 23 Civilians', *Al Jazeera*, 15 July 2022 <www.aljazeera.com/news/2022/7/15/russia-justifies-deadly-attack-on-ukrainian-city-of-vinnytsia>.

[39] See below nn 65–75 and accompanying text.

[40] J Ashley Roach, 'Legal Aspects of Modern Submarine Warfare' (2002) 6 *Max Planck Yearbook of United Nations Law* 367, 368.

[41] Yoram Dinstein, *The Conduct of Hostilities under the Law of International Armed Conflict* (Cambridge University Press, 2022) 23, para. 67 ('*The Conduct of Hostilities*').

instance, the threat or use of nuclear weapons from an undersea platform may implicate the developing body of law concerned with nuclear non-proliferation,[42] and a variety of international agreements prohibit the placement or use of such weapons in certain parts of the ocean.[43] Further, there are international instruments that limit the conduct of hostilities in certain regions, such as in Antarctica,[44] and in the Åland Islands.[45] The discussion in this chapter focuses on the law of the sea, the law of neutrality and law of armed conflict as the most applicable in relation to submarine warfare.

10.2.1 Sources of Law

The 'principal strata' of the law applicable to submarine warfare is treaty and custom.[46] The law of the sea is comprehensively set out in the UN Convention on the Law of the Sea (UNCLOS).[47] Many of the laws of neutrality at sea were codified by the 1907 Hague Conventions,[48] in particular Hague Convention (XIII) of 1907 concerning the Rights and

[42] See generally Anna Hood and Monique Cormier, 'Nuclear Threats under International Law Part I: The Legal Framework' (2024) 7(1) *Journal for Peace and Nuclear Disarmament* 157; Timothy McCormack, 'A *Non Liquet* on Nuclear Weapons: The ICJ Avoids the Application of General Principles of International Humanitarian Law' (1997) 316 *International Review of the Red Cross* 76; Stefan Oeter, 'Methods and Means of Combat' in Dieter Fleck (ed.), *The Handbook of International Humanitarian Law* (2nd ed., Oxford University Press, 2008) paras. 430–435.

[43] For example, the Treaty Banning Nuclear Weapon Tests in the Atmosphere, in Outer Space and Under Water, Moscow, 5 August 1963, entered into force 10 October 1963, 480 UNTS 43; Treaty on the Prohibition of the Emplacement of Nuclear Weapons and Other Weapons of Mass Destruction on the Seabed and the Ocean Floor and in the Subsoil Thereof, Washington, Moscow and London, 11 11 1971, entered into force 18 May 1972, 995 UNTS 115 ('Seabed Arms Control Treaty'), Treaty on the Prohibition of Nuclear Weapons in Latin America and the Caribbean, Mexico City, 14 August 1967, entered into force 22 April 1968, 634 UNTS 281.

[44] Antarctic Treaty, Washington, 23 June 1961, entered into force 23 June 1961, 402 UNTS 71, art. 1. See Newport Manual (n 5) para. 4.2.1.

[45] Treaty of Peace between the Allied and Associated Powers and Finland, Paris, 10 February 1947, 48 UNTS 203, art. 5.

[46] Dinstein, *The Conduct of Hostilities* (n 41) para. 51 (referring to the law of armed conflict generally). Dinstein also observes that the 'bifurcation of [the law of international armed conflict] into treaty law and customary law does not preclude interaction between the two separate strata': para. 59.

[47] UNCLOS (n 6).

[48] International Law Association, 'Helsinki Principles on the Law of Maritime Neutrality' in Dietrich Schindler and Jirí Toman (eds.), *The Laws of Armed Conflict* (Brill, 2024) 1425–1430 ('Helsinki Principles').

Duties of Neutral Powers in Naval War.[49] The law has been further developed by a restatement referred to as the *Helsinki Principles on the Law of Maritime Neutrality* (Helsinki Principles) prepared by the International Law Association's Committee on Maritime Neutrality.[50] These developments were discussed in Chapter 2.

The situation with respect to the law of armed conflict applicable to submarine warfare is more complex for three key reasons. First, the law of armed conflict applicable to submarine warfare is largely derivative of the law of armed conflict applicable to naval warfare. This situation arises in part because, outside the World Wars, there has been limited practice of submarine warfare and also because, in the World Wars, the law of naval warfare was often applied *carte blanche* to all seafaring platforms. The derivative character of the law of submarine warfare will be more fully described in the sections that follow, as it is drawn largely from customary international law.

Second, Dinstein and others have commented that States have been afflicted by a 'treaty making paralysis' in relation to the law of armed conflict since the 1970s.[51] This issue is particularly pronounced in the context of the law of naval and submarine warfare. While there are a limited number of international instruments that concern themselves with the issue of naval warfare,[52] there has been no sustained movement

[49] Phillip Drew, *The Law of Maritime Blockade: Past, Present, and Future* (Oxford University Press, 2017) 19; Bruce A. Harlow, 'The Law of Neutrality at Sea for the 80s and Beyond' (1984) 3(1–2) *UCLA Pacific Basin Law Journal* 42, 42. But see James Farrant, 'Modern Neutrality Law' (2014) 90 *International Law Studies* 198, 201 (observing that Hague XIII 'was a far from comprehensive statement of the law. It included no provisions on the law of blockade, contraband, prize law or belligerent visit and search rights.')

[50] Helsinki Principles (n 48).

[51] Yoram Dinstein, 'Law of Armed Conflict Manuals' (2020) 23 *Yearbook of International Humanitarian Law* 3, 5. See also Dinstein, *The Conduct of Hostilities* (n 41) para. 83 (observing that there has been a 'chilling effect inhibiting any desire to formulate new general [law of international armed conflict] treaties relating to methods of warfare'); Dale Stephens, 'Manuals and Courts: International Humanitarian Law, Informal Law-making and Normativity' in Heike Krieger and Jonas Püschmann (eds.), *Law-Making and Legitimacy in International Humanitarian Law* (Edward Elgar, 2021) 253, 255.

[52] See, e.g., Procès-Verbal relating to the Rules of Submarine Warfare set forth in Part IV of the Treaty for the Limitation and Reduction of Naval Armament of 22 April 1930, London, 6 November 1936, entered into force 6 November 1936, 173 LNTS 353, [1936] ATS 14 ('1936 London Protocol'); Convention (II) for the Amelioration of the Condition of Wounded, Sick and Shipwrecked Members of Armed Forces at Sea, Geneva, 12 August 1949, entered into force 21 October 1950, 75 UNTS 85 ('Geneva II'); Hague Convention (VI) relative to the Legal Position of Enemy Merchant Ships at the Start of Hostilities, The Hague, 18 October 1907, entered into force 26 January 1910; Hague

to codify the customary regime into a comprehensive treaty. Nor do commentators expect there to be any significant push for States to do so in the future.[53] Further, the rapid technological development of submarines and undersea weapons systems arguably does not lend itself to processes of formal, treaty-based law-making, which 'often simply take too long to adapt to changing social and technological realities'.[54]

Third, it is difficult to identify custom in circumstances where there have only been a handful of instances of submarine warfare (and indeed, naval warfare more generally) since the end of WWII. These conflicts have also been limited in geographic scope, which complicates the identification of the general and widespread practice[55] necessary for the crystallisation of new rules of customary international law. The basis of the custom is therefore the submarine warfare activities of WWI and WWII, when submarine warfare was last used in any widespread and sustained capacity. As Fink has observed, 'the law of naval warfare seems to have a long memory, possibly because it cannot rely on a contemporary set of generally accepted rules'.[56] However, the submarines of today are completely foreign to the submarines of WWII. They

Convention (VII) relative to the Conversion of Merchant Ships into War-ships, The Hague, 18 October 1907, entered into force 26 January 1910, 205 CTS 319; Hague Convention (VIII) relative to the Laying of Automatic Submarine Contact Mines, The Hague, 18 October 1907, entered into force 18 October 1907, 205 CTS 331 ('Hague VIII'); Hague Convention (IX) concerning Bombardment by Naval Forces in Time of War, The Hague, 18 October 1907, entered into force 26 January 1910, 205 CTS 345 ('Hague IX'); Hague Convention (X) for the Adaptation to Maritime Warfare of the Principles of the Geneva Convention, The Hague, entered into force 26 January 1910, 18 October 1907, 205 CTS 359; Hague Convention (XI) relative to Certain Restrictions with regard to the Exercise of the Right of Capture in Naval War, The Hague, 18 October 1907, entered into force 26 January 1910, 205 CTS 367; Hague Convention (XIII) concerning the Rights and Duties of Neutral Powers in Naval War, The Hague, 18 October 1907, entered into force 26 January 1910, 205 CTS 395 ('Hague XIII'); Declaration Respecting Maritime Law, Paris, 16 April 1856, entered into force 16 April 1856, 61 BFSP 155.

53 See, e.g., Fink, 'The Ever-Existing "Crisis" of the Law of Naval Warfare' (n 19) 1980.

54 Wouter G. Werner, 'The Law at Hand: Paratext in Manuals on International Humanitarian Law' in Heike Krieger and Jonas Püschmann (eds.), *Law-Making and Legitimacy in International Humanitarian Law* (Edward Elgar, 2021) 217, 221.

55 *Military and Paramilitary Activities in and against Nicaragua* (Nicaragua v. United States) (Judgment of 27 June 1986) [1986] ICJ Rep 14, para. 186.

56 Martin Fink, 'The Newport Manual: The New Kid on the Block on the Laws of Naval Warfare' (2025) 30(1) *Journal of Conflict and Security Law* 139, 144. See also Christopher Greenwood, 'Historical Development and Legal Basis' in Dieter Fleck (ed.), *The Handbook of International Humanitarian Law* (2nd ed., Oxford University Press, 2008) para. 104 ('naval warfare is in other respects subject to a distinct legal regime. The environment in which naval warfare takes place is very different from that of land warfare, its scope for affecting the rights of neutrals is far greater and the rules which

can submerge longer, avoid detection more easily, and are armed with new and complex weapons systems. Their purpose has also shifted during this time of relative naval peace from playing the leading part of 'commerce raider' to undertaking a more diverse set of roles: coastal protection, intelligence gathering and nuclear deterrence to name but a few. This wholesale redevelopment of the role of the submarine in contemporary warfare sits awkwardly with the legal regime of the past. For this reason, the law of naval warfare has been described as 'sometimes astonishing and often outdated'.[57]

These issues present a clear conceptual difficulty for lawyers attempting to determine what is the contemporary law applicable to submarine warfare. Moreover, the situation has led States to express their views on applicable law in the form of national military manuals. These manuals, which vary in their degree of detail, their currency, and the topics considered, guide defence personnel in relation to the law of armed conflict.[58] There is, however, some debate as to whether they may be used as evidence in support of the existence of international rules of custom. Crawford and Brownlie were of the view that manuals of military serve as 'material sources of custom'.[59] The International Criminal Tribunal for the former Yugoslavia, commenting on the difficulties in determining the existence of custom in the context of armed conflict, encouraged reference to military manuals in determining State practice.[60] On the other hand, while these manuals 'may provide important indications of State behavior and *opinio juris*, they cannot be

govern naval warfare have not, for the most part, been the subject of as much attention in recent years as the rules applicable to land warfare').

57 Marco Sassòli, *International Humanitarian Law: Rules, Controversies, and Solutions to Problems Arising in Warfare* (2nd ed., Edward Elgar, 2024) para. 8.432.

58 Or, alternatively, as Boothby puts it, military manuals 'tend to be prepared by individuals employed for that purpose by the relevant state and will be designed to express the view of the relevant state as to the rules of international law that bind it and as to how those rules should be interpreted': William H. Boothby, *Conflict Law: The Influence of New Weapons Technology, Human Rights and Emerging Actors* (Springer, 2014) 65–66.

59 James Crawford, *Brownlie's Principles of Public International Law* (9th ed., Oxford University Press, 2019) 22; Ian Brownlie, *Principles of Public International Law* (5th ed., Clarendon Press, 1998) 5. See also Fink, 'The Newport Manual: The New Kid on the Block on the Laws of Naval Warfare' (n 56) 143 (observing that military manuals 'are generally considered part of the formal State views'); Dinstein, *The Conduct of Hostilities* (n 41) para. 32 ('[a]s for customary international law, it is wrought in the crucible of State practice, predominantly through the actual conduct of armed forces during hostilities and the edicts of military manuals.').

60 *Prosecutor v. Tadic* (Decision on the Defence Motion for Interlocutory Appeal on Jurisdiction of 2 October 1995) International Criminal Tribunal for the Former Yugoslavia, Case No. IT-94-1-AR72 (1996) 35 ILM 32, para. 99.

a replacement for a meaningful assessment of operational State practice in connection with actual military operations'.[61] Some commentators have also expressed the view that certain of these military manuals (in particular, those belonging to the most powerful and active militaries) are likely to be more authoritative in the development of custom.[62] Whatever the true position, it suffices for our purposes to remark that military manuals are, in the absence of other evidence of practice, unlikely to be a panacea in determining custom.[63]

There have also been some attempts by academics and practitioners to codify the law of naval warfare in the form of restatements of the law, which are also referred to as 'manuals'. These manuals, which are prepared by subject matter experts, reflect the collective view of those experts as to the state of the law.[64] The most significant of these efforts is the *San Remo Manual on International Law Applicable to Armed Conflicts at Sea* (San Remo Manual). Completed in 1994, the San Remo Manual aims to 'provide a contemporary restatement of international law applicable to armed conflicts at sea',[65] along with several proposals for the progressive development of the law.[66] More recently, in 2023 a distinguished group of naval warfare experts published the *Newport Manual on the Law of Naval*

[61] This view was that of the Legal Adviser for the US Department of State and the General Counsel of the US Department of Defense: John B, Bellinger III and William J. Haynes II, 'A US Government Response to the International Committee of the Red Cross Study *Customary International Humanitarian Law*' (2007) 89 *International Review of the Red Cross* 443, 445. The Newport Manual authors eschew the use of military manuals on several bases, including that they often reflect the performance of treaty-based obligations as opposed to custom, that they include guidance in military manuals for policy as opposed to legal reasons, and that military manuals exist in varying degrees of formality (in some cases only being used for training purposes): 446–447.

[62] See, for example, Charles J. Dunlap Jr, 'Law of War Manuals and Warfighting: A Perspective' (2012) 47(2) *Texas International Law Journal* 265, 273; Robin Geiß and Anni Pues, 'International Manuals in International Humanitarian Law: A Rejoinder to Wouter G Werner' in Heike Krieger and Jonas Püschmann (eds.), *Law-Making and Legitimacy in International Humanitarian Law* (Edward Elgar, 2021) 232, 239.

[63] See generally David Turns, 'Military Manuals and the Customary Law of Armed Conflict' in Nobuo Hayashi (ed.), *National Military Manuals on the Law of Armed Conflict* (Forum for International Criminal and Humanitarian Law, International Peace Research Institute, Publication Series No. 2, 2008) 64, 72 (observing that 'military manuals at the most could be used as evidence of opinio juris'); Fink, 'The Newport Manual: The New Kid on the Block on the Laws of Naval Warfare' (n 56) 145 (noting that '[a]rguably, one cannot cherry pick one's way through State Manuals as a methodology to find out what the international law is').

[64] Boothby (n 58) 65.

[65] San Remo Manual (n 4) 598.

[66] Ibid.

Warfare (Newport Manual).[67] The *Oslo Manual on Select Topics of the Law of Armed Conflict* (Oslo Manual), published in 2020, is also of note.[68] The San Remo Manual has been greatly influential[69] and has been cited with approval by various international courts, tribunals and commissions.[70] There are a diversity of views among States as to whether the these manuals reflect custom.[71]

These manuals should be approached with some caution. Even if they are expressed to be *lex lata* (and not *lex ferenda*),[72] it remains the fact that they are drafted by experts and therefore do not constitute the State practice necessary to form custom and instead 'reflect what, in the opinions of the contributing experts, the law on the particular matter

[67] Newport Manual (n 5).

[68] Yoram Dinstein and Arne Willy Dahl, *Oslo Manual on Select Topics of the Law of Armed Conflict* (Springer, 2020).

[69] See, e.g., Fink, 'The Newport Manual: The New Kid on the Block on the Laws of Naval Warfare' (n 56) 145; Boothby (n 58) 75–76.

[70] See Constantine Antonopoulos, *Non-Participation in Armed Conflict: Continuity and Modern Challenges to the Law of Neutrality* (Cambridge University Press, 2022) 127–130.

[71] Fink observes:

> A number of States adopted or refer to some rules of the San Remo Manual in their military law manuals, officialising them as a State position. Denmark's military manual notes that the San Remo Manual rules, although not a treaty, 'are widely considered to reflect customary international law' and therefore bind Denmark. Germany's military manual notes more carefully that 'it should not be assumed' that the San Remo Manual's contents 'automatically coincide with the positions of the German Government and/or the Federal Ministry of Defence'. The US Department of Defense Law of War Manual does not refer to the Manual at all. Likewise, the updated US Commander' Handbook on the Law of Naval Operations contains no references to the Manual.

Fink, 'The Ever-Existing "Crisis" of the Law of Naval Warfare' (n 19) 1983. See also Haines (n 17) 434; Stephens (n 51) 264; Michael N. Schmitt, 'Expert Manuals: An Insider's Account' in Sandesh Sivakumaran and Christian R. Burne (eds.), *Making and Shaping the Law of Armed Conflict* (Oxford University Press, 2024) 105, 114; Antonopoulos (n 70) 126.

[72] The difference between a manual expressing *lex lata* and one expressing *lex ferenda* appears to have been brought into issue by the Newport Manual (n 5), which describes itself in opposition to the San Remo Manual as 'the first effort to restate the law of naval warfare as a purely *lex lata* exercise since 1955': xiii. The San Remo Manual (n 4) acknowledges that it 'includes a few provisions which might be considered progressive developments in the law' (in other words, *lex ferenda*): 598. The extent to which it is possible to draft a purely *lex lata* manual has been subject of debate: Geiß and Pues (n 62) 241; Stephens (n 51) 260.

constitutes'.[73] That is not to say that these manuals are incapable of reflecting the substance of customary international law or of influencing the practice of States.[74] Rather, it is sufficient to state that the manuals themselves are not strictly recognised as a primary source of law. They may to some extent constitute the writings of publicists within the meaning of Article 38(1)(d) of the Statute of the International Court of Justice but, ultimately, in determining the content of custom, one must always look to the extent to which the rules within each manual are 'actually followed by the armed forces of states and, thus, are translated into state practice'.[75] Given we have already described the distinct lack of State practice applicable to submarine warfare, that task is not an easy one.

10.2.2 Interaction of the Law of the Sea with the Laws of Neutrality and Armed Conflict

During times of armed conflict, the law of the sea, the law of neutrality and law of armed conflict each operate simultaneously. They each have their own 'work' to do in regulating the conduct of submarine warfare. Consequently, and while it is not always the case, there are instances where the rules cannot all be reconciled and will conflict with each other.

[73] Boothby (n 58) 87. See also Donald R. Rothwell and Tim Stephens, *The International Law of the Sea* (3rd ed., Hart, 2023) 309; Dinstein, 'Law of Armed Conflict Manuals' (n 51) 6–7 (observing that experts 'are able to illuminate the lex lata efficaciously and persuasively. The downside is that mere experts do not possess the required governmental credentials to negotiate a text that transcends the lex lata'); Haines (n 17) 435 ('One does need to be circumspect in assuming that the San Remo Manual is definitive of the law ... It is authoritative, in so far as it is the product of a rigorous process of review, but that authority is limited by the fact that States were not officially represented in the process of consultation, with all officials contributing in their "personal" capacities'). Geiß and Pues ask more simply, 'what is the authority that allows a circle of experts to act as (quasi) lawmakers in international law?': Geiß and Pues (n 62) 236. But see Liesbeth Lijnzaad, 'Going for a Test Drive? Some Observations on the Turn to Informality in the Laws of Armed Conflict' (2022) 104 (920–931) *International Review of the Red Cross* 1930, 1943 (noting that, even though the manuals are drafted by experts, many of these experts have held important military, diplomatic or other governmental roles, and that the drafting process often involves consultation with States, 'albeit in a non-committal manner').

[74] See generally Dinstein, *The Conduct of Hostilities* (n 41) paras. 83, 1194 ('custom is unwritten and its delineation may be blighted by dissension. This is where authoritative (albeit unofficial) restatements or manuals of LOIAC, drawn up by international groups of experts, become (*faute de mieux*) a substitute for treaties by hammering out informal impressions of the present layout of LOIAC'); Geiß and Pues (n 62) ('international manuals inherently tread the fine line between interpretation and law-making').

[75] Boothby (n 58) 89.

One therefore needs to consider how to 'deconflict' these rules of international law.

The primary issue arises in attempting to reconcile the comprehensive regime created by UNCLOS with the sparser rules pertaining to the law of naval warfare. While there has been 'considerable academic debate over the applicability of UNCLOS during times of war and what significance should be accorded to the 'peaceful purposes' provisions of that treaty',[76] there have been few attempts to resolve the interaction of the law of the sea with the law of armed conflict.[77] In this regard, the authors of the Newport Manual suggest that:

> The law of naval warfare is *lex specialis* and prevails over the peacetime international law of the sea. To the extent that peacetime international maritime law as reflected in [UNCLOS] may be inconsistent with the law of naval warfare, the latter prevails during periods of hostility.[78]

The application of the *lex specialis derogate legi generali* principle, in effect, means that the 'special' or more specific rule takes precedence over the more general, as the former 'being more concrete, often takes better account of the particular features of the context in which it is to be applied than any applicable general law'.[79] The interpretive approach requires one to determine the relationship between the two conflicting rules and, 'in the case of conflict, what actually constitutes a contradiction between two rules and if that contradiction exists then the rule that prevails'.[80] There are competing positions on the appropriate interpretive approach with respect to determining how to apply the *lex specialis* principle – in particular, whether each rule should be interpreted individually and compared for conflict, or whether entire bodies of law should be subordinate to others in the event of any

[76] Natalie Klein, *Maritime Security and the Law of the Sea* (Oxford University Press, 2011) 258.

[77] But see David Letts, 'The Law of the Sea and the Law of Naval Warfare: Comfortable Intersection or Irreconcilable Conflict' in Kristina Siig, Brigit Feldtmann and Fenella M. W. Billing (eds.), *The United Nations Convention on the Law of the Sea: A System of Regulation* (Routledge, 2023) 63. There have been several commentaries considering the conflict between the law of armed conflict and international human rights law: Sassòli (n 57) paras. 9.033–9.040 and the sources there cited.

[78] Newport Manual (n 5) para. 1.1.

[79] ILC, 'Conclusions of the Work of the Study Group on the Fragmentation of International Law: Difficulties arising from the Diversification and Expansion of International Law' (2006) 2 *Yearbook of the International Law Commission* 177, 178.

[80] Sassòli (n 57) para. 9.160.

inconsistency.[81] Both interpretations could be accommodated in the wording of the Newport Manual.

In the authors' view, it is the latter approach that should be preferred. It is enough to state that UNCLOS applies in full to the operations of submarines up until the point that an international armed conflict exists.[82] At that time, the law of naval warfare and principles of the law of armed conflict take over as *lex specialis*, but only to the extent that there is inconsistency between the two specific rules. In this way:

> during periods of armed conflict, the law of naval warfare is superimposed on the regimes of peacetime oceans law. So while the provisions of UNCLOS are applicable, in time of war the peacetime rules are calibrated by another set of rules governing the rights and duties of parties to conflict at sea.[83]

This approach, as one of the authors has stated elsewhere, 'is the most tenable view, particularly when account is taken of the efforts to recognize the legal framework created by UNCLOS in modern iterations of the laws of naval warfare'.[84]

10.3 Maritime Zones in Submarine Warfare

The consequence of the development of maritime zones in UNCLOS on modern submarine warfare is that the applicable rules of war and

[81] See, e.g., David T. Lee, 'The Principle of Proportionality in Maritime Armed Conflict: A Comparative Analysis of the Law of Naval Warfare and Modern International Humanitarian Law' (2020) 27 *Southwestern Journal of International Law* 119, 122 ('the law of naval warfare is *lex specialis* and encompasses a significant body of law unique to warfare at sea'); Leslie Green, 'The Environment and the Law of Conventional Warfare' (1991) 29 *Canadian Yearbook of International Law* 222, 226 ('while the Convention is *lex generalis*, the law of war is *lex specialis* and, to the extent that its provisions are contrary to those of the lex generalis, they prevail.'); James Kraska, 'Rule Selection in the Case of Israel's Naval Blockade of Gaza: Law of Naval Warfare or Law of the Sea' (2010) 13 *Yearbook of International Humanitarian Law* 367, 373; Kubo Mačák, 'The Role of International Human Rights Law in the Interpretation of the Fourth Geneva Convention' (2022) *International Yearbook of Human Rights* 219, 231–232; Sassòli (n 57) para. 9.051; Natalie Klein, *Dispute Settlement in the UN Convention on the Law of the Sea* (Cambridge University Press, 2009) 282–283.

[82] As to the question of when an armed conflict exists, see below nn 263–265 and accompanying text.

[83] Kraska, 'Rule Selection' (n 81) 373. See also Antonopoulos (n 70) 87.

[84] Klein, *Maritime Security and the Law of the Sea* (n 76) 259. In Klein's view, 'the maritime rights and duties States enjoy in peacetime continue to exist, with minor exceptions, during armed conflict'. See also Fink, 'The Ever-Existing "Crisis" of the Law of Naval Warfare' (n 19) 1976.

Table 10.1 *Permissibility of submarine warfare in armed conflict*

	Neutral littoral State	Belligerent littoral State
Internal waters	No	Yes
Archipelagic waters	No	Yes
Territorial sea	No	Yes
International strait	No – defensive measures only	Yes
Contiguous zone	Yes – 'due regard'	Yes
Exclusive economic zone	Yes – 'due regard'	Yes
Continental shelf	Yes – 'due regard'	Yes
High seas	*Always permitted*	

neutrality vary with the maritime zone in which the submarine is operating.[85] These variations are summarised in Table 10.1.

10.3.1 Internal Waters, the Territorial Sea and Archipelagic Waters

The quadrupling of the breadth of the territorial sea and the recognition of the concept of archipelagic waters have increased the size of ocean space over which neutrality may be asserted and, consequently, the potential areas in which submarine warfare can be conducted has been reduced.[86] UNCLOS preserves the sovereignty of coastal States over their territorial sea and internal waters.[87] Archipelagic States are also sovereign over their archipelagic waters.[88] In these areas, the regime applicable to submarine warfare has not changed.

While there are no restrictions on the conduct of submarine warfare in the waters of other belligerents,[89] belligerents are strictly prohibited from conducting submarine warfare against both neutrals and other belligerents

[85] Bernard H. Oxman, 'The Regime of Warships Under the United Nations Convention on the Law of the Sea' (1984) 24 *Virginia Journal of International Law* 809, 811.

[86] See generally J. Ashley Roach, 'The Law of Naval Warfare at the Turn of Two Centuries' (2000) 94 *American Journal of International Law* 64.

[87] UNCLOS (n 6) art. 2.

[88] Ibid, arts. 2, 49.

[89] San Remo Manual (n 4) para. 10(a).

while in these zones,[90] which are inviolable and referred to as 'neutral waters'.[91] This prohibition extends to the attack or capture of objects or persons, laying of mines, visit, search, diversion or capture, and the use of neutral waters or territory as a base of operations (including to launch attack or capture operations on objects or territory located outside neutral waters or territory).[92] Consistent with this restriction, belligerent submarines must not use neutral waters as a sanctuary,[93] and are generally not permitted to extend their passage in neutral waters beyond twenty-four hours (except in cases of weather stress or damage, or where exercising the right of archipelagic sea lane passage).[94]

During times of armed conflict, the regime of innocent passage established by UNCLOS gives way to the law of neutrality and, consequently, belligerent warships enjoy only a right of 'mere passage' in neutral waters.[95] The regime of innocent passage continues to apply to neutrals, which may exercise that right through the territorial seas of belligerents. The regimes of innocent and mere passage are similar but there are some critical differences to note. The exercise of the right of mere passage does not affect the neutrality of the State under international law.[96] A neutral State may suspend warships' access to the territorial sea, including submarine access, on a non-discriminatory basis during times of armed conflict.[97] That suspension may be

[90] Hague XIII (n 52) arts. 1–2; Helsinki Principles (n 48) para. 1.4; San Remo Manual (n 4) para. 15; Newport Manual (n 5) para. 11.3.2.3. See also Heintschel von Heinegg, 'Submarine Operations and International Law' (n 5) 151; Sassòli (n 57) para. 8.438; Elmar Rauch, *The Protocol Additional to the Geneva Convention for the Protection of Victims of International Armed Conflicts and the United Nations Convention on the Law of the Sea: Repercussion on the Law of Naval Warfare* (Duncker and Humblot, 1984) 32, cited in Horace B. Robertson Jr, *The 'New' Law of the Sea and the Law of Armed Conflict at Sea* (Naval War College Newport Paper No. 3, October 1992) 16.

[91] San Remo Manual (n 4) para. 14; Newport Manual (n 5) para. 11.3.1; Hague XIII (n 52) art. 1.

[92] Hague XIII (n 52) art. 2; San Remo Manual (n 4) para. 16; Newport Manual (n 5) para. 11.3.2.3.

[93] Hague XIII (n 52) art. 5; San Remo Manual (n 4) para. 17.

[94] Hague XIII (n 52) arts. 12, 14; San Remo Manual (n 4) para. 21. There are some instances in which the 'twenty-four-hour rule' will not apply, see Michael Bothe, 'Neutrality, Concept and General Rules' in Anne Peters and Rüdiger Wolfrum (eds.), *Max Planck Encyclopedia of Public International Law* (Oxford University Press, October 2015) paras. 63–65.

[95] Farrant (n 49) 207, 213; San Remo Manual (n 4) para. 19. See also Chapter 2, Section 2.2.3.

[96] Hague XIII (n 52) art. 10; Newport Manual (n 5) para. 11.3.3.5.

[97] UNCLOS (n 6) art. 25; Newport Manual (n 5) paras. 11.3.3.5, 11.4.1.3; Helsinki Principles (n 48) para. 2.3; San Remo Manual (n 4) para. 19; Farrant (n 49) 211.

temporary or permanent.[98] In fact, both the Australian Law of Armed Conflict manual and the US Commander's Handbook on the Law of Naval Operations suggest that 'general practice has been to close neutral territorial seas to belligerent submarines'.[99] In the territorial sea, UNCLOS requires submarines to show their flag and navigate on the surface when exercising the right of innocent passage:[100] As discussed in Chapter 7, Article 20 of UNCLOS is the only provision of UNCLOS that explicitly regulates the activities of submarines and is therefore of note.[101] In times of armed conflict, belligerent submarines will only be required to surface in the territorial seas of neutral States. Submarines may remain submerged and conduct hostilities in the territorial seas of other belligerents. There is no right of passage in internal waters.[102]

The situation is different with respect to submarines traversing the archipelagic waters of neutral States. Archipelagic States may not avail themselves of the same right to close their archipelagic waters entirely, as the right of archipelagic sea lanes passage is unable to be suspended.[103] When exercising the right of archipelagic sea lanes passage, there is no obligation for belligerent submarines to surface. All vessels (without distinction) are entitled to exercise the right of archipelagic sea lanes passage 'in the normal mode',[104] which for submarines means submerged passage.[105] That right is also unable to be suspended by the archipelagic State.[106]

10.3.2 International Straits

During times of armed conflict, belligerent littoral States are permitted to deny opposing belligerents access to the portions of their territorial sea overlapping with international straits and may conduct

[98] Farrant (n 49) 213.

[99] Commander's Handbook (n 6) para. 7.3.4; Australian Defence Force, *Law of Armed Conflict* (Defence Publishing Service, 2006) para. 11.22 ('Australian Guide'); US Department of Defense, *Law of War Manual* (Department of Defense Office of General Counsel, June 2015, updated July 2023) para. 15.7.4 ('US Law of War Manual').

[100] UNCLOS (n 6) art. 20.

[101] See Chapter 7, Section 7.2.1.

[102] *M/V Norstar* (Panama v. Italy) (Judgment of 10 April 2019) [2019] ITLOS Rep 10, para. 221.

[103] Newport Manual (n 5) paras. 4.1.1.5, 11.3.3.5, 11.3.3.7; San Remo Manual (n 4) para. 29.

[104] UNCLOS (n 6) art. 53(3). See further Chapter 7, Section 7.4.2.

[105] Roach, 'Legal Aspects of Modern Submarine Warfare' (n 40) 372; Ministère des Armées, *Manuel de droit des operations militaires* (French Ministry of the Armed Forces, 2022) para. 1.1.1.2 ('French Manual'); Commander's Handbook (n 6) para. 2.5.4.1.

[106] Newport Manual (n 5) para. 4.1.1.5.

submarine warfare against other belligerents without restriction.[107] However, consistent with the obligations of their neutrality, neutral States may not suspend or hamper the right of transit passage in international straits overlapped by neutral waters where that regime of passage applies.[108] The neutrality of the littoral State is not affected by the transit passage of a belligerent through the international strait.[109] Like the regime governing archipelagic sea lanes passage, belligerent submarines are entitled to exercise the right of transit passage submerged through neutral international straits.[110] Neutral submarines are entitled to exercise the same right through belligerent straits.[111]

The right of a belligerent to transit passage through an international strait during an international armed conflict is subject to certain restrictions. International straits must not be used by belligerents as a sanctuary or a base of operations.[112] Belligerent submarines exercising the right of transit passage are entitled to take defensive measures consistent with their security against other belligerents, but otherwise must refrain from offensive hostilities, activities of war not incident to their transit and any threat or use of force against the neutral State.[113] The scope of these defensive measures in international straits is somewhat broader than that afforded to belligerents in neutral waters, and

[107] Wolff Heintschel von Heinegg, 'The Law of Naval Warfare and International Straits' (1998) 71 *International Law Studies* 263, 264–265.

[108] Newport Manual (n 5) paras. 11.3.2.2, 11.3.3.6; San Remo Manual (n 4) para. 29; Australian Guide (n 99) para. 6.22; Commander's Handbook (n 6) para. 7.3.6; UK Joint Doctrine and Concepts Centre, *The Joint Service Manual of the Law of Armed Conflict* (Joint Service Publication 383, 2004) para. 13.15 ('UK Manual'); Akira Mayama, 'The Influence of the Straits Transit Regime on the Law of Neutrality at Sea' (1995) 26 *Ocean Development and International Law* 1, 5.

[109] Mayama (n 108) 4.

[110] San Remo Manual (n 4) paras. 23, 27–28; Heintschel von Heinegg, 'The Law of Naval Warfare and International Straits' (n 107) 270; Commander's Handbook (n 6) para, 2.5.3.2; French Manual (n 105) para. 1.1.1.2; James Kraska, Raul Pedrozo and Michael N. Schmitt, 'Annotated Supplement to the Commander's Handbook on the Law of Naval Operations' (2024) 102 *International Law Studies* 1, para. 2.5.3.2.

[111] San Remo Manual (n 4) para. 26.

[112] San Remo Manual (n 4) para. 30.

[113] Newport Manual (n 5) paras. 4.1.1.4, 11.3.2.2; San Remo Manual (n 4) para. 30; UNCLOS (n 6) art. 39; Commander's Handbook (n 6) para. 7.3.6; Australian Guide (n 99) para. 11.23; Heintschel von Heinegg, 'The Law of Naval Warfare and International Straits' (n 107) 271.

includes the 'launching and recovery of aircraft, screen formation steaming, and acoustic and electronic surveillance'.[114] While the San Remo Manual appears to indicate that there is a strict prohibition on the conduct of hostilities in international straits,[115] it must be open to belligerent submarines to respond to an attack or imminent risk of attack from an opposing belligerent warship while exercising the right of transit passage. Like the regime governing the conduct of purely defensive hostilities in neutral waters, that response must be proportionate and targeted such that it is truly 'defensive' in nature.

10.3.3 Contiguous Zone, Exclusive Economic Zone and Continental Shelf

In relation to the contiguous zone, exclusive economic zone (EEZ) and continental shelf, there are two points to note. First, even if the coastal State has declared neutrality, these waters are not 'neutral waters' and belligerent acts may be conducted there.[116] Second, unlike the territorial sea, the coastal State does not possess sovereignty in these zones, but rather is afforded the exercise of a limited set of sovereign rights.[117] As discussed in Chapter 8, in conducting activities within these zones, third States are required to have 'due regard' to the exercise of these sovereign rights by coastal States.[118]

The conduct of submarine warfare requires one to consider the interaction of the due regard obligation with belligerency rights. According to the Helsinki Principles, when conducting submarine warfare in the contiguous zone, EEZ and continental shelf, a belligerent must afford due regard to the exercise of sovereign rights in those zones by neutral States.[119] More complicated, however, is discerning the exact substance of the obligation and the steps a belligerent is required to take to comply with it.[120] The lack of an

[114] San Remo Manual (n 4) para. 30; Commander's Handbook (n 6) para. 7.3.6.

[115] San Remo Manual (n 4) para. 30.

[116] Newport Manual [4.1.2.1], [11.3.3.8].

[117] UNCLOS (n 6) art. 56(1).

[118] UNCLOS (n 6) art. 56(2); San Remo Manual (n 4) paras. 12, 34.

[119] See generally Helsinki Principles (n 48) para. 4.

[120] An issue discussed in Chapter 8 in relation to the allocation of authority between States during times of peace. See Chapter 8, Section 8.4.1. See generally James Kraska, 'The Obligation of "Due Regard" in the EEZ During Armed Conflicts at Sea' (2025) 106 *International Law Studies* 116.

adequate definition of the obligation has caused controversy, both in times of war[121] as well as in times of peace.[122]

It is, however, sufficiently certain that the obligation does not operate as a bar to the conduct of hostilities. The obligation, which is recognised in the San Remo Manual[123] and the Newport Manual,[124] likely requires a belligerent to refrain from interfering with the exercise of the neutral State's sovereign rights 'if that is both feasible and reasonable'.[125] In the context of submarine warfare, the obligation would, for instance, extend to refraining from causing destructive undersea explosions in the marine protected areas or designated fisheries of neutral States.[126] A belligerent should also refrain from, through its use of weapons, causing damage to the neutral State's offshore wind farms and oil platforms. The San Remo Manual also suggests that the belligerent must notify the neutral State of any mines laid in these zones (including by submarines)[127] and ensure that the laying of those mines does not unnecessarily interfere with the neutral State's exercise of sovereign rights,[128] though the authors of the Newport Manual have indicated the latter position to be a *lex ferenda* requirement.[129] Certainly, in view of the massive destruction that nuclear weapons are capable of causing, a belligerent intending to launch a nuclear strike in the context of submarine warfare would need to give an exceptional degree of consideration to the impact of that decision on the living and non-living

[121] George V. Galdorisi and Alan G. Kaufman, 'Military Activities in the Exclusive Economic Zone: Preventing Uncertainty and Defusing Conflict' (2002) 32 *California Western International Law Journal* 253, 273; Wolff Heintschel von Heinegg, 'The Current State of the Law of Naval Warfare: A Fresh Look at the *San Remo Manual*' (2006) 82 *International Law Studies* 269, 272 (observing that the lack of specificity in the content of the obligation means that it 'will only be paid lip service or, even worse, it will be abused by coastal States in order to camouflage acts of unneutral service').

[122] See Chapter 8, Section 8.4.1.

[123] San Remo Manual (n 4) para. 12.

[124] Newport Manual (n 5) paras. 4.1.2.1, 11.3.3.8.

[125] Heintschel von Heinegg, 'Submarine Operations and International Law' (n 5) 151. See also Albert J Hoffmann, 'Navigation, Freedom of' in Anne Peters and Rüdiger Wolfrum (eds.) *Max Planck Encyclopedia of Public International Law* (Oxford University Press, April 2011) para. 15 (observing that the obligation requires States to 'refrain from activities that unreasonably interfere with the exercise of the rights of the coastal State').

[126] Sam Bateman, 'Prospective Guidelines for Navigation and Overflight in the Exclusive Economic Zones' (2005) 144 *Maritime Studies* 17, 19.

[127] Hague XIII (n 52) art. 4(2) applies the inverse obligation on neutral States.

[128] San Remo Manual (n 4) para. 35.

[129] Newport Manual (n 5) para. 11.3.3.8.

resources of the EEZ.[130] Conversely, a neutral State is unlikely to be able to complain of breach of the obligation if submarine passage causes accidental damage to marine life.[131] There have further been suggestions that there is nothing inconsistent between the obligation of due regard and a belligerent installing weapons or anti-submarine warfare detection devices on the seabed or continental shelf.[132]

In sum, the due regard obligation alone does not *prevent* a belligerent from infringing the sovereign rights of a neutral State in the contiguous zone, EEZ and continental shelf during submarine warfare. Of course, the demands of warfare are such that consulting with the neutral State[133] or otherwise giving detailed consideration to the impacts of submarine warfare on the third State may not always be possible. The realities of the armed conflict may demand an immediate response and must surely be accommodated within the obligation. The obligation merely requires the belligerent to consider the exercise of the neutral State's sovereign rights as one input in the decision to conduct submarine warfare (and the method of conducting that warfare), as part of a broader balancing exercise.[134]

10.3.4 High Seas

UNCLOS preserves to all States the freedom of the high seas.[135] No State may assert sovereignty in areas beyond national jurisdiction.[136] Consistent with this freedom, belligerents are entitled to conduct submarine warfare on the high seas, subject to any other obligations they may have under international law (such as in relation to the law of

130 A belligerent considering such a course would also need to contend with the more general, live question as to the legality of the threat or use of nuclear weapons, which we do not cover within this book. See generally Charlotte Beaucillon, 'Limiting Third States' Military Activities in the EEZ: Due Regard Obligations and the Law on the Use of Force Applied to Nuclear Weapons' (2019) 34 *International Journal of Marine and Coastal Law* 128.

131 James Kraska, *Maritime Power and the Law of the Sea: Expeditionary Operations in World Politics* (Oxford University Press, 2011) 267.

132 Robertson (n 90) 30.

133 As the *Chagos Marine Protected Area* arbitration tribunal suggested the content of the obligation involved: *Chagos Marine Protected Area Arbitration* (Mauritius v. United Kingdom) (Award of 18 March 2015) (2015) XXXI RIIA 359, para. 519.

134 See Chapter 8, Section 8.4.1.

135 UNCLOS (n 6) art. 87(1); Convention on the High Seas, Geneva, 29 April 1958, entered into force 30 September 1962, 450 UNTS 11, art. 1.

136 UNCLOS (n 6) art. 89. See also *M/V Norstar* (n 102) para. 218.

neutrality and the law of armed conflict).[137] There are two qualifications on the freedom of the high seas within UNCLOS that are of note. First, UNCLOS contains several provisions that require ocean spaces to be used for exclusively peaceful purposes. Article 88 reserves the use of the high seas for 'peaceful purposes',[138] and Article 301 requires States to, in their use of ocean spaces, 'refrain from any threat or use of force against the territorial integrity or political independence of any State, or in any other manner inconsistent with the principles of international law embodied in the Charter of the United Nations'.[139] The latter provision is drawn from Article 2(4) of the Charter of the United Nations and simply requires that any threat or use of force in ocean spaces be 'consistent with the Charter and with other rules of international law'.[140] Accordingly, to the extent that a State legitimately participates in submarine warfare in accordance with established principles of international law, such as the law of neutrality and the law of armed conflict, those activities will not constitute a breach of Articles 88 and 301 of UNCLOS.[141] It suffices to say that despite its insistence on the use of the oceans for peaceful purposes, the obligations contained within UNCLOS do not displace belligerency rights and do not prohibit the conduct of submarine warfare on the high seas.[142]

Second, UNCLOS requires States in the exercise of the freedom of the high seas to have due regard for the interests of other States both on the high seas and in the Area.[143] This language mirrors the due regard obligation in respect of the EEZ and similarly would apply only to a belligerent's interactions with neutral States.[144] The content of this due regard obligation is necessarily of a more limited character than that in the EEZ as UNCLOS imbues no State with sovereign rights on the high seas or in the Area. Accordingly, a belligerent State conducting submarine warfare on the high seas should take care not to damage or

137 San Remo Manual (n 4) para. 10(b).

138 UNCLOS (n 6) art. 88.

139 Ibid, art. 301.

140 *Enrica Lexie* (Italy v. India) (Award of 21 May 2020) PCA Case No. 2015–28, para. 1073.

141 Articles 88 and 301 do not preclude the lawful resort to force in accordance with the law on the use of force (or *jus ad bellum*). The requirements on the lawful resort to force are discussed in Chapter 9.

142 Newport Manual (n 5) para. 4.1.2.2; Heintschel von Heinegg, 'Submarine Operations and International Law' (n 5) 151; David L. Larson, 'Security Issues and the Law of the Sea: A General Framework' (1985) 15 *Ocean Development and International Law* 99, 116.

143 UNCLOS (n 6) art. 87.

144 Helsinki Principles (n 48) para. 3.1.

impede the freedom of navigation of neutral vessels,[145] not to block their participation in the exploration and exploitation of the high seas and the Area,[146] and 'avoid damage to cables and pipelines laid on the sea-bed which do not exclusively serve the belligerents'.[147]

10.4 Law of Maritime Neutrality

The law of neutrality applies to the conduct of submarine warfare during an international armed conflict. This body of law is complex and controversial,[148] and its development has been inextricably tied to economic activity in the oceans. The regulation of neutral commerce at sea has always been of particular import to the law of neutrality, codified in the fourteenth-century *Consolato del Mare*.[149] The most significant role played by submarines in both WWI and WWII was in relation to commerce warfare.[150] Both conflicts were indelibly marked by the practice of unrestricted submarine warfare,[151] which broadly refers to the practice of using submarines and submarine-laid mines to sink merchant vessels on sight and without warning. One of the most notable instances of unrestricted submarine warfare in WWI was the sinking of the British passenger liner *Lusitania* in May 1915.[152]

In WWII, the unrestricted submarine warfare campaigns were split between the Atlantic and Pacific theatres.[153] In the Atlantic theatre, the focus of the German campaign was to 'sink as much Allied tonnage as

[145] Ibid, para. 3.2.
[146] San Remo Manual (n 4) para. 36.
[147] Ibid, para. 37. See generally Raul (Pete) Pedrozo, 'Safeguarding Submarine Cables and Pipelines in Times of Peace and War' (2025) 106 *International Law Studies* 45; Christian Schaller, 'Sabotage of Submarine Cables and Pipelines as a Use of Force and Armed Attack' (2025) 106 *International Law Studies* 173.
[148] See, e.g., Heintschel von Heinegg, 'The Current State of the Law of Naval Warfare' (n 121) 282 (observing that 'the law of neutrality is one of the most disputed aspects of public international law. The diversity of views on the subject makes it almost impossible to establish the continuing validity of that body of law, its scope of applicability, and its content'); Pearce Clancy, 'The Law of Neutrality: *Jus ad Bellum* or *Jus in Bello*?' (2022) 13 *Journal of International Humanitarian Legal Studies* 353, 356 (describing the law of neutrality as 'a fish out of water in contemporary international law').
[149] See Leos Müller, *Neutrality in World History* (Routledge, 2019) 36ff.
[150] See also Chapter 2 and Chapter 4, Section 4.5.
[151] Owen R. Cote Jr, 'The Third Battle: Innovation in the US Navy's Silent Cold War Struggle with Soviet Submarines' (Naval War College Center for Naval Warfare Studies, Newport Paper No. 16, 2003) 2.
[152] See Chapter 2, Section 2.3.
[153] See also Chapter 4, Section 4.4.

possible for the smallest losses to the U-boat force'.[154] By 1943, Germany had over 400 U-boats in commission.[155] The German unrestricted submarine warfare campaign was responsible for the destruction of more than twenty-three million tons of Allied and neutral merchant shipping,[156] though it suffered an estimated loss of 777 U-boats and 30,000 submariners in that effort.[157] The American unrestricted submarine warfare campaign in the Pacific theatre has been described as 'the most successful submarine campaign in history'.[158] Japan's bombing of Pearl Harbor precipitated the entry of the United States into WWII. Within hours of the bombing, the United States ordered 'unrestricted air and submarine warfare against Japan' in reprisal;[159] now conducting the activity to which it went to war over in 1917. The United States sunk over 200 Japanese naval vessels and 1,000 Japanese merchant ships over the course of WWII;[160] nearly 50 per cent of all Japanese merchant vessels were lost to submarines.[161] 603 ships were sunk in 1944 alone, which caused a severe shortage of food and raw materials in Japan.[162] American submarine warfare in the Pacific was so extensive that the Japanese cabinet reported to the National Diet that the greatest cause of its defeat was its loss of shipping.[163] These submarine campaigns conducted in WWI and WWII against neutral merchant vessels, which were among the defining features of both conflicts, demonstrate the specific relationship between the conduct of submarine warfare and the law of neutrality.

In contemporary settings, neutrality has been implicated to a significantly greater extent in maritime conflicts due to the existence of the freedom of navigation, the regimes of innocent and transit passage,

[154] Lautenschläger (n 14) 114.

[155] Ibid 117.

[156] Mallison (n 12) 2.

[157] C. H. Spilman, 'The German Submarine War' (1947) 73(2) *USNI Proceedings* 532. See also Lawrence Sondhaus, *The Great War at Sea: A Naval History of the First World War* (Cambridge University Press, 2014) 276.

[158] Preston (n 9) 60.

[159] See Michael Sturma, 'Atrocities, Conscience, and Unrestricted Warfare: US Submarines during the Second World War' (2009) 16(4) *War in History* 447, 448; Charles J. Weiss, 'Problems of Submarine Warfare under International Law' (1966–1967) 22 *Intermural Law Review of New York University* 136, 140.

[160] Sturma (n 159) 450.

[161] Lautenschläger (n 14) 122.

[162] Joel Ira Holwitt, *Execute Against Japan: The US Decision to Conduct Unrestricted Submarine Warfare* (Texas A&M University Press, 2013) 166.

[163] Ibid, 167. See also Mallison (n 12) 2.

the division of maritime space, and the assignment of sovereign rights within those spaces. For these reasons, 'neutral interests are involved at sea to an infinitely greater extent than is the case with land operations'.[164] It is not the purpose of this section to consider each of the rules of neutrality, which have been considered in detail elsewhere.[165] Instead, the purpose of this section is to focus on the ways in which the law of neutrality applies to the conduct of submarine warfare and to indicate the salient issues that arise as a result.

The law of neutrality is derived from treaty, as well as custom established from centuries of practice of the conduct of war. The law of neutrality is largely codified in Hague Convention (V) of 1907 (Hague V) in relation to neutrality on land and Hague Convention (XIII) of 1907 (Hague XIII) in relation to maritime neutrality. While Hague XIII is most applicable to the conduct of submarine warfare, many of the principles within Hague V are of note (in particular, given the application of the principle of domination).[166] Also influential on the law of neutrality have been the Paris Declaration of 1856,[167] the 1909 London Declaration,[168] the 1949 Geneva Conventions and UNCLOS. However, Hague V and Hague XIII remain 'the only multilateral treaties that have neutrality as their object and are widely accepted as the definitive statement of the law of neutrality'.[169] Hague V and Hague XIII are also widely regarded as representing the customary international law of neutrality and, accordingly, bind all States.[170]

164 San Remo Manual (n 4) 585.

165 See, e.g., Antonopoulos (n 70); James Upcher, *Neutrality in Contemporary International Law* (Cambridge University Press, 2020); Bothe, 'Neutrality, Concept and General Rules' (n 94); Michael Bothe, 'The Law of Neutrality' in Dieter Fleck (ed.), *The Handbook of International Humanitarian Law* (3rd ed., Oxford University Press, 2009) 549; Stephen C. Neff, *The Rights and Duties of Neutrals: A General History* (Manchester University Press, 2000). For an historical example, see Phillip C. Jessup, et al., *Neutrality: Its History, Economics and Law*, 4 vols. (Columbia University Press, 1935–1936).

166 Or, 'the land dominates the sea': *Maritime Delimitation and Territorial Questions between Qatar and Bahrain* (Qatar v. Bahrain) (Judgment of 16 March 2001) [2001] ICJ Rep 40, para. 185. See generally Bing Bing Jia, 'The Principle of the Domination of the Land over the Sea: A Historical Perspective on the Adaptability of the Law of the Sea to New Challenges' (2014) 57 *German Yearbook of International Law* 1.

167 Declaration respecting Maritime Law (n 51).

168 Declaration concerning the Laws of Naval Warfare, London, 26 February 1909, never entered into force, in (1914) 8(S2) *American Journal of International Law* 88 ('London Declaration of 1909').

169 Antonopoulos (n 70) 11.

170 Ibid, 28. See also *Legality of the Threat or Use of Nuclear Weapons* (Advisory Opinion of 8 July 1996) [1996] ICJ Rep 226, 261, para. 89 (observing that 'international law leaves no

Despite the critical importance and extensive practice of the law of neutrality in WWI and WWII, the law has not been the subject of any further codification efforts since the Second Hague Conference.[171] Consequently, the law of neutrality has persisted largely unchanged since 1907 and has acquired 'a slightly musty quality'.[172] In recognition of the need for a modern restatement of the law of neutrality, the International Law Association published the Helsinki Principles, which are the only restatement directed solely towards the topic of neutrality during times of armed conflict at sea. Maritime neutrality has also been given considered treatment in the San Remo Manual, which has been described as reflecting the customary international law of maritime neutrality,[173] as well as in the Newport Manual and the military manuals of various States. However, as mentioned above, restatements and manuals can only have a limited contribution to discerning the *lex lata* in circumstances where the contemporary practice of the law of neutrality has been limited.

Neutrality has been of some consequence in modern conflicts with maritime dimensions, including the Indo-Pakistani War (1971), the Falklands/Malvinas War (1982), and the Iran-Iraq War (1980–1988) and the crisis following the Iraqi invasion of Kuwait (1990–1991), but it has become rare for States extraneous to a conflict to adopt a formal position of neutrality.[174] Neutrality, particularly the status of non-belligerency, has

doubt that the principle of neutrality, whatever its content . . . is applicable (subject to the relevant provisions of the United Nations Charter), to all international armed conflict, whatever weapons might be used'); Heintschel von Heinegg, 'The Current State of the Law of Naval Warfare' (n 121) 283.

[171] See, e.g., Bothe, 'The Law of Neutrality' (n 165) para. 1102 (noting that there has been 'no comprehensive codification of the law of neutrality since the Hague Conventions of 1907. These rules of 1907 have in part been rendered obsolete by later practice. The need for a new codification is urgent'). But see Heintschel von Heinegg, 'Submarine Operations and International Law' (n 5) 161 (arguing that 'any codification would, at best, be counterproductive. It would, according to the position taken here, also be unnecessary because the few parts of the law applicable to submarine operations that may be considered unclear can easily be specified in military manuals or in unilateral declarations of a binding or non-binding character').

[172] Detlev F. Vagts, 'The Traditional Legal Concept of Neutrality in a Changing Environment' (1998) 14(1) *American University International Law Review* 83, 84. See also Peter Seger, 'The Law of Neutrality' in Andrew Clapham and Paolo Gaeta (eds.), *The Oxford Handbook of International Law in Armed Conflict* (Oxford University Press, 2014) 248, 267; Farrant (n 49) 306.

[173] Heintschel von Heinegg, 'The Current State of the Law of Naval Warfare' (n 121) 283, 288.

[174] Georgios C. Petrochilos, 'The Relevance of the Concepts of War and Armed Conflict to the Law of Neutrality' (1998) 31 *Vanderbilt Journal of Transnational Law* 575, 601.

also emerged as a controversial issue in light of the Russo-Ukrainian War considering the substantial military support (including lethal aid) provided to Ukraine by members of the Ukraine Defense Contact Group.[175]

10.4.1 Overarching Principles

In essence, the law of neutrality exists to govern the legal relationship between belligerents and non-participating third States to an international armed conflict.[176] The primary purpose of the law of neutrality is to avoid the escalation of conflict by attempting to confine the number of belligerents.[177] This mission is reflected in the 'cardinal principle of the law of neutrality ... that belligerents may not conduct hostilities in neutral territory, land or sea'.[178] Neither declarations of war nor proclamations of neutrality are required for the law of neutrality to be enlivened. All that is required is the existence of an international armed conflict such that there is 'resort to armed force between States'.[179] In this sense, declarations are not constitutive of neutrality, rather '[o]nce a State is non-participant, its juridical position vis á vis the belligerents is governed by the law of neutrality'.[180] A state of neutrality will end where there has been 'the permanent cessation of active hostilities',[181]

[175] Clancy (n 148) 361; Natalino Ronzitti, 'Neutrality, Non-belligerency, and Permanent Neutrality according to Recent Practice and Doctrinal Views' (2024) 29 *Journal of Conflict and Security Law* 55. Other case studies are considered in Luca Ferro and Nele Verlinden, 'Neutrality During Armed Conflicts: A Coherent Approach to Third-State Support for Warring Parties' (2018) 17 *Chinese Journal of International Law* 15; Giulio Bartolini, 'The Ukrainian-Russian Armed Conflict and the Law of Neutrality: Continuity, Discontinuity, or Irrelevance?' (2024) 71 *Netherlands International Law Review* 281; Raphael van Steenberge, 'Military Assistance to Ukraine: Enquiring the Need for Any Legal Justification under International Law' (2023) 28 *Journal of Conflict and Security Law* 231.

[176] Geneva Convention (I) for the Amelioration of the Condition of the Wounded and Sick in Armed Forces in the Field, Geneva, 12 August 1949, entered into force 21 October 1950, 75 UNTS 31, art. 4 ('Geneva I'); Hitoshi Nasu, 'The Laws of Neutrality in the Interconnected World: Mapping the Future Scenarios' in Matthew C. Waxman and Thomas W. Oakley (eds.), *The Future Law of Armed Conflict* (Oxford University Press, 2022) 122, 125; Antonopoulos (n 70) 1.

[177] William H. Boothby and Wolff Heintschel von Heinegg, *Nuclear Weapons Law: Where Are We Now*? (Cambridge University Press, 2021) 146; Bothe, 'Neutrality, Concept and General Rules' (n 94) para. 4; Newport Manual (n 5) para. 11.1.

[178] Robertson (n 90) 17.

[179] *Prosecutor v. Tadic* (n 60) para. 70.

[180] Antonopoulos (n 70) 20–21; Petrochilos (n 174) 575; Bothe, 'Neutrality, Concept and General Rules' (n 94) paras. 20–21.

[181] Antonopoulos (n 70) 24, 144.

or where the neutral has acted in such a way as to deprive it of its neutrality. This principle highlights the interdependent relationship between the law of neutrality and the law of armed conflict.

The law of neutrality can be fundamentally distilled to two interdependent sets of correlative rights and obligations,[182] which constitute 'a compromise between the belligerents' pursuit of their war aim to overpower their adversary and the neutrals' wish to continue their peaceful relations both with the belligerents and the rest of non-participants in the conflict.'[183] First, the belligerent promises to refrain from any threat or use of force against the neutral, to not breach the inviolability of neutral territory (including neutral waters), and to maintain broadly peaceful relations with the neutral.[184] Second, the neutral promises to act impartially towards each of the belligerents,[185] and to abstain from providing any belligerent with direct or indirect support in relation to the conduct of hostilities.[186] Where these conditions are met, the neutral is entitled to the privileges of neutrality recognised under international law.[187] In effect, the relationship between the neutrals and the belligerent is 'governed by the law of peace, which is modified only in certain respects by the law of neutrality'.[188] One such privilege is the recognition of the inviolability of neutral waters. Another is the right of neutrals to continue to enjoy peaceful relations with other States, which is effectively a right to conduct 'commercial intercourse, among themselves and with each belligerent, in spite and in parallel with the armed conflict in progress at the same time'.[189] The extent to which these privileges are respected is likely to depend on the extent to which the neutral State complies with its duties of neutrality.[190]

An exception to the application of these general principles exists in the form of the collective security mechanism established by the UN Charter.[191] That mechanism provides the UN Security Council with the

[182] Ibid, 75.

[183] Ibid, 74. See also Quincy Wright, 'Effect of the War on International Law' (1920–1921) 5 *Minnesota Law Review* 515, 532.

[184] Hague Convention (V) respecting the Rights and Duties of Neutral Powers and Persons in Case of War on Land, The Hague, 18 October 1907, entered into force 26 January 1910, 205 CTS 299, arts. 1–2 ('Hague V').

[185] Hague XIII (n 52), art. 9.

[186] See, e.g., ibid, art. 6.

[187] See generally Commander's Handbook (n 6) para. 7.2.

[188] Bothe, 'Neutrality, Concept and General Rules' (n 94) para. 2; Farrant (n 49) 202.

[189] Antonopoulos (n 70) 75.

[190] Seger (n 172) 268.

[191] Charter of the United Nations, San Francisco, 26 June 1945, entered into force 24 October 1945, XV UNCIO 335, arts 1(1), 2(5).

authority to determine the existence of a threat to or breach of the peace, or an act of international aggression, and to prescribe measures to maintain or restore international peace or security.[192] All States are required to carry out those measures, which may include the use of force,[193] though such measures have rarely been prescribed. This compulsion to act is fundamentally inconsistent with the maintenance of neutrality and, as such, States are deprived of the ability to rely on the law of neutrality to justify conduct incompatible with the measures prescribed by the UN Security Council.[194] All States will therefore be prohibited from continuing to conduct peaceful relations with the aggressor State. This obligation requires States to prohibit the passage of the aggressor State's warships (including submarines) through neutral waters,[195] as well as to refrain from lending assistance to the aggressor State (other than *bona fide* humanitarian assistance).[196]

There are four main overarching principles. First, neutral States must abstain from the armed conflict to maintain their neutrality. This obligation extends to prohibiting neutrals from engaging in the supply, directly or indirectly, or warships, ammunition or war material of any kind to a belligerent.[197] A neutral State is therefore prohibited from providing a submarine and any submarine-launched weaponry to a belligerent. Neutrals must also take the available means at its disposal to prevent the fit out or arming of a submarine within its jurisdiction if it has a reason to believe that submarine will be used to cruise or engage in hostilities against a belligerent with which the neutral State is at peace.[198] Neutral States are not, however, required to prevent the export of 'arms, ammunition, or . . . anything which could be of use to an army or fleet' by individuals and companies within their jurisdiction.[199] It therefore follows that there is no general rule of international law prohibiting a private sector actor within the jurisdiction of a neutral State from supplying submarine weaponry or other items of use to submarine warfare to a belligerent. It would, however, be open to the neutral State to impose such a ban, subject to that ban being impartial

192 Ibid, art. 39.
193 See generally ibid, ch. VII. See also arts. 48(1), 49; San Remo Manual (n 4) para. 7.
194 San Remo Manual (n 4) para. 8.
195 See generally Antonopoulos (n 70) 62.
196 San Remo Manual (n 4) para. 7(a). See generally Ronzitti (n 175) 58ff.
197 Hague XIII (n 52) art. 6.
198 Ibid, art. 8.
199 Ibid, art. 7.

and non-discriminatory. This historical rule of neutrality may not be of consequence in contemporary conflicts given that States now often exercise strict control over the import and export of arms, including the licensing of defence materiel. Further, private defence contractors now play a significantly greater role in arms manufacture and dealing, and in many cases engage in the financing, production and distribution of submarines and submarine weaponry in conjunction with (whether through a formal joint venture or otherwise) the State.[200]

Second, the neutral must be impartial in their dealings with other belligerents. In the context of submarine warfare, this principle is of particular importance in relation to the passage of submarines through neutral waters. The principle also extends to other matters, for instance in ensuring the neutral does not discriminate between belligerents in their arrangements relating to trade and commerce.[201] The obligation to act impartially 'does not entail a duty of exactly equal treatment . . . a neutral State is under no duty to eliminate differences in commercial relations between itself and each of the parties to the conflict at the time of the outbreak of the armed conflict'.[202]

Third, neutrals are obligated to prevent breaches of their neutrality.[203] This obligation is referred to as the duty of prevention and requires the neutral to prevent and terminate violations of its neutrality by a belligerent, including by building defensive capabilities, conducting surveillance and using force as necessary to bring the breach to an end, subject to what is feasible for the neutral State in the circumstances.[204] The use of force in compliance with the duty of prevention does not cause a State to lose its neutrality and must not be considered as an unfriendly

[200] The German Manual highlights some of the difficulties here, noting that '[i]f the export of war matériel is State controlled, allowing such export is considered an unneutral service': German Directorate-General for Legal Affairs, *Law of Armed Conflict: Manual* (Federal Ministry of Defence, 2013) 1207, 1209. See also Ronzitti (n 175) 57 ('the distinction between State and private supply has become obsolete now that all export of weapons is governmentally licensed'); Walter L. Williams Jr, 'Neutrality in Modern Armed Conflicts: A Survey of the Developing Law' (1980) 90 *Military Law Review* 9, 32–33; Bothe, 'Neutrality, Concept and General Rules' (n 94) paras. 40–44.

[201] Antonopoulos (n 70) 90.

[202] Bothe, 'Neutrality, Concept and General Rules' (n 94) para. 4. See also Seger (n 172) 257.

[203] Hague XIII (n 52) art. 25.

[204] Hague V (n 184) art. 5; Hague XIII (n 52), arts 2, 9, 24; Bothe, 'Neutrality, Concept and General Rules' (n 94) para. 33 (observing that the 'duty of the neutral State to prevent its territory from being used by one of the parties to the conflict as a base for military operations is the corollary of the neutral's right not to be adversely affected by the conflict.'); Seger (n 172) 255–256; Bothe, 'The Law of Neutrality' (n 165) para. 1109.1.

act by a belligerent.[205] For instance, if a belligerent submarine stations itself within the territorial sea of a neutral State and is detected by the neutral State, the neutral State must ask the submarine to depart and, failing that, is obligated to take steps (including the use of force) to remove the belligerent submarine from the territorial sea.[206] If the neutral State fails to adequately discharge the duty of prevention, the opposing belligerent may invoke the right of self-help and take necessary measures in neutral territory to terminate the violation.[207] That use of force will not be governed by the law of neutrality but by the law of armed conflict. Apart from these matters concerning the duty of prevention, Hague V and Hague XIII do not set out the consequences of a violation of neutrality. It is sufficient to note that it will involve the invocation of the rules of State responsibility as well as the laws governing the conduct of hostilities.[208]

Fourth, Hague V is clear that the 'territory of a neutral is inviolable'.[209] This basic principle is universally recognised in national military manuals.[210] As just discussed, this principle indicates that the passage of a belligerent submarine through the waters of a neutral does not jeopardise the coastal State's neutrality.[211] The inviolability of neutral territory requires that submarine warfare not be conducted in neutral waters. Submarines are prohibited from striking land targets in neutral territory from any maritime zone and must ensure that submarine-launched missiles do not travel through neutral airspace.[212] Submarines cannot use neutral waters as a base of operations.[213] The inviolability of the neutral extends to protecting it from 'trans-border incursions of armed forces and to trans-border damage caused to a neutral State by use of a weapon in

205 Hague V (n 184), art. 10; Newport Manual (n 5) para. 14.1.1.1.

206 Mayama (n 108) 17; Boothby and Heintschel von Heinegg (n 177) 150.

207 San Remo Manual (n 4) para. 22; Newport Manual (n 5) para. 11.3.3.1.

208 Antonopoulos (n 70) 235.

209 Hague V (n 184) art. 1.

210 See, e.g., UK Manual (n 108) para. 1.43(b); Australian Guide (n 99) para. 11.8; Canadian Manual at 1304; French Manual (n 105) 66 ('Le territoire des puissances neutres est inviolable'); Newport Manual (n 5) paras. 5.1; 11.3; Defence Command Denmark, *Military Manual on International Law Relevant to Danish Armed Forced in International Operations* (Danish Ministry of Defence, 2016) 62 ('Danish Manual'); Canadian Office of the Judge Advocate General, *Law of Armed Conflict at the Operational and Tactical Levels* (Department of National Defence, 2001) 1304 ('Canadian Manual').

211 Hague XIII (n 52), art. 10; Newport Manual (n 5) para. 11.3.3.5.

212 Ibid, para. 11.3.

213 Hague XIII (n 52), art 5; San Remo Manual (n 4) para. 17.

a belligerent State'.[214] Consequently, the use of submarine-launched missiles to attack land targets will only comply with the law of neutrality to the extent that damage caused by that missile remains exclusively within the land territory of other belligerents.

The inviolability of neutral waters has practical impacts on the ways in which submarines can interact with neutral ports. Neutrals are entitled to close their ports to the submarines of any belligerent State, so long as that closure complies with the duty of impartiality.[215] Belligerent submarines may visit neutral ports for the purpose of replenishing food, water and fuel without compromising the neutral's status. However, no more than three belligerent warships (including submarines), auxiliary vessels and prizes may visit a neutral port at once, the replenishments must not involve munitions, and the quantity of the replenishment must not be greater than that necessary for the submarine to be seaworthy (such that the fighting capacity of the submarine must not be restored or increased).[216] Submarines must not stay more than twenty-four hours in a neutral port unless exceptional circumstances exist.[217] Opposing belligerent submarines may both dock at the same neutral port but there must be twenty-four hours between their departure.[218] It is also prohibited for submarines to complete their crews while at neutral ports or in neutral waters.[219] These specific rules each give content to the general principle of abstention that the territorial sea and ports of the neutral State must not be used for the purpose of gaining a military advantage.[220]

The only exception to the general principle of the inviolability of neutral waters is that a belligerent submarine is entitled to conduct hostilities against other belligerents in neutral waters if it is attacked or if there is a 'serious and immediate threat to the security of the ... belligerent'.[221] That is because the enemy belligerent has breached the

[214] *Legality of the Threat or Use of Nuclear Weapons* (n 170) para. 88; Bothe, 'Neutrality, Concept and General Rules' (n 94) para. 32; Bothe, 'The Law of Neutrality' (n 165) para. 1108.2; Boothby and Heintschel von Heinegg (n 177) 150–151.

[215] Newport Manual (n 5) para. 11.4.1.2.

[216] Hague XIII (n 52), arts. 16–20; San Remo Manual (n 4) para. 20; Newport Manual (n 5) para. 11.3.2.

[217] Hague XIII (n 52), art. 12; San Remo Manual (n 4) para. 21; Helsinki Principles (n 48) para. 2.2.

[218] Hague XIII (n 52), art. 16.

[219] Ibid, art. 18.

[220] Canadian Manual (n 210) para. 810(2).

[221] Newport Manual (n 5) para. 11.3.2.3; Helsinki Principles (n 48) para. 1.4; San Remo Manual (n 4) para. 22; Commander's Handbook (n 6) para. 7.3.4.

law of neutrality, entitling the attacked belligerent to exercise the customary right of self-defence. This exception is narrow in nature. It may only be exercised if the neutral State has failed to bring to an end the violation of its neutrality, or if there is no other 'feasible or timely alternative' to the use of force.[222] The exception also does not imbue belligerents with *carte blanche* authority to conduct hostilities; the use of force must be proportionate to the threat such that the belligerent must only 'use such force as is strictly necessary to respond to the threat posed by the violation'.[223] There will likely be some deference to the commanding officer in determining the level of force necessary to appropriately respond, though that deference exists only within the boundaries of reasonableness.

For example, if a submarine travelling in neutral waters was attacked by a belligerent frigate also travelling in neutral waters, the submarine commander would be entitled to rely on the exception to take the necessary measures to protect the submarine and resolve the breach of neutrality, including by disabling the frigate. It will not be required to seek the permission of the neutral State in this instance due to the immediacy of the threat. With the immediate threat resolved, it would not then be open to the submarine commander to take further steps against the opposing belligerent in neutral waters, such as by launching missiles at military targets on the opposing belligerent's land territory. The attacking belligerent must wait to conduct that activity after it has left neutral waters. A further, more complex example arises where a submarine travelling through neutral waters detects an enemy submarine lying in wait outside neutral waters.[224] The mere presence of the enemy submarine could constitute an immediate threat and international law 'does not require a State to absorb a first blow, which could potentially be fatal, before it may use force in self-defense'.[225] There may be grounds in this scenario for the submarine commander to launch a pre-emptive strike from neutral waters; whether this course of action is reasonable and appropriate is likely to depend significantly on the context and the circumstances. This example is a difficult one to resolve and highlights the complexities of reconciling the law of neutrality to the peculiarities of submarine warfare.

[222] San Remo Manual (n 4) para. 22.
[223] Ibid, para. 22. See also Farrant (n 49) 216.
[224] Farrant (n 49) 218–219.
[225] Ibid.

10.4.2 Neutral Commerce

Submarine warfare has arguably left no greater mark on the law of neutrality than in relation to neutral commerce. The actions of belligerents in WWI and WWII, in particular the use of submarines to conduct unrestricted submarine warfare campaigns that actively targeted neutral commerce, called into question the ongoing validity and utility of the law of neutrality.[226] In particular, the establishment of maritime exclusion zones, in which both neutral and enemy merchant vessels were treated as targets and attacked without prior warning, were grave, serious and continuous breaches of the law of neutrality. This practice was illegal at the time,[227] later condemned by the Nuremberg Tribunal,[228] and remains prohibited in contemporary practice.[229]

The basic principle concerning neutral commerce during times of armed conflict is that a neutral merchant vessel must not be attacked unless it is on unneutral service.[230] That principle arises from the fact that one of the 'fundamental rights of neutral States is to continue to maintain commercial relations with both belligerents as well as other neutral States'.[231] Neutral commerce is highly desirable for both belligerents and neutrals, which explains the great focus on it in the law of neutrality. For neutrals, the opportunity to trade with belligerents and with other neutrals can prove lucrative. For belligerents, neutral trade may be vital in staving off the consequences of armed conflict on the home front and may sustain the war effort.[232] It is for this reason that neutral commerce has attracted so much attention in the context of submarine warfare; it has been the persistent hope of belligerents (though not always the

[226] Following WWI, Hersch Lauterpacht is said to have 'lamented that the law of neutrality had been rendered so uncertain as to be, in effect, non-justiciable by tribunals': Stephen C. Neff, 'Disrupting a Delicate Balance: The Allied Blockade Policy and the Law of Maritime Neutrality during the Great War' (2018) 29(2) *European Journal of International Law* 459, 472.

[227] A. Pearce Higgins, 'Submarine Warfare' (1920–1921) 1 *British Yearbook of International Law* 149, 161.

[228] See generally James Kraska and Raul Pedrozo, *Disruptive Technology and the Law of Naval Warfare* (Oxford University Press, 2022) 155. See also Chapter 5, Section 5.4.1.

[229] In addition to the prohibition on the use of force against neutrals generally and neutral merchant vessels specifically, the San Remo Manual responds to the practice of declaring maritime exclusion zones by indicating that a 'belligerent cannot be absolved of its duties under international humanitarian law by establishing zones which might adversely affect the legitimate uses of defined areas of the sea': San Remo Manual (n 4) para. 105.

[230] San Remo Manual (n 4) para. 67.

[231] Antonopoulos (n 70) 90.

[232] Ibid, 220; Neff, *Rights and Duties of Neutrals* (n 165) 2.

reality) that the interruption of the flow of neutral commerce to an opposing belligerent will have a powerful, and even determinative, effect on the broader hostilities. The protection afforded to neutral commerce is qualified and subject to the several duties owed by a neutral to all belligerents, as well as rights exercisable by belligerents.

The corollary of neutral State's duty of abstention is the right of the belligerent submarine to search and visit merchant vessels in all maritime zones other than neutral waters.[233] The fact that a neutral vessel is flying the flag of a neutral State is prima facie evidence of its neutrality,[234] though a submarine is entitled to exercise the right of search and visit to determine whether the vessel is in reality neutral.[235] There are certain exceptions to the right of search and visit, which include (but are not limited to) where the neutral merchant vessel is travelling to a neutral port, or where it is escorted in a convoy led by a neutral (and not belligerent) warship of the same flag.[236] The purpose of this right is to allow the belligerent to identify whether the vessel is carrying any contraband.[237] If the neutral merchant vessel is carrying contraband, then the belligerent submarine may capture the neutral merchant vessel as a prize for adjudication.[238] In exceptional circumstances, the neutral vessel may be destroyed but only where the safety of the passengers and crew are provided for.[239]

Neutral merchant vessels may also be liable to capture by a belligerent submarine where they are more generally engaged in unneutral service. The types of activity that will constitute unneutral service include where the neutral vessel is engaging in belligerent acts on behalf of the enemy, where it resists search and capture, where it has breached a blockade, where it is incorporated into the enemy belligerent's intelligence system, where it acts as an auxiliary to the enemy belligerent's forces, where it sails under convoy of enemy belligerent warships or aircraft, or where it otherwise makes an effective contribution to the enemy's military action.[240] The attack must be conducted in accordance with the

233 San Remo Manual (n 4) para. 118; Hague XIII (n 52) art. 2.
234 San Remo Manual (n 4) para. 113.
235 Ibid, para. 114.
236 Ibid, para. 120.
237 'Contraband' is defined as 'goods which are ultimately destined for territory under the control of the enemy and which may be susceptible for use in armed conflict': ibid, para. 148.
238 San Remo Manual (n 4) para. 146; Commander's Handbook (n 6) para. 7.10.
239 Among other criteria. San Remo Manual (n 4) para. 151.
240 San Remo Manual (n 4) para. 67.

rules of the law of armed conflict.[241] The same requirements apply to attacks by submarines on neutral civil aircraft.[242]

There is limited contemporary practice of the exercise of the right of visit and search by warships in general. One example is the Iran-Iraq War (1980–1988), where visit and search was conducted and respected by the large number of States that declared themselves neutral.[243] Russia has exercised a belligerent right to visit and search during the Russo-Ukrainian War.[244] In any event, there is cause to doubt the enduring relevance of the law concerning the interdiction of neutral shipping. The rise of flags of convenience, increasing globalisation, the reliance of the global economy on international trade, and the sheer size of modern container ships make the traditional rules of search and visit, contraband and neutral shipping all appear rather quaint.[245] The major shift in the capability and purpose of submarines since the end of WWII has made it increasingly unlikely that States will deploy highly sophisticated and technologically advanced weapons platforms for the purpose of shipping interdiction.[246]

10.5 Law of Armed Conflict

The law of armed conflict, which is also referred to as international humanitarian law, regulates the conduct of hostilities. The law of armed conflict provides several overarching, general principles that apply to the conduct of hostilities wherever they may occur and irrespective of the platform from which an attack is launched. In this sense, the general principles of the law of armed conflict are equally as applicable to the conduct of submarine warfare as they are in relation to traditional land-based warfare. The law of armed conflict also informs a more specific set of rules applicable to the conduct of hostilities at sea. The regime applicable to the conduct of submarine warfare is dictated by several variables, which include the location of the submarine, the type of target to be attacked and whether that target is on land or at sea, as well as

241 Ibid, para. 68.
242 Ibid, para. 70.
243 See generally Petrochilos (n 174) 596–597.
244 Raul (Pete) Pedrozo, 'Russia-Ukraine War at Sea: Naval Blockades, Visit and Search, and Targeting War-Sustaining Objects', *Articles of War*, 25 August 2023 <https://lieber.westpoint.edu/russia-ukraine-war-naval-blockades-visit-search-targeting-war-sustaining-objects/>.
245 See generally Sassòli (n 57) para. 8.461; Haines (n 17) 440.
246 Heintschel von Heinegg, 'Submarine Operations and International Law' (n 5) 143.

the methods and means of warfare utilised. This section clarifies these variables and sets out the legal regime applicable to the conduct of submarine warfare.

10.5.1 *Overarching Principles*

The basic principles of the law of armed conflict apply to 'all methods and means of warfare',[247] whether they occur at sea or on land. There are several different formulations of these principles. The authors of the Newport Manual identify three of them: distinction, humanity and military necessity.[248] First, the principle of distinction has been described as 'the most basic rule of [the law of armed conflict] for submarines'.[249] The principle requires the commander of a submarine to distinguish between protected persons and objects (such as civilians, people *hors de combat*, hospital ships, places of worship and cultural heritage) and legitimate military objectives.[250] The definition of military objectives includes 'those objects which by their nature, location, purpose or use make an effective contribution to military action and whose total or partial destruction, capture or neutralization, in the circumstances ruling at the time, offers a definite military advantage'.[251] If there is any ambiguity as to whether a target is a military objective, then the submarine must refrain from attack.[252] In this sense, the principle requires that precautions be taken in planning for attacks. States must gather information to determine whether or not there are non-military objectives in an area of attack and limit the attack only to military objectives and take precautions to prevent and minimise collateral damage and casualties.[253]

247 Heintschel von Heinegg, 'The Current State of the Law of Naval Warfare' (n 121) 274. See also Newport Manual (n 5) para. 5.1.

248 Newport Manual (n 5) para. 5.1.

249 Kraska and Pedrozo (n 228) 141.

250 Newport Manual (n 5) para. 5.4. See also San Remo Manual (n 4) paras. 39–41; *Legality of the Threat or Use of Nuclear Weapons* (n 170) para. 78 ('States must never make civilians the object of attack and must consequently never use weapons that are incapable of distinguishing between civilian and military targets').

251 Additional Protocol I to the Geneva Conventions of 12 August 1949, and relating to the Protection of Victims of International Armed Conflicts, Geneva, 8 June 1977, entered into force 7 December 1978, 1125 UNTS 3, art. 52(2) ('Additional Protocol I'). See also San Remo Manual (n 4) para. 40; J. Ashley Roach, 'Submarine Warfare' in Anne Peters and Rüdiger Wolfrum (eds.), *Max Planck Encyclopedia of Public International Law* (Oxford University Press, March 2017) para. 15.

252 Newport Manual (n 5) para. 5.4.

253 San Remo Manual (n 4) para. 46.

Indiscriminate attacks that are not directed towards a military objective, or that utilise a method or means of combat that cannot be directed at, or the effects of cannot be limited to, a military objective (such as a biological weapon or contact mine) are prohibited.[254]

Second, the dictates of humanity forbid the 'infliction of suffering, injury or destruction unnecessary to accomplish a legitimate military purpose'.[255] Pursuant to this principle, civilians and enemy combatants *hors de combat* are immune from being made the object of an attack.[256] The incidental or collateral loss of civilian life is not prohibited, subject to that loss of life being proportionate to and justified by military necessity.[257] Belligerents must also not cause unnecessary suffering and superfluous injury in their conduct of submarine warfare.[258] In this sense, an attack must not be launched if it is expected to cause collateral damage excessive in relation to the direct military advantage anticipated from the attack as a whole.[259]

Third, the principle of military necessity, which 'exists in equipoise with the principle of humanity',[260] authorises a belligerent to use means and methods of warfare 'designed and intended to bring about the submission of the adversary's military and other fighting forces at the earliest possible opportunity with the least expenditure of one's own forces'.[261] A belligerent must not use means and methods of warfare that are beyond what is required to achieve the objective and are prohibited from using the concept of military necessity as a 'shield' to excuse breaches of the law of armed conflict. These general principles apply only in situations of armed conflict. The law of armed conflict applies *lex specialis* 'from the initiation of [an] armed conflict and extends beyond the cessation of hostilities until a general conclusion of peace is reached'.[262] Determining whether a state of armed conflict exists is an objective matter;[263] a 'single shot' may qualify as a use of

254 Newport Manual (n 5) para. 8.5. See also Additional Protocol I (n 251) art. 4.

255 Newport Manual (n 5) para. 5.2. See also Additional Protocol I (n 251) art. 35(2).

256 Newport Manual (n 5) para. 5.2.

257 Ibid, para. 5.5.1.

258 Newport Manual (n 5) para. 5.5.2; San Remo Manual (n 4) paras. 42–43.

259 San Remo Manual (n 4) para. 46(d).

260 Michael N. Schmitt, 'Military Necessity and Humanity in International Humanitarian Law: Preserving the Delicate Balance' (2010) 50(4) *Virginia Journal of International Law* 796, 796.

261 Newport Manual (n 5) para. 5.3.

262 *Prosecutor v. Tadic* (n 60) para. [70].

263 ILA Committee on the Use of Force, *Final Report on the Meaning of Armed Conflict in International Law* (Hague Conference, 2010) 33.

force,[264] and, as such, 'the use of force against a foreign warship, whether manned or unmanned, may bring an [international armed conflict] into existence'.[265]

The specific legal regime applicable to the conduct of submarine warfare will depend on the location of the target, considering that submarines are capable of striking both targets at sea (and in the suprajacent airspace) and on land. The former category of attack is largely regulated by rules of customary international law as well as the London Protocol of 1936, which is the only international instrument dedicated to the conduct of submarine warfare. The rules applicable to the latter category of attack are drawn not only from custom, but also from Hague Convention (IX) of 1907,[266] Hague Convention (IV) of 1907[267] and Additional Protocol I of 1977.[268] The discussion immediately below considers each category of attack in turn.

10.5.2 Attacks on Targets at Sea

The rules applicable to the conduct of submarine warfare at sea differ based on the status of the target as a military objective. In this discussion, we consider attacks on the enemy, attacks on protected vessels and aircraft, attacks on merchant vessels and finally, attacks on land.

10.5.2.1 Attacks on the Enemy

Enemy warships and naval auxiliaries qualify as military objectives and are always liable to attack,[269] save for limited circumstances such as when they have surrendered or are in the process of surrendering (which, in the case of submarines, is signalled by surfacing).[270] Those attacks must be performed in accordance with the general principles described above. For instance, even if it is permissible under the law of armed conflict for a submarine to attack an enemy frigate, it must not cause superfluous or

264 See Chapter 9, Section 9.3 on what may constitute a violation of the prohibition on the use of force.

265 Newport Manual (n 5) para. 2.1.2.1. See also Klein, *Maritime Security and the Law of the Sea* (n 76) 258; San Remo Manual (n 4) para. 1.

266 Hague IX (n 52).

267 Hague Convention (IV) respecting the Laws and Customs of War on Land, The Hague, 18 October 1907, entered into force 26 January 1910, [1910] ATS 8.

268 Additional Protocol I (n 251).

269 Newport Manual (n 5) para. 8.6.1.

270 Ibid, paras. 8.6.6–8.6.8; US Law of War Manual (n 99) para. 13.3.5; Roach (n 251) [20]; Commander's Handbook (n 6) para. 8.7.

gratuitous harm to the crew of the frigate when conducting that attack. Two examples illustrate these issues.[271]

The first took place in the 1971 Indo-Pakistani War. On 9 December 1971, two Indian anti-submarine frigates, INS *Khurki* and INS *Kirpan*, were on patrol off the Kathiawar coast in the Arabian Sea. The frigates were hunting PNS *Hangor*, a French-built Pakistani submarine of the *Daphné*-class.[272] The frigates were unaware that their target was, in a game of cat and mouse, already tracking the two vessels. *Hangor* fired a tracking torpedo at the *Kirpan*, which evaded attack with the assistance of the ship's sonar. The *Khurki* approached to launch an attack on behalf of the *Kirpan*, but a torpedo fired by the *Hangor* struck the *Khurki* first. The *Khurki* quickly sank, taking with it eighteen officers and 176 sailors.[273] The *Hangor* evaded the ensuing search for it, which saw it attacked by over 150 depth charges, and returned to Karachi.[274] The sinking of the *Khurki*, which has been described as 'the greatest achievement of the Pakistan Navy till date',[275] was of immense strategic benefit to the Pakistani forces and 'turned around Pakistan's flailing war effort at sea'.[276] Concerned about the risk of further losses that could be caused by a Pakistani submarine loose in the Arabian Sea, India cancelled a planned missile strike on Karachi Harbour.[277] The short-lived war ended a few days later.

A second incident of modern submarine warfare occurred in the context of the Falklands/Malvinas War of 1982. On 2 May 1982, HMS *Conqueror*, a British nuclear-powered submarine, fired three Mark 8 Mod 4 torpedoes[278] at ARA *General Belgrano*, an Argentine light cruiser.[279] The *Belgrano* responded in turn, dropping depth charges in

[271] See also the discussion of the *Cheonan* in Chapter 9, Section 9.3.

[272] Adam Kok Wey Leong, '*Are Two Subs Enough?* Malaysia's Small Submarine Force and Lessons from Strategic History' (2016) 8(4) *Australian Journal of Maritime and Ocean Affairs* 298, 300–301.

[273] Kraska and Pedrozo (n 228) 157.

[274] Leong (n 272) 300–302.

[275] Tariq Rahman, *Pakistan's Wars: An Alternate History* (Taylor and Francis, 2022) 111.

[276] Kraska and Pedrozo (n 228) 157.

[277] Leong (n 272) 304; Kraska and Pedrozo (n 228) 157.

[278] Despite the fact that the *Conqueror* was equipped with newer and more sophisticated Mark 24 Tigerfish torpedoes, the decision was made to use the WWII-era Mark 8, which possessed an explosive charge of some 350kg: Desmond Rice and Arthur Gavshon, *The Sinking of the Belgrano* (Secker and Warburg, 1984) 55.

[279] See David Letts, 'The Sinking of *ARA General Belgrano*' in David Letts and Rob McLaughlin (eds.), *Maritime Operations Law in Practice* (Routledge, 2023) 191, 195, 198–199.

an attempt to destroy the *Conqueror*. Ultimately, the *Belgrano* sank resulting in the death of 323 Argentine sailors out of a complement of 1,093.[280] The British position was that the attack 'took the heart out of the Argentinian Navy',[281] with Britain's retrospective analysis of the war recording that '[o]ur nuclear-powered submarines (SSN) played a crucial role. After the sinking of the *Belgrano*, the Argentine surface fleet effectively took no further part in the Campaign.'[282] The effective immobilisation of the Argentine fleet by the actions of a single British submarine represented a crucial turning point in the conflict and demonstrated the immense strategic power of submarine warfare. The incident marked the first use of a nuclear submarine in combat,[283] and only the second time a submarine had sunk a warship since the end of WWII.

10.5.2.2 Protected Vessels and Aircraft

Submarines are prohibited from attacking protected vessels or protected aircraft regardless of the flag that they fly and whether it is of an enemy character. The types of vessel and aircraft that fall within the scope of this blanket prohibition include hospital ships and medical transports, medical aircraft, rescue ships, passenger vessels carrying civilian passengers and civilian airliners, small coastal fishing vessels, vessels that have surrendered, aircraft granted safe conduct by the parties to the conflict and vessels engaged in humanitarian missions.[284] Protected vessels may lose their status if they are not innocently employed,[285] do not submit to identification[286] or intentionally hamper the movement of combatants.[287] Protected vessels that have lost their exemption from

280 Lawrence Freedman, *The Official History of the Falklands Campaign* (Routledge, 2005) vol. 2, 250.

281 Memo from Commander-in-Chief Fleet (Admiral Sir John Fieldhouse) to HMS Conqueror, extracted in Rice and Gavshon (n 278) 166.

282 'The Falklands Campaign: The Lessons', Cmnd. 8758, December 1982, para. 211, extracted in Rice and Gavshon (n 278) 165.

283 Kraska and Pedrozo (n 228) 158–159.

284 San Remo Manual (n 4) para. 47. Protected aircraft are listed in para. 53, and the regime governing their protection provided for in paras. 54–58. The regime governing enemy civil aircraft is outlined in paras. 62–64. Passenger vessels carrying civilian passengers have been described as exempt from attack as a rule of customary international law: Louise Doswald-Beck, 'The San Remo Manual on International Law Applicable to Armed Conflicts at Sea' (1995) 89(1) *American Journal of International Law* 192, 202.

285 San Remo Manual (n 4) para. 48(a).

286 Ibid, para. 48(b).

287 Ibid, para. 48(c).

attack may only be attacked in limited circumstances and, generally speaking, only as a matter of last resort.[288]

10.5.2.3 Merchant Vessels

There is a complex series of rules concerning attacks by submarines on merchant vessels. The law governing attacks on merchant vessels at sea has been described as 'one of the least developed areas of the law of armed conflict'.[289] It is, however, the only part of the law of armed conflict that explicitly regulates the conduct of submarine warfare. The London Protocol of 1936, which regulates interactions between submarines and merchant vessels, provides two rules. First, in their interactions with merchant vessels, 'submarines must conform to the rules of international law to which surface vessels are subject'.[290] As a result, submarines are generally prohibited from attacking merchant vessels as they do not, as a matter of course, qualify as a legitimate military objective.[291] While it is permissible for enemy merchant vessels to be captured and taken as a prize for adjudication,[292] some action is required on the part of the merchant vessel to render it a legitimate military objective. For instance, the merchant vessel may engage in belligerent acts (such as laying mines or attacking a submarine), it may carry troops, assist the enemy's intelligence system, resist visit and search, sail under convoy with enemy warships or aircraft, be armed beyond the extent required to defend itself, and engage in any other activity that may bring them within the definition of a military objective (such as shielding enemy warships).[293] A broadly similar regime applies to attacks on civil aircraft.[294] A merchant vessel or civil aircraft engaged in these activities is liable to attack without prior warning as, absent special circumstances, the attack is likely to provide the belligerent with a definite military advantage.[295] Further, in accordance with the right of self-defence, a submarine may protect itself and launch an attack on a vessel when it itself is attacked.[296] Its exercise of that right must be

[288] San Remo Manual (n 4) para. 52. Hospital ships are subject to a more restrictive regime: San Remo Manual (n 4) paras. 49–51.
[289] Roach, 'Legal Aspects of Modern Submarine Warfare' (n 40) 379.
[290] 1936 London Protocol (n 52) art. 1. See also Chapter 4, Section 4.3.
[291] San Remo Manual (n 4) para. 59.
[292] Ibid, paras. 135, 136, 138.
[293] Newport Manual (n 5) para. 8.6.3; San Remo Manual (n 4) para. 60.
[294] Newport Manual (n 5) para. 8.6.4; San Remo Manual (n 4) paras. 62–63.
[295] Heintschel von Heinegg, 'Submarine Operations and International Law' (n 5) 158. See also Commander's Handbook (n 6) para. 8.7.1; German Manual (n 200) para. 1054.
[296] San Remo Manual (n 4) para. 3.

in accordance with the principles of necessity and proportionality such that they should not exceed the degree and kind of force required to repel the attack and restore security.[297] Following an attack, Geneva Convention II of 1949 requires all possible measures for search and rescue operations to be undertaken by the attacker.[298] This obligation applies to attacks on both warships and merchant vessels without distinction.[299]

The complexity concerning attacks on merchant vessels by submarines is introduced because of the second rule set out in the London Protocol, which prohibits a submarine from conducting an attack on a merchant vessel 'without having first placed passengers, crew and ship's papers in a place of safety'.[300] Submarines are, generally speaking, 'ill-suited to fulfill the legal obligation to protect merchantmen and civilian passengers during armed conflict'.[301] They are unlikely to have the space to take on passengers.[302] Compliance would also require the submarine to surface, therefore rendering it extremely vulnerable to attack.[303] Similar issues arise in relation to the practicalities of a submarine exercising the rights of visit and search,[304] as well as in undertaking search and rescue missions for the shipwrecked. Accordingly, strict compliance with these rules of international law would result in the submarine losing 'a great part of its effectiveness as an offensive weapon for the destruction of commerce'.[305]

There is a diversity of opinion as to how the unique design features of submarines should be reconciled against the requirements of the London Protocol and customary international law. The London Protocol was roundly ignored during WWII with the conduct of unrestricted submarine warfare,[306] leading commentators to suggest that the 'rule is more likely to be followed in war at sea, is more limited and applies only to the extent that military exigencies permit'.[307] The position of the United

[297] San Remo Manual, arts 4–5.
[298] Geneva II (n 52) art. 18.
[299] Heintschel von Heinegg, 'The Law of Military Operations at Sea' (n 5) para. 20.11(j).
[300] 1936 London Protocol (n 52) art. 2.
[301] Kraska and Pedrozo (n 228) 156.
[302] Weiss (n 159) 138.
[303] Heintschel von Heinegg, 'Submarine Operations and International Law' (n 5) 159; Weiss (n 159) 138.
[304] Sassòli (n 57) para. 8.466. See also Haines (n 17) 433.
[305] Weiss (n 159) 138.
[306] Haines (n 17) 437.
[307] Roach, 'Legal Aspects of Modern Submarine Warfare' (n 40) 378; Roach, 'Submarine Warfare' (n 270) para. 21; Weiss (n 159) 143–144.

States is that 'one cannot lay down an absolute rule that the commander of a warship must engage in rescue operations if, by doing so, he would expose his vessel to attack'.[308] To this end, submarines are required to act in accordance with the London Protocol unless compliance would subject the submarine to imminent danger or otherwise preclude mission accomplishment. In these circumstances, the location of survivors should be communicated by the submarine commander to a surface ship or other facility capable of conducting the search and rescue operation.[309] The Danish position is broadly similar, providing that only in 'exceptional cases will submarines ... be required to take part in rescue operations after having been involved in attacks'.[310] The German position appears to indicate stricter compliance with the London Protocol and provides that the legality of an attack is contingent on the submarine's capacity to first bring the passengers, crew and papers to a safe location.[311] This position is also adopted in the French Manual.[312] The US and Danish viewpoints run counter to the finding of the International Military Tribunal in the trial of German Admiral Dönitz, which held that 'the Protocol is explicit. If the commander cannot rescue, then under its terms he cannot sink a merchant vessel and should allow it to pass harmless before his periscope.'[313]

10.5.2.4 Attacks on Land Targets

The advent of submarine-launched missiles has provided undersea platforms with the ability to launch attacks on land targets from some distance. The use of submarines as a platform for conducting attacks on land is a relatively new one.[314] The rules of the law of armed conflict, including in relation to targeting, apply equally in relation to attacks from

308 US Law of War Manual (n 99) para. 7.4.4.2.

309 See Roach, 'Submarine Warfare' (n 270) para. 21. US Law of War Manual (n 99) para. 13.7.2. See also Commander's Handbook (n 6) para. 8.7; Heintschel von Heinegg, 'The Development of the Law of Naval Warfare (n 7) 72–82; Heintschel von Heinegg, 'The Law of Military Operations at Sea' (n 5) para. 20.11(j).

310 Danish Manual (n 210) para. 4.8.

311 German Manual (n 200) para. 1054.

312 French Manual (n 105) para. 1.2.3.1.3.

313 International Military Tribunal at Nuremberg, 'Dönitz' (1947) 41(1) *American Journal of International Law* 302, 305. See also Chapter 5, Section 5.4.1.

314 Roach, 'Legal Aspects of Modern Submarine Warfare' (n 40) 383; Heintschel von Heinegg, 'Submarine Operations and International Law' (n 5) 152.

sea as they do attacks on land. As such, if the land target is a legitimate military objective, 'a submarine bombardment will, in the main, be as lawful as any other attack'.[315] As a matter of customary international law,[316] submarines are prohibited from attacking undefended ports, towns, villages, dwellings or buildings;[317] medical facilities, vehicles, stores and equipment that are not used for military purposes;[318] and sacred edifices, buildings used for artistic, scientific or charitable purposes and historic monuments.[319] States that are party to the 1977 Additional Protocol I to the Geneva Conventions are further prohibited from conducting attacks on religious and cultural buildings and monuments;[320] dams, dykes and nuclear electrical generating stations;[321] and objects indispensable to the civilian population for survival, such as the intentional (as opposed to incidental) destruction of food, crops, livestock and drinking water.[322] Compliance with these rules of international law is unlikely to be a major impediment to the use of submarines to attack land targets considering the sophistication of submarine-launched missiles, which are generally able to strike targets with a high degree of accuracy.[323]

10.5.3 Means of Warfare

The 'means of warfare' are the weapons and weapons systems used to conduct an attack. The starting position is that States 'do not have unlimited freedom of choice of means in the weapons they use'.[324] Their use of submarine weaponry will therefore be constrained by the general principles earlier described.[325] It is therefore prohibited to use a submarine to launch a weapon that causes superfluous injury or unnecessary suffering, though the application of this principle in relation to submarine warfare is likely to be limited given that attacks made by

315 Jacobson (n 20) 226.

316 Heintschel von Heinegg, 'Submarine Operations and International Law' (n 5) 152–153.

317 Hague IX (n 52) art. 1. See Newport Manual (n 5) para. 8.7.1.

318 Newport Manual (n 5) para. 8.7.2, citing Geneva I (n 176) art. 23; Hague IX (n 52) art. 5.

319 Newport Manual (n 5) para. 8.7.3, citing Hague IX (n 52) art. 5.

320 Newport Manual (n 5) para. 8.7.4.1, citing Additional Protocol I (n 251) art. 53.

321 Newport Manual (n 5) para. 8.7.4.2, citing Additional Protocol I (n 251) art. 56.

322 Newport Manual (n 5) para. 8.7.4.3, citing Additional Protocol I (n 251) art. 54(1).

323 Heintschel von Heinegg, 'Submarine Operations and International Law' (n 5) 153.

324 *Legality of the Threat or Use of Nuclear Weapons* (n 170) para. 78. See also San Remo Manual (n 4) para. 38.

325 See generally San Remo Manual (n 4) paras. 38–42.

submarines 'are directed against platforms' as opposed to individuals.[326] To comply with this obligation, modern submarine-launched weapons, such as missiles, torpedoes and mines must be (and generally are) capable of identifying or being programmed to identify military objectives.[327]

The use of submarine weaponry is generally restrained to accommodate the principle of discrimination. Compliance with the requirements of discrimination is unlikely to greatly impede the conduct of submarine warfare considering that modern submarine-launched missiles, torpedoes and mines tend to be able to discriminate against targets.[328] Consistent with that principle, it is prohibited for a submarine to make use of a weapon that is unable to discriminate between military objectives and civilians. There are certain weapons that intrinsically offend the principle of discrimination. The use of these weapons is therefore prima facie prohibited. One example is automatic submarine contact mines, which detonate upon contact with any vessel that strikes it. The use of these mines are 'generally a thing of the past', with modern naval mines 'capable of identifying even specific ships and can, therefore, be programmed not to respond to vessels that are protected civilian objects'.[329] In view of their historical use, the use of automatic contact mines has been heavily restricted and regulated.[330] In a similar fashion, customary international law requires that submarine-launched torpedoes sink or otherwise become harmless after their run to avoid them later harming a merchant or protected vessel.[331]

The use of a submarine-launched biological weapon would also offend the principle of discrimination. Biological weapons are, by their very nature, incapable of distinguishing between military objectives, civilians and protected objects.[332] The Japanese Navy made plans during WWII, which were never acted upon, to attack Southern California with submarine-launched aircraft carrying bombs containing bubonic plague.[333] This plan, if executed,

326 Newport Manual (n 5) para. 6.2.1.

327 Chapter 14, Section 14.4 addresses legal principles associated with underwater autonomous systems that are used in naval warfare.

328 Heintschel von Heinegg, 'Submarine Operations and International Law' (n 5) 153; Heintschel von Heinegg, 'The Law of Military Operations at Sea' (n 5) para. 20.11(j).

329 Steven Haines, '1907 Hague Convention VIII Relative to the Laying of Automatic Submarine Contact Mines' (2014) 90 *International Law Studies* 412, 444.

330 Hague VIII (n 52). See generally Haines (n 329) 422–425. See also Newport Manual (n 5) para. 7.2.3.

331 San Remo Manual (n 4) para. 79; Hague VIII (n 52) art. 1(3); Newport Manual (n 5) para. 6.6.

332 Newport Manual (n 5) paras. 6.2.2–6.2.3.

333 Samuel J. Cox, 'H-057-2: I-400 and Operation Cherry Blossoms at Night: Japanese Plan for Biological Warfare – September 1945', *Naval History and Heritage Command*,

would have been an undeniable breach of international law. The position with respect to nuclear weapons is more complicated. In its Advisory Opinion on the *Threat or Use of Nuclear Weapons*, the International Court of Justice declined to declare an outright ban on the threat or use of nuclear weapons.[334] It is beyond the scope of this chapter to resolve this debated question of international law. It suffices to say that the extent to which the threat or use of submarine-launched nuclear weapons is permissible is likely to depend heavily on context.[335] Their use will undoubtedly be restrained by the requirement to comply with the general principles of the law of armed conflict, particularly those relating to target discrimination. It is further prohibited to lay any other weapon of mass destruction, or facility for launching, storing or testing of such weapons, on the seabed and ocean floor of areas beyond the territorial sea.[336]

10.5.4 Methods of Warfare

'Methods of warfare' refers to the tactics and specific strategies implemented to facilitate attacks in times of armed conflict. There are several methods of warfare that have been intrinsically tied to the use of submarines.

First, in modern maritime conflicts it has been common practice for belligerents to declare maritime exclusion zones policed by submarines, as well as surface vessels. The practice of belligerents in relation to maritime exclusion zones is mixed and the consequences imposed by the belligerent on vessels present within the zone have varied. In several armed conflicts, belligerents have warned that any vessel, regardless of its status, travelling through the maritime exclusion zone is liable to attack by a submarine or other warship without warning. In this sense, the belligerent declares that the mere presence of a vessel within the boundaries of the zone renders that vessel a legitimate military objective. Such zones were declared during WWI and WWII, as well as by the United Kingdom during the Falklands/Malvinas War.[337] This practice has been

January 2021 <www.history.navy.mil/about-us/leadership/director/directors-corner/h-grams/h-gram-057/h-057-2.html>.

334 *Legality of the Threat or Use of Nuclear Weapons* (n 170).

335 Newport Manual (n 5) para. 6.10. See, for example, Dale Stephens and Michael W. Lewis, 'The Law of Armed Conflict: A Contemporary Critique' (2005) 6 *Melbourne Journal of International Law* 55, 68. See also Jacobson (n 20) 227.

336 Seabed Arms Control Treaty (n 43).

337 As to the practice in the latter conflict, see Roach, 'Legal Aspects of Modern Submarine Warfare' (n 40) 375.

controversial, considering that the declaration of a maritime exclusion zone does not absolve a belligerent of its obligations under the law of armed conflict,[338] including in relation to target discrimination. It is therefore prohibited for a State to use maritime exclusion zones to avoid undertaking the task of target discrimination,[339] or to otherwise permit one of its submarines to attack a vessel that it would otherwise be prohibited from attacking.

Maritime exclusion zones that impose consequences other than attack on vessels travelling through the zone are permitted in 'exceptional circumstances'.[340] These maritime exclusion zones, which are a prima facie imposition on the freedom of navigation, must bend to the requirements of the peacetime law of the sea, including by not infringing the legitimate uses of the seas.[341] The same law therefore applies inside the zone as outside it.[342] They might be beneficial when they enable the separation of neutral and enemy shipping and therefore 'safeguard merchant ships and crews'.[343] Belligerents must apply the same body of law inside and outside the zone. They must also ensure that the size of the zone and the measures implemented within it not exceed what is strictly required by military necessity and the principles of proportionality, afford due regard to the rights of neutral States including by ensuring safe passage for neutral vessels and aircraft and ensure proper declaration and notification of the commencement, duration, location, restrictions applicable in and extent of the zone.[344]

As discussed above, submarines were deployed by the United Kingdom and Argentina in the 1982 conflict between the two States over the Falklands/Malvinas islands.[345] Argentina had just four diesel-powered submarines, only two of which were operational in the conflict – one of these being captured early on after disembarking troops and supplies in South Georgia.[346] British SSNs played an important role in

338 San Remo Manual (n 4) para. 105.
339 Heintschel von Heinegg, 'Submarine Operations and International Law' (n 5) 155.
340 San Remo Manual (n 4) para. 105.
341 Ibid.
342 Kraska and Pedrozo (n 228) 159–160.
343 Ibid.
344 San Remo Manual (n 4) para. 106; Newport Manual, para. 7.2.1.
345 Peter Henessy and James Jinks, *The Silent Deep: The Royal Navy Submarine Service since 1945* (2016, Penguin) ch. 7.
346 Steven R. Harper, *Submarine Operations in the Falklands War* (Tannenberg Publishing, 2014) 9–11.

maintaining an exclusion zone around the Falklands. The sinking of the Argentinian *Belgrano* by the SSN HMS *Conqueror* occurred outside the exclusion zone. In his analysis of the exclusion zone, Letts correctly notes that the declaration of such a zone cannot authorise attacks within it or outlaw those beyond it; instead, '[t]he legality of attacking a target either inside or outside the zone is governed by the same rules of international humanitarian law – in this case, the law of naval warfare – that would apply in any armed conflict'.[347]

A second method of warfare to consider is blockades. Submarines have often been used to police blockades declared by States, such as those declared around the British Isles by Germany in WWI and WWII. A blockade is intended to 'prevent vessel traffic from all States from entering or leaving specific coastal areas that are under the sovereignty, occupation or control of an enemy'.[348] These blockades must be notified,[349] applied impartially regardless of flag State, be maintained effectively[350] and must not bar access to the ports and coasts of neutral States.[351] Consistent with the overarching principles of discrimination and the prevention of superfluous suffering, blockades must not be conducted for the sole purpose of starving or causing excessive damage to the civilian population.[352] The breach or attempted breach of a blockade may lead to a neutral vessel losing its neutrality and therefore being liable to capture.[353] It is suggested that developments in military technology, particularly submarines, 'have rendered the in-shore blockade exceedingly difficult, if not impossible, to maintain during anything other than a local or limited armed conflict'.[354] The possibility of underwater maritime autonomous vehicles being deployed for blockades is discussed in Chapter 14.

Third, it is generally permissible for submarines to engage in a ruse, including by flying a false flag.[355] This general regime is subject to some caveats: submarines are prohibited from engaging in perfidy by feigning

347 Letts, 'The Sinking of ARA *General Belgrano*' (n 279) 199–200.
348 Newport Manual (n 5) para. 7.4.1.
349 Ibid, para. 7.4.2. See also London Declaration of 1909 (n 168) arts. 8–9, 11, 16.
350 Newport Manual (n 5) para. 7.4.3. See also London Declaration of 1909 (n 168) art. 2.
351 San Remo Manual (n 4) para. 99; Newport Manual (n 5) para. 7.4.6.
352 San Remo Manual (n 4) para. 102; Newport Manual (n 5) para. 7.4.5. See also San Remo Manual (n 4) paras. 103–104.
353 Commander's Handbook (n 6) para. 7.4.7.
354 Ibid, para. 7.7.5.
355 San Remo Manual (n 4) para. 110; Newport Manual (n 5) para. 7.5.3.1.

protected or neutral status when launching an attack.[356] Also, it is unlawful for a submarine to feign distress.[357] A further caveat is that the improper use by a submarine of a flag of truce, the flag or insignia of the United Nations or the distinctive emblems of the Geneva Conventions is a war crime.[358] For States that are party to Additional Protocol I, it is also prohibited to feign protected status to capture a vessel, such as by feigning surrender.[359]

A final point to observe is that States Party to Additional Protocol I of 1977 are prohibited from employing 'methods or means of warfare which are intended, or may be expected, to cause widespread, long-term and severe damage to the natural environment'.[360] This prohibition sets a rather high bar for environmental damage and is therefore unlikely to prohibit the use of all but the most destructive weapons. The San Remo Manual 'encourages' belligerents to agree that hostilities will not be conducted in areas containing rare or fragile ecosystems or the habitat of depleted, threatened or endangered species or other forms of marine life.[361] It further provides that States should employ methods and means of warfare 'with due regard for the natural environment' and prohibits '[d]amage or destruction of the natural environment not justified by military necessity or carried out wantonly'.[362] However, the authors of the Newport Manual consider these rules to be merely 'aspirational' and not reflective of treaty or custom.[363] Rules protecting the marine environment have very limited applicability to military submarines, as discussed in Chapter 12.

10.6 Conclusion

The international legal regime governing the conduct of submarine warfare draws primarily from three distinct but interrelated bodies of international law: the law of the sea, the law of neutrality and the law of armed conflict. The law of the sea is largely directed to regulating peaceful uses of the ocean. However, the maritime zones created by UNCLOS and

356 San Remo Manual (n 4) paras. 109–111; Newport Manual, para. 7.5.2.1.
357 Newport Manual (n 5) para. 7.5.2.
358 Rome Statute of the International Criminal Court, Rome, 17 July 1998, entered into force 1 July 2002, 2187 UNTS 3, art. 2(b)(vii). See also Newport Manual (n 5) para. 7.5.3.3.
359 Additional Protocol I (n 251) art. 85(3)(f); Newport Manual (n 5) para. 7.5.2.1.
360 Additional Protocol I (n 251) art. 35(3).
361 San Remo Manual (n 4) para. 11.
362 Ibid, para. 44.
363 Newport Manual (n 5) para. 6.3.

the concomitant rights and responsibilities of States within those zones inform inter alia the areas in which hostilities can be conducted. The law of neutrality is governed by a bundle of interdependent obligations and rights, which regulate the interactions between belligerents and neutrals during an international armed conflict. The law of armed conflict regulates interactions between belligerents. In this respect, the law of armed conflict applicable to submarine warfare is largely derivative of the law of armed conflict applicable to naval warfare. The principles of humanity, military necessity and proportionality balance the State's interest in the achievement of legitimate military objectives against the desire to prevent superfluous injury and unnecessary suffering. The interaction of these three bodies of law results in a regime in which the specific rules applicable to the conduct of submarine warfare will depend inter alia on the location of the submarine, as well as the location (at sea or on land) and character (neutral or belligerent) of the target.

This chapter has highlighted some difficulties in the practical application of these rules to the conduct of modern submarine warfare. Those difficulties arise at least in part considering there is a distinct lack of 'hard' international law that specifically regulates the conduct of hostilities at sea. Further, the identification of applicable rules of custom has been complicated by a distinct lack of contemporary practice of naval warfare generally and submarine warfare specifically. Chief among the challenges for submarines specifically is the ongoing debate as to the content and application of the obligation of a submarine commander to place a ship's passengers, crew and papers in a place of safety before launching an attack, and to search for survivors after such an attack.

Despite these challenges, the international legal regime governing the conduct of hostilities at sea has been subject to only limited development since the conclusion of WWII. Moreover, since that time, submarines have become significantly larger, quieter and more sophisticated. They are armed with increasingly devastating forms of weaponry, including nuclear weapons. Their purpose in a modern navy has moved away from 'commerce raiding' and towards a more diverse set of roles, including coastal protection, intelligence gathering, posturing and nuclear deterrence. These developments have made the legal regime governing the conduct of submarine warfare, including rules concerning search and visit as well as the capture of prizes for adjudication, look increasingly dated. In addition, the derivative nature of the international legal regime governing the conduct of submarine warfare presents some challenges in view of the unique and intrinsic design features of submarines. While it is unlikely that any new treaty will emerge setting out contemporary norms of naval warfare, the varied purposes and distinct features of submarines should prompt greater attention in the articulation of rules in different manuals so as to update current understandings and practices in relation to submarine warfare.

11

Navigational Safety and Sunken Submarines

11.1 Introduction

Since the turn of the century, the significant maritime incidents involving submarines have concerned accidents or collisions and occasionally resulted in the loss of the submarine and those onboard. This chapter draws out the relevant international laws that may be applicable to ensure the navigational safety of submarines and to establish what laws apply when a submarine is ultimately lost at sea. The discussion is concerned with both military and private submarines that are operating during times of peace. Technological advances have been critical in the development of submarines and the earliest accidents and loss of life were largely attributable to design flaws.[1] Notably, the loss of USS *Thresher* prompted the development of the US Navy's SUBSAFE programme, which was intended as a quality assurance mechanism for nuclear submarines.[2] Damage and loss of submarines have not only spurred innovations in engineering, but also raised questions as to the relevant rules and procedures in place to prevent and respond to submarine casualties.

The need for international safety regulations for private submarines was highlighted in 2023 following the implosion of the *Titan* submersible. Privately owned submersibles used for transporting civilian passengers are more commonly subject to national regulations and have classification or certification requirements that must be met when operating in the waters of a particular State or entering or leaving a port of

[1] Tingle has commented: 'the data suggest that a submarine was almost three times more likely to sink at sea during the period 1946 to 1974 than during the subsequent period. That coupled with a similar improvement in fatality statistics can only yield the conclusion that submarines have been designed better and operated more safely in the past 30 years': Christopher Tingle, 'Submarine Accidents: A 60-Year Statistical Assessment' (2009) 54(9) *Professional Safety* 31, 31.

[2] Ibid.

that State.[3] Certification may be undertaken by industry third parties, such as the American Bureau of Shipping or the European company DNV,[4] which may be a precondition for obtaining insurance.[5] The certification process is typically an annual requirement and may involve different inspections as well as timelines for tests and checks.[6] OceanGate, the company owner of the *Titan* submersible, had opted not to be certified, against industry advice,[7] as the certification process was considered an impediment to rapid innovation and did not align with OceanGate's own (supposedly higher) safety standards.[8] Certification may not be required in relation to submersibles that are tethered to the operating ship and considered part of the equipment of this ship.[9] Given the increase in privately owned and operated submarines, and incidents like the *Titan* implosion, it may now be timely to establish international standards on construction, equipment and seaworthiness of all privately owned and operated submarines.[10]

Beyond (or because of) design flaws, collisions involving submarines have been one of the greatest causes of accidents involving submarines. Following a review of all submarine accidents from 1945 to 2005, Tingle observed the potential contribution of international regulations in reducing submarine accidents:

> Unlike floods, the causes behind collisions involve human factors (operator error and/or an aggressive party) or a less-than-adequate capability to effectively detect (or be detected as the situation warrants) and quickly

[3] See Daiana Seabra Venancio, 'Law of the Sea and the *Titan* Incident: The Legal Loophole for Underwater Vehicles', *EJIL: Talk!*, 14 July 2023 <www.ejiltalk.org/law-of-the-sea-and-the-titan-incident-the-legal-loophole-for-underwater-vehicles/>.

[4] Brad Brooks and Daniel Trotta, 'Titanic Sub: How is Submersible Tourism Regulated and What's Next for Industry?', *Reuters*, 24 June 2023 <www.reuters.com/world/after-titanic-sub-disaster-industry-faces-scrutiny-2023-06-23/>. The Maritime Safety Committee of the International Maritime Organisation (IMO) has adopted guidelines that are intended to inform these certification processes. IMO, 'Guidelines for the Design, Construction and Operation of Passenger Submersible Craft', IMO Doc. MSC/Circ. 981, 29 January 2001.

[5] Clio Chang, 'The Murky Regulations Governing Submersibles', *Curbed.com*, 21 June 2023 <www.curbed.com/2023/06/oceangate-titan-submarine-unregulated-tourism.html>.

[6] Ibid.

[7] Ibid. See also Brooks and Trotta (n 4).

[8] Simmone Shah, 'The Titan Sub and the Dangers of Unregulated Deep-Sea Tourism', *Time Magazine*, 23 June 2023 <https://time.com/6289279/titanic-tourism-sub-deep-sea-regulation/> (referring to a 2019 blogpost from OceanGate that has since been removed).

[9] Fiona Carruthers, 'Push for Tougher "Tourist Sub" Rules after Titan Tragedy', *Australian Financial Review*, 23 June 2023 <www.afr.com/world/north-america/push-for-tougher-tourist-sub-rules-after-titan-tragedy-20230622-p5dinc> (citing a maritime law practitioner).

[10] An option canvassed by Brooks and Trotta (n 4).

> maneuver to avoid striking. Indeed, sensor and navigational capability for submarines and their surface counterparts have improved considerably during the period of study. That coupled with the fall of the Iron Curtain and the introduction of regulatory instruments such as IMO's collision regulations have likely contributed to the 40% to 50% reduction in the number of catastrophic submarine collisions observed since 1988.[11]

Rules for collision avoidance are especially important in maritime areas with higher density maritime traffic and where the proximity between vessels requires greater mutual regard in steering and sailing decisions. Where a submarine is in distress and ultimately sinks, consideration is further needed as to international law rules on search and rescue, distress and possible salvage. The question of salvage also brings to the fore the issue of immunity for State-owned submarines and the scope of that immunity for sunken submarines. These issues are the focus of this chapter.

A primary site of regulation on questions of navigational safety is the International Maritime Organization (IMO). Acting under the auspices of the IMO, States have adopted treaties and other international instruments addressing diverse facets of navigational safety. For example, the International Code of Signals (INTERCO), which has been developed through the Maritime Safety Committee of the IMO, sets out an internationally accepted, common system for communication at sea. Some of the IMO treaties pre-dated the UN Convention on the Law of the Sea (UNCLOS)[12] and have been updated following the adoption and entry into force of UNCLOS. The INTERCO falls into this category because it was adopted in 1965 and has since been updated.[13] The amendment procedure at the IMO allows for technological advancements to be incorporated into the rules and permits engagement with and feedback from key industry and government stakeholders as to what international standards best promote maritime safety and security.[14]

11 Tingle (n 1) 37.

12 United Nations Convention on the Law of the Sea, Montego Bay, 10 December 1982, entered into force 16 November 1994, 1833 UNTS 397 ('UNCLOS').

13 Substantive updates have occurred on four occasions. For the most recent version, see International Maritime Organization, *International Code of Signals* (4th rev. ed., IMO, 2021) ('INTERCO').

14 The IMO typically allows for a 'tacit acceptance' procedure, which allows for amendments to come into force automatically for all States party to the amended treaty after a designated period of time, unless a certain number of States have expressly objected to the amendment: see International Maritime Organization, 'Conventions' <www.imo.org/en/About/Conventions/Pages/Default.aspx>.

The requirements laid out in these IMO treaties are incorporated into UNCLOS through rules of reference.[15] Notably, Article 94 of UNCLOS, which sets out the duties of flag States, requires every State to take measures to ensure safety at sea.[16] Navigational safety obligations include requirements for steering and sailing, which also relate to safe speeds, avoiding collisions and navigating too near other vessels, as well as the lights and sound signals that are required and used on a vessel. These core international rules are set out in the International Regulations for Preventing Collisions at Sea (COLREGs) and cover over 98 per cent of the world's shipping tonnage.[17] The COLREGs reflect 'generally agreed international rules and standards' for the purposes of UNCLOS provisions on navigational safety.[18] As such, even when a State is not a party to the COLREGs, if the State is a party to UNCLOS, it is also bound by the COLREGs because of the rules of reference in UNCLOS.[19] The COLREGs and other navigational safety rules, which were developed with surface vessels in mind, are explored in Section 11.2 below and focus particularly on collision avoidance for submerged vessels.

Despite the requirements of navigational safety, accidents involving submarines have nonetheless occurred, necessitating the rescue of the boat and its crew. 'One study of 60 years (1946–2005) of submarine accidents which led to the vessels being sunk or significantly damaged found that the "greatest source of loss for submarines was a flood (21%) followed closely by collision (18%)".'[20] Explosions and fires are the other main causes of damage to submarines. While difficult to be definitive, there have been several dozen incidents involving submarines since the year 2000.[21] Section 11.3 examines the obligations to render assistance

[15] Rules of reference are provisions of UNCLOS that require the parties to take into account or give effect to rules and standards set out in other international agreements, regardless of whether the parties to UNCLOS are also parties to those other international agreements.

[16] UNCLOS (n 12) art. 94(3).

[17] Convention on the International Regulations for Preventing Collisions at Sea, London, 20 October 1972, entered into force 15 July 1977, 1050 UNTS 16 ('COLREGs').

[18] This position was reflected in the *South China Sea* arbitration: *South China Sea Arbitration* (Philippines v. China) (Award of 12 July 2016) PCA Case No. 2013–19, para. 1083.

[19] Ibid.

[20] Zia Mian, M. V. Ramana and Abdul H. Nayyara, 'Nuclear Submarines in South Asia: New Risks and Dangers' (2019) 2(1) *Journal for Peace and Nuclear Disarmament* 184, 189 (citing Tingle's 2009 study).

[21] Lists of submarine accidents have been compiled by various authors. See, e.g., Hans Liwång, 'The Interconnectedness between Efforts to Reduce the Risk Related to

and the duty to rescue those in distress. These obligations are set out in UNCLOS,[22] and elaborated upon in the Safety of Life at Sea Convention (SOLAS)[23] and the Search and Rescue Convention (SAR Convention).[24]

When a submarine has sunk, an initial question concerns whether the wreck is a hazard and requires removal. A further consideration in this instance may be the applicability of the law of salvage. Briefly stated, the law of salvage concerns the rescue of a ship and its cargo and consequent entitlement to remuneration for that effort. Salvage is not, however, available in relation to State-owned vessels and prompts a question as to the extent of immunities enjoyed by sunken military submarines. Where wrecks have been on the seabed for many decades, they may constitute underwater cultural heritage (UCH). The 2001 Convention on the Protection of Underwater Heritage (2001 UNESCO Convention) sets out when a wreck may be considered as UCH and what rights and duties apply to States party depending on where the wreck is located.[25] Again, the sovereign immunity of a submarine may hold implications for the protection of a submarine wreck as UCH. Environmental risks may also emerge with a sunken submarine, especially for submarines with nuclear reactors on board. These concerns and the applicable rules of international environmental law are addressed in Chapter 12.[26] Section 11.4 of this chapter is

Accidents and Attacks: Naval Examples' (2020) 13 *Journal of Transportation Security* 245, 268 for a list of identified submarine incidents between 2000 and 2015. See also Handan Tanyildizi-Kökkülünk, Görkem Kökkülünk and John Settles, 'Probabilistic Risk Framework for Nuclear- and Fossil-Powered Vessels: Analyzing Casualty Event Severity and Sub-Causes' (2025) 13 *Journal of Marine Science and Engineering* 1, 16 which provides a list of accidents involving nuclear-powered vessels between 1960 and 2024, most of which are submarines. While not renowned as a scholarly source, a list of submarine accidents has been compiled on Wikipedia: 'List of Submarine and Submersible Incidents Since 2000', *Wikipedia* <https://en.wikipedia.org/wiki/List_of_submarine_and_submersible_incidents_since_2000>.

22 UNCLOS (n 12) art. 98.

23 International Convention for the Safety of Life at Sea, London, 1 November 1974, entered into force 25 May 1980, 1184 UNTS 1 ('SOLAS Convention').

24 International Convention on Maritime Search and Rescue, Hamburg, 27 April 1979, entered into force 22 June 1985, 1184 UNTS 278 ('SAR Convention').

25 Convention on the Protection of the Underwater Cultural Heritage, Paris, 2 November 2001, entered into force 2 January 2009, 2562 UNTS 3 ('2001 UNESCO Convention').

26 In relation to nuclear submarine accidents up until 2005, Tingle observed that 'nuclear accidents have not dominated the accident record, a testament to the scale of safe design, built-in redundancy, and operational effectiveness stemming from a near-zero tolerance of such incidents': Tingle (n 1) 37.

more focused on the rights and duties for retrieving a submarine or parts thereof, or its treatment when it has sunk and rests on the seabed.

This chapter demonstrates that the submerged passage of submarines does give rise to distinct issues in collision avoidance. However, once a submarine has sunk, the existing international law framework largely does not raise special questions for submarines. Instead, it is nonetheless notable for enduring questions as to the applicable international law, especially in relation to sunken warships.

11.2 Navigational Safety

The COLREGs are considered the 'rules of the road' for the oceans and provide detailed rules to avoid collisions, developed from traditional principles of 'good seamanship'.[27] The COLREGs have also been affirmed in bilateral treaties that govern incidents at sea, most notably the Incidents at Sea Agreement between the United States and then Soviet Union.[28] Aspects of the COLREGs have further been adopted into non-legally binding instruments as a way to better manage interactions between navies in different maritime areas. China and the United States have adopted a bilateral Memorandum of Understanding that incorporates key elements of the COLREGs[29] and navies of the Western Pacific adopted the Code for Unplanned Encounters at Sea (CUES).[30] The Association of Southeast Asian Nations (ASEAN) and China also adopted the CUES to apply in the South China Sea.[31] The acceptance of the COLREGs is thus manifest as a general matter, but

[27] For a discussion on the evolution of the 'rules of the road', see Alfredo C. Robles Jr, *Vessel Collisions in the Law of the Sea: The South China Sea Arbitration* (Springer, 2022) 43–47.

[28] Agreement between the Government of the United States of America and the Government of the Union of Soviet Socialist Republics on the Prevention of Incidents on and over the High Seas, Moscow, 25 May 1972, entered into force 25 May 1972, 852 UNTS 151.

[29] Memorandum of Understanding between the Department of Defense of the United States of America and the Ministry of National Defense of the People's Republic of China Regarding the Rules of Behavior for Safety of Air and Maritime Encounters, Washington and Beijing, 10 November 2014.

[30] Western Pacific Naval Symposium, 'Code for Unplanned Encounters at Sea: Version 1.0', 22 April 2014 <www.ions.global/sites/default/files/CUES-10-Approvedat-the-14th-WPNS-2014422.pdf>.

[31] Joint Statement on the Application of the Code for Unplanned Encounters at Sea in the South China Sea, Vientiane, 7 September 2016 <https://asean.org/wp-content/uploads/2016/09/Joint-Statement-on-the-Application-of-CUES-in-the-SCS-Final.pdf>.

determining their applicability to submarine operations may prompt questions given the absence of rules explicitly addressing submerged operations.

The COLREGs 'apply to all vessels upon the high seas and in all waters connected therewith navigable by seagoing vessels'.[32] The scope of the rules thereby encompasses both State-owned submarines and private submarines operating in areas both under and beyond national jurisdiction.[33] The term 'vessels' is also defined broadly in the COLREGs to include 'every description of water craft . . . used or capable of being used as a means of transportation on water'.[34] Possibly excluded from this definition may be small, uncrewed submersibles that are operated for research or commercial purposes and may not be considered as a 'means of transportation'.[35] Their size and scale of operation may mean that their operation does not typically jeopardise navigational safety and the COLREGs are more likely applicable to any parent ship that deploys these craft.

There may be instances where submarines, due to their particular characteristics, may be able to deviate from the specific requirements of the COLREGs so as to avoid immediate danger.[36] However, where submarines are submerged and have the benefit of periscopes and radars to detect other maritime traffic, it is the submarine that must take steps to avoid collisions with other vessels, especially when surfacing.[37] Surfacing has been considered a dangerous manoeuvre as a general matter,[38] with the danger

32 COLREGs (n 17) r. 1(a).

33 Robin Churchill, Vaughan Lowe and Amy Sander, *The Law of the Sea* (4th ed., Manchester University Press, 2022) 501. Plant doubted the applicability of the COLREGs to submerged submarines but only on the basis that it was difficult to conceive of the rules applying across three planes: Glent Plant, 'The Collision Avoidance Regulations as a Regulator of International Navigation Rights: Underlying Principles and their Adequacy for the Twenty-first Century' (1996) 49(3) *Journal of Navigation* 377, 382 and n 59.

34 COLREGs (n 17) r. 3(a). Warships and other government-owned vessels are clearly within the scope of COLREGs, especially when regard is had to the inclusion of specific rules regulating their operations (such as Rule 1(c) and Rule 3(g)): Robles (n 27) 61–62.

35 See further Chapter 14, Section 14.2.

36 COLREGs (n 17) r. 2(b).

37 John Paul Jones, 'Marine Collisions in the Vertical: Submarines Surfacing' (2002) *Military Law News* 1, citing *Woodbury v. United States*, 75 F. Supp. 829 (D. Mass. 1948), vacated and remanded, 175 F.2d 854 (1st Cir. 1949).

38 The danger is due to the fact that obstacles above the submarine can be hard to detect. Ice is particularly difficult for sonars to hear: David Adam, 'Why Do Our Submarines Keep Bumping into Things', *The Guardian*, 29 May 2003 <www.theguardian.com/science/2003/may/29/thisweekssciencequestions3>. In 2015, HMS *Talent* sustained significant damage after colliding with floating ice despite being equipped with advanced sonar

intensifying for other vessels when a submarine surfaces in an emergency and hence with less control over speed and steering.[39] The latter situation occurred when USS *Greeneville*, a nuclear submarine, collided with the *Ehime Maru* in waters off Hawai'i in 2001, causing nine deaths on the Japanese fishing and training vessel.[40] The US Navy's court of inquiry that subsequently investigated the incident determined that '[h]ad *Greeneville's* CO and crew been practicing the basic tenants [sic] of ORM [Operational Risk Management], the collision may have been avoided'.[41] The relevant crew members of USS *Greeneville* were subject to disciplinary proceedings,[42] a suite of changes was introduced to submarine operations,[43] and the US Navy paid compensation to the Japanese prefecture of the vessel, as well as to the families of the victims of the accident.[44]

Underlying the key requirements of navigational safety is the concept of 'good seamanship', which reflects the practice of masters of ships and is said to have a residual application either where the COLREGs leave a gap or otherwise inform the interpretation and application of the rules.[45] Core requirements for navigational safety include maintaining look-out,[46] operating at a safe speed so as to avoid collision,[47] using all available means to determine if there is a risk of collision,[48] and taking action to avoid collision.[49] Actions to reduce the likelihood of collision include changing course or reducing speed and acting 'with due regard to the observance of good seamanship'.[50] The COLREGs further provide rules to be followed when vessels are navigating in a narrow channel or

systems: see Maya Carlin, '6 Foot "Hole": A Nuclear Submarine was "Severely Damaged" Tracking Russian Ships', *The National Interest*, 18 October 2024 <https://nationalinterest.org/blog/buzz/6-foot-hole-nuclear-submarine-was-severely-damaged-tracking-russian-ships-213187>.

[39] Jones (n 37) citing *Brodosplas v. United States*, 1975 AMC 117 (S.D.N.Y. 1975).

[40] US National Transportation Safety Board, *Marine Accident Brief*, 29 September 2005 (Doc. NTSB/MAB-05/01) <www.ntsb.gov/investigations/AccidentReports/Reports/MAB0501.pdf> 24.

[41] Ibid, 40.

[42] Ibid, 35.

[43] Ibid, 36–41.

[44] Howard W. French, 'Japanese Accept US Offer in Ship Accident', *New York Times*, 15 November 2022 <www.nytimes.com/2002/11/15/world/japanese-accept-us-offer-in-ship-accident.html>.

[45] Plant (n 33) 377.

[46] COLREGs (n 17) r. 5.

[47] Ibid, r. 6.

[48] Ibid, r. 7(a).

[49] Ibid, r. 8.

[50] Ibid, r. 8.

through traffic separation schemes, indicating which surface vessels may have priority in any given situation as well as the steps for overtaking a vessel or otherwise progressing through such waters.[51]

The COLREGs provide the requirements for vessel responses when there is a risk of head-on collision,[52] when vessels are crossing in front of each other,[53] and the responsibilities of each vessel as either the vessel passing or the one being passed.[54] Jones refers to the relative relationship of vessels as being either burdened or privileged, and that the 'burdened vessel is always obliged to maneuver so as to avoid a privileged vessel, and failure of avoidance generally leaves the burdened vessel at least partially, if not exclusively, at fault and liable for the damages ensuing'.[55] Operating submerged, submarines are the 'burdened' vessel and are responsible for avoiding collisions with surface vessels. This paradigm is evident in the 2016 collision of HMS *Ambush* with a Panamanian merchant ship during a training exercise in the Strait of Gibraltar.[56] The collision occurred when HMS *Ambush* attempted to surface.[57] The commander in charge of the submarine was found responsible for the error in not keeping sufficient watch during the training exercise.[58]

Additionally, to further reduce the risk of accidents at sea, there are requirements as to the display of lights,[59] or sounding of whistles, bells or gongs, to signal what action a vessel is planning to take.[60] Submarines

[51] Ibid, rr. 9, 10, addressing, respectively, narrow channels and traffic separation schemes.

[52] Ibid, r. 14. In this situation, each vessel is to alter course to starboard to pass each other on the port side: ibid, r. 14(a).

[53] Ibid, r. 15.

[54] Ibid, rr. 16, 17.

[55] Jones (n 37). See also Plant (n 33) 381 (discussing consequences of privileged vessels in navigation).

[56] Royal Navy, 'Royal Navy Statement: 20 July 2016' (Media Release, 20 July 2016) <www.gov.uk/government/news/royal-navy-statement-20-july-2016>.

[57] Sam LaGrone, 'U.K. Nuclear Submarine HMS Ambush Collides with Merchant Vessel', *USNI News*, 20 July 2016 <https://news.usni.org/2016/07/20/u-k-nuclear-submarine-hms-ambush-collides-merchant-vessel>.

[58] 'Nuclear Submarine Commander "Took Eye Off Ball" before Collision', *The Guardian*, 15 February 2018 <www.theguardian.com/uk-news/2018/feb/15/nuclear-submarine-commander-admits-hazarding-ship-after-collision>.

[59] See COLREGs (n 17) r. 23. An amber flashing light may be used by submarines as an aid to identification, in addition to other navigation lights. See A. N. Cockcroft and J. N. F. Lameijer, *A Guide to the Collision Avoidance Rules: International Regulations for Preventing Collisions at Sea* (7th ed., Elsevier, 2012) 110.

[60] COLREGs (n 17) r. 34. Annex I of the COLREGs contains more technical requirements, including in relation to 'vessels engaged in underwater operations': COLREGs (n 17) annex I, s. 4.

should normally signal when they are surfacing in an emergency.[61] The INTERCO provides the relevant codes to indicate if there has been a collision with a submarine,[62] or that submarines are operating in the area and other vessels should proceed with caution.[63] Although a submarine can signal that it is involved in survey work in accordance with the INTERCO, the COLREGs still apply to its operations.[64] Even submersibles involved in diving operations are required to have specific lights and shapes that are applicable between sunset and sunrise.[65] There have, however, been concerns raised that aspects of the COLREGs relating to lights, shapes and sound signals are inadequate or outdated.[66]

There have been at least nine collisions involving submarines reported since 2000, with collisions occurring underwater between two submarines or otherwise between a submarine and a surface vessel. For example, in 2020, a Norwegian car carrier, *Hoegh London*, collided with a submerged South Korean Navy submarine.[67] In some instances, it is not immediately known that a submarine has collided with another vessel or whether it has hit an inanimate object. For example, USS *Oklahoma City* collided with a Norwegian liquefied natural gas tanker, *Norman Lady*, in 2002 when surfacing,[68] but the precise vessels involved were only determined in the days following the incidents in light of the respective damage reports.[69]

[61] Under an Australian notice to mariners, red pyro flames are used to indicate an emergency surfacing procedure with the intention that all vessels should clear the area but stand by in case assistance is needed: see Australian Hydrographic Office, 'Information Concerning Submarines' (Notice to Mariners 612/2014).

[62] INTERCO (n 13) code HW 2.

[63] Ibid, code NE 2. Code NE6 indicates that a hostile submarine has been sighted.

[64] Ibid, code IR.

[65] COLREGs (n 17) rr. 20, 27(d), 27(e), 27(g).

[66] See Wenhai Dong, Jie Li and Xinghua Tu, 'A Study on the Development and Trend of COLREGs: A Broader Perspective' (2023) 76(4–5) *Journal of Navigation* 577, 584–585.

[67] 'Norwegian Car Carrier Collided with Korean Submarine', *Maritime News* <www.fleetmon.com/maritime-news/2020/30285/norwegian-car-carrier-collided-korean-submarine/>; Changeun Ji, 'Analysis of Submarine-Civilian Vessel Collision Cases and Investigation of Collision Avoidance Technology' (2024) 25(5) *Journal of the Korea Academia-Industrial Cooperation Society* 99, 101–102.

[68] Harrison Kass, 'A US Nuclear Attack Submarine Crashed Into an Oil Tanker', *The National Interest*, 3 October 2024, <https://nationalinterest.org/blog/buzz/us-nuclear-attack-submarine-crashed-oil-tanker-211432>; Lesley A. Whyborn et al., 'A Critical Review of Casualties from Non-Combat Submarine Incidents and Current US Navy Medical Response Capability with Specific Focus on the Application of Prolonged Field Care to Disabled Submarine Survival and Rescue', *Naval Submarine Medical Research Laboratory*, 16 April 2019, B-3.

[69] 'Nuclear Sub "Collides" with Tanker', *CNN*, 15 November 2002 <https://edition.cnn.com/2002/WORLD/europe/11/15/norway.tanker/>. Similarly, a collision between

Submarines operating on the surface must adhere to the COLREGs in line with other surface vessels. USS *Philadelphia* collided with a Turkish merchant ship during surface operations in 2005 when it was located 30 miles from the Bahraini coast.[70] A US veteran involved in the incident described the situation as follows:

> We were doing a surface transit at night into Bahrain and a Turkish merchant ship was mistaken for a stationary rig. By the time the ship's control party finally realized that it was in fact a ship, it had turned and was headed on a course straight at us. We were not running sub ID lighting due to security concerns in the area we were operating. The merchant thought we were going to give way and ended up running over us. The merchant got stuck on top of the sub and our fairwater plane put a huge gash down their side just above the water line.[71]

While the submarine was not operating its lights, a further problem appears to have been that the surfaced submarine did not show on the freighter's radar until it was too late to avoid the collision.[72] Although the damage to each vessel was minimal, the submarine commander was relieved of duty.[73]

More complicated under the COLREGs is when a submarine is submerged and risks collision with a surface vessel. USS *Newport News* collided with a Japanese supertanker, *Mogamigawa*, in 2007 while transiting the Strait of Hormuz. The submarine was submerged at the time and hit the stern of the *Mogamigawa* with its bow.[74] The US Navy

British and French nuclear submarines in 2009 was only determined when reports of damage from each Navy were compared: Sebastien Roblin, 'The Nightmare Scenario: 2 NATO Submarines Packed with Nuclear Weapons Slammed Into Each Other', *The National Interest*, 29 September 2024 <https://nationalinterest.org/blog/the-buzz/2009-two-nuclear-submarines-collided-under-the-sea-they-were-18690>.

70 AFP, 'US Submarine Collides with Cargo Ship', *Al Jazeera*, 5 September 2005 <www.aljazeera.com/news/2005/9/5/us-submarine-collides-with-cargo-ship>.

71 Z. Smith, 'USS Philadelphia (SSN-690) Collision in 2005', *US Militaria* Forum, 1 September 2016 <www.usmilitariaforum.com/forums/index.php?/topic/274358-uss-philadelphia-ssn-690-collision-in-2005/>. See also Lyle Goldstein and William Murray, 'International Submarine Rescue: A Constructive Role for China?' (2008) 5 *Asia Policy* 167, 171.

72 'Submarines: Details of a Collision in the Persian Gulf', *Strategy Page*, 3 October 2005 <www.strategypage.com/htmw/htsub/articles/20051003.aspx>.

73 US Navy, 'USS Philadelphia Command Operations Report', 17 October 2006 <www.history.navy.mil/content/dam/nhhc/research/archives/command-operation-reports/ship-command-operation-reports/p/philadelphia-ssn-690-vi/pdf/2005.pdf> 5.

74 'Sub Accident: How Could This Happen?', *ABC News*, 10 January 2007 <https://abcnews.go.com/Technology/story?id=2781756&page=1>.

reportedly paid the ship owners compensation for the collision.[75] In the collision between USS *Newport News* and the *Mogamigawa*, it appears that the submarine did not pass under the supertanker at sufficient depth. The depth maintained by a submarine is important to avoid the so-called venturi effect, which is a 'partial vacuum . . . created as the water passing under the ship changes velocity and pressure', and can cause a submarine to be sucked up into the hull of the vessel.[76] Moreover, submarines may not be using radar equipment and have passive sonar in operation when submerged so as to avoid detection; which also makes it easier for a collision to occur as another ship is unaware of the submarine's presence.[77]

Submerged passage in a narrow, busy strait may be difficult when the submarine has to be sufficiently deep to avoid ships passing overhead but not so deep as to hit the seafloor. For example, two US warships, one a submarine and the other an amphibious ship, collided in the Strait of Hormuz in 2009. The nuclear-powered submarine was submerged at the time, and a subsequent investigation revealed the submarine to be at fault because of 'personnel failures'.[78] In these types of maritime areas, further consideration is needed as to the applicability of routeing measures, either to confine submerged submarines to the deepest areas or as a means of a submerged submarine knowing where not to voyage given the likely presence of many surface vessels navigating along a particular route.

Reported collisions between submerged submarines are infrequent but do occur. While operating submerged, the key submarine strategy is to be undetected. This strategy is especially true in relation to ballistic submarines that are intended to have a second-strike capability in the event of a nuclear attack. To remain undetectable, submarines will operate passive sonar so that they can listen to the surrounding area, rather than active

[75] 'SSN 750 – USS Newport News', *Seaforces Online: Naval Information* <www.seaforces.org/usnships/ssn/SSN-750-USS-Newport-News.htm>.

[76] Sam Bateman, 'Perils of the Deep: The Dangers of Submarine Operations in Asia', *RSIS Commentaries*, 21 February 2007 <www.rsis.edu.sg/rsis-publication/idss/895-perils-of-the-deep-the-danger/>. See also 'SSN 750 – USS Newport News', *Seaforces Online: Naval Information* <www.seaforces.org/usnships/ssn/SSN-750-USS-Newport-News.htm>.

[77] 'Sub Accident: How Could This Happen?', *ABC News*, 10 January 2007 <https://abcnews.go.com/Technology/story?id=2781756&page=1>.

[78] Ben Werner, 'Navy Punishes Negligence at Sea But Rarely Secures Criminal Convictions', *US Naval Institute News*, 25 January 2023 <https://news.usni.org/2018/01/22/30725>; Grace V. Jean, 'Submariners Going "Back to Basics"' (2010) 94(674) *National Defense* 26, 26.

sonar, which may provide more information to the submarine but also increase the likelihood of the submarine being detected. It has been suggested that French and British nuclear submarines collided in 2009 because both were using passive sonar at the time and were thus unable to detect the other.[79] While NATO members are to advise each other of the location of submerged submarines as part of 'water space management' agreements, ballistic submarines are excluded from these notices.[80]

NATO has adopted 'water space management', which is intended to allocate space to facilitate differentiation between allied and enemy submarines,[81] as well as 'prevention of mutual interference' in relation to areas of operation.[82] More specifically, water space management 'is a set of operating areas and attack rules specifically defined for submarine and Anti-Submarine Warfare (ASW) assets'.[83] To coordinate, NATO allies use a regional Submarine Operating Authority (SUBOPAUTH) to ensure no overlap of submarine operations and is a 'de-confliction agency for underwater movements'.[84] As a risk management approach, the SUBOPAUTH can advise re-routing of submarines or changing the time and/or the space required for an activity.[85] The United States also utilises risk management during its military exercises, albeit with occasional failures. In 2012, two US warships, USS *Montpelier* and USS *San Jacinto*, collided off the coast of Florida during an anti-submarine warfare exercise. USS *Montpelier* ascended to periscope depth immediately in front of USS *San Jacinto* and the vessel was unable to avoid striking the submarine. A subsequent investigation determined that USS *Montpelier* had not followed basic procedures designed to ensure ship safety in operating at that depth.[86]

79 Roblin (n 69).

80 John F. Burns, 'French and British Subs Collide', *New York Times*, 17 February 2009 <www.nytimes.com/2009/02/17/world/europe/17submarine.html>.

81 NATO, IFB-CO-13859-TRITON, Amd.2 <www.gdaee.mil.gr/wp-content/uploads/2021/09/4_2.pdf> 188.

82 Ibid, 188–191. Prevention of mutual interference 'provides the authorised user to avoid the risk of submerged interference between friendly submarines, between submarines and friendly ship-towed bodies or between submarines and any other underwater or surface objects': ibid, 193.

83 Ibid, 194.

84 Chris Walter, 'The Prevention of Mutual Interference Within the Subsea Littoral: The Need for a Co-operative Approach with Non-military Users', *Hydro International*, 2 November 2010 <www.hydro-international.com/content/article/the-prevention-of-mutual-interference-within-the-subsea-littoral>.

85 Ibid.

86 US Department of Navy, 'Command Investigation into the Collision Involving USS San Jacinto (CG 56) and USS Montpelier (SSN 765)', 3 January 2013 <https://media.defense

Moreover, the operational risk management had been flawed in failing to plan for hazards and to mitigate for those risks.[87]

Several commentators have indicated that there is a need for an international authority, either multilateral or regional, to better coordinate the movement of submarines.[88] Such an organisation could also assist in managing private submarine uses, including underwater maritime autonomous vehicles that may be deployed for research purposes, and that operate in the same spaces as military submarines.[89] The International Civil Aviation Organization has a role in managing different airspace use and a comparable system could be developed for underwater space use.[90]

Bateman has proposed several practical steps that could be implemented on a regional basis, as follows:

> Those might include regional protocols for dealing with unidentified submarines detected in the territorial sea, including the procedures to be followed and the signals to be used. Such protocols might include an agreement that in normal circumstances, the submarine shouldn't be attacked with potentially lethal force. Government to government 'hotlines' between national submarine operating authorities to deal specifically with submarine incidents might also be considered.[91]

In line with Bateman's comment on the use of protocols, it may be noted that the United States and Russia entered into an additional agreement for signalling in relation to the operation of naval vessels, as a supplement to INTERCO. These additional signals include indications that submarines are planning to surface and other vessels are requested to stay clear, as well as warning signals to foreign submarines that are submerged in national waters.[92] There is a clear need for specific rules to be in place to better manage navigational safety in the operation of submarines, especially when submerged and surfacing. Improving the use of signals is an

.gov/2020/Jun/06/2002311740/-1/-1/1/MONTPELIER-SANJACINTO-INVRESRPT.PDF> 6, para. 1.

87 Ibid, 10.

88 Bateman for example, proposed a regional submarine Movement Advisory Authority: Sam Bateman, 'The Perils of Submarine Operations', *ASPI The Strategist*, 10 April 2014 <www.aspistrategist.org.au/the-perils-of-submarine-operations-2/>.

89 Walter (n 84).

90 Ibid.

91 Bateman (n 88).

92 'US/Russia Supplementary Signals for Naval Vessels' in National Geospatial Intelligence Agency, *International Code of Signals for Visual, Sound and Radio Communications: United States Edition* (Lighthouse Press, 1969 ed., 2005).

important first step but clearer identification of what vessels are burdened or impeded in the application of the COLREGs would also be beneficial.

11.3 Search and Rescue

While submarines have collided with other submarines and surface vessels, submarines have also collided with stationary objects, such as seamounts,[93] ice[94] and sunken oil rig platforms,[95] resulting in damage. Further, accidents due to equipment failure or damage have occurred on submarines resulting in floods, fires or the release of poisonous gases, and imperilling the lives of the crew on board. For example, in 2003, the Chinese submarine *No. 361* was believed to have suffered a mechanical failure that killed all seventy crew on board.[96]

When a vessel is in distress,[97] the COLREGs set out the required signals to indicate distress and the need for assistance.[98] The master of a ship has a duty 'to render assistance to any person found at sea in danger of being lost',[99] and such assistance should be rendered to another ship and its crew following a collision.[100] If submarines are involved in a collision, there are thus requirements under international law to provide assistance. Obligations to render assistance to vessels and crew in distress are not

[93] USS *San Francisco* struck a seamount south of Guam in 2005: Sam Bateman, 'Perils of the Deep: The Dangers of Submarine Operations in Asia', *RSIS Commentaries*, 21 February 2007 <www.rsis.edu.sg/rsis-publication/idss/895-perils-of-the-deep-the-danger/>.

[94] Carlin (n 36) (also noting that the Royal Navy had claimed that submarines struck ice when they had instead collided with Soviet submarines during the Cold War).

[95] In 2021, it was reported that USS *Connecticut* collided with an abandoned oil rig: Kristin Huang, 'US Nuclear Sub "May Have Hit an Oil Rig" in South China Sea', *South China Morning Post*, 13 November 2021 <www.scmp.com/news/china/military/article/3155777/us-nuclear-sub-may-have-hit-oil-rig-south-china-sea>. However, a US investigation indicated that the collision occurred against an uncharted seamount: Sam LaGrone, 'Investigation Concludes USS Connecticut Grounded on Uncharted Seamount in South China Sea', *USNI News*, 1 November 2021 <https://news.usni.org/2021/11/01/investigation-concludes-uss-connecticut-grounded-on-uncharted-seamount-in-south-china-sea>.

[96] John Pomfret, 'Chinese Submarine Accident Kills 70', *Washington Post*, 2 May 2003 <www.washingtonpost.com/archive/politics/2003/05/03/chinese-submarine-accident-kills-70/755b8587-e1b2-4eba-a1fc-e88e4eb9c016/>.

[97] A distress phase for search and rescue emerges when a person or vessel is in danger and in immediate need of assistance. SAR Convention (n 24) art. 4.4.3.1.

[98] COLREGs (n 17) r. 37 and annex IV.

[99] UNCLOS (n 12) art. 98(1)(a).

[100] Ibid, art. 98(1)(c).

absolute, however, but depend on whether the assistance is within the capability of the vessel as assessed by the master of that vessel.[101] The design of a submarine may mean that it does not have the capacity to undertake rescues at sea.[102] A rescue involves providing medical and other assistance as may be needed and delivering people rescued to a place of safety.[103]

Rather than submarines being involved in a rescue operation, it may instead be the case that a mishap aboard a submarine necessitates a rescue of the submarine. Following the sinking of USS *Thresher* in 1963, the US Navy recommended developing a submarine rescue system from collapse depth, a deep-ocean search system with investigation and recovery capability to 20,000 feet, and a 'man-in-the-sea program with 600 foot operations for long duration'.[104] Notable among these proposals was the need to develop deep-sea submersibles that could be used in the context of providing assistance and / or surveying wrecks.[105] The Russian *Mir* submersibles were deployed to support Russia's remediation efforts for a sunken nuclear submarine.[106] Several navies have developed portable rescue capabilities, which may include remotely operated vehicles (ROVs) and submersibles being deployed to develop rescue strategies and potentially serving as escape craft to bring submariners to the surface.[107]

In recent years, Indonesia[108] and Argentina[109] have engaged in search and rescue operations following the disappearance of their submarines. The Indonesian submarine KRI *Nanggala-402* went missing during a training exercise in April 2021, prompting a rescue operation involving Indonesia, Australia and Singapore.[110] ARA *San Juan* went missing in

[101] Ibid, arts. 98(1), 98(1)(b).

[102] This issue has arisen under the law of armed conflict as well. See Chapter 10, Section 10.5.2.3.

[103] SAR Convention (n 24) art. 1.3.2.

[104] William Kohnen, 'Human Exploration of the Deep Seas: Fifty Years and the Inspiration Continues' (2009) 43(5) *Marine Technology Society Journal* 42, 53.

[105] Ibid.

[106] Ibid, 61.

[107] For discussion on the different rescue modalities deployed currently and historically, see Nick Stewart, 'Submarine Escape and Rescue: A Brief History', *Sea Power Centre* <https://seapower.navy.gov.au/history/feature-histories/submarine-escape-and-rescue-brief-history>.

[108] 'Indonesian Navy Submarine Found Split into Three on Sea Bed', *BBC News*, 25 April 2021 <www.bbc.com/news/world-asia-56879933>.

[109] 'Argentina Submarine: ARA San Juan Found', *BBC News*, 17 November 2018 <www.bbc.com/news/world-latin-america-46245686>.

[110] Associated Press, 'Indonesian Navy Submarine Goes Missing with 53 People Onboard', *The Guardian*, 22 April 2021 <www.theguardian.com/world/2021/apr/21/indonesian-navy-submarine-missing-bali-kri-nanggala>.

the Atlantic Ocean in November 2017, which prompted a rescue operation involving twenty-eight ships and nine airplanes from eleven countries.[111] The Argentine submarine was located a year later by a US company contracted by the Argentine government to search for the wreck.[112] A Russian nuclear-powered submarine, *Kursk K-141*, sank following two explosions in 2000 in the Barents Sea. Although some crew members initially survived, the Russian search and rescue mission was unable to save them.[113]

The disappearance of private submarines may also prompt search and rescue missions. In 2023, the disappearance of OceanGate's *Titan* submersible en route to visit the wreckage of the *Titanic* gave rise to an extensive search and rescue operation. Around ten vessels were engaged in the search and rescue operation for the five-person submersible, including vessels with ROVs that could be deployed to search deep underwater for the missing submersible as well as the release of sonar buoys to detect sound and movement in deep ocean.[114] While the equipment needs may be distinct when managing responses to distressed submarines, the legal framework remains essentially the same.

Beyond reflecting the customary international law duty to render assistance to vessels and crew in distress, UNCLOS also imposes an obligation on coastal States to 'promote the establishment, operation and maintenance of an adequate and effective search and rescue

111 Laura Smith-Spark et al., 'Argentina's Missing Submarine Found a Year after it Vanished with 44 Aboard', *CNN*, 17 November 2018 <https://edition.cnn.com/2018/11/17/americas/argentina-missing-submarine-found-intl/index.html>. The United States reportedly deployed underwater maritime autonomous vehicles as part of the search effort: Sanjeet Ruhal, 'The Evolving Seascape of Naval Warfare: Unmanned Underwater Vehicles and the Challenges for International Law' (2024) *Journal of Conflict and Security Law* 1, 4 (referring to US Department of Defense news release).

112 Smith-Spark et al. (n 111).

113 For a general overview, see George Sviatov, 'The Kursk's Loss Offers Lessons' (2003) 129(6) *US Naval Institute Proceedings* 1204. There was controversy over Russia's handling of the search and rescue operation, with initial refusals of assistance from other states. Norwegian divers were able to open the hatch but the remaining crew members had died. See Ingar Amundsen et al., 'The Kursk Accident' (Strålevern Rapport No. 5, Norwegian Radiation Protection Authority, 2001) 7–8 <https://dsa.no/en/publications/stralevernrapport-the-kursk-accident/straalevernrapport-2001-5-the-kursk-accident.pdf>.

114 'The Search for the Missing Titanic Sub in Maps and Graphics', *BBC News*, 23 June 2023 <www.bbc.com/news/world-us-canada-65965665>. For a detailed account of the rescue effort and the resources brought to bear, see Willem Marx, 'Inside the Titan Sub Recovery: A Hopeful Rescue Turned Tragic Mission', *Vanity Fair*, 18 June 2024 <www.vanityfair.com/news/story/inside-titan-titanic-recovery>.

service'.[115] The details of this obligation have been set out in the SOLAS Convention[116] and the Search and Rescue Convention.[117] In accordance with the SAR Convention, the IMO's Maritime Safety Committee divided ocean spaces into thirteen SAR areas, and in these areas, States have established search and rescue regions, which may be aligned differently to their juridical maritime zones.[118] Search and rescue regions are to be notified to the IMO, and there are instances where the search and rescue regions of coastal States overlap.[119]

For each State that has declared a search and rescue region, it must provide search and rescue services in accordance with the requirements set out in the SAR Convention.[120] Search and rescue services may entail responding to distress calls, locating nearby vessels to proceed to the vessel in need of assistance and coordinating rescue efforts.[121] A rescue operation for a submarine may involve the deployment of uncrewed submersibles to scan the ocean floor and, when a sunken submarine is located, a submarine rescue chamber may be used to retrieve crew members.[122] States party to the SAR Convention are required to coordinate their search and rescue organisations,[123] but are not required to accept assistance from other rescue coordination centres.[124] NATO has developed an International Submarine Escape and Rescue Liaison Office, which aims to facilitate and coordinate assistance to distressed submarines.[125] Although established by NATO, the Office is intended

[115] UNCLOS (n 12) art. 98(2).

[116] SOLAS Convention (n 23).

[117] SAR Convention (n 24).

[118] International Maritime Organization, 'International Convention on Maritime Search and Rescue (SAR)' <www.imo.org/en/about/Conventions/Pages/International-Convention-on-Maritime-Search-and-Rescue-(SAR).aspx>.

[119] See, e.g., US Coast Guard, 'IMO Maritime SAR Regions' <www.dco.uscg.mil/Portals/9/CG-5R/nsarc/IMO%20Maritime%20SAR%20Regions.pdf>.

[120] SAR Convention (n 24) art. 2.3.1.

[121] Ibid, art. 1.3.3.

[122] 'Argentina Sub: What Happens When a Submarine Vanishes', *BBC News*, 24 November 2017 <www.bbc.com/news/world-latin-america-42057864>. Australian rescue procedures also note the desirability to have a diver's decompression chamber on scene to assist mariners rescued from the submarine: Australian Hydrographic Office (n 61).

[123] SAR Convention (n 24) art. 3.1.1.

[124] Ibid, art. 3.1.6.1 (States 'should' do so, however).

[125] See 'International Submarine Escape and Rescue Liaison Office' <https://ismerlo.org/>. No distinction is made between military and private submarines, although ISMERLO is referred to as 'a military organisation operating in an international environment focused on the humanitarian objective of saving lives at sea'.

to provide assistance to any State.[126] While the legal framework for search and rescue is relatively strong in relation to submarines, national security concerns may impede States from seeking assistance or even acknowledging that an accident has occurred.[127]

11.4 Sunken Submarines under International Law

In situations where submarines are lost at sea, a variety of international laws may still be applicable in relation to that submarine. In the immediate aftermath of a submarine sinking during times of peace, the wreck may constitute a hazard to the safe navigation of other vessels or a threat to the marine environment. For submarines lost at sea in times past and recently discovered, questions relating to the international laws of salvage and UCH in relation to historic submarines may arise. Laws of salvage may also be at play for recent submarine losses.

Yet it is important to acknowledge at the outset that cutting across laws relating to wreck removal, salvage and cultural heritage is the status of submarines as either military submarines, which are entitled to sovereign immunity, or private submarines. At present, the sovereign immune status of submarines that are warships or other government vessels operated on non-commercial service will potentially render nugatory laws concerning wrecks, salvage and UCH. The latter laws remain applicable for private submarines and submersibles and may otherwise only be relevant to military submarines where the flag State is so willing.

126 Ibid. For example, although not a member of NATO, Australia is a member of this Office: Andrew McLaughlin, 'Australia's Submarine Rescue System Certified for Another Year after Successful Demonstration', *PS News*, 3 January 2024 <https://psnews.com.au/australias-submarine-rescue-system-certified-for-another-year-after-successful-demonstration/125080/>.

127 See, e.g., Tom Balmforth and Victoria Klesty, 'Russia Accused of Cover-up over Lethal Submarine Fire' *Reuters*, 4 July 2019 <www.reuters.com/article/world/russia-accused-of-cover-up-over-lethal-submarine-fire-idUSKCN1TY1C1/>; 'China Covered Up Sinking Of Newest Submarine: US Official', *Barron's*, 26 September 2024 <www.barrons.com/news/china-covered-up-sinking-of-newest-submarine-us-official-aa50ae23>; Charles Digges, 'Italy Furious after US Navy Tried to Cover Up Sub Accident', *Bellona*, 13 November 2003 <https://bellona.org/news/nuclear-issues/nuclear-usa/2003-11-italy-furious-after-us-navy-tried-to-cover-up-sub-accident>; Hether Mongilio, 'Pentagon Denies Chinese Accusation of Cover-Up in Nuclear Attack Submarine Crash', *USNI News*, 12 October 2021 <https://news.usni.org/2021/10/12/pentagon-denies-chinese-accusation-of-cover-up-in-nuclear-attack-submarine-crash>. Not all submarine accidents necessitate a search and rescue, however.

11.4.1 Sovereign Immunity of Sunken Military Submarines

As discussed in Chapter 1, submarines are primarily, albeit not exclusively, warships. The sovereign immunity of warships is clearly established under UNCLOS and customary international law.[128] A question of concern in the context of sunken submarines is whether any immunity enjoyed by a submarine persists when it has sunk. The United States has a clear and long-held policy that its warships and other government vessels operated on non-commercial service retain their immunity even when sunken and may not be salvaged in the absence of the consent of the United States.[129] Russia shares this position,[130] and bilateral agreements between States in relation to specific wrecks have asserted sovereign immunity or the status of the wreck as State property.[131] Spain argued in domestic proceedings in the United States that the sunken status of a warship had no effect on its protected status under international law; a position recognised by 'sea-going nations' and necessitating that 'the site of a sunken warship may not be disturbed without the express permission of the warship's sovereign owner'.[132] Tuckett has described the retention of sovereign immune status for warships even when resting on the seabed as 'the prevailing view'.[133]

[128] UNCLOS (n 12) arts. 32, 95, 58(2). The immunity of warships was described as 'general international law' in *ARA Libertad* (Argentina v. Ghana) (Provisional Measures Order of 15 December 2012) [2012] ITLOS Rep 332, para. 95. For further discussion on sovereign immunity, see Chapter 1, Section 1.3.

[129] Michael G Collins, 'The Salvage of Sunken Military Vessels' (1976) 10(4) *The International Lawyer* 681, 693–694. A position reinforced by President Bill Clinton: Bill Clinton, 'Statement on United States Policy for the Protection of Sunken Warships' in (2001) 37 *Weekly Compilation of Presidential Documents* 195 (22 January 2001).

[130] 'Communication from the Government of the Russian Federation to the US State Department', 3 October 2003, cited in Valentina S. Vadi, 'International Law and the Uncertain Fate of Military Sunken Vessels' (2009) 14 *Italian Yearbook of International Law* 253, 262. See also Mariano J. Aznar-Gomez, 'Treasure Hunters, Sunken State Vessels and the 2001 UNESCO Convention on the Protection of Underwater Cultural Heritage (2010) 25 *International Journal of Marine and Coastal Law* 209, 222.

[131] Aznar-Gomez (n 130) 221–222; Vadi (n 130) 262.

[132] Cited in Vadi (n 130) 264. Japan, Germany and the United Kingdom have also articulated this view: see Craig Forrest, 'Culturally and Environmentally Sensitive Sunken Warships' (2012) 26 *Australian and New Zealand Maritime Law Journal* 80, 84.

[133] Caroline Tuckett, 'Sunk in Battle, But the War is Not Over: Who Owns the Moskva?' (2025) 106 *International Law Studies* 66, 75. China's position is unclear, however. It has asserted rights over UCH in its territorial waters but there are instances of China seemingly disregarding sovereign immune status of sunken ships: see Zhen Lin, 'Legal Status of Sunken Warships That Meet the Definition of Underwater Cultural Heritage in Territorial Waters: Legislations of China and ASEAN State' (2018) 1 *China Oceans Law Review* 13, 22–23. China does, however, assert jurisdiction over underwater relics originating from China: Anastasia Strati, 'Protection of the Underwater Cultural

The Institut de Droit International (IDI) has studied the legal status of warship wrecks, and concluded 'sunken state ships' and their cargo are immune from the jurisdiction of any State other than the flag State.[134]

The counter-argument is that the sovereign immunity enjoyed by warships and other government vessels operated on non-commercial service is based on the functions that those vessels perform; once sunken, the vessel no longer performs those functions.[135] The sunken vessels cannot be considered warships on the basis that they no longer meet the definition of warships in Article 29 of UNCLOS, because they are not 'under the command' or crewed by official naval officers.[136] Tuckett considers these arguments run against the weight of case law and State practice on the issue, as well as disregarding the immunity of warships recognised in the 2001 UNESCO Convention and the 1989 Salvage Convention.[137] The key inquiry is the use of the vessel at the time it sank, and not when it is a wreck on the ocean floor.[138] Moreover, immunity is just one dimension to sunken warships, including submarines, as there are other considerations including cultural heritage and potentially protection of war graves,[139] which are discussed in Section 11.4.4 below.

Heritage: From the Shortcomings of the UN Convention on the Law of the Sea to the Compromises of the UNESCO Convention' in Anastasia Strati, Maria Gavouneli and Nikos Skourtos (eds.), *Unresolved Issues and New Challenges to the Law of the Sea* (Brill Nijhoff, 2006) 21, 30–31.

134 IDI Resolution on the Legal Regime of Wrecks of Warships and Other State-Owned Ships in International Law, Tallinn, 29 August 2015 <www.idi-iil.org/en/publications/le-regime-juridique-des-epaves-des-navires-de-guerre-et-des-epaves-des-autres-navires-detat-en-droit-international/>.

135 Vadi (n 130) 265.

136 Jason R. Harris, 'Protecting Sunken Warships as Objects Entitled to Sovereign Immunity' (2002) 33 *University of Miami Inter-American Law Review* 101, 111; Marlène M. Losier, 'The Conflict between Sovereign Immunity and the Cargo of Sunken Colonial Vessels' (2018) 33 *International Journal of Marine and Coastal Law* 528, 535–536.

137 Tuckett (n 133) 76. Underlying some arguments that counter ongoing State immunity for sunken warships are concerns about colonial actions removing cultural property. For discussion, see Losier (n 136). 2001 UNESCO Convention (n 25); International Convention on Salvage, London, 28 April 1989, entered into force 14 July 1996, 1953 UNTS 165 ('Salvage Convention').

138 Richard Garnett, 'Foreign State Immunity and Marine Wrecks' (2021) 35 *Australian and New Zealand Maritime Law Journal* 1, 18.

139 Vadi (n 130) 266. The situation of immunity of sunken warships during times of armed conflict will also trigger different legal considerations. See Tuckett (n 133) 79–83.

11.4.2 Submarine Wrecks as Hazards

When submarines sink, the wreckage may pose a risk to the marine environment, especially if fuel or other chemicals leak – or may potentially leak – from the submarine. The distinct threat posed by nuclear-powered or nuclear-armed submarines to the marine environment is acute in this regard and is addressed in Chapter 12 on international marine environmental law. Beyond environmental harms, sunken submarines may create navigational hazards to other submarines or surface vessels or may interfere with the laying or operation of submarine cables and pipelines in areas under and beyond national jurisdiction. For example, a sunken U-boat in the Dover Strait had to be moved with considerable care ninety years after its demise because of the risk it posed to modern vessels traversing the Strait.[140] Within a coastal State's exclusive economic zone (EEZ) or territorial sea, a sunken submarine may prejudice the economic or security interests of that coastal State.

UNCLOS does not address the question of wrecks specifically,[141] with no treaty obligation on States to render wrecks harmless nor authority granted to a coastal State to require that another State ensure that wrecks are removed or rendered harmless within its EEZ. At most, the principle articulated in the *Corfu Channel* case that States must warn of navigational hazards within its territorial sea (or at least in an international strait) so as not to prejudice other States' rights would be applicable by analogy to any wrecks.[142] In this vein, the SOLAS Convention requires a ship's master to report 'dangerous derelicts' to competent authorities and ships in the vicinity.[143] An obligation to notify or warn also arises when there is actual or threatened damage to the marine environment.[144] However, an obligation to warn to ensure the safety of ships may not necessarily extend to a requirement to remove a wreck. States are allowed to take measures to avoid pollution that may eventuate due to maritime

[140] Care was needed because of the ammunitions that remained onboard, as well as respect for the deceased crew members: Forrest (n 132) 81.

[141] Gaskell and Forrest observe that UNCLOS only addresses wrecks implicitly in discussing intervention following maritime casualties and in relation to underwater cultural heritage. Nicholas Gaskell and Craig Forrest, *The Law of Wreck* (Routledge, 2019) 306.

[142] According to the International Court of Justice, it is 'every State's obligation not to allow knowingly its territory to be used for acts contrary to the rights of other States': *Corfu Channel* (United Kingdom v. Albania) [1949] ICJ Rep 4, 22.

[143] SOLAS Convention (n 23) ch. V/31, discussed in Gaskell and Forrest (n 141) 312.

[144] UNCLOS (n 12) art. 198. See further UNCLOS (n 12) art. 211(7).

casualties.[145] Such measures may include the removal of any hazard posed by a wreck.

The 2007 Nairobi International Convention on the Removal of Wrecks (Nairobi Convention) may be applicable to private submarines and submersibles that pose a hazard to navigational safety or the marine environment in the EEZ.[146] Article 4(2) of the Nairobi Convention excludes warships and other government vessels operated on non-commercial service from its scope of application, unless a State decides otherwise. At time of writing, the Nairobi Convention has forty-one State parties, including China, France and the United Kingdom, but not including either Russia or the United States. To date, no State party has issued a declaration applying the Nairobi Convention to its warships,[147] but this decision could be made when needed in a specific incident. The requirements under the Nairobi Convention are thus legally binding for a limited number of States in relation to private submarines flagged to that State, or if a State so decides in relation to its warships.[148] Otherwise, the process and requirements set out in the Nairobi Convention may be considered indicative of what standards might be expected of States in dealing with submarine wrecks that constitute a hazard but not impose legal obligations.

[145] Ibid, art. 221(1). Maritime casualty is defined in UNCLOS as 'a collision of vessels, stranding or other incident of navigation, or other occurrence on board a vessel or external to it resulting in material damage or imminent threat of material damage to a vessel or cargo': art. 221(2). See further 1969 International Convention on Civil Liability for Oil Pollution Damage, Brussels, 29 November 1969, entered into force 27 June 1975, 973 UNTS 319. For discussion on maritime casualties under UNCLOS, see Gaskell and Forrest (n 141) 318–320.

[146] Nairobi Convention on the Removal of Wrecks, Nairobi, 18 May 2007, entered into force 14 April 2015, [2023] ATNIF 8 ('Nairobi Convention'). States party to the treaty have the option of extending its application to their territorial sea under the conditions set forth in the Nairobi Convention: art. 3(2). States are encouraged by the IMO to extend the application of the treaty to promote consistency throughout ocean space and a 'significant number' of States party to the Nairobi Convention have done so. See Colin de la Rue and Charles Anderson, *Shipping and the Environment: Law and Practice* (3rd ed., 2022, Routledge) 1128, 1140–1141.

[147] See 'Nairobi International Convention on the Removal of Wrecks', *UN Treaty Series* <https://treaties.un.org/Pages/showDetails.aspx?objid=080000028053c3a0>.

[148] It should also be noted that the Nairobi Convention does not likely apply to vessels that have sunk prior to the entry into force of the treaty. Sarah Dromgoole, 'The Legal Regime of Wrecks of Warships and Other State-Owned Ships in International Law: The 2015 Resolution of the Institut de Droit International' (2015) 25 *Italian Yearbook of International Law* 181, 184.

Where the Nairobi Convention is applicable to submarine wrecks in the EEZ of a coastal State, that coastal State may set a deadline for the owner of a sunken submarine to prevent, mitigate or eliminate the hazard posed by that vessel.[149] The hazard could be to navigational safety, the environment or other interests of the coastal State, including its tourism trade, fisheries or offshore infrastructure.[150] Where a wreck constitutes a hazard, the master or operator of the vessel concerned must notify the affected coastal State,[151] and thereby enable that State to determine if it constitutes a hazard requiring removal.[152] If so, the registered owner has the responsibility to remove that hazard.[153] The Nairobi Convention further establishes the liability of the registered owner for locating, marking and removing the wreck.[154] The Nairobi Convention has been viewed as 'a modest extension to the EEZ rights of coastal States bestowed by UNCLOS'.[155]

The Nairobi Convention will most likely have relevance for submarines in instances where flag States are willing to apply its procedures and principles on an ad hoc basis to military submarines that would otherwise be outside the scope of application. It may also well be the case that naval forces will seek to recover lost submarines irrespective of the Nairobi Convention. Nonetheless, the application of the Nairobi Convention should be seriously considered as the relevant legal framework when the hazard posed by a sunken submarine is manifest in relation to navigational safety (e.g., where a submarine has sunk in a relatively shallow channel). It should further be an additional factor in meeting due diligence requirements of international environmental obligations, which are discussed further in Chapter 12.

149 For a detailed discussion on the Nairobi Convention see de la Rue and Anderson (n 146) 1127–1142; Gaskell and Forrest (n 141) pt. II.

150 Nairobi Convention (n 146) arts. 1(5)–(6).

151 Ibid, art. 5(1). The information required in a report is set out in Article 5 of the Nairobi Convention.

152 Ibid, art. 6. Article 6 lists a range of criteria that may be considered in assessing whether the sunken vessel is a hazard or not.

153 Ibid, art. 9(2). Removing the hazard may not mean the wreck itself has to be removed or moved but rather the focus is on what constitutes the hazard itself (such as oil or other hazardous cargo).

154 Ibid, arts. 10, 11 (the latter provision includes exceptions to liability, which primarily relate to liability otherwise arising under other international civil liability regimes).

155 Churchill, Lowe and Sander (n 33) 276.

11.4.3 *Salvage of Submarines*

The law of salvage has developed from national laws and early customs founded on the basic premise that those who saved another vessel at sea would be rewarded for their efforts.[156] It is primarily of relevance in the context of surface vessels that are in distress at sea where the salvage efforts will return the distressed vessel to commercial service. The three key elements of salvage have thus been identified as 'marine peril, voluntary assistance, and success in whole or in part'.[157] Compensation for salvage efforts will also be available where the action is taken to prevent or minimise harm to the marine environment, even if a ship is not saved.[158] Under the 1989 Salvage Convention,[159] although sunken ships (or wrecks) are not specifically mentioned, international salvage law is considered to be applicable to sunken vessels,[160] albeit not necessarily certain historic shipwrecks.[161]

In contemporary salvage operations, 'the right to salvage arises when a person, acting as a volunteer, preserves or contributes to preserving at sea any vessel, cargo, freight or other recognised subject of salvage in danger'.[162] The act of salvage involves assistance to a vessel or its cargo when there is peril of loss or damage at sea.[163] Salvage is further concerned with the rights of private individuals, usually professional salvors, who seek to be compensated in situations where a ship is saved.[164] It is the master of a vessel who has authority to conclude contracts for salvage operations on behalf of the owner of the vessel.[165]

156 Roberta Garabello, 'Salvage' in Anne Peters and Rüdiger Wolfrum (eds.), *Max Planck Encyclopedia of Public International Law* (Oxford University Press, March 2013) para. 2; Archie Bishop, 'Law of Salvage' in David Joseph Attard et al. (eds.), *The IMLI Manual on International Maritime Law* (Oxford University Press, 2016) vol. 2, 474, para. 18.1.2.

157 Garabello (n 156) para. 4. The law of salvage is distinct from the law of finds, which applies in relation to abandoned property and permits claims of ownership, but the latter has influenced the former in national decision-making. See Elizabeth Barrowman, 'The Recovery of Shipwrecks in International Waters: A Multilateral Solution' (1987) 8(1) *Michigan Journal of International Law* 231, 238–239.

158 Salvage Convention (n 137) art. 14.

159 Ibid.

160 Garabello (n 156) para. 14.

161 Salvage Convention (n 137) art. 30(1)(d). The 2001 UNESCO Convention (n 25) is more explicit in its exclusion of the law of salvage unless specific conditions are met: art. 4.

162 John Reeder, *Brice on Maritime Law of Salvage* (5th ed., Sweet & Maxwell, 2012), cited in Bishop (n 156) vol. 2, 474, para. 18.1.3.

163 Collins (n 129) 685.

164 Salvage Convention (n 137) art. 12.

165 Ibid, art. 6(2).

The salvor obtains a lien over the ship and may seek compensation before an admiralty court, but does not gain ownership rights in the property.[166] The compensation is calculated by reference to a number of criteria set out in Article 13 of the Salvage Convention. Individuals who have a duty to rescue persons in distress at sea fall outside the scope of salvage law.[167]

Submarines do fall within the scope of the definition of property subject to salvage,[168] but submarines subject to sovereign immunity are not regulated by the Salvage Convention unless the flag State waives that immunity.[169] As discussed above, States have opposed any attempts to salvage their sunken warships on the basis of the immunity enjoyed by those vessels.[170] Even if a sunken warship was salvaged, recovery for a salvage claim may be prevented before admiralty courts with foreign immunity preventing the claim from being heard or enforced.[171] While national courts have grappled with questions as to the applicable immunity enjoyed by government vessels and whether they are on commercial or non-commercial service following salvage,[172] international law is clear as to the sovereign immunity of warships.[173]

Prior to the adoption of the Salvage Convention, the United States undertook a salvage operation in 1974 of a Soviet nuclear-armed submarine that had sunk in 1968 in a high seas area of the Pacific Ocean.[174] The Soviet Union did not protest the US actions, though it has been speculated that such restraint was due to the failure of the Soviet Union to acknowledge the loss of its submarine officially.[175] At the time of the operation, the United States and the Soviet Union were both parties to a 1910 treaty on salvage, which, like its modern equivalent, excluded

166 Collins (n 129) 684. See also Barrowman (n 157) 237.

167 Bishop (n 156) vol. 2, 474, para. 18.4.1.3.1.

168 Salvage Convention (n 137) art. 1.

169 Ibid, art. 4.

170 See above notes 129–134 and accompanying text.

171 How sovereign immunity claims may be raised before national courts in salvage proceedings is discussed in Garnett (n 138).

172 The position in Australia, the United Kingdom and the United States for salvage of government vessels is discussed by Garnett: ibid, 3–11.

173 A position also set out in the Convention on State Immunities (albeit a treaty not presently in force): United Nations Convention on the Jurisdictional Immunities of States and Their Property, New York, 2 December 2004, not in force (UN Doc. A/59/508), art. 16(1).

174 For discussion, see Collins (n 129).

175 Ibid, 683.

sovereign immune warships from its scope.[176] The United States' salvage operation of parts of the Soviet submarine would be considered unlawful under modern law (and was arguably unlawful at the time of its occurrence as well).

Salvage operations will be undertaken in some situations to retrieve bodies of those lost at sea. For example, following USS *Greeneville*'s collision with the *Ehime Maru*, the sunken vessel was lifted from the ocean floor so that Japanese and US Navy divers were able to search for and surface the accident victims for return to Japan.[177] Where bodies are not retrieved, there are only basic rules under international law requiring respect and the treatment of gravesites with sanctity.[178] This aspect is discussed immediately below.

11.4.4 Underwater Cultural Heritage Law and Submarines

There are general obligations of both protection and cooperation imposed on all States in relation to 'objects of an archaeological or historical nature'.[179] Sunken submarines located within the territorial sea, or contiguous zone,[180] fall within the coastal State's jurisdiction.[181] The coastal State is therefore entitled to limit the flag State's access to its wreck when located in that maritime area.[182] However, under UNCLOS, any right that the coastal State may assert is subject to inter alia the rights of an identifiable owner, the law of salvage and rules relating to the protection of UCH.[183] The 2001 UNESCO Convention accords the coastal State a possible coordination role to protect UCH located in its EEZ,[184] but its terms are otherwise subject to the rights and duties allocated under UNCLOS.[185]

176 Convention pour l'Unification de certaines Règles en matière d'Assistence et de Sauvetage maritimes, Brussels, 23 September 1910, entered into force 1 March 1913, 103 BSP 434, art. 14.

177 US National Transportation Safety Board (n 40) 31.

178 Dromgoole (n 148) 195–196. See further below nn 209–217 and accompanying text.

179 UNCLOS (n 12) art. 303(1).

180 Ibid, art. 303(2).

181 For discussion of this regime, see Strati (n 133) 28–31.

182 Dromgoole (n 148) 192.

183 UNCLOS (n 12) arts. 303(3)–(4).

184 2001 UNESCO Convention (n 25) arts. 9, 10. See further, discussion in Chapter 8, Section 8.3.3.3. See also Zhen Sun, *Finding a Balance in the Exclusive Economic Zone Conflict and Stability in the Law of the Sea* (Cambridge University Press, 2025) 341–345.

185 2001 UNESCO Convention (n 25) art. 3.

Article 149 of UNCLOS provides that objects of 'an archaeological and historical nature' located on the deep seabed are to be preserved or disposed of for the benefit of all humankind; whichever entity undertakes the preservation or disposal is to pay 'particular regard' to the 'preferential rights of the State or country of origin, or the State of cultural origin, or the State of historical and archaeological origin'.[186] No definition is provided as to the meaning of either archaeological or historical objects (and indeed whether the terms are cumulative or separate criteria)[187] but would presumably include wrecks. Nor does the text provide any sense of prioritisation between those States with preferential rights.[188]

Although there is no detail within UNCLOS as to how this provision is to be operationalised, the International Seabed Authority has since addressed this question. Obligations to notify have been set out in its regulations for exploration and prospecting.[189] Within the context of the development of regulations for the exploitation of the deep seabed, Draft Regulation 35 has provided a process for notifying the Secretary-General in the event that any archaeological or historical object is found and setting out the need to preserve and protect the object or site.[190] Proposals to revise this regulation predominantly aim to clarify the process and its scope, but not in essence changing the requirement of notification and avoiding the disturbance of the site until the International Seabed Authority's Council has acted.[191]

What constitutes UCH has been defined in the 2001 UNESCO Convention as: 'all traces of human existence having a cultural, historical or archaeological character which have been partially or totally under

[186] UNCLOS (n 12) art. 149.

[187] Tullio Scovazzi, 'Article 149' in Alexander Proelß (ed.), *The United Nations Convention on the Law of the Sea: A Commentary* (CH Beck; Hart; Nomos, 2017) 1052, para. 9.

[188] Ibid, para. 14.

[189] See, e.g., International Seabed Authority, 'Regulations on Prospecting and Exploration for Polymetallic Nodules in the Area', 13 July 2000 (ISA Doc. ISBA/6/A/18) regs. 8, 34; International Seabed Authority, 'Regulations on Prospecting and Exploration for Polymetallic Sulphides in the Area', 7 May 2010 (ISA Doc. ISBA/16/A/12/Rev.1) regs. 8, 37; International Seabed Authority, 'Regulations on Prospecting for Cobalt-rich Ferromanganese Crusts in the Area', 22 July 2013 (ISA Doc. ISBA/19/C/17) regs. 8, 37.

[190] International Seabed Authority, Draft Regulations on Exploitation of Mineral Resources in the Area, 28 March 2025 (ISA Doc. ISBA/30/C/CRP.11) reg. 35.

[191] See, e.g., International Institute for Sustainable Development, 'Summary of the Twenty-eighth Annual Session of the International Seabed Authority (First Paty): 16–31 March 2023' (2023) 25(251) *Earth Negotiations Bulletin* 1. An approach focused on intangible cultural heritage has been mooted as an alternative during discussions at the International Seabed Authority: see Julian Arato, Aline Jaeckel and Lucas Lixinski, 'On the Cultural Stakes of Deep Seabed Mining' (2024) 118 *AJIL Unbound* 67–71.

water, periodically or continuously, for at least 100 years such as . . . (ii) vessels, aircraft, other vehicles or any part thereof, their cargo or other contents, together with their archaeological and natural context'.[192]

At time of writing, the 100-year timeframe effectively excludes submarines that have sunk after World War I. However, the requirements under UNCLOS do not specify any time limit, and it is arguable as to whether sunken submarines that have rested on the seabed for less than 100 years may still fall within the basic requirements of UNCLOS even if not falling within the more detailed requirements set out in the 2001 UNESCO Convention.[193] In this vein, Forrest has observed that '[i]t is axiomatic that remains of State-owned vessels of the past may fall within the broader term "cultural heritage" and should therefore be recovered in an archaeologically sound manner'.[194] Yet even if submarines were sufficiently old to fall within the protection regime established under the 2001 UNESCO Convention, that agreement still preserves the sovereign immunity of State vessels and defers to the view of the flag State.[195]

Forrest is critical of the exclusion of warships from consideration as UCH under the 2001 UNESCO Convention for the following reasons:

> Application of the principle of State immunity to vessels of antiquity is particularly problematic, not only because Article 29 of UNCLOS, which defines warship for the purposes of that Convention, is inappropriate as a definition for warships of earlier centuries, but also because it may be difficult to determine whether a particular historic wreck was in fact a 'State owned vessel'. There could be a number of reasons for this. A wreck site may be so old that it predates any conception of 'the State' in international law, and no existing State can claim to be the flag State. Alternatively, the original flag State may no longer exist as a separate entity, but has been broken up into smaller nation-States or subsumed within a larger State. It may also be that there is simply no historic evidence available to determine ownership of the vessel.[196]

[192] 2001 UNESCO Convention (n 25) art. 1(a). For detailed discussions of the 2001 UNESCO Convention, see Craig Forrest, 'A New International Regime for the Protection of Underwater Cultural Heritage' (2002) 51 *International and Comparative Law Quarterly* 511; Sarah Dromgoole, *Underwater Cultural Heritage and International Law* (Cambridge University Press, 2013).

[193] See Dromgoole (n 148) 188.

[194] Forrest (n 192) 526.

[195] 2001 UNESCO Convention (n 25) arts. 2(8), 12(7).

[196] Forrest (n 192) 527–528 (citations omitted). Dromgoole has also noted that a 'substantial proportion' of wrecks are State vessels: Dromgoole (n 148) 187.

This reasoning is compelling when considering the age of the wrecks to garner status as UCH, especially under the 2001 UNESCO Convention, and the diminution in strategic or military advantages that may be achieved in investigating such old warships. It is not, however, the view that prevailed in the 2001 UNESCO Convention. The critical determination under Article 1(8) is whether the State vessel is identifiable as a warship of that State and whether it meets the definition of UCH in the 2001 UNESCO Convention.[197] If a submarine meets the definition of UCH and cannot be identified as a warship of a particular State, then it should be considered as UCH in accordance with the 2001 UNESCO Convention.

Flag States may occasionally choose to waive or relinquish their immunity over sunken warships that are located in another State's jurisdiction. The United Kingdom, for example, relinquished sovereignty over the warships HMS *Erebus* and HMS *Terror*, which were lost in the 1840s, to Canada.[198] This approach may be favoured by a State when there is no strategic advantage to be maintained, or when seeking to redress colonial legacies,[199] and the protection of UCH is the paramount consideration. For all States party to the 2001 UNESCO Convention, *in situ* preservation is 'the first option before allowing or engaging in any activities directed at this heritage'.[200]

For submarines that are protected under the 2001 UNESCO Convention as UCH, State parties are to cooperate to protect UCH, as well as 'ensure and strengthen' the protection of UCH.[201] Central to the 2001 UNESCO Convention is the preservation of UCH, which Forrest describes as 'the safeguarding and conservation of the physical integrity of the UCH and the archaeological value derived therefrom'.[202] UCH is not to be commercially exploited.[203] As discussed in Chapter 8,[204] this prohibition does not preclude tourism to sites of UCH,[205] but is more directed at preventing removal of objects from wrecks. More specific requirements are set out in the 2001 UNESCO Convention in relation to

[197] Forrest (n 192) 528.
[198] Tuckett (n 133) 77.
[199] Lucas Lixinski, *A Research Agenda for Cultural Heritage Law* (Edward Elgar, 2024) 135.
[200] 2001 UNESCO Convention (n 25) art. 2(5).
[201] Ibid, art. 2(1) and (2)
[202] Forrest (n 192) 520. See 2001 UNESCO Convention (n 25) art. 2(3).
[203] UNESCO Convention (n 25) art. 2(7) and annex, r. 2.
[204] See Chapter 8, Section 8.3.3.3.
[205] See 2001 UNESCO Convention (n 25) art. 2(10).

each of the maritime zones.[206] States are also to take measures to ensure their 'nationals and vessels flying their flag do not engage in any activity directed at underwater cultural heritage in a manner not in conformity with this Convention'.[207] If a submarine subject to sovereign immunity discovers a wreck, it is not necessarily bound to report the discovery under the 2001 UNESCO Convention, although, when practicable and not impairing the submarine's operations, the flag State of the submarine should comply with those notice requirements.[208]

A further consideration for sunken submarines is the status of the humans who have lost their lives in the incident. The UN General Assembly regularly expresses concern in relation to the desecration of graves at sea, as well as the looting of wrecks, and calls on States to prevent such desecration and 'ensure that proper respect is given to all human remains located in maritime waters'.[209] While the General Assembly indicates that such respect is required under international law, no specific rules are referenced in this context and are somewhat obscure in times of peace.

Sunken warships lost during times of armed conflict may be considered as war graves.[210] A 1995 statement of France, Germany, Japan, Russia, the United Kingdom and the United States recognised sunken warships as sailors' gravesites that should not be disturbed but protected from disturbance or salvage.[211] The IDI, in its resolution on sunken State ships, addresses war graves as follows:

> Due respect shall be shown for the remains of any person in a sunken State ship. This obligation may be implemented through the establishment of the wreck as a war cemetery or other proper treatment of the remains of

[206] 2001 UNESCO Convention (n 25) arts. 7–12. See further Chapter 8, Section 8.3.3.3 for discussion on submersibles used in relation to UCH in the EEZ and continental shelf.

[207] Ibid, art. 16.

[208] Ibid, art. 13. The language of this provision is similar to the due diligence obligation set out in Article 236 of UNCLOS in relation to adherence to international environmental law.

[209] See, e.g., 'Oceans and the Law of the Sea', 11 December 2023, UNGA Res. 78/69 (UN Doc. A/Res/78/69) para. 363.

[210] International humanitarian law sets out a number of rules relating to the treatment of dead persons and their gravesites. For discussion, see Anna Petrig, 'The War Dead and their Gravesites' (2009) 91 (874) *International Review of the Red Cross* 341. See also Jason R. Harris, 'The Protection of Sunken Warships as Gravesites at Sea' (2001) 7 *Ocean and Coastal Law Journal* 75 (considering US law as well as international law).

[211] Robert S Neyland, 'Sovereign Immunity and the Management of United States Naval Shipwrecks', *Naval Historical Center Homepage* <www.history.navy.millbrancheslorgl2-7h.htm>, cited in Harris (n 210) 124–135.

> deceased persons and their burial when the wreck is recovered. States concerned should provide for the establishment of war cemeteries for wrecks.[212]

Although there has been greater attention and emphasis on sunken warships, similar principles are arguably just as pertinent for civilian deaths at sea.[213] Notably, the UN General Assembly resolution does not distinguish between the treatment of naval crew and civilians.

The 2001 UNESCO Convention requires that 'proper respect' is accorded to human remains located in maritime waters.[214] Dromgoole has observed that:

> there is a wealth of State practice indicating a general acceptance that human remains found on State wrecks should be treated with appropriate respect and that sites that represent substantial gravesites should be treated as places of sanctity. The exact bounds of this practice are hard to gauge, however, although it does seem to extend beyond the confines of lives lost in direct wartime combat.[215]

She further considers that the IDI's work confirms that there is 'a customary rule of international law that appropriate respect must be shown for human remains present in any sunken State ship, whatever the context of its loss'.[216] The reality of human decomposition in seawater has led to a proposal that sunken ships should be reconsidered as reflecting intangible heritage to account for the persons who died.[217] At a minimum, it seems that the presence of humans on a vessel (at least while in operation) reflects a further consideration in determining the status and extent of protection that must be afforded a sunken ship and may further influence the content of any duty of cooperation in relation to UCH.

While the 2001 UNESCO Convention sets out important regulations to preserve and protect UCH, it has several critical limitations in relation to sunken submarines. First, the 2001 UNESCO Convention does not enjoy universal membership and as such, there is scope to debate the

[212] IDI Resolution on the Legal Regime of Wrecks of Warships and Other State-Owned Ships in International Law (n 134) art. 12.

[213] See Tullio Scovazzi, 'Human Remains as Cultural Heritage' in Lucas Lixinski and Lucie K. Morisset (eds.), *The Routledge Handbook of Heritage and the Law* (Routledge, 2024) 456, 467–469.

[214] 2001 UNESCO Convention (n 25) art. 2(9).

[215] Dromgoole (n 148) 195.

[216] Ibid, 196.

[217] See Elena Perez Alvaro, 'Shipwrecks and Graves: Their Treatment as Intangible Heritage' (2022) 17 *International Journal of Intangible Heritage* 184.

extent that its requirements reflect customary international law.[218] Second, the designation of a wreck as UCH is age dependent and an arbitrary timeframe of 100 years is established in the definition of UCH in the 2001 UNESCO Convention. Submarines that have sunk during and subsequent to World War II do not (yet) fall within the definition of UCH under the 2001 UNESCO Convention. As a result, the main international requirements for States to cooperate or to ensure that sunken submarines are protected or preserved are those articulated in UNCLOS or considered as customary international law. Further, where submarines have sunk more recently, the status of these sites as graves and what ensuring respect for human remains actually entails in any given situation is obscure. Finally, sunken submarines will most commonly be military submarines (despite the navigational safety concerns that have arisen more recently following the *Titan* disaster) and subject to sovereign immunity. That sovereign immunity may ultimately be the deciding factor for State actions on what steps may be taken to remove or move a wreck or to remove objects on that wreck. The existence of sovereign immunity is expected to provide the core international right to provide protection for security, social or cultural reasons against looting, desecration, salvage or espionage.[219] The sufficiency of this rule for flag States seeking to prevent coastal State or others' actions appears to be under challenge in some scenarios, as is seemingly the case currently in southeast Asian waters.[220]

11.5 Conclusion

The construction and design of submarines are the foremost critical elements in ensuring the safety of submarines. As Tingle's study

[218] It has however been noted that 'Australia, Canada, China, Germany, Greece, Russia, the Netherlands, the United Kingdom, the United States and Türkiye generally support the principles and standards' in the 2001 UNESCO Convention, even though these States are not formally parties to the treaty. See Sun (n 184) 329.

[219] This position is manifest in the practice of the United States and was reflected in a statement by former US President Bill Clinton: Clinton (n 129). For discussion of US position, see, e.g., Michael White, 'Sea Hunt, Inc. v. Unidentified Shipwrecked Vessel or Vessels, 221 F.3d 634 (2000), cert. denied, 121 S.Ct. 1079 (2001)' (2001) 95 *American Journal of International Law* 678; W. Gomez Pretel et al., 'Preserving Sunken Military Vessels as Underwater Cultural Heritage in Colombia: Legal Challenges and Prospects for the USS Kearsarge Wreck Site' (2023) 6 *Heritage* 4843–4863.

[220] See, e.g., Zhen Lin, 'The Protection of Sunken WWII Warships Located in Indonesian or Malaysian Territorial Waters' (2020) 113 *Marine Policy* 103804.

demonstrated, submarine accidents declined as engineering advanced.[221] Yet it is also important to recall that the introduction of the COLREGs was viewed as another contributing factor to the reduction of accidents. While the COLREGs provide valuable rules for reducing the risk of collisions when vessels are operating on the surface, their applicability to manage navigational safety when submarines are submerged or surfacing is less evident. These aspects of submarine operations likely require explicit attention, potentially by articulating precise rules beyond relying on signals and assessing which vessels are burdened or privileged.

It is possibly the case that the accidents caused when surfacing or when submerged may not be resolved through a multidimensional rendering of the COLREGs (as Plant suspected).[222] An initial step forward would require greater transparency as to what submarines are operating where and when. Clearly for military submarines, that very information is antithetical to the point of their operations. There have been some efforts of coordination, as apparent between NATO members but when coordination is limited as between allies, that effort may be insufficient in solving emerging problems in other parts of the world. Notably, as Bateman discussed, the growth in submarine deployments in waters throughout the Indo-Pacific may necessitate greater cooperation; informal agreements may be the first useful tool rather than expecting anything as formal as an amendment or addition to the COLREGs, especially when high-stakes military craft are at issue. Developing legal rules around notice and consultation may be as high as the legal bar might be set at present, but even then seems unlikely for military submarines.

Once sunk, the situation of submarines is not noticeably different to any other vessel, particularly no different to any other warship. Dromgoole has noted a difficult tension in regulating sunken vessels, as there may be competing regimes that aim to preserve the wreck as cultural heritage, or that aim to remove it as a hazard or that recognise the value of the wreck to allow for it to be salvaged for commercial benefit.[223] These tensions prompt questions as to how to manage the interaction of these regimes (such as when there is a wreck that is a hazard but must still be protected). Cutting across these different regimes is the core protection afforded to military submarines, as warships, by sovereign immunity. The work of the IDI sought to establish

[221] Tingle (n 1) 37. See above n 11 and accompanying text.
[222] See n 33 and accompanying text.
[223] Dromgoole (n 148) 184.

a clear statement of law on the sovereign immune status of sunken warships. This work has drawn together existing State practice and may support better harmonisation of national court decisions when relevant.

Nonetheless, the rules in place to deal with submarines that are not protected by sovereign immunity could, and should, still usefully inform State decision-making on managing issues related to submarines that are wrecks, may benefit from salvage, or where their age renders them worthy of designation as UCH under either UNCLOS or the 2001 UNESCO Convention. In the more immediate aftermath of a submarine catastrophe, rescue and salvage and minimising hazards (whether environmental or to other vessels or activities in the area) will be the key international law rules at stake. Where questions emerge in relation to submarines that sank in an earlier era, the international laws relating to cultural heritage will be applicable. Whether a submarine sank recently or long ago, a further guiding principle of respect for human remains should also be factored into State decision-making.

12

Submarines and the Protection of the Marine Environment

12.1 Introduction

The core obligation to protect and preserve the marine environment applies in all maritime zones,[1] necessarily including under the ocean's surface. When submarines sink, the remaining wreckage may pose environmental risks. For example, a World War II German submarine that sank near Norway 'had a payload of 67 tons of mercury stored in steel containers', and prompted the cessation of fishing activities in the area.[2] Norwegian authorities determined that the preferred response was to stabilise the wreck on the ocean floor, cover it and prevent further sediment contamination.[3] Constant environmental monitoring was considered an essential element of this operation.[4] In 2021, a US nuclear submarine collided with a seamount (or possibly a sunken oil rig) in the South China Sea, prompting concerns about possible environmental damage.[5] This chapter is concerned with the international environmental law obligations relevant to the use of submarines.

Although the obligation to protect and preserve the marine environment is a central facet of international marine environmental law, this duty has varied applicability in relation to submarines. Under Article 236 of the UN Convention on the Law of the Sea (UNCLOS),[6] the

[1] *South China Sea* (Philippines v. China) (Award of 12 July 2016) PCA Case No. 2013–19, para. 940.

[2] Markus Motze and Thomas Radtke, 'Stabilizing a Toxic WWII Submarine Wreck: Monitoring System Detects Possible Mercury Contamination' (2017) 58(2) *Sea Technology* 23.

[3] Ibid.

[4] Ibid.

[5] Mohd Hazmi Mohd Rusli, 'The Legality of Passage of Nuclear-Powered Submarines: Are Malaysia and Indonesia in Catch-22' (2022) 4 *Moscow Journal of International Law* 34, 41.

[6] United Nations Convention on the Law of the Sea, Montego Bay, 10 December 1982, entered into force 16 November 1994, 1833 UNTS 397 ('UNCLOS').

requirements associated with this obligation do not directly apply to submarines entitled to sovereign immunity.[7] This provision does not just exclude sovereign-immune vessels from the enforcement jurisdiction of another State, but stops the *application* of UNCLOS provisions on the protection and preservation of the marine environment. Rather, each State is to ensure that these submarines 'act in a manner consistent' with UNCLOS. This due diligence requirement allows the flag State significant discretion as obligations arising under international environmental law may be modified by considerations as to what impairs the 'operations or operational capabilities' of sovereign-immune submarines and what is 'reasonable and practicable'.[8]

This chapter therefore proceeds on the basis that States must 'do their utmost'[9] to act consistently with international environmental law obligations associated with the protection and preservation of the marine environment in relation to sovereign-immune submarines (described in this volume as 'military submarines'). Further, while international marine environmental obligations under UNCLOS may not apply fully to military submarines, which is a large body of law, there will remain some small number of treaty rules that do apply to military submarines. The operation of private (commercial or research) submarines must still align with obligations to protect and preserve the marine environment.

In light of these parameters, this chapter first articulates in Section 12.2 the core principles of international marine environmental law that are applicable to private submarines and with which flag States of military submarines should act consistently. International environmental law sets out important principles that apply to a State's conduct at sea, including the duties of prevention, cooperation, to undertake an environmental impact assessment and the precautionary principle.[10] Further, in relation

[7] Article 236 refers to 'any warship, naval auxiliary, other vessels or aircraft owned or operated by a State and used, for the time being, only on government non-commercial service': ibid, art. 236.

[8] Ibid, art. 236.

[9] Consistent with the due diligence standard as explained by the International Court of Justice and endorsed by the International Tribunal for the Law of the Sea: see *Request for Advisory Opinion Submitted by the Sub-Regional Fisheries Commission* (Advisory Opinion of 2 April 2015) [2015] ITLOS Rep 41, para. 131 ('*SRFC Advisory Opinion*'), quoting *Pulp Mills on the River Uruguay* (Argentina v. Uruguay) (Judgment of 20 April 2010) [2010] ICJ Rep 14, para. 197.

[10] See generally Yoshifumi Tanaka, 'Basic Principles of International Marine Environmental Law' in Rosemary Rayfuse, Aline Jaeckel and Natalie Klein (eds.), *Research Handbook on International Marine Environmental Law* (2nd ed., Edward Elgar, 2023) 81.

to the marine environment, there are obligations to prevent, reduce and control marine pollution, as well as obligations to conserve and protect living marine resources and the ecosystems in which they live.[11] The latter duties are included in Part XII of UNCLOS, and international marine environmental law is further set out in different multilateral and regional treaties and reflected in customary international law.[12] Consideration is needed as to how flag States may be able to ensure that they act consistently with these requirements when operating in areas beyond the territorial sea, bearing in mind the discretionary framework available for those decisions in respect of military submarines.

The typology of submarines in Chapter 1 explained that submarines are most typically powered with diesel and gasoline engines, as well as battery-operated electrical engines.[13] The way submarines are powered has implications for the possible threat that they pose to the marine environment. The introduction of nuclear-powered submarines from the mid-1950s has augmented these concerns due to the potential risk to the marine environment from radioactive materials. Section 12.3 of this chapter addresses the potential international obligations that arise from an environmental perspective when submarines are either nuclear-powered or armed with nuclear weapons ('nuclear submarines'). The immunity of Article 236 of UNCLOS remains applicable for military submarines. Yet, the duty to ensure that a State acts consistently with marine environmental obligations should also contemplate requirements arising from laws associated with nuclear waste and liability for nuclear accidents. The third section in this chapter is a complement to the chapter on navigational safety and sunken submarines in addressing the environmental harms and associated obligations to prevent or reduce the impact of accidents and sinkings involving nuclear submarines.

Section 12.4 of the chapter deals with concerns regarding noise pollution and most particularly the effects that submarine detection equipment, notably sonar, may have on living marine resources. In concluding, we observe the existing limitations for the operation of international environmental law when addressing the conduct of military submarines. Not only do these submarines enjoy sovereign immunity, but these

[11] This core obligation is articulated in Article 194 of UNCLOS.

[12] Rosemary Rayfuse, Aline Jaeckel and Natalie Klein, 'International Marine Environmental Law in the 21st Century' in Rosemary Rayfuse, Aline Jaeckel and Natalie Klein (eds.), *Research Handbook on International Marine Environmental Law* (2nd ed., Edward Elgar, 2023) 2, 6–14.

[13] See Chapter 1, Section 1.4.

vessels are most commonly excluded from the scope of international treaties intended to regulate nuclear materials. By contrast, the operation of private submarines, especially for research purposes or in connection with commercial activities will need to be consistent with applicable principles of international environmental law.

This chapter shows that international environmental law and international nuclear law provide rules, albeit not without some ambiguous content, that impinge on submarine operations. However, the limited applicability of those rules to military submarines may prompt concerns on accountability and the availability of clear benchmarks for moderating State actions. To date, mutual interests in preventing environmental harm have allowed for cooperative actions.[14] The terms of Article 236 of UNCLOS will otherwise continue to provide the key legal parameters in regulating military submarines' adherence to international environmental law.

12.2 Core Principles Relevant to Protection of the Marine Environment

Every State is bound by a general obligation to protect and preserve the marine environment, which includes a positive obligation to protect as well as a 'negative obligation not to degrade the marine environment'.[15] From the corpus of international environmental law, States must have regard to their duty of prevention whereby States should refrain from activities within their jurisdiction that will cause harm in the territory of other States.[16] Further, the International Tribunal for the Law of the Sea (ITLOS) has remarked that the 'duty to co-operate is a fundamental principle in the prevention of pollution of the marine environment under Part XII of the Convention and general international law'.[17] This

[14] Most notably in the context of sunken Soviet and Russian submarines. See S. V. Antipov and N. S. Moroleva, 'International Collaboration on Salvaging Nuclear-Powered Submarines' (2004) 97(5) *Atomic Energy* 796.

[15] *South China Sea* (n 1) para. 941 (assessing the meaning of Article 192 of UNCLOS).

[16] Declaration of the United Nations Conference on the Human Environment, Stockholm, 16 June 1972 (UN Doc. A/Conf.48/14/Rev.1) principle 21 ('Stockholm Declaration'); *Legality of the Threat or Use of Nuclear Weapons* (Advisory Opinion of 8 July 1996) [1996] ICJ Rep 226, para. 29.

[17] *MOX Plant* (Ireland v. United Kingdom) (Provisional Measures Order of 3 December 2001) [2001] ITLOS Rep 95, para. 82 ('*MOX Plant*, Provisional Measures'); *Land Reclamation by Singapore in and around the Straits of Johor* (Malaysia v. Singapore) (Provisional Measures, Order of 8 October 2003) [2003] ITLOS Rep 10 [92] ('*Land*

obligation, as well as the duty of prevention, should be considered where a submarine flagged to one State is damaged or has sunk in another State's maritime zones.[18]

In addition, the deployment of submarines, or of equipment to detect submarines in specific locations, may warrant consideration as to whether an environmental impact assessment is required. Under UNCLOS, States must assess the potential effects of their activities when there are reasonable grounds for believing that they may cause 'substantial pollution of or significant and harmful changes to the marine environment'.[19] An environmental impact assessment may be especially important in the context of any operations undertaken in connection with sunken submarines, as was the situation in Norway's response to the sinking of a Soviet nuclear submarine.[20] In addition, the conduct of military exercises in a specific area that may greatly increase the likelihood of striking whales or other protected species (such as the whale shark) should warrant a prior assessment to determine the timing or location of the exercises at issue.

The precautionary approach may also be relevant for States in deciding when or how to undertake specific submarine operations that may cause harm to the marine environment. The content and status of the precautionary approach has been debated in different contexts.[21] In 2024,

Reclamation, Provisional Measures'). The duty to cooperate to protect the environment is further reflected in Principle 24 of the Stockholm Declaration (n 16) and in Principle 27 of the Rio Declaration: Rio Declaration on Environment and Development, Rio de Janeiro, 13 June 1992 (UN Doc. A/Conf.151/26 (Vol. I)) principle 27 ('Rio Declaration').

[18] The relevant maritime zones include the EEZ, as well as the territorial sea or internal waters, in light of the coastal State's exclusive jurisdiction or sovereignty over these areas.

[19] UNCLOS (n 6) art. 206. The customary law status of this obligation was confirmed in the *Responsibilities and Obligations of States with Respect to Activities in the Area* (Advisory Opinion of 1 February 2011) [2011] ITLOS Rep 10, para. 145 ('*Seabed Advisory Opinion*').

[20] See further discussion below notes 46–47 and accompanying text.

[21] See, e.g., David L. VanderZwaag, 'The ICJ, ITLOS and the Precautionary Approach: Paltry Progressions, Jurisprudential Jousting' (2013) 35 *University of Hawai'i Law Review* 617; Rosemary Rayfuse, 'Precaution and the Protection of Marine Biodiversity' in David Freestone (ed.), *Areas beyond National Jurisdiction in The 1982 Law of the Sea Convention at 30* (Brill, 2013) 99–107; Daniel Kazhdan, 'Precautionary Pulp: Pulp Mills and the Evolving Dispute between International Tribunals over the Reach of the Precautionary Principle' (2011) 38 *Ecology Law Quarterly* 527; Abdullah Al Arif, 'Legal Status of the Precautionary Principle in International Fisheries Law and Its Application in the Marine Fisheries Regime of Bangladesh' (2018) 3 *Asia Pacific Journal of Ocean Law and Policy* 95; Ida Lauridsen, 'Precautionary Action: Study on the Status and Implications of the Precautionary Principle in International Environmental Law' (2014) 19 *Eastern and Central European Journal of Environmental Law* 9.

ITLOS indicated that States must apply a precautionary approach when the pollution of the marine environment 'encompasses potential deleterious effects'.[22] The precautionary approach anticipates that '[w]here there are threats of serious or irreversible damage, lack of full scientific certainty shall not be used as a reason for postponing cost-effective measures to prevent environmental degradation'.[23] The precautionary approach would usually need to be considered in connection with the other core principles of international environmental law and have bearing on the interpretation of those principles in specific situations.

States must also ensure that they act consistently with requirements relating to the prevention, reduction and control of marine pollution associated with submarines. While military submarines are not bound by specific requirements that are set out in the multilateral treaties adopted under the auspices of the International Maritime Organization (IMO) to protect the marine environment and ensure the safety of vessels,[24] the standards in those agreements are arguably indicative of what should be taken into account by individual flag States. Private submarines, which do not enjoy sovereign immunity, are required to comply with environmental obligations established by their flag State. The flag State has a due diligence obligation to ensure the actions of private submarines align with international obligations to prevent, reduce and control marine pollution.

Furthermore, there are specific international obligations relating to the conservation and protection of different marine species, especially in relation to marine mammals, which have most notably been affected by noise pollution.[25] Coastal States have the right to adopt laws for the conservation of marine species within their territorial sea[26] and their

[22] *Request for an Advisory Opinion submitted by the Commission of Small Island States on Climate Change and International Law* (Advisory Opinion of 21 May 2024) ITLOS Case No. 31, para. 213.

[23] Rio Declaration (n 17) principle 15.

[24] Tim Stephens, 'Article 236' in Alexander Proelss (ed.), *United Nations Convention on the Law of the Sea: A Commentary* (CH Beck; Hart; Nomos, 2017) 1592, para. 3. For example, MARPOL does 'not apply to any warship, naval auxiliary or other ship owned or operated by a State and used, for the time being, only for government non-commercial service': International Convention for the Prevention of Pollution from Ships, London, 2 November 1973, entered into force 2 October 1983, 1340 UNTS 62, art 3(3) ('MARPOL Convention'). Navigational safety requirements are further addressed in Chapter 11, Section 11.2.

[25] See Section 12.4 below.

[26] UNCLOS (n 6) art. 21(1)(f).

exclusive economic zone (EEZ).[27] Coastal State laws seeking to restrict the movement of submarines, or the operation of submarine detection equipment, to protect the marine environment in the EEZ must do so with due regard to the rights of other users, including the freedom of navigation and other internationally lawful uses related to navigational rights.[28] States are also required to conserve the living resources of the high seas, although arguably the provisions of UNCLOS setting out these requirements (Articles 117 to 119) are directed more so towards the management of fishing activities rather than striving to reduce noise pollution that harms marine species.[29]

These core principles will govern the conduct of private submarines, including those deployed for research, leisure activities, to repair maritime infrastructure and to facilitate resource exploration and exploitation. In some of these situations, the deployment of a submersible tethered to a larger ship will be subject to international environmental obligations in the context of the specific activities being undertaken by the parent ship.[30] Any assessment will depend on the specific function that the submarine is undertaking; deploying a submersible to repair submarine cables would require regard to environmental obligations for this function whereas the use of a submersible in the course of a wider mining operation may mean the use of the submarine is not problematic in itself, but the other activities of which it is part is the broader assessment for meeting environmental requirements.

As noted at the outset, State decision-making on the deployment of military submarines must 'ensure' they act 'consistently' with UNCLOS

[27] Ibid, art. 56(1).

[28] Ibid, art. 56(3). See further Chapter 8, Section 8.4.1.

[29] The establishment of marine protected areas on the high seas may have implications for submarine operations that prejudice the conservation and management of marine living resources. Such areas may be established through procedures set out in the Agreement to Protect Biodiversity in Areas Beyond National Jurisdiction: Agreement under the United Nations Convention on the Law of the Sea on the Conservation and Sustainable Use of Marine Biological Diversity of Areas beyond National Jurisdiction, New York, 19 June 2023, entered into force 17 January 2026 (UN Doc. A/CONF.232/2023/4). It will fall to the Conference of Parties to determine precise rules for such areas and it remains to be seen whether any such areas impose restrictions on submarine operations (if even contemplated).

[30] For some of the uses of private submarines for ocean research, see Bryan Zhang, 'Submersibles for Deep Sea Exploration', *Tufts Electrical and Computer Engineering Design Handbook*, 2015 <https://sites.tufts.edu/eeseniordesignhandbook/2015/submersibles-for-deep-sea-exploration/>. See further Chapter 8, Section 8.3.3 for discussion of the regulation of submersibles in commercial activities in the EEZ.

provisions to protect and preserve the marine environment. Yet, in doing so, the applicable obligations arising under international environmental law are modified by considerations as to what impairs the 'operations or operational capabilities' of submarines and what is 'reasonable and practicable'.[31] There are thus specific considerations that further temper the application of the international environmental law principles outlined in this section. A balance is to be struck between the due diligence obligation to act consistently with international marine environmental law, and the operations or operational capabilities of submarines and a non-specific assessment of what is 'reasonable and practicable'. The weight of considerations is clearly in favour of the flag State of the military submarine but does not allow for complete disregard of international environmental law. Nonetheless, even if a military submarine does cause environmental damage, UNCLOS does not explicitly recognise that international responsibility for loss or damage accrues (in distinction to the situation of damage or loss caused during passage in the territorial sea under Article 31 of UNCLOS).[32] The absence of such a provision may not be decisive, however, in relation to nuclear submarines, which are next discussed.

12.3 International Environmental Law Issues in the Operation of Nuclear Submarines

Since the mid 1950s, nuclear-powered submarines have been commissioned as a complement to conventional diesel-electric submarines.[33] It is estimated that there are more than 160 ships, most of which are submarines, powered by over 200 nuclear reactors.[34] In addition, conventionally powered submarines may be armed with nuclear weapons.[35] Both are termed here as 'nuclear submarines' when considered collectively or will otherwise be differentiated as nuclear-powered or nuclear-armed submarines where relevant for specific laws. The environmental hazards

[31] UNCLOS (n 6) art. 236.

[32] Stephens (n 24) 1595, para. 20.

[33] See Chapter 1, Section 1.4.1.2.

[34] World Nuclear Association, 'Nuclear-Powered Ships', 4 February 2025 <https://world-nuclear.org/information-library/non-power-nuclear-applications/transport/nuclear-powered-ships>. Nuclear propulsion in surface ships is predominantly used in ice-breakers operating in the Arctic: ibid.

[35] Dimitrios Mitsopoulos, 'All the Nuclear Missile Submarines in the World in One Chart', *Popular Mechanics*, 8 June 2018 <www.popularmechanics.com/military/navy-ships/a21204892/nuclear-missile-submarines-chart/>.

posed by nuclear submarines are due to the risk of radiation pollution, both into marine areas as well as in the atmosphere. The increased production of nuclear submarines, which is occurring among a growing number of countries,[36] should increasingly give rise to environmental concerns due to the risk of accidents. A study from 2019 observed '[o]f the total of 41 accidents recorded in 36 [nuclear] submarines, 12 related to nuclear reactors, resulting in the release of radioactivity within the vessel as well as in the sea, and radiation poisoning as well as the death of the crews in some cases'.[37] The International Atomic Energy Agency (IAEA) has reported on the release of radioactive materials into the water column as well as the air consequent to these accidents.[38]

A significant majority of these accidents involved Soviet/Russian submarines.[39] For example, the explosion of a Soviet submarine in 1985 (which was revealed only seven years later) in Chazma Bay has been highly detrimental to the surrounding maritime areas, as well as affecting the health of individuals living in adjacent towns.[40] The explosion occurred in a shipyard during nuclear fuel reloading operations and has been described as 'the largest nuclear accident in the history of the nuclear fleet'.[41] While different remedial action was undertaken, commentators have observed that '[t]he bay was not cleaned, a portion of the fuel, fission products, and activation products remains in the bottom deposits'.[42]

[36] As noted in Chapter 1, China, France, India, Russia, the United Kingdom and the United States all have such submarines. They are also either deployed, under construction or planned for Australia, South Korea and Brazil. See Chapter 1, Section 1.4.1.2. For discussion on the different nuclear submarines previously and currently in operation, see World Nuclear Association (n 34).

[37] Zia Mian, M. V. Ramana and Abdul H. Nayyara, 'Nuclear Submarines in South Asia: New Risks and Dangers' (2019) 2 *Journal for Peace and Nuclear Disarmament* 184, 189. See further ibid, Appendix 1. Table of Nuclear Submarine Accidents.

[38] International Atomic Energy Agency, 'Inventory of Accidents and Losses at Sea Involving Radioactive Material', September 2001 (IAEA Doc. IAEA-TECDOC-1242).

[39] Mian, Ramana and Nayyara (n 37) 190.

[40] International Physicians for the Prevention of Nuclear War, 'Chazhma Bay, Russia', *Hibakusha Worldwide*, 2024 <https://hibakusha-worldwide.org/en/locations/chazhma-bay>. The extent of harm caused appears to be disputed: see Yu. V. Sivintsev, V. L. Vysotskii and V. A. Danilyan, 'Radioecological Consequences of a Radiation Accident in a Nuclear-powered Submarine in Chazhma Cove' (1994) 76 *Atomic Energy* 157.

[41] A. A. Sarkisov et al., 'Damaging Factors of a Nuclear Accident at the Nuclear Submarine K-431 in the Chazhma Bay' (2021) 129(3) *Atomic Energy* 169, 169.

[42] Ibid, 173.

In relation to the 1989 sinking of a Russian nuclear submarine, corrosion of the construction materials, as well as corrosion associated with the nuclear fuel and the nuclear weapons have all presented risks. In this instance, scientists estimated that the damage sustained would result in very slow rates of corrosion,[43] and that the release of radionuclides would not increase significantly for a thousand years.[44] Nonetheless, plutonium is not an element that dissolves easily in sea water. Of great concern is Cesium-137, which is one of the most significant long-term contaminants in the event of an accident involving a nuclear reactor.[45] In 2019, a joint Russian-Norwegian project estimated that a sunken nuclear submarine 'was leaking radiation up to 800,000 times above normal levels'.[46] Scientists have observed, however, that the amount of plutonium on board a Russian nuclear submarine was much smaller than the quantity of plutonium released into oceans from reprocessing plants or during nuclear weapon tests.[47] Nonetheless, the presence of any radionuclides in the marine ecosystem will result in their ingestion by fish with flow on consequences up the food-chain, including to human consumption.

Chapter 7 discussed the special rules that may be applicable to nuclear submarines during passage in the territorial sea, as UNCLOS allows for the passage of 'nuclear-powered ships and ships carrying nuclear or other inherently dangerous or noxious substances' to exercise the right of innocent passage in the territorial sea of another State.[48] However, such vessels must 'carry documents and observe special precautionary measures established for such ships by international agreements'.[49] The standards imposed under UNCLOS are 'international' rather than allowing each individual State to formulate its own restrictions independently.[50] Under the auspices of the IAEA, a suite of treaties has been adopted to

[43] Steinar Høibråten, Per E. Thoresen and Are Haugan, 'The Sunken Nuclear Submarine *Komsomolets* and its Effects on the Environment' (1997) 202 *Science of the Total Environment* 67, 72.

[44] Ibid, 74.

[45] Centers for Disease Control and Prevention, 'Radioisotope Brief: Cesium-137 (Cs-137)', 4 April 2018 <www.cdc.gov/nceh/radiation/emergencies/isotopes/cesium.htm>; Teppei J. Yasunari, et al., 'Cesium-137 Deposition and Contamination of Japanese Soils due to the Fukushima Nuclear Accident' (2011) 108 *PNAS* 19530.

[46] Rusli (n 5) 40.

[47] Høibråten, Thoresen and Haugan (n 43) 76.

[48] UNCLOS (n 6) art. 23. See Chapter 7, Section 7.2.2.

[49] UNCLOS (n 6) art. 23.

[50] John Astley II and Michael N. Schmitt, 'The Law of the Sea and Naval Operations' (1997) 42 *Air Force Law Review* 119, 132 (noting that, as of time of writing, five States – Djibouti,

address safety and security concerns associated with nuclear materials.[51] These treaties are considered in this section where relevant and applicable to submarines.

12.3.1 Nuclear Submarines and Liability for Ultrahazardous Activities

Beyond the specific concerns associated with passage that are identified in relation to the law of the sea, the catastrophic environmental (and human health) consequences that are risked in relation to nuclear substances have prompted a distinct area of regulation in relation to what are termed 'ultrahazardous activities'.[52] These activities may be lawful in their own right but nonetheless pose risks of grave transboundary harm.

The ultrahazardous nature of nuclear submarines may influence assessments of what actions are 'necessary and practicable' in protecting the marine environment in accordance with Article 236 of UNCLOS. However, the international laws relating to nuclear safety generally exempt military or defence uses of nuclear substances. For example, Article 3(3) of the Joint Convention on the Safety of Spent Fuel Management and on the Safety of Radioactive Waste Management reads:

> This Convention shall not apply to the safety of management of spent fuel or radioactive waste *within military or defence programmes*, unless declared as spent fuel or radioactive waste for the purposes of this Convention by the Contracting Party. However, this Convention shall apply to the safety of management of spent fuel and radioactive waste from military or defence programmes if and when such materials are transferred permanently to and managed within exclusively civilian programmes.[53]

Egypt, Oman, Pakistan and Yemen – had established special requirements for nuclear-powered craft).

51 See generally, International Atomic Energy Agency, 'Treaties' <www.iaea.org/resources/legal/treaties>. See also Elena Bernini, 'Small Modular Reactors and Transportable Nuclear Power Plants' in James Kraska and Young-Kil Park (eds.), *Emerging Technology and the Law of the Sea* (Cambridge University Press, 2022) 108, 119–120.

52 The International Law Commission (ILC) has defined 'ultrahazardous activity' as 'an activity with a danger that is rarely expected to materialize but might assume, on that rare occasion, grave (more than significant, serious or substantial) proportions': ILC, 'Draft Articles on Prevention of Transboundary Harm from Hazardous Activities, with Commentaries' in *Report of the International Law Commission on the Work of its 53rd Session (23 April–1 June and 2 July–10 August 2001)* (UN Doc. A/56/10) 149, para. 2 (commentary to art. 1) ('Draft Articles on Prevention of Transboundary Harm').

53 Joint Convention on the Safety of Spent Fuel Management and on the Safety of Radioactive Waste Management, Vienna, 9 May 1997, entered into force 18 June 2001, 2153 UNTS 303, art. 3(3) (emphasis added).

The Convention on the Physical Protection of Nuclear Material initially limited its scope to nuclear materials 'for peaceful purposes',[54] but amendments to that treaty in 2005 clarified the non-applicability of the treaty to armed forces nor to nuclear materials used or retained for military purposes.[55] The IMO's Code for the Safe Carriage of Irradiated Nuclear Fuel, Plutonium and High-Level Radioactive Wastes in Flasks Onboard Ships specifies how certain nuclear materials should be carried by sea, but excludes warships, naval auxiliaries and other sovereign-immune vessels from its scope.[56] Peace-time uses of nuclear submarines that are also warships are thus often excluded from international obligations that apply to civilian uses of nuclear materials, particularly in relation to nuclear energy. The nuances to this general position are slight and identified immediately below. At present, private submarines are not used for the transport of nuclear materials. If they were to be so utilised, rules relating to transport of ultrahazardous and radioactive substances would apply similarly to those rules governing surface ships that transport nuclear waste or other nuclear materials.[57]

For ultrahazardous activities, international law establishes a standard of strict liability on an operator to remedy damage caused by such

[54] Convention on the Physical Protection of Nuclear Material, New York and Vienna, 3 March 1980, entered into force 8 February 1987, 1456 UNTS 101, art. 2.

[55] Amendment to the Convention on the Physical Protection of Nuclear Material, Vienna, 8 July 2005, entered into force 8 May 2016, 3132 UNTS 136, amended arts. 2(4)–(5).

[56] International Maritime Organization, Code for the Safe Carriage of Irradiated Nuclear Fuel, Plutonium and High-Level Radioactive Wastes in Flasks Onboard Ships, London, 27 May 1999, para. 1.2.1 ('INF Code'), referring to International Convention for the Safety of Life at Sea, London, 1 November 1974, entered into force 25 May 1980, 1194 UNTS 278, ch. VII, reg. 15.2 ('SOLAS Convention'), which excludes the application of the Code to warships. Similar to Article 236 of UNCLOS, regulation 15.2 reads:

> This part and the INF Code do not apply to warships, naval auxiliary or other vessels owned or operated by a Contracting Government and used, for the time being, only on government noncommercial service; however, each Administration shall ensure, by the adoption of appropriate measures not impairing operations or operational capabilities of such ships owned or operated by it, that such ships carrying INF cargo act in a manner consistent, so far as reasonable and practicable, with this part and the INF Code.

[57] For discussion on transport of nuclear material and other ultrahazardous substances generally, see, e.g., Cathy Suykens, 'Globalisation of the Nuclear Fuel Cycle and Maritime Carriage of Radioactive Materials: Review of the Legal Regime' (2011) 26(3) *International Journal of Marine and Coastal Law* 385; Duncan E. J. Currie and Jon M. van Dyke, 'Recent Developments in the International Law Governing Shipments of Nuclear Materials and Wastes and their Implications for SIDS' (2005) 14(2) *Review of European Community and International Environmental Law* 117.

activities.[58] An argument may be raised that this standard applies in relation to the operation of nuclear submarines. Not long after the development of nuclear submarines, efforts were undertaken to extend strict liability to inter alia operators of nuclear submarines, as the Convention on the Liability of Operators of Nuclear Ships applies to nuclear-powered warships.[59] This treaty was drafted at a time when it was envisaged that there would be an increasing number of commercial ships operated with nuclear power and that this industry would be encouraged if a regulatory regime was developed to ensure it would not be decimated by claims for damage in the event of an accident.[60] However, that 1962 treaty is yet to enter into force as it has only garnered seven ratifications to date.[61] Similar with other civil liability regimes established in relation to maritime pollution,[62] the treaty anticipates that a nuclear ship operator will be absolutely liable for any nuclear damage upon proof that such damage has been caused by a nuclear

[58] ILC, 'Draft Principles on the Allocation of Loss in the Case of Transboundary Harm Arising out of Hazardous Activities, with Commentaries' (2006) 2 *Yearbook of the International Law Commission* 59, principle 4(2).

[59] Convention on the Liability of Operators of Nuclear Ships, Brussels, 25 May 1962, not entered into force, 57 *American Journal of International Law* 268, art. 2(1). The United States and the Soviet Union voted against the adoption of this treaty because of the inclusion of nuclear warships within its terms. Michael Hardy, 'The Liability of Operators of Nuclear Ships' (1963) 12 *International and Comparative Law Quarterly* 778, 787.

[60] Hardy (n 59) 778.

[61] Under Article XXIV(1), the Convention shall come into force three months after the deposit of an instrument of ratification by at least one licensing State and one other State; a 'licensing state' is defined in Article I(2) as being a contracting state that 'operates or has authorised the operation of a nuclear ship under its flag': Convention on the Liability of Operators of Nuclear Ships (n 59).

[62] See, e.g., International Convention on Civil Liability for Oil Pollution Damage, Brussels, 29 November 1969, entered into force 19 June 1975, 973 UNTS 3; International Convention on the Establishment of an International Fund for Compensation for Oil Pollution Damage, Brussels, 18 December 1971, entered into force 16 October 1978, 1110 UNTS 57 ('Fund Convention'); Protocol of 1992 to Amend the International Convention on Civil Liability for Oil Pollution Damage, London, 27 November 1996, entered into force 30 May 1996, 1956 UNTS 258; Protocol of 1992 to Amend the International Convention on the Establishment of an International Fund for Oil Pollution Damage, London, 27 November 1992, entered into force 30 May 1996, 1956 UNTS 255. For discussion, see Louise Angélique de La Fayette, 'New Approaches for Addressing Damage to the Marine Environment' (2005) 20 *International Journal of Marine and Coastal Law* 167; Gaetano Librando, 'Influence of the Torrey Canyon Incident on the Liability and Compensation Regimes Developed under the Auspices of the IMO' in Norman A. Martínez Gutiérrez (ed.), *Serving the Rule of International Maritime Law: Essays in Honour of Professor David Joseph Attard* (Routledge, 2009) 315.

incident.[63] Such liability does not arise if the damage was caused directly by an act of war or hostilities.[64] Moreover, while the operator may be liable, no enforcement jurisdiction is recognised in relation to warships.[65] In the absence of a binding treaty but strong counter-practice to uphold the sovereign immunities of warships, it could not be reasonably argued that the operator of a military nuclear submarine would be held civilly liable as a matter of customary international law.

A more general civil liability regime has been established to compensate victims for damage following nuclear incidents.[66] However, Bernini has observed that '[m]any states have not signed or ratified these agreements, impeding recognition of a global, uniform civil nuclear liability regime'.[67] This complex web of treaties provides for different geographic scope of application depending on the treaty (and depending on whether a State is a party to the treaty or not); the Amended Vienna Convention allows for the possibility of compensating victims for damage 'wherever suffered', which could include maritime areas,[68] whereas the Amended Paris Convention does not.[69] The courts of the coastal State have

63 Convention on the Liability of Operators of Nuclear Ships (n 61) art. 2(1).

64 Ibid, art. 8.

65 Ibid, art. 10.

66 See Vienna Convention on Civil Liability for Nuclear Damage, Vienna, 21 May 1963, entered into force 12 November 1977, 1063 UNTS 266 ('1977 Vienna Convention'), as amended by the Protocol to amend the Vienna Convention on Civil Liability for Nuclear Damage, Vienna, 12 September 1997, entered into force 4 October 2003, 2241 UNTS 270 ('Amended Vienna Convention'); Paris Convention on Third Party Liability in the Field of Nuclear Energy, Paris, 29 July 1960, entered into force 1 April 1968, 956 UNTS 251, as amended by the Protocol to Amend the Convention on Third Party Liability in the Field of Nuclear Energy as amended by the Additional Protocol of 28 January 1964 and by the Protocol of 16 November 1982, Paris, 12 February 2004, entered into force 1 January 2022 ('Amended Paris Convention'); Brussels Convention Supplementary to the Convention on Third Party Liability in the Field of Nuclear Energy, Brussels, 31 January 1963, entered into force 4 December 1974, 1041 UNTS 358, as amended by the Protocol to Amend the Convention on Third Party Liability in the Field of Nuclear Energy of 29 July 1960 as amended by the Additional Protocol of 28 January 1964 and by the Protocol of 16 November 1982, Paris, 12 February 2004, entered into force 1 January 2022 ('Amended Brussels Convention').

67 Bernini (n 51) 125.

68 Including maritime areas of non-contracting parties to that treaty, subject to requirements about those States' national legislation: Amended Vienna Convention (n 66) art. IA.

69 Amended Paris Convention (n 66). As discussed in Johan G. Lammers, 'Compensation for Nuclear Damage under the Paris, Brussels and Vienna Conventions' (2003) 16 *Hague Yearbook of International Law* 47, 57. It should further be acknowledged that the Paris Convention is open to OECD countries, but a 1988 joint protocol relating to the Vienna

jurisdiction in relation to nuclear incidents that occur within its EEZ.[70] However, the civil liability regime under the Amended Vienna Convention does not otherwise apply to nuclear-powered submarines in light of the scope of application covering 'any nuclear reactor other than one with which a means of sea or air transport is equipped for use as a source of power, whether for propulsion thereof or for any other purpose'.[71] Further, nuclear damage directly due to an act of armed conflict or hostilities is also excluded from the civil liability regime.[72] Arguably, damage caused by a nuclear incident during peace-time operations involving a nuclear-armed submarine may still fall within this civil liability regime.[73] Such applicability is implicit rather than explicit.[74] Otherwise, in the absence of a civil liability regime, transnational environmental harm caused by a nuclear incident at sea must be resolved at the inter-State level as a question of State responsibility.[75]

Nuclear-powered submarines may also be regulated in relation to treaties dealing with notification of and assistance with nuclear accidents. For instance, the Convention on Early Notification of a Nuclear Accident has a scope of application that includes 'the transport and storage of nuclear fuels', as well as 'any nuclear reactor wherever located', and is concerned with accidents that may cause transboundary harm.[76] In the event of a nuclear accident, there are notification and information

and Paris Conventions allow for parties to that protocol to be treated as if parties to both conventions: see Bernini (n 51) 125–126 and fn 66.

70 In accordance with the 1997 Protocol: Amended Vienna Convention (n 66) art. 7.

71 1977 Vienna Convention (n 66) art. 1(1)(j). This language was retained in the Amended Vienna Convention (n 66).

72 Amended Vienna Convention (n 66) art. IV(3).

73 The Amended Vienna Convention does anticipate the possibility of a State being an 'operator': see International Atomic Energy Agency, 'The 1997 Vienna Convention on Civil Liability for Nuclear Damage and the 1997 Convention on Supplementary Compensation for Nuclear Damage – Explanatory Texts' (IAEA International Law Series No. 3 (Rev. 2), 2020) <www-pub.iaea.org/MTCD/Publications/PDF/P1906_web.pdf> 24 para. 2.2.1.

74 Bernini (n 51) argues that warships or military activities may be covered by the nuclear liability conventions as the Vienna Convention only purports to exclude 'nuclear installations used for non-peaceful purposes' (Art. 1B), which excludes actions in violation of the prohibition on the use of force and not all military activities: 131–132.

75 Article XVIII, which, as amended by the 1997 Protocol, now reads as follows: 'This Convention shall not affect the rights and obligations of a Contracting Party under the general rules of public international law': Amended Vienna Convention (n 66) art. XVIII.

76 Convention on Early Notification of a Nuclear Accident, Vienna, 27 October 1986, entered into force 27 October 1986, 1439 UNTS 275, art. 1.

obligations that are owed to States that may be physically affected.[77] Further, there is no limitation on the scope of application of a multilateral agreement concerning any assistance that may be afforded in the event of a nuclear accident or radiological emergency.[78] While the scope of this treaty does not exclude warships or nuclear-armed vessels, Article 3 provides that States 'may' notify of other nuclear accidents that do not expressly fall within the scope of the treaty. This treaty has 132 parties, including the permanent members of the UN Security Council, India, Israel and Pakistan, but not North Korea.[79] However, as noted above,[80] Russia has not always provided prompt notice of accidents involving its nuclear submarines.

12.3.2 Nuclear Submarines and Environmental Protection in Nuclear Free Zones

Protection of the marine environment from the risks associated with nuclear submarines may further emerge from regional treaties that establish nuclear free zones. The 1985 South Pacific Nuclear Free Zone Treaty (Treaty of Raratonga) has the aim of keeping the region 'free of environmental pollution by radioactive wastes and other radioactive matter'.[81] Such zones have also been created under regional treaties for Latin America and the Caribbean,[82] as well as Africa,[83] Southeast Asia[84] and Central Asia,[85] but are focused on nuclear

[77] Ibid, art. 2.

[78] Convention on Assistance in the Case of a Nuclear Accident or Radiological Emergency, Vienna, 26 September 1986, entered into force 26 February 1987, 1457 UNTS 133.

[79] International Atomic Energy Agency, 'Convention on Early Notification of a Nuclear Accident: Status' <www.iaea.org/sites/default/files/22/06/cenna_status.pdf>.

[80] See above nn 39–41 and accompanying text.

[81] South Pacific Nuclear Free Zone Treaty, Rarotonga, 6 August 1985, entered into force 11 December 1986, 1445 UNTS 177, preamble ('Treaty of Rarotonga').

[82] Treaty for the Prohibition of Nuclear Weapons in Latin America, Mexico City, 14 February 1967, entered into force 22 April 1968, 1894 UNTS 335.

[83] Treaty on the Nuclear-Weapon-Free Zone in Africa, Cairo, 1 April 1996, entered into force 15 July 2009 (1996) 35 ILM 698 ('Treaty of Pelindaba').

[84] Southeast Asia Nuclear Weapon-Free Zone Treaty, Bangkok, 15 December 1995, 1981 UNTS 129 ('Treaty of Bangkok').

[85] Central Asian Nuclear-Weapon-Free Zone Treaty, Semipalatinsk, 8 September 2006, 2970 UNTS 91 ('Treaty of Semipalatinsk'). This treaty is of marginal relevance for present purposes as its scope of application is limited to the 'waters' of the States party, which are described as 'harbors, lakes, rivers and streams'. See ibid, art. 2(a) and seemingly would not include the Aral Sea or Caspian Sea.

weapons specifically. Within each of these zones, there are comprehensive prohibitions relating to nuclear explosive devices.

While States party to these treaties are to prevent the stationing of nuclear explosive devices in their territory, each State typically retains the right to decide on the passage or visit of foreign ships beyond the navigational rights enjoyed by these ships for innocent passage, transit passage or archipelagic sea lanes passage.[86] These restrictions only apply to the EEZ and continental shelves for those States that are party to the Southeast Asia treaty;[87] whereas no comparable term is included in the other nuclear-free-zone treaties.[88] In any event, the Southeast Asia treaty further seeks to preserve navigational rights set out in UNCLOS for other States,[89] while denying themselves the right to transport nuclear weapons within the designated zone.[90] Consequently, the relevance of these treaties for nuclear submarines is reduced.

It is important to underline that these nuclear-free-zone treaties would be primarily targeted at nuclear-armed submarines, rather than nuclear-powered submarines given that the treaties are directed to 'nuclear explosive devices', including when unassembled, and not all nuclear materials more broadly. For example, the Treaty of Raratonga excludes from the definition of nuclear explosive devices 'the means of transport or delivery of such a weapon or device if separable from and not an

[86] See, e.g., Treaty of Rarotonga (n 81) art. 5. Stationing is defined as 'emplantation, emplacement, transportation on land or inland waters, stockpiling, storage, installation and deployment': ibid, art. 1(d). See also Treaty of Bangkok (n 85) art. 7; Treaty of Semipalatinsk (n 85) art. 4. During negotiations of the Treaty for the Prohibition of Nuclear Weapons in Latin America (n 85), debates ensued as to the legality of maritime transit, but drafters considered 'existing international law and norms guaranteed state parties' right to allow or deny passage rights to non-signatories in the free exercise of their sovereignty': J. Luis Rodriguez and Elizabeth Mendenhall, 'Nuclear Weapon-free Zones and the Issue of Maritime Transit in Latin America' (2022) 98 *International Affairs* 819.

[87] Treaty of Bangkok (n 85) art. 2(1).

[88] The Treaty for the Prohibition of Nuclear Weapons in Latin America (n 85) purports to apply to high seas areas in accordance with Article 4(2). As this treaty was adopted prior to the negotiation of UNCLOS, there is no reference to or alignment with currently existing EEZ boundaries. By contrast, the Treaty of Pelindaba (n 85) is limited to territorial seas, archipelagic waters and internal waters of the States party to that treaty: art. 1(b).

[89] 'Nothing in this Treaty shall prejudice the rights or the exercise of these rights by any State under the provisions of the United Nations Convention on the Law of the Sea of 1982, in particular with regard to freedom of the high seas, rights of innocent passage, archipelagic sea lanes passage or transit passage of ships and aircraft, and consistent with the Charter of the United Nations': Treaty of Bangkok (n 85) art. 2(2).

[90] Ibid, art. 3(1)(b).

indivisible part of it'.[91] While the nuclear-free-zone treaties arguably contribute to the protection of the marine environment in purporting to reduce the occurrence of nuclear weapons within different maritime areas and hence possible contamination of the marine environment, these treaties are more so directed at the purpose of nuclear non-proliferation and nuclear disarmament – as evident in the preambles to the treaties – rather than marine environmental protection.

12.3.3 *Environmental Obligations when Decommissioning Nuclear Submarines*

A final concern that may emerge for the marine environment in relation to nuclear submarines arises at the point that these craft are no longer operational. When nuclear-powered submarines reach the end of their operations, the decommissioning must further consider the defueling and safe disposal of nuclear reactors. Nuclear submarines are estimated to have an operational life of between twenty and thirty years; 'operational life ends when the military capability does not justify the cost of continued operation'.[92] In the regular decommissioning process, the reactor compartments are removed from nuclear submarines and a site for their storage on land must then be determined and will be subject to national laws governing such activities, albeit subject to international safety standards.[93]

In the early 1980s, the US Navy contemplated the possibility of dumping decommissioned nuclear submarines at sea.[94] The extent of possible radioactive pollution was calculated to be unacceptably high at this time, as it was anticipated that radioactive material would leak from the

[91] Treaty of Raratonga (n 81) art. 1(c). See also Treaty for the Prohibition of Nuclear Weapons in Latin America (n 85) art. 5 ('An instrument that may be used for the transport or propulsion of the device is not included in this definition if it is separable from the device and not an indivisible part thereof').

[92] Yran Leite Maia et al. 'Decommissioning of Nuclear Submarines and the Interim Storage of their Reactor Compartments' (2022) 8 *ASCE-ASME Journal of Risk and Uncertainty in Engineering Systems, Part B: Mechanical Engineering* 041103–1, 1–2, citing United States Department of Navy, 'US Naval Nuclear Powered Ship Inactivation, Disposal, and Recycling', 2019 <www.energy.gov/nepa/doeeis-0524-disposal-decommissioned-defueled-ex-enterprise-cvn-65-and-its-associated-naval>.

[93] See, e.g., International Atomic Energy Agency, 'Disposal of Radioactive Waste, Specific Safety Requirements', 2011 (IAEA Doc. IAEA-SSR-5).

[94] United States Navy, 'Draft Environmental Impact Statement on the Disposal of Decommissioned Defueled Naval Submarine Reactor Plants' (1982), cited in W. Jackson Davis and Jon M. van Dyke, 'Dumping of Decommissioned Nuclear Submarines at Sea: A Technical and Legal Analysis' (1990) 14 *Marine Policy* 467, 467.

corroded walls of the reactor's pressure vessel and bulkheads.[95] Further, the projected duration of radioactive material in the marine environment could be measured in centuries.[96] When the US Navy decommissions a nuclear submarine, the nuclear fuel is removed from the reactor and sent for processing, and the nuclear reactor compartments are cut out, sealed and transported to an approved site for disposal.[97] In the early 1960s, accidents on two Soviet submarines prompted the disposal of the nuclear reactors at sea with the damaged fuel.[98] Soviet nuclear submarines disposed of at sea have raised concerns about pollution of the Arctic Ocean,[99] prompting Russia to commit in 2020 to programmes to raise two Soviet nuclear submarines and four reactor compartments.[100] The project is currently delayed due to the Russo-Ukrainian war.[101]

While there are international requirements restricting the dumping of nuclear waste at sea,[102] a nuclear submarine is still protected by sovereign immunity and the requirements of the London Dumping Convention would not therefore be applicable to it.[103] Davis and van Dyke have

95 For extent of possible harm envisaged from fifteen nuclear submarines being dumped per year in the late 1980s, see Davis and van Dyke (n 94) 469–470.

96 Ibid, 470.

97 Environmental Protection Agency, 'Nuclear Submarines and Aircraft Carriers', *RadTown*, 3 May 2023 <www.epa.gov/radtown/nuclear-submarines-and-aircraft-carriers>.

98 Mian, Ramana and Nayyara (n 37) 190.

99 Beyond the Arctic, Van Dyke reported that between '1973 and 1979, Russia dumped four nuclear ship reactors in the East Sea (off North Korea), and they continued dumping nuclear wastes in the years that followed, culminating in a dump of 900 tons of low-level waste generated by nuclear submarines of the Russian navy directly into East Sea in October 1993': Jon M. Van Dyke, 'Whither the UNEP Regional Seas Programmes?' in Harry N. Scheiber and Jin-Hyun Paik (eds.), *Regions, Institutions and the Law of the Sea* (Martinus Nijhoff, 2013) 89, 106. The policies and environmental implications with regards to dumping of nuclear materials at sea during the Cold War have been examined by Vartanov and Hollister. Raphael Vartanov and Charles D. Hollister, 'Nuclear Legacy of the Cold War. Russian Policy and Ocean Disposal' (1997) 21(1) *Marine Policy* 1.

100 Alec Luhn, 'Russia's 'Slow-motion Chernobyl' at Sea', *BBC News*, 2 September 2020 <www.bbc.com/future/article/20200901-the-radioactive-risk-of-sunken-nuclear-soviet-submarines>.

101 Charles Digges, 'War Puts Cleanup of Russia's Radioactive Wrecks on Ice', *Bulletin of the Atomic Scientists*, 28 November 2022 <https://thebulletin.org/2022/11/war-puts-cleanup-of-russias-radioactive-wrecks-on-ice/>.

102 The act of 'dumping' includes 'any deliberate disposal at sea of vessels, aircraft, platforms or other man-made structures at sea': Convention on the Prevention of Marine Pollution by Dumping of Wastes and Other Matter, London, 29 December 1972, entered into force 30 August 1975, 1046 UNTS 120, art. III(l)(a)(ii) ('London Dumping Convention'). See also UNCLOS (n 6) art. 1(1)(5)(a)(ii) (which includes an identical definition).

103 London Dumping Convention (n 102) art. VII(4).

argued that a decommissioned, defueled, deactivated nuclear submarine is no longer subject to sovereign immunity.[104] Even if sovereign immunity was still claimed, the State seeking to dump a nuclear submarine would need to adhere to general obligations to protect and preserve the marine environment and to show due diligence in assessing what is 'reasonable and practicable' in line with Article 236 of UNCLOS.

12.4 Noise Pollution

Noise (or acoustic) pollution may be problematic in relation to the protection of the marine environment because of the potential impacts of this pollution on marine species – particularly cetaceans as species that use sound to communicate or navigate – as well as marine ecosystems.[105] The UN General Assembly has repeatedly called upon States to assess and address anthropogenic underwater noise in light of both socioeconomic and environmental impacts.[106] There are diverse sources of underwater noise, not specific to submarines, that may impact negatively on marine mammals in particular and other marine species more generally.[107] 'At high levels and/or at frequencies where marine species have developed particular sensitivity, noise can lead to physical injuries, negatively affect species' ability to hear other sounds, disrupt their behaviour, or increase their sensitivity'.[108] As a result, the production of underwater noise should be addressed within a frame that accounts for international environmental law, and thus holds implications for the navigational rights of submarines.

To be considered in the context of international law rules concerned with the prevention, reduction and control of marine pollution, a preliminary question is whether underwater noise constitutes 'pollution'. Pollution is defined in UNCLOS as

[104] Davis and van Dyke (n 94) 474–475.

[105] The possible harms caused to marine species and ecosystems are set out in Harm M. Dotinga and Alex G. Oude Elferink, 'Acoustic Pollution in the Oceans: The Search for Legal Standards' (2000) 31 *Ocean Development and International Law* 151, 154–156.

[106] See, e.g., 'Oceans and the Law of the Sea', 12 December 2024, UNGA Res. 79/114 (UN Doc. A/RES/79/144) paras. 280–285.

[107] Jeremy Firestone and Christina Jarvis, 'Response and Responsibility: Regulating Noise Pollution in the Marine Environment' (2007) 10 *Journal of International Wildlife Law and Policy* 109, 116–118. See generally Jon M. van Dyke, Emily A. Gardner and Joseph R. Morgan, 'Whales, Submarines, and Active Sonar' (2004) 18 *Ocean Yearbook* 330.

[108] Dotinga and Elferink (n 105) 152.

> the introduction by man, directly or indirectly, of substances or energy into the marine environment, including estuaries, which results or is likely to result in such deleterious effects as harm to living resources and marine life, hazards to human health, hindrance to marine activities, including fishing and other legitimate uses of the sea, impairment of quality for use of sea water and reduction of amenities.[109]

Noise pollution arguably falls within this definition as a form of energy that potentially produces or does produce deleterious effects to marine species and ecosystems.[110] Some consideration as to whether the noise pollution reaches a threshold of 'deleterious' or not could be debated.

Submarines prompt concerns with regards to noise pollution in two ways: first, as a source of noise pollution, potentially in relation to diesel-powered submarines, or in the operation of certain equipment on submarines, and, second, the use of sonar for anti-submarine warfare and more generally as a security measure for the detection of submarines. As a source of anthropogenic pollution, the noise from submarines may be similar to noise that emanates from surface vessels.[111] These noises, especially at low frequencies, are considered a 'significant anthropogenic contributor to underwater noise'.[112] It has, though, been the case that the diesel-electric submarines have become quieter,[113] especially when running submerged on electricity.[114] Navies are also seeking ways to render nuclear submarines quieter and thus less detectable.[115] Technology has advanced to the development of 'silent submarines'.[116] While the contribution of submarines to noise pollution has thus (significantly) diminished, the technology used to detect submarines has progressed from passive sonar to active sonar.[117]

109 UNCLOS (n 6) art. 1(1)(4).

110 See Karen N. Scott, 'International Regulation of Undersea Noise' (2004) 53 *International and Comparative Law Quarterly* 287, 293.

111 For a description of the noise generated from commercial shipping, see, e.g., Michael T. Palmer, 'Regulating Ocean Noise: A Non-traditional Threat to Maritime Security' (2010) 5 *Maritime Affairs* 86, 90.

112 Firestone and Jarvis (n 107) 116.

113 van Dyke, Gardner and Morgan (n 107) 341.

114 Ryan White, 'Why are Diesel-electric Submarines Quieter than Nuclear Submarines?', *Naval Post*, 14 March 2021 <https://navalpost.com/nuclear-submarines-diesel-electric-submarines-noise-level/>.

115 Ibid.

116 James Kraska, 'Seabed Technology and Naval Operations on the Continental Shelf' in James Kraska and Young-Kil Park (eds.), *Emerging Technology and the Law of the Sea* (Cambridge University Press, 2022) 301, 318. Palmer describes them as 'ultra quiet': Palmer (n 111) 92.

117 van Dyke, Gardner and Morgan (n 107) 341–342.

The use of sonar has been posited as a cause of (or at least contributing to) the mass stranding of whales on beaches at diverse locations around the world.[118] Palmer has described sonar as: 'a method or device for "seeing" underwater to detect and locate objects by either intercepting the acoustic waves of an object's natural-borne sound (passive sonar) or by emitting pulses of sound and receiving the reflecting acoustic waves that bounce off an object as echoes (active sonar).'[119] Active sonar systems were developed to respond to the need to detect quiet enemy submarines.[120]

Active sonar, especially military sonar, will vary in the frequency and intensity of sounds transmitted through the ocean in seeking to ascertain if submarines are present.[121] Evidence that the use of high-intensity active sonar was detrimental to marine species prompted the European Parliament to adopt a resolution in 2004 calling for a moratorium on its use 'until a global assessment of their cumulative environmental impact on marine mammals, fish and other marine life has been completed'.[122] The United States did not support this position,[123] nor did Australia.[124] Within the UN, there has been encouragement for further research into concerns that anthropogenic ocean noise negatively impacts marine living resources.[125] The International Union for Conservation of Nature (IUCN) adopted a resolution that requested governments to

[118] See Firestone and Jarvis (n 107) 109; van Dyke, Gardner and Morgan (n 107) 335–338; Scott (n 110) 290–292.

[119] Palmer (n 111) 91.

[120] Scott (n 110) 289.

[121] Palmer describes mid-frequency active sonar as a primary tool in anti-submarine warfare. He further notes that low-frequency sonar is ideal for long-range search and surveillance of submarines: Palmer (n 111) 92.

[122] Resolution on the Environmental Effects of High-Intensity Active Naval Sonars, Strasbourg, 28 October 2004 (Doc. B6-0089/2004) para. K.1.2 (European Parliament). The European Commission did not proceed to a ban but subsequently urged member States to regulate anthropogenic noise, such as Low Frequency Active Sonar, in the context of the Marine Strategy Framework Directive: Karmenu Vella, Answer Given on Behalf of European Commission, 12 June 2016 (Doc. E-003049/2016).

[123] Firestone and Jarvis (n 107) 140–141 (noting that the United States 'strongly opposes any international regulatory framework addressing military use of active sonar because of the potential to restrict the ability of individual States to balance the relevant security and environmental interests').

[124] 'Hill Defends Use of Active Sonar', *Sydney Morning Herald*, 2 December 2004 <www.smh.com.au/national/hill-defends-use-of-active-sonar-20041202-gdk8cq.html>.

[125] See, e.g., 'Report on the Work of the United Nations Open-ended Informal Consultative Process on Oceans and the Law of the Sea at its 6th Meeting', 7 July 2005 (UN Doc. A/60/99) 8; 'Oceans and the Law of the Sea: Report of the Secretary General' (Addendum),

act urgently in relation to military sonar, by limiting training to 'low-risk areas' and 'working diligently toward the development of international standards that regulate its use'.[126]

The US tests of anti-submarine technology have been the subject of national litigation.[127] Initially, a settlement was reached that allowed 'sonar exercises to proceed, but require[d] the [US] Navy to undertake certain mitigation measures to safeguard marine mammals including the establishment of buffer zones and marine mammal monitoring'.[128] Yet subsequent legislative changes strengthened the US Navy's ability to undertake the sonar operations with only small modifications to account for protection of marine mammals.[129] A 2008 US Supreme Court decision then concluded that the US Navy's need to conduct realistic training with the use of sonar outweighed environmental concerns.[130] Subsequent decisions in lower courts have reached mixed results in further cases that have sought to limit the US Navy's use of active sonar for marine mammal protection.[131] The exigencies of maritime security have clearly been factors in resisting any prohibition on active sonar.

Dotinga and Oude Elferink have suggested that 'regulation at the national level in many cases will be sufficient to address acoustic

15 July 2005 (UN Doc A/60/63/Add.1); Oceans and the Law of the Sea, 16 March 2007, UNGA Res. 61/222 (UN Doc. A/RES/61/222).

126 International Union for the Conservation of Nature, 'Undersea Noise Pollution', 17–25 November 2004 (Res. Res 3.068) <https://portals.iucn.org/library/sites/library/files/resrecfiles/WCC_2004_RES_68_EN.pdf> para. 5(d).

127 *Natural Resources Defense Council v. United States Department of Navy*, unreported, 2002 U.S. Dist Lexis 26360, 17 September 2002. For further discussion of the litigation, see Firestone and Jarvis (n 107) 141–143; van Dyke, Gardner and Morgan (n 107) 331–333.

128 'Court Allows Sonar in RIMPAC War Games with New Restrictions', *Environment News Service*, 7 September 2006 <www.ens-newswire.com/ens/jul2006/2006-07-09-01.asp>, cited in Firestone and Jarvis (n 107) 143.

129 Firestone and Jarvis (n 107) 144. However, Kraska and Pedrozo have argued that the US Navy's mitigation measures during sonar operations 'represent the most extensive measures undertaken by any civilian or naval force to ameliorate the potential effects of underwater sound on marine mammals': James Kraska and Raul Pedrozo, *International Maritime Security Law* (Brill, 2013) 154.

130 *Natural Resources Defense Council v. Winter*, 555 US 7 (2008).

131 See, e.g., *Strahan v. Roughead*, 910 F. Supp. 2d 358 (2012); *Natural Resources Defense Council, Inc v. Pritzker*, 838 F.3d 1125 (2016). See further Michael Jasny, 'Major Victory on Low-Frequency Sonar', *Natural Resources Defense Council*, 18 July 2016 <www.nrdc.org/bio/michael-jasny/major-victory-low-frequency-sonar>; 'US Navy Banned from Using Sonar that Harms Dolphins and Walruses, *The Guardian*, 16 July 2016 <www.theguardian.com/us-news/2016/jul/16/us-navy-banned-from-using-sonar-that-harms-dolphins-and-walruses>.

pollution', but also acknowledge that international law standards continue to have relevance.[132] Notably, the precautionary principle would at least be at stake even when it is argued that the scientific results of studies on the impact on marine mammals and other marine living resources is unclear.[133] Commentators have further argued how noise pollution must be addressed under existing international treaties that deal with the conservation and management of marine mammals and other marine living species, and in relation to pollution control.[134]

The impact of noise pollution caused by equipment for detecting submarines may be mitigated through construction and design so as to minimise the frequency and intensity of sounds,[135] or if regard is given to where such sources of noise pollution emanate from so as to avoid specific areas where vulnerable species are known to be located;[136] a factor that could be relevant in establishing marine protected areas. As Scott has observed, in such areas 'it may be possible to regulate particularly noisy activities much more stringently or even prohibit them altogether and, in co-operation with the IMO, regulate shipping so as to minimize their impact on vulnerable species'.[137] The IMO has adopted non-mandatory guidelines in 2014 for reducing underwater noise,[138] which were subsequently revised and updated in 2023.[139] This instrument is focused on commercial shipping, however, and the revised guidelines explicitly exclude 'the introduction of noise from warships and

[132] Dotinga and Elferink (n 105) 151.

[133] Palmer argues that maritime security issues are indeed at stake in opposition to environmental concerns: Palmer (n 111) 102–104.

[134] See, e.g., Karen N. Scott, 'International Regulation of Undersea Noise' (2004) 53 *International and Comparative Law Quarterly* 287, 292–302.

[135] Dotinga and Elferink (n 105) 156.

[136] An approach considered by the Scientific Committee of the International Whaling Commission. See, e.g., International Whaling Commission, 'Report of the Scientific Committee', 24 May 1999 (IWC Doc. IWC/51/4) para. 11.4.1 and annex. H, para. 7.1. As of 2022, '[r]esearch is ongoing to understand the impact of noise on cetaceans and the effectiveness of various approaches to reducing exposure': International Whaling Commission, 'Report of the Intersessional Work on Anthropogenic Underwater Noise', April 2023 (IWC Doc. IWC/SC/69A/E/11) para. 14.5.

[137] Scott (n 110) 312–313.

[138] IMO, 'Guidelines for the Reduction of Underwater Noise from Commercial Shipping to Address Adverse Impacts on Marine Life', 22 August 2023 (IMO Doc. MEPC.1/Circ.833)..

[139] IMO, 'Revised Guidelines for the Reduction of Underwater Radiated Noise from Shipping to Address Adverse Impacts on Marine Life', 22 August 2023 (IMO Doc. MEPC.1/Circ.906).

naval auxiliaries and the deliberate introduction of noise for other purposes such as sonar or seismic activities'.[140]

The standards for establishing any international law violation because of noises generated from submarines or from submarine detection equipment are thus very discretionary. If a naval force is sufficiently cognisant of the risks posed by operations in a particular location and takes steps to reduce the impact (e.g., cutting back the length of time of the operations, or moving the location) then the due diligence standard to protection and preserve the marine environment is arguably met.

12.5 Conclusion

International marine environmental law consists of an extensive and complex regime of multilateral and regional treaties, customary international law and intergovernmental organisational endeavours, which all contribute to the core obligation imposed on States in Article 192 of UNCLOS to protect and preserve the marine environment. The content of that obligation, as well as the core obligation to prevent, reduce and control marine pollution, have been progressively developed in the jurisprudence of international courts and tribunals established under the UNCLOS dispute settlement regime.[141] These rules must be accounted for in the operations of private submarines – such as in the laying of submarine cables or when deployed for marine scientific research. The sovereign immunity of military submarines is otherwise a considerable limitation in how rules of international marine environmental law apply to those submarines.

Despite the significant risks posed by nuclear submarines for polluting the marine environment, especially following accidents and sinkings, there is limited applicability of international environmental law given that nuclear submarines are almost uniformly (if not entirely all) warships.[142] As warships are subject to sovereign immunity and there is extremely limited application of nuclear safety and liability treaties to

[140] Ibid, para. 2.2.

[141] See Natalie Klein and Kate Parlett, *Judging the Law of the Sea: Judicial Contributions to the UN Convention on the Law of the Sea* (Oxford University Press, 2022) 342–353.

[142] If nuclear-powered submarines were ever deployed by governments for commercial purposes or were privately owned (both scenarios highly unlikely at present), it can still be acknowledged there are concerns about the existing régime if applied to nuclear merchant ships and similar concerns would extend to submarines. See Qiuwen Wang, Hu Zhang and Puxin Zhu, 'Using Nuclear Energy for Maritime Decarbonization and Related Environmental Challenges: Existing Regulatory Shortcomings and

warships, the absence of clear international standards to which nuclear submarines must adhere to protect the marine environment is palpable. States operating nuclear submarines instead have caveated due diligence obligations to align with international obligations.[143] At most, notification obligations apply in the event of an accident involving a nuclear reactor further to the Convention on Early Notification of a Nuclear Accident. The existence of nuclear free zones in different regions sends strong messaging about nuclear non-proliferation and State concerns to minimise the presence of nuclear weapons in their regions. They hold only marginal relevance for the possible operations of nuclear-powered and conventionally armed submarines. The sufficiency of these existing (minimal) rules will continue to be tested as States advance technological developments in the application of nuclear weaponry and nuclear power, including to underwater maritime autonomous vehicles.[144]

International laws relating to noise pollution vis-à-vis submarines may be described as nascent at most. There must first be an assessment as to whether the noise in question produces sufficiently 'deleterious effects' to be defined as pollution under Article 1 of UNCLOS. Second, where naval submarines or other government vessels operated for non-commercial purposes are at issue, the immunities enjoyed by these vessels will only require an assessment as to whether any restrictions on the noise produced impair 'operations or operational capabilities' and otherwise align with what a flag State considers as 'reasonable and practicable'. Finally, even if it could be argued that the noise has deleterious effects and is not reasonable and practicable in the submarines' operations, a State must take steps to prevent, reduce and control the noise pollution; not eliminate the pollution.

Sovereign immunity and exclusions of warships from many of the legal regimes relevant to the protection of marine environment undoubtedly reduce the regulations imposed on military submarines. It is, however, important to recall that in relation to the core obligations to protect and preserve the marine environment and to prevent, reduce and control

Improvements' (2023) 20 *International Journal of Environmental Research Public Health* 2993.

143 UNCLOS (n 6) art. 236.

144 See Brad Lendon and Yoonjung Seo, 'North Korea Claims to Have Tested a Nuclear Capable Underwater Drone. Analysts are Skeptical', *CNN*, 24 March 2023 <https://edition.cnn.com/2023/03/23/asia/north-korea-underwater-drone-test-intl-hnk-ml/index.html>; Brad Lendon, 'Russian Navy's Massive Submarine Could Set the Stage for "A New Cold War" in the Oceans', *CNN*, 24 July 2022 <https://edition.cnn.com/2022/07/23/europe/russia-belgorod-submarine-nuclear-torpedo-intl-hnk-ml/index.html>.

marine pollution, there is an extensive body of law and it remains incumbent on the flag State to ensure that their vessels act consistently with those requirements, even if that due diligence obligation is tempered by operational considerations and what is reasonable and practical. The latter two factors may not necessarily be entirely self-judging given that they imply some level of objectivity in making such an assessment. The caveat set out in Article 236 of UNCLOS seemingly prevents wholesale disregard of environmental standards and arguably a State proceeding in its submarine operations in the absence of due consideration to environmental obligations risks violating the requirement of non-abuse of rights.[145]

[145] For discussion on abuse of rights, see Chapter 8, Section 8.4.2.

13

Submarines and Criminal Activity

13.1 Introduction

The previous chapters have reflected how the warship status of many submarines has influenced the international regulation of submarine activity. Yet as recognised in Part I of the book, even when the first military submarines were developed, it was also anticipated that commercial uses of submarines would equally evolve. In the previous chapters of Part II, the discussion has sought to recognise that submarines may also be privately owned or deployed for commercial purposes (including for tourism or other leisure purposes) and hence bound by rules relating to inter alia navigational rights, navigational safety and marine environmental protection. Private uses of submarines for scientific research and to facilitate commercial activities, such as the laying of submarine cables or exploitation of seabed resources, may also be regulated in accordance with the allocations of authority within the exclusive economic zone (EEZ); these private uses of submarines have been explored in Chapter 8. The use of submarines, submersibles and semi-submersibles[1] by private actors to perpetrate different crimes, predominantly smuggling offences, are the focus of this chapter.

The international law of the sea has core principles relating to maritime law enforcement and there are also legal regimes relating to drug-trafficking that will be assessed for their applicability to the use of submersibles or semi-submersibles. The chapter begins with a short explanation of laws of criminal jurisdiction in Section 13.2, noting the infamous Danish incident of a murdered journalist aboard a private submarine.

In the following sections, we consider the conduct of maritime law enforcement either *by* submarines or *against* submarines. Most typically, submarines, as warships and significant military assets, form part of

[1] 'Semi-submersibles' are low-profile vessels that are designed to run low in the water to minimise detection but do not submerge fully. For further discussion on these definitional issues, see Chapter 1, Section 1.2.

a State's naval forces and will not be deployed for policing purposes. Section 13.3 will discuss the limited instances where submarines may contribute to and are regulated under international laws pertaining to maritime law enforcement. The latter situation may be relevant where a coastal State deploys submarines and information is obtained about criminal activity or when a delinquent ship is identified during submarine activities and efforts at law enforcement commence.

Section 13.4 examines international laws relevant to maritime law enforcement operations against submarines. In relation to the commission of crimes involving submarines, the use of submarines and semi-submersibles for drug-trafficking has increased in the last thirty years. Wilson has observed that '[a]lthough the cost of constructing a submersible vessel is high – around $2 million – those costs are mitigated by the fact that such vessels can transport several tons of cocaine in one voyage'.[2] While the international drug trade is lucrative, it must be anticipated that other illicit contraband may be transported via submarines and semi-submersibles. Colombia, Ecuador and the United States, among others, have been involved operationally in the seizure of submersibles in countering illicit trafficking operations.[3] For example, Colombian authorities seized an electric 'narco-sub' in 2020 that could have transported six tonnes of cocaine (valued at US$120 million at the time).[4] In 2025, a semi-submersible was interdicted on the high seas, travelling from South America to Europe, with 6.5 tonnes of cocaine (now valued at US$1.1 billion) amid concerns that the Atlantic is increasingly being used for the trafficking of drugs into Europe by submarines.[5] Finally, in light of the use of submarines by the Tamil Tigers during the Sri Lankan civil war, we address the international laws relating to terrorism.[6] It will be seen that international law provides a strong framework for the regulation of submarines engaged

[2] Brian Wilson, 'Submersibles and Transnational Criminal Organizations' (2011) 17(1) *Ocean and Coastal Law Journal* 35, 40.

[3] Ibid, 47. See also James Orange, 'Spanish Police Recover Suspected Drug Submarine Off North Coast', *Euro Weekly News*, 16 March 2023 <https://euroweeklynews.com/2023/03/15/spanish-police-recover-suspected-drug-submarine-off-north-coast/>; Sally Rawsthorne, 'Submarines the New Threat in Fight against Cocaine Smugglers', *Sydney Morning Herald*, 3 February 2025.

[4] It was designed to be towed for part of the journey and then travel fully submerged to the destination. See H. I. Sutton, 'Rare Electric Narco Submarine Seized in Colombia', *USNI News*, 16 November 2020.

[5] Harriet Barber, 'Submarine Carrying Tonnes of Cocaine Seized in Atlantic', *Australian Financial Review*, 31 March 2025.

[6] The Tamil Tigers may not necessarily be considered as terrorists but insurgents participating in a non-international armed conflict. Their conduct is referenced as terrorism in this chapter only for illustrative purposes. See further nn 81–86 and accompanying text.

in criminal activities. The legal complications instead emerge in States' domestic laws in ensuring the relevant authority is accorded to law enforcement officials to arrest and prosecute alleged offenders.

13.2 Criminal Jurisdiction under International Law

States may exercise criminal jurisdiction at sea depending on where an activity is occurring and what is occurring. The exercise of criminal jurisdiction at sea falls within States' maritime law enforcement authority and is deployed against private or commercial vessels (i.e., those vessels not subject to sovereign immunity) for violation of the State's laws proscribing or otherwise regulating the conduct of maritime activities. As a foreground to the discussion on maritime law enforcement operations by or against submarines, this section briefly sets out key rules of criminal jurisdiction under international law that inform the allocation of authority between States during maritime law enforcement operations.

Coastal States have specific law enforcement authority when operating in their territorial sea, contiguous zone and EEZ. In the territorial sea, the United Nations Convention on the Law of the Sea (UNCLOS) recognises the powers of the coastal State to exercise both criminal and civil jurisdiction, which aligns with the sovereignty that the coastal State exercises over that maritime zone.[7] Yet the coastal State's exercise of criminal jurisdiction is permitted against a foreign-flagged ship in its territorial sea only in the following circumstances under Article 27(1) of UNCLOS:

> (a) if the consequences of the crime extend to the coastal State;
> (b) if the crime is of a kind to disturb the peace of the country or the good order of the territorial sea;
> (c) if the assistance of the local authorities has been requested by the master of the ship or by a diplomatic agent or consular officer of the flag State; or
> (d) if such measures are necessary for the suppression of illicit traffic in narcotic drugs or psychotropic substances.[8]

The remit of authority is clearly broad under this provision. In addition, a coastal State may exercise criminal jurisdiction against

[7] United Nations Convention on the Law of the Sea, Montego Bay, 10 December 1982, entered into force 16 November 1994, 1833 UNTS 397, art. 2(1) ('UNCLOS').

[8] Ibid, art. 27(1).

foreign-flagged vessels in the territorial sea when those vessels have exited its internal waters.[9] The authority to exercise criminal jurisdiction over non-sovereign-immune vessels in port or in the internal waters of a coastal State is plenary in light of the full sovereignty exercised over those areas.

Within the contiguous zone, the coastal State is granted specific powers under UNCLOS (and recognised as part of customary international law)[10] to take policing actions in relation to fiscal, immigration, sanitation and customs concerns.[11] Coastal States may 'take the control necessary' to prevent and punish infringements that may occur, or have occurred, within its territory or territorial sea.[12] This authority may have most relevance for submarines that are being used for illicit smuggling activities in violation of customs laws.

In the EEZ, the coastal State has specific law enforcement authority in relation to its fisheries laws and regulations under Article 73 of UNCLOS, and implicitly for the exploration and exploitation of the natural resources of the seabed.[13] As discussed in Chapter 8, the coastal State also has exclusive jurisdiction over marine scientific research in the EEZ.[14] The coastal State has authority to suspend or require cessation of marine scientific research in specific circumstances,[15] though it would not normally be anticipated that criminal jurisdiction would flow from scientific research activities.

On the high seas, and within the EEZ in line with Article 58(1) of UNCLOS, it is the flag State that has exclusive jurisdiction over its vessels and that may exercise, or consent to another State exercising, law enforcement powers over those ships.[16] While the flag State thus has a primary role in exercising enforcement jurisdiction against its vessels, it

[9] Article 27(2) refers to 'the right of the coastal State to take any steps authorized by its laws for the purpose of an arrest or investigation on board a foreign ship passing through the territorial sea after leaving internal waters': ibid, art. 27(2). See further Chapter 7, Section 7.2.4.

[10] *Alleged Violations of Sovereign Rights and Maritime Spaces in the Caribbean Sea* (Nicaragua v. Colombia) (Judgment of 21 April 2022) [2022] ICJ Rep 266, para. 155.

[11] UNCLOS (n 7) art. 33(1).

[12] Ibid.

[13] *Arctic Sunrise* (Netherlands v. Russia) (Award on the Merits of 14 August 2015) PCA Case No. 2014–02, para. 284.

[14] UNCLOS (n 7) art. 56(1). See also Chapter 8, Section 8.3.2.

[15] Ibid, art. 253.

[16] Ibid, art. 92(1). There has been debate as to whether a flag State has exclusive prescriptive and enforcement jurisdiction over its vessels on the high seas. See, e.g., Aaron H. N. Honniball, 'The Exclusive Jurisdiction of Flag States: A Limitation on Proactive Port States' (2016) 31 *International Journal of Marine and Coastal Law* 499, 508. The current discussion is centred on enforcement jurisdiction and does not weigh into this debate.

may be noted that the delinquent submarines and submersibles used in criminal operations are not typically registered to a particular State. A warship or any other government vessel on non-commercial service and clearly identified as a law enforcement vessel may conduct the right of visit to verify the nationality of a vessel.[17] In the event the vessel is stateless,[18] one view is that any State may exercise jurisdiction over that vessel.[19] Another view is that for the exercise of criminal jurisdiction over a stateless vessel, there must still be some other jurisdictional link (e.g., the people on board are nationals of the policing State).[20]

The exercise of criminal jurisdiction at sea predominantly flows from core concepts of territorial and nationality jurisdiction. Further to territorial jurisdiction, a State may generally exercise enforcement jurisdiction over people and conduct within its sovereign territory.[21] In accordance with nationality jurisdiction, a State may exercise enforcement jurisdiction over its nationals in relation to their conduct, which includes not only individuals but also the vessels flagged to that State. States may occasionally seek to exercise criminal jurisdiction over individuals who have harmed their nationals (which is referred to as passive personality jurisdiction) and may be relevant in the maritime context when nationals are the victims of terrorism at sea.[22] Additional bases of

[17] UNCLOS (n 7) art. 110(1)(d).

[18] A vessel may be considered without nationality where it is unable to meet the burden of demonstrating its nationality; does not claim nationality; its purported flag State denies that the vessel has its nationality or is lawfully registered in that State; the vessel changes flag mid-journey or flies more than one flag: see Juliana Gonzalez-Pinto, 'Interdiction of Narcotics in International Waters' (2008) 15 *University of Miami International and Comparative Law Review* 443, 457.

[19] The United States aligns its practice with this view: United States Navy, United States Marine Corps and United States Coast Guard, *The Commander's Handbook on the Law of Naval Operations* (Naval War College, March 2022) para. 3.11.2.3.

[20] Robin Churchill, Vaughan Lowe and Amy Sander, *The Law of the Sea* (4th ed., Manchester University Press, 2022) 405.

[21] Subject to the recognition of immunity from enforcement jurisdiction.

[22] As was the situation for the United States following the *Achille Lauro* hijacking and murder of a US national. For discussion, see Malvina Halberstam, 'Terrorism on the High Seas: The *Achille Lauro*, Piracy and the IMO Convention on Maritime Safety (1988) 82 *American Journal of International Law* 269. Passive personality jurisdiction is reflected in Article 6(2)(b) of the Protocol of 2005 to the Convention for the Suppression of Unlawful Acts against the Safety of Maritime Navigation, London, 14 October 2005, entered into force 28 July 2010, [2005] ATNIF 31 ('2005 SUA Protocol'). The 2005 SUA Protocol amended the Convention for the Suppression of Unlawful Acts against the Safety of Maritime Navigation, Rome, 10 March 1988, entered into force 1 March 1992, 1678 UNTS 201 ('1988 SUA Convention'). The 1988 SUA Convention and the 2005 SUA Protocol are referred to together as the 2005 SUA Convention.

jurisdiction under international law are the protective principle and universal jurisdiction. The protective principle allows States to exercise criminal jurisdiction over extraterritorial actions that are considered as harmful to the security interests of the State. Universal jurisdiction may be exercised by any State over crimes that are considered as heinous to the international community; acts of piracy fall within universal jurisdiction.[23]

The operation of these principles in relation to submarines are readily illustrated through the 2017 murder of a Swedish journalist aboard a submersible. Danish inventor Peter Madsen was found guilty of premeditated murder, aggravated sexual assault and desecrating a corpse and sentenced to life in prison in Denmark.[24] The submersible had been constructed by Madsen and his company Copenhagen Orbitals,[25] and the crime was committed in the Oresund strait between Denmark and Sweden.[26] It appears that the submarine sank in Danish waters and Madsen was rescued by nearby fishers.[27] Sweden may have potentially asserted criminal jurisdiction on the basis of passive personality jurisdiction in light of the victim's nationality. Denmark had jurisdiction in light of the nationality of the perpetrator, the apparent nationality of the submarine and the location of the events. International law does not have any established hierarchy between the bases of jurisdiction in the situation where more than one State has authority to exercise jurisdiction.[28] However, as a matter of practicality, the State with custody of the alleged offender will often exercise jurisdiction or may otherwise

[23] As recognised under customary international law, as well as reflected in UNCLOS: see UNCLOS (n 7) art. 105.

[24] Jon Henley, 'Danish Killer Confesses to Murder of Kim Wall for First Time', *The Guardian*, 9 September 2020, <www.theguardian.com/world/2020/sep/09/danish-killer-peter-madsen-confesses-to-murder-of-kim-wall-for-first-time>. See further May Jeong, 'The Final, Terrible Voyage of the Nautilus', *Wired*, 15 February 2018 <www.wired.com/story/final-terrible-voyage-nautilus/>.

[25] Sean Gallagher, 'Biggest Amateur-built Sub Sinks: Owner is Suspected of Killing Passenger', *Ars Technia*, 8 December 2017 <https://arstechnica.com/gadgets/2017/08/biggest-amateur-built-sub-sinks-owner-is-suspected-of-killing-passenger/>.

[26] 'Kim Wall: What We Know About Danish Submarine Death', *BBC News*, 25 April 2018 <www.bbc.com/news/world-europe-40922750>.

[27] Ibid.

[28] In some instances, the substantive law may indicate which jurisdictional basis might prevail. Otherwise, there may be a view that territorial jurisdiction (i.e., where a particular act has occurred) is the primary consideration. See Bernard H. Oxman, 'Jurisdiction of States' in Anne Peters and Rüdiger Wolfrum (eds.), *Max Planck Encyclopedia of International Law* (Oxford University Press, November 2007) paras. 50–56.

consider extradition to a State that also has jurisdiction.[29] While the location of a submerged submarine may obscure a basis for the exercise of criminal jurisdiction, the international law principles to exercise jurisdiction over crimes on submarines are otherwise the same as with surface vessels.

13.3 Submarine Involvement in Maritime Law Enforcement

As noted in the Introduction to this chapter, submarines will not typically be deployed for the purposes of maritime law enforcement operations. However, there are instances where their operation may nonetheless contribute to policing against crimes at sea. Two such scenarios that implicate international law concern intelligence-gathering and the right of hot pursuit.

A critical role for submarines includes enhancing a State's maritime domain awareness and gathering information in relation to conditions and activities at sea.[30] While such information may be collected for defence purposes, the information may also indicate the conduct of illegal activities in different maritime zones. The advanced sonar of submarines can identify and track vessels from long distances.[31] This information can be provided to relevant policing authorities either of the adjacent coastal State or to the State's own policing authorities. States are frequently subject to requirements to share information for law enforcement purposes.[32]

Maritime law enforcement activities usually proceed against a private vessel on the basis of reasonable suspicions. For the interdiction of a vessel, a warship or other government vessel operated on non-commercial service must reasonably suspect that a vessel is in violation of relevant prescriptions. The standard of reasonable suspicion emerges in relation to the right of visit under UNCLOS and other multilateral

[29] Under counter-terrorism treaties, there may be an obligation to extradite an alleged offender if a State opts not to prosecute under the principle of *aut dedere aut judicare*. Extradition is otherwise dependent on the existence of an extradition treaty between the States concerned.

[30] See Chapter 8, Section 8.3.1.1.

[31] H. I. Sutton, '5 Ways The Military Hunts Narco Submarines You Don't Hear About', *Forbes*, 4 June 2020 <www.forbes.com/sites/hisutton/2020/06/04/5-unseen-eyes-helping-the-navy-hunt-narco-submarines/>.

[32] See, e.g., United Nations Convention against Illicit Traffic in Narcotic Drugs and Psychotropic Substances, Vienna, 20 December 1988, entered into force 11 November 1990, 1582 UNTS 95, art. 20(1)(b) ('1998 Vienna Convention').

treaties setting out a right of visit. For example, Article 8(1) of the Migrant Smuggling Protocol refers to a State having 'reasonable grounds to suspect' that a vessel is engaged in migrant smuggling.[33] The exercise of the right of hot pursuit similarly anticipates that a delinquent vessel is reasonably suspected of violating the laws of the particular maritime zone in which it is located at the start of the pursuit.[34]

Acknowledging the ambiguity as to what a 'reasonable' suspicion might entail, what is clear for present purposes is that there is no stipulation that the determination of the 'reasonable suspicion' must originate within the vessel that undertakes the maritime law enforcement operation. In the context of port inspections in relation to illegal, unreported or unregulated (IUU) fishing under the Port State Measures Agreement, the port State may act on 'such other information as it may require to determine whether the vessel requesting entry into its port has engaged in IUU fishing'.[35] Seemingly, information forming the grounds of the reasonable suspicion may come from any source and hence include information gathered by submarines in the course of their patrolling.

If a submarine encounters a vessel that is reasonably suspected of violating laws applicable to the maritime zone in which it is operating, and the submarine is a 'warship or other government vessel operated for non-commercial purposes', it may potentially engage in maritime law enforcement as a matter of international law.[36] A further requirement is that the submarine is 'clearly marked and identifiable' as on government service. If these criteria are met, a submarine may have the legal authority to engage in maritime law enforcement. Whether this activity is one that a submarine

[33] Protocol against the Smuggling of Migrants by Land, Sea and Air, supplementing the United Nations Convention against Transnational Organized Crime, New York, 15 November 2000, entered into force 28 January 2004, 2241 UNTS 507. See also 1988 Vienna Convention (n 32) art. 17(2) (referring to 'reasonable grounds to suspect').

[34] UNCLOS (n 7) art. 111(1) (referring to 'good reason to believe').

[35] Agreement on Port State Measures to Prevent, Deter and Eliminate Illegal, Unreported and Unregulated Fishing, Rome, 22 November 2009, entered into force 5 June 2016, 3161 UNTS 377, art. 9(1).

[36] The engagement of submarines in constabulary operations will otherwise be a decision under national laws that set out the division of policing powers and the relevant command structure. See, e.g., Cameron Moore, 'Act of State Doctrine in the Antipodes: The Intersection of National and International Law in Naval Constabulary Operations' in Natalie Klein, Joanna Mossop and Donald R. Rothwell (eds.), *Maritime Security: International Law and Policy Perspectives from Australia and New Zealand* (Routledge, 2010) 172, 173.

either physically can undertake, is duly authorised by domestic law to conduct, or is disposed to engage in, are separate matters.[37]

A submarine seeking to engage lawfully in the right of hot pursuit must be able to provide a visual or audible signal to stop to the delinquent vessel within the maritime zone in which the offending conduct has occurred.[38] Requirements for the conduct of lawful hot pursuit are cumulative.[39] Any hot pursuit must be continuous and can only be undertaken in waters beyond the territorial sea of any State other than the flag State of the submarine.[40] If a submarine lawfully commences a hot pursuit, it may be preferable for a surface vessel to complete the pursuit and undertake the right of visit. While UNCLOS anticipates that hot pursuit may be commenced by aircraft,[41] there is no such anticipation of submarines starting a hot pursuit and that pursuit being transferred to a surface vessel. Moreover, there remains uncertainty as to whether hot pursuit by relays (where the pursuit is undertaken by several warships in sequence during a lengthy pursuit) is lawful.[42]

The international regulation of maritime law enforcement operations does not have any specific rights or duties in relation to submarines. Rather, the existing laws are to be applied where submarines are considered analogous to any surface warship or other government vessel. This lack of distinction is presently unproblematic given the exceptional engagement of submarines in such operations. Where their operation may be most relevant, which is in relation to information-gathering, international law does not create any barriers to the use of such intelligence by surface warships or other government vessels. The difficult and presently unresolved questions that may emerge in relation to the right of hot pursuit concern pursuit by relay and varied technologies for signalling. These issues equally concern surface ships' operations.

[37] There are reports of US and Dutch submarines contributing to counter-narcotics operations: Sutton (n 31).

[38] UNCLOS (n 7) art. 111(1).

[39] *M/V Saiga (No. 2)* (Saint Vincent and the Grenadines v. Guinea) (Judgment of 1 July 1999) [1999] ITLOS Rep 10, para. 146; *Arctic Sunrise* (n 13) para. 246.

[40] UNCLOS (n 7) art. 111(3).

[41] Ibid, art. 111(6).

[42] For discussion, see Churchill, Lowe and Sander (n 20) 407 (noting that in terms of transfer from ship to ship, it would 'seem reasonable to allow this'). See also Erik J. Molenaar, 'Multilateral Hot Pursuit and Illegal Fishing in the Southern Ocean: The Pursuits of the Viarsa 1 and the South Tomi' (2004) 19 *International Journal of Marine and Coastal Law* 19.

13.4 Submarine Use in Criminal Activities

The utility of submerged vessels for the transport of illicit goods was recognised as early as the Prohibition Era in the United States when attempts were made to smuggle alcohol through US waters. Interestingly, rumours of rum-smuggling submarines were common in the 1920s – it was even claimed that German U-boats were involved in such operations.[43] Such claims have never clearly been proven as no such vessels were apprehended, though NicKenzie Lawson has shown in a recent history of the Prohibition Era that an image of two large commercial submarines in the Hudson River was captured by a commercial mapping company and passed onto the US Navy in 1924.[44] There is also evidence that liquor was smuggled into the United States in submerged containers towed by surface vessels – a technology described by Canadian Customs officials in 1926 as 'a submarine without motors' including 'a device for submerging and rising to the surface'.[45]

From the start of this century, maritime law enforcement officials became keenly aware of the use of submersibles and semi-submersibles for drug-trafficking and other smuggling activities. In addition, policy-makers and analysts have linked the deployment of submarines for drug-trafficking with terrorist operations.[46] The criminal motivation for using submarines and semi-submersibles rests in the reduced detection of such vehicles. This advantage is being further capitalised with the development of autonomous underwater vehicles for illicit trafficking of goods[47] and is discussed further in the next chapter.

For present purposes, it is important to set out the core legal framework that allows for maritime law enforcement operations against

[43] See e.g., 'Rum Runners Use German Submarine', *New York Times*, 3 August 1924.

[44] E. NicKenzie Lawson, *Smugglers, Bootleggers, and Scofflaws: Prohibition and New York City* (SUNY Press, 2013) 12.

[45] See 'Prohibition in USA: Submarines are Used by Border Rumrunners', *Barrier Miner*, 15 November 1926; Sarah Laskow, 'Did German U Boats Smuggle Alcohol into the US during Prohibition?' *Atlas Obscura*, 29 August 2017 <www.atlasobscura.com/articles/rum-running-submarines-german-uboats-prohibition-smuggling>.

[46] See, e.g., Terrance G. Lichtenwald, Mara H. Steinhour and Frank S. Perri, 'A Maritime Threat Assessment of Sea Based Criminal Organizations and Terrorist Operations' (2012) 8(13) *Homeland Security Affairs* 1; Michelle Jacome Jaramillo, 'The Revolutionary Armed Forces of Colombia (FARC) and the Development of Narco-Submarines' (2016) 9(1) *Journal of Strategic Security* 49.

[47] See, e.g., Leo Sands, 'Drug Smuggling: Underwater Drones Seized by Spanish Police', *BBC News*, 4 July 2022 <www.bbc.com/news/world-europe-62040790> (Spanish police seized three underwater drones capable of carrying up to 200 kilograms of cargo and built to smuggle drugs across the sea from Morocco).

delinquent submarines, considering if there are any points of difference to the enforcement of criminal jurisdiction against surface vessels. Sub-section 13.4.1 below considers whether the existing international law rules are sufficient when contemplating the criminal use of submarines for drug-trafficking. Sub-section 13.4.2 studies the US Drug Trafficking Vessel Interdiction Act (DTVIA) given that the United States has been especially responsive to the criminal threats posed by submarines and semi-submersibles pursuant to its national 'war on drugs' policy. US officials have estimated that 30 per cent of the supply of illicit drugs is delivered via 'narco-submarines'.[48] Finally, the legal regime for the prevention and suppression of maritime terrorism is addressed in light of the possible, and actual, deployment of submarines and semi-submersibles for such purposes.

13.4.1 *International Regulation of Drug-Trafficking*

The international legal framework for the prevention and suppression of trafficking in narcotic drugs and psychotropic substances does not differentiate between surface vessels engaged in this illegal conduct and underwater vehicles. As noted above, coastal States may exercise criminal jurisdiction, consistent with their domestic laws and regulations, over drug-trafficking in their internal waters, territorial sea and potentially prevent and punish this conduct in the contiguous zone, if the coastal State has claimed that zone. Beyond the territorial sea, there are different international treaties (multilateral, regional and bilateral) that set out the rights and duties of States seeking to respond to drug-trafficking at sea. As an initial matter, Article 108 of UNCLOS requires all States to cooperate in the suppression of illicit drug-trafficking.

There are three multilateral treaties that reflect the international agreement reached on what substances and conduct are to be regulated by States to suppress international trade in drugs.[49] Most importantly, the 1988 Vienna Convention against Illicit Traffic in Narcotic Drugs and Psychotropic Substances articulates the most serious drug-trafficking offences,[50] requires States to establish jurisdiction over those offences

[48] Jaramillo (n 46) 51.

[49] Single Convention on Narcotic Drugs, New York, 30 March 1961, entered into force 13 December 1964, 520 UNTS 151; Convention on Psychotropic Substances, Vienna, 21 February 1971, entered into force 16 August 1976, 1019 UNTS 175; 1988 Vienna Convention (n 32).

[50] 1988 Vienna Convention (n 32) art. 3.

when committed on board one of its vessels,[51] and allows for the flag State to consent to interdiction of that vessel when outside the territorial sea.[52] Where a vessel is without nationality, the 1988 Vienna Convention simply provides that a State 'may request the assistance of other Parties in suppressing its use for that purpose'.[53] Parties are to 'render such assistance within the means available to them' in relation to stateless vessels.[54] Obligations to cooperate are further reflected in requirements concerning mutual legal assistance[55] and information exchange.[56] The latter obligations underline the potential role for submarines in gathering and sharing information concerning illicit activities at sea.

Similar legal regimes have been created at the regional level. The 1995 Council of Europe Agreement on Illicit Traffic by Sea allows for the parties to interdict vessels flagged to other parties with their consent,[57] and supports the sharing of information to suppress illicit trafficking.[58] Of interest in relation to the Council of Europe Agreement is that it includes 'submersible craft' within the definition of 'vessel'.[59] In relation to stateless vessels, the Council of Europe Agreement requires that 'each Party shall take such measures as may be necessary to establish its jurisdiction over the relevant offences committed on board a vessel which is without nationality, or which is assimilated to a vessel without nationality under international law'.[60] Under Article 5(1), when law enforcement officials suspect that a vessel is without nationality, they 'shall inform such other Parties as appear most closely affected and may request the assistance of any such Party in suppressing its use for that purpose'. This clause appears to satisfy the two views on assertions of jurisdiction over stateless vessels;[61] the parties may interdict the vessel and exercise jurisdiction, but regard must still be had to any other party that 'appear[s] most closely affected', which would likely include a party

[51] Ibid, art. 4. The 1988 Vienna Convention does not provide a definition of 'vessel' so it must be assumed that submarines will be 'vessels' for the purposes of this treaty.
[52] Ibid, art. 17(3) and (4).
[53] Ibid, art. 17(2).
[54] Ibid.
[55] Ibid, art. 8.
[56] Ibid, art. 9(1)(a).
[57] Agreement on Illicit Traffic by Sea, Implementing Article 17 of the United Nations Convention against Illicit Traffic in Narcotic Drugs and Psychotropic Substances, Strasbourg, 31 January 1995, entered into force 1 May 2000, 2136 UNTS 61, arts. 7–10.
[58] Ibid, art. 2(5).
[59] Ibid, art. 1(c).
[60] Ibid, art. 3(3).
[61] See above notes 17–19 and accompanying text.

that has nationals aboard the interdicted craft.[62] It thus seems that the Council of Europe Agreement provides a basis under international law for the interdiction of stateless submersibles beyond the territorial sea and the exercise of jurisdiction over those vessels and individual offenders.

The 2003 Caribbean Agreement is more ambitious than the Council of Europe Agreement in implementing Article 17 of the 1988 Vienna Convention, as it potentially allows for law enforcement operations in the territorial seas of States party to the treaty,[63] as well as incorporating the possibility of ship-riders, who are embarked law enforcement officials sailing with law enforcement officials of another State to provide the necessary consent for law enforcement actions against vessels flagged to that embarked official's State.[64] The 2003 Caribbean Agreement does not provide for a general definition of vessels and so its applicability to submersibles would need to be assumed as falling within the scope of a 'suspect vessel'.[65] This agreement requires State parties to assume jurisdiction over vessels without nationality suspected of offences listed in the 1988 Vienna Convention.[66]

The United States has also concluded a suite of bilateral agreements that are intended to enhance law enforcement efforts against drug-trafficking.[67] For example, a 1981 Exchange of Notes with the United Kingdom granted the United States permission to interdict British-flagged vessels suspected of drug-trafficking in specific areas of the Caribbean, Gulf of Mexico and Atlantic Oceans.[68] This Exchange of Notes does not explicitly refer to submersibles, only 'vessels' and is

[62] Gilmore considers that this affected State might be 'a state which was well positioned to initiate law enforcement action or that of the next known port of call': William C. Gilmore, 'Narcotics Interdiction at Sea: The 1995 Council of Europe Agreement' (1996) 20(1) *Marine Policy* 3, 5.

[63] Agreement concerning Co-operation in Suppressing Illicit Maritime and Air Trafficking in Narcotic Drugs and Psychotropic Substances in the Caribbean Area, San Jose, 10 April 2003, not entered into force, arts. 8(2), 11.

[64] Ibid, art. 9.

[65] The definition of a 'suspect vessel' is 'any vessel in respect of which there are reasonable grounds to suspect that it is engaged in illicit traffic': ibid, art. 1(l).

[66] Ibid, arts. 23, 24.

[67] Gonzalez-Pinto (n 18) 453, 472–478.

[68] Agreement between the Government of the United States and the Government of the United Kingdom of Great Britain and Northern Ireland to Facilitate the Interdiction by the United States of Vessels of the United Kingdom which are Suspected of being Engaged in Trafficking in Drugs, London, 13 November 1981, entered into force 13 November 1981 (1981) 33 UST 4224 (TIAS No. 10296).

concerned with British-flagged vessels rather than stateless craft. A model maritime agreement that the United States may use as a basis for negotiations with another State does not address explicitly the definition of vessels and applicability to submersibles, nor does it deal with authority over vessels without nationality.[69] The latter feature is not surprising in the context of a bilateral agreement that is focused on regulating the relations between two States with regards to their respective vessels.

These international agreements, in conjunction with the customary international law principles for the exercise of criminal jurisdiction, thereby create the international legal authority for a State to act in maritime areas beyond national jurisdiction against illicit drug-trafficking. As submarines are presumably included in any reference to 'vessels', the existing international laws apply irrespective of whether they operate on or below the ocean surface. In light of the existing international law authority accorded to States to prevent and suppress drug-trafficking, it is critical that national laws are adopted to authorise law enforcement officials to interdict and arrest individuals and their vessels suspected of illegal drug-trafficking. One of the few (if not only) examples of national legislation explicitly addressing criminal activities undertaken with submarines is in place in the United States and is discussed next.

13.4.2 *Example of National Regulation: The US DTVIA*

The US Constitution grants the US Congress power to 'define and punish Piracies and Felonies committed on the high Seas, and Offences against the Law of Nations'.[70] Under this authority, the United States has progressively asserted greater law enforcement authority by adopting legislation to enable the interdiction of vessels engaged in drug smuggling where those vessels are 'subject to the jurisdiction of the United States', which has included stateless vessels.[71] The Maritime Drug Law Enforcement Act (MDLEA),[72] which was adopted in 1986, set out

[69] Reproduced in Joseph E. Kramek, 'Bilateral Maritime Counter-Drug and Immigrant Interdiction Agreements: Is This the World of the Future?' (2000) 31(1) *University of Miami Inter-American Law Review* 121, 152–160.

[70] Constitution of the United States of America, art. I(8)(10).

[71] See, e.g., Marijuana on the High Seas Act, Pub. L. No. 96–350, 94 Stat. 1159 (1980) (United States); Maritime Drug Law Enforcement Act, 46 U.S.C. § 705 (2006) (United States). See discussion in Ann Marie Brodarick, 'High Seas, High Stakes: Jurisdiction over Stateless Vessels and an Excess of Congressional Power under the Drug Trafficking Vessel Interdiction Act' (2012) 67(1) *University of Miami Law Review* 255, 257–263.

[72] 46 U.S.C. §§ 70501–70507 (United States).

jurisdictional authority for US law enforcement in relation to US flagged vessels, foreign-flagged vessels where the flag State had consented to boarding, and stateless vessels, as well as over trafficking offences on the high seas and in the territorial sea of other States if that State so consents. One problem emerging in the operation of this Act was that drugs would be pitched overboard at the prospect of interdiction and, especially with the use of submersibles, the vessel would be scuttled following detection and thereby minimise, if not eliminate, the likelihood of successful prosecution.

In 2008, the United States adopted the DTVIA to address specifically the use of stateless submarines and semi-submersible craft, given their increasing use to transport drugs into the United States. This legislation criminalises their operation when they are without nationality and navigate outside of the territorial sea with intent to evade detection.[73] This assertion of jurisdiction avoids the scenarios of drugs being disposed of or vessels scuttled. Rather, irrespective of any drugs on board, merely being stateless and seeking to evade detection are criminalised and may thus be relevant for crimes other than drug-trafficking.[74] Bennet has observed that the DTVIA makes the 'operation of a stateless vessel a key component of the substantive crime it proscribes', rather than just using statelessness as a 'jurisdictional hook'.[75] In focusing on the statelessness of the vessel and its evasive actions alone, concerns have thus been raised that the assertion of jurisdiction has extended beyond the bounds of US authority under international law.[76] The criminalisation of the particular operation of the stateless vessel is said to be

[73] The DTVIA reads:

> Whoever knowingly operates, or attempts or conspires to operate, by any means, or embarks in any submersible vessel or semi-submersible vessel that is without nationality and that is navigating or has navigated into, through, or from waters beyond the outer limit of the territorial sea of a single country or a lateral limit of that country's territorial sea with an adjacent country, with the intent to evade detection, shall be fined under this title, imprisoned not more than 15 years, or both.

18 U.S.C. § 2285.

[74] *United States v. Ibarguen-Mosquera*, 634 F.3d 1370 (11th Cir. 2011) 1381.

[75] Allyson Bennett, 'That Sinking Feeling: Stateless Ships, Universal Jurisdiction, and the Drug Trafficking Vessel Interdiction Act' (2012) 37(2) *Yale Journal of International Law* 433, 435, 447.

[76] See, e.g., Brodarick (n 71); Bennett (n 75).

tantamount to creating a crime of universal jurisdiction,[77] and could thus have far-reaching implications for other maritime activities, including migration.[78]

To prevent the criminalisation of lawful activities using submarines under the DTVIA, there is allowance for affirmative defences, which include being 'classed by and designed in accordance with the rules of a classification society' and 'lawfully operated in government-regulated or licensed activity, including commerce, research, or exploration'.[79] Further, another affirmative defence may be proffered if the submarine is equipped with tracking equipment, such as a vessel monitoring system, an automatic identification system or long range information and tracking.[80]

While quite exceptional in its approach, the DTVIA is legally responsive to the core issue of unregistered submersibles used for illicit activities. If States consider the assertion of jurisdiction objectionable over their nationals who are arrested under this legislation, it is incumbent on those States to engage in the appropriate diplomatic protests. Those protests would likely need to assert that the United States has abused its rights of law enforcement authority beyond its territorial sea (and contiguous zone), and that the State of nationality of the alleged offender has the primary obligation to investigate and prosecute illicit conduct that occurs in areas beyond national jurisdiction.

13.4.3 Submarines Deployed for Terrorist Activities

During the Sri Lankan civil war (1983–2009), the Liberation Tigers of Tamil Eelam (LTTE) developed submarines,[81] semi-submersibles and craft described as 'human torpedoes', which were 'one-man semi-submersible craft designed to ram and destroy the enemy'.[82] As a preliminary point, it may be observed that the conflict between the LTTE and the Sri Lankan defence force could be considered a non-international armed conflict and governed by the law of armed conflict

[77] Bennett (n 75) 448–454.
[78] Ibid, 454–456.
[79] 18 U.S.C.A. § 2285(e) (United States).
[80] Ibid.
[81] Martin N. Murphy, *Contemporary Piracy and Maritime Terrorism: The Threat to International Security* (Routledge, 2013) 54.
[82] H. I. Sutton, 'LTTE Sea Tigers Sneak Attack Craft and Midget Subs', 24 April 2016 <www.hisutton.com/LTTE%20Sea%20Tigers%20sneak%20attack%20craft%20and%20midget%20subs.html>.

rather than counter-terrorism laws.[83] The actions of the LTTE are considered within the frame of terrorism for the purposes of discussion in this chapter, without engaging with the question as to whether there was a non-international armed conflict or not, as illustrative of the possible use of submarines to advance terrorist goals.[84]

The LTTE primarily deployed 'snorkel subs'.[85] The tactics of the maritime element of the LTTE, the Sea Tigers, were described as follows:

> The Sea Tigers' suicide craft are almost impossible to detect. They are dark, sit low in the water and cannot be detected by radar. The only way for the Sri Lankan navy to find them is through heat-detecting systems, but even then they travel at such speed that they are very difficult to shoot at. The boats, packed with explosives, are modelled on an American stealth bomber, but a more recent development is a human torpedo craft designed especially for suicide attacks.[86]

The LTTE was reported as claiming inspiration from al-Qaeda's suicide attacks on vessels like USS *Cole*.[87] The Sea Tigers' suicide attacks were in addition to the use of low-profile vessels for ship protection, control of certain maritime areas, transporting fighters and supplies, as well as carrying out raids.

Beyond the LTTE Sea Tigers, the potential uses of submarines to achieve terroristic aims have been the source of some speculation. It has been claimed that North Korea has used 'mini-submarines to insert terrorist kill teams into South Korea'.[88] Further possibilities range from submarine use to attack ports and ships (not only as suicide missions) to

83 For discussion on this point, see, e.g., Suthaharan Nadarajah and Dhananjayan Sriskandarajah, 'Liberation Struggle or Terrorism? The Politics of Naming the LTTE' in Michael Bhatia (ed.), *Terrorism and the Politics of Naming* (Routledge, 2013) 83–96; Muttukrishna Sarvananthan, '"Terrorism" or "Liberation"? Towards a Distinction: A Case Study of the Armed Struggle of the Liberation Tigers of Tamil Eelam (LTTE)' (2018) 12(2) *Perspectives on Terrorism* 1.

84 Lichtenwald and colleagues have observed that the development of narco-submarines in Colombia occurred in an area controlled by the Colombian Revolutionary Armed Forces, FARC, and argue that despite different motives, there are connections between drug-trafficking operations and terrorism: see Lichtenwald, Steinhour and Perri (n 46).

85 Sutton (n 82).

86 Tom Birtley, 'Sri Lanka Battles Tigers at Sea', *Al Jazeera*, 11 June 2007, cited in Peter Lehr, 'Maritime Terrorism: Locations, Actors, and Capabilities' in Rupert Herbert-Burns, Sam Bateman and Peter Lehr (eds.), *Lloyd's MIU Handbook of Maritime Security* (Routledge, 2009) 56, 61.

87 Sudha Ramachandran, 'The Sea Tigers of Tamil Eelam,' *Asia Time Online*, 31 August 2006, cited in Lichtenwald, Steinhour and Perri (n 46).

88 Lichtenwald, Steinhour and Perri (n 46).

the hijacking of a nuclear-powered or nuclear-armed submarine belonging to the armed forces of a State.[89] The discussion immediately below considers the applicability of the international law framework available to States to prevent and suppress maritime terrorism involving submarines.

The primary international law instrument addressing maritime terrorism is the 2005 Convention for the Suppression of Unlawful Acts against the Safety of Maritime Navigation ('2005 SUA Convention').[90] The 2005 SUA Convention consists of the 1988 SUA Convention and amendments to that convention through a 2005 Protocol. States that are parties to the 1988 SUA Convention must also separately sign and ratify or accede to the 2005 SUA Protocol.[91] At time of writing, 166 States are parties to the 1988 SUA Convention whereas only 53 States are parties to the 2005 SUA Protocol.[92] The reasons for the slower uptake of the 2005 SUA Protocol are multiple,[93] and resistance to the new instrument has been especially strong in Asia.[94]

As an initial matter, it is clear that the 2005 SUA Convention extends to submarines (and not just surface craft) in light of the broad definition of ships. Article 1 affirms the definition of 'ships' as meaning 'a vessel of any type whatsoever not permanently attached to the sea-bed, including dynamically support craft, *submersibles*, or any other floating craft'.[95] However, it is also clear that the 2005 SUA Convention is concerned with

[89] KG Weiss, 'The Enemy is Still Below: The Global Diffusion of Submarines and Related Technology' (Workshop Paper, Lawrence Livermore National Laboratory, 12 July 2012). See also Joshua Sinai, 'Future Trends in Worldwide Maritime Terrorism' (2004) 3(1) *Connections* 49, 65–66.

[90] 2005 SUA Convention (n 22).

[91] For the sake of completeness, it should be observed that there is a separate protocol adopted in 1988 that addressed the suppression of terrorist acts against fixed platforms: Protocol to the Convention of 10 March for the Suppression of Unlawful Acts Against the Safety of Fixed Platforms Located on the Continental Shelf, Rome, 10 March 1988, entered into force 1 March 1992, 1678 UNTS 201, as amended by the Protocol of 2005 to the Protocol for the Suppression of Unlawful Acts against the Safety of Fixed Platforms Located on the Continental Shelf, London, 14 October 2005, entered into force 28 July 2010 (IMO Doc. LEG/CONF.15/22). These instruments are not the focus of the current analysis.

[92] IMO, 'Status of Conventions' <www.imo.org/en/About/Conventions/Pages/StatusOfConventions.aspx>.

[93] See generally Scott D. MacDonald, 'The SUA 2005 Protocol: A Critical Reflection' (2013) 28(3) *International Journal of Marine and Coastal Law* 485.

[94] See Natalie Klein, 'Responding to Maritime Terrorism in Southeast Asia: What are the Alternatives to the 2005 SUA Protocol?' (2023) 8 *Asia Pacific Journal of Ocean Law and Policy* 221.

[95] 2005 SUA Convention (n 22) art. 1(1)(a) (emphasis added).

the actions of private vessels, as the actions of warships and naval auxiliaries are outside the scope of the treaty and the sovereign immunities enjoyed by those vessels are also maintained.[96] States have, though, described certain attacks on their warships as a terrorist attack.[97]

For present purposes, it may be noted that the 2005 SUA Convention aligns with other counter-terrorism treaties in that it sets out a series of offences that States are to criminalise within their national laws, indicates what States have authority to prosecute alleged offenders and creates a basis for extradition of alleged offenders. The number of possible offences to be criminalised was expanded with the adoption of the 2005 SUA Protocol.[98] In relation to submarines, an offence is established if that submarine is used 'in a manner that causes death or serious injury or damage' when 'the purpose of the act, by its nature or context, is to intimidate a population or to compel a government . . . to do or to abstain from doing any act'.[99] A crime is also to be established for persons who commit different acts that endanger the safe navigation of ships.[100] Further, if a submarine is used to transport any explosive or radioactive material for the purposes of terrorist acts on land, such an act may also be criminalised under the 2005 SUA Convention.[101] The revisions to the original 1988 SUA Convention greatly expanded the range of criminal acts that are to be articulated in State parties' domestic legislation and, provided a State is party to the 2005 SUA Convention and has fully implemented that treaty, it is highly likely that any violent act involving the use of a submarine would fall within the terms of the 2005 SUA Convention.

96 Ibid, art. 2.

97 For example, the attack on USS *Cole* is commonly described as a terrorist attack in the United States. See, e.g., Raphael Perl and Ronald O'Rourke, 'Terrorist Attack on USS Cole: Background and Issues for Congress', *Naval History and Heritage Command*, 30 January 2001 <www.history.navy.mil/browse-by-topic/ships/modern-ships/uss-cole/terrorist-attack-on-uss-cole-background-and-issues-for-congress.html>; United States Senate Committee on Armed Services, *Lessons Learned from the Attack on U.S.S. Cole, on the Report of the Crouch-Gehman Commission, and on the Navy's Judge Advocate General Manual Investigation into the Attack, Including a Review of Appropriate Standards of Accountability for U.S. Military Services* (US Government Printing Office, 2002).

98 For discussion, see Natalie Klein, 'The Right of Visit and the 2005 Protocol on the Suppression of Unlawful Acts against the Safety of Maritime Navigation' (2007) 35(2) *Denver Journal of International Law and Policy* 287.

99 2005 SUA Convention (n 22), art. 3*bis* (1)(a)(iii).

100 Ibid, art. 3(1).

101 Ibid, art. 3*bis*(1)(b)(i).

States party to the 2005 SUA Convention are to establish jurisdiction over these broad offences in instances where they are committed against or on board a ship flying the State's flag, or when the offence occurs in the territory of that State (including its territorial sea) or where the alleged offender is a national of the State.[102] Jurisdiction may also be established on the basis of passive personality (the victim is a national of the State), where the alleged offender is stateless but a habitual resident of a State, and if the act 'is committed in an attempt to compel that State to do or abstain from doing any act'.[103] A significant addition to the 2005 SUA Convention was the inclusion of a boarding provision, which allows for a right of visit against a suspect ship with the flag State's consent.[104] In line with other counter-terrorism treaties, if a State does not prosecute an alleged offence, the 2005 SUA Convention provides a basis for the extradition of that offender to a State that has a basis of jurisdiction to pursue prosecution.[105] States are also subject to obligations with regards to information sharing and mutual legal assistance in responding to unlawful acts against the safety of maritime navigation under the 2005 SUA Convention.

There are undoubtedly questions regarding the interpretation and application of various provisions of the 2005 SUA Convention, especially with the more recently introduced amendments. One question of relevance may be the application of the 2005 SUA Convention in the context of a warship that has been the victim of a violent attack by a private group. This action may be piracy under the classic definition of piracy set out in UNCLOS.[106] However, if a submarine is hijacked by persons who were able to stowaway on the submarine, there may be an argument that the exclusion of warships from the scope of the 2005 SUA Convention is not limited to actions *by* warships but may also include actions *against* warships. Factually, it may be difficult to contemplate the possibility of private individuals secreting themselves away on a naval submarine as it would reflect a definite lack of security on the part of that military force. If the individuals taking control of

[102] Ibid, art. 6(1).
[103] Ibid, art. 6(2).
[104] Ibid, art. 8*bis*.
[105] Ibid, art. 10(1).
[106] Piracy consists of: 'any illegal acts of violence or detention, or any act of depredation, committed for private ends by the crew or the passengers of a private ship or a private aircraft, and directed: (i) on the high seas, against another ship or aircraft, or against persons or property on board such ship or aircraft; (ii) against a ship, aircraft, persons or property in a place outside the jurisdiction of any State': UNCLOS (n 7) art. 101(a).

a naval submarine were part of the armed forces of that submarine, a situation of mutiny would instead arise.

Mutiny is most commonly defined under domestic laws and involves individuals on board a vessel (including a submarine) taking command and control of the vessel away from the master or commanding officer.[107] A mutiny on a warship will be subject to the military law of the flag State concerned. One infamous mutiny concerned the Soviet anti-submarine frigate *Storozhevoy*: the political officer seised control of the ship because he 'was upset by the privilege and corruption of the Soviet bureaucratic elite in a supposedly classless society' and sought a new Leninist revolution.[108] The incident was later fictionalised as occurring on a Soviet submarine in the Tom Clancy novel, *The Hunt for Red October*.[109] For present purposes, the incident is relevant for demonstrating that mutiny is an act regulated by a State's national laws, as the officers involved in the mutiny were ultimately tried and convicted under Russian law.[110]

If a mutiny occurred on a private submarine, seizing control of the ship constitutes an offence under the 2005 SUA Convention.[111] Mutiny has been considered a serious crime because of the potential risks to safe navigation that may follow a mutiny, causing dangers to those on board as well as creating a hazard to other vessels in the vicinity.[112] Where the mutiny results in an unlawful act against the safety of maritime navigation, an offence under the 2005 SUA Convention may also arise in addition to any violation of national law for the mutiny itself. While Lauterpacht has argued that a mutinous act may also be an act of piracy, this position is not widely accepted,[113] and is not reflected in UNCLOS, which anticipates two ships are involved in an act of piracy. If the mutiny results in an act of piracy then jurisdiction may be asserted on the basis of

[107] See, e.g., Criminal Code Act 1995 (Cth) s. 83.1 (Australia); 18 US § 2193 (1982) (United States); Armed Forces Act 2006, s. 6 (United Kingdom).

[108] Sebastien Roblin, 'In 1975, a Russian Navy Frigate Mutinied. And It Made Tom Clancy's Career', *The National Interest*, 1 August 2018 <https://nationalinterest.org/blog/buzz/1975-russian-navy-frigate-mutinied-and-it-made-tom-clancys-career-27472>.

[109] Boris Gindin and David Hagberg, *Mutiny: The True Events That Inspired The Hunt For Red October* (Tor Publishing Group, 2008).

[110] Roblin (n 108).

[111] 2005 SUA Convention (n 22) art. 3(1)(a).

[112] See George P Smith II, 'From Cutlass to Cat-O'-Nine Tails: The Case for International Jurisdiction of Mutiny on the High Seas' (1989) 10(1) *Michigan Journal of International Law* 277, 285.

[113] Ibid, 295 (referring to Hersch Lauterpacht, *Oppenheim's International Law: A Treatise* (8th ed., Longman, 1955) vol. 1, 608–609).

the piratical acts.[114] Otherwise the act of mutiny on board a private vessel could be prosecuted potentially as a violation of the 2005 SUA Convention, if the relevant State is a party and has implemented the treaty into its national laws.

13.5 Conclusion

The international law framework affirming the authority of States to take action against criminal activity at sea largely applies equally to surface vessels as it does to submarines. The use of submarines for criminal activity and the increased difficulty of detection prompts greater policing challenges and underlines the need for cooperation among States in addressing transnational crime. One of the main international law issues spotlighted by the deployment of submarines for criminal activities is the authority that may be exercised over stateless vessels. The fact that vessels are stateless and so not protected by any State, as well as the possibility that the nationals aboard are likely guilty of criminal offences and perhaps provide less incentive for States to act on their behalf, perpetuate the differing views on legal authority over these vessels. Even if a State proceeds against a stateless vessel on the basis that the vessel's lack of nationality so allows, the State engaging in law enforcement still owes human rights obligations to the individuals within their effective control.[115]

In light of the existing legal framework responding to maritime terrorism, it is evident that the types of attacks perpetrated by private actors using submarines or submersibles would likely fall within the scope of the 2005 SUA Convention. For example, the use of explosive-laden submarines for suicide attacks against other ships or ports, the hijacking of submarines – particularly nuclear submarines – with the intention of using the weapons or radioactive material on board for a terrorist attack, and potentially the transport of a person involved in

[114] Article 102 of UNCLOS (n 7) reads: 'The acts of piracy, as defined in article 101, committed by a warship, government ship or government aircraft whose crew has mutinied and taken control of the ship or aircraft are assimilated to acts committed by a private ship or aircraft.'

[115] *Hirsi Jamaa v. Italy* (2012) II Eur Court HR 97 (App No 27765/09, 23 February 2012); UN Human Rights Committee, *General Comment No. 31: Nature of the General Legal Obligation Imposed on States Parties to the Covenant*, 26 May 2004 (UN Doc. CCPR/C/21/Rev.1/Add.13) para. 10; UN Committee Against Torture, *Concluding Observations: United States of America*, 25 July 2006 (UN Doc. CAT/C/USA/C/2) para. 20.

terrorist activity[116] will all fall within the scope of offences of the 2005 SUA Convention. As a consequence, these scenarios will trigger the State obligations to exercise jurisdiction, assist States with investigations and generally to cooperate to prevent and suppress these acts.

While the international law framework is largely in place, there remain various hurdles in relation to its effective operation. Foremost is the extent of participation in the treaty regime, especially in relation to the expanded version of that regime from the adoption of the 2005 SUA Protocol. The slow uptake of States in becoming parties to the 2005 SUA Protocol has been attributed to a range of factors, including that it is too expansive, that it is not broad enough, that there are risks of criminalising seafarers' acts in the ordinary course of their duties, and that flag State authority over ships is jeopardised.[117] Another important element for the successful operation of the 2005 SUA Convention is its full implementation into the national laws of a State. The role of national law is critical to ensure that criminal offences are established so that a State does have the necessary authority to either prosecute or extradite alleged offenders or otherwise engage in the cooperative actions expected to prevent and suppress terrorist acts against the safety of maritime navigation. These points hold true for both surface vessels as well as submarines. An appreciation of the potential criminal uses of submarines should render these law reform requirements as more pressing for States.

116 Article 3*ter* reads: 'Any person commits an offence … if that person unlawfully and intentionally transports another person on board a ship knowing that the person has committed an act [of terrorism] … and intending to assist that person to evade criminal prosecution': 2005 SUA Convention (n 22) art. 3*ter*.

117 See Klein, 'Responding to Maritime Terrorism in Southeast Asia' (n 94) 226–229.

14

Underwater Maritime Autonomous Vehicles and the Future of Submarines

14.1 Introduction

As indicated at the start of this book, submarines have greatly evolved over the last century.[1] Technological innovations have now led to the development of underwater vehicles that can be operated remotely or run autonomously. The extent of human engagement ranges across a spectrum from contemporaneous remote control to minimal or no active human engagement while a vehicle operates in accordance with its programming. In the context of shipping generally, the International Maritime Organization (IMO) has differentiated between four levels of autonomy in its consideration of Maritime Autonomous Surface Ships (MASS): (1) ships with automated processes and decision support; (2) remotely controlled ships with seafarers on board; (3) remotely controlled ships without seafarers on board; and (4) fully autonomous ships, which have an 'operating system . . . able to make decisions and determine actions by itself'.[2] This differentiation in the extent of autonomy provides a starting point for a legal assessment of underwater maritime autonomous vehicles (UMAVs).

There are a variety of UMAVs currently in operation, which differ in their size and functionality.[3] Remote-controlled submersibles have been

[1] See Chapter 1, Section 1.4, which sets out a legal taxonomy of submarines.

[2] IMO, 'Outcome of the Regulatory Scoping Exercise for the Use of Maritime Autonomous Surface Ships (MASS)', 3 June 2021 (IMO Doc. MSC.1/Circ.1638) annex, para. 3.4 ('MASS Outcome'). There have been proposals at the IMO that a different set of degrees of autonomy may be needed. See ibid, para. 5.8. Lloyd's Register has instead identified six levels of autonomy. Lloyd's Register, 'ShipRight Design and Construction, Additional Design Procedures, Design Code for Unmanned Marine Systems', February 2017, 1–2.

[3] Andrew H. Henderson, 'Murky Waters: The Legal Status of Unmanned Undersea Vehicles' (2006) 53 *Naval Law Review* 55, 57. See further National Research Council, *Autonomous Vehicles in Support of Naval Operations* (The National Academies Press, 2005) 124–128.

deployed to assist in submarine cable repair, as part of the exploration and exploitation of seabed resources and in the course of marine scientific research.[4] Remotely operated vehicles (ROVs) that are tethered to another (crewed) vessel are usually seen as an extension of the support vessel;[5] tethered UMAVs are not addressed further in this chapter given this connection.[6] Gliders, which are small, remotely controlled or fully autonomous underwater vehicles, have been deployed for research purposes, as well as for intelligence, reconnaissance and surveillance (ISR) missions. The use of gliders has already prompted consideration as to what legal regime applies, and caused controversy in inter-State relations when deployed for ISR in the exclusive economic zone (EEZ) of another State. These aspects of gliders are discussed in this chapter.

In addition, States are developing 'extra-large uncrewed underwater vehicles' (XLUUVs), which can be armed, have a range of up to 3,000 miles and are 30 metres long.[7] They can dive to a depth of 6,000 metres and are considered an important element in deterring aggression.[8] The US Navy's thirty-year shipbuilding plan envisages a fleet with eighteen to fifty-one XLUUVs, which 'will potentially have the capability to deliver multiple payloads at extended ranges'.[9] These vehicles, which are yet to be delivered and cost some US$115 million each, are too large

[4] See discussion in Chapter 8, Section 8.3.3.2.

[5] Henderson (n 3) 65.

[6] Their operations are discussed in Chapter 8, Section 8.3.3.

[7] H. I. Sutton, 'Royal Navy To Get First Large Autonomous Submarine' *Forbes*, 5 March 2020 </www.forbes.com/sites/hisutton/2020/03/05/royal-navy-to-get-first-large-autonomous-submarine/>. XLUUVs have been described as 'roughly the size of a subway car'; Ronald O'Rourke, *Navy Large Unmanned Surface Vehicles: Background and Issues for Congress* (Congressional Research Service Report R45757, 19 December 2024) 15.

[8] Tory Shepherd, 'Robotic Submarines Fast-Tracked for Build at Site on Sydney Harbour to Plug Capability Gap' *The Guardian*, 17 August 2022 <www.theguardian.com/australia-news/2022/aug/17/robotic-submarines-fast-tracked-for-sydney-harbour-to-bridge-defence-capability-gap>.

[9] Office of the Chief of Naval Operations, *Report to Congress on the Annual Long-Range Plan for Construction of Naval Vessels for Fiscal Year 2023* (April 2022) 4, 6. This figure does not include smaller UMAVs. As O'Rourke observed:

> The Navy has operated smaller unmanned surface vehicles (USVs) and unmanned underwater vehicles (UUVs) for many years, but because these unmanned vehicles (UVs) are launched from manned ships to act essentially as extensions of the manned ships, they have not been considered ships in their own right and consequently have not been included in the top-level expression of the Navy's force-level goal or the publicly cited figure for the number of ships in the Navy.

to be launched from submarines.[10] The British Royal Navy envisages building a similar set of XLUUVs,[11] as does the Royal Australian Navy.[12] The United Kingdom announced it would use an unarmed XLUUV for deterrence and detection of attacks, such as that perpetrated against the Nord Stream gas pipelines in 2022.[13] The potential legal ramifications for the deployment of armed XLUUVs have already been recognised, and distinguished from the advent of aerial drones on the basis that '[a]erial drones generally have a human in the loop before the weapon is fired, but this may not be practical for an autonomous submarine'.[14] Instead, crewed vessels may be needed to work in tandem with XLUUVs.[15]

As with other aspects of submarine operations, there are legal issues that arise in relation to UMAVs that are shared with maritime autonomous vehicles (MAVs) that operate on the surface. Yet some legal issues are more acute in relation to UMAVs or, indeed, unique to these vehicles.

Ronald O'Rourke, *Navy Force Structure and Shipbuilding Plans: Background and Issues for Congress* (Congressional Research Service Report RL32665, 20 October 2022) 3.

10 See generally O'Rourke (n 7) 15–19 and the sources cited therein. See also US Department of the Navy, *Unmanned Campaign Framework*, 16 March 2021, 16.

11 Dominic Nicholls, 'New Drone Submarines Will Protect Britain's Underwater Infrastructure after Nord Stream Attacks', *The Telegraph*, 2 December 2022. <www.telegraph.co.uk/world-news/2022/12/01/new-drone-submarine-will-protect-britainsunderwater-infrastructure/>. See also Lee Willett, 'UK XLUUV Trials Demonstrate Towed Array Sonar Deployment', 23 May 2022, *Janes*; Lee Willett, 'Doing the Dull, Dirty, or Dangerous: UK Builds UUV Operational Capability', 20 May 2022, *Janes*.

12 Oishee Majumdar, 'Cellula, TAS Partner to Develop XLUUV for RAN', 31 May 2022, *Janes* (describing the RAN's 'SeaWolf XLUUV project', which is currently in the prototype phase with a vehicle measuring 12m in length and 1.7m in diameter); Nishant Kumar, 'Anduril to Develop XL-AUVs for Australian Navy', 6 May 2022, *Janes*. It may further be noted that the AUKUS members are collaborating through the AUKUS Undersea Robotics Autonomous Systems (AURAS) project, in which the States will further develop UMAV technology: 'Fact Sheet: Implementation of the Australia–United Kingdom–United States Partnership (AUKUS)', *The White House*, 5 April 2022 <https://bidenwhitehouse.archives.gov/briefing-room/statements-releases/2022/04/05/fact-sheet-implementation-of-the-australia-united-kingdom-united-states-partnership-aukus/>.

13 Nicholls, (n 11). Though the UMAVs being developed for the Royal Navy also include vessels that can carry payload. See 'Manta – The Royal Navy Gets its First Extra-Large Autonomous Submarine'. *Navy Lookout*, 31 March 2020 <www.navylookout.com/manta-the-royal-navy-gets-its-first-extra-large-autonomous-submarine/>.

14 Sutton, 'Royal Navy To Get First Large Autonomous Submarine' (n 7).

15 Shepherd (n 8).

The focus of this chapter is on the legal differences that emerge when a craft operates underwater and is uncrewed.[16]

A first issue of difference relates to definitions and is considered in Section 14.2: it is necessary to consider whether there may be legally relevant distinctions as to whether UMAVs are ships and vessels or not. As with surface vessels, it is also necessary to determine when a UMAV is a 'warship' – an assessment that traditionally refers to how a ship is commanded and crewed in accordance with Article 29 of the United Nations Convention on the Law of the Sea (UNCLOS).[17]

Section 14.3 is concerned with the navigational rights and duties of UMAVs, which may need to account for their autonomous status. Questions on this issue concern the legal challenges that arise in relation to the passage regimes through the territorial sea or international straits and archipelagic sea lanes, as well as the freedom of navigation enjoyed in the EEZ and on the high seas. Are there, or should there be, situations where the autonomous or remotely controlled nature of the UMAV changes the legal assessment of the exercise of different navigational rights and duties? The very fact that UMAVs operate underwater and autonomously must be accounted for in assessing navigational rights and duties.[18]

Another issue, addressed in Section 14.4, concerns possible implications for the law of naval warfare when regard is had to the use of UMAVs in the course of an armed conflict. Their underwater status invites comparisons to torpedoes and mines in some instances. Finally, the illicit use of UMAVs to smuggle goods, such as drugs, weapons and cash, prompts queries in Section 14.5 as to whether existing criminal offences under international law are sufficient and how criminal jurisdiction may be lawfully exercised by States in these situations. The submerged operation of UMAVs will be especially appealing in criminal contexts as these craft are less likely to be detected as compared to surface vehicles but do not risk team members being apprehended at sea. In this chapter, we aim to flag gaps and

16 Under the IMO schemata, we are referring to UMAVs that have levels 3 or 4 autonomy. See above n 2 and accompanying text.

17 United Nations Convention on the Law of the Sea, Montego Bay, 10 December 1982, entered into force 16 November 1994, 1833 UNTS 397 ('UNCLOS').

18 The navigational rights and duties of crewed submarines in contemporary law are explored in earlier chapters, especially Chapters 7 and 8.

ambiguities that exist within international law and conclude in Section 14.6 with proposals on how to move forward to enhance the regulation of submarines in international law when operated remotely or without crew. Just as submarines constituted new technology to which international law needed to respond when introduced over a century ago, the advent of UMAVs again brings into sharp relief the need for rights and duties under international law to be clearly articulated, both to guide the development of this technology and to regulate its use once deployed. Section 14.7 concludes Part II of the book.

14.2 Questions of Definition

It is almost inevitable that a 'one size fits all' approach to UMAVs will not work because of their diverse characteristics and uses. The US Navy has defined a UMAV as a 'self-propelled submersible whose operation is either fully autonomous (pre-programmed or operated under real-time adaptive mission control) or under minimal supervisory control and is untethered except, possibly, for data links such as a fiber optic cable'.[19] Allan has rightly argued that it will be important to assess the context and application of any MAV, with consideration accorded to the purpose of classifying the MAV a certain way as well as the consequences of such a classification.[20]

In line with Allan's observation, smaller submersible vehicles deployed for marine research may need to be legally defined to determine the rights and duties of the users of such devices, especially if these vehicles inadvertently enter the territorial sea or internal waters of a State. Floats and gliders, which are used for marine scientific research as well as for military research, have been defined in work undertaken by the International Oceanographic Commission's Advisory Body of Experts on the Law of the Sea. A float was defined as: 'an autonomous vehicle . . . floating passively at a preprogrammed pressure level until at predetermined time intervals rising to the ocean surface to broadcast its position and, as the case may be, collected data to a satellite'.[21] Gliders are ballasted vehicles and so may ascend and descend through the water

[19] Craig H. Allen, 'Determining the Legal Status of Unmanned Maritime Vehicles: Formalism vs Functionalism' (2018) 49 *Journal of Maritime Law and Commerce* 477, 485.

[20] Ibid 493.

[21] Intergovernmental Oceanographic Commission of UNESCO, Draft (Practical) Guidelines of the Intergovernmental Oceanographic Commission, within the Context

column, as well as pursue a pre-determined horizontal movement, but may also be affected in their positioning through ocean currents.[22] The legal significance of these definitions is considered further below in this section.

For larger vehicles, the work of the IMO in relation to MASS may hold relevance for questions of definition. In 2018, the IMO commenced a Regulatory Scoping Exercise in relation to MASS with the purpose of assessing the existing IMO agreements and determining what changes may be needed to account for the operation of such ships. In undertaking this study, the purpose was to ascertain in what instances the existing agreements remained fit for purpose, whether amendment was necessary or whether a new instrument may be needed.[23] In the course of the Regulatory Scoping Exercise, IMO members discerned a need to devise common definitions of certain terms, such as 'master' and 'seafarer', and to account for possible meanings of a remote control centre or a remote operator.[24] Policy decisions within the IMO as to terminology and the development of a MASS Code may prove influential for future State practice, and be reflected within national laws (including criminal law).[25] Such decisions should be expected to hold implications for some of the legal questions that arise in relation to UMAVs. Yet one issue that has not been highlighted for priority consideration at the IMO is any further definition of 'ship' or 'vessel'. The usage of the term 'MASS' indicates that IMO members agree that at least some portion of MAVs may be considered 'ships'.[26]

Given the smaller size of some UMAVs, such as floats and gliders, and their different uses, it should be asked whether they fall within the

of UNCLOS, for the Collection of Oceanographic Data by Specific Means, Paris, 19 February 2007 (UNESCO Doc. IOC/ABE-LOS VII).

22 Katharina Bork et al., 'The Legal Regulation of Floats and Gliders: In Quest of a New Regime?' (2008) 39(3) *Ocean Development and International Law* 298, 300–301. But see Tobias Hofmann and Alexander Proelss, 'The Operation of Gliders under the International Law of the Sea' (2015) 46(3) *Ocean Development and International Law* 167, 175 (disputing that navigation through the application of an algorithm is sufficient and contesting the ability of gliders to navigate).

23 IMO, 'MASS Outcome' (n 2) annex, para. 3.12.

24 Ibid, annex, paras. 5.5–5.8.

25 At time of writing, the IMO plans to adopt the MASS Code to operate on a voluntary basis in 2026 with work on a mandatory code starting in 2028 for implementation by 2032: IMO, 'Autonomous Shipping', <www.imo.org/en/MediaCentre/HotTopics/Pages/Autonomous-shipping.aspx>.

26 Allen (n 19) 503.

rules regulating 'ships' and 'vessels'.[27] UNCLOS uses the terms 'ship' and 'vessels' interchangeably, without providing a formal definition. Treaties adopted under the auspices of the IMO have adopted different definitions of 'ships' relative to the issues being addressed in each treaty.[28] Letts and Pedrozo have noted that the 'key takeaway' from the different IMO definitions is that the presence or otherwise of crew is not 'an essential characteristic' of a ship.[29] The attribution of 'vessel' or 'ship' carries legal significance as 'vessels' have nationality and must be properly registered or otherwise associated with a State that exercises effective control over that vessel.[30] Equally, a coastal State will be entitled to exercise prescriptive and enforcement jurisdiction over 'vessels' engaged in different activities within its maritime zones.[31] These rights and duties regarding nationality and the exercise of jurisdiction may differ in relation to UMAVs that are not 'vessels' or 'ships'. There are also references in UNCLOS to 'underwater vehicles',[32] 'boats'[33] and 'devices'[34] that may be relevant to UMAVs in different contexts. Characteristics of 'ships' or 'vessels' include that they are human-made, floating (i.e., not attached to the seabed) and are intended to provide transportation.[35] This last element may prove

27 This issue in relation to MAVs generally (surface or underwater) has been explored in Klein's earlier work. See Natalie Klein, 'Maritime Autonomous Vehicles within the International Law Framework to Enhance Maritime Security' (2019) 95 *International Law Studies* 244–271; Natalie Klein et al., 'Maritime Autonomous Vessels: New Frontiers in the Law of the Sea' (2020) 69(3) *International and Comparative Law Quarterly* 719.

28 Eric Van Hooydonk, 'The Law of Unmanned Merchant Shipping: An Exploration' (2014) 20 *Journal of International Maritime Law* 403, 406–407.

29 David Letts and Raul (Pete) Pedrozo, 'Maritime Drones at War: Legal Issues Affecting Characterization and Use' in Natalie Klein et al. (eds.), *Maritime Autonomous Vehicles and International Law: Maritime Security Perspectives* (Routledge, 2025) 103, 113.

30 Further to Articles 90–94 of UNCLOS (n 17). See Allen (n 19) 490. However, a difficulty of this assumption is that small UMAVs may not be subject to the formalities of registration in a State: see Rob McLaughlin, 'Some Rules Applicable to Use of Long-Range Underwater Maritime Autonomous Vehicles for Intelligence, Surveillance and Reconnaissance Purposes' in Natalie Klein et al. (eds.), *Maritime Autonomous Vehicles and International Law: Maritime Security Perspectives* (Routledge, 2025) 145, 151. See further Chapter 11, Section 11.1.

31 See, e.g., UNCLOS (n 17) arts. 27, 28, 56, 73, 110.

32 Ibid, art. 20.

33 Ibid, art. 111.

34 Ibid, art. 60.

35 See, e.g., Oliver Daum, 'The Implications of International Law on Unmanned Naval Craft' (2018) 49 *Journal of Maritime Law and Commerce* 71, 80.

problematic with some UMAVs, especially floats and gliders. One of the simplest definitions is that a vessel is 'a human-made device, including submersible vessels, capable of traversing the sea'.[36] Whether such an inclusive definition is politically acceptable and legally plausible remains an open question. In the absence of resolution of this point, a difficulty that emerges is that if UMAVs are not considered as 'ships' then they are potentially unregulated by a variety of international laws that otherwise have bearing on safe navigation and ocean use.

When smaller UMAVs are used for military missions (such as the gliders that are approximately two metres in length), their torpedo-like appearance may also prompt questions as to whether they may be characterised as 'ships' and what legal consequences follow as a result of this determination. These naval UMAVs may be used to detect mines or submarines, or to undertake ISR, and may potentially be armed for attack or defence purposes.[37] It has been suggested that even small military UMAVs will meet the definition of a 'ship' and enjoy the rights and entitlements, as well as the obligations, that flow from that status, as they are human-made, floating craft and transport their own weapons or sensors.[38] However, Daum has argued that small 'naval drones' are not 'ships' on the basis that the definition criterion of transportation concerns the movement of objects that are external or not connected to the craft itself, as is the case with sensors, equipment or weapons on military UMAVs; the latter equipment is inherent to its operation and reflects the human-made nature of the craft instead.[39] If the requirement of transportation was aligned more with navigation,[40] so that transportation concerned movement rather than an ability to

[36] George K. Walker, 'Defining Terms in the 1982 Law of the Sea Convention III: The International Hydrographic Organization ECDIS Glossary' (2004) 34 *California Western International Law Journal* 211, 238.

[37] Letts and Pedrozo (n 29) note that UMAVs, along with uncrewed surface vessels, 'will augment the force to increase the fleet's capacity for distributed operations, expand its ISR capabilities, add depth to its missile magazines, supplement logistics, and enhance its survivability', as well as providing 'additional warfighting capabilities and capacity to augment the manned fleet': 105.

[38] See James Kraska, 'The Law of Umanned Naval Systems in War and Peace' (2010) 5 *Journal of Ocean Technology* 44, 52; Rob McLaughlin, 'Umanned Naval Crafts at Sea: USVs, UUVs, and the Adequacy of the Law' (2011) 21 *Journal of Law Information and Science* 100, 112.

[39] Daum (n 35) 83.

[40] Bork, et al. (n 22) note that international conventions do sometimes align means of transportation and purpose of navigation: 307.

carry items through the ocean, then this criterion would be less problematic for 'ship' status. The gliders' ability to navigate may differentiate these craft from floats and, if navigation is an essential criterion, create a stronger case for gliders to fall within a definition of 'ship' or 'vessel'.[41] Bork and others have assessed the characteristics of floats and gliders and concluded that they should fall within the meaning of 'equipment' under Article 258 of UNCLOS.[42] Hofmann and Proelss also conclude that gliders are not ships.[43] If small, military UMAVs do not meet the definition of 'ship', this characterisation prompts questions about their rights of passage and immunity status.[44]

Where UMAVs are used for military purposes, a related question is whether UMAVs fall within the definition of a 'warship' or not.[45] As discussed in Chapter 1, military submarines (with humans onboard) are commonly considered to be 'warships'.[46] UNCLOS defines a warship in Article 29 as follows:

> For the purposes of this Convention, "warship" means a ship belonging to the armed forces of a State bearing the external marks distinguishing such ships of its nationality, under the command of an officer duly commissioned by the government of the State and whose name appears in the appropriate service list or its equivalent, and manned by a crew which is under regular armed forces discipline.

This definition reflects an earlier version that was decided in the 1900s, with the elements of being under command and crewed by members of the regular armed forces of a State intended to distinguish warships from privateering vessels.[47] Those same elements of the warship definition are problematic for UMAVs. Even if the vehicle is remotely controlled, and hence ostensibly 'under the command' of an official, there is no crew on

41 Ibid, 308.

42 Ibid, 309. Article 258 of UNCLOS (n 17) reads: 'The deployment and use of any type of scientific research installations or equipment in any area of the marine environment shall be subject to the same conditions as are prescribed in this Convention for the conduct of marine scientific research in any such area.'

43 Hofmann and Proelss (n 22) 177.

44 Issues discussed in Daum (n 35) 85–101.

45 See generally, Malgorzata Materna, 'Adjusting the Aperture: The International Law Case for Qualifying Unmanned Vessels as Warships' (2023) 100 *International Legal Studies* 475.

46 Louise Doswald-Beck (ed.), *San Remo Manual on International Law Applicable to Armed Conflicts at Sea* (Cambridge University Press, 1995) 90 ('San Remo Manual').

47 Klein et al. (n 27) 723–724.

board the vehicle itself. At most, engineers and other staff may be controlling its navigation from a remote location, but the vehicle may otherwise be operating autonomously. It is certainly arguable that this remote crew would be sufficient to meet the definitional requirements, provided a dynamic interpretation of Article 29 of UNCLOS is accepted.[48]

State practice will likely prove influential in advancing the interpretation of Article 29 of UNCLOS as States make decisions as to which of their naval vessels are registered as warships and which are listed as auxiliaries.[49] The question of whether a UMAV is a warship or not matters in the context of the law of naval warfare. Only warships have belligerent rights and may use force aggressively in an armed conflict.[50] If the UMAV is not a 'warship' it may be classed as a 'naval auxiliary'.[51] An auxiliary may be deployed for defensive purposes but does not have belligerent rights.[52] Alternatively, if the military UMAV is a weapon system, it may then be used offensively during an armed conflict, albeit subject to the requirements of the law of armed conflict.[53] These matters are discussed further in Section 14.4 below.

[48] For further discussion, see Sanjeet Ruhal, 'The Evolving Seascape of Naval Warfare: Unmanned Underwater Vehicles and the Challenges for International Law' (2024) *Journal of Conflict and Security Law* 1, 12–13. For the counter position, see Chenhong Liu and Song Pan, 'Regulations of International Humanitarian Law and Naval Warfare Law on UUVs Operations at Sea' in Haiwen Zhang, Yao Huang and Lijuan Xing (eds.), *Uncrewed Vessels and International Law* (Brill, 2024) 22, 26–30.

[49] This decision rests with each State and, similarly to questions of the grant of nationality to merchant vessels, it is up to individual States to determine the conditions of nationality. See UNCLOS (n 17) art. 91(1). See also Letts and Pedrozo (n 29) 117 (citing *Muscat Dhows Case* (France v. Great Britain) (1905) Scott Hague Court Rep 93, 96, PCA Case No. 1904-01).

[50] Klein et al. (n 27) 725.

[51] Defined in the San Remo Manual as: 'a vessel, other than a warship, that is owned by or under the exclusive control of the armed forces of a State and used for the time being on government non-commercial service': San Remo Manual (n 46) para. 13(h).

[52] Apart from firing weapons, most of the activities that fall within 'belligerent rights' are those that most typically assume humans will be involved, such as capturing enemy merchant vessels, or enforcing a blockade by checking which vessels may enter and which may not. Potentially, the enforcement of an exclusion zone may be accomplished with the use of UMAVs. At present, it may be expected that UMAVs will most likely work in tandem with crewed naval vessels during an armed conflict.

[53] Daum (n 35) 100. The regulation of lethal autonomous weapon systems has prompted considerable discussion and holds implications for the Convention on Certain Conventional Weapons which may be deemed to be Excessively Injurious or to Have Indiscriminate Effects, Geneva, 10 October 1980, entered into force 2 December 1983, 1342 UNTS 137.

14.3 Navigational Rights and Duties

Chapter 7 explored the legal rights and obligations applicable to submarines in the exercise of navigational rights in areas under national jurisdiction, and Chapter 8 addressed the exercise of the freedom of navigation in the EEZ. As an initial point, it may be asked if all UMAVs have comparable rights of navigation. In this regard, it can be observed that the freedom of navigation is accorded to States to bestow on ships rather than it being a right granted directly to a vessel itself.[54] Even if it was the case that a UMAV is not a 'ship', the freedom to use such a craft would fall within the freedoms of the high seas, given the inclusive nature of such freedom,[55] with core restrictions being a requirement of showing due regard to other users,[56] safe navigation[57] and not operating in violation of the prohibition on the threat or use of force.[58] States may potentially agree on restrictions or standards of operations to limit their uses of the high seas in relation to UMAVs.[59]

The right of innocent passage is accorded exclusively to 'ships'.[60] Thus if a UMAV is not a 'ship', a fortiori the UMAV does not have a right of innocent passage. Any passage of a non-ship UMAV within the territorial sea of a coastal state is bound by the legislative authority of the coastal State. The non-ship UMAV would similarly be subject to the enforcement jurisdiction of the coastal State if the non-ship UMAV is not entitled to sovereign immunity.[61] Where the UMAV has a right of innocent passage, it must exercise that right consistent with the

[54] See UNCLOS (n 17) arts. 87, 90. The right of innocent passage is bestowed directly on ships: art. 17.

[55] As evident in the inclusive listing of freedoms in UNCLOS, which include navigation, scientific research and the laying of submarine cables and pipelines: ibid, art. 87(1). For more discussion on the freedom of navigation in relation to submarines, see Chapter 8.

[56] UNCLOS (n 17) art. 87(2).

[57] Either not posing a risk to navigation (if not a ship) or navigating safely (if a ship): McLaughlin (n 30) 155.

[58] UNCLOS (n 17) art. 301; Charter of the United Nations, San Francisco, 26 June 1945, entered into force 24 October 1945, XV UNCIO 335, art. 2(4).

[59] Prior to formal adoption of international rules and standards at the inter-State level, there have been initiatives among civil society to guide practice. For example, the Society for Underwater Technology has developed a Code of Practice for the Operation of Autonomous Marine Vehicles, as a self-regulation tool designed for use and adoption as a community standard. See C. Carleton et al., *The Operation of Autonomous Underwater Vehicles* (SUT, 2000) vol. 1.

[60] UNCLOS (n 17) art. 17.

[61] The question of sovereign immunity is considered below nn 63–71 and accompanying text.

requirements set out in UNCLOS and under customary international law. As discussed in Chapter 7, Article 21 of UNCLOS allows the coastal State to impose requirements to ensure safe navigation through the territorial sea. However, Article 21(2) limits a coastal State's authority in relation to 'design, construction, *manning* or equipment of foreign ships' unless the laws and regulations are consistent with 'generally accepted international rules or standards'.[62] Consequently, the coastal State may not limit the right of innocent passage on the basis that the ship in question is uncrewed in the absence of any international standard to this effect.[63]

Most significantly for UMAVs, the obligation to surface in the territorial sea of another State clearly applies given the reference in Article 20 of UNCLOS to '[s]ubmarines and *other underwater vehicles*'.[64] The use of this broad terminology permits no doubt that all UMAVs would fall within this provision,[65] unless it is disputed that a UMAV does not even constitute a 'vehicle'.[66]

The requirements of Article 20 require closer scrutiny in the context of UMAVs in that the obligation necessitates surfacing and 'show[ing] the flag' of the vehicle. While it may not be possible to conform literally to an obligation to 'show the flag',[67] the clear import of the obligation is to provide visible information to the coastal State as to the nationality of the UMAV. To this end, McKenzie has argued:

62 UNCLOS (n 17) art. 21(2) (emphasis added).

63 Simon McKenzie, 'The Future of Ocean Technology and Navigational Rights in the International Law of the Sea' in Natalie Klein et al., *Maritime Autonomous Vehicles and International Law: Maritime Security Perspectives* (Routledge, 2025) 125, 136. McKenzie further notes that the prohibition on discrimination in Article 24 of UNCLOS would also limit coastal State actions against UMAVs: 137.

64 UNCLOS (n 17) art. 20 (emphasis added).

65 It could be argued that the placement of Article 20 within a section that refers to 'rules applicable to all ships' indicates that 'underwater vehicles' must still be interpreted to refer only to vehicles that may also be classified as ships. Daum (n 35) considered that the term 'vehicles' still anticipates transportation and this criterion is not met by small, military UMAVs: 93–94. However, Allen instead argued that because Article 20 is within a section referring to 'all ships' that necessarily 'underwater vehicles' must be understood to be 'ships' precisely because of their inclusion in such a section: Allen (n 19) 507.

66 A position taken by Hofmann and Proelss in relation to gliders: Hofmann and Proelss (n 22) 177–178. Their approach emphasises that a vehicle must be a means of transportation.

67 There may also be a technical difficulty in UMAVs having the capability to navigate to the surface. Arguably, however, this design element needs to be considered and potentially rectified so as to meet existing legal requirements. See McKenzie (n 63) 135.

> The fact that equipping a MAV with the capacity to travel on the surface of the ocean might be unnecessary for its mission or purpose or that travelling underwater might be faster, more efficient or even safer is not a sufficient reason to treat them differently from other underwater maritime vehicles, particularly when this requirement is for the benefit of the coastal state.[68]

Thus, for a UMAV to exercise its right to traverse a State's territorial sea lawfully, it must have markings on it that will allow the coastal State to contact relevant authorities of the flag State to enquire as to the purpose of the passage or otherwise determine means to communicate with the UMAV as to any possible requirements for navigational safety to which the UMAV must adhere. UMAVs subject to requirements under the Convention on the International Regulations for Preventing Collisions at Sea[69] would further be required to have appropriate lights and to make certain sound signals.[70]

As discussed in Chapter 7, there is no requirement for a submarine to surface when it is exercising the right of transit passage through international straits.[71] Equally, no such requirement pertains in relation to archipelagic sea lane passage.[72] The situation does not change in the event that a submarine is uncrewed. Any UMAV would be authorised to traverse a strait or archipelagic waters consistent with those passage regimes provided that it is operating in 'normal' mode.[73] The passage must be continuous and expeditious, as well as not constitute

[68] Ibid, 135.

[69] Convention on the International Regulations for Preventing Collisions at Sea, London, 20 October 1972, entered into force 15 July 1977, 1050 UNTS 16 ('COLREGs'). See further Chapter 11, Section 11.2.

[70] In this regard, Henderson has written that under the COLREGs:

> Rule 22, for example, requires an inconspicuous, partly submerged vessel to display a white, all-round light visible for three miles. [UMAVs] over 12 meters in length would have to display lights on the side, stern, and on a masthead. Under rule 33, vessels are also required to make various sound signals, depending on their size.

Henderson (n 3) 71 (citations omitted).

[71] See Chapter 7, Section 7.3.1.

[72] See Chapter 7, Section 7.4.2.

[73] And provided it is a 'ship': UNCLOS (n 17) arts. 38(1)–(2); 52(1)–(3). It may be noted that under Article 38(3), which addresses the right of transit passage, '[a]ny activity which is not an exercise of the right of transit passage through a strait remains subject to the other applicable provisions of this Convention'. If the UMAV is not a 'ship', its activities would instead be subject to the coastal State's sovereignty as an activity in the territorial sea of that State.

a prohibited threat or use of force.[74] The latter assessment involves a consideration of whether there are characteristics of a hostile relationship between the parties concerned to warrant a characterisation of an unlawful threat of force.[75] The collection of information during such a passage may well be part of that 'normal' mode, but no research or survey activities may be carried out during transit passage without the prior consent of the littoral States.[76] Debates may emerge as to whether some information collection constitutes research or survey activities or not, and if not, whether the collection of information goes beyond what is 'normal' may be a question of degree.[77] The level of autonomy of a UMAV may influence the extent of data that is collected and processed for its operation while navigating through an international strait or an archipelagic sea lane. A ship launching or collecting a UMAV while in transit or archipelagic sea lane passage would not be acting in accordance with that passage regime if the launch or collection involved stopping or slowing the vessel, as those actions would be inconsistent with the requirements of continuous and expeditious transit.[78]

The operation of UMAVs in another State's EEZ prompts two main questions. First, if the UMAV is undertaking military activities, most likely ISR, are the coastal State's rights being violated? At first blush, the legal assessment for UMAVs is no different to the assessment as to crewed submarines as discussed in Chapter 8 and in relation to the possible prohibited threat or use of force, as outlined in Chapter 9. Whether the fact of autonomy or remote control changes the assessment will depend on the specific and further circumstances that emerge during those activities.

Second, a question arises as to whether the coastal State's exclusive jurisdiction with regards to marine scientific research in the EEZ is being infringed when UMAVs are deployed by another State.[79] This issue is acute in relation to floats and gliders and the International Oceanographic Commission adopted guidelines for the use of such

[74] Ibid, art. 38(2) and Art 39(1).

[75] The requirements are discussed further in Chapter 9, Section 9.2.1.

[76] UNCLOS (n 17) art. 40. This restriction applies in relation to archipelagic sea lane passage as well: art. 54.

[77] See discussion in Chapter 7, Section 7.3.1.

[78] Henderson (n 3) 70.

[79] The marine scientific research regime in relation to submarines is discussed further in Chapter 8.

vehicles in an ocean monitoring project (known as the Argo Project).[80] While non-binding, the guidelines provide that a coastal State must be informed in advance of the deployment of a project float if the float might enter its EEZ.[81] Military floats or gliders are outside the scope of these guidelines, however. Under UNCLOS, there is a requirement to seek prior consent or otherwise implied consent for the conduct of marine scientific research in a coastal State's EEZ.[82] Consent may, though, be withheld if the scientific research has direct significance for the exploration and exploitation of natural resources.[83] The consent requirements may be difficult to meet in relation to floats and gliders where there is insufficient control in relation to the geographic area of coverage.[84] This consent regime does not apply to military research in any event.[85]

A final issue to consider in relation to navigation is whether a military UMAV is entitled to sovereign immunity.[86] As previously discussed in this book, under the law of the sea, warships and other government vessels operated on non-commercial service enjoy sovereign immunity throughout the oceans.[87] Military UMAVs will similarly enjoy such immunity as government vessels, but reliance on these UNCLOS provisions again raises the spectre of whether sovereign immunity is enjoyed by small, military UMAVs that are not 'ships'. While the immunity of warships and of government vessels operated on non-commercial service is recognised as part of customary international law,[88] it does not immediately follow that any State property enjoys the same immunity.[89] Some States consider that the immunity is derived from the ship that has

[80] International Oceanographic Commission, Guidelines for the Implementation of Resolution XX-6 of the IOC Assembly regarding the Deployment of Profiling Floats in the High Seas within the Framework of the Argo Programme (Resolution EC-XLI.4). The Argo Project includes an array of almost 4,000 active free-floating ocean monitoring devices.

[81] Ibid, guideline 1.

[82] See UNCLOS (n 17) arts. 246(2)–(3), 252. See further Chapter 8, Section 8.3.2.

[83] UNCLOS (n 17) art. 246(5)(a).

[84] Bork et al. (n 22) 312.

[85] The United Kingdom and the United States have also argued that the marine scientific research is inapplicable in relation to operational oceanography. Hofmann and Proelss (n 22) 173. However, other States have disagreed: ibid.

[86] Such immunity derives from the sovereign equality of States, which is enshrined in Article 2(1) of the UN Charter.

[87] UNCLOS (n 17) arts. 32, 95, 96. See further Chapter 1, Section 1.3.

[88] *ARA Libertad* (Argentina v. Ghana) (Provisional Measures Order of 15 December 2012) [2012] ITLOS Rep 332, para. 95 (referring to 'general international law').

[89] Kraska argues that State property does have sovereign immunity: James Kraska, 'Sovereign Immunity of Unmanned Maritime Vehicles' in Natalie Klein et al., *Maritime*

launched the small, military UMAV.[90] However, the fact that States such as Iran,[91] Indonesia,[92] the Philippines[93] and China[94] have seized small, military UMAVs suggests that no immunity is recognised for these craft. The United States has protested the seizure of its military UMAVs to both China and Iran.[95] Some US commentators have argued that these craft enjoy immunity,[96] whereas others acknowledge disagreement on this point.[97] Regard may also be had to the Convention on Jurisdictional Immunities of States and Their Property, which provides in Article 21 that State property used for 'government non-commercial purposes' includes 'property of a military character or used or intended for use in the performance of military functions'.[98] The Jurisdictional Immunities

Autonomous Vehicles and International Law: Maritime Security Perspectives (Routledge, 2025) 77, 83–84. See further Chapter 1, Section 1.3.

[90] Henderson (n 3) 67; McLaughlin (n 30) 157. Contra Daum (n 35) 98.

[91] Barbara Starr, Mostafa Salem and Oren Liebermann, 'Iranian Navy Seized 2 US Navy Maritime Drones on Thursday', *CNN*, 2 September 2022 <https://edition.cnn.com/2022/09/02/politics/iran-navy-us-maritime-drones/index.html>.

[92] Andrew Greene, 'Suspected Chinese Submarine Drone Found by Indonesian Fishermen in Crucial Maritime Passage to Australia', *ABC News*, 31 December 2020 <www.abc.net.au/news/2020-12-31/suspected-chinese-submarine-drone-found-by-indonesian-fishermen/13022488>.

[93] Jeoffrey Maitem, 'Armed Forces of the Philippines Investigate Chinese Submarine Drone', *Naval News*, 3 January 2025 <www.navalnews.com/naval-news/2025/01/armed-forces-of-the-philippines-investigate-chinese-submarine-drone/>.

[94] A well-known example is when a Chinese Navy Dalang-III-class ship seized a US Navy 'ocean glider' that was being operated from USNS *Bowditch* in the South China Sea on 15 December 2016.

[95] See US Department of Defense, 'Statement by Pentagon Press Secretary Peter Cook on Incident in South China Sea', 16 December 2016 <www.defense.gov/Newsroom/Releases/Release/Article/1032611/statementby-pentagon-press-secretary-peter-cook-on-incident-in-south-china-sea/>; Starr, Salem and Liebermann (n 91).

[96] James Kraska and Raul 'Pete' Pedrozo, 'China's Capture of US Underwater Drone Violates Law of the Sea', *Lawfare*, 16 December 2016 <www.lawfareblog.com/chinas-capture-us-underwater-drone-violates-law-sea> (reflecting view of the Pentagon Press Secretary). See also James Kraska, 'Sovereign Immunity of Unmanned Maritime Vehicles' (n 89) 77. But see Mark J. Valencia, 'US-China Underwater Drone Incident: Legal Grey Areas', *The Diplomat*, 11 January 2017 <https://thediplomat.com/2017/01/us-china-underwater-drone-incident-legal-grey-areas/>.

[97] Andrew Norris, *Legal Issues Relating to Unmanned Maritime Systems* (US Naval War College, 2013) 45–46. In relation to the discussion on immunity of State property in the context of the Tallinn Manual, it was commented that the International Group of Experts could not reach consensus on this point. See Michael N. Schmitt (ed.), *Tallinn Manual on the International Law Applicable to Cyber Warfare* (Cambridge University Press, 2013) commentary to r. 4, para. 6.

[98] United Nations Convention on Jurisdictional Immunities of States and Their Property, New York, 2 December 2004, not yet entered into force (UN Doc. A/59/508) art. 21.

Convention provides robust protection for State property from enforcement jurisdiction.[99] However, the Jurisdictional Immunities Convention has not entered into force and it remains a matter of debate as to the extent it reflects customary international law.[100] State action on this question would be beneficial to bring greater clarity as to the protection available to State property at sea, including UMAVs.

The confiscations of UMAVs highlight the competing understandings of States as to how UMAVs ought to be defined and characterised, and how the classification of a UMAV as a vehicle lesser than a ship has substantial implications on the ability and freedom of the UMAV to operate unimpeded. The seizure of small UMAVs being used for ISR (typically gliders) may indicate that sovereign immunity does not extend to non-ship UMAVs, or that those States seizing the property have violated sovereign immunity. The confiscation of State property by another State may still otherwise be legally challenged if it is possible to draw from other, more general, international law principles, such as respect for State sovereignty and non-abuse of rights. The latter principles may affirm a preferred position that State property is immune from enforcement actions (such as seizure or arrest) by other States.

14.4 Law of Naval Warfare

Beyond initial questions of definition in classifying UMAVs, further consideration should be afforded to the deployment of UMAVs under the law of naval warfare. A distinction may be necessary as to whether the UMAV is a 'ship' or 'system'.[101] The term 'system' is most commonly used in this context as referencing a 'weapons system'.[102] A system would not necessarily have the same navigational rights as bestowed on ships, as

[99] Ibid, arts. 18, 19 (covering pre- and post-judgment immunity, which anticipates exceptions for adjudicative jurisdiction but not enforcement jurisdiction). This position is reinforced by the comments of the International Court of Justice in *Jurisdictional Immunities*, where it was stated, 'the immunity from enforcement enjoyed by States in regard to their property situated on foreign territory goes further than the jurisdictional immunity enjoyed by those same States before foreign courts': *Jurisdictional Immunities of the State* (Germany v. Italy; Greece intervening) (Judgment of 3 February 2012) [2012] ICJ Rep 99, para. 113.

[100] In favour of this position, see Ruhal (n 48) 17.

[101] See discussion in Hitoshi Nasu and Dave Letts, 'The Legal Characterization of Lethal Autonomous Systems: Warship, Torpedo, or Naval Mine?' (2020) 96 *International Law Studies* 79.

[102] Ibid.

discussed above in Section 14.3. A recent commentary on the law of armed conflict, the Oslo Manual, has sought to define 'unmanned maritime systems' as 'self-propelled or remotely-navigated craft that are normally recoverable and designed to perform functions at sea by operating on the surface, semi-submerged or undersea' and are either remotely controlled/operated or autonomous.[103] This definition does not differentiate between UMAVs that are unarmed, such as the XLUUV being developed in Project Cetus in the United Kingdom,[104] and UMAVs that carry weapons.[105]

If the UMAV is not a ship but an object that navigates underwater and detonates upon impact, this weapon system may be classed as a torpedo or a naval mine. The traditional distinction between torpedoes and naval mines was that torpedoes were designed to be harmless upon missing their target whereas mines caused an indefinite threat.[106] Naval mines were regulated under Hague Convention (VIII) of 1907.[107] Customary international law regulating the use of mines has since evolved, and for present purposes it may be noted that the San Remo Manual defined mines as an 'explosive device laid in the water, on the sea-bed, or in the subsoil thereof, with the intention of damaging or sinking ships or of deterring ships from entering the area'.[108] Technological advances make the distinction between torpedoes and naval mines less meaningful, however, as the self-navigation systems may create uncertainty as to the endpoint for a torpedo.[109] Nasu and Letts suggest that lethal autonomous maritime systems are torpedoes when they are designed for one instance of detonation rather than recovery for further use.[110] The 'system' definition set out in the Oslo Manual would preclude torpedoes because they are not 'normally recoverable'. Mines would need to be assessed on the basis of whether

103 Yoram Dinstein and Arne Willy Dahl, *Oslo Manual on Select Topics of the Law of Armed Conflict* (Brill, 2020) r. 46(a) ('Oslo Manual').

104 Nicholls (n 11).

105 The latter have been developed for Ukraine's use in its war against Russia: see Joshua Cheetham, 'Sea Drones: What Are They and How Much Do They Cost?', *BBC News*, 2 August 2023 <www.bbc.com/news/world-europe-66373052>.

106 Nasu and Letts (n 101) 87–88.

107 Hague Convention (VIII) relative to the Laying of Automatic Submarine Contact Mines, The Hague, 18 October 1907, entered into force 26 January 2010, 205 CTS 331.

108 San Remo Manual (n 46) para. 79.2. The San Remo Manual does not define torpedoes, but stipulates a prohibition on using torpedoes that 'do not sink or otherwise become harmless when they have completed their run': para. 77.

109 Nasu and Letts (n 101) 88.

110 Ibid.

they are 'self-propelled or remotely-navigated'. How the UMAV is used may thus be influential in determining what body of law applies.

Where a UMAV is deployed during an armed conflict, questions of the law of armed conflict come to the fore.[111] Each UMAV used for this purpose would need to be assessed as to whether it causes unnecessary suffering, widespread and severe harm to the marine environment, or is indiscriminate.[112] Part of this assessment may depend on whether there is a 'human in the loop' (i.e., human intervention is necessary for the system to operate), as is discussed in relation to the use of any lethal autonomous weapons systems.[113] UMAVs are more likely to operate autonomously without such human involvement because of communication limitations when submerged.[114]

Where a UMAV is not a ship, and hence not a 'warship' under the terms of Article 29 of UNCLOS, the UMAV would lack belligerent rights and could only be utilised for defensive purposes. This interpretation may limit the deployment of UMAVs to enforce blockades (as may be intended with the deployment of swarms of UMAVs[115]), especially if the UMAVs are not designed to discriminate between merchant and enemy vessels.[116] Nonetheless, commentary in the Oslo Manual suggests that emerging State practice reflects 'that they [autonomous maritime systems] are, and will be, used not only for attack purposes but also for the exercise of other belligerent rights, such as inspection of vessels'.[117] The Newport Manual asserts that the 'classic definition of a "warship" is evolving in light of contemporary technologies' and if a MAV 'can be

111 Laws of naval warfare in relation to submarines are discussed in Chapter 10, Section 10.5.

112 Daum (n 35) 99–100.

113 For example, the UN Secretary General has recommended that States conclude a treaty prohibiting lethal autonomous weapon systems that function without human control or oversight and cannot be used in compliance with international humanitarian law: UN Secretary General, *A New Agenda For Peace* (Our Common Agenda Policy Brief No. 9, July 2023) 27.

114 Allen (n 19) 485. Ruhal also raises questions about the ability of UMAVs to 'comply with the principle of distinction, particularly when it comes to the identification of military objectives': Ruhal (n 48) 23.

115 See Letts and Pedrozo (n 29) 120.

116 Lin considers that the question of whether a UMAV can 'independently and correctly characterize a breach of zonal controls, and conduct responsive measures that are necessary and proportionate' is a technical issue rather than a legal one. Zhaoran Lin, 'Forcing Their Way Out at Sea: UMS in the Law of Naval Warfare' in Haiwen Zhang, Yao Huang, Lijuan Xing (eds.), *Uncrewed Vessels and International Law* (Brill Nijhoff, 2024) 47, 69.

117 Oslo Manual (n 103) r. 52, para. 1.

a ship, then it can also be designated a "warship" by the flag State'.[118] If all autonomous maritime systems are deployed for the exercise of belligerent rights,[119] many requirements of warships, such as clear military markings and under the command of a commissioned officer (even if not physically present), would apply equally to such systems.[120] An XLUUV should thus be marked accordingly and its actions would further be required to align with the rights and duties of crewed submarines. It may thus be more the case that UMAVs should be developed so as to conform to existing legal standards in the law of armed conflict, as set out in Chapter 10, rather than the availability of new technology necessitating new rules.

14.5 Criminal Policing and Criminal Use

UMAVs may not only be deployed by the State for military purposes or for scientific research but may also be utilised in relation to the policing and commission of criminal acts at sea. Policing by UMAVs engages questions concerning ISR in the different maritime zones; the legality of these operations by submarines is addressed in the discussion on transnational crime in Chapter 13.[121] This assessment changes only to the extent that information sharing from UMAVs is necessitated for a crewed law enforcement vessel to take action. For example, information acquired by UMAVs may be shared with law enforcement officials as a type of mutual legal assistance and law enforcement officials may thereby form the 'reasonable suspicion' to warrant exercising the right of visit.[122] Provided there is no legal impediment under national criminal laws for information to be obtained from a source other than the officers on the vessel who effect the arrest, UMAVs could well be anticipated to support policing efforts.

In relation to criminal acts involving UMAVs, two scenarios are assessed in this section to highlight key legal questions with regards to the criminal use of UMAVs.[123] One possible use may be reflected in the

[118] James Kraska et al., 'The Newport Manual on the Law of Naval Warfare' (2023) 101 *International Law Studies* 1, 44.

[119] Rule 57 of the Oslo Manual, for example, refers to hostile actions by belligerent autonomous systems being undertaken in neutral waters and ports: Oslo Manual (n 103) r. 57.

[120] Ruhal (n 48) 11.

[121] See Chapter 13, Section 13.3.

[122] See, e.g., UNCLOS (n 17) art. 110(1).

[123] The possible scenarios are greater in relation to surface MAVs but the focus in this part is on the potential criminal use of UMAVs for terrorist and smuggling purposes.

2017 deployment of remote-controlled boats packed with explosives by Houthi rebels off the coast of Yemen with the intention of targeting Saudi commercial shipping.[124] Houthi rebels have since deployed UMAVs to similar end.[125] The conduct of the Houthi rebels may be assessed as part of a non-international armed conflict in Yemen;[126] the actions nonetheless provide an exemplar of a possible terrorist attack and the legal dimensions of this action may be explored under the Convention for the Suppression of Unlawful Acts against the Safety of Maritime Navigation (2005 SUA Convention).[127]

The 2005 SUA Convention defines 'ship' broadly to mean 'a vessel of any type whatsoever not permanently attached to the sea-bed, including dynamically supported craft, submersibles, or any other floating craft' and may thus include a UMAV as a submersible or other floating craft.[128] States parties to the 2005 SUA Convention are to adopt national legislation that creates an offence where an alleged offender 'uses a ship in a manner that causes death or serious injury or damage' for a terrorist purpose.[129] Any terrorist deployment of a UMAV would thus likely constitute one of the offences under the 2005 SUA Convention that is to be implemented into a State's domestic law. Such liability would also extend to cover individuals who attempt, aid, organise or direct others or participate in such acts.[130] The latter offences will be especially important

[124] Sam LaGrone, 'Navy: Saudi Frigate Attacked by Unmanned Bomb Boat, Likely Iranian', *USNI News*, 20 February 2017 <https://news.usni.org/2017/02/20/navy-saudi-frigate-attacked-unmanned-bomb-boat-likely-iranian>.

[125] H. I. Sutton, 'Houthi Lethal Underwater Drones Adds New Threat to Red Sea', *USNI News*, 19 February 2024 <https://news.usni.org/2024/02/19/houthi-lethal-underwater-drones-adds-new-threat-to-red-sea>.

[126] 'Situation of Human Rights in Yemen, including Violations and Abuses since September 2014: Report of the Detailed Findings of the Group of Eminent International and Regional Experts on Yemen', 3 September 2019 (UN Doc. A/HRC/42/CRP.1) para. 46.

[127] The 2005 Convention for the Suppression of Unlawful Acts against the Safety of Maritime Navigation combines a 1998 Treaty and a 2005 Protocol (together, the '2005 SUA Convention'): Convention for the Suppression of Unlawful Acts against the Safety of Maritime Navigation, Rome, 10 March 1988, entered into force 1 March 1992, 1678 UNTS 201; Protocol of 2005 to the Convention for the Suppression of Unlawful Acts against the Safety of Maritime Navigation, London, 14 October 2005, entered into force 28 July 2010. See also Chapter 13, Section 13.4.3.

[128] 2005 SUA Convention (n 127) art. 1.

[129] A terrorist purpose arises when 'the purpose of the act, by its nature or context, is to intimidate a population, or to compel a government or an international organization to do or to abstain from doing any act': ibid, art. 3*bis* (1)(a)(iii).

[130] Ibid, art. 3*quater*.

in the context of UMAVs given that individuals will not be arrested on the UMAV used to cause death, serious injury or damage. Rather, the remote-control operators and individuals who participate in planning and implementation may instead be found criminally responsible under national legislation, assuming the 2005 SUA Convention is fully implemented into a State party's domestic law.[131]

A second scenario concerns the potential use of UMAVs to transport illicit goods, such as drugs, weapons and cash. This scenario is no longer hypothetical following the 2022 seizure of 'narco drone submarines', being semi-submersible UMAVs capable of holding a 200 kilogram payload.[132] Important questions of jurisdiction arise under international law, especially when an operator is located in one State and goods are being shipped between two (or more) other States. As with offences arising under the terms of the 2005 SUA Convention, the exercise of criminal jurisdiction may further need to consider participatory offences.

For States party to the 1988 United Nations Convention against Illicit Traffic in Narcotic Drugs and Psychotropic Substances (1988 Vienna Convention),[133] national laws are to reflect drug trafficking offences that include 'delivery on any terms whatsoever, . . ., dispatch, dispatch in transit, transport, importation or exportation of any narcotic drug or any psychotropic substance'.[134] No special definitions are provided in relation to the transportation of drugs, although there are references to offences involving 'vessels'.[135] Provided the UMAV is considered a vessel, the use of UMAVs for drug trafficking should normally fall within the offences a State may set out in its domestic law. The offences outlined in the 1988 Vienna Convention extend to '[p]articipation in, association or conspiracy to commit, attempts to commit and aiding,

[131] When the SUA Convention was discussed at the IMO as part of the Regulatory Scoping Exercise, the Legal Committee determined that changes to the SUA Convention should not be undertaken within the IMO but could be more properly resolved within State parties' national laws: see IMO, 'MASS Outcome' (n 2).

[132] H. I. Sutton, 'Elusive Narco Drone Submarines Surface in Spain', 5 July 2022 <www.hisutton.com/Narco-Drone-Submarine-Found-In-Spain.html>. See also 'La droga? La consegna il barchino con il pilota automatico', *Metropolinotizie*, 22 June 2019 <www.metropolinotizie.it/la-droga-la-consegna-il-barchino-con-il-pilota-automatico/> (reporting on an Italian interdiction).

[133] United Nations Convention against Illicit Traffic in Narcotic Drugs and Psychotropic Substances, Vienna, 20 December 1988, entered into force 11 November 1990, 1582 UNTS 95, art. 20(1)(b) ('1998 Vienna Convention').

[134] Ibid, art. 3(1)(a)(i).

[135] Ibid, in conjunction with art. 4(1)(a)(ii).

abetting, facilitating and counselling the commission' of drug trafficking,[136] as well as the 'organization, management or financing' of such activities.[137] Thus, to the extent the State exercising jurisdiction has enacted the relevant 1988 Vienna Convention offences, an individual who may arrange for the operation of the UMAV, be responsible for its remote control, or otherwise contribute to the drug trafficking operation should still fall within existing criminal laws irrespective of whether the drugs are shipped in a UMAV or another vehicle.[138]

For the exercise of criminal jurisdiction, flag States may be requested to consent to the exercise of enforcement jurisdiction against one of its vessels in accordance with Article 17 of the 1988 Vienna Convention. Practically speaking, law enforcement officials will seek to hail, warn or stop a UMAV, but may be restricted from communicating with the vessel where there is no master or crew aboard. The 1988 Vienna Convention explicitly asserts jurisdiction over 'a vessel concerning which that Party has been authorized to take appropriate action pursuant to article 17' to the extent that such action has been authorised by the flag State.[139] If a UMAV is intercepted and there is no possibility of connecting it to specific humans (assuming it is not flagged or branded or otherwise has the markings of the criminal organisation), law enforcement officials may have to decide what steps to take in relation to the UMAV and its contents. Article 17 of the 1988 Vienna Convention allows for a process for law enforcement officials to request permission to board a suspect vessel, carry out a search and potentially assert further jurisdiction for the purposes of prosecution.[140] Unlike an illegal fishing vessel or a crewed drug-trafficking vessel, where there are people onboard to arrest and transfer to land for prosecution, and whose presence may change any assessment of what is necessary or reasonable force in a law enforcement operation, these factors are absent for UMAVs. Law enforcement officials may opt to confiscate the UMAV and the goods it

[136] Ibid, art. 3(1)(c)(iv).

[137] Ibid, art. 3(1)(a)(v).

[138] For considerations as to possible prosecutions of individuals involved in drug trafficking with MAVs generally, see Rob McLaughlin and Natalie Klein, 'Maritime Autonomous Vessels and Drug Trafficking, by Sea: Some Legal Issues' (2021) 36 *International Journal of Marine and Coastal Law* 389.

[139] 1988 Vienna Convention (n 133) art. 4(1)(b)(ii).

[140] Ibid, art. 17, in conjunction with Article 4(1)(b)(ii) in relation to jurisdiction over the apprehended vessel.

carries, consistent with domestic law requirements, or otherwise seek to dispose of the UMAV at sea.[141]

14.6 Future Directions for UMAVs

The regulatory framework for the operations of UMAVs largely depends on questions of definition (especially as to what constitutes a ship or warship), as well as national actions in the adoption of laws that may classify the UMAVs or establish jurisdiction over UMAVs in different settings. As discussed in this chapter, whether a UMAV is a ship or not will be relevant for navigational rights and claims to sovereign immunity. Military UMAVs may be classified as warships under a State's domestic law if analogies to the command and crew requirements in the warship definition are accepted in instances of remote operation. For example, the US Commander's Handbook provides:

> In all cases, U.S. Navy UMSs [unmanned maritime systems] are the sovereign property of the United States and immune from foreign jurisdiction. When flagged as a ship, a UMS may exercise the navigational rights and freedoms and other internationally lawful uses of the seas related to those freedoms. Unmanned systems may be designated as USS [United States Ship] if they are under the command of a commissioned officer and manned by a crew under regular armed forces discipline, by remote or other means.[142]

While State practice may assist in the interpretation of Article 29 of UNCLOS,[143] or in understandings of what constitutes a vessel or not, whether one State accepts another State's designation of a UMAV as a 'ship' or 'warship' must also be taken into account. The International Tribunal for the Law of the Sea (ITLOS) has held that the criteria for granting nationality to a ship rests within the exclusive jurisdiction of the flag State.[144] The same reasoning may exist for designation of what may be classified as a ship and what is classified as a warship. ITLOS has also

[141] McLaughlin and Klein (n 138) 408–410.

[142] United States Navy, United States Marine Corps and United States Coast Guard, *The Commander's Handbook on the Law of Naval Operations* (Naval War College, March 2022) para 2.3.5.

[143] State practice being a consideration in treaty interpretation: Vienna Convention on the Law of Treaties, Vienna, 23 May 1969, entered into force 27 January 1980, 1155 UNTS 331, art. 31(3)(b). Though it may be recalled in this instance that the United States is not a party to UNCLOS.

[144] *M/V Saiga (No. 2)* (Saint Vincent and the Grenadines v. Guinea) (Judgment of 1 July 1999) [1999] ITLOS Rep 10, paras. 63–65.

resisted claims that a State may opt to challenge the validity of registration of a ship,[145] which may further support the view that a flag State's decision as to the status of a UMAV will be enforceable against all other States.

Outside a military setting, UMAVs are predominantly used for research purposes. UMAVs such as floats and gliders that are utilised for marine scientific research (as opposed to military research) will be subject to coastal State jurisdiction in that State's EEZ and the coastal State's sovereignty when in its territorial sea. Where research UMAVs are classified as equipment, the consent regime under UNCLOS will be applicable to their deployment in another State's EEZ. The deployment of research UMAVs classified as equipment is not permissible in another State's territorial sea, in international straits subject to the regime of transit passage or in archipelagic waters in light of the prohibition on surveys and research in these maritime zones. A remaining difficulty arises where a UMAV accidentally enters the sovereign waters of another State without authorisation, raising questions regarding the steps that may be taken by the coastal State in this situation. If a coastal State cannot communicate with a UMAV, it may be unable to ascertain the national status of the UMAV to follow up with the flag State or to otherwise confirm the legality of the UMAV's conduct.

The inability to communicate with a UMAV may also cause difficulties in relation to law enforcement processes where there are reasonable suspicions that a UMAV is engaged in illicit smuggling. Given the submerged operation of a UMAV, law enforcement officials may not be able to establish the nationality of the UMAV to seek consent to detain or inspect the UMAV.[146] Rather than arresting a UMAV, a coastal State's law enforcement officials may instead opt to interfere with its electronics, if possible,[147] or otherwise cause its destruction at sea. This latter response may be a simple way to hinder transnational crime but may create inter-State tensions if it is subsequently discovered that the UMAV was a research vehicle or if law enforcement authority was otherwise

[145] Ibid, paras. 79–83.

[146] A surface MAV may still bear markings indicating nationality, especially in relation to cargo ships that may have both legal and illicit items on board and allow for the consent regime associated with the right to visit to operate similarly to situations of crewed surface vessels.

[147] On jamming the electromagnetic spectrum, see Tracy L. Reynolds and Hitoshi Nasu, 'The Legality of Electromagnetic Interference with Maritime Autonomous Vehicles' in Natalie Klein et al. (eds.) *Maritime Autonomous Vehicles and International Law: Maritime Security Perspectives* (Routledge, 2025) 160.

exerted wrongfully. States will need to ensure that domestic rules of engagement provide processes to address encounters with UMAVs, including confirmation that the vehicle is indeed crewless before it is destroyed on reasonable suspicion of being a UMAV engaged in unlawful activities.

UMAVs reflect a new frontier in the regulation of submarines in international law. While in many respects, UMAVs will be bound by the same duties and have the same rights as crewed submarines, their operation prompts questions because of their distinctive characteristics. The absence of a crew affects questions of definition and may render the exercise of UMAVs' rights and duties more difficult when interaction with other vessels or with coastal and other State authorities is needed. Communication with other States about the UMAV prior to its operations may alleviate and resolve questions as to the legality of its conduct; communications while the UMAV is in operation may equally provide a means to prevent confrontation and misunderstandings as to the exercise of international law rights and duties. These practicalities do not resolve the gaps and legal ambiguities that have been presented in this chapter in relation to UMAVs. It is, though, an area where State practice will be especially influential in determining the future international regulatory regime in relation to this type of submarine.

14.7 Conclusion to Part II

When contemplating submarines in international law, it may well be difficult to imagine that a specific type of vessel warrants consideration separate to any other vessel. States are required to regulate all their ships, and the allocation of authority to States depends on what activities are occurring and where they are occurring rather than necessarily pondering what rights and duties are held by a particular type of ship. There is of course validity to this view. Yet what we have sought to show in this book is that, within the allocation of State authority across maritime zones and in relation to varied maritime activities, sometimes the fact that it is a submarine matters. Our study has indicated that there are instances when it matters more than may have initially been anticipated, and that the international legal system may need to say more about States' rights and duties when it comes to submarines.

Part I of this book reflected on how the steady, sometimes rapid, development of submarine technology challenged existing international law rules. Implications for the law of naval warfare and the operation of neutrality were initial concerns, and these issues were often folded into bigger questions concerning the scope of coastal State authority over the territorial sea and what rights and duties the vessels of other States held therein. The experience of military submarines during World War I (WWI) prompted the creation of a specific disarmament regime; submarines held such strategic importance and caused such damage that States contemplated (fleetingly) the abolition of submarines and otherwise sought to curtail the numbers of submarines. Yet because of their military significance, there was no way to return the proverbial genie to the bottle. The State responses following WWI may similarly be detected after World War II with the advent of nuclear submarines. As a platform for delivery of nuclear bombs as well as enjoying enhanced operation through nuclear power, rules were again sought to prevent nuclear proliferation and to safeguard against the multiple risks posed by nuclear powered submarines. Submarines have not been the only consideration as States have jostled in the formulation of rules and other standards for the conduct of maritime activities across the oceans, as an array of economic, social and other political interests have also been at play. Yet the evasive nature of submarines should not also mean that they elude international law.

In Part II, we have demonstrated how there are many areas of international law that apply to submarine operations, highlighting specific instances of regulation. We have also acknowledged how some rules generally apply but that there are settings where the failure to consider submarines specifically raises questions and may lead to potential disputes. In concluding the book, we highlight below some of the areas of international law where more attention is warranted in articulating precise rules, clarifying positions or in closing gaps that exist because of insufficient attention to the distinct characteristics of submarines.

In this regard, the passage of foreign-flagged military submarines through a State's territorial waters has garnered the most attention under international law. As we explained in Chapter 7, it is in relation to this navigational activity that the most explicit rule pertaining to submarines exists: submarines must surface and show their flag when exercising the right of innocent passage. This rule is set out in Article 20 of UNCLOS, building on legal developments that began with the deployment of submarines in WWI, and arguably reflects customary international law. This view on the customary law status of the rule could be articulated by States in the instances that they protest submerged passage of submarines in their territorial seas.

A working assumption in relation to transit passage and archipelagic sea lane passage is that submarines may remain submerged as their normal mode of continuous and expeditious transit. Language in UNCLOS that refers to refraining from activities other than those incidental to normal mode provides some flexibility and accounts for emerging technologies. The widely accepted understanding of submarines travelling submerged during transit and archipelagic sea lanes passage does not seem problematic even if not explicitly stated. Where clarity may well be needed in the future is whether submarines may stay submerged in the approaches to international straits subject to transit passage or archipelagic sea lanes. As discussed in Chapter 7, the United States supports such a view, and it does not appear to have been contested by littoral States.

Coastal State responses to illegal passage in territorial waters are tempered under international law because of the sovereign immunity enjoyed by warships, which prevents their detention or arrest by other States. What amount of force is acceptable in a request to a foreign-flagged warship to leave the territorial sea has uncertain limits. It is nonetheless notable that State practice has shown tolerance for the release of low-power depth charges to signal to submerged submarines that they are in violation of international law and required to leave the territorial sea.

For submarine operations beyond territorial waters and in the EEZ of another State, the debate as to the legality of military research, as distinct to the marine scientific research subject to coastal State consent, is especially acute for submarines, which may engage in varied activities in one mission. The SCience ICe EXercise (SCICEX) missions, discussed in Chapter 8, provide an interesting study of how military submarines may engage with the science community to foster research and what parameters are put on those engagements to ensure the integrity of their respective endeavours: research that has security implications and is retained by a country's defence forces and research that may be made publicly available to further knowledge about the oceans. The former is military research and not subject to a coastal State's consent whereas the latter is governed by rules of marine scientific research set out in UNCLOS. Maintaining a distinction is not an obvious task, however.

Chapter 8 discussed how private submarines have an increasing presence across the exploration and exploitation of natural resources, the laying and repair of submarine cables and pipeline, and in the leisure industry. They may be regulated as part of those activities, but there may be other instances (especially in relation to safety standards) where discrete regulation is warranted. Certification schemes run by industry organisations may be an inadequate panacea for ensuring maritime safety for submersibles and other small submarines operated privately or commercially. As we considered in Chapter 11, rules relating to navigational safety reflect an area of international law where more singular focus on submarines may be warranted. The 'rules of the road' set out in the International Regulations for Preventing Collisions at Sea (COLREGs) anticipate procedures and requirements for surface navigation with less specificity as to what vessel is burdened or privileged when submarines are submerged or when surfacing. These issues will become more pressing as the number of submarines increase and may require, at least in first instance, greater coordination and communication. Securing cooperation in relation to military submarines is not an obvious path forwards, however, when part of the appeal of submarines is their hidden location.

Nuclear submarines pose a distinct set of risks, including to the marine environment as well as the security of other States. While the transfer, development and disposal of nuclear materials and technology on land is subject to a range of international requirements and processes through the International Atomic Energy Agency (IAEA), once a nuclear submarine is deployed at sea, the regulatory seascape is markedly different. Nuclear liability treaties routinely exclude warships and other government vessels operated on non-commercial service, as well as excluding more generally nuclear materials that are part of a country's defence or military programme. At most, notification obligations apply in the event of a nuclear reactor accident where there is a risk of transboundary harm.[148] There is a strong trend to exclude warships, including military submarines and hence nuclear submarines, from the application of international rules and standards intended to promote maritime safety and the protection of the marine environment. Instead, more general international law principles, perhaps drawn from international disaster law, or from core principles of State sovereignty, non-abuse of rights, or the protection principle will be available to States that may be prejudiced through the functioning (or malfunctioning) of a nuclear submarine.

Chapter 10 highlighted the role that submarines have played in armed conflict throughout history. Submarines have always been closely

[148] Convention on Early Notification of a Nuclear Accident, Vienna, 26 September 1986, entered into force 27 October 1986, 1439 UNTS 275, art. 2. See Chapter 12, Section 12.3.1.

associated with armed conflict and it remains the case that the largest and most powerful submarines remain in the almost exclusive domain of the world's navies. This association has not, however, produced clarity in the law applicable to the conduct of submarine warfare. This lacuna in the law arises from the happy fact that contemporary practice of submarine warfare is rather limited. The limited practice of submarine warfare heightens the risk that questions will emerge as to the exact law applicable to the conduct of submarine warfare, which may potentially be taken advantage of in a future international armed conflict at sea. A key issue is the difficulty in applying the law that has governed the conduct of warfare in relation to surface vessels to the unique design features of submarines. The significant debate over the extent to which a submarine is required to place passengers, crews and papers in a place of safety before conducting an attack remains a key and unresolved issue. The conduct of anti-submarine warfare will also remain a key issue. The techniques and tools used to conduct anti-submarine warfare have evolved rapidly with technological advancement. While anti-submarine warfare has largely been beyond the focus of this book, reconciling the key principles governing the law of armed conflict with these techniques and tools should be an ongoing priority.

The advent of MAVs has concentrated attention on ambiguities or absences in definitions (what is a ship?) and prompted consideration as to how flexible existing rules may be in catering for new technology. With its focus on UMAVs, this chapter has especially demonstrated the regulatory gaps in relation to gliders: what actions can gliders lawfully undertake and what actions can States lawfully take against them? As underscored at the start of this book, the sovereign immunity enjoyed by most submarines (as military submarines) has far-reaching implications for the application and enforcement of international law. If a glider is not a warship or even a ship, does it still have sovereign immunity as State property? The direction of international law indicates that the answer is affirmative, but greater certainty is needed, as well as greater clarity as to the scope of the immunity from enforcement (and not just adjudicative) jurisdiction.

Beyond assessments of the legality of submarine operations, it is important to note that there is a counter-interest in the detection of submarines, which may carry its own implications for international law. Maritime domain awareness, which includes both maritime intelligence and situational awareness, has become a key concept in connection with maritime security.[149] National and regional initiatives emphasise the need to overcome 'sea blindness'[150] and enhance ocean 'transparency'.[151] Detecting submarines and submarine activity are inevitably part of this goal of ocean transparency.

The technologies for increasing ocean transparency are diverse and evolving. According to Friedman, '[c]urrent submarine silencing seems to have defeated the sound surveillance systems used during the Cold War'.[152] Contemporary anti-submarine warfare (ASW) at its best combines 'satellite capabilities, strategic towed arrays, seabed arrays, tactical towed arrays, maritime patrol aircraft, ASW helicopters, submarines and information sharing with like-minded partners'.[153] Quantum sensing is also being explored by some States as an aspect of ASW; however, a key challenge in this context, and in any complex system of sensors, is distinguishing submarines from other undersea phenomena.[154] The

149 The IMO has described this concept as 'the effective understanding of anything associated with the maritime domain that could impact security, safety, the economy or the marine environment': IMO, 'Maritime Domain Awareness' <www.imo.org/en/OurWork/Security/Pages/Maritime-DomainAwareness.aspx>.

150 See IMO, 'Enhancing Maritime Domain Awareness in West Indian Ocean and Gulf of Aden', 14 November 2018 <www.imo.org/en/MediaCentre/Pages/WhatsNew-1203.aspx>.

151 See, e.g., US Maritime Domain Awareness Executive Steering Committee, *National Strategy for Maritime Security: National Maritime Domain Awareness Plan* (January 2023) <https://nmio.ise.gov/Media-Publications/National-Maritime-Domain-Awareness-Plan/>. The Quadrilateral Security Dialogue between Australia, India, Japan, and the United States known as QUAD announced a new Indo-Pacific Partnership for Maritime Domain Awareness (IPMDA) at the Tokyo Summit (May 2022). According to the White House Press Release, '[i]n close consultations with regional partners, IPMDA will offer a near-real-time, integrated, and cost-effective maritime domain awareness picture. This initiative will transform the ability of partners in the Pacific Islands, Southeast Asia, and the Indian Ocean region to fully monitor the waters on their shores and, in turn, to uphold a free and open Indo-Pacific': 'Fact Sheet: Quad Leaders' Tokyo Summit 2022', *The White House*, 23 May 2022 <https://bidenwhitehouse.archives.gov/briefing-room/statements-releases/2022/05/23/fact-sheet-quad-leaders-tokyo-summit-2022/>.

152 Norman Friedman, 'Strategic Submarines and Strategic Stability: Looking Towards the 2030s' in Rory Medcalf et al. (eds.), *The Future of the Undersea Deterrent: A Global Survey* (ANU National Security College, 2020) 69, 76.

153 See Jennifer Parker, 'Effective Anti-Submarine Warfare Requires Much More than Submarines', *ASPI: The Strategist*, 7 August 2023 <www.aspistrategist.org.au/effective-anti-submarine-warfare-requires-much-more-than-submarines/>.

154 Sydney J Freedberg Jr, 'Transparent Sea: AUKUS Looks to AI, Quantum in Hunt for Chinese Submarines', *Breaking Defense*, 29 January 2024 <https://breakingdefense.com/2024/01/transparent-sea-aukus-looks-to-ai-quantum-in-hunt-for-chinese-submarines/>.

United States has developed a 'continuous trail unmanned vessel (ACTUV)' operating 'primarily to detect enemy diesel-electric submarines in shallow waters'.[155] Moreover, UMAVs, including XLUUVs, will also be increasingly deployed to determine what is happening where and in what conditions. Ensuring there is a strong legal frame in place for these activities should reduce disputes over competing rights and duties.

Recent technological advances increasing ocean transparency suggest that these developments may have consequences for the further progress of submarines as well as the nature of submarine operations. What has been presented here as the current body of international law regulating submarines will no doubt require further refinement and elaboration as submarines and their operations evolve. There is a clear imperative to ensure that international law keeps apace. International law must occupy a place of importance in State decision-making about submarines rather than being obscured in the depths of ocean governance.

[155] 'Sea Hunter ASW Continuous Trail Unmanned Vessel (ACTUV)', *Naval Technology*, 17 April 2016 <www.naval-technology.com/projects/sea-hunter-asw-continuous-trail-unmanned-vessel-actuv/>.

INDEX

CAMBRIDGE STUDIES IN INTERNATIONAL AND COMPARATIVE LAW

Books in the Series

197 *Submarines in International Law* Natalie Klein, Kate Purcell and Jack McNally

196 *The Classical Doctrine of Civil War in International Law* Ville Kari

195 *Adjudicating over Anarchy: Judicial Remedies, Compliance, and Enforcement in International Law* Geraldo Vidigal

194 *Regional Trade Agreements, Prosperity and the Global South: Normative Beliefs and Interests* Yenkong Ngangjoh Hodu and Collins Chikodili Ajibo

193 *A Theory of International Organizations in Public International Law* Orfeas Chasapis Tassinis

192 *The Individual in the Law and Practice of the International Court of Justice* Yusra Suedi

191 *Ghosts of International Law: The Figure of the Foreign Fighter in a Cultural Perspective* Alberto Rinaldi

190 *Merchants of Legalism: A History of State Responsibility (1870–1960)* Alan Tzvika Nissel

189 *The Functions of International Adjudication and International Environmental Litigation* Joshua Paine

188 *Demystifying Treaty Interpretation* Andrea Bianchi and Fuad Zarbiyev

187 *International Law-Making by the International Court of Justice and International Law Commission: Partnership for Purpose in a Decentralized Legal Order* Omri Sender

186 *The Rebirth of Territory* Gail Lythgoe

185 *Reimagining Sustainable Development in International Law: Perspectives from African Legal Cosmologies* Godwin Eli Kwadzo Dzah

184 *Collective Self-Defence in International Law* James A. Green

183 *Weaponising Evidence: A History of Tobacco Control in International Law* Margherita Melillo

182 *The Justice Factory: Management Practices at the International Criminal Court* Richard Clements

181 *A Communitarian Theory of WTO Law* Chi Carmody

180 *Drones and International Law: A Techno-Legal Machinery* Rebecca Mignot-Mahdavi

179 *The Necessity of Nature: God, Science and Money in 17th Century English Law of Nature* Mónica García-Salmones

178 *Making the World Safe for Investment: The Protection of Foreign Property 1922–1959* Andrea Leiter

177 *National Governance and Investment Treaties* Josef Ostřanský and Facundo Pérez Aznar

176 *Who Owns Outer Space? International Law, Astrophysics, and the Sustainable Development of Space* Michael Byers and Aaron Boley

175 *Intervening in International Justice: Third States before Courts and Tribunals* Brian McGarry

174 *Reciprocity in Public International Law* Arianna Whelan

173 *When Environmental Protection and Human Rights Collide* Marie-Catherine Petersmann

172 *The International Law of Sovereign Debt Dispute Settlement* Kei Nakajima

171 *The Everyday Makers of International Law: From Great Halls to Back Rooms* Tommaso Soave

170 *Virtue in Global Governance: Judgment and Discretion* Jan Klabbers

169 *The Effects of Armed Conflict on Investment Treaties* Tobias Ackermann

168 *Investment Law's Alibis: Colonialism, Imperialism, Debt and Development* David Schneiderman

167 *Negative Comparative Law: A Strong Programme for Weak Thought* Pierre Legrand

166 *Detention by Non-State Armed Groups under International Law* Ezequiel Heffes

165 *Rebellions and Civil Wars: State Responsibility for the Conduct of Insurgents* Patrick Dumberry

164 *The International Law of Energy* Jorge Viñuales

163 *The Three Ages of International Commercial Arbitration* Mikaël Schinazi

162 *Repetition and International Law* Wouter Werner

161 *State Responsibility and Rebels: The History and Legacy of Protecting Investment Against Revolution* Kathryn Greenman

160 *Rewriting Histories of the Use of Force: The Narrative of 'Indifference'* Agatha Verdebout

159 *The League of Nations and the Protection of the Environment* Omer Aloni

158 *International Investment Law and Legal Theory: Expropriation and the Fragmentation of Sources* Jörg Kammerhofer

157 *Legal Barbarians: Identity, Modern Comparative Law and the Global South* Daniel Bonilla Maldonado

156 *International Human Rights Law Beyond State Territorial Control* Antal Berkes

155 *The Crime of Aggression under the Rome Statute of the International Criminal Court* Carrie McDougall

154 *Minorities and the Making of Postcolonial States in International Law* Mohammad Shahabuddin

153 *Preclassical Conflict of Laws* Nikitas E. Hatzimihail

152 *International Law and History: Modern Interfaces* Ignacio de la Rasilla

151 *Marketing Global Justice: The Political Economy of International Criminal Law* Christine Schwöbel-Patel

150 *International Status in the Shadow of Empire* Cait Storr

149 *Treaties in Motion: The Evolution of Treaties from Formation to Termination* Edited by Malgosia Fitzmaurice and Panos Merkouris

148 *Humanitarian Disarmament: An Historical Enquiry* Treasa Dunworth

147 *Complementarity, Catalysts, Compliance: The International Criminal Court in Uganda, Kenya, and the Democratic Republic of Congo* Christian M. De Vos

146 *Cyber Operations and International Law* François Delerue

145 *Comparative Reasoning in International Courts and Tribunals* Daniel Peat

144 *Maritime Delimitation as a Judicial Process* Massimo Lando

143 *Prosecuting Sexual and Gender-Based Crimes at the International Criminal Court: Practice, Progress and Potential* Rosemary Grey

142 *Capitalism As Civilisation: A History of International Law* Ntina Tzouvala

141 *Sovereignty in China: A Genealogy of a Concept Since 1840* Adele Carrai

140 *Narratives of Hunger in International Law: Feeding the World in Times of Climate Change* Anne Saab

139 *Victim Reparation under the Ius Post Bellum: An Historical and Normative Perspective* Shavana Musa

138 *The Analogy between States and International Organizations* Fernando Lusa Bordin

137 *The Process of International Legal Reproduction: Inequality, Historiography, Resistance* Rose Parfitt

136 *State Responsibility for Breaches of Investment Contracts* Jean Ho

135 *Coalitions of the Willing and International Law: The Interplay between Formality and Informality* Alejandro Rodiles

134 *Self-Determination in Disputed Colonial Territories* Jamie Trinidad

133 *International Law as a Belief System* Jean d'Aspremont

132 *Legal Consequences of Peremptory Norms in International Law* Daniel Costelloe

131 *Third-Party Countermeasures in International Law* Martin Dawidowicz

130 *Justification and Excuse in International Law: Concept and Theory of General Defences* Federica Paddeu

129 *Exclusion from Public Space: A Comparative Constitutional Analysis* Daniel Moeckli

128 *Provisional Measures before International Courts and Tribunals* Cameron A. Miles

127 *Humanity at Sea: Maritime Migration and the Foundations of International Law* Itamar Mann

126 *Beyond Human Rights: The Legal Status of the Individual in International Law* Anne Peters

125 *The Doctrine of Odious Debt in International Law: A Restatement* Jeff King

124 *Static and Evolutive Treaty Interpretation: A Functional Reconstruction* Christian Djeffal

123 *Civil Liability in Europe for Terrorism-Related Risk* Lucas Bergkamp, Michael Faure, Monika Hinteregger and Niels Philipsen

122 *Proportionality and Deference in Investor-State Arbitration: Balancing Investment Protection and Regulatory Autonomy* Caroline Henckels

121 *International Law and Governance of Natural Resources in Conflict and Post-Conflict Situations* Daniëlla Dam-de Jong

120 *Proof of Causation in Tort Law* Sandy Steel

119 *The Formation and Identification of Rules of Customary International Law in International Investment Law* Patrick Dumberry

118 *Religious Hatred and International Law: The Prohibition of Incitement to Violence or Discrimination* Jeroen Temperman

117 *Taking Economic, Social and Cultural Rights Seriously in International Criminal Law* Evelyne Schmid

116 *Climate Change Litigation: Regulatory Pathways to Cleaner Energy* Jacqueline Peel and Hari M. Osofsky

115 *Mestizo International Law: A Global Intellectual History 1842–1933* Arnulf Becker Lorca

114 *Sugar and the Making of International Trade Law* Michael Fakhri

113 *Strategically Created Treaty Conflicts and the Politics of International Law* Surabhi Ranganathan

112 *Investment Treaty Arbitration As Public International Law: Procedural Aspects and Implications* Eric De Brabandere

111 *The New Entrants Problem in International Fisheries Law* Andrew Serdy

110 *Substantive Protection under Investment Treaties: A Legal and Economic Analysis* Jonathan Bonnitcha

109 *Popular Governance of Post-Conflict Reconstruction: The Role of International Law* Matthew Saul

108 *Evolution of International Environmental Regimes: The Case of Climate Change* Simone Schiele

107 *Judges, Law and War: The Judicial Development of International Humanitarian Law* Shane Darcy

106 *Religious Offence and Human Rights: The Implications of Defamation of Religions* Lorenz Langer

105 *Forum Shopping in International Adjudication: The Role of Preliminary Objections* Luiz Eduardo Salles

104 *Domestic Politics and International Human Rights Tribunals: The Problem of Compliance* Courtney Hillebrecht

103 *International Law and the Arctic* Michael Byers

102 *Cooperation in the Law of Transboundary Water Resources* Christina Leb

101 *Underwater Cultural Heritage and International Law* Sarah Dromgoole

100 *State Responsibility: The General Part* James Crawford

99 *The Origins of International Investment Law: Empire, Environment and the Safeguarding of Capital* Kate Miles

98 *The Crime of Aggression under the Rome Statute of the International Criminal Court* Carrie McDougall

97 *'Crimes against Peace' and International Law* Kirsten Sellars

96 *Non-Legality in International Law: Unruly Law* Fleur Johns

95 *Armed Conflict and Displacement: The Protection of Refugees and Displaced Persons under International Humanitarian Law* Mélanie Jacques

94 *Foreign Investment and the Environment in International Law* Jorge E. Viñuales

93 *The Human Rights Treaty Obligations of Peacekeepers* Kjetil Mujezinović Larsen

92 *Cyber Warfare and the Laws of War* Heather Harrison Dinniss

91 *The Right to Reparation in International Law for Victims of Armed Conflict* Christine Evans

90 *Global Public Interest in International Investment Law* Andreas Kulick

89 *State Immunity in International Law* Xiaodong Yang

88 *Reparations and Victim Support in the International Criminal Court* Conor McCarthy

87 *Reducing Genocide to Law: Definition, Meaning, and the Ultimate Crime* Payam Akhavan

86 *Decolonising International Law: Development, Economic Growth and the Politics of Universality* Sundhya Pahuja

85 *Complicity and the Law of State Responsibility* Helmut Philipp Aust

84 *State Control over Private Military and Security Companies in Armed Conflict* Hannah Tonkin

83 *'Fair and Equitable Treatment' in International Investment Law* Roland Kläger

82 *The UN and Human Rights: Who Guards the Guardians?* Guglielmo Verdirame

81 *Sovereign Defaults before International Courts and Tribunals* Michael Waibel

80 *Making the Law of the Sea: A Study in the Development of International Law* James Harrison

79 *Science and the Precautionary Principle in International Courts and Tribunals: Expert Evidence, Burden of Proof and Finality* Caroline E. Foster

78 *Transition from Illegal Regimes under International Law* Yaël Ronen

77 *Access to Asylum: International Refugee Law and the Globalisation of Migration Control* Thomas Gammeltoft-Hansen

76 *Trading Fish, Saving Fish: The Interaction between Regimes in International Law* Margaret A. Young

75 *The Individual in the International Legal System: Continuity and Change in International Law* Kate Parlett

74 *'Armed Attack' and Article 51 of the UN Charter: Evolutions in Customary Law and Practice* Tom Ruys

73 *Theatre of the Rule of Law: Transnational Legal Intervention in Theory and Practice* Stephen Humphreys

72 *Science and Risk Regulation in International Law* Jacqueline Peel

71 *The Participation of States in International Organisations: The Role of Human Rights and Democracy* Alison Duxbury

70 *Legal Personality in International Law* Roland Portmann

69 *Vicarious Liability in Tort: A Comparative Perspective* Paula Giliker

68 *The Public International Law Theory of Hans Kelsen: Believing in Universal Law* Jochen von Bernstorff

67 *Legitimacy and Legality in International Law: An Interactional Account* Jutta Brunnée and Stephen J. Toope

66 *The Concept of Non-International Armed Conflict in International Humanitarian Law* Anthony Cullen

65 *The Principle of Legality in International and Comparative Criminal Law* Kenneth S. Gallant

64 *The Challenge of Child Labour in International Law* Franziska Humbert

63 *Shipping Interdiction and the Law of the Sea* Douglas Guilfoyle

62 *International Courts and Environmental Protection* Tim Stephens

61 *Legal Principles in WTO Disputes* Andrew D. Mitchell

60 *War Crimes in Internal Armed Conflicts* Eve La Haye

59 *Humanitarian Occupation* Gregory H. Fox

58 *The International Law of Environmental Impact Assessment: Process, Substance and Integration* Neil Craik

57 *The Law and Practice of International Territorial Administration: Versailles to Iraq and Beyond* Carsten Stahn

56 *United Nations Sanctions and the Rule of Law* Jeremy Matam Farrall

55 *National Law in WTO Law: Effectiveness and Good Governance in the World Trading System* Sharif Bhuiyan

54 *Cultural Products and the World Trade Organization* Tania Voon

53 *The Threat of Force in International Law* Nikolas Stürchler

52 *Indigenous Rights and United Nations Standards: Self-Determination, Culture and Land* Alexandra Xanthaki

51 *International Refugee Law and Socio-Economic Rights: Refuge from Deprivation* Michelle Foster

50 *The Protection of Cultural Property in Armed Conflict* Roger O'Keefe

49 *Interpretation and Revision of International Boundary Decisions* Kaiyan Homi Kaikobad

48 *Multinationals and Corporate Social Responsibility: Limitations and Opportunities in International Law* Jennifer A. Zerk

47 *Judiciaries within Europe: A Comparative Review* John Bell

46 *Law in Times of Crisis: Emergency Powers in Theory and Practice* Oren Gross and Fionnuala Ní Aoláin

45 *Vessel-Source Marine Pollution: The Law and Politics of International Regulation* Alan Khee-Jin Tan

44 *Enforcing Obligations* Erga Omnes *in International Law* Christian J. Tams

43 *Non-Governmental Organisations in International Law* Anna-Karin Lindblom

42 *Democracy, Minorities and International Law* Steven Wheatley

41 *Prosecuting International Crimes: Selectivity and the International Criminal Law Regime* Robert Cryer

40 *Compensation for Personal Injury in English, German and Italian Law: A Comparative Outline* Basil Markesinis, Michael Coester, Guido Alpa and Augustus Ullstein

39 *Dispute Settlement in the UN Convention on the Law of the Sea* Natalie Klein

38 *The International Protection of Internally Displaced Persons* Catherine Phuong

37 *Imperialism, Sovereignty and the Making of International Law* Antony Anghie

36 *Principles of the Institutional Law of International Organizations* C. F. Amerasinghe

35 *Necessity, Proportionality and the Use of Force by States* Judith Gardam

34 *International Legal Argument in the Permanent Court of International Justice: The Rise of the International Judiciary* Ole Spiermann

33 -

32 *Great Powers and Outlaw States: Unequal Sovereigns in the International Legal Order* Gerry Simpson

31 *Local Remedies in International Law* (second edition)Chittharanjan Felix Amerasinghe

30 *Reading Humanitarian Intervention: Human Rights and the Use of Force in International Law* Anne Orford

29 *Conflict of Norms in Public International Law: How WTO Law Relates to Other Rules of International Law* Joost Pauwelyn

28 -

27 *Transboundary Damage in International Law* Hanqin Xue

26 -

25 *European Criminal Procedures* Edited by Mireille Delmas-Marty and J. R. Spencer

24 *Accountability of Armed Opposition Groups in International Law* Liesbeth Zegveld

23 *Sharing Transboundary Resources: International Law and Optimal Resource Use* Eyal Benvenisti

22 *International Human Rights and Humanitarian Law* René Provost

21 *Remedies against International Organisations* Karel Wellens

20 *Diversity and Self-Determination in International Law* Karen Knop

19 *The Law of Internal Armed Conflict* Lindsay Moir

18 *International Commercial Arbitration and African States: Practice, Participation and Institutional Development* Amazu A. Asouzu

17 *The Enforceability of Promises in European Contract Law* James Gordley

16 *International Law in Antiquity* David J. Bederman

15 *Money Laundering: A New International Law Enforcement Model* Guy Stessens

14 *Good Faith in European Contract Law* Reinhard Zimmermann and Simon Whittaker

13 *On Civil Procedure* J. A. Jolowicz

12 *Trusts: A Comparative Study* Maurizio Lupoi and Simon Dix

11 *The Right to Property in Commonwealth Constitutions* Tom Allen

10 *International Organizations before National Courts* August Reinisch

9 *The Changing International Law of High Seas Fisheries* Francisco Orrego Vicuña

8 *Trade and the Environment: A Comparative Study of EC and US Law* Damien Geradin

7 *Unjust Enrichment: A Study of Private Law and Public Values* Hanoch Dagan

6 *Religious Liberty and International Law in Europe* Malcolm D. Evans

5 *Ethics and Authority in International Law* Alfred P. Rubin

4 *Sovereignty over Natural Resources: Balancing Rights and Duties* Nico Schrijver

3 *The Polar Regions and the Development of International Law* Donald R. Rothwell

2 *Fragmentation and the International Relations of Micro-States: Self-Determination and Statehood* Jorri C. Duursma

1 *Principles of the Institutional Law of International Organizations* C. F. Amerasinghe

Printed by Integrated Books International,
United States of America